Prefixes

and Other Word-Initial Elements of English

Prefixes

and Other Word-Initial Elements of English

*A Compilation of Nearly 3,000 Common and
Technical Free Forms, Bound Forms, and Roots
That Frequently Occur at the Beginnings of Words,
Accompanied by a Detailed Description of Each,
Showing Its Origin, Meanings,
History, Functions, Uses and Applications,
Variant Forms, and Related Forms,
Together with Illustrative Examples,
the Whole Arranged in Alphabetical Order
with Entries Numbered for Easy Reference,
Supplemented by a Detailed Index Containing All
Sample Words, Variants, and Etymological Source
Words and Roots Described in the Text.*

Laurence Urdang
EDITORIAL DIRECTOR

Alexander Humez
EDITOR

Gale Research Company
BOOK TOWER • DETROIT, MICHIGAN 48226

Editorial Staff:

Laurence Urdang, *Editorial Director*

Alexander Humez, *Editor*

Frank R. Abate, *Managing Editor*

Linda M. D. Legassie, *Editorial Associate*

Programming, Data Processing, and Typesetting by
Alexander Typesetting, Inc., Indianapolis, Indiana

Typographic and Systems Design by Laurence Urdang

Library of Congress Cataloging in Publication Data

Main entry under title:

Prefixes and other word-initial elements of English.

Includes index.
1. English language—Suffixes and prefixes.
2. English language—Word formation. I. Urdang, Laurence.
II. Humez, Alexander.
PE1175.P68   1983   425   83-20662
ISBN 0-8103-1548-3

Contents

Introduction and
How To Use This Book

Speakers of English are aware that the elements that make up the words of the language fall into several categories. They may occur as free-standing roots, like *take, run, house,* and many others, almost all of which can be used in close combination with other words or word elements, as in *intake, uptake, take-off, rerun, runabout, housekeeping, lighthouse, greenhouse,* and so on. Another category includes word elements that appear frequently or solely as combining forms, like the *a-* of *abed,* the *corneo-* of *corneosclera,* the *-ful* of *helpful,* the *-ly* of *graciously,* the *pre-* of *prefix,* the *re-* of *retread,* and so on. Some of these, like *a-, -ful, -ly, pre-,* were once free forms, that is, free-standing words; others, like *corneo-,* are transparent alterations of free-standing words for use in combination with other linguistic elements; and others, like *re-,* have always occurred, as far as one can tell, exclusively prefixally, never in isolation.

In *Prefixes,* we have listed nearly 3,000 word-initial forms that are either always or frequently encountered in combination with other words or word elements. Some of these, like *ameba-, blue-,* and *check-,* occur as words in the language: they are listed and described for convenience, chiefly because they often occur in combination with other elements. The rest, like *ab-, recti-,* and *zygo-,* which rarely or never occur in isolation, are the mainstay of this book.

It will be noted that certain formulaic terminology to which precisionists may object has been employed for the sake of uniformity and clarity of treatment in the descriptions. The phrase "word-initial combining element" has been adopted to describe what people loosely refer to as a "prefix," mainly because a prefix is properly a form that cannot stand on its own, and *Prefixes* lists many forms that function as independent words. The element to which the "word-initial element" is attached is called the "combining

7

root," despite the fact that "root" is a misnomer in those instances where the "prefix" is attached to a "suffix." This terminology has been used for the sake of simplicity and, in certain cases, to avoid specific commitment as to the classification of the element.

With few exceptions, the prefixes described have been selected because the editor found at least five examples of their use—albeit at times in technical language. In certain instances, forms appearing in word-initial position in fewer than five words have been included either because of the comparatively high frequency of the words in which they occur or because of their resemblance to (homographic) forms of more frequent occurrence. Thus, for example, the relatively rare **col-¹** of *collate, collect,* and *collocation* is included, along with the more frequently occurring **col-²** of *colalgia, colitis,* and the like.

Many such homographs are listed. Like **col-¹** and **col-²**, these are forms with identical spellings but different etymologies. (**Col-¹** is derived from Latin *col-*, a combining form of the preposition *cum* 'with,' while **col-²** is derived from Greek *kól(on)* 'colon.') Other examples are **a-¹, a-², a-³; for-¹, for-²; ulo-¹, ulo-², ulo-³**, and so forth, all fully distinguished in the text.

Many word-initial combining elements are themselves combinations: *cholecyst-* is a combination of *chole-* and *cyst-, dinitro-* is a combination of *di-* and *nitro-*, and so on. Each such combination is listed, but those with meanings transparent from the meanings of the component parts are simply given as cross references to the main entries where their components are described. Thus, under the entry for **dinitro-** (whose meaning of 'having two (NO_2) groups' is obvious from the meanings of **di-¹** 'two' and **nitro-** 'containing the group (NO_2)'), the reader is directed to "See **di-¹** and **nitro-**." By contrast, **cholecyst-** (whose meaning of 'of or pertaining to the gallbladder' is not immediate from the meanings of **chole-** 'gall, bile' and **cyst-** 'sac') gets a full entry (at the end of which the reader is directed to "Compare **chole-** and **cyst-**").

Each full entry consists of the following information:

1. a sequential number for each word-initial element, in **bold** type;
2. the entry form itself, in **bold** type;
3. descriptive text detailing the etymon or etyma (in *italic* type), meaning(s) (enclosed in single quotation marks), and use(s) of the form;
4. examples, in **bold** type, illustrating actual words in which the combining form appears in attested sources;
5. variant forms or spellings, in **bold** type, given under the heading "Also" (and listed in alphabetical order elsewhere in the text with the designation "A variant of [the main entry]," as: "**amoeb-** A variant of **ameba-**."
6. closely related forms, in **bold** type, given under the heading "Com-

pare" (and listed as full entries in alphabetical order elsewhere in the text, as **cancer-** and **chancr-**, (the latter being derived from the former), or **set-** and **sit-**, (both being derived from the same Old English verb, *sittan* 'to be seated'));

7. cognate forms, in **bold** type, given under the heading "Related forms" (and listed as full entries in alphabetical order in the text, as **cornu-** and **horn-**, (the former being derived from Latin and the latter from Old English, both from a common Proto-Indo-European root meaning 'head, horn')).

For the convenience of the user, the letter ȝ (yogh), which appears in some Old and Middle English texts, has been uniformly transcribed in this book as ġ.

An Index at the end of the text contains, in alphabetical order, all variant and related forms, all cross references within entries, all sample words, all etymological elements, that is, all forms from which the entry forms are derived, and all (basic) meanings to be found in the text. The numbers in the Index refer to the entries in which these forms can be found.

No honest person claims to be omniscient or infallible: some likely candidates for inclusion as entry forms in this book may have been omitted through editorial oversight. We should be grateful for information from readers regarding omissions or suggestions on how we might improve the content or usefulness of *Prefixes*.

Alexander Humez

Somerville, Massachusetts
September 1983

Prefixes

and Other Word-Initial Elements of English

A

1   **A-**   A word-initial combining element, an abbreviation of English *atomic* (from Greek *a-* 'not, un-, without' plus *tóm(os)* 'cut; piece cut off' plus the adjective-forming suffix *-ic*, the whole combination meaning 'indivisible'), used in the specialized sense of 'using *atomic energy*, energy resulting from nuclear fission or fusion' in combination with other English elements: **A-bomb, A-plant, A-ship.** Compare **a-¹** and **tomo-.**

2   **a-¹**   A word-initial combining element, derived from Greek *a(n)-* 'without, lacking, un-,' used in its etymological sense in borrowings from Greek and in Neo-Greek combinations in which the element to which it is joined begins with a consonant other than *h:* **amorphous, aphasia, asymmetry.** Compare **an-¹.** Related forms: **i-, il-¹, im-¹, in-¹, ir-¹, non-¹, neutro-, never-, no-, nulli-, un-¹.**

3   **a-²**   A word-initial combining element, derived from Latin *a-,* a combining form of *a(b)* 'from, away from,' appearing in its etymological sense in inherited combinations in which the element to which it is joined begins with *p* or *v:* **aperture, avert, avoid.** Compare **ab-, abs-.** Related forms: **after-, apo-, of-¹, off-.**

4   **a-³**   A word-initial combining element, a reduced form of the Old English preposition *æf, of* 'of,' appearing in its etymological and extended senses in a few forms inherited from Middle English: **afresh, akin, anew.**

13

5 **a-⁴** A word-initial combining element, a reduced form of the Old English preposition *an, on* 'on, in, into, to, toward,' appearing as a word-initial combining element in two main types of combination with other English elements:
  1. In words inherited from Middle English, in which **a-⁴** has its etymological sense: **abed, asleep, asunder.**
  2. In words in which **a-⁴** plus an infinitival form yields a present participial sense of the combining root: **agape, astride, awash.** Compare **on-**.

6 **a-⁵** A word-initial combining element, derived from Latin *a-*, a combining form of *ad* 'to, toward, near,' appearing in its etymological sense in inherited combinations in which the element to which it is joined begins with *b, sc, sp,* or *st:* **abate, ascend, aspiration, astringent.** Compare **ac-, ad-, af-, ag-, al-², an-², ap-², ar-, as-, at-**.

7 **a-⁶** A word-initial combining element, derived from Old English *ā-* 'away, out,' formerly used as an intensifier of the sense of the verbal roots to which it was joined: **abide, arise, ashamed.**

8 **ab-** A word-initial combining element, derived from Latin *ab* 'from, away from,' used in its etymological sense in inherited combinations in which the element to which it is joined begins with a vowel or with a consonant other than *c, p, t,* or *v:* **abject, abrasive, absorb.** Compare **a-², abs-**. Related forms: **after-, apo-, of-¹, off-**.

9 **abdomino-** A word-initial combining element, derived from Latin *abdōmen, abdōmin(is)* 'belly, abdomen, the part of the body between the thorax and the pelvis' (of ultimately uncertain origin, though possibly from the verb *abdere* 'to put away, to hide') plus the combining vowel *-o-,* used in its etymological sense in biomedical terminology: **abdominocentesis, abdominogenital, abdominothoracic.** Also, **abdomin-: abdominalgia.**

10 **abs-** A word-initial combining element, derived from Latin *abs-*, a combining form of *ab* 'away, away from,' appearing in its etymological sense in inherited combinations in which the element to which it is joined begins with *c* or *t:* **abscess, abstain, abstract.** Compare **a-², ab-**. Related forms: **after-, apo-, of-¹, off-**.

11 **ac-** A word-initial combining element, derived from Latin *ac-*, a combining form of *ad* 'to, toward, near,' appearing in its etymological sense in inherited combinations in which the element to which it is joined begins with *c* or *qu:* **accumulate, accord, acquire.** Compare **a-⁵, ad-, af-, ag-, al-², an-², ap-², ar-, as-, at-**.

12   **acantho-**   A word-initial combining element, derived from Greek
     ákanth(a) 'thorn, pricker' (from an Indo-European root meaning
     'pointed, sharp') plus the combining vowel *-o-*, used in the sense of
     'spiny' in Neo-Greek combinations: **acanthocarpous, acanthocla-
     dous, acanthopterygian.** Also, **acanth-: acanthite.** Related forms:
     **aceto-, acetyl-, acid-, acro-, acu-, acuti-, edge-, keto-, oxal-, oxy-[1],
     oxy-[2].**

13   **acardio-**   A word-initial combining element, derived from Greek
     a(n)- 'not, lacking, without' plus *kardí(a)* 'heart' plus the combining
     vowel *-o-*, used to denote 'the heart's lack' of that which is named
     by the combining root in biomedical terminology: **acardiohemia,
     acardionervia, acardiotrophia.** Compare **a-[1]** and **cardio-.**

14   **acaro-**   A word-initial combining element, derived from Greek
     ákar(i) 'maggot, mite' plus the combining vowel *-o-*, used in the
     sense of 'of or pertaining to mites' in Neo-Greek combinations:
     acarodermatitis, acarophobia, acarotoxic. Also, **acar-, acari-, acarin-:
     acariasis, acariosis, acarinosis.**

15   **acephalo-**   See **a-[1]** and **cephalo-.**

16   **aceto-**   A word-initial combining element, derived from Latin
     acēt(um) 'vinegar' (from an Indo-European root meaning 'pointed,
     sharp') plus the combining vowel *-o-*, used in the extended sense of
     'containing *acetic acid* or belonging to the *acetyl group*' in chemical
     terminology: **acetonitrile, acetophenone, acetostearin.** Also, **acet-:
     acetaldehyde.** Compare **acetyl-, keto-.** Related forms: **acantho-,
     acid-, acro-, acu-, acuti-, edge-, oxal-, oxy-[1], oxy-[2].**

17   **acetyl-**   A word-initial combining element, also occurring as a word,
     derived from **acet-** plus the suffix *-yl* (which is used in naming
     chemical radicals), used in the sense of 'containing or derived from
     acetic acid' in chemical terminology: **acetylcholine, acetyloxyphe-
     nol, acetylsulfathiazole.** Compare **aceto-.**

18   **achroa-**   A variant of **achroo-.**

19   **achroma-**   A variant of **achromo-.**

20   **achromato-**   A variant of **achromo-.**

21   **achromo-**   See **a-[1]** and **chromo-.**

22   **achroo-**   A word-initial combining element, derived from Greek
     áchroo(s) 'colorless' (from *a(n)-* 'not, without, un-' plus *chrõs* 'outer

layer, surface, color'), used in its etymological and extended senses in Neo-Greek combinations: **achrooamyloid, achroocytosis, achroodextrin.** Also, **achroa-: achroacytosis.** Related form: **achromo-.**

23 **acid-** A word-initial combining element, also occurring as a word, derived from Latin *acīd(us)* 'sour' (from an Indo-European root meaning 'pointed, sharp'), used chiefly in the extended sense of 'of, pertaining to, or containing an *acid,* a compound of an electronegative element with one or more hydrogen atoms which may be replaced by electropositive atoms' in biochemical terminology: **acidalbumin, acid-fast, acidosis.** Also, **acidi-, acido-: acidimeter, acidocytopenia.** Related forms: **acantho-, aceto-, acetyl-, acro-, acu-, acuti-, edge-, keto-, oxal-, oxy-[1], oxy-[2].**

24 **acou-** A word-initial combining element, derived from Greek *akoú(ein)* 'to hear,' used in the sense of 'of or pertaining to hearing' in Neo-Greek combinations: **acouesthesia, acoulalion, acoumeter.** Also, **acouo-, acouto-: acouophonia, acoutometer.**

25 **acro-** A word-initial combining element, derived from Greek *ákro(s)* 'outermost, topmost, extreme' (from an Indo-European root meaning 'pointed, sharp'), used in its etymological and extended senses, chief among these being 'of or pertaining to the extremities of the body,' in Neo-Greek combinations: **acro-ataxia, acroparalysis, acrophobia.** Also, **acr-: acronyx.** Related forms: **acantho-, aceto-, acetyl-, acid-, acu-, acuti-, edge-, keto-, oxal-, oxy-[1], oxy-[2].**

26 **acromio-** A word-initial combining element, derived from Greek *akrōmio(n)* 'upper arm, shoulder' and, by extension, 'the *acromion,* the point of the shoulder which is formed by the outward extension of the spine of the scapula' (from *ákr(os)* 'high, topmost' plus *ōm(os)* 'shoulder' plus the noun-forming suffix *-ion*), used in its etymological sense in biomedical combinations: **acromioclavicular, acromiohumeral, acromiothoracic.** Compare **acro-** and **omo-.**

27 **actino-** A word-initial combining element, derived from Greek *aktís, aktîn(os)* 'ray (of light)', used in its etymological and extended senses in Neo-Greek and Neo-Latin combinations: **actinochemistry, actinogenesis, actinotoxemia.** Also, **actin-, actini-: actinism, actiniform.**

28 **acu-** A word-initial combining element, derived from Latin *acu(s)* 'needle' (from an Indo-European root meaning 'pointed, sharp'), used in its etymological sense in Neo-Latin combinations:

acuclosure, acupuncture, acusection. Related forms: **acantho-, aceto-, acetyl-, acid-, acro-, acuti-, edge-, keto-, oxal-, oxy-[1], oxy-[2].**

29 **acuti-** A word-initial combining element, derived from Latin *acūt(us)*, the past participle of the verb *acūere* 'to sharpen' (from an Indo-European root meaning 'pointed, sharp'), plus the combining vowel *-i-*, used in the sense of 'sharp, sharpened' in Neo-Latin combinations: **acutifoliate, acutilingual, acutilobate.** Related forms: **acantho-, aceto-, acetyl-, acid-, acro-, acu-, edge-, keto-, oxal-, oxy-[1], oxy-[2].**

30 **ad-** A word-initial combining element, derived from Latin *ad* 'to, toward, near,' appearing in its etymological sense in inherited forms in which the element to which it is joined begins with a vowel or with *d, h, j, m,* or *v:* **adopt, address, adhere, adjective, admire, advertise.** Compare **a-[5], ac-, af-, ag-, al-[2], an-[2], ap-[2], ar-, as-, at.**

31 **adeno-** A word-initial combining element, derived from Greek *adēn, adén(os)* 'acorn' and, by extension, 'gland' plus the combining vowel *-o-*, used in the sense of 'of or pertaining to a gland or glands' in biomedical terminology: **adenocarcinoma, adenology, adenovirus.** Also, **aden-: adenoid.**

32 **adia-** See **a-[1]** and **dia-.**

33 **adipo-** A word-initial combining element, derived from Latin *adep(s), adip(is)* 'lard, fat' plus the combining vowel *-o-*, used in the sense of 'of or pertaining to fat; fleshy' in Neo-Latin and Neo-Greek combinations: **adipocellular, adipofibroma, adipolysis.** Also, **adip-, adipos-: adipic, adiposuria.**

34 **adnex-** A word-initial combining element, derived from Scientific Latin *adnex(a)* 'appendages, esp. of the uterus' (from the past participle of the Latin verb *adnectere* 'to attach,' itself a combination of *ad* 'to, toward, near' and *nectere* 'to fasten, connect') plus the combining vowel *-o-*, used in its Scientific Latin sense in biomedical terminology: **adnexectomy, adnexitis, adnexorganogenic.** Also, **adnexo-: adnexogenesis.**

35 **adreno-** A word-initial combining element, derived from Latin *ad* 'to, toward, near' plus *rēn(ēs)* 'kidneys' plus the combining vowel *-o-*, used in the sense of 'of or pertaining to the *adrenal glands* (which are so named because of their proximity to the kidneys)' in biomedical terminology: **adrenocortical, adrenopause, adrenotoxin.** Also, **adren-: adrenic.** Compare **ad-** and **reni-.**

36 aedoeo- A word-initial combining element, derived from Greek *aidoî(a)* 'genitals' (literally, 'those things that are regarded with reverence or awe') plus the combining vowel *-o-*, used in its etymological and extended senses in Neo-Greek combinations: **aedoeocephalus, aedoeoptosis, aedoeotomy.**

37 aego- A word-initial combining element, derived from Greek *aí(x)*, *aig(ós)* 'goat' plus the combining vowel *-o-*, used in its etymological and extended senses in Neo-Greek combinations: *Aegocerus,* **aegobronchophony, aegophonic.** Also, **ego-²: egobronchophony.**

38 aeluro- A word-initial combining element, derived from Greek *aíl(o)uro(s)* 'cat,' used in its etymological sense in Neo-Greek combinations: **aelurophile, aelurophobia, aeluropodous.** Also, **aelur-, eluro-, ailuro-: aeluropsis, elurophobia, ailurophobia.**

39 aero- A word-initial combining element, derived from Greek *aĕr*, *aér(os)* and Latin *āēr, āer(is)*, both meaning 'air, atmosphere,' plus the combining vowel *-o-*, used in the sense of 'of or pertaining to air or gas' in Neo-Greek and Neo-Latin combinations: **aerocystography, aero-embolism, aeropause.** Also, **aer-, aeri-: aerenchyma, aeriform.** Compare **air-.**

40 aetio- A variant of **etio-.**

41 af- A word-initial combining element, derived from Latin *af-*, a combining form of *ad-* 'to, toward, near,' appearing in its etymological sense in inherited combinations in which the element to which it is joined begins with *f:* **affect, affiliate, affluence.** Compare **a-⁵, ac-, ad-, ag-, al-², an-², ap-², ar-, as-, at-.**

42 after- A word-initial combining element, derived from Old English *æfter* '(from) behind, following,' used in its etymological sense in combination with other English elements: **afterbirth, after-care, afterimage.** Related forms: **a-², ab-, abs-, apo-, of-¹, off-.**

43 ag- A word-initial combining element, derived from Latin *ag-*, a combining form of *ad* 'to, toward, near,' appearing in its etymological sense in inherited combinations in which the element to which it is joined begins with *g:* **agglomerate, agglutination, aggrandize.** Also, **a-⁵, ac-, ad-, af-, al-², an-², ap-², ar-, as-, at-.**

44 agamo- A word-initial combining element, derived from Greek *ágamo(s)* 'unmarried, celibate' (from *a(n)-* 'not, un-' plus *gámos* 'marriage, sexual intercourse'), used in the sense of 'of, pertaining to, or characterized by a state of asexual development' in Neo-

Greek and Neo-Latin combinations: **agamobium, agamogenesis, agamocytogeny.** Also, **agam-: agamont.** Compare **a-¹** and **gamo-.**

45 agglutino- A word-initial combining element, derived from Latin *agglutin(āre)* 'to glue to, stick onto' (from Latin *ad* 'to, toward, near' plus *glūten, glūtinis* 'beeswax, glue' plus the verbal endings of the first conjugation class) plus the combining vowel *-o-,* used in the general sense of 'of or pertaining to the action of adhesion' and in the specific sense of 'of or pertaining to *agglutinin,* an antibody responsible for the aggregation of a particulate antigen' in biomedical terminology: **agglutinogenic, agglutinophilic, agglutinoscope.** Also, **agglutin-, aggluto-: agglutination, agglutometer.**

46 agito- A word-initial combining element, derived from Latin *agit(āre)* 'to excite' plus the combining vowel *-o-,* used in the sense of 'of or characterized by abnormal rapidity or restlessness' in Neo-Latin and Neo-Greek combinations: **agitographia, agitolalia, agitophasia.** Also, **agit-: agitation.**

47 agro- A word-initial combining element, derived from Greek *agró(s)* 'countryside, field' (c.f. Latin *ag(e)r, agr(ī)* 'field, cultivated land'), used in its etymological and extended senses chiefly in Neo-Greek combinations: **agrology, agromania, agronomy.** Also, **agri-: agriculture.**

48 air- A word-initial combining element, also occurring as a word, derived through Old French from Latin *āēr* 'air, atmosphere,' used in its etymological sense in combination with other English elements: **aircraft, air-dry, airline.** Compare **aero-.**

49 al-¹ A word-initial combining element, derived from the Arabic definite article *al,* appearing with no discernible sense of its own in borrowings from Arabic (often via one or another of the Romance languages): **algebra, alembic, alcohol.**

50 al-² A word-initial combining element, derived from Latin *al-,* a combining form of *ad* 'to, toward, near,' appearing in its etymological sense in inherited combinations in which the element to which it is joined begins with *l:* **alleviate, allow, alloy.** Compare **a-⁵, ac-, ad-, af-, ag-, an-², ap-², ar-, as-, at-.**

51 al-³ A variant of **alcoholo-.**

52 al-⁴ A variant of **aldo-.**

53 albumino- A word-initial combining element, derived from Latin *albūmen, albūmin(is)* 'egg white' (cf. Latin *albus* 'white') plus the combining vowel *-o-*, used in the extended sense of 'of or pertaining to *albumin*, a water-soluble protein (of which the white of an egg is a prime example) widely found in plant and animal tissues' and in extensions of this sense in Neo-Latin and Neo-Greek combinations: **albuminocholia, albuminoptysis, albuminoreaction.** Also, **albumi-, albumin-, albumini-, albumo-: albumimeter, albuminemia, albuminiferous, albumoscope.**

54 **alcoholo-** A word-initial combining element, derived from Arabic *al-koh'l* 'antimony sulfide (a metallic powder used as a cosmetic),' later, 'powder derived by sublimation (as was antimony sulfide)' and, by further extension, 'liquid obtained by distillation, esp. (C_2H_5OH)' plus the combining vowel *-o-*, used in the sense of 'of or pertaining to *alcohol* (C_2H_5OH)' in biochemical combinations: **alcoholomania, alcoholometer, alcoholophilia.** Also, **al-[3], alcoho-, alcohol-: alinjection, alcohometry, alcoholism.** Compare **alk-[1].**

55 **aldo-** A word-initial combining element, derived from English *ald(ehyde)* 'substance containing the chemical group (CHO), derived from one of the primary alcohols by oxidation' (from Scientific Latin *al(cohol) dēhyd(rogenātum)* 'dehydrogenated alcohol') plus the combining vowel *-o-*, used in the sense of 'of, pertaining to, containing, or derived from an *aldehyde*' in chemical terminology: **aldohexose, aldoketomutase, aldopentose.** Also, **al-[4], ald-: alanine, aldol.** Compare **alcoholo-, de-[2], and hydro-.**

56 **alexo-** A word-initial combining element, derived from Greek *aléx(ein)* 'to ward off, keep away' plus the combining vowel *-o-*, used in its etymological and extended senses in biomedical terminology: **alexocyte, alexofixagen, alexofixin.** Also, **alex-, alexi-: alexin, alexipyretic.**

57 **algesi-** A word-initial combining element, derived from Greek *álgēsi(s)* 'sense of pain' (from the verb *algeîn* 'to feel pain' (from *álgos* 'pain')), used in the sense of 'of or pertaining to sensitivity to pain or to pain itself' in Neo-Greek and Neo-Latin combinations: **algesichronometer, algesimeter, algesireceptor.** Also, **alges-, algesio-: algesia, algesiometer.** Compare **algo-.**

58 **algio-** A word-initial combining element, derived from Greek *álg(os)* 'pain' plus *-io-* (whose precise origin open to debate), used in the sense of 'pertaining to or resulting from painful stimulation or activity' in biomedical terminology: **algiometabolic, algiometer, algiovascular.** Compare **algo-.**

59 **algo-** A word-initial combining element, derived from Greek *álgo(s)* 'pain,' used in its etymological sense in Neo-Greek combinations: **algolagnia, algometer, algophobia.** Also, **alg-: alganesthesia.** Compare **algesi-, algio-.**

60 **ali-** A word-initial combining element, derived from Latin *āl(a)* 'wing' (from unattested **axla,* a form cognate with English *axle* and related to the form underlying French *aisselle* 'armpit,' Proto-Indo-European **ax-* having originally meant something on the order of 'pivotal point, pivot') plus the combining vowel *-i-,* used in its etymological and extended senses in Neo-Latin and Neo-Greek combinations: **aliform, alinasal, alisphenoid.** Related forms: **axio-, axo-.**

61 **alipo-** See **a-**[1] and **lipo-.**

62 **alk-**[1] A word-initial combining element, derived from German *Alk(ohol)* 'alcohol' (from Arabic *al-kohʻl* 'antimony sulfide (a metallic powder used as a cosmetic),' later, 'powder derived by sublimation (as was antimony sulfide),' and, by further extension, 'liquid obtained by distillation, esp. $(C_2H_5OH_5)$'), used in its etymological and extended senses in chemical terminology: **alkamine, alkozide, alkyl.** Compare **alcoholo-.**

63 **alk-**[2] A variant of **alkali-.**

64 **alkali-** A word-initial combining element, also occurring as a word, derived from Arabic *al-qalīy* 'saltwort ash, potash, soda ash' (from the verb *qalay* 'to fry'), used in the sense of 'of, pertaining to, or composed of an *alkali,* one of a number of hydroxide compounds' in biochemical terminology: **alkaligenous, alkalimeter, alkalipenia.** Also, **alk-**[2]**, alkal-, alkalo-: alkargen, alkalemia, alkalotherapy.** Compare **al-**[1] and **kali-.**

65 **all-**[1] A word-initial combining element, also occurring as a word, derived from Old English *(e)all* 'every, whole, entire,' used in its etymological and extended senses in combination with other English elements: **allheal, all-important, all-purpose.**

66 **all-**[2] A variant of **allo-.**

67 **allanto-** A word-initial combining element, derived from Greek *allâ(s), allânt(os)* 'sausage' plus the combining vowel *-o-,* used both in its etymological sense and in the extended sense of 'of or pertaining to the *allantois,* a sausage-shaped diverticulum' in Neo-

Greek combinations: **allantochorion, allantoinuria, allantotoxicon.**
Also, **allant-: allantiasis.**

68 allelo-   A word-initial combining element, derived from Greek
allḗlō(n) 'to one another, of one another, one another' (from Greek
állos 'other, another'), used in Neo-Greek combinations to denote
'a relationship of contrast or mutuality': **allelocatalysis, allelomorph, allelotaxis.** Compare **allo-.**

69 allo-   A word-initial combining element, derived from Greek *állo(s)*
'other, another,' used in its etymological and extended senses, chief
among these being 'abnormal, reversed,' in Neo-Greek and Neo-
Latin combinations: **allocentric, allolalia, allotransplantation.** Also,
all-[2]: allergy. Compare **allelo-, allotrio-.** Related forms: **alter-, ultra-.**

70 allotrio-   A word-initial combining element, derived from Greek
allótrio(s) 'of or belonging to another; foreign' (from Greek *állos*
'other, another'), used in the sense of 'foreign, abnormal' in Neo-
Greek combinations: **allotriogeustia, allotriolith, allotriophagy.**
Also, **allotri-: allotriuria.** Compare **allo-.**

71 alpha- (A, α)   A word-initial combining element, the first letter of
the Greek alphabet, used to designate, variously, 'the first member
of a series; the carbon atom to which the principal group (or its
substitute) is attached in a straight chain compound; the carbon
atom closest to any other carbon atom shared by two rings in a
polycyclic compound; the carbon atom closest to the carboxyl
group in a compound; the stereoisomer of a sugar; the group of
atoms occupying the first of two or more possible positions in a
molecule; the first of a number of co-occurring substances of
unidentified constitution' in scientific terminology: **alpha-brass,
α-dinitrophenol, alpha-ray.** Note: Like **alpha-** (A, α), each of the
other letters of the Greek alphabet (usually in lower-case form)
may be used in chemical terminology to designate 'the *n*th carbon
atom in a straight chain compound or a derivative thereof in which
the substitute group is attached to that atom (when *n* corresponds
to the numerical position in the (Greek) alphabet of the letter in
question)':

A, α (alpha-) 1	I, ι (iota-) 9	P, ρ (rho-) 17
B, β (beta-) 2	K, κ (kappa-) 10	Σ, σ (sigma-) 18
Γ, γ (gamma-) 3	Λ, λ (lambda-) 11	T, τ (tau-) 19
Δ, δ (delta-) 4	M, μ (mu-) 12	Υ, υ (upsilon-) 20
E, ε (epsilon-) 5	N, ν (nu-) 13	Φ, φ (phi-) 21
Z, ζ (zeta-) 6	Ξ, ξ (xi-, ksi-) 14	X, χ (chi-) 22
H, η (eta-) 7	O, o (omicron-) 15	Ψ, ψ (psi-) 23
Θ, θ (theta) 8	Π, π (pi-) 16	Ω, ω (omega-) 24

Thus: **λ-hydroxy, ζ-carotene, χ-carrageenan.**

72 **alter-** A word-initial combining element, derived from Latin *alter* 'other,' used in its etymological and extended senses in borrowings from Latin and in Neo-Latin combinations: **altercation, alterative, alteregoism.** Related forms: **allelo-, allo-, allotrio-, ultra-.**

73 **alti-** A word-initial combining element, derived from Latin *alt(us)* 'high, lofty' (from an Indo-European root meaning 'grow') plus the combining vowel *-i-*, used in its etymological sense in Neo-Latin and Neo-Greek combinations: **altigraph, altimeter, altivolant.** Also, **alt-, alto-: altazimuth, altocumulus.** Related form: **old-.**

74 **alumin-** A word-initial combining element, derived from Neo-Latin *alumin(um)* (from Latin *alūm(en), alūmin(is)* 'alum, a double sulfate of a trivalent metal such as aluminum' plus the noun-forming suffix *-um*), used in the sense of 'of, composed of, or containing *aluminum*' in scientific terminology: **aluminate, aluminite, aluminize.** Also, **alumino-: aluminosilicate.**

75 **alveolo-** A word-initial combining element, derived from Latin *alveol(us)* 'small cavity, vessel' plus the combining vowel *-o-*, used in the sense of 'small cavity, cell' in Neo-Latin and Neo-Greek combinations: **alveoloclasia, alveolodental, alveolotomy.** Also, **alveol-: alveolectomy.**

76 **am-** A variant of **em-²**.

77 **ambi-** A word-initial combining element, derived from the Latin prefix *ambi-* 'around' and, by confusion with Latin *ambō* 'both, the two,' 'on both sides, both,' appearing in all of these senses in borrowings from Latin and in Neo-Latin combinations: **ambidextrous, ambilateral, ambivalent.** Also, **amb-: ambient.** Compare **ambo-.** Related form: **amphi-.**

78 **ambly-** A word-initial combining element, derived from Greek *amblý(s)* 'dull, blunt,' used in its etymological and extended senses in Neo-Greek combinations: **amblyaphia, amblygeustia, amblypod.**

79 **ambo-** A word-initial combining element, derived from Latin *ambō* 'both, the two,' used in its etymological sense in Neo-Latin and Neo-Greek combinations: **amboceptor, ambomalleal, ambosexual.** Compare **ambi-.** Related form: **ampho-.**

80 **ameba-** A word-initial combining element, also occurring as a word, derived from Greek *amoibḗ* 'return, exchange, change,' used in the extended sense of 'of or pertaining to a one-celled protozoan (which changes shape as it moves and feeds)' in Neo-Greek and Neo-Latin combinations: **amebacide, amebadiastase, amebaism.** Also, **ameb-, amebi-, amebo-, amoeb-, amoeba-, amoebi-, amoebo-: amebiasis, amebiform, amebocyte, amoeboid, amoeba-movement, amoebiform,** *Amoebobacter.*

81 **amelo-**   A word-initial combining element, derived from Norman French *amail* 'enamel' plus the combining vowel *-o-*, used in its etymological sense in biomedical terminology: **ameloblast, amelodental, amelogenesis.**

82 **amido-**   A word-initial combining element, derived from English *am(monia)* plus the chemical compound-naming suffix *-id(e)* plus the combining vowel *-o-*, used in chemical terminology in the sense of 'containing the chemical radical ($=NH_2$), (that of *ammonia* being ($=NH_3$), one of its hydrogen atoms being replaced by a metal, group of atoms, or acid 'stem' to form an *amide*)': **amidobenzene, amidohexose, amidopyrine.** Also, **amid-: amidase.** Compare **amino-, ammoni-, imido-.**

83 **amino-**   A word-initial combining element, derived from English *am(monia)* plus the suffix *-in(e)* (used in naming basic chemical substances) plus the combining vowel *-o-*, used in chemical terminology in the sense of 'containing the chemical radical ($=NH_2$) (that of *ammonia* being ($=NH_3$), one or more of its hydrogen atoms being replaced by a hydrocarbon or other organic group or groups to form an *amine*)': **aminoacidemia, aminobenzene, aminopeptidase.** Also, **amin-: aminase.** Compare **amido-, ammoni-, imino-.**

84 **ammo-**   A word-initial combining element, derived from Greek *ámmo(s)* 'sand,' used in its etymological and extended senses in Neo-Greek combinations: *Ammobium,* **ammochryse,** *Ammocrypta.* Related forms: **psammo-, sand-.**

85 **ammoni-**   A word-initial combining element, derived from Scientific Latin *(sal) ammoni(acus)* 'ammonium chloride (NH_4Cl)' (so named because it was obtained from the region of Lybia in which the temple of the Egyptian god *Amūn* (Greek *Ámmōn*) was situated), used in chemical terminology in the sense of 'of, pertaining to, or composed of *ammonia* ($=NH_3$)': **ammoniemia, ammonification, ammonirrhea.** Also, **ammon-, ammono-: ammonemia, ammonolysis.** Compare **amido-, amino-.**

86 **amnio-**   A word-initial combining element, derived from Greek

amnio(n) 'bowl in which to catch the blood of a sacrificial victim' (cf. Greek *amnós* 'lamb,' the classical sacrificial victim) and, by extension, 'membrane surrounding the fetus in utero,' used in this latter sense in Neo-Greek combinations: **amniocentesis, amnioplastin, amniorrhexis.** Also, **amnion-: amnionitis.**

87 **amoeb-** A variant of **ameba-.**

88 **amphi-** A word-initial combining element, derived from Greek *amphi* 'around, about, on both sides' and, by confusion with Greek *ámphō* 'both, the two,' 'both, two, double,' used in all of these senses in Neo-Greek combinations: **amphibious, amphiblastic, amphicentric.** Also, **amph-: ampheclesis.** Compare **ampho-.** Related form: **ambi-.**

89 **ampho-** A word-initial combining element, derived from Greek *ámphō* 'both, the two,' used in its etymological sense in Neo-Greek combinations: **amphodiplopia, amphogenic, amphotony.** Compare **amphi-.** Related form: **ambo-.**

90 **amyel-** See **a-¹** and **myelo-.**

91 **amygdalo-** A word-initial combining element, derived from Greek *amygdál(ē)* 'almond' plus the combining vowel *-o-*, used both in its etymological sense and in the extended sense of 'tonsil, an almond-shaped organ' in Neo-Greek combinations: **amygdalolith, amygdalophenin, amygdalothrypsis.** Also, **amygdal-: amygdalase.**

92 **amylo-** A word-initial combining element, derived from Latin *amyl(um)* 'starch' (from Greek *ámylos* 'nonmilled substance' (from *a(n)-* 'not, un-' plus *mýlē* 'mill')) plus the combining vowel *-o-*, used in its etymological and extended senses, chief among these being 'belonging to the *amyl* group' (from *am(ylum)* plus the chemical radical-naming suffix *-yl*), in biochemical terminology: **amyloclastic, amylodextrin, amyloprolamine.** Also, **amyl-: amylemia.** Compare **a-¹** and **mylo-.**

93 **amyo-** A word-initial combining element, derived from Greek *a(n)-* 'not, lacking, without, un-' plus *mý(s)* 'muscle' plus the combining vowel *-o-*, used to denote 'a muscle's lack' of that which is named by the combining root in biomedical terminology: **amyoesthesis, amyoplasia, amyostasia.** Compare **a-¹** and **myo-.**

94 **an-¹** A word-initial combining element, derived from Greek *a(n)-* 'not, without, lacking, un-,' used in its etymological sense in Neo-Greek combinations in which the element to which it is joined

begins with a vowel or *h:* **analgesic, anarchy, anodyne.** Compare **a-¹.** Related forms: **i-, il-¹, im-¹, in-¹, ir-¹, neutro-, never-, no-, non-¹, nulli-, un-¹.**

95 **an-²** A word-initial combining element, derived from Latin *an-,* a combining form of *ad* 'to, toward, near,' appearing in its etymological and extended senses in inherited combinations in which the element to which it is joined begins with *n:* **annihilate, annotate, announce.** Compare **a-⁵, ac-, ad-, af-, ag-, al-², ap-², ar-, as-, at-.**

96 **an-³** A variant of **ana-.**

97 **ana-** A word-initial combining element, derived from Greek *aná* 'up, back, again,' used in its etymological and extended senses and as an intensifier in borrowings from Greek and in Neo-Greek combinations: **anabiosis, anabolism, anachoresis.** Also, **an-³:** **anerythropsia.** Compare **ano-¹.** Related forms: **a-⁴, on-.**

98 **anaero-** See **an-¹** and **aero-.**

99 **anaphylacto-** A word-initial combining element, derived from Greek *aná* (in its use as an intensifier) plus *phylact(ḗr)* 'sentinel, guard' plus the combining vowel *-o-,* used in the sense of 'of or pertaining to *anaphylaxis,* the extreme reaction of an organism to foreign protein' in Neo-Greek combinations: **anaphylactogen, anaphylactogenesis, anaphylactotoxin.** Also, **anaphylact-:** **anaphylactia.**

100 **anatomico-** A word-initial combining element, derived from Greek *anatomikó(s)* 'of or pertaining to *anatomy'* (ultimately from the verb *anatémnein* 'to cut up, dissect,' hence the sense of 'science of the parts of the body and their interrelationships'), used in its etymological sense in Neo-Greek and Neo-Latin combinations: **anatomicomedical, anatomicopathological, anatomicosurgical.** Compare **ana-** and **tomo-.**

101 **anchylo-** A variant of **ankylo-.**

102 **ancylo-** A variant of **ankylo-.**

103 **andro-** A word-initial combining element, derived from Greek *an(ḗr), andr(ós)* 'man (as contrasted with woman), male' plus the combining vowel *-o-,* used in its etymological sense in Neo-Greek combinations: **androgalactozemia, androgen, andrology.** Also, **andr-:** **andranatomy.**

104 **anemo-** A word-initial combining element, derived from Greek *ánemo(s)* 'breath, wind,' used in its etymological senses in borrowings from Greek and in Neo-Greek combinations: **anemopathy, anemophilous, anemophobia.**

105 **anerythro-** See **an-¹** and **erythro-**.

106 **aneurysmo-** A word-initial combining element, derived from Greek *aneúrysm(a)* '(a) widening' (ultimately from *aná* (in its use as an intensifier) plus *eurýs* 'wide, broad') plus the combining vowel *-o-*, used in the specialized sense of 'of or pertaining to an *aneurysm*, a sac formed by the dilation of a blood-filled vein or artery' in Neo-Greek combinations: **aneurysmograph, aneurysmoplasty, aneurysmotomy.** Also, **aneurysm-: aneurysmectomy.** Compare **ana-** and **eury-**.

107 **angio-** A word-initial combining element, derived from Greek *ang(e)îo(n)* 'vessel,' used in its etymological sense and, more commonly, in the extended sense of 'blood vessel' in Neo-Greek combinations: **angioblast, angiocarditis, angioscopy.** Also, **angi-: angiectomy.**

108 **Anglo-** A word-initial combining element, derived from Latin *Angl(us)* 'member of a Germanic tribe living in the *Angul* region' (so named because the territory was shaped like a fishhook (cf. Old High German *angul* 'fishhook')) and, by extension, 'a Briton (of Germanic stock),' used in the further extended sense of 'English, English-speaking' in a variety of combinations: **Anglo-American, Anglophobe, Anglo-Saxon.** Related forms: **ankylo-, onco-², unci-**.

109 **anhydro-** See **an-¹** and **hydro-¹**.

110 **aniso-** See **an-¹** and **iso-**.

111 **ankylo-** A word-initial combining element, derived from Greek *ankýl(ē)* 'that which is bent or crooked; a loop' plus the combining vowel *-o-*, used in the sense of 'hook-shaped, joint, adhesion' in Neo-Greek combinations: **ankylochilia, ankyloglossia, ankylomele.** Also, **anchyl-, anchylo-, ancyl-, ancylo-, ankyl-: anchylosis, anchyloblepharon, ancylotic, ancyclostomiasis, ankylurethria.** Related forms: **Anglo-, onco-², unci-**.

112 **annul-** A word-initial combining element, derived from Latin *annul(us)* 'ring' (from *ān(us)* 'ring' plus the diminutive suffix *-ulus*), used in its etymological and extended senses in a variety of combinations: **Annulaceae, annulet, annulose.** Compare **ano-²**.

113   ano-¹   A word-initial combining element, derived from the Greek adverb *ánō* 'up, upward, above' (from the preposition *aná* 'up, back, again' plus the adverb-forming suffix *-ō*), used in its etymological and extended senses in Neo-Greek combinations: **anoneme, anoopsia, anotropia.** Compare **ana-**.

114   ano-²   A word-initial combining element, derived from Latin *ān(us)* 'ring' and, by extension, 'the ring-shaped opening at the distal end of the alimentary canal' plus the combining vowel *-o-*, used in this latter sense in biomedical terminology: **anoderm, anoperineal, anorectal.** Also, **ani-: anilinction.** Compare **annul-**.

115   anomalo-   A word-initial combining element, derived from Greek *anŏmalo(s)* 'irregular, uneven' (from *a(n)-* 'not, lacking, un-' plus *(h)omalós* 'smooth, balanced, even'), used in its etymological and extended senses in Neo-Greek combinations: **anomalogonatous, anomaloscope, anomalotrophy.** Also, **anomal-: anomalopia.** Compare **an-¹** and **homalo-**.

116   anomo-   A word-initial combining element, derived from Greek *ánomo(s)* 'lawless' (from *a(n)-* 'not, lacking, un-' plus *nómos* 'law, rule'), used in the sense of 'irregular' in Neo-Greek combinations: **anomocarpous, Anomoean, anomophyllous.** Compare **a-¹** and **nomo-**.

117   ant-   A variant of **anti-**.

118   ante-   A word-initial combining element, derived from Latin *ante* 'before, in front of,' used in its etymological sense in Neo-Latin combinations: **antefebrile, antenuptial, anteposition.** Compare **antero-**. Related forms: **anti-, end-², un-²**.

119   antero-   A word-initial combining element, derived from Latin *anter(ior)*, the comparative form of *ante* 'before, in front of,' plus the combining vowel *-o-*, used in the sense of 'before, front' in Neo-Latin combinations: **anterograde, antero-internal, anteroposterior.** Compare **ante-**.

120   antho-   A word-initial combining element, derived from Greek *ántho(s)* 'that which buds, sprouts, or flowers; a flower, bloom,' used in its etymological and extended senses in Neo-Greek combinations: **anthobian, anthocarpous, anthophore.** Also, **anth-: anthema.**

121   anthraco-   A word-initial combining element, derived from Greek *ánthra(x)*, *ánthrak(os)* 'coal, charcoal, carbuncle' plus the combining vowel -*o*-, used in its etymological senses and in the sense of 'carbon' in Neo-Greek combinations: **anthracometer, anthraconecrosis, anthracosilicosis.** Also, **anthra-, anthrac-: anthraquinone, anthracene.**

122 **anthropo-**   A word-initial combining element, derived from Greek *ánthrōpo*(*s*) 'human being,' used in its etymological sense in Neo-Greek combinations: **anthropogenesis, anthropolatry, anthropophage.**

123 **anti-**   A word-initial combining element, derived from Greek *anti* 'before, against, opposing, opposite to,' used in its etymological senses in a variety of combinations: **antiblastic, anti-intellectual, antimatter.** Also, **ant-: antacid.** Related forms: **ante-, antero-, end-², un-².**

124 **antro-**   A word-initial combining element, derived from Greek *ántro*(*n*) 'cave, cavern,' used in the sense of 'of or pertaining to a (bodily) cavity or sinus' in biomedical combinations: **antrodynia, antronasal, antroscope.** Also, **antr-: antritis.**

125 **any-**   A word-initial combining element, also occurring as a word, derived from Old English *æniġ* 'any' (from *ān* 'one' plus the suffix -*iġ* 'having the character of'), used in its etymological sense in a number of inherited combinations: **anybody, anyhow, anyway.** Compare **one-.**

126 **aorto-**   A word-initial combining element, derived from Greek *aort*(*ē̆*) 'lower extremity of the windpipe' and, by extension, 'extremity of the heart, the great artery' plus the combining vowel -*o*-, used in this latter sense in biomedical terminology: **aortoclasia, aortolith, aortosclerosis.** Also, **aort-, aortico-: aortarctia, aorticorenal.** Related form: **arterio-.**

127 **ap-¹**   A variant of **apo-.**

128 **ap-²**   A word-initial combining element, derived from Latin *ap*-, a combining form of *ad* 'to, toward, near,' appearing in its etymological and extended senses in inherited combinations in which the element to which it is joined begins with *p*: **apparatus, append, approve.** Compare **a-⁵, ac-, ad-, af-, ag-, al-², an-², ar-, as-, at-.**

129 **api-**   A word-initial combining element, derived from Latin *api*(*s*) 'bee,' used in its etymological sense in Neo-Latin combinations: **apiary, apicosan, apiculture.**

130 apico-   A word-initial combining element, derived from Latin *ap(ex)*, *apic(is)* 'top, cap, tip' plus the combining vowel *-o-*, used in its etymological and extended senses in Neo-Latin and Neo-Greek combinations: **apicoectomy, apicostome, apicotomy.** Also, **apic-: apical.**

131 apo-   A word-initial combining element, derived from Greek *apó* 'from, away from,' used in the sense of 'separate from, derived from' in Neo-Greek combinations: **apoatropine, apocoptic, apolegamy.** Also, **ap-[1]: apandria.** Related forms: **a-[2], ab-, abs-, after-, of-[1], off-.**

132 aponeuro-   A word-initial combining element, derived from Greek *aponeúrō(sis)* 'tendinous end of a muscle' (from *apó* 'from' plus *neûr(on)* 'sinew, tendon, nerve' plus the noun-forming suffix *-ōsis*), used in its etymological sense in Neo-Greek combinations: **aponeurology, aponeurorrhaphy, aponeurotomy.** Also, **aponeur-: aponeurectomy.** Compare **apo-** and **neuro-.**

133 appendico-   A word-initial combining element, derived from Latin *appendi(x)*, *appendic(is)* 'supplement' (literally, 'that which hangs to or upon something' (from *ap-* '**ap-[2]**' plus *pend(ere)* 'to hang')) plus the combining vowel *-o-*, used chiefly in the extended sense of 'organic appendage' or, more specifically, 'vermiform appendix' in biomedical combinations: **appendicocecostomy, appendicolithiasis, appendicopathy.** Also, **append-, appendic-: appendalgia, appendicitis.**

134 apter-   See **a-[1]** and **pter-.**

135 aqua-   A word-initial combining element, derived from Latin *aqua* 'water,' used in its etymological sense in a variety of combinations: **aquacade, aqualung, aquaplane.** Also, **aqu-, aqui-: aqueduct, aquifer.**

136 ar-   A word-initial combining element, derived from Latin *ar-*, a combining form of *ad* 'to, toward, near,' appearing in its etymological and extended senses in inherited combinations in which the element to which it is joined begins with *r:* **arraign, arrange, arrest.** Compare **a-[5], ac-, ad-, af-, ag-, al-[2], an-[2], ap-[2], as-, at-.**

137 arachno-   A word-initial combining element, derived from Greek *aráchn(ē)* 'spider' plus the combining vowel *-o-*, used in its etymological and extended senses in Neo-Greek combinations: **arachnodactylia, arachnogastria, arachnolysin.** Also, **arachn-: arachnid.**

138 arch-[1]   A variant of **arche-[1].**

31   argent- 149

139 arch-² A word-initial combining element, derived from Greek *arch(ós)* 'leader, chief' (literally, 'first, foremost person'), used in its etymological senses in a variety of combinations: **archangel, archdeacon, archenemy.** Also, **archi-²: architect.** Compare **archaeo-, arche-¹, archo-.**

140 archaeo- A word-initial combining element, derived from Greek *archaîo(s)* 'from the first, from the beginning, ancient,' used in its etymological and extended senses in Neo-Greek combinations: **archaeological, archaeopteryx, Archaeozoic.** Also, **archa-, archae-, arche-², archeo-: archaic, archaeal, archetype, archeology.** Compare **arch-², arche-¹, archo-.**

141 arche-¹ A word-initial combining element, derived from Greek *archḗ* 'beginning, origin,' used in the sense of 'original, primitive, first, formative' in Neo-Greek combinations: **archebiosis, archecentric, archespore.** Also, **arch-¹, archi-¹: archamphiaster, archiblast.** Compare **arch-², archaeo-, archo-.**

142 arche-² A variant of **archaeo-.**

143 archeo- A variant of **archaeo-.**

144 archi-¹ A variant of **arche-¹.**

145 archi-² A variant of **arch-².**

146 archo- A word-initial combining element, derived from Greek *archó(s)* 'leader, chief' (literally, 'first, foremost person') and, by extension, 'fundament, rectum,' used in this latter sense in Neo-Greek combinations: **archocele, archoptoma, archorrhea.** Compare **arch-², archaeo-, arche-¹.**

147 areo-¹ A word-initial combining element, derived from Greek *araió(s)* 'thin, slight, weak,' used in its etymological and extended senses in Neo-Greek combinations: **areocardia, areometry, areostyle.**

148 areo-² A word-initial combining element, derived from Greek *Arē(s)* 'the god of war; the planet Mars' plus the combining vowel -*o*-, used in the sense of 'of or pertaining to the planet Mars' in Neo-Greek combinations: **areocentric, areographic, areology.**

149 argent- A word-initial combining element, derived from Latin *argent(um)* 'silver,' used in its etymological sense in Neo-Latin and

Neo-Greek combinations: **argentaffine, argentic, argentite.** Also, **argenti-, argento-: argentiferous, argentophil.**

150 **argyr-** A word-initial combining element, derived from Greek *árgyr(os)* 'silver,' used in its etymological sense in Neo-Greek combinations: **argyranthous, argyremia, argyron.** Also, **argyro-: argyrophil.**

151 **aristo-** A word-initial combining element, derived from Greek *áristo(s)* 'best' (from an Indo-European root meaning something on the order of 'hold together, attach'), used in its etymological and extended senses in Neo-Greek combinations: **aristocrat, aristogenics, aristotype.**
Related forms: **arm-¹, arm-², arthro-, arti-.**

152 **arm-¹** A word-initial combining element, also occurring as a word, derived from Old English *(e)arm* 'upper limb of the body; arm' (from an Indo-European root meaning something on the order of 'hold together, attach'), used in its etymological and extended senses in combination with other English elements: **armband, armchair, armhole.** Related forms: **aristo-, arm-², arthro-, arti-.**

153 **arm-²** A word-initial combining element, also occurring as a word, derived through Old French *arm(er)* from Latin *arm(āre)* 'to equip with weapons' (from Latin *arma* 'tools, weapons' (from an Indo-European root meaning something on the order of 'hold together, attach')), used in its etymological and extended senses in inherited combinations: **armiger, armistice, army.** Related forms: **aristo-, arm-¹, arthro-, arti-.**

154 **arrheno-** A word-initial combining element, derived from Greek *árrhēn, árrhen* 'masculine, male' plus the combining vowel *-o-*, used in its etymological and extended senses in Neo-Greek combinations: **arrhenoblastoma, arrhenogenic, arrhenotoky.**

155 **arseno-** A word-initial combining element, derived through Greek *arsen(ikón)* from Arabic *azzernīkh* 'orpiment, yellow sulfuret of arsenic' (from the Arabic definite article *al-* plus Persian *zarnīkh* (cf. Persian *zar,* Avestan *zaranya* 'gold')) plus the combining vowel *-o-*, used in the sense of 'of or pertaining to *arsenic,* belonging to the *arseno* group (-As=As)' in chemical terminology: **arsenoautohemotherapy, arsenobenzol, arsenoresistant.** Also, **ars-, arsen-: arsphenamine, arsenic.** Related forms: **chlor-¹, chlor-², chole-, choler-, gall-, glass-, gold-, golden-, yellow-.**

156 **arterio** A word-initial combining element, derived from Greek

artēri(a) 'windpipe, artery' plus the combining vowel *-o-*, used in the sense of 'of or pertaining to an artery' in Neo-Greek combinations: **arterioatony, arteriogenesis, arteriosclerosis.** Also, **arteri-: arteriectasia.** Related form: **aorto-.**

157 **arthro-**   A word-initial combining element, derived from Greek *árthro(n)* 'joint' (from an Indo-European root meaning something on the order of 'hold together, attach'), used in its etymological sense in Neo-Greek combinations: **arthroclasia, arthroendoscopy, arthropathy.** Also, **arthr-: arthritis.** Related Forms: **aristo-, arm-¹, arm-², arti-.**

158 **arti-**   A word-initial combining element, derived from Latin *ar(s)*, *art(is)* 'workmanship, art' (from an Indo-European root meaning something on the order of 'hold together, attach') plus the combining vowel *-i-*, used in the sense of 'made by a human being' in inherited combinations: **artifact, artificial, artifex.** Related forms: **aristo-, arm-¹, arm-², arthro-.**

159 **as-**   A word-initial combining element, derived from Latin *as-*, a combining form of *ad* 'to, toward, near,' appearing in its etymological and extended senses in inherited combinations in which the element to which it is joined begins with *s* plus a vowel: **assemble, assent, assimilate.** Compare **a-⁵, ac-, ad-, af-, ag-, al-², an-², ap-², ar-, at-.**

160 **ascari-**   A word-initial combining element, derived from Greek *askarí(s)*, *askarí(dos)* 'maw-worm, intestinal worm,' used in its etymological sense in Neo-Greek and Neo-Latin combinations: **ascariasis, ascaricide, ascariosis.** Also, **ascarid-: ascaridosis.**

161 **asco-**   A word-initial combining element, derived from Greek *askó(s)* 'sack, bag,' used in the specialized sense of 'sack in which spores are formed' in botanical terminology: **ascocarp, ascogonium, *Ascomycetes*.**

162 **asept-**   See **a-¹** and **septico-.**

163 **aspergill-**   A word-initial combining element, ultimately derived from Latin *asperg(ere)* 'to sprinkle, scatter' plus the diminutive noun-forming suffix *-ill(us)*, used in Neo-Latin and Neo-Greek combinations in reference to 'the *Aspergillus* genus of fungi and to the diseases to which they give rise': **aspergillar, aspergillin, aspergillosis.** Also, **aspergillo-: aspergillomycosis.**

164 **astheno-**   A word-initial combining element, derived from Greek

asthen(ḗs) 'lacking strength' (from *a(n)-* 'without, lacking' plus *sthénos* 'strength') plus the combining vowel *-o-*, used in the sense of 'of, pertaining to, or characterized by weakness' in Neo-Greek combinations: **asthenobiosis, asthenocoria, asthenophobia.** Also, **asthen-: asthenopia.** Compare **a-¹** and **stheno-.**

165 **astigm-**   A word-initial combining element, derived from Greek *a(n)-* 'without, lacking' plus *stígm(a)*, *stígm(atos)* 'mark, brand, spot, dot' and, by extension, 'focus, focal point' (from *stízein* 'to prick, mark with a pointed instrument; to tattoo'), used in the specialized sense of 'of, pertaining to, or characterized by *astigmatism*, an abnormal curvature of the eye's refractive surfaces which results in the diffusion (rather than sharp focusing) of light rays on the retina' in Neo-Greek combinations: **astigmagraph, astigmia, astigmic.** Also, **astigmat-, astigmato-, astigmo-: astigmatism, astigmatoscope, astigmometer.**

166 **astragalo-**   A word-initial combining element, derived from Greek *astrágalo(s)* 'ankle bone, talus' and, by extension, 'die' (because the earliest Greek dice were made from ankle bones), used in reference both to 'the ankle bone, talus' and to 'dice' in Neo-Greek and Neo-Latin combinations: **astragalocalcanean, astragalomancy, astragaloscaphoid.** Also, **astragal-: astragalar.** Related forms: **osseo-, ossi-, osteo-.**

167 **astro-**   A word-initial combining element, derived from Greek *ástro(n)* 'star,' used in its etymological and extended senses in Neo-Greek combinations: **astrocyte, astrology, astrophysics.** Related form: **star-.**

168 **at-**   A word-initial combining element, derived from Latin *at-*, a combining form of *ad* 'to, toward, near,' appearing in its etymological and extended senses in inherited combinations in which the element to which it is joined begins with *t:* **attempt, attend, attract.** Compare **a-⁵, ac-, ad-, af-, ag-, al-², an-², ap-², ar-, as-.**

169 **ataxia-**   A word-initial combining element, also occurring as a word, derived from Greek *ataxía* 'disorder' (from *a(n)-* 'lacking, without' plus *táx(is)* 'order, arrangement' plus the noun-forming suffix *-ia-*), used in the specialized sense of 'of, pertaining to, or characterized by a lack of coordination' in Neo-Greek combinations: **ataxiadynamia, ataxiagraph, ataxiaphasia.** Also, **atax-, ataxi-, ataxio-, ataxo-: ataxaphasia, ataxiamnesic, ataxiophemia, ataxophobia.** Compare **a-¹** and **taxi-².**

170 **atelo-**   A word-initial combining element, derived from Greek

atel(ḗs) 'without end, imperfect, incomplete' (from *a(n)*- 'without, lacking, un-' plus *tél(os)* 'end, accomplishment' plus the adjective-forming suffix *-ēs*) plus the combining vowel *-o-*, used in the sense of 'incomplete, imperfect' in Neo-Greek combinations: **atelocardia, ateloencephalia, ateloprosopia.** Also, **atel-: atelectasis.** Compare **a-**[1] and **telo-**[1].

171   **athero-**   A word-initial combining element, derived from Greek *athḗr(ē)* 'groats, porridge' plus the combining vowel *-o-*, used in the extended senses of 'of or pertaining to a sebaceous cyst' and 'of or pertaining to arteriosclerosis, the 'thickening' of the arteries' in Neo-Greek combinations: **atherocheuma, atherogenesis, atheronecrosis.** Also, **ather-: atheroma.**

172   **atlanto-**   A word-initial combining element, derived from Greek *Atlas, Atlant(os)* 'Atlas, the god who was assigned the task of bearing the heavens on his shoulders' plus the combining vowel *-o-*, used in the extended sense of 'of or pertaining to that which acts as a support, specifically, the first cervicle vertebra' in biomedical combinations: **atlantoaxial, atlantodidymus, atlantomastoid.** Also, **atlant-, atlo-: atlantal, atlodidymus.**

173   **atmo-**   A word-initial combining element, derived from Greek *atmó(s)* 'smoke, vapor,' used in the sense of 'of or pertaining to vapor, steam' and in the extended sense of 'of or pertaining to air, gas, respiration' in Neo-Greek combinations: **atmocausis, atmograph, atmosphere.** Also, **atm-: atmiatrics.**

174   **atreto-**   A word-initial combining element, derived from Greek *átrēto(s)* 'imperforate,' literally, 'lacking a hole' (from *a(n)*- 'not, lacking, without' plus *trētos* 'bored through, having a hole'), used in its etymological sense in Neo-Greek combinations: **atretocephalus, atretogastria, atretometria.** Also, **atret-: atretopsia.**

175   **atrio-**   A word-initial combining element, derived from Latin *ātri(um)* 'main hall, main room' plus the combining vowel *-o-*, used in the extended sense of 'of or pertaining to the *atrium,* the upper chamber of the heart or the main part of the tympanic chamber' in biomedical terminology: **atrionector, atriotomy, atrioventricular.**

176   **attico-**   A word-initial combining element, derived from English *attic* (which originally meant 'a building's uppermost story enclosed by a decorative architectural structure' (from Latin *Attic(us)* 'Athenian,' the Athenians having been the presumptive originators of this kind of architectural embellishment), then, by extension, 'uppermost floor of a house,' and, by further extension, 'the part of

the tympanum which is located above the atrium') plus the combining vowel -o-, used in this last sense in biomedical terminology: **atticoantrotomy, atticomastoid, atticotomy.** Also, **attic-:** **atticitis.**

177   **audio-**   A word-initial combining element, derived from Latin *audī(re)* 'to hear' plus the combining vowel -o-, used in the sense of 'of or pertaining to hearing' in Neo-Latin and Neo-Greek combinations: **audiology, audiometry, audio-visual.** Also **audi-: audiclave.**

178   **aur-[1]**   A variant of **auri-[1].**

179   **aur-[2]**   A variant of **auri-[2].**

180   **auri-[1]**   A word-initial combining element, derived from Latin *auri(s)* 'ear,' used in its etymological and extended senses, chief among these being 'of or pertaining to hearing,' in Neo-Latin and Neo-Greek combinations: **aurilave, auripuncture, auriscope.** Also, **aur-[1], auro-[1]: aural, aurometer.** Compare **auriculo-.** Related forms: **ear-, oto-.**

181   **auri-[2]**   A word-initial combining element, derived from Latin *aur(um)* 'gold' plus the combining vowel -i-, used in its etymological sense and in the extended sense of 'yellow' in Neo-Latin and Neo-Greek combinations: **auriargentiferous, auriphrygia, aurivorous.** Also, **aur-[2], auro-[2], ori-[2], oro-[2]: auride, aurocephalous, oriole, oroide.**

182   **auriculo-**   A word-initial combining element, derived from Latin *auricul(a)* 'the external ear; the ear' (from *auri(s)* 'ear' plus the diminutive noun-forming suffix *-cula*) plus the combining vowel -o-, used in its etymological sense in biomedical terminology: **auriculocranial, auriculotemporal, auriculoventricular.** Also, **auricul-: auriculid.** Compare **auri-[1].**

183   **auro-[1]**   A variant of **auri-[1].**

184   **auro-[2]**   A variant of **auri-[2].**

185   **Austr-[1]**   A variant of **Austro-[1].**

186   **Austr-[2]**   A variant of **Austro-[2].**

187   **Austro-[1]**   A word-initial combining element, derived from English *Austr(ia)*, an Anglicization of German *Österreich*, literally, 'Eastern Kingdom' (from Old High German *ōstar* 'eastern' plus *rīhhi*

'kingdom', the region in question having been to the east of
Charlemagne's western dominions) plus the combining vowel *-o-*,
used in the sense of 'of or pertaining to Austria' in combination
with other English elements: **Austro-Germanic, Austro-Hungarian,
Austro-Prussian.** Also, **Austr-[1]: Austrasia.** Related form: **eo-.**

188   **Austro-[2]**   A word-initial combining element, derived from Latin
auster, austr(ī) 'south wind' and, by extension, 'south(ern)' plus the
combining vowel *-o-*, used in its etymological and extended senses
in a variety of combinations: **Austro-Asiatic, Austrocolumbia,
Austronesian.** Also, **Austr-[2], austro-: Australia, austromancy.**

189   **auto-[1]**   A word-initial combining element, derived from the Greek
reflexive pronoun *autó(s)*, used in the sense of 'self, native, natural'
in a variety of combinations: **autoanalysis, autoblood, autologous.**
Also, **aut-: autarcesis.** Compare **auto-[2], tauto-.**

190   **auto-[2]**   A word-initial combining element, also occurring as a word,
derived from English *auto(mobile)* (from a combination of Greek
autó(s) 'self' and Latin *mōbil(is), mōbile* 'movable'), used in the
sense of 'automotive' in combination with other English elements:
autobus, autocade, autotruck. Compare **auto-[1].**

191   **aux-**   A variant of **auxo-.**

192   **auxano-**   A word-initial combining element, derived from Greek
auxán(ein) 'to increase, grow' (from *aúxein* 'to increase, grow') plus
the combining vowel *-o-*, used in the sense of 'of or pertaining to
growth' in Neo-Greek combinations: **auxanogram, auxanography,
auxanology.** Compare **auxo-.**

193   **auxo-**   A word-initial combining element, derived from Greek
aúx(ein) 'to increase, grow' plus the combining vowel *-o-*, used in
the sense of 'of or pertaining to growth or acceleration or to that
which stimulates growth or acceleration' in Neo-Greek and Neo-
Latin combinations: **auxocardia, auxodrome, auxoflore.** Also, **aux-,
auxi-: auxesis, auxilytic.** Compare **auxano-.** Related form (?):
waist-.

194   **avi-**   A word-initial combining element, derived from Latin *avi(s)*
'bird,' used in its etymological and extended senses, chief among
these being 'of or pertaining to flight,' in Neo-Latin combinations:
aviation, aviculture, avifauna. Related forms: **egg-, oo-, ovario-,
ovo-.**

195   **axio-**   A word-initial combining element, derived from Latin *axi(s)*

'axle, axis' plus the combining vowel -*o*-, used in the sense of 'of or pertaining to an *axis* or *axon,* the spinal axis of the body or the central conducting portion of a nerve fiber' in Neo-Latin and Neo-Greek combinations: **axiobuccal, axiolemma, axiomesial.** Also, axi-: **axifugal.** Related forms: **ali-, axo-.**

196 axo-   A word-initial combining element, derived from Greek *áxō(n)*, *áxo(nos)* 'axle, axis,' used in the sense of 'of or pertaining to an *axis* or *axon,* the spinal axis of the body or the central conducting portion of a nerve fiber' in Neo-Greek and Neo-Latin combinations: **axodendrite, axofugal, axograph.** Also, **axon-, axono-: axonal, axonotmesis.** Related forms: **ali-, axio-.**

197 azo-   A word-initial combining element, derived from French *azo(te)*, a term coined by Lavoisier to name the element now known as *nitrogen* (N) (from a combination of Greek *a(n)*- 'not, lacking, without' and *zōt(ikós)* 'preserving or giving life'), used in chemical terminology to designate 'the presence of nitrogen or of the group (-N:N-)': **azobenzine, azocarmine, azochloramid.** Also, **azot-, azoto-: azotase, azotometer.** Compare **a-**[1] and **zoo-.**

B

198   **bacci-**   A word-initial combining element, derived from Latin *bacc(a)* 'berry' plus the combining vowel *-i-*, used in its etymological sense in Neo-Latin combinations: **bacciferous, bacciform, baccivorous.**

199   **bacilli-**   A word-initial combining element, derived from Latin *bacill(us)* 'rod, staff' plus the combining vowel *-i-*, used in the extended sense of 'of or pertaining to a *bacillus*, a rod-shaped bacterium' in Neo-Latin and Neo-Greek combinations: **bacillicide, bacilliculture, bacilligenic.** Also, **bacill-, bacillo-: bacillemia, bacillotherapy.** Related form: **bacterio-.**

200   **back-**   A word-initial combining element, also occurring as a word, derived from Old English *bæc* 'hind surface of the human trunk,' used in its etymological and extended senses in combination with other English elements: **backbone, backstroke, back-up.**

201   **bacterio-**   A word-initial combining element, derived from Neo-Latin *bactēri(um)* 'rod-shaped microorganism' (from Greek *baktḗri(on)* '(little) rod, staff') plus the combining vowel *-o-*, used in its Neo-Latin sense in biomedical terminology: **bacterio-erythrin, bacteriogenic, bacteriopexy.** Also, **bacter-, bacteri-: bacteremia, bactericide.** Related form: **bacilli-.**

202   **bad-**   A word-initial combining element, also occurring as a word, derived from Middle English *bad(de)* 'not good,' used in its

39

etymological and extended senses in combination with other English elements: **badlands, badman, bad-mouth.**

203 bag-   A word-initial combining element, also occurring as a word, derived from Middle English *bag(ge)* 'sack,' used in its etymological and extended senses in combination with other English elements: **bagman, bagpipe, bagworm.**

204 balano-   A word-initial combining element, derived from Greek *bálano(s)* 'acorn' and, by extension, 'glans penis,' used in this latter sense in Neo-Greek combinations: **balanoplasty, balanorrhagia, balanorrhea.**

205 ball-   A word-initial combining element, also occurring as a word, derived from Middle English *bal(le)* 'spherical body (used in play)' (cf. Old English *bealluc* 'testicle'), used in its etymological and extended senses in combination with other English elements: **ball-carrier, ballflower, ball-peen (hammer).** Related form: **phallo-.**

206 balneo-   A word-initial combining element, derived from Latin *balne(us)* 'bath' plus the combining vowel *-o-*, used in its etymological sense in Neo-Latin and Neo-Greek combinations: **balneography, balneology, balneotherapy.** Also, **balne-: balneary.**

207 bar-¹   A word-initial combining element, derived from Greek *báro(s)* 'weight,' used in its etymological and extended senses, chief among these being 'of, pertaining to, or composed of *barium,* the element (Ba) (which has a substantial atomic weight)' in Neo-Greek combinations: **baragnosis, baresthesia, barite.** Compare **baro-, bary-.**

208 bar-²   A word-initial combining element, also occurring as a word, derived from Middle English *bar(re)* 'rod (for fastening a gate),' used chiefly in the sense of 'counter (at which alcoholic beverages are offered)' and in extensions of this sense in combination with other English elements: **barfly, barhop, barstool.**

209 bare-   A word-initial combining element, also occurring as a word, derived from Old English *bær* 'naked, uncovered,' used in its etymological and extended senses in combination with other English elements: **bareback, barefaced, bareheaded.**

210 barley-   A word-initial combining element, also occurring as a word, derived from Old English *bærlī(c)* 'of the cereal *Hordeum sativum*' (from *ber(e)* 'the cereal *Hordeum sativum*' plus the adjective-forming suffix *-līc*), used in its etymological and extended senses in combination with other English elements: **barley-bree, barleycorn, barley-sugar.** Compare **barn-**.

211 barn- A word-initial combining element, also occurring as a word, derived from Old English *ber(e)n* 'building in which to store grain' (from *ber(e)* 'barley' plus *(er)n* 'house'), used in its etymological and extended senses in combination with other English elements: **barndoor, barnstorm, barnyard.** Compare **barley.**

212 baro- A word-initial combining element, derived from Greek *báro(s)* 'weight,' used in the sense of 'of or pertaining to weight or pressure' in Neo-Greek combinations: **baroagnosis, barometer, barophilic.** Compare **bar-¹, bary-.**

213 bary- A word-initial combining element, derived from Greek *barý(s)* 'heavy,' used in its etymological sense and in the extended sense of 'difficult, slow' in Neo-Greek combinations: **barycentric, baryesthesia, barythymia.** Compare **bar-¹, baro-.**

214 base- A word-initial combining element, also occurring as a word, derived through Old French from Latin *basis* 'foundation' (from Greek *básis* 'step; foot, i.e., that with which one steps; ground, foundation, i.e., that upon which one steps' (from the verb *baínein* 'to step, go')), used in its Latin and extended senses in combination with other English elements: **baseboard, basecoat, baseline.** Compare **basi-, baso-.**

215 basi- A word-initial combining element, derived from Latin *basi(s)* 'foundation' (from Greek *básis* 'step; foot, i.e., that with which one steps; ground, foundation, i.e., that upon which one steps' (from *baínein* 'to step, go')), used in its Latin and extended senses in Neo-Latin and Neo-Greek combinations: **basicranial, basifacial, basilemma.** Also, **basio-: basioglossus.** Compare **base-, baso-.**

216 baso- A word-initial combining element, derived from Greek *bás(is)* 'step; foot, i.e., that with which one steps; ground, foundation, i.e., that upon which one steps' (from the verb *baínein* 'to step, go') plus the combining vowel *-o-*, used in both the sense of 'step(ping), walk(ing)' and 'fundamental, basic' in Neo-Greek combinations: **basograph, basophilic, basoplasm.** Compare **base-, basi-.** Related form: **come-.**

217 bat- A word-initial combining element, also occurring as a word, derived by alteration of Middle English *backe* 'winged nocturnal mammal resembling a mouse,' used in its etymological and extended senses in combination with other English elements: **batfowl, bat-eared, batwing.**

218 bathy- A word-initial combining element, derived from Greek *bathý(s)* 'deep,' used in its etymological and extended senses in Neo-Greek combinations: **bathycentesis, bathypnea, bathysphere.** Also, **batho-: bathomorphic.**

219 be- A word-initial combining element, derived from Old English *bī* 'by, near,' appearing in its etymological and extended senses (which are many and varied) in inherited combinations: **befoul, behead, bejewel.** Compare **by-.**

220 beach- A word-initial combining element, also occurring as a word, derived from Middle English *bache, baich* 'seashore,' used in its etymological and extended senses in combination with other English elements: **beachcomber, beachhead, beachwear.**

221 bead- A word-initial combining element, also occurring as a word, derived from Middle English *bede* 'prayer' (from Old English *(ġe)bed* 'prayer' (cf. Modern English *bid*)), used (rarely) in its etymological sense and, more commonly, in the extended sense of '(prayer) *bead*, a small, round, perforated object which may be strung together with others to form a rosary, necklace, or the like' in combination with other English elements: **beadeye, beadhouse, beadwork.**

222 bean- A word-initial combining element, also occurring as a word, derived from Old English *bēan* 'seed of certain leguminous plants,' used in its etymological and extended senses in combination with other English elements: **bean-bag, beanfeast, beanpole.**

223 bear- A word-initial combining element, also occurring as a word, derived from Old English *ber(a)* 'quadruped belonging to the genus *Ursus*' (possibly from the same Indo-European root which underlies Modern English *brown*), used in its etymological and extended senses in combination with other English elements: **bearcat, bear-leader, bearskin.** Related form(?): **brown-.**

224 bed- A word-initial combining element, also occurring as a word, derived from Old English *bed(d)* 'couch to accommodate a body asleep or at rest,' used in its etymological and extended senses in combination with other English elements: **bedbug, bedrock, bed-roll.**

225 beef- A word-initial combining element, also occurring as a word, derived through Old French from Latin *bō(s)*, *bov(is)* 'ox, cow,' used in its etymological and extended senses in combination with other English elements: **beefcake, beefsteak, beefwood.** Related forms: **bou-, bov-, cow-.**

226 **bell-**   A word-initial combining element, also occurring as a word, derived from Old English *bell(e)* 'cup-shaped metal instrument which resonates when struck' (akin to Old English *bellan* 'to roar, bellow'), used in its etymological and extended senses in combination with other English elements: **bellhop, bellman, bellwether.**

227 **belly-**   A word-initial combining element, also occurring as a word, derived from Old English *belliġ* 'bag' and, by extension, 'stomach,' used in this latter and extended senses in combination with other English elements: **bellyache, bellybutton, bellyful.**

228 **bene-**   A word-initial combining element, derived from Latin *bene* 'well, good' (from an Indo-European root meaning something on the order of 'do, do well, favor'), appearing in its etymological sense in inherited combinations: **benediction, benefactor, benevolent.** Related form: **dynamo-.**

229 **benz-**   A word-initial combining element, derived from English *benz(oin)* 'aromatic resin obtained from a variety of Javanese tree' (ultimately from Arabic *(lu)bān j(āwi)* 'frankincense of Java'), used in the sense of 'containing (the benzoin-derivative) *benzoic acid* (C_6H_5COOH) or *benzene* (C_6H_6)' in chemical terminology: **benzaldehyde, benzene, benzidine.** Also, **benzo-: benzonitrile.**

230 **beta-** (B, β)   A word-initial combining element, the second letter of the Greek alphabet, used to designate, variously, 'the second member of a series; the carbon atom next to the carbon atom to which the principal group (or its substitute) in a straight chain compound is attached; a carbon atom which is separated by one ring carbon atom from any other carbon atom shared by two rings in a polycyclic compound; a group of atoms in the second of two or more possible positions in a molecule; the second of a number of co-occurring substances of unidentified constitution' in scientific terminology: **beta-brass, beta-naphthol, beta-ray.** See **alpha-.**

231 **between-**   A word-initial combining element, also occurring as a word, derived from Old English *betwēon, betwēon(um)* 'in the middle of two' (from *bī, be* 'by' plus the dative-case form of the word for 'two'), used in its etymological and extended senses in combination with other English elements: **betweenbrain, betweenmaid, betweentimes.** Compare **be-** and **two-.**

232 **bi-¹** A word-initial combining element, derived from Latin *bi-*, a combining form of *bis* 'twice, doubly, double, twofold,' used in its etymological and extended senses in Neo-Latin combinations: **bicameral, biennial, bigeminy.** Compare **bin-, bis-.** Related forms: **di-¹, dicho-, diplo-, dis-¹, double-, dui-, duo-, twelve-, twi-, twin-, two-.**

233 **bi-²** A variant of **bio-.**

234 **biblio-** A word-initial combining element, derived from Greek *biblío(n)* 'book,' used in its etymological and extended senses in Neo-Greek combinations: **bibliomancy, bibliophile, bibliopole.**

235 **big-** A word-initial combining element, also occurring as a word, derived from Middle English *big(ge)* 'large,' used in its etymological and extended senses in combination with other English elements: **bighead, big-name, bigwig.**

236 **bilharzi-** A word-initial combining element, derived from Scientific Latin *Bilharzi(a)* 'genus of flukes now known as *Schistosoma*' (from (*Theodor Maximilian*) *Bilharz* plus the genus-naming suffix *-ia*), used in the sense of 'relating to or caused by *Bilharzia* (*Schistosoma*)' in Neo-Latin and Neo-Greek combinations: **bilharzial, bilharzioma, bilharziosis.** Also, **bilharz-: bilharziasis.**

237 **bili-** A word-initial combining element, derived from Latin *bili(s)* 'bile,' used in its etymological and extended senses in Neo-Latin and Neo-Greek combinations: **biliary, bilirubin, bilitherapy.**

238 **bin-** A word-initial combining element, derived from Latin *bīn(ī)* 'two (together), two by two, double, pair(ed),' used in its etymological and extended senses in Neo-Latin and Neo-Greek combinations: **binauricular, biniodide, binophthalmoscope.** Also, **bino-: binoscope.** Compare **bi-¹, bis-.** Related forms: **di-¹, dicho-, diplo-, dis-¹, dui-, duo-, twelve-, twi-, twin-, two-.**

239 **bio-** A word-initial combining element, derived from Greek *bío(s)* 'life,' used in its etymological and extended senses in a variety of combinations: **bio-assay, biogenesis, biomutation.** Also, **bi-²: biorgan.** Related forms: **quick-, vita-¹, vivi-, zoo-.**

240 **bird-** A word-initial combining element, also occurring as a word, derived from Old English *brid(d)* 'chick, young bird,' used in its etymological and extended senses in combination with other English elements: **birdbath, birdbrain, bird-dog.** Compare **bird's-.**

241 **bird's-** A word-initial combining element, the possessive form of the English noun *bird* (from Old English *brid(d)* 'chick, young bird' plus the singular genitive-case ending), used chiefly in extensions of its etymological sense in combination with other English elements: **bird's-eye, bird's-foot, bird's-mouth.** Compare **bird-.**

242 birth-   A word-initial combining element, also occurring as a word, derived through Middle English from Old Norse *byrth* 'nativity, descent,' used in its etymological sense in combination with other English elements: **birthday, birthright, birthstone.** Related form: **phoro-.**

243 bis-   A word-initial combining element, derived from Latin *bis* 'twice, doubly, double, twofold,' used in its etymological and extended senses in Neo-Latin and Neo-Greek combinations: **bisacromial, bisferious, bishydroxycoumarin.** Compare **bi-¹, bin-.** Related forms: **di-¹, dicho-, diplo-, dis-¹, dui-, duo-, twelve-, twi-, twin-, two-.**

244 bismuth-   A word-initial combining element, also occurring as a word, derived from Georg Agricola's 1530 Latinization of German *Wismut(h)* 'the metallic element (Bi),' *bis(e)mūt(h)(um),* used in its etymological sense in biochemical terminology: **bismuthic, bismuthine, bismuthosis.** Also, **bismut-, bismutho-, bismuto-: bismutite, bismuthotartrate, bismutosphaerite.**

245 bite-   A word-initial combining element, also occurring as a word, derived from Old English *bīt(an)* 'to seize with the teeth,' used chiefly in extensions of this sense in combination with other English elements in the terminology of dentistry: **bitegage, bitelock, bite-wing.** Compare **bitter-.**

246 bitter-   A word-initial combining element, derived from Old English *biter* 'biting,' hence, 'harsh, acrid,' used in these latter and extended senses in combination with other English elements: **bitterender, bitternut, bittersweet.** Compare **bite-.**

247 black-   A word-initial combining element, also occurring as a word, derived from Old English *blæc* 'inky; the opposite of white,' used in its etymological and extended senses in combination with other English elements: **blackball, blackberry, blackout.** Related forms: **blue-, flame-, flavo-, phlogo-.**

248 blasto-   A word-initial combining element, derived from Greek *blastó(s)* 'bud, shoot, germ,' used in its etymological and extended senses, chief among these being 'of or pertaining to an embryonic or germinal stage of development' in Neo-Greek combinations: **blastoderm, blastogenic, blastolysis.** Also, **blast-: blastema.**

249 **blenno-** A word-initial combining element, derived from Greek *blénn(a)* 'phlegm, mucus' plus the combining vowel *-o-*, used in its etymological sense in Neo-Greek combinations: **blennorrhagia, blennorrhea, blennothorax.** Also, **blenn-: blennadenitis.**

250 **blepharo-** A word-initial combining element, derived from Greek *blépharo(n)* 'eyelid,' used in the sense of 'of or pertaining to the eyelid(s) or eyelash(es)' in Neo-Greek combinations: **blepharoadenoma, blepharochalasis, blepharospasm.** Also, **blephar-: blepharitis.**

251 **block-** A word-initial combining element, also occurring as a word, derived from Middle English *blok* 'solid mass of wood,' used in its etymological and extended senses in combination with other English elements: **blockade, blockbuster, blockhead.**

252 **blood-** A word-initial combining element, also occurring as a word, derived from Old English *blōd* 'the fluid that circulates through the cardiovascular system in living animals,' used in its etymological and extended senses in combination with other English elements: **bloodflower, bloodline, bloodsucker.**

253 **blow-** A word-initial combining element, also occurring as a word, derived from Old English *blāw(an)* 'to produce a current of air,' used in its etymological and extended senses in combination with other English elements: **blowball, blowfish, blow-hard.**

254 **blue-** A word-initial combining element, also occurring as a word, derived through Middle English from Old French *bleu(e)* 'the primary color that contrasts with red and yellow,' used in its etymological and extended senses in combination with other English elements: **blueberry, blue-chip, bluegrass.** Related forms: **black-, flame-, flavo-, phlogo-.**

255 **boat-** A word-initial combining element, also occurring as a word, derived from Old English *bāt* 'small sea-going vessel,' used in its etymological and extended senses in combination with other English elements: **boatbill, boatload, boatswain.**

256 **body-** A word-initial combining element, also occurring as a word, derived from Old English *bodi(g)* 'frame of a creature,' used in its etymological and extended senses in combination with other English elements: **bodycheck, bodyguard, bodywork.**

257 **bolo-** A word-initial combining element, derived from Greek *bol(is)* 'a throw; that which is thrown' and, by extension, 'a ray (of light' (from the verb *bállein* 'to throw') plus the combining vowel *-o-*, used in this last and extended senses in Neo-Greek combinations: **bolograph, bolometer, boloscope.**

258 **bomb-** A word-initial combining element, also occurring as a word, derived, ultimately, from Greek *bómb(os)* 'booming, buzzing, humming sound,' used in the extended sense of 'explosive device' in combination with other English elements: **bombload, bombproof, bombshell.**

259 **bond-** A word-initial combining element, formerly occurring as a word, derived from Middle English *bond(e)* 'serf' (from Old English *bōnd(a)* 'householder' (from an Indo-European root meaning 'exist, grow')), appearing in the sense of '(in) servitude, serfdom' and in extensions of this sense in a handful of inherited combinations: **bondland, bondmaid, bondservant.** Related forms: **phylo-, physali-, physico-, physio-, phyto-.**

260 **bone-** A word-initial combining element, also occurring as a word, derived from Old English *bān* 'the material of the skeleton of most vertebrates,' used in its etymological and extended senses in combination with other English elements: **bonehead, bonesetter, boneyard.**

261 **book-** A word-initial combining element, also occurring as a word, derived from Old English *bōc* 'written document' (from the Proto-Germanic form which underlies Modern English *beech*, it having been an early practice to inscribe runes on beech tablets), used in its etymological and extended senses in combination with other English elements: **bookbinder, bookmaker, bookworm.**

262 **boot-** A word-initial combining element, also occurring as a word, derived from Old French *bot(e)* 'covering for the foot and lower leg,' used in its etymological and extended senses in combination with other English elements: **bootjack, bootleg, boottopping.**

263 **boro-** A word-initial combining element, derived from English *boro(n)* 'the nonmetallic element (B)' (from *bor(ax)* plus *(carb)on)*, used in its etymological sense in chemical terminology: **boroglyceride, borohydride, borosilicate.** Also, **bor-: boride.**

264 **botano-** A word-initial combining element, derived from Greek *botán(ē)* 'grass, herb, plant, fodder' plus the combining vowel *-o-*, used in the sense of 'of or pertaining to plant life' in Neo-Greek

and Neo-Latin combinations: **botanology, botanomancy, botanophily.** Also, **botan-: botanist.**

265 **bothr-** A word-initial combining element, derived from Greek *bóthr(os)* 'pit, ditch,' used in the sense of 'pitted, grooved' in Neo-Greek combinations: **bothrenchyma, bothridium, Bothrops.**

266 **botryo-** A word-initial combining element, derived from Greek *bótry(s)* 'cluster of grapes' plus the combining vowel *-o-,* used in its etymological and extended senses in Neo-Greek combinations: **botryogen, botryomycosis, botryotherapy.** Also, **botry-: botryose.**

267 **bou-** A word-initial combining element, derived from Greek *boû(s)* 'cow, ox,' used in its etymological and extended senses in Neo-Greek combinations: **boulemia, bouphonia, boustrophedon.** Also, **bu-: bulemia.** Related forms: **beef-, bov-, cow-.**

268 **bov-** A word-initial combining element, derived from Latin *bō(s), bov(is)* 'ox, cow,' used in its etymological and extended senses in Neo-Latin combinations: **bovid, bovine, Bovril.** Also, **bovi-, bovo-: boviculture, bovovaccination.** Related forms: **beef-, bou-, cow-.**

269 **bow-[1]** A word-initial combining element, also occurring as a word, derived from Old English *bo(ga)* 'arch; rainbow; curved strung device for shooting arrows,' used in this last and extended senses in combination with other English elements: **bowdrill, bowknot, bowstring.**

270 **bow-[2]** A word-initial combining element, also occurring as a word, derived from either Low German *bo(og)* or Dutch *bo(eg)* 'forward end of a boat' (originally, 'limb, shoulder'), used in its etymological sense in combination with other English elements: **bowgrace, bowman, bowsprit.**

271 **box-** A word-initial combining element, also occurring as a word, derived through Old English from Latin *bux(is)* 'lidded or otherwise covered container made of wood' (cf. Latin *buxus* 'box-tree, boxwood'), used in its etymological and extended senses in combination with other English elements: **boxcar, boxhead, box-spring.**

272 **brachio-** A word-initial combining element, derived from Greek *brachiō(n)* 'arm' (originally, apparently, 'upper, shorter part of the arm' (cf. Greek *brachýs* 'short')), used in its etymological and extended senses in Neo-Greek and Neo-Latin combinations: **brachiocrural, brachiocyrtosis, brachiopod.** Also, **brachi-: brachialgia.** Related forms: **brachy-, brevi-, merry-(?).**

273   **brachy-**   A word-initial combining element, derived from Greek *brachý(s)* 'small, short,' used in the sense of 'abnormally small, short' in Neo-Greek combinations: **brachybasia, brachydactylia, brachymorphic.** Related forms: **brachio-, brevi-, merry-(?).**

274   **brady-**   A word-initial combining element, derived from Greek *bradý(s)* 'slow, heavy,' used in the sense of 'abnormally slow' in Neo-Greek combinations: **bradycardia, bradycrotic, bradylexia.**

275   **brain-**   A word-initial combining element, also occurring as a word, derived from Old English *bræ(ge)n* 'mass of nervous tissue contained in the cranium,' used in its etymological and extended senses in combination with other English elements: **brainchild, brainpan, brainwash.**

276   **branchio-**   A word-initial combining element, derived from Greek *bránchi(a)* 'gills' plus the combining vowel *-o-*, used in its etymological and extended senses in Neo-Greek and Neo-Latin combinations: **branchiogenous, branchiopneustic, branchiostegal.** Also, **branchi-: branchiform.**

277   **bread-**   A word-initial combining element, also occurring as a word, derived from Old English *brēad* 'fragment, morsel (of food)' and, by extension, 'a food made by baking dough,' used in this latter and extended senses in combination with other English elements: **breadbasket, breadboard, breadfruit.**

278   **break-**   A word-initial combining element, also occurring as a word, derived from Old English *brec(an)* 'to fragment,' used in its etymological and extended senses in combination with other English elements: **breakdown, breakthrough, breakwater.**

279   **breast-**   A word-initial combining element, also occurring as a word, derived from Old English *brēost* 'anterior surface of the chest,' used in its etymological and extended senses in combination with other English elements: **breastbone, breast-feed, breast-hook.**

280   **breech-**   A word-initial combining element, also occurring as a word, derived from Old English *brēc* 'trousers,' used in the extended sense of 'covering of the lower part of the body; lower (hind) part of the body; hind part of something, esp. a gun' in combination with other English elements: **breechblock, breechcloth, breechloader.**

281   **brepho-**   A word-initial combining element, derived from Greek *brépho(s)* 'fetus; infant,' used in the sense of 'of or pertaining to an

embryo, infant, or early stage of development' in Neo-Greek combinations: **brephoplastic, brephopolyscaria, brephotrophic.** Also, **breph-: brephic.**

282 **brevi-**   A word-initial combining element, derived from Latin *brevi(s)* 'short,' used in its etymological sense in Neo-Latin combinations: **brevicaudate, brevicollis, brevipennate.** Related forms: **brachio-, brachy-**.

283 **bridge-**   A word-initial combining element, also occurring as a word, derived from Old English *brycg* 'structure allowing passage over an obstacle which it spans,' used in its etymological and extended senses in combination with other English elements: **bridgehead, bridgeman, bridgework.**

284 **broad-**   A word-initial combining element, also occurring as a word, derived from Old English *brād* 'wide,' used in its etymological and extended senses in combination with other English elements: **broadax, broadband, broadside.**

285 **bromato-**   A word-initial combining element, derived from Greek *brôma, brômat(os)* 'food' (from the verb *(bi)brô(skein)* 'to eat' plus the noun-forming suffix *-ma* plus the combining vowel *-o-*, used in its etymological sense in Neo-Greek combinations: **bromatology, bromatotherapy, bromatotoxin.** Also, **broma-: bromatherapy.**

286 **bromo-[1]**   A word-initial combining element, derived from Greek *brômo(s)* 'stench, stink,' used in the sense of 'unpleasant (bodily) odor' in Neo-Greek combinations: **bromohyperhidrosis, bromomenorrhea, bromopnea.** Also, **brom-[1]: bromidrosis.** Compare **bromo-[2].**

287 **bromo-[2]**   A word-initial combining element, derived from English *brom(ine)* 'the (extremely unpleasant-smelling) element (Br)' (from Greek *brôm(os)* 'stench, stink' plus the suffix *-ine* which is used in naming (usually basic) chemical substances) plus the combining vowel *-o-*, used in the sense of 'of, pertaining to, containing, or derived from *bromine*' in chemical terminology: **bromobenzylcyanide, bromomethylethyl, bromophenol.** Also, **brom-[2]: bromacetone.** Compare **bromo-[1].**

288 **bronch-**   A variant of **broncho-.**

289 **bronchi-**   A variant of **broncho-.**

290 **bronchio-**   a variant of **broncho-.**

291   **bronchiol-**   A word-initial combining element, derived from Neo-Latin *bronchi(um)* 'ramification of a *bronchus,* one of the two main branches of the trachea' (from Greek *brónchos* 'windpipe') plus the diminutive noun-forming suffix *-ol(us),* used in the sense of 'of or pertaining to a small end branch or end branches of the bronchia' in biomedical terminology: **bronchiolar, bronchiolectasis, bronchiolitis.** Compare **broncho-.**

292   **broncho-**   A word-initial combining element, derived from Greek *bróncho(s)* 'windpipe,' used in the sense of 'of or pertaining to the two main branches of the trachea or to their various ramifications, or both' in biomedical terminology: **bronchoclysis, bronchomotor, bronchospasm.** Also, **bronch-, bronchi-, bronchio-: bronchadenitis, bronchiarctia, bronchiospasm.** Compare **bronchiol-.**

293   **bronto-**   A word-initial combining element, derived from Greek *bront(ḗ)* 'thunder' plus the combining vowel *-o-,* used in its etymological and extended senses in Neo-Greek combinations: **brontology, brontophobia, Brontosaurus.**

294   **broom-**   A word-initial combining element, also occurring as a word, derived, ultimately, from Old English *brōm* 'broom plant (*Cytisus scoparius*),' whence Middle English *brom(e)* 'sweeping device (made from the twigs of the *Cytisus scoparius*),' used in both its Old and Middle English senses in combination with other English elements: **broomcorn, broomrape, broomsquire.**

295   **brown-**   A word-initial combining element, also occurring as a word, derived from Old English *brūn* 'the color produced by mixing orange and black,' used in its etymological and extended senses in combination with other English elements: **brownie, brown-nose, brownout.** Related form(?): **bear-.**

296   **brush-**   A word-initial combining element, also occurring as a word, derived from the crossing of two related Old French words, *bro(i)sse* 'device for sweeping or scrubbing' and *broce* 'dense undergrowth (suitable for making a sweeping or scrubbing device)', used in its etymological and extended senses in combination with other English elements: **brush-off, brushup, brushwood.**

297   **bryo-**   A word-initial combining element, derived from Greek *brýo(n)* 'moss; clustering (male) blossom; blossom' (from *brýein* 'to be full, swell, bloom, cause to burst forth'), used chiefly in the sense of 'of or pertaining to moss' in Neo-Greek combinations: **bryology, bryophyte, bryozoan.** Compare **embryo-.**

298 **bu-** A variant of **bou-**.

299 **bucco-** A word-initial combining element, derived from Latin *bucc(a)* 'cheek' and, by extension in Proto-Romance, 'mouth' plus the combining vowel *-o-*, used in both of these senses in biomedical terminology: **buccoaxial, buccolabial, buccopharyngeal.**

300 **buck-** A word-initial combining element, also occurring as a word, derived from the crossing of Old English *buc* 'male deer' and *buc(ca)* 'he-goat,' used chiefly in the former and extended senses in combination with other English elements: **buckeye, buckshot, bucktooth.**

301 **bufo-** A word-initial combining element, derived from Latin *būfō* 'toad,' used in its etymological and extended senses in Neo-Latin and Neo-Greek combinations: **bufotherapy, bufothionine, bufotoxin.**

302 **bug-** A word-initial combining element of obscure origin, also occurring as a word, used in the sense of 'small insect' and in extensions of this sense in combination with other English elements: **bugbane, bug-eyed, bugseed.**

303 **bulbo-** A word-initial combining element, derived through Latin from Greek *bolbó(s)* 'onion, bulbous root, bulb,' used in the sense of 'bulb, bulb-shaped mass' in Neo-Greek and Neo-Latin combinations: **bulboatrial, bulbocavernous, bulbourethral.**

304 **bull-** A word-initial combining element, also occurring as a word, derived from Old English *bul(a)* 'male of the bovine family,' used in its etymological and extended senses in combination with other English elements: **bullbat, bulldog, bullhead.**

305 **bur-** A word-initial combining element, also occurring as a word, derived from Middle English *bur(re)* 'prickly seed case of certain plants,' used in its etymological and extended senses in combination with other English elements: **burdock, burstone, burweed.**

306 **burso-** A word-initial combining element, derived from Latin *burs(a)* 'bag, pouch, purse' (from Greek *býrsa* 'animal hide, leather') plus the combining vowel *-o-*, used chiefly in the specialized sense of 'of or pertaining to a synovial sac' in biomedical terminology: **bursolith, bursopathy, bursotomy.** Also, **burs-: bursitis.**

307 **bush-** A word-initial combining element, also occurring as a word, derived from Middle English *bu(s)sh(e)* 'shrub,' used in its etymological and extended senses in combination with other English elements: **bushbuck, bush-league, bushranger.**

308 **but-** A word-initial combining element, derived through Latin from Greek *b(o)út(yron)* 'butter' (from *boû(s)* 'ox, cow' plus *tyró(s)* 'cheese'), used in the specialized sense of 'containing or derived from *butyric* acid (which is typically found in rancid butter)' in chemical terminology: **butane, butethal, butyl.** Compare **butter-, butyro-.**

309 **butter-** A word-initial combining element, also occurring as a word, derived through Latin from Greek *b(o)útyr(on)* 'fatty milk solid' (from *boû(s)* 'ox, cow' plus *tyró(s)* 'cheese'), used in its etymological and extended senses in combination with other English elements: **buttercup, butterfly, buttermilk.** Compare **but-, butyro-.**

310 **butyro-** A word-initial combining element, derived through Latin from Greek *b(o)útyro(n)* 'butter' (from *boû(s)* 'ox, cow' plus *tyró(s)* 'cheese'), used in its etymological and extended senses in Neo-Greek combinations: **butyromel, butyrometer, butyroscope.** Also, **butyr-: butyric.** Compare **bou-, tyro-.**

311 **by-** A word-initial combining element, also occurring as a word, derived from Old English *bī* 'alongside, according to,' used in its etymological and extended senses in combination with other English elements: **bygone, bylaw, by-line.** Also, **bye-: bye-election.** Related form: **be-.**

312 **bysso-** A word-initial combining element, derived from Greek *býsso(s)* 'flax,' used in its etymological and extended senses in Neo-Greek and Neo-Latin combinations: **byssocausis, byssolite, byssophthisis.** Also, **biss-: bissaceous.**

C

313 **caco-** A word-initial combining element, derived from Greek *kakó*(*s*) 'bad,' used in its etymological and extended senses in Neo-Greek combinations: **cacoethic, cacography, cacology**. Also, **cac-, kak-, kako-: cacexia, kakergasia, kakotrophy**.

314 **caeco-** A variant of **ceco-**.

315 **caeno-** A variant of **ceno-¹**.

316 **caino-** A variant of **ceno-¹**.

317 **calcaneo-** A word-initial combining element, derived from Latin *calcāne*(*um*) 'heel' (from *cal*(*x*), *calc*(*is*) 'heel' plus the adjective-forming suffix *-āneum*) plus the combining vowel *-o-*, used in the sense of 'of or pertaining to the heel bone' and, by extension, 'of or pertaining to clubfoot (in which only the heel touches the ground)' in biomedical terminology: **calcaneo-astragaloid, calcaneofibular, calcaneovalgocavus**. Also, **calcane-: calcaneitis**. Compare **calcar-¹, calce-**.

318 **calcar-¹** A word-initial combining element, also occurring as a word, derived from Latin *calcar* 'spur' (from *cal*(*x*), *calc*(*is*) 'heel' plus the noun-forming suffix *-ar*), used in its etymological and extended senses in Neo-Latin combinations: **calcarate, calcarine**. Also, **calcari-¹: calcariform**. Compare **calcaneo-, calce-**.

55

319   calcar-²   A variant of **calcareo-**.

320   calcareo-   A word-initial combining element, derived from Latin *calcāri(us)* 'of or pertaining to lime' (from *cal(x)*, *calc(is)* 'lime, limestone' plus the adjective-forming suffix *-ārius*) plus the combining vowel *-o-*, used in its etymological and extended senses, chief among these being 'of, pertaining to, or containing *calcium* (Ca) (which is a basic component of lime),' in Neo-Latin and Neo-Greek combinations: **calcareo-argillaceous, calcareobituminous, calcareosiliceous**. Also, **calcar-², calcare-, calcari-²: calcaroid, calcareous, calcariferous**. Compare **calci-**.

321   calce-   A word-initial combining element, derived from Latin *calce(us)* 'shoe' (from *cal(x)*, *calc(is)* 'heel' plus the adjective-forming suffix *-eus*), used in the sense of '(resembling a) shoe, slipper' in Neo-Latin combinations (generally with the combining vowel *-i-* or *-o-*): **calceamentum, calceiform, calceolate**. Compare **calcaneo-, calcar-¹**.

322   calci-   A word-initial combining element, derived from Latin *cal(x)*, *calc(is)* 'lime, limestone' plus the combining vowel *-i-*, used in its etymological and extended senses, chief among these being 'of, pertaining to, or containing *calcium* (Ca) (which is a basic component of lime),' in Neo-Latin and Neo-Greek combinations: **calcigerous, calciphilia, calciprivia**. Also, **calc-, calcio-, calco-: calcemia, calciotropisim, calcoglobule**. Compare **calcareo-, chalk-¹**.

323   cale-   A variant of **calori-**.

324   cali-¹   A variant of **calli-**.

325   cali-²   A variant of **calyc-**.

326   call-   A word-initial combining element, also occurring as a word, derived from Middle English *call(en)* 'to cry out, summon by crying out,' used in its etymological and extended senses in combination with other English elements: **call-board, callboy, callfire**.

327   calli-   A word-initial combining element, derived from Greek *kalli-*, a combining form of *kalós* 'beautiful' (cf. *kállos* 'beauty'), used in its etymological and extended senses in inherited and Neo-Greek combinations: **calligraphy, calliopsis, callipygian**. Also, **cali-¹, callo-, calo-¹: caligraphy, callomania, calotype**.

328   callo-   A variant of **calli-**.

329 **calo-¹** A variant of **calli-**.

330 **calo-²** A variant of **calori-**.

331 **calori-** A word-initial combining element, derived from Latin *calor, calōr(is)* 'heat' plus the combining vowel *-i-*, used in its etymological and extended senses in Neo-Latin and Neo-Greek combinations: **calorigenic, calorimeter, caloripuncture**. Also, **cale-, calo-², calor-**: **calefaction, caloreceprot, calorose**.

332 **calyc-** A word-initial combining element, derived from Greek *kály(x), kályk(os)* 'shell; husk; cup (of a flower),' used chiefly in the specialized senses of 'of or pertaining to a cup-shaped bodily organ or cavity) and 'cup-shaped ring of sepals encasing a flower bud' in Neo-Greek and Neo-Latin combinations: **calycanthemy, calycectomy, calycine**. Also, **calyci, cali-²**: **calyciform, caliectasis**.

333 **calypto-** A word-initial combining element, derived from Greek *kalyptó(s)* 'covered, hidden' (from *kalýptein* 'to cover, hide'), used in its etymological and extended senses in Neo-Greek combinations: **calyptoblastic, calyptobranchiate, calyptomerous**.

334 **camber-** A word-initial combining element, also occurring as a word, derived from dialectal Old French *cambre* 'arch(ed), curve(d)' (either from Latin *camera* 'vault, arched roof, arch' (from Greek *kamára* 'anything with a vaulted or arched covering') or from Latin *camurus* 'bent, crooked, turned inward' (of obscure origin)), used in its Old French and extended senses in combination with other English elements: **camber-beam, camber-keeled, camber-slip**. Compare **camera-, chamber-**.

335 **camel-** A word-initial combining element, also occurring as a word, derived, ultimately, from one of the Semitic languages (cf. Hebrew *gāmāl* 'ruminant of the family *Camelidae*'), used in its etymological and extended senses in combination with other English elements: **camelback, camelbird, camel-grass**. Also, **camelo-**: **camelopard**.

336 **cameo-** A word-initial combining element, also occurring as a word, derived from Late Latin *cam(m)oe(us), cama(h)u(tus)* 'engraving in relief on a stone, usually of differently colored layers' (of obscure origin), used in its etymological and extended senses in combination with other English elements: **cameoglass, cameopress, cameoware**.

337 **camera-** A word-initial combining element, also occurring as a word, derived from Neo-Latin *camera (obscura)* 'light-free device

used for recording photographic images,' literally, '(dark) chamber,' used in the sense of 'of or pertaining to a device for recording photographic images' and extensions of this sense in combination with other English elements: **cameraman, camera-ready, camera-shy.** Compare **camber-, chamber-.**

338   **camp-**   A word-initial combining element, also occurring as a word, derived from Latin *camp(us)* 'field' and, by extension, 'field of military action,' used in its etymological and extended senses in combination with other English elements: **campfire, camp-follower, campsite.** Also, **campi-: campimeter.**

339   **camphor-**   A word-initial combining element, also occurring as a word, derived from Late Latin *camphor(a)* 'the (white) substance $(C_{10}H_{16}O)$' (through Arabic from Malay *kāpūr* 'chalk'), used in its Late Latin and extended senses in a variety of combinations: **camphorate, camphoronic, camphorweed.** Also, **camph-, campho-: camphene, camphopyrazolon.**

340   **campo-[1]**   A word-initial combining element, derived from Greek *kamp(ḗ)* 'caterpillar' (from a Greek root meaning 'bend, curve') plus the combining vowel *-o-*, used in its etymological sense chiefly in Linnaean nomenclature: **campophagine, Campophilus, Campostoma.** Compare **campto-, campylo-.**

341   **campo-[2]**   A variant of **campto-.**

342   **campto-**   A word-initial combining element, derived from Greek *kamptó(s)* 'bent, curved' (from *kámptein* 'to bend, curve'), used in its etymological and extended senses in Neo-Greek combinations: **camptocormia, camptodactylia, camptospasm.** Also, **campo-[2]: campospasm.** Compare **campo-[1], campylo-.**

343   **campylo-**   A word-initial combining element, derived from Greek *kampýlo(s)* 'crooked, bent,' used in its etymological and extended senses in Neo-Greek combinations: **campylognathia, campylometer, campylotropal.** Compare **campo-[1], campto-.**

344   **cancer-**   A word-initial combining element, also occurring as a word, derived from Latin *canc(e)r, cancr(ī)* 'crab' and, by extension, 'malignant tumor (the swollen veins surrounding which, according to Galen, resemble the legs of a crab),' used in its etymological and extended senses in a variety of combinations: **cancerite, cancer-mushroom, cancerphobia.** Also, **canceri-, cancero-, cancri-, cancro-: cancericidal, canceroderm, cancriform, cancrocirrhosis.** Compare **chancr-.** Related forms: **carcino-, hard-, karyo-.**

345   **candle-**   A word-initial combining element, also occurring as a word, derived from Latin *candēl(a)* 'taper,' used in its etymological and extended senses in combination with other English elements: **candlebeam, candleberry, candlepin.**

346   **cane-**   A word-initial combining element, also occurring as a word, derived, ultimately, from one of the Semitic languages (cf. Hebrew *qāneh* 'reed'), used in the sense of 'woody stem (as of a large reed)' and in extensions of this sense in combination with other English elements: **canebrake, cane-killer, canework.**

347   **cannab-**   A word-initial combining element, derived from Greek *kánnab(is)* 'hemp,' used in its etymological and extended senses, chief among these being 'of or pertaining to hemp's chemical components or derivatives,' in ·biochemical terminology: **cannabene, cannabine, cannabism.** Also, **cannabi-: cannabitetanine.**

348   **cant-**   A word-initial combining element, also occurring as a word, derived through Latin from Greek *kánth(os)* 'corner of the eye,' used in the extended sense of 'angle(d), slant(ed)' in combination with other English elements: **cant-hook, cant-fall, cant-timber.** Compare **cantho-.**

349   **cantho-**   A word-initial combining element, derived from Greek *kántho(s)* 'corner of the eye,' used in its etymological sense in Neo-Greek combinations: **cantholysis, canthoplasty, canthotomy.** Also, **canth-: canthectomy.** Compare **cant-.**

350   **capillar-**   A word-initial combining element, derived from Latin *capillār(is)* 'of, pertaining to, or resembling hair' (from *capill(us)* 'hair (of the head)' plus the adjective-forming suffix *-āris*), used in its etymological and extended senses, chief among these being 'of or pertaining to *capillaries,* minute (hairlike) blood vessels that connect the arterioles and the venules,' in Neo-Latin and Neo-Greek combinations: **capillarectasia, capillaritis, capillarity.** Also, **capillario-, capillaro-: capillariomotor, capillaroscopy.** Compare **capilli-.**

351   **capilli-**   A word-initial combining element, derived from Latin *capill(us)* 'hair (of the head)' (possibly from *caput, capit(is)* 'head') plus the combining vowel *-i-,* used in its etymological and extended senses in Neo-Latin combinations: **capilliculture, capillifolious, capilliform.** Compare **capillar-.** Related forms(?): **capit-, head-, scape-.**

352   **capit-**   A word-initial combining element, derived from Latin *caput,*

capit(is) 'head,' used in its etymological and extended senses in inherited and Neo-Latin combinations, generally with the combining vowel *-i-* or *-o-:* **capital, capitibranchiate, capitopedal.** Related forms: **capillar-(?), capilli-(?), head-, scape-.**

353   capno-   A word-initial combining element, derived from Greek *kapnó(s)* 'smoke, vapor,' used in its etymological and extended senses in Neo-Greek combinations: **capnomancy, capnomor, capnophilic.**

354   capri-   A word-initial combining element, derived from Latin *cap(e)r, capr(ī)* 'goat' plus the combining vowel *-i-,* used in its etymological and extended senses in inherited and Neo-Latin combinations: **capricious, Capricorn, caprigenous.** Also, **capr-: capric.**

355   capsulo-   A word-initial combining element, derived from Scientific Latin *capsul(a)* 'enveloping structure' (from Latin *caps(a)* 'box' plus the diminutive suffix *-ula*) plus the combining vowel *-o-,* used in its Scientific Latin sense in biomedical terminology: **capsulolenticular, capsuloplasty, capsulorrhaphy.** Also, **capsul-: capsulitis.** Compare **case-², cash-.**

356   Car-   A word-initial combining element, derived from Welsh *ca(e)r* 'castle, (walled) city,' appearing in its etymological and extended senses in a number of Anglo-Welsh place names: **Cardiff, Carlisle, Carnarvon.** Also, **Caer-: Caerleon.**

357   car-   A word-initial combining element, also occurring as a word, derived, ultimately, from one of the Celtic languages (cf. Old Irish *carr* 'wheeled vehicle') through Latin *car(rus)* 'wagon,' used in the sense of 'wheeled vehicle, esp. an automobile or train' in combination with other English elements: **carload, carman, carport.** Compare **carry-.**

358   carbo-   A word-initial combining element, derived from Latin *carbō, carbō(nis)* 'charcoal,' used chiefly in the extended sense of 'of, pertaining to, or containing the element *carbon* (C) (which appears in its nearly pure form in charcoal)' in biochemical terminology: **carbocyclic, carbogen, carbohydrate.** Also, **carb-, carbon-, carbono-: carbamide, carbonuria, carbonometer.** Compare **carbol-.**

359   carbol-   A word-initial combining element, derived from Latin *carbō* 'charcoal' and, by extension, 'the element *carbon* (C)' plus the suffix *-ol* (from Latin *ol(eum)* 'oil') which is used in chemical terminology in naming oils or oillike substances, used in the sense of 'of, pertaining to, or containing *phenol* (otherwise known as *carbolic acid*)' in biochemical terminology: **carbolfuchsin, carbolism, carbollysoform**. Compare **carbo-, oleo-**.

360   **carcino-**   A word-initial combining element, derived from Greek *karkíno(s)* 'crab,' used chiefly in the extended sense of 'malignant tumor (the swollen veins surrounding which, according to Galen, resemble the legs of a crab)' in Neo-Greek combinations: **carcinogenic, carcinology, carcinolysin**. Also, **carcin-: carcinemia**. Related forms: **cancer-, chancr-, hard-, karyo-**.

361   **card-**   A word-initial combining element, also occurring as a word, derived through Middle English *card(e)* 'small rectangular piece of pasteboard used in playing games' from Greek *chárt(ēs)* 'piece of papyrus, paper,' used in its Middle English and extended senses in combination with other English elements: **cardboard, card-carrying, cardsharp**. Compare **carto-**.

362   **cardio-**   A word-initial combining element, derived from Greek *kardi(a)* 'heart' plus the combining vowel *-o-*, used in its etymological and extended senses in Neo-Greek and Neo-Latin combinations: **cardio-accelerator, cardiocentesis, cardiokinetic**. Also, **card-, cardi-: carditis, cardialgia**. Related forms: **cordate-, core-[1], heart-**.

363   **care-**   A word-initial combining element, also occurring as a word, derived from Old English *c(e)ar(u)* 'grief, worry,' used in its etymological and extended senses in combination with other English elements: **carefree, caretaker, careworn**.

364   **carni-**   A word-initial combining element, derived from Latin *car(ō), carn(is)* 'flesh, meat' (from an Indo-European root meaning 'cut,' the idea being, presumably, that meat was one's 'portion' or 'cut') plus the combining vowel *-i-*, used in its etymological and extended senses in Neo-Latin and Neo-Greek combinations: **carniferrin, carnigen, carnivorous**. Also, **carn-, carne-, carno-: carnine, carneous, carnophobia**. Related forms: **core-[2], cork-(?), cortico-, score-, screw-, scrofulo-, sharp-, shirt-, short-**.

365   **caroten-**   A word-initial combining element, derived from English *caroten(e)* 'orange or red pigment ($C_{40}H_{56}$) (found in carrots)' (from Latin *carōt(a)* 'carrot' (from an Indo-European root meaning 'head, horn') plus the suffix *-ene* which is used in naming hydrocarbons), used in the sense of 'of, pertaining to, containing, or resembling *carotene*' in biochemical terminology: **carotenemia, carotenoid, carotenosis**. Also, **carotin-: carotinase**. Related forms:

cerebello-, cerebro-, cervi-[2], cervico-, corneo-, corner-, cornu-, cranio-, ginger-, hart's-, horn-, keratin-, kerato-.

366 carp- A variant of **carpo-[1]**.

367 carpet- A word-initial combining element, derived from Late Latin *carpet(a)* 'woven covering for a floor' (from Latin *carpere* 'to card wool'), used in its etymological and extended senses in combination with other English elements: **carpetbag, carpet-cut, carpetweed.**

368 carpho- A word-initial combining element, derived from Greek *kárpho(s)* 'straw, dry stock' (from *kárphein* 'to wither, wrinkle, dry'), used in a variety of extensions of its etymological sense in Neo-Greek combinations: **carpholite, carphology, carphosiderite.**

369 carpo-[1] A word-initial combining element, derived from Greek *karpó(s)* 'wrist' (from an Indo-European root meaning 'turn, twist'), used in its etymological sense in Neo-Greek and Neo-Latin combinations: **carpocarpal, carpopedal, carpoptosis.** Also, **carp-: carpitis.** Related form: **whirl-.**

370 carpo-[2] A word-initial combining element, derived from Greek *karpó(s)* 'fruit,' used in its etymological and extended senses in Neo-Greek combinations: **carpogonium, carpophore, carpophagous.**

371 carry- A word-initial combining element, also occurring as a word, derived from dialectal Old French *cari(er)* 'to cart, bear by vehicle' (from Latin *car(rus)* 'wagon'), used in its etymological and extended senses in combination with other English elements: **carry-all, carry-back, carry-over.** Compare **car-.**

372 cart- A word-initial combining element, also occurring as a word, derived from Old English *cræt* 'carriage,' used in the sense of 'nonautomotive vehicle in which to transport things' in combination with other English elements: **cart-horse, cartload, cartwright.**

373 carto- A word-initial combining element, derived through Latin from Greek *c(h)árt(ēs)* 'piece of papyprus, paper,' used chiefly in the extended senses of '(playing) card' and 'map' in Neo-Greek combinations: **cartogram, cartography, cartomancy.** Also, **charto-: chartographic.** Compare **card-.**

374 caryo- A variant of **karyo-.**

375 case-[1] A word-initial combining element, also occurring as a word, derived from Latin *cās(us)* '(a) fall, happening, event' (from *cadere* 'to fall, befall'), used in the sense of 'event' and in extensions of that sense in combination with other English elements: **casebook, caseload, caseworker.**

376   **case-²**   A word-initial combining element, also occurring as a word, derived from Latin *ca(p)s(a)* 'box' (from *capere* 'to take, accept, hold'), used in its etymological and extended senses in combination with other English elements: **casebound, caseharden, caseworm.** Compare **capsulo-, cash-.** Related form: **catch-.**

377   **case-³**   A word-initial combining element, derived from Latin *cāse(us)* 'cheese,' used in its etymological and extended senses in Neo-Latin and Neo-Greek combinations: **casefy, casein, caseose.** Also, **caseo-: caseogenous.** Compare **cheese-.**

378   **cash-**   A word-initial combining element, also occurring as a word, derived from Middle French *cass(ier)* 'money-box' (from Latin *ca(p)s(a)* 'box' plus the French noun-forming suffix *-ier*), used in the sense of 'money' in combination with other English elements: **cashbook, cashbox, cashdrawer.** Compare **capsulo-, case-².** Related form: **catch-.**

379   **cast-**   A word-initial combining element, also occurring as a word, derived from Middle English *cast(en)* 'to throw,' used in its etymological and extended senses in combination with other English elements: **castaway, cast-iron, cast-off.**

380   **cat-¹**   A word-initial combining element, also occurring as a word, derived from Old English *cat(t)* '*Felis domesticus,*' used in its etymological and extended senses in combination with other English elements: **catcall, catfish, catnap.**

381   **cat-²**   A variant of **cata-.**

382   **cata-**   A word-initial combining element, derived from Greek *katá* 'down, back, against,' used in its etymological and extended senses in inherited and Neo-Greek combinations: **catabatic, catalysis, cataphasia.** Also, **cat-², kata-: catamnesis, kataphylaxis.** Compare **kato-.**

383   **catch-**   A word-initial combining element, also occurring as a word, derived through dialectal Old French *cach(ier)* 'to chase, capture' (cf. Latin *capere* 'to take' from which Old French *cachier* is ultimately derived), used in its etymological and extended senses in

combination with other English elements: **catchall, catch-as-catch-can, catch-cord.** Related forms: **capsulo-, case-², cash-.**

384 **caten-** A word-initial combining element, derived from Latin *catēn(a)* 'chain,' used in its etymological and extended senses in Neo-Latin and Neo-Greek combinations: **catenane, catenate, catenoid.** Compare **chain-.**

385 **cato-** A variant of **kato-.**

386 **catoptro-** A word-initial combining element, derived from Greek *kátoptro(n)* 'mirror' (from *kat(á)* 'against, back' plus *op(tós)* 'seen' plus the noun-forming suffix *-tron*), used in its etymological and extended senses in Neo-Greek combinations: **catoptromancy, catoptrophobia, catoptroscope.** Compare **cata-** and **optico-.**

387 **caulo-** A word-initial combining element, derived from Greek *kauló(s)* (cf. Latin *caulis*) 'stock, stem,' used in its etymological and extended senses in Neo-Greek and Neo-Latin combinations: *Caulobacteriineae,* **caulophyllum,** *Caulopteris.* Also, **caul-, cauli-: caulescent, cauliform.**

388 **cauter-** A word-initial combining element, also occurring as a word, derived from Greek *kautḗr* 'branding iron' (from *kaiein* 'to burn' (from which *causalgia* 'burning pain' and *caustic* 'burning' are also both derived) plus the agentive noun-forming suffix *-tēr*), used in the sense of 'of or pertaining to the application of a caustic device' in a variety of combinations: **cauterant, cauterize, cautery.** Related form: **ink-.**

389 **cav-** A word-initial combining element, derived from Latin *cav(us)* 'hollow,' used in its etymological and extended senses in inherited and Neo-Latin and Neo-Greek combinations: **caval, cavern, cavitis.** Also, **cava-, cavi-, cavo-: cavascope, cavicorn, cavovalgus.** Compare **cavern-, jail-.** Related forms: **celio-, celo-¹.**

390 **cavern-** A word-initial combining element, also occurring as a word, derived from Latin *cavern(a)* 'hole, hollow, cavity' (from *cav(us)* 'hollow' plus the noun-forming suffix *-erna*), used chiefly in the sense of 'of or pertaining to a bodily cavity' in Neo-Latin and Neo-Greek combinations: **cavernitis, cavernoma, cavernose.** Also, **caverni-, caverno-: caverniloquy, cavernoscopy.** Compare **cav-, jail-.** Related forms: **celio-, celo-¹.**

391 **ceco-** A word-initial combining element, derived from Latin *caec(us)* 'blind' plus the combining vowel *-o-*, used in its etymologi-

cal and extended senses, chief among these being 'of or pertaining
to an anatomical cul-de-sac' (from Latin (*intestinum*) *caecum* 'blind
(gut)'), in Neo-Latin and Neo-Greek combinations: **cecocolon,
cecoileostomy, cecopexy.** Also, **caec-, caeco-, cec-: caecal,
caecotomy, cecal.**

392   **cel-¹**   A variant of **celo-¹.**

393   **cel-²**   A variant of **celo-².**

394   **celio-**   A word-initial combining element, derived from Greek
koili(a) 'belly' (from *koîl(os)* 'hollow' plus the noun-forming suffix
-ia) plus the combining vowel *-o-*, used in the sense of 'of or
pertaining to the abdomen' in Neo-Greek combinations: **ce-
liocolpotomy, celio-enterotomy, celiomyositis.** Also, **celi-, coeli-:
celialgia, coeliac.** Compare **celo-¹.** Related forms: **cav-, cavern-,
jail-.**

395   **celli-**   A word-initial combining element, derived from Latin *cell(a)*
'storeroom, chamber, closet' (from an Indo-European root mean-
ing 'conceal(ed), cover(ed)') plus the combining vowel *-i-*, used in
the sense of 'small closed space' and, by extension, 'of or pertaining to a *cell,* a microscopic protoplasmic mass made up of a
nucleus enclosed in a semipermeable membrane' in Neo-Latin
combinations: **cellicolous, celliform, cellifugal.** Compare **cello-,
cellulo-.** Related forms: **cilio-, coleo-, color-, hell-, hollow-.**

396   **cello-**   A word-initial combining element, derived from English
cell(ulose) 'the carbohydrate ($C_6H_{10}O_5$) (of which the cell walls of
most plants are made)' (from Latin *cellul(a)* 'small storeroom,'
later, 'small cell' plus the suffix *-ose* which is used in naming
carbohydrates) plus the combining vowel *-o-*, used in the sense of
'of, pertaining to, containing, or derived from cellulose' in chemical
terminology: **cellobiase, cellohexose, cellophane.** Also, **cell-, cellu-:
cellase, celluflor.** Compare **celli-, cellulo-.**

397   **cellulo-**   A word-initial combining element, derived from Latin
cellul(a) 'small storeroom' (from *cell(a)* 'storeroom, chamber,
closet' plus the diminutive suffix *-ul(a)*) plus the combining vowel
-o-, used in the extended sense of 'of or pertaining to *cells*
—microscopic protoplasmic masses, each made up of a nucleus
enclosed in a semipermeable membrane—or to cell tissue' in
biochemical terminology: **cellulocutaneous, cellulofibrous, cel-
luloneuritis.** Also, **cellul-, celluli-: cellulitis, cellulipetal.** Compare
celli-, cello-.

398   celo-¹   A word-initial combining element, derived from Greek *koîlo(s)* 'hollow,' used chiefly in the sense of 'concave; of or pertaining to a bodily cavity' in Neo-Greek combinations: **celophlebitis, celoschisis, celoscope.** Also, **cel-¹, coel-, coelo-, coil-, koil-, koilo-: celonychia, coeloma, coeloblastule, coilonychia, koilonychia, koilosternia.** Compare **celio-**. Related forms: **cav-, cavern-, jail-**.

399   celo-²   A word-initial combining element, derived from Greek *kēl(ē)* 'tumor, hernia' plus the combining vowel *-o-*, used in its etymological senses in Neo-Greek combinations: **celology, celosomia, celotomy.** Also, **cel-², kel-, kelo-: celectomy, kelectome, kelotomy.**

400   Celto-   A word-initial combining element, derived from Greek *Kelt(oi)* 'certain people living to the west of Greece' through Latin *Celt(ae)* 'Bretonese,' later, 'people belonging to the same linguistic stock as the Bretonese' plus the combining vowel *-o-*, used in this last sense in combination with other English elements: **Celto-Germanic, Celto-Frankish, Celto-Iberian.**

401   cemento-   A word-initial combining element, derived from Neo-Latin *cement(um)* 'layer of hard tissue which covers the root of a tooth' (from Latin *caementum* 'quarry-stone, uncut stone') plus the combining vowel *-o-*, used in its Neo-Latin sense in biomedical combinations: **cementoblast, cementoclasia, cementoexostosis.** Also, **cement-: cementitis.**

402   ceno-¹   A word-initial combining element, derived from Greek *kainó(s)* 'new, recent, fresh,' used in its etymological and extended senses in Neo-Greek combinations: **cenogenesis, cenopsychic, Cenozoic.** Also, **caeno-, caino-, kaino-: Caenozoic, Cainozoic, kainophobia.**

403   ceno-²   A word-initial combining element, derived from Greek *koinó(s)* 'common, shared,' used in its etymological and extended senses in Neo-Greek combinations: **cenobite, cenosite, cenotype.** Also, **cen-, coen-, coeno-, koino-: cenadelphus, coenenchyma, coenocyte, koinotropic.**

404   ceno-³   A word-initial combining element, derived from Greek *kenó(s)* 'empty,' used in its etymological and extended senses in Neo-Greek combinations: **cenophobia, cenotaph, cenotoxin.** Also, **keno-: kenophobia.**

405   centi-   A word-initial combining element derived from Latin *cent(um)* 'hundred' plus the combining vowel *-i-*, used in its etymological sense and in the extended sense of 'hundredth' in Neo-Latin and Neo-Greek combinations: **centibar, centimeter, centinormal.** Also, **cent-: centuple.** Related forms: **hecto-, hundred-.**

406   center-   A word-initial combining element, also occurring as a word, derived through Old French from the Latin borrowing of Greek *kéntr(on)* 'point; point of a compass; point around which a circle may be described,' used in this last and extended senses in combination with other English elements: **centerboard, centerline, centerpiece.** Also (chiefly British), **centre-: centreboard.** Compare **centro-.**

407   centro-   A word-initial combining element, derived through Latin from Greek *kéntr(on)* 'point; point of a compass; point around which a circle may be described,' used in this last and extended senses in Neo-Greek and Neo-Latin combinations: **centrocecal, centrodorsal, centroosteosclerosis.** Also, **centr-, centri-, kentro-: central, centrifugal, kentrokinesia.** Compare **center-.**

408   cephalo-   A word-initial combining element, derived from Greek *kephal(ē̆)* 'head,' used in its etymological and extended senses in Neo-Greek and Neo-Latin combinations: **cephalodymia, cephalogyric, cephalomotor.** Also, **cephal-, kephal-, kephalo-: cephalalgia, kephalin, kephalogram.**

409   cer-[1]   A variant of **cero-.**

410   cer-[2]   A word-initial combining element, derived from Latin *Cer(ēs)* 'Ceres, the goddess of agriculture,' appearing in the extended senses of 'of or pertaining to grain' and 'of or pertaining to the rare-earth mineral (Ce)' in a variety of combinations: **cereal, cerite, cerium.**

411   cerato-   A variant of **kerato-.**

412   cerco-   A word-initial combining element, derived from Greek *kérko(s)* 'tail,' used in its etymological and extended senses in Neo-Greek combinations: **cercocystitis, cercolabine, cercomonad.**

413   cerebello-   A word-initial combining element, derived from Latin *cerebell(um)* 'little brain' (from *cereb(rum)* 'brain' plus the diminutive suffix *-ellum*) plus the combining vowel *-o-,* used in the sense of 'of or pertaining to the little brain or hind brain, the three-lobed portion of the brain which is connected to the cerebrum, pons, and medulla' in Neo-Latin combinations: **cerebelloolivary, cerebello-**

pontile, cerebellospinal. Also, **cerebell-, cerebelli-: cerebellar, cerebellifugal.** Compare **cerebro-.**

414 **cerebro-** A word-initial combining element, derived from Latin *cerebr(um)* 'brain' (from an Indo-European root meaning 'head, horn') plus the combining vowel *-o-,* used in its etymological and extended senses, chief among these being 'of or pertaining to the main (anterior) part of the brain,' in biomedical terminology: **cerebrocentric, cerebrology, cerebroocular.** Also, **cerebr-, cerebri-: cerebrasthenia, cerebriform.** Compare **cerebello-.** Related forms: **caroten-, cervi-², cervico-, corneo-, corner-, cornu-, cranio-, ginger-, hart's-, horn-, keratin-, kerato-.**

415 **cero-** A word-initial combining element, derived from Greek *kēró(s)* 'wax,' used in its etymological and extended senses in Neo-Greek and Neo-Latin combinations: **cerolysin, ceromel, ceroplasty.** Also, **cer-¹, keri-, kero-: ceraceous, keritherapy, kerosene.**

416 **cervi-¹** A variant of **cervico-.**

417 **cervi-²** A word-initial combining, derived from Latin *cerv(us)* 'deer' (from an Indo-European root meaning 'head, horn') plus the combining vowel *-i-,* used in its etymological sense in Neo-Latin and Neo-Greek combinations: **cervicaprine, cervicide, cervicorn.** Also, **cerv-: cervanthropy.** Related forms: **caroten-, cerebello-, cerebro-, cervico-, corneo-, corner-, cornu-, cranio-, ginger-, horn-, keratin-, kerato-.**

418 **cervico-** A word-initial combining element, derived from Latin *cervi(x), cervīc(is)* 'head-joint, neck, throat' (from an Indo-European root meaning 'head, horn') plus the combining vowel *-o-,* used in the sense of 'neck' and, by extension, 'constricted part (of the body), esp. of the uterus' in biomedical combinations: **cervicoaxillary, cervicobuccal, cervicoplasty.** Also, **cervi-¹, cervic-, cervici-: cervimeter, cervical, cerviciplex.** Related forms: **caroten-, cerebello-, cerebro-, cervi-², corneo-, corner-, cornu-, cranio-, ginger-, hart's-, horn-, keratin-, kerato-.**

419 **cess-** A word-initial combining element, derived either from Italian *cess(o)* 'privy' (from Latin *(sē)cess(us)* 'retreat, hiding-place, deep recess, ravine') or else from Gaelic *sos* 'mess,' used in the sense of 'bodily waste' in combination with other English elements: **cesspipe, cesspit, cesspool.**

420 **cet-** A word-initial combining element, derived from Greek *kêt(os)* 'sea monster, large fish, whale,' used in the sense of 'whale' and in the extended sense of 'of, pertaining to, containing, or derived from the chemical ($C_{16}H_{33}$) (which appears as a major constituent of spermaceti)' in Neo-Greek combinations: **cetacean, cetane, cetyl.** Also, **ceto-: cetochelid.**

421 **chaeto-** A word-initial combining element, derived from Neo-Latin *chaet(a)* 'bristle' (from Greek *chaítē* 'flowing hair, mane') plus the combining vowel *-o-*, used in its Neo-Latin and extended senses in in Neo-Greek and Neo-Latin combinations: **chaetognath, chaetophorous, chaetotaxy.** Also, **chaet-, chaeti-: chaetodont, chaetiferous.**

422 **chaff-** A word-initial combining element, also occurring as a word, derived from Old English *ćeaf, ćæf* 'husk (of grain),' used in its etymological and extended senses in combination with other English elements: **chaff-flower, chaff-seed, chaffweed.**

423 **chain-** A word-initial combining element, also occurring as a word, derived through Old French from Latin *catēn(a)* 'fetter, shackle, flexible series of links in a single line,' used in its etymological and extended senses in combination with other English elements: **chainbreak, chainsmoke, chainstitch.** Compare **caten-.**

424 **chalc-** A word-initial combining element, derived from Greek *chalk(ós)* 'copper, brass,' used in its etymological and extended senses in Neo-Greek combinations: **chalcanthite, chalcone, chalcosis.** Also **chalco-, chalk-²: chalcopyrite, chalkitis.**

425 **chalk-¹** A word-initial combining element, also occurring as a word, derived through Old English from Latin *cal(x), calc(is)* 'lime, limestone,' used in the sense of 'powdery white limestone' and in extensions of this sense in combination with other English elements: **chalkboard, chalk-line, chalkstone.** Compare **calci-.**

426 **chalk-²** A variant of **chalc-.**

427 **chamae-** A word-initial combining element, derived from Greek *chamaí* 'on the ground, low,' used in its etymological and extended senses, chief among these being 'dwarflike,' in Neo-Greek combinations: **chamaecephaly, chamaelirium, chamaeprosopy.** Also, **chame-: chamecephalous.**

428 **chamber-** A word-initial combining element, also occurring as a word, derived from Old French *chambre* 'room' (through Latin from Greek *kamára* 'anything with a vaulted or arched covering'), used in its Old French and extended senses in a variety of

combinations: **chamberlain, chambermaid, chamber-pot.** Compare **camber-, camera-.**

429 **chame-** A variant of **chamae-.**

430 **chancr-** A word-initial combining element, derived through Middle French *chancr(e)* 'canker, ulcer' (from Latin *canc(e)r, cancr(ī)* 'crab' and, by extension, 'malignant tumor, ulcer'), used in the sense of 'canker, (syphilitic) ulcer' in a few biomedical terms: **chancrelle, chancroid, chancrous.** Also, **chancri-: chancriform.** Compare **cancer-.**

431 **change-** A word-initial combining element, also occurring as a word, derived through Old French from Latin *cambi(āre)* 'to exchange,' used in its etymological and extended senses in combination with other English elements: **changeling, changemaker, changeover.**

432 **charto-** A variant of **carto-.**

433 **chasmo-** A word-initial combining element, derived from Greek *chásm(a), chásm(atos)* '(wide) opening or hollow' plus the combining vowel *-o-,* used in its etymological and extended senses in Neo-Greek combinations: **chasmogony, chasmophyte, *Chasmorhynchus.*** Also, **chasmato-: chasmatoplasson.**

434 **cheap-** A word-initial combining element, also occurring as a word, derived by abstraction from such Middle English expressions as *at good cheape* 'at a good price, at a good bargain' and *at greate cheape* 'at a great price, at a great bargain' (cf. Old English *ćeap* 'trade, bargain, price'), used chiefly in the sense of 'inexpensive' and 'stingy' in combination with other English elements, though a few relic forms preserve the older senses: **cheap-jack, Cheapside, cheapskate.**

435 **check-** A word-initial combining element, also occurring as a word, derived through Old French *(es)chec* 'threat to the king (in the game of chess)' from Persian *shāh* 'king,' used first in Middle English in its Old French sense, then in the extended sense of 'attack' and 'arrest, stop,' now used in this last and extended senses in combination with other English elements: **checkbook, checkmark, checkpoint.** [Note: *checkmate* is not, etymologically, **check-** plus English *mate* 'companion' but, rather, the reflex of Persian *shāh māt* 'the king dies.'] Compare **checker-.**

436 **checker-** A word-initial combining element, also occurring as a word, derived from Old French (*es*)*chequ*(*i*)*er* 'chessboard' (from (*es*)*chec* 'threat to the king (in the game of chess)'—from Persian *shāh* 'king'—plus the noun-forming suffix *-ier*), used in a variety of extensions of its Old French sense in combination with other English elements: **checkerboard, checkerspot, checkerwork**. Compare **check-**.

437   **cheese-**   A word-initial combining element, also occurring as a word, derived through Old English from Latin *cās*(*eus*) 'milk curd prepared as food,' used in its etymological and extended senses in combination with other English elements: **cheeseburger, cheesecake, cheesecloth**. Compare **case-³**.

438   **cheilo-**   A word-initial combining element, derived from Greek *cheîlo*(*s*) 'lip,' used in its etymological and extended senses in Neo-Greek combinations: **cheiloangioscopy, cheilognathoschisis, cheilophagia**. Also, **cheil-, chil-, chilo-: cheilectomy, chilitis, *Chilopoda***. Related form: **gill-**.

439   **cheiro-**   A word-initial combining element, derived from Greek *cheir* 'hand' (perhaps from an Indo-European root meaning 'to grasp') plus the combining vowel *-o-*, used in its etymological and extended senses in Neo-Greek combinations: **cheirokinesthetic, cheiropompholyx, cheirospasm**. Also, **cheir-, chir-, chiro-: cheiragra, chiragra, chirospasm**. Related form(?): **heredo-**.

440   **cheli-**   A word-initial combining element, derived from Greek *chēl*(*ḗ*) 'hoof, claw, talon' plus the combining vowel *-i-*, used in the sense of 'claw' in Neo-Greek and Neo-Latin combinations: **cheliferous, cheliform, cheliped**. Also, **chel-, chelo-: chelate, *Chelophora***.

441   **chelono-**   A word-initial combining element, derived from Greek *chelṓn*(*ē*) 'tortoise' plus the combining vowel *-o-*, used in its etymological sense in Neo-Greek combinations: ***Chelonobatrachia*, chelonography, chelonologist**. Also, **chelon-: chelonite**.

442   **chemo-**   A word-initial combining element, derived through Late Latin and Old French from Arabic (*al*)*kīm*(*īyā*) '(the) art of combining base metals (to make gold)' (from Greek *Chēmía* 'Egypt, the presumptive place of origin of the art of transmuting metals into gold' (cf. Old Egyptian *khmi* 'land of black earth, Egypt') with the influence of Greek *chymeîa* 'mixture' (from *chéai* 'to pour')) plus the combining vowel *-o-*, used in the sense of 'of or pertaining to the basic elements which form matter, to their combination, or to their scientific study' in Neo-Greek and Neo-

Latin combinations: **chemobiotic, chemoreflex, chemotherapy.** Also, **chem-, chemi-: chemasthenia, chemiluminescence.** Compare **chemico-.**

443 **chemico-** A word-initial combining element, derived from **chem(o)-** plus the adjective-forming suffix *-ic* plus the combining vowel *-o-,* used in the sense of 'of or pertaining to the basic elements which form matter, to their combination, or to their scientific study' in Neo-Greek and Neo-Latin combinations: **chemicobiological, chemicogenesis, chemicovital.** Compare **chemo-.**

444 **chi-** (X, χ) A word-initial combining element, the twenty-second letter of the Greek alphabet, used chiefly to designate 'the twenty-second carbon atom in a straight chain compound or a derivative thereof in which the substitute group is attached to that atom' in chemical terminology. See **alpha-.** Compare **chiasto-.**

445 **chiasto-** A word-initial combining element, derived from Greek *chiastó(s)* 'crossed, laid crosswise' (from *chiázein* 'to make in the shape of the letter *chi* (χ)'), used in several extensions of its etymological sense, all having to do with 'crossing' or 'being crossed,' in Neo-Greek combinations: **chiastolite, chiastometer,** *Chiastoneura.* Compare **chi.**

446 **chicken-** A word-initial combining element, also occurring as a word, derived from Old English *čīcen* 'young fowl,' used in its etymological and extended senses, chief among these being 'insignificant' and 'cowardly,' in combination with other English elements: **chicken-hearted, chicken-livered, chickenshit.**

447 **chil-** A variant of **cheilo-.**

448 **child-** A word-initial combining element, also occurring as a word, derived from Old English *čild* 'young person,' used in its etymological and extended senses in combination with other English elements: **childbed, childbirth, childcare.**

449 **chili-** A word-initial combining element, derived from Greek *chíli(oi)* 'thousand,' appearing in its etymological sense in a few late Greek combinations: **chiliad, chiliarch, chiliasm.** Also, **chilia-: chiliagon.** Compare **kilo-.**

450 **chilo-** A variant of **cheilo-.**

451 **chin-**[1] A word-initial combining element, also occurring as a word, derived from Old English *cin(n)* 'extremity of the lower jaw,' used

in its etymological and extended senses in combination with other English elements: **chinbeak, chinfest, chin-up.** Related forms: **genio-, geny-.**

452   **chin-**[2]   A variant of **quin-**[2].

453   **chip-**   A word-initial combining element, derived from Old English *ćyp, ćip(p)* 'beam' (cf. Old English *forćyppian* 'to hew, cut off'), used in the sense of 'flake, particle' in combination with other English elements: **chipboard, chip-blower, chip-proof.**

454   **chiro-**   A variant of **cheiro-**.

455   **chito-**   A word-initial combining element, derived from Greek *chitŏ(n)* 'tunic, covering,' used in several extensions of its etymological sense, chief among these being 'of, pertaining to, containing, or derived from the polysaccharide ($C_{30}H_{50}O_{19}N_4$) (which is the main constituent of crab and lobster shells),' in Neo-Greek combinations: **chitobiose, chitoneure, chitotriose.** Also, **chit-, chiton-: chitose, chitonitis.**

456   **chlamydo-**   A word-initial combining element, derived from Greek *chlamý(s), chlamýd(os)* 'cloak, mantle' plus the combining vowel *-o-*, used in several extensions of its etymological sense, chief among these being 'ensheathed,' in Neo-Greek and Neo-Latin combinations: *Chlamydobacteriales*, **chlamydospore**, *Chlamydozoa*.

457   **chlor-**[1]   A word-initial combining element, derived from Greek *chlōr(ós)* 'pale green, yellow-green,' used in its etymological and extended senses in Neo-Greek combinations: **chlorastrolite, chlorine, chlorosis.** Also, **chloro-**[1]**: chlorophyll.** Compare **chlor-**[2]. Related forms: **arseno-, chole-, choler-, gall-, glass-, gold-, golden-, yellow-.**

458   **chlor-**[2]   A word-initial combining element, derived from English *chlor(ine)* 'the gaseous yellow-green element (Cl)' (from Greek *chlōr(ós)* 'pale green, yellow-green' plus the noun-forming suffix *-ine* which is used in naming basic chemical substances), used in the sense of 'of, pertaining to, containing, or derived from *chlorine*' in chemical terminology: **chloramine, chlordiazepoxide, chloride.** Also, **chloro-**[2]**: chlorobenzene.** Compare **chlor-**[1], **chloral-**.

459   **chloral-**   A word-initial combining element, also occurring as a word, derived from English *chlor(ine)* plus the noun-forming suffix *-al* (from English *al(dehyde)*), used in the sense of 'of, pertaining to, containing, or derived from the liquid ($Cl_2C \cdot CHO$)' in chemical

terminology: **chloralcaffeine, chloralcamphoroxim, chloralose.** Compare **chlor-², aldo-.**

460   **choano-**   A word-initial combining element, derived from Greek *choan(ē̆)* 'funnel' plus the combining vowel *-o-*, used in its etymological and extended senses in Neo-Greek and Neo-Latin combinations: **choanocyte, choanophorous, choanosome.** Also, **choan-: choanal.**

461   **cholangio-**   A word-initial combining element, derived from Greek *chol(ē̆)* 'bile, gall' plus *ang(e)îo(n)* 'vessel,' used in the sense of 'bile duct, bile capillary' in biomedical terminology: **cholangio-enterostomy, cholangiohepatoma, cholangiojejunostomy.** Also, **cholang-, cholange-, cholangi-: cholangitis, cholangeitis, cholangiectasis.** Compare **chole-, angio-.**

462   **chole-**   A word-initial combining element, derived from Greek *cholē̄* 'bile, gall,' used in its etymological and extended senses in Neo-Greek and Neo-Latin combinations: **cholechromeresis, choleglobin, choleprasin.** Also, **chol-, cholo-: choline, choloplania.** Compare **choler-.** Related forms: **arseno-, chlor-¹, chlor-², gall-, glass-, gold-, golden-, yellow-.**

463   **cholecyst-**   A word-initial combining element, also occurring as a word, derived from Greek *cholē̄* 'bile, gall' plus *kýst(is)* 'bladder, sac,' used in the sense of 'gallbladder' in biomedical terminology: **cholecystatony, cholecystendysis, cholecystnephrostomy.** Also, **cholecysto-: cholecystoptosis.** Compare **chole-, cyst-.**

464   **choledocho-**   A word-initial combining element, derived from Greek *cholē̄* 'bile, gall' plus *dochó(s)* 'receptacle,' used in the sense of 'common bile duct' in biomedical terminology: **choledochoenterostomy, choledocholith, choledochorrhaphy.** Also, **choledoch-: choledochectomy.** Compare **chole-.**

465   **cholelitho-**   A word-initial combining element, derived from Greek *cholē̄* 'bile, gall' plus *litho(s)* 'stone,' used in the sense of 'gallstone(s)' in biomedical terminology: **cholelithophone, cholelithotomy, cholelithotrity.** Also, **cholelith-: cholelithiasis.** Compare **chole-.**

466   **choler-**   A word-initial combining element, derived from Greek *cholér(a)* 'disease in which the bodily humors (biles) are subject to violent discharge' (from *cholē̄* 'bile, gall' plus the noun-forming suffix *-ra*), used in the sense of 'of or pertaining to *cholera,* an infectious disease characterized by severe vomiting and diarrhea' in biomedical terminology: **cholerase, cholerine, choleroid.** Also, **chol-**

era-, choleri-, cholero-: choleraphage, choleriform, cholerophobia. Compare chole-.

467   cholester-   A word-initial combining element, derived from Greek *cholē* 'bile, gall' plus *ster(eós)* 'solid,' used chiefly in the sense of 'of, pertaining to, or containing the sterol ($C_{27}H_{45}OH$) (*cholesterol*)' in Neo-Greek combinations: cholesteremia, cholesterinuria, cholesterol. Also, cholestero-: cholesterohistechia. Compare chole- and stereo-.

468   chondro-   A word-initial combining element, derived from Greek *chóndro(s)* 'groat, grain, any small rounded mass; gristle, cartilage (which resembles washed groats in appearance),' used in both the sense of 'granular' and 'of or pertaining to cartilage' in Neo-Greek and Neo-Latin combinations: chondrodystrophy, chondroendothelioma, chondrosternal. Also, chondr-, chondri-, chondrio-: chondralgia, chondrification, chondriosome.

469   chord-   A word-initial combining element, also occurring as a word, derived from Greek *chord(ē)* 'gut string (of a lyre)' plus the combining vowel -*o*-, used chiefly in the extended sense of 'sinew, flexible rod-shaped organ, esp. the *notochord*' in biomedical terminology: chordectomy, chorditis, chordoma. Also, chordo-, cord-¹, cordo-: chordoskeleton, cordectomy, cordopexy. Compare cord-². Related form: hernio-.

470   choreo-   A word-initial combining element, derived from Greek *chore(ía)* 'dance' plus the combining vowel -*o*-, used in its etymological and extended senses, chief among these being 'of or pertaining to *St. Vitus' dance*,' in Neo-Greek and Neo-Latin combinations: choreography, choreomania, choreophrasia. Also, chore-, chorei-, choro-¹: choreal, choreiform, choromania.

471   chorio-   A word-initial combining element, derived from Greek *chório(n)* 'skin, membrane, leather' used in the sense of 'of or pertaining to the *corium* (dermis, true skin), to the *chorion* (outermost covering of a zygote), or to the *choroid* (vascular coating of the eye)' in Neo-Greek and Neo-Latin combinations: chorioadenoma, choriocapillaris, chorioplaque. Also (in the sense of 'of or pertaining to the *chorion*'), chorion-: chorionepithelioma. Compare choroid-.

472   choro-¹   A variant of choreo-.

473   choro-²   A word-initial combining element, derived from Greek *chôro(s)* 'place, space, land,' used in its etymological and extended

senses in Neo-Greek combinations: **chorography, chorology, chorometry.**

474 **choroid-** A word-initial combining element, also occurring as a word, derived from Greek *chór(ion)* 'skin, membrane, leather' plus the adjective-forming suffix *-o(e)id(ēs)* '-like,' used in the sense of 'of or pertaining to the *choroid,* the vascular coating of the eye between the sclera and the retina' in biomedical terminology: **choroidectomy, choroideremia, choroiditis.** Also, **choroido-: choroidoretinitis.** Compare **chorio-.**

475 **Christ-** A word-initial combining element, also occurring as a word, derived from Greek *Christ(ós)* 'Anointed One,' a loan translation of Hebrew *Māshīah* 'Anointed One, Messiah,' used to refer to 'Jesus of Nazareth' in a variety of combinations: **Christhood, Christian, Christmas.** Also, **Christo-: Christology.** Related form: **cream-.**

476 **chrom-** A word-initial combining element, derived from Greek *chrõm(a), chrõm(atos)* 'color, pigment,' used in its etymological and extended senses, chief among these being 'stainable' and 'of, pertaining to, containing, or derived from *chromium* (Cr) (which forms the basis of several pigments),' in Neo-Greek and Neo-Latin combinations: **chromaffin, chromagogue, chromopsia.** Also, **chromat-, chromato-, chromo-: chromaturia, chromatometer, chromogenesis.**

477 **chrono-** A word-initial combining element, derived from Greek *chróno(s)* 'time,' used in its etymological and extended senses in Neo-Greek combinations: **chronobiology, chronognosis, chronophobia.** Also, **chron-: chronaxy.**

478 **chryso-** A word-initial combining element, derived from Greek *chrysó(s)* 'gold,' used in its etymological and extended senses, chief among these being 'golden, yellow,' in Neo-Greek combinations: **chrysocreatinine, chrysoderma, chrysotherapy.** Also, **chrys-: chrysanthemum.**

479 **chuck-** A word-initial combining element of obscure origin, also occurring as a word, first used in sixteenth-century English in the sense of 'tap under the chin with the hand, throw with the hand,' appearing in the sense of 'throw(n)' in a few inherited combinations: **chuck-a-luck, chuck-farthing, chuckhole.**

480 **church-** A word-initial combining element, also occurring as a word, derived from Greek *kyr(ia)k(ón) (dõma)* '(house) of the

Lord,' used in the sense of 'building in which Christians worship' and in extensions of this sense in combination with other English elements: **churchgoer, churchman, churchwarden.**

481 **chylo-** A word-initial combining element, derived from Greek *chyló(s)* 'juice' (from *chéai* 'to pour'), used chiefly in the specialized sense of 'of or pertaining to *chyle,* the milky fluid consisting of lymph and emulsified fat which is a product of the digestive process' in biomedical terminology: **chylocyst, chyloderma, chylomediastinum.** Also, **chyl-, chyli-: chylemia, chylifaction.** Compare **chymo-.** Related form: **gut-.**

482 **chymo-** A word-initial combining element, derived from Greek *chymó(s)* 'juice, liquid' (from *chéai* 'to pour'), used chiefly in the specialized sense of 'of or pertaining to *chyme,* the semifluid material resulting from the partial digestion of food' in biomedical terminology: **chymopapain, chymorrhea, chymotrypsin.** Also, **chym-, chymi-: chymase, chymification.** Compare **chylo-.** Related form: **gut-.**

483 **ciconi-** A word-initial combining element, derived from Latin *cicōni(a)* 'stork,' used in its etymological sense in Neo-Latin and Neo-Greek combinations: *Ciconiidae,* **ciconiiform, ciconiine.** Also, **cicon-: ciconine.**

484 **cider-** A word-initial combining element, also occurring as a word, derived, ultimately, from Hebrew *shēkār* 'intoxicating beverage' (from *shākar* 'to become intoxicated'), used in the specialized sense of 'juice of pressed apples (which, if allowed to ferment and consumed in sufficient quantity, is an intoxicant)' in combination with other English elements: **cider-brandy, cider-mill, cider-press.**

485 **cilio-** A word-initial combining element, derived from Latin *cili(um)* 'eyelid, eyelash' (from an Indo-European root meaning 'conceal(ed), cover(ed)') plus the combining vowel -*o-*, used in its etymological and extended senses in Neo-Latin and Neo-Greek combinations: **ciliogenesis, cilioretinal, ciliospinal.** Also, **cili-: ciliectomy.** Related forms: **celli-, cello-, cellulo-, coleo-, color-, hell-, hollow-.**

486 **cimic-** A word-initial combining element, derived from Latin *cīm(ex), cīmic(is)* 'bedbug,' used in its etymological and extended senses in Neo-Latin and Neo-Greek combinations: **cimicid, cimicine, cimicosis.** Also, **cimici-: cimicifugin.**

487 **cin-** A variant of **kino-.**

488 **cinchon-** A word-initial combining element, derived from Neo-Latin *cinchon(a)* 'rubiaceous tree which is native to the Andes and from whose bark quinine and related alkaloids may be extracted' (said to be named after the Countess of *Chinchón* who, while serving as vice-queen in Peru in the seventeenth century, was said to have been cured of a fever through the ingestion of the bark of this tree), used in the sense of 'of, pertaining to, or derived from the bark of one or another of the trees of the genus *Cinchona*' in Neo-Latin and Neo-Greek terminology: **cinchonamine, cinchonate, cinchonine.** Also, **cinch-, cincho-, cinchon-, cinchono-: cinchamidine, cinchophen, cinchonism, cinchonology.**

489 **cine-¹** A variant of **kino-.**

490 **cine-²** A word-initial combining element, derived from English *cine(matograph)* 'motion picture camera or projector' (through French from Greek *kínēma, kinēmat(os)* 'motion, movement' (from *kineîn* 'to move, set in motion') plus the combining vowel -*o*- plus the suffix -*graph* 'device for recording, reproducing, or transmitting verbal or visual information' (from Greek *gráph(ein)* 'to engrave, write, draw')), used in the sense of 'of or pertaining to motion picture photography' in a variety of combinations: **cine-fluorography, cineradiography, cineroentgenography.** Also, **cinema-, cinemat-, cinemato-, kine-², kinemato-: cinemascopia, cinematic, cinematoradiography, kinescope, kinematograph.** Compare **kinesi-, kineto-, kino-.** Related form: **exacto-.**

491 **cines-** A variant of **kinesi-.**

492 **cinnam-** A word-initial combining element, derived, ultimately, from one of the Semitic languages (cf. Hebrew *qinnāmōn* 'aromatic bark of the East Indian tree of the genus *Cinnamomum*'), used in its etymological and extended senses, chief among these being 'of, pertaining to, containing, or derived from *cinnamic acid* ($C_6H_5CH=CHCOOH$) (which is derived from the bark of the *Cinnamomum*)': **cinnamate, cinnamol, cinnamyl.** Also, **cinn-, cinnamo-: cinnaldehydum, cinnamoyl.**

493 **cino-** A variant of **kino-.**

494 **cinque-¹** A word-initial combining element, also occurring as a word, derived through Old French from Latin *quinque* 'five,' appearing in its etymological sense in a few borrowings from French: **cinquefoil, cinque-pace, cinque-port.** Also, **cinq-: cinqfoil.** Compare **quinque-.**

495   **cinque-**[2]   A word-initial combining element, derived through Italian from Latin *quinque* 'five,' appearing in its etymological sense in borrowings from Italian: **cinquecento, cinquedea.** Compare **quinque-**.

496   **ciono-**   A word-initial combining element, derived from Greek *kiōn* 'uvula' plus the combining vowel *-o-*, used in its etymological sense in biomedical terminology: **cionoptosis, cionorrhaphy, cionotome.** Also, **cion-, kio-, kiono-: cionectomy, kiotome, kionocranial.**

497   **circum-**   A word-initial combining element, derived from Latin *circum* 'around, about, surrounding' (cf. Latin *circus* 'circle'), used in its etymological and extended senses in borrowings from Latin and in Neo-Latin combinations: **circumcorneal, circumnavigate, circumvallate.** Related form: **crico-**.

498   **cirro-**   A word-initial combining element, derived from Latin *cirr(us)* 'tuft of hair, fringe' and, by extension (in Neo-Latin), 'filament, tendril' plus the combining vowel *-o-*, used in its etymological and extended senses in Neo-Latin and Neo-Greek combinations: **cirrocumulus, cirropodous, cirrostomous.** Also, **cirr-, cirri-: cirrose, cirrigerous.**

499   **cirso-**   A word-initial combining element, derived from Greek *kirsó(s)* 'varix,' used in its etymological sense in biomedical terminology: **cirsocele, cirsodesis, cirsotome.** Also, **cirs-: cirsomphalos.**

500   **cis-**   A word-initial combining element, derived from Latin *cis* 'on this side, on the near side' (from the Proto-Indo-European demonstrative pronoun which underlies English *he* and *hind*), used in its etymological and extended senses in Neo-Latin combinations and in combination with other English elements: **cisalpine, cisatlantic, cisvestitism.** Related forms: **he-, hind-.**

501   **citr-**   A word-initial combining element, derived from Latin *citr(us)* 'thuja, lemon tree' (cf. Greek *kédros* 'cedar (tree)'), used in the sense of 'of or pertaining to a rutaceous tree of the genus *Citrus*, to its fruit, to their color, or to their chemical derivatives' in Neo-Latin and Neo-Greek combinations: **citrate, citrine, citronellol.**

502   **city-**   A word-initial combining element, also occurring as a word, derived through Old French *cite(t)* 'large town' from Latin *cīvitās* 'citizenship, community of citizens,' used in its Old French and extended senses in combination with other English elements: **cityscape, city-state, cityward.**

503   clack-   A word-initial combining element, also occurring as a word, derived from Middle English *clack(en)* 'to make a quick clapping sound or a series of such sounds,' used in its etymological and extended senses in combination with other English elements: **clack-box, clack-dish, clack-valve.**

504   clado-   A word-initial combining element, derived from Greek *kládo(s)* 'shoot, young branch,' used in its etymological and extended senses in Neo-Greek combinations: **cladocarpous, *Cladocera*, cladophyll.** Also, **clad-: cladenchyma.**

505   clair-   A word-initial combining element, derived from French *clair* 'clear(ly)' (from Latin *clārus* 'clear'), used in the specialized sense of 'perceiving through extrasensory powers' in a few French borrowings and Neo-Latin combinations: **clairaudience, clairsentience, clairvoyant.** Compare **clar-, clear-.**

506   clam-   A word-initial combining element, also occurring as a word, derived by abstraction from early Modern English *clam(shell)*, literally, 'a shell that clamps shut' (cf. Old English *clam* 'bond, clamp'), used in the sense of 'bivalve mollusk' and in extensions of this sense in combination with other English elements: **clambake, clamshell, clamworm.** Related form: **clamp-.**

507   clamp-   A word-initial combining element, also occurring as a word, derived from Middle Dutch *klamp(e)* 'tenon, press, cleat,' used in its etymological and extended senses in combination with other English elements: **clamp-cell, clamp-dog, clampdown.** Related form: **clam-.**

508   clap-   A word-initial combining element, also occurring as a word, derived from Old English *clæp(pian)* 'to beat, throb,' used in the sense of 'beat or strike (so as to produce a quick, sharp sound)' and in extensions of this sense in combination with other English elements: **clap-sill, clap-stick, claptrap.**

509   clar-   A word-initial combining element, derived from Latin *clār(us)* 'clear,' used in its etymological and extended senses in Neo-Latin combinations and in borrowings from Latin and French: **claret, clarite, clarion.** Also, **clari-: clarification.** Compare **clair-, clear-.**

510   clasmato-   A word-initial combining element, derived from Greek *klásma, klásmat(os)* 'fragment, piece broken off' plus the combining vowel *-o-*, used in its etymological and extended senses in Neo-Greek combinations: **clasmatocyte, clasmatocytosis, clasmatodendrosis.** Also, **clasmat-: clasmatosis.**

511   **clasp-**   A word-initial combining element, also occurring as a word, derived from Middle English *clasp(en)* 'to grasp firmly,' used its etymological and extended senses in combination with other English elements: **clasp-hook, clasp-knife, clasp-nail.**

512   **class-**   A word-initial combining element, also occurring as a word, derived from Latin *class(is)* 'division (of the Roman citizenry), army, fleet,' used in the sense of 'division, categorization' and in extensions of that sense in combination with other English elements: **classbook, classical, classmate.** Also, **classi-: classification.**

513   **clathr-**   A word-initial combining element, derived through Latin from Greek *klêthr(a)* 'bars, lattice, grate,' used in the sense of 'lattice(d), latticelike' in Neo-Greek and Neo-Latin combinations: **clathrate, clathrose, clathrulate.** Also, **clathro-:** *Clathrocystis.*

514   **claustro-**   A word-initial combining element, derived from Latin *claustr(a)* 'lock, barrier' (from *claudere* 'to close, enclose, hem in') plus the combining vowel *-o-,* used in the sense of 'being enclosed, shut in' in a few Neo-Latin and Neo-Greek combinations: **claustrophilia, claustrophobia, claustrophobic.** Also, **claustr-: claustral.** Related forms: **clavi-¹, cleido-, cleisto-, clitorid-, close-.**

515   **clavi-¹**   A word-initial combining element, derived from Latin *clāvi(s)* 'key' (from *claudere* 'to close, enclose, hem in'), used in its etymological and extended senses, chief among these being 'of or pertaining to the collar bone, or *clavicle* (which is so named because of its keylike shape),' in Neo-Latin and Neo-Greek combinations: **clavichord, clavicylinder, clavipectoral.** Also, **clavo-: clavomastoid.** Related forms: **claustro-, cleido-, cleisto-, clitorid-, close-.**

516   **clavi-²**   A word-initial combining element, derived from Latin *clāv(a)* 'knotty stick, club' plus the combining vowel *-i-,* used in its etymological and extended senses in Neo-Latin combinations: *Claviceps,* **clavicorn, claviform.** Also, **clav-: clavate.**

517   **claw-**   A word-initial combining element, also occurring as a word, derived from Old English *clēa, claw(u)* 'toenail, talon,' used in its etymological and extended senses in combination with other English elements: **clawfoot, claw-hammer, clawhand.**

518   **clean-**   A word-initial combining element, also occurring as a word, derived from Old English *clæn(e)* 'pure, fine, clear,' used in its etymological and extended senses in combination with other English elements: **clean-cut, clean-living, cleanup.**

519 **clear-**   A word-initial combining element, also occurring as a word, derived through Old French from Latin *clār(us)* 'bright, not obscure, light,' used in its etymological and extended senses in combination with other English elements: **clear-cut, clearheaded, clearstarch.** Compare **clair-, clar-.**

520 **cleido-**   A word-initial combining element, derived from Greek *klei(s), kleidó(s)* 'key' and, by extension, 'collar bone,' used in its etymological and extended senses in Neo-Greek and Neo-Latin combinations: **cleidocostal, cleidocranial, cleidotomy.** Also, **cleid-, clid-, clido-: cleidarthritis,** *Clidastes,* **clidomancy.** Related forms: **claustro-, clavi-¹, cleisto-, clitorid-, close-.**

521 **cleisto-**   A word-initial combining element, derived from Greek *kleistó(s)* 'closed, shut,' used in its etymological and extended senses in Neo-Greek combinations: **cleistocarpous, cleistogamy, cleistothecium.** Also, **clisto-: clistocarp.** Related forms: **claustro-, clavi-¹, cleido-, clitorid-, close-.**

522 **clepto-**   A variant of **klepto-.**

523 **clero-**   A word-initial combining element, derived from Greek *klêro(s)* 'lot, allotment, inheritance,' used in its etymological and extended senses in borrowings from Greek and in Neo-Greek combinations: ***Clerodendron,* cleromancy, cleronomy.** Also, **cler-: cleruchy.**

524 **click-**   A word-initial combining element of onomatopoeic origin, also occurring as a word, used in the sense of 'making a ticking sound' in combination with other English elements: **click-beetle, click-pulley, click-wheel.**

525 **clido-**   A variant of **cleido-.**

526 **cliff-**   A word-initial combining element, also occurring as a word, derived from Old English *clif* 'steep face of rock,' used in its etymological sense in combination with other English elements: **cliff-brake, cliff-hanger, cliff-swallow.**

527 **climato-**   A word-initial combining element, derived from Greek *klíma, klímat(os)* 'inclination, slope; the (supposed) slope of the earth from the equator towards the poles,' hence, '(latitudinal) zone of the earth' and 'prevailing weather (in a given zone)' plus the combining vowel *-o-*, used in this last sense in Neo-Greek combinations: **climatography, climatology, climatometer.** Also, **climo-: climograph.** Related forms: **clino-¹, clino-², ladder-.**

528   **climbing-**   A word-initial combining element, also occurring as a word, the present participle of the English verb *climb* (from Old English *climb(an)* 'to ascend'), used in the sense of 'that which climbs' and 'that which facilitates climbing' in combination with other English elements: **climbing-fern, climbing-fish, climbing-irons.**

529   **clino-¹**   A word-initial combining element, derived from Greek *klin(esthai)* 'to slope, incline, decline, lie down, be bent' plus the combining vowel *-o-*, used in its etymological and extended senses in Neo-Greek combinations: **clinodactyly, clinoscope, clinostatism.** Compare **clino-².** Related forms: **climato, ladder-.**

530   **clino-²**   A word-initial combining element, derived from Greek *klin(ē)* 'bed' (from *klinesthai* 'to slope, incline, decline, lie down') plus the combining vowel *-o-*, used in its etymological and extended senses, chief among these being 'sick bed, of or pertaining to the sick,' in Neo-Greek combinations: *Clinocoris,* **clinomania, clinotherapy.** Also, **clin-: clinic.** Compare **clino-¹.**

531   **clip-**   A word-initial combining element, also occurring as a word, derived from Old English *clyp(pan)* 'to embrace,' used in several extensions of its etymological sense, all having to do with 'holding,' in combination with other English elements: **clipboard, clip-fed, clip-on.**

532   **clisto-**   A variant of **cleisto-.**

533   **clitorid-**   A word-initial combining element, derived from Greek *kl(e)itori(s), kl(e)itorid(os)* 'clitoris' (cf. Greek *kleiein* 'to close, enclose' and *kleis* 'key'), used in its etymological sense in biomedical combinations: **clitoridauxe, clitoridectomy, clitoriditis.** Also, **clitor-, clitoro-: clitorism, clitorotomy.** Related forms: **claustro-, clavi-¹, cleido-, cleisto-, close-.**

534   **cloak-**   A word-initial combining element, also occurring as a word, derived from Late Latin *cloc(ca)* 'bell' and, by extension, '(bell-shaped) mantle or cape,' used in the sense of 'cape, coat, outer garment' in combination with other English elements: **cloak-and-dagger, cloak-bag, cloakroom.** Compare **clock-.**

535   **clock-**   A word-initial combining element, also occurring as a word, derived from Middle Dutch *klock(e)* 'time-keeping device' (from Late Latin *clocca* 'bell'), used in its Middle Dutch and extended senses in combination with other English elements: **clockmaker, clockwise, clockwork.** Compare **cloak-.**

536   clod-   A word-initial combining element, also occurring as a word, derived from Middle English *clod(de)* 'lump (of dirt),' used in its etymological and extended senses, chief among these being 'dolt,' in combination with other English elements: **clodhopper, clodpate, clodpoll.** Related forms: **cloud-, club-, gli-, globe-.**

537   clog-   A word-initial combining element, also occurring as a word, derived from Middle English *clog(ge)* 'block of wood,' used in its etymological and extended senses in combination with other English elements: **clog-almanac, clog-burnisher, clog-dance.**

538   close-   A word-initial combining element, also occurring as a word, derived through Old French from Latin *claus(us)*, the past participle of the verb *claudere* 'to shut, hem in,' used in its etymological and extended senses in combination with other English elements: **close-fertilization, closefisted, close-fitting.** Related forms: **claustro-, clavi-[1], cleido-, cleisto-, clitorid-.**

539   cloth-   A word-initial combining element, also occurring as a word, derived from Old English *clāth* 'woven fabric, garment (made of woven fabric),' used in the sense of 'woven fabric' in combination with other English elements: **clothbound, cloth-stitch, cloth-yard.** Compare **clothes-.**

540   clothes-   A word-initial combining element, also occurring as a word, derived from Old English *clāthas,* the nominative-accusative plural form of *clāth* 'woven fabric, garment (made of woven fabric,' used in the sense of 'garments' in combination with other English elements: **clotheshorse, clothesline, clothespin.** Compare **cloth-.**

541   cloud-   A word-initial combining element, also occurring as a word, derived from Old English *clūd* 'rock, hill' (cf. Middle English *clod(de)* 'lump (of earth)'), later, 'mass of water or ice particles in the air,' used in this latter and extended senses in combination with other English elements: **cloudburst, cloud-capped, cloudland.** Related forms: **clod-, club-, gli-, globe-.**

542   club-   A word-initial combining element, also occurring as a word, derived from Old Norse *klub(ba)* 'cudgel,' used in its etymological and extended senses, chief among these being 'group of people organized around a common interest' (perhaps because a conglomeration of people may be likened in form to the lumpy end of a cudgel), in combination with other English elements: **clubfoot, clubhouse, clubroot.** Related forms: **clod-, cloud-, gli-, globe-.**

543   cnem-   A word-initial combining element, derived from Greek *knēm(ē)* 'the part of the leg between the knee and the ankle,' used in its etymological sense in biomedical terminology: **cnemapophysis, cnemidium, cnemitis.** Also, **cnemi-, cnemo-: cnemial, cnemoscoliosis.**

544   **cnido-**   A word-initial combining element, derived from Greek *knid(ē)* 'nettle' plus the combining vowel *-o-*, used in its etymological and extended senses in Neo-Greek combinations: **cnidoblast, cnidocyst, cnidophore.** Also, **cnid-: cnidosis.**

545   **co-**   A word-initial combining element, derived from Latin *co-*, a combining form of *cum* 'with, together,' appearing in Latin in combinations in which the element to which it is joined begins with a vowel, *h*, or *gn*, but now used in English in its etymological and extended senses without restriction as to the phonetic shape of the elements to which it may be joined: **coactive, coconsciousness, coworker.** Compare **col-[1], com-, con-, cor-.**

546   **coach-**   A word-initial combining element, also occurring as a word, derived from Hungarian *kocs(i czeker)* '(car, cart) of the town of *Kocs*,' used in early Modern English in the sense of '(horse-drawn) carriage' and, by extension (in British university slang), 'private tutor,' now used in these and extended senses in combination with other English elements: **coach-and-four, coachman, coachwork.**

547   **coagul-**   A word-initial combining element, derived from Latin *coāgul(āre)* 'to curdle' (from *coāgulum* 'that which causes curdling; rennet' (from a verb meaning 'to bring together')), used chiefly in the sense of 'of, pertaining to, or facilitating clotting of the blood' in biomedical terminology: **coagulability, coagulin, coagulose.** Also, **coagulo-: coaguloviscosimeter.**

548   **coal-**   A word-initial combining element, also occurring as a word, derived from Old English *col* 'glowing piece of wood,' later, 'burned wood suitable for fuel (*charcoal*)' and 'black fossil fuel,' used in this last and extended senses in combination with other English elements: **coalbin, coalfish, coalmouse.** Compare **coke-.**

549   **coast-**   A word-initial combining element, also occurring as a word, derived through Middle English *cost(e)* 'side, seashore' from Latin *cost(a)* 'rib, side,' used in the sense of 'seashore' in combination with other English elements: **coastguardsman, coastline, coastward.** Compare **costo-.**

550   **coat-**   A word-initial combining element, also occurring as a word, derived from Late Latin *cot(a)* 'tunic,' used in the sense of 'outer garment or covering' in combination with other English elements: **coatdress, coatroom, coattail.**

551 cocain-   A word-initial combining element, derived from English *cocain(e)* 'the alkaloid *methyl benzoyl ecgonine*' (from the Spanish borrowing of Quechua *kuka* 'plant of the genus *Erythroxylon*' plus the suffix *-ine* which is used in naming basic chemical substances), used in the sense of 'of, pertaining to, containing, or derived from *cocaine*' in biochemical terminology: **cocainidine, cocainine, cocainism.** Also, **cocaino-: cocainomaniac.**

552 cocco-   A word-initial combining element, derived through Latin from Greek *kókko(s)* 'kernel, berry,' used in its etymological and extended senses, chief among these being 'spherical or ovoid bacterium,' in Neo-Greek and Neo-Latin combinations: **coccobacillus, *Coccoloba*, coccomelasma.** Also, **cocc-, cocci-: coccal, coccigenic.**

553 coccy-   A word-initial combining element, derived from Greek *kókky(x), kókky(gos)* 'cuckoo,' used chiefly in the extended sense of 'shaped like a cuckoo's bill,' most frequently in reference to 'the *coccyx*, the triangular bone which forms the caudal extremity of the human spinal column,' in Neo-Greek and Neo-Latin combinations: **coccyalgia, coccycephalus, coccydynia.** Also, **coccyg-, coccyge-, coccygo-, coccyo-: coccygerector, coccygeal, coccygotomy, coccyodynia.**

554 cochle-   A word-initial combining element, derived through Latin from Greek *kochlí(as)* 'snail with a spiral shell,' used in its etymological and extended senses, chief among these being 'of or pertaining to the *cochlea*, the spiral tube in the inner ear,' in Neo-Latin and Neo-Greek combinations: **cochleate, cochleitis, cochleoid.** Also, **cochl-, cochleo-, cochlio-: cochlitis, cochleovestibular, *Cochliomyia*.**

555 cock-   A word-initial combining element, also occurring as a word, derived through Old English from Late Latin *coc(cus)* 'male gallinaceous fowl,' used in its etymological and extended senses in combination with other English elements: **cock-and-bull, cockpit, cocksure.**

556 cod-   A word-initial combining element, also occurring as a word, derived from Middle English *cod* 'fish of the family *Gadidae*' (possibly from Old English *cod(d)* 'bag, husk'), used in its etymological sense in combination with other English elements: **codfish, codline, codliver (oil).**

557   **coel-**   A variant of **celo-¹**.

558   **coeli-**   A variant of **celi-**.

559   **coelo-**   A variant of **celo-¹**.

560   **coeno-**   A variant of **ceno-²**.

561   **coffee-**   A word-initial combining element, also occurring as a word, derived through Dutch (via Turkish) from Arabic *qahwah* 'beverage made from the seeds of the *Coffea arabica*' (perhaps from *Kaffa*, an Abyssinian region to which the *Coffea arabica* is native), used in its etymological and extended senses in combination with other English elements: **coffeecake, coffeehouse, coffeepot.**

562   **coffin-**   A word-initial combining element, also occurring as a word, derived through Late Latin from Greek *kóphin(os)* 'basket,' used in the extended sense of 'box in which a corpse is placed for burial or cremation' and in further extensions of this sense in combination with other English elements: **coffin-bearer, coffin-end (spoon), coffinite.**

563   **cog-**   A word-initial combining element, also occurring as a word, derived from Middle English *cog(ge)* 'tooth on a gear' (possibly from Scandinavian or Celtic, there being cognates of *cogge* in languages of each of these families), used in its etymological and extended senses in combination with other English elements: **cog-rail, cogwheel, cogwood.**

564   **coke-**   A word-initial combining element, also occurring as a word, derived from Middle English *co(l)ke* 'solid residue of the process of dry distillation of coal' (from Old English *col* 'coal' plus the descriptive noun-forming suffix *-(o)ca*), used in its etymological sense in combination with other English elements: **coke-barrow, coke-oven, coke-tower.** Compare **coal-.**

565   **col-¹**   A word-initial combining element, derived from Latin *col-*, a combining form of *cum* 'with, together,' appearing in its etymological sense in borrowings from Latin in which the element to which it is joined begins with *l:* **collate, collect, colliquation.** Compare **co-, com-, con-, cor-¹.**

566   **col-²**   A word-initial combining element, derived through Latin from Greek *kól(on)* 'food, fodder' and, by extension, 'the part of the large intestine which extends from the cecum to the rectum,' used in this latter sense in biomedical terminology: **colalgia,**

colauxe, colitis. Also, **coli-²**, **colo-²**, **colon-**, **colono-**: **colipuncture, colohepatopexy, colonitis, colonorrhagia.** Compare **coli-¹**.

567 **cold-** A word-initial combining element, also occurring as a word, derived from Old English *cald* 'of low temperature,' used in its etymological and extended senses in combination with other English elements: **cold-draw, cold-hearted, cold-shoulder.** Related forms: **cool-, gelo-².**

568 **cole-¹** A variant of **coleo-**.

569 **cole-²** A word-initial combining element, also occurring as a word, derived through Old English from Latin *caul(is)* 'cabbage,' used in the sense of 'plant of the genus *Brassica*' in combination with other English elements: **colerape, coleseed, coleslaw.**

570 **coleo-** A word-initial combining element, derived from Greek *koleó(s)* 'sheath, covering,' used in its etymological and extended senses, chief among these being 'of or pertaining to the vagina,' in Neo-Greek combinations: **coleocele, *Coleoptera*, coleoptosis.** Also, **cole-¹: coleitis.** Related forms: **celli-, cello-, cellulo-, cilio-, color-, hell-, hollow-.**

571 **coli-¹** A word-initial combining element, derived from Neo-Latin (*Escherichia*) *coli* 'species of bacillus which is characteristically found in the lower intestinal track' (cf. Latin *colon*, a borrowing of Greek *kólon* 'the part of the large intestine which extends from the cecum to the rectum'), used in the sense of 'of, pertaining to, or caused by *E. coli*' in Neo-Latin and Neo-Greek combinations: **coliform, colicolitis, colipyuria.** Compare **col-²**.

572 **coli-²** A variant of **col-²**.

573 **coll-¹** A word-initial combining element, derived from Greek *kóll(a)* 'glue,' used in its etymological and extended senses in Neo-Greek combinations: **collemia, collenchyma, collidine.** Also, **collo-¹: colloxylin.** Compare **colloido-**.

574 **coll-²** A word-initial combining element, derived from Latin *coll(um)* 'neck' (from an Indo-European root meaning 'rotate, turn,' the neck being 'that which allows the head to turn'), occurring with the combining vowel *-i-* or *-o-* in biomedical combinations: **collifixation, collodiaphysical, collopexia.** Compare **collar-**. Related forms: **cyclo-, palin-, polari-, teleo-³, telo-¹, wheel-**.

575 **collar-** A word-initial combining element, also occurring as a word,

derived through dialectal Old French from Latin *collār(e)* 'neck chain' (from Latin *collum* 'neck'), used in the sense of 'that which is worn around the neck' and in extensions of this sense in combination with other English elements: **collarbone, collar-cell, collarwork.** Compare **coll-².**

576 **collo-¹** A variant of **coll-¹.**

577 **collo-²** A variant of **colloido-.**

578 **colloido-** A word-initial combining element, derived from Greek *kóll(a)* 'glue' plus the adjective-forming suffix *-o(e)id(ēs)* '-like' plus the combining vowel *-o-*, used in the sense of 'of or pertaining to a *colloid,* a gelatinous (gluelike) substance in which particle matter is suspended' in Neo-Greek combinations: **colloidoclasia, colloidogen, colloidophagy.** Also, **collo-², colloid-: collochemistry, colloidin.** Compare **coll-¹.**

579 **colo-¹** A word-initial combining element, derived from Greek *kólo(s)* 'curtailed, docked, mutilated,' used in its etymological and extended senses in Neo-Greek and Neo-Latin combinations: **coloboma, colobrachiate, colocephalous.**

580 **colo-²** A variant of **col-².**

581 **colon-** A variant of **col-².**

582 **color-** A word-initial combining element, also occurring as a word, derived from Latin *color* 'tint, hue, complexion' (from an Indo-European root meaning 'conceal(ed), cover(ed),' tint being a covering of sorts), used in its etymological and extended senses in combination with other English elements: **colorbearer, color-blind, colorfast.** Related forms: **celli-, cello-, cellulo-, cilio-, coleo-, hell-, hollow-.**

583 **colpo-** A word-initial combining element, derived from Greek *kólpo(s)* 'bosom, lap, bosomlike hollow, womb,' used in the sense of 'vagina' in Neo-Greek combinations: **colpocystocele, colpohyperplasia, colpoperineoplasty.** Also, **colp-: colpatresia.**

584 **columb-** A word-initial combining element, derived from Neo-Latin *Columb(ia)* 'the United States of America' (from (*Christopher*) *Columb(us)* plus the noun-forming suffix *-ia*), used chiefly in the sense of 'of, pertaining to, containing, or derived from the element *niobium* (Nb) (which was formerly called *columbium* because of its having been first discovered in the United States)' in

scientific terminology: **columbate, columbite, columbium.** Also, **columbi-: columbiferous.**

585 coly- A variant of **koly-.**

586 com- A word-initial combining element, derived from Latin *com-*, a combining form of *cum* 'with, together,' appearing in its etymological sense and as an intensifier in borrowings from Latin in which the element to which it is joined begins with *b, p,* or *m* and in a few borrowings from French in which the element to which it is joined begins with *f:* **combine, comfort, compare.** Compare: **co-, col-¹, con-, cor-¹.**

587 comb- A word-initial combining element, also occurring as a word, derived from Old English *camb, comb* 'cock's crest' and, by extension, 'toothed device (suggestive in shape of a cock's crest) for untangling hair,' used in its etymological and extended senses in combination with other English elements: **comb-bearer, combfish, comb-jelly.**

588 come- A word-initial combining element, also occurring as a word, derived from Old English *cum(an)* 'to approach, arrive,' used in its etymological and extended senses in combination with other English elements: **comeback, come-on, comeuppance.** Related forms: **base-, basi-, baso-.**

589 common- A word-initial combining element, also occurring as a word, derived through Old French from Latin *commūn(is)* 'belonging equally to two or more; universal,' used in its etymological and extended senses in combination with other English elements: **common-law, commonplace, commonweal.**

590 compass- A word-initial combining element, also occurring as a word, derived from Old French *compas* 'measure; pair of dividers' (from unattested Late Latin **compāssus* 'a measuring off by paces' (from *com-* 'with' plus *pāssus* 'step')), used in the sense of '(measured) area, circle, dividers,' and in the extended sense of 'mariner's (circular) instrument for determining position' as well as in extensions of this sense in combination with other English elements: **compass-bowl, compass-brick, compass-saw.** Compare **com-, pass-.**

591 composing- A word-initial combining element, also occurring as a word, the present participle of the English verb *compose* 'to put together, arrange,' derived through Middle French from Latin *com-* 'with, together' plus the past tense stem of the verb *ponere* 'to put, place,' used chiefly in the specialized sense of 'of or pertaining to the setting up (putting together) of print type' in combination with other English elements: **composing-frame, composing-room, composing-stick.**

592 **con-**[1] A word-initial combining element, derived from Latin *con-*, a combining form of *cum* 'with, together,' occurring in its etymological sense and as an intensifier in borrowings from Latin in which the element to which it is joined begins with a consonant other than *b, p, m, h, l:* **condense, confirm, convection.** Compare **co-, col-**[1], **com-, cor-**[1].

593 **con-**[2] A variant of **cone-.**

594 **con-**[3] A variant of **conio-.**

595 **concert-** A word-initial combining element, also occurring as a word, derived through French from Italian *concert(o)* 'musical composition for orchestra and solo instrument' (from Italian *concertare* 'to bring into agreement or harmony'), used in the extended sense of 'musical performance or recital' in combination with other English elements: **concertgoer, concertmaster, concert-pitch.**

596 **conch-** A word-initial combining element, also occurring as a word, derived through Latin from Greek *kónch(ē)* 'mussel, cockle' and, by extension, 'mussel-shaped shell or vessel; shell-like bone or cavity of the body,' used in its etymological and extended senses in Neo-Greek and Neo-Latin combinations: *Conchacea,* **conchfish, conchitic.** Also, **conchi-, concho-: conchiform, conchoscope.** Compare **conchylio-.**

597 **conchylio-** A word-initial combining element, derived through Latin from Greek *conchýlio(n)* 'mussel, cockle, mussel shell, cockle shell,' appearing in its etymological and extended senses in largely obsolete Neo-Greek and Neo-Latin combinations: **conchyliology, conchyliometer, conchyliomorphite.** Also, **conchyli-: conchyliated.** Compare **conch-.**

598 **condyl-** A word-initial combining element, derived from Greek *kóndyl(os)* 'knuckle' and, by extension, 'knucklelike knob,' used in its etymological and extended senses in Neo-Greek combinations: **condylarthrosis, condylectomy, condyloma.** Also, **condylo-: condylotomy.**

599 **cone-** A word-initial combining element, also occurring as a word,

derived through Latin from Greek *kôn(os)* 'something whose base is a circle and whose apex is a point,' used in its etymological and extended senses in combination with other English elements: **coneflower, cone-in-cone, conenose**. Also, **con-², coni-¹, cono-: conophthalmus, conirostral, conomyoidin**.

600   **coni-¹**   A variant of **cone-**.

601   **coni-²**   A variant of **conio-**.

602   **conio-**   A word-initial combining element, derived from Greek *kóni(s)* 'dust' plus the combining vowel -*o*-, used in its etymological and extended senses in Neo-Greek and Neo-Latin combinations: **coniofibrosis, coniophage, coniotoxicosis**. Also, **con-³, coni-², koni-, konio-, kono-: coniasis, coniosis, konimeter, koniocortex, konometer**.

603   **conjunctiv-**   A word-initial combining element, derived from Late Latin (*membrāna*) *conjunctīv(a)* 'connective (membrane),' used in the sense of 'of or pertaining to the *conjunctiva*, the mucous membrane which lines the eyelids and covers the surface of the eyeball' in biomedical terminology: **conjunctival, conjunctivitis, conjunctivoma**. Also, **conjunctivi-, conjunctivo-: conjunctiviplasty, conjunctivoplasty**.

604   **cono-**   A variant of **cone-**.

605   **contra-**   A word-initial combining element, derived from Latin *contrā* 'in opposition to, facing, against,' used in its etymological and extended senses in a variety of combinations: **contradiction, contraparetic, contrarotating**. Compare **contre-, counter-¹, country-**.

606   **contre-**   A word-initial combining element, derived from French *contre* 'against, in opposition to' (from Latin *contrā* 'in opposition to, against, facing'), appearing in its etymological sense in a few borrowings from French: **contrecoup, contre-lettre, contretemps**. Compare **contra-, counter-¹**.

607   **convexo-**   A word-initial combining element, derived from Latin *convex(us)* 'arched, rounded' (after Latin *convehere* 'to draw together') plus the combining vowel -*o*-, used in the sense of 'rounded outward' in a few Neo-Latin combinations: **convexo-concave, convexo-convex, convexo-plane**.

608   **cook-**   A word-initial combining element, also occurring as a word, derived through Old English from Late Latin *coc(us)*, a variant of

Latin *coquus* 'one who prepares food (by heating it),' used in its etymological and extended senses, chief among these being 'of, pertaining to, or facilitating the preparation of food,' in combination with other English elements: **cookbook, cookout, cookstove.** Related forms: **pepto-¹, pepto-².**

609 cool- A word-initial combining element, also occurring as a word, derived from Old English *cōl* 'chilly,' used in its etymological and extended senses in combination with other English elements: **cool-cup, cool-headed, coolweed.** Related forms: **cold-, gelo-².**

610 coon- A word-initial combining element, also occurring as a word, derived from English (*rac*)*coon* 'the mammal *Procyon lotor*' (from Virginian Algonquian *àràhkunem* 'he who scratches with his hands'), used in its etymological and extended senses in combination with other English elements: **cooncat, coonhound, coonskin.**

611 copper- A word-initial combining element, also occurring as a word, derived through Old English from late Latin *cupr*(*um*), *copr*(*um*) (from Latin (*aes*) *Cyprium* '(base metal) from Cyprus,' specifically, 'the reddish-brown metal (Cu) (of which Cyprus was a major source in Roman times)'), used in the sense of 'composed of or resembling the metal (Cu)' in combination with other English elements: **copperhead, copperplate, coppersmith.** Compare **cupro-, cyprido-.**

612 copro- A word-initial combining element, derived from Greek *kópro*(*s*) 'dung, feces,' used in its etymological and extended senses in Neo-Greek combinations: **coprolalomania, coprophobia, coprostasis.** Also, **copr-, kopr-, kopro-: copremesis, kopratin, koprosterin.**

613 copy- A word-initial combining element, also occurring as a word, derived through Old French from Latin *cōpi*(*a*) 'abundance,' hence, 'means, power' and, in Late Latin, 'transcript' (whether as an extension of the sense of 'abundance' or as the result of reanalysis of *cōpia* in such an expression as *copiam describendi facere* 'to grant the power to transcribe'), used in the sense of 'transcript, reproduction' and in the extended sense of 'something (written) which is intended to be reproduced' in combination with other English elements: **copybook, copyreader, copyright.**

614 cor-¹ A word-initial combining element, derived from Latin *cor-*, a combining form of *cum* 'together, with,' appearing in its etymological sense and as an intensifier in borrowings from Latin in which the element to which it is joined begins with *r:* **correlate, correspond, corrode.** Compare **co-, col-¹, com-, con-.**

615   **cor-²**   A variant of **core-²**.

616   **coraco-**   A word-initial combining element, derived from Greek *korako(eidēs)* 'crowlike' (from *kórax, kórak(os)* 'crow' plus the adjective-forming suffix *-oeidēs* '-like'), used in the specialized sense of 'of, pertaining to, or connected to the *coracoid*, the bony process which forms part of the scapular arch (and is so named because its shape resembles that of a crow's beak)' in biomedical terminology: **coracobrachialis, coracoclavicular, coracohumeral**. Also, **corac-**: **coracoid**.

617   **coral-**   A word-initial combining element, also occurring as a word, derived, ultimately, from one of the Semitic languages (cf. Hebrew *gōrāl* 'pebble') through Greek and Latin (cf. Greek *korállion* and Latin *corallium* 'red calcareous skeleton secreted by certain marine polyps'), used in its Greek and Latin and extended senses in combination with other English elements: **coralberry, coralfish, coralroot**. Compare **coralli-**.

618   **coralli-**   A word-initial combining element, derived, ultimately, from one of the Semitic languages (cf. Hebrew *gōrāl* 'pebble') through Greek *korálli(on)* and Latin *coralli(um)* 'red calcareous skeleton secreted by certain marine polyps,' used in its etymological and extended senses in Neo-Greek and Neo-Latin combinations: **coralliferous, coralliform, coralligerous**. Also, **corall-, corallo-**: **corallite**, *Corallorhiza*. Compare **coral-**.

619   **cord-¹**   A variant of **chord-**.

620   **cord-²**   A word-initial combining element, also occurring as a word, derived from Late Latin *cord(a)* 'string, rope' and, by extension, 'measure of wood' (from Latin *chorda*, a direct borrowing of Greek *chordē* 'gut string (of a lyre)'), used in its Late Latin and extended senses in combination with other English elements: **cord-stitch, cordwood, cordwork**. Compare **chord-**. Related form: **hernio-**.

621   **cordate-**   A word-initial combining element, also occurring as a word, derived from Neo-Latin *cordāt(us)* 'heart-shaped' (from Latin *cor, cord(is)* 'heart' plus the adjective-forming suffix *-ātus* '-possessing'), used in its etymological sense in botanical terminology: **cordate-lanceolate, cordate-oblong, cordate-sagittate**. Compare **core-¹**. Related forms: **cardio-, heart-**.

622   **core-¹**   A word-initial combining element, also occurring as a word, derived through Old French from Latin *cor, cor(dis)* 'heart,' used in the extended sense of 'central part' in combination with other

English elements: **core-barrel, coremaker, core-print.** Compare **cordate-**. Related forms: **cardio-, heart-**.

623 core-² A word-initial combining element, derived from Greek *kórē* 'pupil of the eye,' used in its etymological sense in Neo-Greek combinations: **coredialysis, coremorphosis, coretomy.** Also, **cor-², coreo-, coro-, koro-: corectopia, coreoplasty, corodiastasis, korometer.** Related forms: **carni-, cork-(?), cortico-, score-, screw-, scrofulo-, sharp-, shirt-, short-**.

624 cork- A word-initial combining element, also occurring as a word, derived either from Latin *querc(us)* 'oak' (through Arabic, Spanish, and Dutch) or from the etymologically unrelated Latin *cor(tex)*, *cor(ti)c(is)* 'bark, esp. of the oak (*Quercus suber*)' (through Spanish and Dutch), used in the sense of 'bark of the *Quercus suber*' and in extensions of this sense in combination with other English elements: **corkboard, corkbrain, corkscrew.** Related forms(?): **carni-, core-², cortico-, score-, screw-, scrofulo-, sharp-, shirt-, short-**.

625 cormo- A word-initial combining element, derived from Greek *kormó(s)* 'trunk (of a tree),' used chiefly in extensions of its etymological sense in Neo-Greek combinations: **cormogeny, cormophyte, *Cormostomata*.**

626 corn- A word-initial combining element, also occurring as a word, derived from Old English *corn* 'seed, grain,' used chiefly in the sense of 'maize' and in extensions of this sense in combination with other English elements: **cornbread, corncrib, cornflakes.** Related form: **granulo-**.

627 corneo- A word-initial combining element, derived from Latin *corne(us)* 'horny, hornlike' (from Latin *corn(ū)* 'horn' plus the adjective-forming suffix *-eus*) plus the combining vowel *-o-*, used in its etymological sense and in the extended sense (from Late Latin *cornea* (*tēla*) 'horny (tissue)') of 'of or pertaining to the *cornea*, the horny transparent anterior portion of the external covering of the eye' in Neo-Latin and Neo-Greek combinations: **corneocalcareous, corneo-iritis, corneosclera.** Compare **cornu-**.

628 corner- A word-initial combining element, also occurring as a word, derived from Old French *corn(i)er* 'horn; point at which two converging lines or planes meet' (from Latin *corn(ū)* 'horn' and, by extension, 'pointed protuberance, point' plus the noun-forming suffix *-ārius*), used in the sense of 'point at which two converging lines or planes meet' and in extensions of this sense in combination with other English elements: **corner-cutter, corner-plate, corner-stone.** Compare **cornu-.**

629 cornu- A word-initial combining element, derived from Latin *cornū* 'horn,' used in its etymological sense in Neo-Latin combinations: **cornulite, cornupete, *Cornuspira.*** Also, **corni-: corniform.** Compare **corneo-, corner-.** Related forms: **caroten-, cerebello-, cerebro-, cervi-[2], cervico-, cranio-, ginger-, hart's-, horn-, keratin-, kerato-.**

630 coro- A variant of **core-[2].**

631 corpse- A word-initial combining element, also occurring as a word, derived through Old French from Latin *corp(u)s* 'body,' used in the specialized sense of 'dead body' in combination with other English elements: **corpse-candle, corpse-light, corpse-sheet.**

632 cortico- A word-initial combining element, derived from Latin *cort(ex), cortic(is)* 'bark (of a tree), hull, shell' (from an Indo-European root meaning 'cut, scrape' bark being 'that which may be scraped off a tree') plus the combining vowel *-o-,* used in its etymological and extended senses, chief among these being 'of or pertaining to the outer layer of a bodily organ, esp. the brain,' in Neo-Latin and Neo-Greek combinations: **corticobulbar, corticopetal, corticosuprarenoma.** Also, **cortici-, corti-, cortic-: corticifugal, cortiadrenal, corticate.** Related forms: **carni-, core-[2], cork-(?), score-, screw-, scrofulo-, sharp-, shirt-, short-.**

633 cory- A word-initial combining element, derived from Neo-Latin *Cory(dalis)* 'genus of papaveraceous plants (so named because the spur of the plant is said to resemble that of a lark)' (from Greek *korydallís* 'crested lark' (cf. Greek *kórys* 'helmet, crest')), used in the extended sense of 'of, pertaining to, containing, or derived from an alkaloid derived from the *Corydalis*' in chemical terminology: **corybulbine, corycavine, corytuberine.**

634 coscino- A word-initial combining element, derived from Greek *kóskino(n)* 'sieve,' used in its etymological and extended senses in Neo-Greek and Neo-Latin combinations: **coscinomancy, coscinoporid, Coscinoptera.**

635 cosmo- A word-initial combining element, derived from Greek *kósmo(s)* 'world, universe,' used in its etymological sense in Neo-Greek combinations: **cosmochemistry, cosmology, cosmopolitan.**

636 cost-[1] A variant of **costo-.**

637   cost-²   A word-initial combining element, also occurring as a word, derived through Old French from Latin *co(n)st(āre)* 'to agree' (literally, 'to stand together'), 'to be resolved,' and, in Late Latin, 'to stand at a price,' used in this last and extended senses in combination with other English elements: **cost-account, cost-effective, cost-plus.**

638   costo-   A word-initial combining element, derived from Latin *cost(a)* 'rib, side' plus the combining vowel *-o-*, used in the sense of 'of or pertaining to a rib or the ribs' in biomedical terminology: **costocentral, costotomy, costovertebral.** Also, **cost-¹, costi-: costalgia, costicervical.** Compare **coast-.**

639   cotton-   A word-initial combining element, also occurring as a word, derived through Old Italian and Middle French from Arabic *quṭun* 'soft, white, fleecy substance which covers the seeds of plants of the genus *Gossypium*,' used in its etymological and extended senses in combination with other English elements: **cottonseed, cottontail, cottonweed.**

640   cotylo-   A word-initial combining element, derived from Greek *kotýl(ē)* 'something hollow, esp. a cup,' used in the sense of 'cup-shaped (esp. with reference to the *acetabulum*)' in Neo-Greek and Neo-Latin combinations: ***Cotylogonimus,* cotylopubic, cotylosacral.** Also, **cotyl-, cotyli-: cotyloid, cotyligerous.**

641   council-   A word-initial combining element, also occurring as a word, derived through Old French from Latin *concil(ium)* 'assembly of people, esp. for the purpose of consultation,' used in its etymological and extended senses in combination with other English elements: **council-book, councilman, council-manager.**

642   counter-¹   A word-initial combining element, also occurring as a word, derived through Old French from Latin *contrā* 'in opposition to, against,' used in its etymological and extended senses in combination with other English elements: **countercharge, counterinsurgency, countersink.** Compare **contra-, contre-.**

643   counter-²   A word-initial combining element, also occurring as a word, derived from Old French *conte(oi)r* 'counting-room, counting-table' (from Late Latin *computātōrium* 'place for computation, esp. for monetary reckoning'), used in the extended sense of 'table on which goods for sale may be presented for consumption or over which monetary transactions may take place between buyer and seller' and in extensions of this sense in combination with other English elements: **counterman, counterjumper, countertop.**

644 country- A word-initial combining element, also occurring as a word, derived through Old French from Latin (*regiō* or *terra*) *contrāta* '(territory) opposite, facing,' used in the sense of '(one's) land' and, by extension, 'rural land' in combination with other English elements: **country-bred, countryman, countryside.** Compare **contra-.**

645 coupling- A word-initial combining element, also occurring as a word, the present participle of the English verb *to couple,* derived through Middle French from Latin *cōp(u)l(a)* 'tie, fastening, bond,' used in the sense of 'joining, connecting' in combination with other English elements: **coupling-link, coupling-pin, coupling-valve.**

646 court- A word-initial combining element, also occurring as a word, derived through Old French from Latin *co(h)or(s), co(h)ort(is)* 'enclosure, yard,' and, by extension, 'crowd, (organized) group, retinue,' used in the sense of 'enclosed yard' and, by extension, 'royal dwelling or retinue; place where justice is meted out' in combination with other English elements: **court-dance, courthouse, courtyard.**

647 cover- A word-initial combining element, also occurring as a word, derived through Old French from Latin *c(o)op(er)īr(e)* 'to bury, conceal by placing something over the thing to be concealed,' used in the sense of 'concealment' and 'that which is placed over something else' in combination with other English elements: **coverall, cover-girl, cover-up.**

648 cow- A word-initial combining element, also occurring as a word, derived from Old English *cū* 'female bovine animal,' used in its etymological and extended senses in combination with other English elements: **cowboy, cowcatcher, cowfish.** Related forms: **bou-, bov-.**

649 cox- A word-initial combining element, derived from Latin *cox(a)* 'hip, hip-bone, hip joint,' used in its etymological sense in biomedical terminology: **coxankylometer, coxarthritis, coxarthropathy.** Also, **coxo-: coxotuberculosis.**

650 crab-[1] A word-initial combining element, also occurring as a word, from Old English *crab(ba)* 'crustacean of the suborder *Brachyura*' (from an Indo-European root meaning 'to scratch'), used in its etymological and extended senses in combination with other English elements: **crabeater, crab-louse, crabstone.** Related forms: **gram-, grapho-.**

651   crab-²   A word-initial combining element, also occurring as a word, possibly derived from one of the Scandinavian languages (cf. Swedish *skrabbe* 'wild apple') or perhaps through a specialized use of **crab-¹**, used in the sense of 'sour wild apple or the tree on which it grows' and in extensions of this sense in combination with other English elements: **crabstick, crabstock, crabwood.** Compare **crab-¹.**

652   crack-   A word-initial combining element, also occurring as a word, derived from Old English *crac(ian)* 'to resound,' used in a variety of extensions of its etymological sense in combination with other English elements: **crackdown, crack-off, crack-up.**

653   cradle-   A word-initial combining element, also occurring as a word, derived from Old English *cradol* 'child's bed, usually basket-shaped and built on rockers' (cf. Old High German *cratto* 'basket', the Indo-European root underlying *cradle* and *cratto* having meant something on the order of 'curved, bent'), used in its etymological and extended senses in combination with other English elements: **cradle-cap, cradle-scythe, cradlesong.** Related forms: **cramp-¹, cramp-², crank-, creeping-, crochet-, crook-, crop-, grape-.**

654   cramp-¹   A word-initial combining element, also occurring as a word, derived from Middle Dutch *kramp(e)* 'hook' (from an Indo-European root meaning something on the order of 'curved, bent'), used in the extended sense of 'clamp, i.e., a metal bar which is bent at each end' and in extensions of this sense in combination with other English elements: **cramp-iron, cramp-drill, cramp-joint.** Compare **cramp-².** Related forms: **cradle-, crank-, creeping-, crochet-, crook, crop-, grape-.**

655   cramp-²   A word-initial combining element, also occurring as a word, derived through Old French from Middle Dutch or Middle Low German *kramp(e)* 'hook' (from an Indo-European root meaning something on the order of 'curved, bent'), used in the extended sense of 'severe muscle contraction' and in extensions of this sense in combination with other English elements: **cramp-bark, cramp-bone, cramp-stone.** Compare **cramp-¹.** Related forms: **cradle-, crank-, creeping-, crochet-, crook-, crop-, grape-.**

656   crane-   A word-initial combining element, also occurring as a word, derived from Old English *cran* 'bird of the family *Gruidae*,' used in its etymological and extended senses, chief among these being 'device for lifting and lowering heavy objects (which is so named because its shape resembles that of the bird's neck),' in combination with other English elements: **crane-fly, crane-ladle, crane-necked.**

657 cranio- A word-initial combining element, derived through Late Latin from Greek *kranio(n)* 'skull,' used in its etymological sense and in the specialized sense of 'the part of the skull which encloses the brain' in biomedical combinations: **cranio-acromial, craniobuccal, craniodidymus.** Also, **crani-: craniamphitomy.** Related forms: **caroten-, cerebello-, cerebro-, cervi-², cervico-, corneo-, corner-, cornu-, ginger-, hart's-, horn-, keratin-, kerato-.**

658 crank- A word-initial combining element, also occurring as a word, derived through Middle English from Old English *cranc-* (as in *crancstæf* 'weaver's tool') (from an Indo-European root meaning something on the order of 'crooked, bent'), used in the sense of 'device for imparting rotary or oscillatory motion to a connecting shaft' in combination with other English elements: **crankcase, crankpin, crankshaft.** Related forms: **cradle-, cramp-¹, cramp-², creeping-, crochet-, crook-, crop-, grape-.**

659 crash- A word-initial combining element, also occurring as a word, derived from Middle English *cras(c)h(en)*, a blend of Middle English *cra(sen)* 'to shatter' and *(d)as(c)h(en)* 'to strike, throw with force' or *(me)sh(en)* 'to mash' (or both), used in the sense of 'smash, (cause to) collapse suddenly' and in extensions of this sense in combination with other English elements: **crash-dive, crash-land, crash-pad.** Compare **crazy-** and **dash-.**

660 crauno- A variant of **creno-.**

661 crazy- A word-initial combining element, also occurring as a word, derived from Middle English *cras(en)* 'to shatter,' hence, 'to break down in physical or mental health' plus the adjective-forming suffix *-y*, used in extensions of the sense of 'suffering from a breakdown in mental health' in combination with other English elements: **crazy-bone, crazyweed, crazywork.** Compare **crash-.**

662 cream- A word-initial combining element, also occurring as a word, derived from Old French *cre(s)m(e)* 'the fatty part of milk,' a blend of Late Latin *chrisma* 'consecrated oil' (from Greek *chrîsma* 'unguent, consecrated oil' (from *chriein* 'to anoint')) and Late Latin *crāma* 'the fatty part of milk' (probably of Gaulish origin), used in its Old French and extended senses in combination with other English elements: **cream-colored, creamcups, creamware.** Related form: **Christ-.**

663 creatin- A word-initial combining element, derived as though from Greek *kréa(s)*, **kréat(os)* 'flesh, meat' (cf. *kréas. kréōs* 'flesh, meat') plus the noun-forming suffix *-ine* (which is used in naming basic chemical substances), used in the sense of 'of, pertaining to, containing, or derived from methyl-quanidine-acetic acid (which is found in the muscle tissue of vertebrates)' in biochemical terminology: **creatinase, creatinemia, creatinuria.** Compare **creo-**.

664 creato-   A variant of **creo-**.

665 creeping-   A word-initial combining element, also occurring as a word, the present participle of the English verb *to creep,* from Old English *crēop(an)* 'to move with the body close to the ground' (from an Indo-European root meaning something on the order of 'bent, crooked'), used in its etymological and extended senses in combination with other English elements: **creeping-disk, creeping-jenny, creeping-sailor.** Related forms: **cradle-, cramp-¹, cramp-², crank-, crochet-, crook-, crop-, grape-**.

666 creno-   A word-initial combining element, derived from Greek *krēn(ē)* 'well, spring' plus the combining vowel *-o-,* used in its etymological and extended senses in Neo-Greek combinations: **crenology, crenotherapy, *Crenothrix.*** Also, **crauno-: craunotherapy.**

667 creo-   A word-initial combining element, derived as though from Greek *kré(as), *kré(atos)* 'flesh, meat' (cf. *krás, kréōs* 'flesh, meat') plus the combining vowel *-o-,* used in its etymological and extended senses in Neo-Greek combinations: **creophagy, creosote, creotoxin.** Also, **cre-, crea-, creato-, kreo-: creodont, creatoxin, creatotoxism, kreotoxin.** Compare **creatin-**. Related form: **raw-**.

668 crest-   A word-initial combining element, also occurring as a word, derived through Old French from Latin *crist(a)* 'tuft, comb (on an animal's head),' used in its etymological and extended senses in combination with other English elements: **crestfallen, crestfish, crest-tile.**

669 crib-   A word-initial combining element, also occurring as a word, derived from Old English *crib* 'manger, rack for storing grain,' used in its etymological and extended senses in combination with other English elements: **crib-dam, crib-strap, cribwork.**

670 crico-   A word-initial combining element, derived from Greek *kríko(s)* 'ring,' used in its etymological and extended senses, chief among these being 'of or pertaining to the (ring-shaped) cartilage which forms the back and lower part of the laryngeal cavity,' in Neo-Greek combinations: **cricoarytenoid, cricoderma, cricotracheotomy.** Also, **cric-: cricoid.** Related form: **circum-**.

671 crio- A word-initial combining element, derived from Greek *krió(s)* 'ram,' used in its etymological sense in a few Neo-Greek combinations: **criocephalous, criocerate, criosphinx.**

672 crochet- A word-initial combining element, also occurring as a word, derived from French *crochet* 'small hook (used in knitting)' (from one of the Scandinavian languages (cf. Old Norse *krókr* 'hook, bend')), used in its French and extended senses in combination with other English elements: **crochet-needle, crochet-type, crochetwork.** Related forms: **cradle-, cramp-¹, cramp-², crank-, creeping-, crook-, crop-, grape-.**

673 crook- A word-initial combining element, also occurring as a word, derived from Old Norse *krókr* 'hook, bend,' used in its etymological and extended senses in combination with other English elements: **crookback, crookneck, crook-rafter.** Related forms: **cradle-, cramp-¹, cramp-², crank-, creeping-, crochet-, crop-, grape-.**

674 crop- A word-initial combining element, also occurring as a word, derived from Old English *crop(p)* 'craw of a bird; top of a plant' (from an Indo-European root meaning something on the order of 'bent, curved, bulging'), used in a variety of extended senses, chief among these being 'cultivated produce,' in combination with other English elements: **crop-duster, crop-eared, cropland.** Related forms: **cradle-, cramp-¹, cramp-², crank-, creeping-, crochet-, crook-, grape-.**

675 cross- A word-initial combining element, also occurring as a word, derived through Old Norse or Old Irish from Latin *crux, cruc(is)* 'gallows tree; manmade structure consisting of a horizontal piece of wood affixed to a vertical one on which convicts may be impaled as a means of execution,' used in this latter sense and in a variety of extensions of this sense, most referring to the original structure's shape, in combination with other English elements: **cross-bearer, crossbones, crosscurrent.** Compare **cruci-.**

676 crow- A word-initial combining element, also occurring as a word, derived from Old English *cräw(e)* 'black bird of the genus *Corvus*,' used in its etymological and extended senses in combination with other English elements: **crowbar, crowfoot, crowhop.**

677 crown- A word-initial combining element, also occurring as a word, derived through Anglo-Norman from Latin *c(o)rōn(a)* 'garland, diadem' (from Greek *korōnē* 'having a crooked beak,' hence, 'something crooked or bent, esp. a garland or wreath'), used in the sense of 'diadem' and in extensions of this sense, chief among these being 'of or pertaining to royalty' and 'crest, top,' in combination with other English elements: **crown-of-jewels, crownpiece, crown-work.** Related forms: **curb-, curvi-, ring-.**

678 **cruci-** A word-initial combining element, derived from Latin *cru(x), cruc(is)* 'gallows tree; cross' plus the combining vowel *-i-*, used in the sense of 'cross, crosslike' in Neo-Latin combinations: **cruciferous, crucifix, cruciform.** Compare **cross-.**

679 **cry-** A variant of **cryo-.**

680 **crymo-** A word-initial combining element, derived from Greek *krymó(s)* 'chill, cold, frost' (from *krý(os)* '(icy) cold, frost,' perhaps by analogy to *théros* 'summer' and *thermós* 'warm' (both from *thérein* 'to heat')), used in the sense of 'of or pertaining to coldness' in Neo-Greek combinations: **crymoanesthesia, crymophilia, crymotherapy.** Also, **krymo-: krymotherapy.** Compare **cryo-, crystallo-.**

681 **cryo-** A word-initial combining element, derived from Greek *krýo(s)* 'chill, (icy) cold, frost,' used in the sense of 'of or pertaining to coldness, esp. extreme coldness' in Neo-Greek and Neo-Latin combinations: **cryocautery, cryogenic, cryotolerant.** Also, **cry-, kryo-: cryalgesia, kryoscopy.** Compare **crymo-, crystallo-.**

682 **crypto-** A word-initial combining element, derived from Greek *kryptó(s)* 'hidden, secret,' used in its etymological and extended senses, chief among these being 'microscopic' and 'of or pertaining to a small (esp. glandular) cavity,' in a variety of combinations: **crypto-fascist, cryptogram, cryptometer.** Also, **crypt-, krypto-: cryptanalysis, kryptomnesic.**

683 **crystallo-** A word-initial combining element, derived from Greek *krýstallo(s)* '(clear) ice' (from Greek *krýos* '(icy) cold'), used in the sense of 'icelike; transparent (esp. in reference to a mineral or glass); of or pertaining to a mineral body whose internal structure is composed of symmetrical planes' in Neo-Greek combinations: **crystallogram, crystallography, crystallophobia.** Also, **crystall-: crystalluria.** Compare **crymo-, cryo.**

684 **cteno-** A word-initial combining element, derived from Greek *kté(is), kte(i)nó(s)* 'comb, rake,' used in the sense of 'comblike, comb-shaped' in Neo-Greek combinations: **ctenobranch, ctenocyst, ctenodactyl.** Also, **cten-: ctenodont.**

685 **cubo-** A word-initial combining element, derived from Greek *kýbo(s)* 'six-sided solid, each side of which is a square; die' (from an Indo-European root meaning 'bend,' hence, 'something bent or

empty, as a cup'), used in its etymological and extended senses in Neo-Greek and Neo-Latin combinations: **cubocube, cubocuneiform, cubomancy.** Also, **cub-, cubi-: cuboctahedral, cubicontravariant.** Related forms: **cup-, hip-, hop-¹.**

686 cuckoo- A word-initial combining element, also occurring as a word, derived from (onomatopoeic) Middle English *cuc(c)u* 'bird of the family *Cuculidae,*' used in its etymological and extended senses in combination with other English elements: **cuckoo-ale, cuckooclock, cuckoopint.**

687 cultri- A word-initial combining element, derived from Latin *cult(e)r, cultr(ī)* 'knife' plus the combining vowel *-i-*, used in its etymological and extended senses in Neo-Latin combinations: **cultriform, cultrirostral, cultrivorous.** Also, **cultr-: cultrate.**

688 cumulo- A word-initial combining element, derived from Latin *cumul(us)* 'heap, mass' plus the combining vowel *-o-*, used chiefly in the sense of 'thick, heaplike cloud' in Neo-Latin combinations: **cumulocirrus, cumulonimbus, cumulostratus.** Also, **cumul-, cumuli-: cumulate, cumuliform.**

689 cuneo- A word-initial combining element, derived from Latin *cune(us)* 'wedge' plus the combining vowel *-o-*, used in its etymological and extended senses, chief among these being 'wedge-shaped bone (of the human foot or wrist),' in Neo-Latin and Neo-Greek combinations: **cuneo-avicular, cuneocuboid, cuneoscaphoid.** Also, **cune-, cunei-: cuneate, cuneiform.**

690 cup- A word-initial combining element, also occurring as a word, derived from Late Latin *cup(pa)* 'bowl, drinking vessel' (from Latin *cūpa* 'vat, cask' (from an Indo-European root meaning 'bend,' hence, 'something bent or empty')), used in its Late Latin and extended senses in combination with other English elements: **cupbearer, cupboard, cupcake.** Related forms: **cubo-, hip-, hop-¹.**

691 cupro- A word-initial combining element, derived from late Latin *cupr(um)* 'copper' (from Latin *(aes) Cypr(i)um* '(base metal) from Cyprus,' specifically, 'copper') plus the combining vowel *-o-*, used in its etymological sense in metallurgical terminology: **cupromagnesite, cupronickel, cuproscheelite.** Also, **cupr-, cupri-: cuprammonium, cupriferous.** Compare **copper-, cyprido-.**

692 curb- A word-initial combining element, also occurring as a word, derived through Middle French from Latin *curv(us)* 'crooked, bent,' used in its etymological and extended senses in native combinations: **curb-chain, curb-roof, curbstone.** Compare **curvi-.**

693 curvi- A word-initial combining element, derived from Latin *curv(us)* 'crooked, bent' plus the combining vowel *-i-,* used in its etymological and extended senses in Neo-Latin combinations: **curvicaudate, curvifoliate, curvilinear.** Compare **curb-.** Related forms: **crown-, ring-.**

694 cut-¹ A variant of **cuti-.**

695 cut-² A word-initial combining element, also occurring as a word, derived from Middle English *cut(te)* 'slice,' used in its etymological and extended senses in combination with other English elements: **cut-and-cover, cutaway, cutoff.**

696 cuti- A word-initial combining element, derived from Latin *cuti(s)* 'skin,' used in its etymological sense in biomedical terminology: **cuticolor, cutireaction, cutisector.** Also, **cut-¹: cutitis.**

697 cyan-¹ A variant of **cyano-¹.**

698 cyan-² A variant of **cyano-².**

699 cyan-³ A variant of **cyano-³.**

700 cyano-¹ A word-initial combining element, derived from Greek *kýano(s)* '(dark) blue substance,' used in the sense of 'blue, bluish' in Neo-Greek combinations: **cyanochroia, cyanoderma, cyanometer.** Also, **cyan-¹, kyan-, kyano-: cyanosis, kyanopsia, kyanophane.** Compare **cyano-², cyano-³.**

701 cyano-² A word-initial combining element, also occurring as a word, derived from English *cyano(gen)* 'the chemical radical (CN)' (from **cyano-¹** plus the suffix *-gen* '-producing' (because (CN) is a major constituent of Prussian blue pigment)), used in its etymological sense in chemical terminology: **cyanocobalamine, cyanohydrin, cyanophoric.** Also, **cyan-²: cyanide.** Compare **cyano-¹, cyano-³.**

702 cyano-³ A word-initial combining element, derived from English *cyanide* 'binary compound of cyanogen' (from **cyan(o)-²** plus the suffix *-ide* (which is used in naming binary compounds)), used in its etymological sense in chemical terminology: **cyanocuprol, cyanoguanidine, cyanoplatinite.** Also, **cyan-³: cyanamide.** Compare **cyano-¹, cyano-².**

703 **cyatho-** A word-initial combining element, derived from Greek *kýatho(s)* 'cup,' used in its etymological and extended senses in Neo-Greek and Neo-Latin combinations: **cyathocrinite, cyatholith, cyathozooid.** Also, **cyath-, cyathi-: cyathoid, cyathiform.**

704 **cyclo-** A word-initial combining element, derived from Greek *kýklo(s)* 'ring, circle,' used in its etymological and extended senses in Neo-Greek combinations: **cyclodialysis, cyclograph, cyclometer.** Also, **cycl-: cyclops.** Related forms: **coll-², collar-, palin-, polari-, teleo-³, telo-¹, wheel-.**

705 **cylindro-** A word-initial combining element, derived from Greek *klindro(s)* 'roller, roller-shaped figure' (from *kylíndein* 'to roll'), used in the sense of 'roller-shaped, column-shaped' in Neo-Greek and Neo-Latin combinations: **cylindrocellular, cylindrodendrite, cylindrosarcoma.** Also, **cylindr-, cylindri-: cylindrarthrosis, cylindriform.**

706 **cym-** A variant of **kymo-.**

707 **cymato-** A variant of **kymo-.**

708 **cymo-** A variant of **kymo-.**

709 **cyno-** A word-initial combining element, derived from Greek *ký(ō)n, kyn(ós)* 'dog' plus the combining vowel -*o*-, used in its etymological and extended senses in Neo-Greek combinations: **cynobex, cynocephalic, cynophobia.** Also, **cyn-, kyn-, kyno-: cynanthropy, kynurin, kynophobia.**

710 **cyo-** A word-initial combining element, derived from Greek *kýo(s)* 'embryo, fetus' (from *kýein* 'to contain, be pregnant, swell'), used in the sense of 'of or pertaining to pregnancy or to a fetus' in Neo-Greek combinations: **cyogenic, cyophoric, cyotrophy.** Also, **kyo-: kyogenic.** Compare **cyst-, cyto-, kymo-.**

711 **cyprido-** A word-initial combining element, derived from Greek *Kýpri(s), Kýprid(os)* 'Cyprus' and, by extension, 'Aphrodite (who, as the goddess of love, was first worshiped on Cyprus)' plus the combining vowel -*o*-, used in the extended sense of 'of or pertaining to sexual intercourse' in Neo-Greek combinations: **cypridology, cypridopathy, cypridophobia.** Also, **cipri-: cipriphobia.** Compare **copper-, cupro-.**

712 **cyrto-** A word-initial combining element, derived from Greek *kyrtó(s)* 'bent, curved,' used in its etymological and extended senses

in Neo-Greek combinations: **cyrtograph, cyrtometer, cyrtostyle.** Also, **cyrt-, kyrto-:** *Cyrtonyx,* **kyrtorrhachic.**

713 cyst- A word-initial combining element, also occurring as a word, derived from Greek *kýst(is)* 'bladder, sac, pouch' (from *kýein* 'to contain, swell'), used in its etymological and extended senses in Neo-Greek and Neo-Latin combinations: **cystadenoma, cystectomy, cystencephalus.** Also, **cysti-, cystido-, cysto-: cystifelleotomy, cystidoparalysis, cystoneuralgia.** Compare **cyo-, cyto-, kymo-.**

714 cyto- A word-initial combining element, derived from Greek *kýto(s)* 'container, hollow vessel' (from *kýein* 'to contain, swell'), used chiefly in the extended sense of 'animal or plant cell' (because cells were originally thought to be hollow) in Neo-Greek and Neo-Latin combinations: **cytoblast, cytodiagnosis, cytoinhibition.** Also, **cyt-, cytio-: cythemolysis, cytioderm.** Compare **cyo-, cyst-, kymo-.**

D

715   **D-**   A word-initial combining element, an abbreviation of **d(extro)-**, used to designate 'the 'right-handed' enantiomer of an optical isomer,' as, e.g., **D-glyceraldehyde;** 'the highest-numbered asymmetric carbon atom in a carbohydrate,' as, e.g., **D-glucose;** and 'the lowest-numbered asymmetric carbon atom in an amino acid,' as, e.g., **D-threonine.** Compare D_g-, D_s-, **d-, dextro-**.

716   **D_g-**   A variant of **D-,** used in carbohydrate nomenclature in naming substances 'of the same configurational family as **D-glyceraldehyde,'** as, e.g., **D_g-glucosaminic acid.** Compare **D-, d-, dextro-**.

717   **D_s-**   A variant of **D-,** used in amino acid nomenclature in naming substances 'of the same configurational family as **D-serine,'** as, e.g., **D_s-threonine.** Compare **D-, d-, dextro-**.

718   **d-**   A word-initial combining element, an abbreviation of **d(extro)-**, used in two kinds of chemical terms:
1.   those in which **d-** refers to the 'clockwise direction in which the plane of polarized light rotates when passed through the substance named by the combining root,' e.g., **d-menthol.**
2.   those in which **d-**, followed by (+) or (−), refers to the 'clockwise or counterclockwise configurational family to which the substance named by the combining root belongs,' e.g., **d(+)-cystine, d(−)-alaine.** Compare **D-, D_g-, D_s-, dextrose-**.

109

719 dacryo-   A word-initial combining element, derived from Greek *dákryo(n)* 'tear(drop),' used in its etymological and extended senses in Neo-Greek combinations: **dacryoadenalgia, dacryocele, dacryolith.** Also, **dacry-: dacryagogue.** Related forms: **lacrimo-, tear-.**

720 dacryocyst-   A word-initial combining element, also occurring as a word, derived from Greek *dákryo(n)* 'tear(drop)' plus *kýst(is)* 'container, sac,' used in the sense of 'lacrimal sac' in biomedical terminology: **dacryocystalgia, dacryocystectomy, dacryocystitis.** Also, **dacryocysto-: dacryocystoptosis.** Compare **dacryo-** and **cyst-.**

721 dactylo-   A word-initial combining element, derived from Greek *dáktylo(s)* 'finger, toe,' used in its etymological and extended senses in Neo-Greek combinations: **dactylogram, dactylology, dactylomegaly.** Also, **dactyl-: dactyledema.**

722 dad-   A word-initial combining element, an Anglo-Irish euphemistic substitution for English *gad* (a euphemistic substitution for *God*), used in combination with other English elements in mild expletives of recent coinage: **dad-blamed, dad-blasted, dad-burned.** Compare **God-.**

723 dairy-   A word-initial combining element, also occurring as a word, derived from Middle English *dayerie,* an equivalent of Middle English *daye* 'female servant,' later, 'farm servant; milkmaid' (from old English *dǽǧe* 'kneader (of bread)'), used in the sense of 'of or pertaining to the production of milk, cream, butter, and cheese' in combination with other English elements: **dairy-farm, dairymaid, dairyman.** Compare **lady-, lady's-.** Related form: **thigmo-.**

724 dark-   A word-initial combining element, also occurring as a word, derived from Old English *deorc* 'not light,' used in its etymological and extended senses in combination with other English elements: **dark-field, darkroom, dark-trace (tube).**

725 dash-   A word-initial combining element, also occurring as a word, derived from Middle English *das(c)h(en)* 'to strike, throw with force,' used in its etymological and extended senses in combination with other English elements: **dashboard, dashpot, dash-wheel.** Compare **crash-.**

726 dasy-   A word-initial combining element, derived from Greek *dasý(s)* 'thick, shaggy,' used in its etymological and extended senses in Neo-Greek combinations: **dasymeter, *Dasypus,* dasypose.**

727   date-   A word-initial combining element, also occurring as a word, derived through Middle French from Late Latin *dat(a)* 'specific time (day) of an event's occurrence' (by reanalysis of Latin expressions such as *data* (*Romae*) 'given (at Rome),' customarily used in recording the place of origin and the day on which a letter was given to a messenger for delivery, *data* being a form of the past participle of the verb *dare* 'to give'), used in its Late Latin and extended senses in combination with other English elements: **datebook, dateline, date-mark.** Related form: **die-².**

728   day-   A word-initial combining element, also occurring as a word, derived from Old English *dæġ* 'interval between two successive nights,' used in its etymological and extended senses in combination with other English elements: **daybook, daydream, daytime.**

729   de-¹   A word-initial combining element, derived from Latin *dē* 'from, away (from),' used in its etymological sense and as an intensifier in borrowings from Latin and in the sense of 'negation, reversal, or removal' of that which is named by the combining root in borrowings from Romance and in combination with other English elements: **de-emphasize, denude, depart.**

730   de-²   A word-initial combining element, derived through French from Latin *dis-* 'apart, asunder, not, utterly,' appearing in its etymological sense in borrowings from French: **decry, deface, defame.** Compare **des-, di-², dif-, dis-².**

731   dead-   A word-initial combining element, also occurring as a word, derived from Old English *dēad* 'no longer alive,' used in its etymological and extended senses in combination with other English elements: **deadbeat, deadfall, deadline.** Related forms: **death-, die-¹.**

732   death-   A word-initial combining element, also occurring as a word, derived from Old English *dēaþ* 'end of life; act of ceasing to be alive,' used in its etymological and extended senses in combination with other English elements: **deathbed, deathblow, deathtrap.** Related forms: **dead-, die-¹.**

733   deca-   A word-initial combining element, derived from Greek *déka* 'ten,' used in its etymological sense in Neo-Greek and Neo-Latin combinations: **decagram, decahydrate, decanormal.** Also, **dec-, dek-, deka-: decare, dekare, dekadrachm.** Related forms: **deci-, ten-¹.**

734   deci-   A word-initial combining element, derived from Latin *deci(mus)* 'one tenth,' used in its etymological sense in Neo-Latin and Neo-Greek combinations: **decibel, decimeter, decinormal.** Related forms: **deca-, ten-**[1].

735 deck- A word-initial combining element, also occurring as a word, derived from Middle Dutch *dec* 'roof, covering,' used chiefly in the extended sense of 'of or pertaining to the floorlike surface on a ship' and in extensions of this sense in combination with other English elements: **deckhead, deckhouse, deckpipe.**

736 deep- A word-initial combining element, also occurring as a word, derived from Old English *dē(o)p* 'profound,' used in its etymological and extended senses in combination with other English elements: **deep-dish, deep-seated, deepwater.** Related forms: **dip-, dipping-, diving-.**

737 deer- A word-initial combining element, also occurring as a word, derived from Old English *dē(o)r* 'animal, beast' (from an Indo-European root meaning 'breath, smoke, dust,' an animal being 'that which breathes'), used in the specialized sense of 'animal of the family *Cervidae*' in combination with other English elements: **deerhound, deerskin, deerstalker.** Related forms: **dust-, thio-, thym-**[1]**, thymo-**[2]**, typhl-**[1]**, typhlo-**[2]**, typho-.**

738 dehydro- See **de-**[1] and **hydro-.**

739 deka- A variant of **deca-.**

740 delta- (Δ, δ) A word-initial combining element, the fourth letter of the Greek alphabet, used chiefly to designate 'the fourth carbon atom in a straight chain compound or a derivative thereof in which the substitute group is attached to that atom' in chemical terminology. See **alpha-.**

741 dem- A variant of **demo-.**

742 demi- A word-initial combining element, derived through French from Latin *dīmi(dius)* 'cut in half; half' (from *dis-* 'apart, asunder' plus *medium* 'middle'), used in the sense of 'half' in a variety of combinations: **demibath, demigauntlet, demimonstrosity.** Compare **de-**[2] and **medio-.**

743 demo- A word-initial combining element, derived from Greek *dêmo(s)* 'territory,' hence, 'people (inhabiting a territory); common people,' used in this latter and extended senses in borrowings from

Greek and in Neo-Greek combinations: **democracy, demography, demophobia.** Also, **dem-: demagogue.** Related forms: **tide-, time-.**

744 demono- A word-initial combining element, derived from Late Latin *demon(ium)* 'evil spirit, devil' (from Greek *daimōn* '(lesser) god or goddess' and, in New Testament Greek, 'evil spirit, devil') plus the combining vowel *-o-,* used in its New Testament Greek and Late Latin sense in Neo-Greek combinations: **demonography, demonolatry, demonophobia.** Also **demon-: demonize.**

745 dendro- A word-initial combining element, derived from Greek *déndro(n)* 'tree' (from an Indo-European root meaning 'strong, steadfast'), used in its etymological and extended senses in Neo-Greek and Neo-Latin combinations: **dendrochronology, dendrophagous, dendrophilia.** Also, **dendr-, dendri-: dendraxon, dendriform.** Related forms: **duro-, tree-, true-.**

746 denti- A word-initial combining element, derived from Latin *den(s), dent(is)* 'tooth' plus the combining vowel *-i-,* used in its etymological and extended senses in Neo-Latin and Neo-Greek combinations: **dentibuccal, dentilabial, dentilingual.** Also, **dent-, denta-, dentia-, dento-: dentalgia, dentaphone, dentiaskiascope, dentomechanical.** Compare **dentin-.** Related forms: **odonto-, tooth-.**

747 dentin- A word-initial combining element, also occurring as a word, derived from Latin *den(s), dent(is)* 'tooth' plus the noun-forming suffix *-in,* used in the sense of 'of or pertaining to the substance which immediately surrounds the tooth pulp and makes up the major part of the tooth' in biomedical terminology: **dentinalgia, dentinitis, dentinosteoid.** Also **dentini-, dentino-: dentinification, dentinoblast.** Compare **denti-.**

748 deorsum- A word-initial combining element, also occurring as a word, derived from Latin *deorsum* 'downwards,' used in its etymological sense in Neo-Latin combinations: **deorsumduction, deorsumvergence, deorsumversion.**

749 deoxy- See **de-²** and **oxy-².**

750 der- A word-initial combining element, derived from Greek *dér(ē)* 'neck,' used in its etymological and extended senses in Neo-Greek combinations: **deradenitis, deranencephalia, derencephalocele.** Also, **dero-: derodidymus.**

751 derma- A word-initial combining element, also occurring as a word, derived from Greek *dérma, dérma(tos)* 'skin,' used in its etymological and extended senses in biomedical terminology: **dermagraphy, dermahemia, dermalaxia.** Also, **derm-, dermat-, dermato-, dermo-: dermanaplasty, dermataneuria, dermatocellulitis, dermophylaxis.**

752　**dero-**　A variant of **der-.**

753　**des-**　A word-initial combining element, derived through Old French from Latin *dis-* 'asunder, away, not, utterly,' used in its etymological sense in borrowings from French and, in biochemical terminology, as though a variant of **de-**[1] in combinations in which the element to which it is joined begins with *h* or a vowel: **desamydase, descant, deshydremia.** Compare **de-**[1], **de-**[2], **di-**[2], **dif-**, **dis-**[2].

754　**desmo-**　A word-initial combining element, derived from Greek *desmó(s)* 'bond,' used in its etymological and extended senses in Neo-Greek combinations: **desmoenzyme, desmoneoplasm, desmopexia.** Also, **desm-: desmepithelium.**

755　**desoxy-**　See **des-** and **oxy-**[2].

756　**deutero-**　A word-initial combining element, derived from Greek *deútero(s)* 'second' (from *deúein* 'to fail to reach; to fall behind'), used in the sense of 'second; derived from' and, in chemical terminology, 'containing *deuterium,* heavy hydrogen, the mass two isotope of hydrogen': **deuteroalbuminose, deuteroconidium, deuterofat.** Also, **deut-, deuter-, deuto-: deutencephalon, deuteranomalopia, deutochloride.**

757　**devil-**　A word-initial combining element, also occurring as a word, derived through Old English from Late Latin *diabol(us),* a borrowing of New Testament Greek *diábol(os)* 'slanderer, Satan' (from *diabállein* 'to throw or carry across; to cross; to slander'), used in the sense of 'Satan' and in extensions of this sense in combination with other English elements: **devilfish, devil-may-care, devilwood.** Compare **devil's-.**

758　**devil's-**　A word-initial combining element, also occurring as a word, the possessive singular form of *devil,* derived through Old English and Late Latin from New Testament Greek *diábol(os)* 'slanderer, Satan' (from *diabállein* 'to throw or carry across; to cross; to slander'), used in the sense of 'Satan's' and in extensions of this sense in combination with other English elements: **devil's-food, devil's-mark, devil's-pincushion.** Compare **devil-.**

759   **dew-**   A word-initial combining element, derived from Old English *dē(a)w* 'condensed moisture appearing as water droplets on any cool surface,' used in its etymological and extended senses in combination with other English elements: **dewberry, dewdrop, dewfall.**

760   **dextro-**   A word-initial combining element, derived from Latin *dext(e)r, dext(e)r(a), dext(e)r(um)* 'right-hand; on or to the right-hand side' plus the combining vowel *-o-*, used in its etymological and extended senses, chief among these being 'of or pertaining to an enantiomorph which rotates towards the right,' in Neo-Latin and Neo-Greek combinations: **dextroduction, dextroglucose, dextropedal.** Also, **D-, d-, dextr-: D-glyceraldehyde, d-menthol, dextrocular.**

761   **di-**[1]   A word-initial combining element, derived from Greek *di-*, a combining form of *dís* 'twice, double,' appearing in its etymological and extended senses in borrowings from Greek in which the element to which it is joined begins with a consonant other than *ch, m, p, s, t,* or *th* and in Neo-Greek combinations in which the element to which it is joined may begin with any (Greek) consonant or vowel: **diacid, dicalcic, dihysteria.** Compare **dicho-, diplo-, dis-**[1]. Related forms: **bi-**[1]**, bin-, bis-, double-, dui-, duo-, twelve-, twi-, twin-, two-.**

762   **di-**[2]   A word-initial combining element, derived from Latin *dī-*, a combining form of *dis-* 'asunder, away, not, utterly,' appearing in one or another of its etymological senses in borrowings from Latin in which the element to which it is joined begins with a voiced consonant: **digress, diligent, divest.** Compare **de-**[2]**, des-, dif-, dis-**[2]**.** Related forms(?): **di-**[3]**, dia-.**

763   **di-**[3]   A variant of **dia-.**

764   **dia-**   A word-initial combining element, derived from Greek *diá* 'through, across, between, opposing, one from another, utterly,' appearing in one or another of its etymological senses in borrowings from Greek and in Neo-Greek combinations: **diagnosis, dialysis, diathermy.** Also, **di-**[3]**: dielectrolysis.** Related forms(?): **de**[2]**, dēs-, di-**[2]**, dis-**[2]**.**

765   **diamido-**   See **di-**[1] and **amido-.**

766   **diamino-**   See **di-**[1] and **amino-.**

767   **diamond-**   A word-initial combining element, also occurring as a word, derived from Late Latin (*a*)*diama*(*s*), (*a*)*diamant*(*is*) 'extremely hard form of nearly pure carbon' (from Latin *adamās*, *adamant*(*is*) 'hardest metal; any hard substance; a diamond,' a borrowing of Greek *adámas*, *adámant*(*os*), literally, 'unconquerable' (from *a*- 'not' plus *damân* 'to conquer'), but also used in the senses found in Latin), used in its Late Latin and extended senses in combination with other English elements: **diamondback, diamond-cutter, diamond-leaf.**

768 **diaphano-** A word-initial combining element, derived from Greek *diaphan*(*ḗs*) 'transparent' (from *diá* 'through, across' plus *phaneîn* 'to show, display') plus the combining vowel -*o*-, used in its etymological and extended senses in Neo-Greek combinations: **diaphanometer, diaphanoscope, diaphanotype.** Compare **dia-** and **pheno-¹.**

769 **diastemato-** A word-initial combining element, derived from Greek *diástēma*, *diastḗmat*(*os*) 'interval' (from *diastênai* 'to set apart, divide' (from *diá* 'through, across, opposing' plus *stênai* 'to stand')) plus the combining vowel -*o*-, used in the sense of '(congenital) fissure or division' in Neo-Greek combinations: **diastematocrania, diastematomyelia, diastematopyelia.** Compare **dia-** and **stato-.**

770 **diazo-** See **di-¹** and **azo-.**

771 **dichlor-** See **di-¹** and **chlor-².**

772 **dicho-** A word-initial combining element, derived from Greek *dích*(*a*) 'divided in two,' hence, 'unalike' plus the combining vowel -*o*-, used in its etymological and extended senses in Neo-Greek combinations: **dichogamous, dichogeny, dichotomy.** Compare **di-¹.**

773 **dictyo-** A word-initial combining element, derived from Greek *diktyo*(*n*) 'net,' used in the sense of 'netlike' in Neo-Greek and Neo-Latin combinations: ***Dictyocysta, Dictyophyllum,*** **dictyoxylon.**

774 **die-¹** A word-initial combining element, also occurring as a word, derived from Middle English *deġ*(*en*) 'to cease to live,' used in its etymological and extended senses in combination with other English elements: **die-away, dieback, die-hard.** Related forms: **dead-, death-.**

775 **die-²** A word-initial combining element, also occurring as a word, derived from Middle English *dē* 'marked cube used in games of chance' (through Old French from Latin *datum* 'that which is given,' hence, 'that which is cast, thrown'), used chiefly in the

extended sense of 'device for cutting or stamping a design on metal' in combination with other English elements: **die-holder, diesinker, diestock.** Compare **date-.**

776 **dif-** A word-initial combining element, derived from Latin *dif-,* a combining form of *dis-* 'asunder, away, not, utterly,' appearing in one or another of its etymological senses in borrowings from Latin in which the element to which it is joined begins with *f:* **different, diffraction, diffuse.** Compare **di-², de-², des-, dis-².** Related forms(?): **di-³, dia-.**

777 **digi-** A word-initial combining element, derived from English *digi(talis)* 'dried leaves of the foxglove, esp. as used medicinally' (from Scientific Latin *Digitalis* (*purpurea*) 'foxglove,' literally, 'finger-shaped (purple plant)'), used in the sense of 'of, pertaining to, or effected by *digitalis*' in biochemical terminology: **digifolin, digiglusin, diginutin.** Also, **dig-, digit-², digital-, digito-: digoxin, digitin, digitalose, digitophyllin.** Compare **digiti-.**

778 **digit-¹** A variant of **digiti-.**

779 **digit-²** A variant of **digi-.**

780 **digiti-** A word-initial combining element, derived from Latin *digit(us)* 'finger, toe' plus the combining vowel *-i-,* used in its etymological and extended senses in Neo-Latin combinations: **digitiform, digitigrade, digitipennate.** Also, **digit-¹: digitate.** Compare **digi-.**

781 **dihydro-** See **di-¹** and **hydro-.**

782 **diiodo-** See **di-¹** and **iodo-.**

783 **dimethyl-** See **di-¹** and **methyl-.**

784 **dinitro-** See **di-¹** and **nitro-.**

785 **dino-** A word-initial combining element, derived from Greek *d(e)inó(s)* 'fearful, terrible,' used in its etymological and extended senses in Neo-Greek and Neo-Latin combinations: **dinoflagellate, dinosaur, dinothere.**

786 **dioxy-** See **di-¹** and **oxy-².**

787 **dip-** A word-initial combining element, also occurring as a word, derived from Old English *dyp(pan)* 'to plunge into water,' used in

its etymological and extended senses in combination with other English elements: **dip-bucket, dip-net, dip-stick.** Compare **dipping-.** Related forms: **deep-, diving-.**

788 diphenyl- See **di-¹** and **phenyl-.**

789 diplo- A word-initial combining element, derived from Greek *dipló(os)* 'double,' literally, 'twofold,' used in its etymological and extended senses in Neo-Greek and Neo-Latin combinations: **diplobacillus, diplogaster, diploneural.** Also, **dipl-: diplopia.** Compare **di-¹.**

790 dipping- A word-initial combining element, also occurring as a word, the present participle of the English verb *to dip* (from Old English *dyp(pan)* 'to plunge into water'), used both in the sense of 'that which dips' and 'that into which something may be dipped' in combination with other English elements: **dipping-compass, dipping-tube, dipping-vat.** Compare **dip-.**

791 dipso- A word-initial combining element, derived from Greek *dips(a)* 'thirst' plus the combining vowel *-o-*, used in its etymological and extended senses in Neo-Greek combinations: **dipsomania, dipsopathy, dipsotherapy.** Also, **dips-: dipsesis.**

792 direct- A word-initial combining element, also occurring as a word, derived from Latin *dīrect(us)*, a variant of *dērect(us)* 'straight, straightforward, plain' (from *dērigere* 'to lay straight; to form, define, guide'), used in its etymological and extended senses in combination with other English elements: **direct-acting, direct-examine, direct-vision (prism).** Compare **de-¹** and **recti-; dress-, dressing-.**

793 dirt- A word-initial combining element, also occurring as a word, derived from Middle English *drit* 'excrement' (from Old Norse *drit* 'excrement'), used in its etymological and extended senses in combination with other English elements: **dirt-bed, dirt-cheap, dirt-eating.**

794 dis-¹ A word-initial combining element, derived from Greek *dís* 'twice, double,' appearing in its etymological and extended senses in borrowings from Greek: **disdiaclast, dissyllabic, districhiasis.** Compare **di-¹, dicho-, diplo-.** Related forms: **bi-¹, bin-, bis-, double-, dui-, duo-, twelve-, twi-, twin-, two-.**

795 dis-² A word-initial combining element, derived from Latin *dis-* 'asunder, away, not, utterly,' appearing in one or another of its

etymological senses in borrowings from Latin in which the element
to which it is joined begins with an unvoiced stop consonant or
with *s* and, chiefly in the sense of 'not, un-,' in a variety of more
modern combinations in which the element to which it is joined
may begin with any (English) consonant or vowel: **disagree,
disband, discolor.** Compare **de-², des-, di-², dif-.** Related forms(?):
di-³, dia-.

796   **disco-**   A word-initial combining element, derived from Greek
dísko(s) 'round plate thrown in athletic competitions' (from *diskeîn*
'to throw'), used chiefly in the extended sense of 'something shaped
like a round plate' in Neo-Greek and Neo-Latin combinations:
discoblastula, discography, discoplacenta. Also, **disc-, disk-, disko-:**
discoid, diskitis, diskography. Compare **dish-.**

797   **disem-**   See **dis-²** and **em-².**

798   **disen-**   See **dis-²** and **en-².**

799   **dish-**   A word-initial combining element, also occurring as a word,
derived through Old English from Latin *disc(us)*, a direct borrowing of Greek *disk(os)* 'round plate thrown in athletic competitions'
(from *diskeîn* 'to throw'), used in the extended sense of 'plate or
bowl on or in which food is served' in combination with other
English elements: **dishcloth, dishpan, dishwasher.** Compare **disco-.**

800   **disin-**   See **dis-²** and **in-².**

801   **disko-**   A variant of **disco-.**

802   **disre-**   See **dis-²** and **re-.**

803   **disto-**   A word-initial combining element, derived from English
dist(al) 'situated or directed away from a point of reference' (from
Latin *dīstāre* 'to stand away; to be remote' (from *dis-* 'apart' plus
stāre 'to stand') plus the adjective-forming suffix *-al*) plus the
combining vowel *-o-*, used in the sense of 'more remote, farther
away from a point of reference, esp. a dental surface, wall, or
cavity' in Neo-Latin combinations: **distobuccal, distoceptor, disto-
labial.** Compare **di-²** and **state-.**

804   **diversi-**   A word-initial combining element, derived from Latin
dīvers(us) 'different, separate, opposite,' literally, 'turned away
(from each other)' (from *dīvertere* 'to turn away, go in different
directions') plus the combining vowel *-i-*, used in its etymological

sense in Neo-Latin combinations: **diversiflorous, diversifolious, diversiform.** Related form: **diverticul-.**

805 diverticul- A word-initial combining element, derived from Latin *dīverticul(um)* 'by-road, digression, deviation' (from *dīvertere* 'to turn away, go in different directions'), used in the specialized sense of 'tubular pocket or pouch that branches off from a bodily cavity or canal' in biomedical terminology: **diverticulectomy, diverticulitis, diverticulosis.** Also, **diverticulo-: diverticulopexy.** Related form: **diversi-.**

806 diving- A word-initial combining element, also occurring as a word, the present participle of the English verb *to dive,* derived from Old English *dȳf(an)* 'to dip, plunge (into water),' used in its etymological and extended senses in combination with other English elements: **diving-beetle, diving-bell, diving-board.** Related forms: **deep-, dip-, dipping-.**

807 do- A word-initial combining element, also occurring as a word, derived from Old English *dō(n)* 'to accomplish, perform,' used in its etymological and extended senses in combination with other English elements: **do-gooder, do-it-yourself, do-nothing.** Related forms: **face-, facio-, thec-.**

808 dock- A word-initial combining element, also occurring as a word, derived from Middle Dutch *dock(e)* 'furrow made by a ship running aground,' used in the extended sense of 'wharf' in combination with other English elements: **dockside, dockwalloper, dockyard.**

809 dodeca- A word-initial combining element, derived from Greek *d(u)ṓdeka* 'twelve' (from *dúō* 'two' plus *déka* 'ten'), used in its etymological sense in Neo-Greek combinations: **dodecahedron, dodecapetalous, dodecasyllabic.** Also, **dodec-, duodec-: dodecarchy, duodecahedral.** Compare **duo-** and **deca-.**

810 dog- A word-initial combining element, also occurring as a word, derived from Old English *do(c)g(a)* '(large) member of the genus *Canis,*' used in its etymological and extended senses in combination with other English elements: **dogbane, dogcatcher, dogtooth.**

811 dolicho- A word-initial combining element, derived from Greek *dolichó(s)* 'long,' used in its etymological and extended senses, chief among these being 'abnormally long,' in Neo-Greek and Neo-Latin combinations: **dolichocephalic, dolichofacial, dolichosigmoid.** Also, **dolich-: dolichuranic.**

812   dollar-   A word-initial combining element, also occurring as a word, derived through Dutch or Low German from German (*Joachims*)*t*(*h*)*aler* '(silver coin minted in) the city of Joachimsthal,' used in the extended sense of 'currency coin or bill (having different values from country to country)' and in extensions of this sense in combination with other English elements: **dollar-a-year** (**man**), **dollarbird, dollarfish.**

813   donkey-   A word-initial combining element, also occurring as a word, derived perhaps from English *dun* 'brown' plus the diminutive double suffix *-k-ie* (as in dialectal English *horsikie* 'little horse') or perhaps from the diminutive form of such a name as *Duncan* or even, though this would seem rather unlikely, from *Don Qui*(*xote*), used in the sense of 'ass (*Equus asinus*)' and in extensions of this sense in combination with other English elements: **donkey-engine, donkey-pump, donkey-rest.**

814   door-   A word-initial combining element, also occurring as a word, derived from Middle English *dor*(*e*) 'movable barrier which closes off an entranceway' (from a blend of Old English *dur*(*u*) 'door' and *dōr* 'gate'), used in its etymological and extended senses in combination with other English elements: **doorbell, doorstop, door-to-door.** Related forms: **for-², thyro-.**

815   dorso-   A word-initial combining element, derived from Latin *dors*(*um*) 'back' plus the combining vowel *-o-*, used in its etymological and extended senses in Neo-Latin and Neo-Greek combinations: **dorsoanterior, dorsolumbar, dorsomesial.** Also, **dors-, dorsi-: dorsalgia, dorsiflexion.**

816   double-   A word-initial combining element, also occurring as a word, derived through Old French from Latin *dupl*(*us*) 'twice as much, twice as large,' literally, 'twofold,' used in its etymological and extended senses in combination with other English elements: **double-barreled, double-decker, doublethink.** Compare **duo-.**

817   dove-   A word-initial combining element, also occurring as a word, derived from Middle English *duve, dofe* 'bird of the family *Columbidae*' (said to be derived, variously, from the verb *to dive* (in reference to the bird's flight), from *dun* 'brown' (in reference to the bird's color), and by imitation of the bird's call), used in its etymological and extended senses in combination with other English elements: **dovecote, dovetail, dovewood.** Related forms(?): **deep-, dip-, dipping-, dive-; donkey-.**

818   down-   A word-initial combining element, also occurring as a word, derived from Old English (*a*)*dūn*(*e*) '(off the) hill,' used in the extended sense of 'toward or at a lower position' and in extensions of this sense in combination with other English elements: **downfall, downhearted, downwind.**

819 **draft-** A word-initial combining element, also occurring as a word, derived from Middle English *draht* 'that which is drawn or pulled' (cf. Old English *dragan* 'to draw, drag'), used in a variety of extensions of its etymological sense, chief among these being 'that which pulls or facilitates pulling,' in combination with other English elements: **draft-hole, draft-hook, draft-horse.** Compare **drag-, draw-.**

820 **drag-** A word-initial combining element, also occurring as a word, derived either from Old English *drag*(*an*) 'to pull' or from its Old Norse cognate, *drag*(*a*), used in its etymological and extended senses in combination with other English elements: **drag-chain, draghound, dragnet.** Compare **draft-, draw-.**

821 **dragon-** A word-initial combining element, also occurring as a word, derived through Latin from Greek *drákōn* 'serpentine monster,' used in its etymological and extended senses in combination with other English elements: **dragonfly, dragonhead, dragonroot.**

822 **drain-** A word-initial combining element, also occurring as a word, derived from Old English *drēa*(*h*)*n*(*ian*) 'to remove liquid a little at a time,' used in its etymological and extended senses in combination with other English elements: **drainboard, drainfield, drainspout.** Related form: **dry-².**

823 **draw-** A word-initial combining element, also occurring as a word, derived from Old English *drag*(*an*) 'to drag, pull,' used in its etymological and extended senses in combination with other English elements: **drawbridge, drawknife, draw-sheet.** Compare **draft-, drag-.**

824 **dream-** A word-initial combining element, also occurring as a word, derived from Middle English *drēm* 'vision in sleep' (from a Germanic root meaning something on the order of 'deception' (cf. Modern German *trügen* 'to deceive')), used in its etymological and extended senses in combination with other English elements: **dreamboat, dreamland, dream-world.**

825 **dress-** A word-initial combining element, derived from Middle French *dress*(*er*) 'to put in order, arrange, prepare' (from unattested Late Latin *directiāre* 'to order, direct' (from Latin *dīrectus,*

the past participle of *dīrigere,* a variant of *dērigere* 'to lay straight; to form; to direct')), used chiefly in the extended sense of 'put in order (by putting on clothes)' and, by further extension, 'of or pertaining to clothes, esp. formal or feminine' in combination with other English elements: **dressmaker, dress-up, dress-spur.** Compare **direct-, dressing-.**

826 dressing- A word-initial combining element, also occurring as a word, the present participle of the English verb *to dress,* derived from Middle French *dress(er)* 'to put in order, arrange, prepare' (through Late Latin from Latin *dērigere* 'to lay straight; to form; to direct'), used in a variety of extended senses, chief among these being 'adjunct to preparing something or to clothing someone,' in combination with other English elements: **dressing-gown, dressing-knife, dressing-room.** Compare **direct-, dress-.**

827 drift- A word-initial combining element, also occurring as a word, variously derived from cognate Old English *drīfan* 'to drive,' Old Norse *drift* 'mound of driven snow,' and Middle Dutch *drift* 'driven herd; impetus; course,' used in the sense of 'driven' and in extensions of this sense in combination with other English elements: **driftbolt, driftfish, driftwood.** Related forms: **drive-, driving-.**

828 drill- A word-initial combining element, also occurring as a word, derived from Middle Dutch *drill(en)* 'to turn in a circle; to bore (a hole)' and, by extension, 'to train soldiers (by having them perform repeated precise movements),' used in its etymological and extended senses in combination with other English elements: **drill-master, drill-press, drillstock.** Related forms: **thread-, traumato-, trypano-, turn-.**

829 drive- A word-initial combining element, also occurring as a word, derived from Old English *drīf(an)* 'to propel,' used in its etymological and extended senses in combination with other English elements: **drive-in, driveway, drive-wheel.** Compare **driving-.** Related form: **drift-.**

830 driving- A word-initial combining element, also occurring as a word, the present participle of the English verb *to drive,* derived from Old English *drīf(an)* 'to propel,' used in the sense of 'propelling' and in extensions of this sense in combination with other English elements: **driving-axle, driving-chisel, driving-wheel.** Compare **drive.** Related form: **drift-.**

831 dromo- A word-initial combining element, derived from Greek *drómo(s)* 'course, race, racecourse' (from *drameîn* 'to run'), used in its etymological and extended senses in Neo-Greek combinations: **dromograph, dromophobia, dromotropic.** Related forms: **trade-, trap-.**

832 drop- A word-initial combining element, also occurring as a word, derived from Old English *drop(a)* 'globule of water (which falls from the sky),' used in its etymological and extended senses, chief among these being 'globule of liquid' and 'that which falls or is made to fall,' in combination with other English elements: **drop-kick, dropout, dropwort.**

833 drum- A word-initial combining element, also occurring as a word, derived from Middle English *drom(slade),* a borrowing of Low German *trommelslag* 'drumbeat' (from *trommel* 'drum' plus *slag* 'beat'), used in the sense of 'percussive instrument consisting of a skin stretched over an opening in a hollow vessel' in combination with other English elements: **drumbeat, drumfish, drumstick.**

834 dry-¹ A variant of **dryo-.**

835 dry-² A word-initial combining element, also occurring as a word, derived from Old English etymological and extended senses in combination with other English elements: **drybrush, dry-clean, dry-gulch.** Related form: **drain-.**

836 dryo- A word-initial combining element, derived from Greek *drý(s)* 'oak tree' and, by extension, 'tree' plus the combining vowel *-o-*, used in this latter and extended senses chiefly in Linnaean nomenclature: **Dryobalanops, Dryocopus,** dryodrome. Also, **dry-¹:** *Dryophis.*

837 du- A variant of **duo-.**

838 duck- A word-initial combining element, also occurring as a word, derived from Old English *dūc(e)* 'aquatic bird of the family *Anatidae*' (from *dūcan* 'to dive'), used in its etymological and extended senses in combination with other English elements: **duckbill, duckpin, ducktail.**

839 dui- A word-initial combining element, derived from Sanskrit *dvi-*, a combining form of *dvāu* 'two,' used to designate 'a hypothetical chemical element which should have the same properties as the group named by the combining root and from which it is separated by one element in the Mendelejeff periodic system': **dui-fluorine.** Related forms: **bi-¹, bin-, bis-, di-¹, dicho-, diplo-, dis-¹, double-, duo-, twelve-, twi-, twin-, two-.**

840   dumb-   A word-initial combining element, also occurring as a word, derived from Old English *dumb* 'mute,' used in its etymological and extended senses in combination with other English elements: **dumbbell, dumbstruck, dumbwaiter.**

841   dung-   A word-initial combining element, also occurring as a word, derived from Old English *dung* 'manure,' used in its etymological sense in combination with other English elements: **dung-beetle, dunghill, dung-hunter.**

842   duo-   A word-initial combining element, also occurring as a word, derived from Latin *duo* and Greek *dýō* 'two,' used in its etymological sense in Neo-Latin and Neo-Greek combinations: **duodiode, duoliteral, duotone.** Also, **du-, dy-: duplex, dyad.** Related forms: **bi-[1], bin-, bis-, di-[1], dicho-, diplo-, dis-[1], double-, dui-, twelve-, twi-, twin-, two-.**

843   duodeca-   A variant of **dodeca-.**

844   duodecim-   A word-initial combining element, derived from Latin *duodecim* 'twelve' (from *duo* 'two' plus *decem* 'ten'), used in its etymological sense in Neo-Latin combinations: **duodecimal, duodecimfid, *Duodecimpennatae.*** Also, **duodec-: duodecuple.** Compare **duo-** and **deci-.**

845   duodeno-   A word-initial combining element, derived from Late Latin *duoden(um)* 'proximal part of the small intestine' (so named, from Latin *duodēnī*, the distributive form of *duodecim* 'twelve,' because its length is approximately twelve finger-breadths) plus the combining vowel *-o-,* used in its etymological sense in biomedical terminology: **duodenogram, duodenoileostomy, duodenopancreatectomy.** Also, **duoden-: duodenectomy.** Compare **duodecim-.**

846   duro-   A word-initial combining element, derived from Latin *dūr(us)* 'hard' (from an Indo-European root meaning 'strong, steadfast') plus the combining vowel *-o-,* used in its etymological and extended senses, chief among these being 'of or pertaining to the *dura mater* (literally, 'hard mother'), the hard outermost membrane of the brain and spinal cord,' in Neo-Latin and Neo-Greek combinations: **duroarachnitis, durometer, durosarcoma.** Also, **dur-, dura-: durematoma, duraplasty.** Related forms: **dendro-, tree-, true-.**

847   dust-   A word-initial combining element, also occurring as a word, derived from Old English *dūst* 'particles of solid matter' (from an Indo-European root meaning 'breath, smoke, dust'), used in its etymological and extended senses in combination with other English elements: **dustcloth, dustman, dustup.** Related forms: **deer-, thio-, thym-¹, thymo-², typhl-¹, typhlo-², typho-.**

848   Dutchman's-   A word-initial combining element, also occurring as a word, the possessive singular form of English *Dutchman,* a combination of English *Dutch* 'of or pertaining to the Netherlands' (from Middle Dutch *Dutsch* 'Netherlandish, German,' the original sense having been 'Germanic (language),' later, 'people speaking a Germanic language') plus *man* 'adult (male) person' (from Old English *man(n)* 'adult person'), used in extensions of its etymological sense in combination with other English elements: **Dutchman's-breeches, Dutchman's-laudanum, Dutchman's-pipe.**

849   dy-   A variant of **duo-.**

850   dye-   A word-initial combining element, also occurring as a word, derived from Old English *dēag* 'coloring matter' (from the verb *dēagian* 'to color'), used in its etymological and extended senses in combination with other English elements: **dyestuff, dyeweed, dyewood.** Compare **dyer's-.**

851   dyer's-   A word-initial combining element, also occurring as a word, the possessive singular form of English *dyer* 'one who colors cloth, paper, or the like' (from Old English *dēag(ian)* 'to color' plus the agentive suffix *-er*), used chiefly in the extended sense of 'yielding coloring matter' in combination with other English elements: **dyer's-broom, dyer's-weed, dyer's-woodruff.** Compare **dye-.**

852   dynamo-   A word-initial combining element, also occurring as a word, derived from Greek *dýnam(is)* 'strength, power' plus the combining vowel *-o-,* used in its etymological and extended senses in Neo-Greek combinations: **dynamogenesis, dynamograph, dynamoneure.** Also, **dynam-: dynamization.** Related form: **bene-.**

853   dys-   A word-initial combining element, derived from the Greek prefix *dys-* 'ill-, bad-, faulty-, difficult-,' used in its etymological sense in Neo-Greek and Neo-Latin combinations: **dysanagnosia, dysfunction, dyspeptic.**

E

854 **e-¹** A word-initial combining element, derived from Latin *ē-*, a combining form of *ex* 'out of, out from, away from, from,' appearing in its etymological and extended senses in borrowings from Latin in which the element to which it is joined begins with a voiced consonant: **educate, emission, enumeration.** Compare **ef-, ex-¹.** Related forms: **ec-, ecto-, ex-², exo-.**

855 **e-²** An excrescent vowel, appearing word-initially in the borrowed French, Spanish, and Portuguese reflexes of Latin words beginning with *s* plus a consonant: **especial, esquire, estate.**

856 **eagle-** A word-initial combining element, also occurring as a word, derived through Old French from Latin *aquil(a)* 'large bird belonging to the family *Accipitridae*' (said by some to be derived from Latin *(avis) aquila* 'dark brown (bird),' though others hold that the use of *aquila* as a color term is secondary, an extension of its use as a name for the (brown) bird in question), used in its etymological and extended senses in combination with other English elements: **eagle-eyed, eagle-ray, eaglestone.**

857 **ear-** A word-initial combining element, also occurring as a word, derived from Old English *ēar(e)* 'organ of hearing,' used in its etymological and extended senses in combination with other English elements: **earache, earflap, earshot.** Related forms: **auri-¹, auriculo-, oto-.**

127

858 earth- A word-initial combining element, also occurring as a word, derived from Old English *eorþ(e)* 'world, ground,' used in its etymological and extended senses in combination with other English elements: **earthmover, earthquake, earthwork.**

859 ec- A word-initial combining element, derived from Greek *ek-*, a combining form of *ex* 'from, out of,' appearing in its etymological and extended senses in borrowings from Greek in which the element to which it is joined begins with a consonant: **eccentric, ecphylactic, ecthyreosis.** Compare **ecto-, ex-[2].** Related forms: **e-[1], ef-, ex-[1], extra-.**

860 echidno- A word-initial combining element, derived from Greek *échidn(a)* 'viper' plus the combining vowel *-o-*, used in its etymological and extended senses in Neo-Greek and Neo-Latin combinations: *Echidnophaga,* **echidnotoxin, echidnovaccine.** Also, **echidn-: echidnase.**

861 echino- A word-initial combining element, derived from Greek *echîno(s)* 'sea urchin; hedgehog; (spiny) seed husk,' used in the sense of 'of, pertaining to, or derived from sea urchins' and in the more general sense of 'spiny, spinelike' in Neo-Greek combinations: **echinochrome, echinococciasis,** *Echinodermata.* Also, **echin-: echinophthalmia.**

862 echo- A word-initial combining element, also occurring as a word, derived from Greek *ēchṓ* 'sound, esp. a returned sound,' used in its etymological and extended senses, chief among these being 'repetition, imitation,' in Neo-Greek combinations: **echoacousia, echomimia, echopraxis.** Also, **eco-[2]: ecophony.**

863 eco-[1] A word-initial combining element, derived from Greek *oîko(s)* 'house, dwelling, household,' used in its etymological and extended senses, chief among these being 'environment,' in borrowings from Greek and in Neo-Greek combinations: **economy, ecophobia, ecosphere.** Also, **oiko-,** (rarely) **oeco-: oikophobia, oecology.**

864 eco-[2] A variant of **echo-.**

865 ecto- A word-initial combining element, derived from Greek *ektó(s)* 'outside, beyond' (from *ek-* 'from, out of' plus the adverbial suffix *-tos*), used in its etymological and extended senses in Neo-Greek and Neo-Latin combinations: **ectodermal, ectoglobular, ectonuclear.** Also, **ect-: ectethmoids.** Compare **ec-.**

866   **ectro-**   A word-initial combining element, derived from Greek *éktrō(ma)* 'abortion; untimely birth' or *éktrō(sis)* 'miscarriage' (from *ektitróskein* 'to miscarry' (from *ek-* 'from, resulting from' plus *titróskein* 'to wound, hurt')), used chiefly in the extended sense of 'congenital absence or defect' of that which is named by the combining root, in Neo-Greek combinations: **ectrodactylia, ectrogenic, ectromelic.**

867   **Ed-**   A word-initial combining element, derived from Old English *ē(a)d-* 'prosperity, happiness,' appearing in its etymological sense in a number of English proper nouns: **Edmund, Edward, Edwin.**

868   **edge-**   A word-initial combining element, also occurring as a word, derived from Old English *e(ċ)g* 'sharp side (of a blade),' used in its etymological and extended senses in combination with other English elements: **edge-grained, Edgewater, Edgewood.** Related forms: **acantho-, aceto-, acetyl-, acid-, acro-, acu-, acuti-, keto-, oxal-, oxy-¹, oxy-².**

869   **eel-**   A word-initial combining element, also occurring as a word, derived from Old English *ǣl, ēl* 'fish of the genus *Anguilla*,' used in its etymological and extended senses in combination with other English elements: **eelback, eelgrass, eelpout.**

870   **ef-**   A word-initial combining element, derived from Latin *ef-*, a combining form of *ex* 'out of, out from, from,' appearing in its etymological and extended senses in borrowings from Latin (sometimes via French) in which the element to which it is joined begins with *f:* **efflorescence, effort, effusion.** Compare **e-¹, ex-¹.** Related forms: **ec-, ecto-, ex-², exo-.**

871   **egg-**   A word-initial combining element, also occurring as a word, derived from Old Norse *egg* 'thin-shelled avian ovum,' used in its etymological and extended senses in combination with other English elements: **eggbeater, eggnog, eggplant.** Related forms: **avi-, oo-, ovario-, ovo-.**

872   **ego-¹**   A word-initial combining element, also occurring as a word, derived from Greek *egṓ* and Latin *egō* 'I,' used in the sense of 'self' in Neo-Greek and Neo-Latin combinations: **egoaltruistic, egocentric, egotheism.**

873   **ego-²**   A variant of **aego-.**

874   **eido-**   A word-initial combining element, derived from Greek *eîdo(s)* 'form, shape,' literally, 'that which is seen' (from the verb *ideîn* 'to see' and, in the medio-passive, 'to be seen; to appear'), used in its etymological and extended senses in Neo-Greek combinations: **eidogen, eidograph, eidoscope.** Also, **eid-: eidoptometry.** Compare **ideo-.** Related forms: **guide-, story-, video-, visuo-.**

875 **eigen-** A word-initial combining element, derived from German *eigen* 'own, particular, peculiar,' used in the sense of 'characteristic' in mathematical terminology: **eigenfunction, eigenvalue, eigenvector.**

876 **eight-** A word-initial combining element, also occurring as a word, derived from Old English *eht(a)* 'the cardinal number between seven and nine,' used in its etymological sense in combination with other English elements and, as the numeral 8, to designate 'the eighth carbon atom in an aliphatic compound' in chemical terminology: **eightball, eightfoil, eightscore.** Related form: **octo-.**

877 **eis-** A word-initial combining element, derived from Greek *eis* 'into' (by contraction from *en* 'in, at, near' plus *-s*), used in its etymological and extended senses in Neo-Greek combinations: **eisanthema, eisegesis, eisodic.** Compare **em-¹, en-¹, eso-.** Related forms: **em-², en-², entre-, il-², im-², in-², in-³, inter-, intero-, intra-, intro-, ir-².**

878 **eka-** A word-initial combining element, derived from Sanskrit *eka* 'one,' used to designate 'an unknown element which might be expected to occur next in the same group in the periodic system of Mendelejeff' as that named by the combining root: **eka-iodine.** Related forms: **any-, inch-, one-, uni-.**

879 **elaeo-** A variant of **eleo-.**

880 **elaio-** A variant of **eleo-.**

881 **elasmo-** A word-initial combining element, derived from Greek *elasmó(s)* 'beaten metal, metal plate' (from *elaúnein* 'to drive, strike, beat out'), used in its etymological and extended senses in Neo-Greek combinations: **elasmobranch, elasmognathous, *Elasmosaurus.***

882 **elbow-** A word-initial combining element, also occurring as a word, derived from Old English *el(n)bo(ga)* 'bend in the arm between the forearm and the upper arm' (from *eln* 'ell' (with which Old Norse *oln* 'cubit, forearm' and Latin *ulna* 'elbow, arm, ell' are cognate) plus *boga* 'bow, bend'), used in its etymological and extended

senses in combination with other English elements: **elbow-board, elbow-grease, elbowroom.**

883 **electro-**   A word-initial combining element, derived from English *electr*(*ic*) (from Greek *ēlektr*(*on*)) 'amber' (which, when vigorously rubbed, produces the effect of static electricity, as first described by Dr. William Gilbert in 1600) plus the adjective-forming suffix *-ic*) plus the combining vowel *-o-*, used in the sense of 'of, pertaining to, or resulting from electricity' in a variety of combinations: **electroacoustics, electrocoagulation, electrojet.** Also, **electr-**, **electri-**: **electrode, electrify.**

884 **eleo-**   A word-initial combining element, derived from Greek *élai*(*a*) '(olive) oil' plus the combining vowel *-o-*, used in the sense of 'oil' in Neo-Greek combinations: **eleometer, eleotherapy, eleothorax.** Also, **elaeo-**, **elaio-**: **elaeoplast, elaiopathy.** Compare **oil-, oleo-, olive-.**

885 **elephant-**   A word-initial combining element, also occurring as a word, derived through Latin from Greek *elépha*(*s*), *eléphant*(*os*) 'ivory; large ivory-tusked mammal of the family *Elephantidae*' (probably of Near Eastern origin (cf. Hamitic *elu*, Coptic *ebu*, and Egyptian *abu* 'ivory; elephant')), used in the sense of 'mammal of the family *Elephantidae*' and in extensions of this sense chiefly in combination with other English elements: **elephantiasis, elephant-leg, elephant-mouse.** Related form(?): **ivory-.**

886 **eleuthero-**   A word-initial combining element, derived from Greek *eleúthero*(*s*) 'free,' used in its etymological and extended senses in Neo-Greek combinations: **eleutherodactyl, eleutheromania, Eleutherozoa.**

887 **elf-**   A word-initial combining element, also occurring as a word, derived from Old English *ælf, elf* 'sprite, incubus, (small) supernatural creature,' used in this last and extended senses in combination with other English elements: **elf-bolt, elfland, elflock.**

888 **elk-**   A word-initial combining element, also occurring as a word, derived from Old English *e*(*o*)*lk* 'the deer *Aces aces*,' used in its etymological and extended senses in combination with other English elements: **elk-grass, elkhound, elkwood.**

889 **eluro-**   A variant of **aeluro-.**

890 **elytro-**   A word-initial combining element, derived from Greek *élytro*(*n*) 'covering, wrapping' and, by extension, 'sheath, casing'

and, by further extension (in Scientific Greek), 'vagina,' used in the sense of 'sheath, vagina' in Neo-Greek and Neo-Latin combinations: **elytrocele, elytroplastic, elytroprosis.** Also, **elytr-, elytri-: elytroid, elytriform.**

891 **em-¹** A word-initial combining element, derived from Greek *em-*, a combining form of *en* 'in, at, near,' appearing in its etymological and extended senses in borrowings from Greek and in Neo-Greek combinations in which the element to which it is joined begins with *b, m, p,* or *ph:* **embiotocid, emplastic, emphractic.** Compare **eis-, en-¹.** Related forms: **em-², en-², entre-, il-², im-², in-², in-³, inter-, intero-, intra-, intro-, ir-².**

892 **em-²** A word-initial combining element, derived through French from Latin *im-*, a combining form of *in* 'in, into,' appearing in its etymological and extended senses in borrowings from French and in combination with other English elements, often as an intensifier or as a marker of transitivity, when the element with which it is joined begins with *b, m,* or, *p:* **embed, emmarble, employ.** Also, **am-, im-³: ambush, imbed.** Compare **im-².**

893 **embolo-** A word-initial combining element, derived from Greek *émbolo(s)* 'that which is thrust into something; wedge, stopper' (from *embállein* 'to throw in' (from *em-* 'in' plus *bállein* 'to throw')), used in the sense of 'interpolation, obstruction' in Neo-Greek and Neo-Latin combinations: **embolomycotic, embololalia, embolophrasia.** Also, **embol-, emboli-: embolism, emboliform.** Compare **em-¹, bolo-.**

894 **embryo-** A word-initial combining element, also occurring as a word, derived from Greek *émbryo(s)* 'that which grows in another body; fetus' (from *em-* 'in' plus *brý(ein)* 'to swell, bloom'), used in the sense of 'of or pertaining to an organism in its early or rudimentary state of development' and in extensions of this sense in Neo-Greek combinations: **embryogenic, embryograph, embryoplastic.** Also, **embry-, embryon-: embryectomy, embryonic.** Compare **em-¹** and **bryo-.**

895 **emeto-** A word-initial combining element, derived from Greek *émeto(s)* 'vomiting' (from *emeîn* 'to vomit'), used in its etymological and extended senses in Neo-Greek combinations: **emetocathartic, emetomorphine, emetophobia.** Also, **emet-: emetatrophia.**

896 **emotio-** A word-initial combining element, derived from French *émotio(n)* 'agitation, esp. of one's feelings' (from Latin *ēmōt(us)*, the past participle of the verb *ēmovēre* 'to move out or away; to stir'

(from *ē-* 'from, away from' plus *movēre* 'to move') plus the noun-forming suffix *-iō, -ion(is)*), used in the sense of 'of, pertaining to, or resulting from one's feelings' in Neo-Latin and Neo-Greek combinations: **emotiometabolic, emotiomotor, emotiovascular.** Compare **e-¹** and **motor-.**

897 **en-¹** A word-initial combining element, derived from Greek *en* 'in, at, near, among,' appearing in its etymological and extended senses in borrowings from Greek and in Neo-Greek combinations: **enanthesis, encelialgia, engram.** Compare **eis-, em-¹, endo-, entero-, ento-, eso-.** Related forms: **em-², en-², entre-, il-², im-², in-², in-³, inter-, intero-, intra-, intro-, ir-².**

898 **en-²** A word-initial combining element, derived through French from Latin *in* 'into, in,' appearing in its etymological and extended senses in borrowings from French and (often as an intensifier or marker of transitivity) in combination with other English elements: **enable, enchant, endear.** Compare **il-².**

899 **enantio-** A word-initial combining element, derived from Greek *enantio(s)* 'opposite, opposing, over against' (from *en* 'in, at, near' plus *antios* 'against' (from *anti* 'opposing, against')), used in its etymological and extended senses in Neo-Greek combinations: **enantiobiosis, enantiomorph, enantiopathia.** Compare **en-¹** and **anti-.**

900 **encephalo-** A word-initial combining element, derived from Greek *enképhalo(s)* 'that which is inside the head; the brain' (from *en* 'in' plus *kephal(ḗ)* 'head'), used in the sense of 'of or pertaining to the brain' in biomedical terminology: **encephaloarteriography, encephalocystocele, encephalomyelitis.** Also, **encephal-: encephalatrophy.** Compare **en-¹** and **cephalo-.**

901 **end-¹** A variant of **endo-.**

902 **end-²** A word-initial combining element, also occurring as a word, derived from Old English *end(e)* 'extremity, terminus,' used in its etymological and extended senses in combination with other English elements: **end-all, end-blown, endnote.** Related forms: **ante-, antero-, anti-, un-².**

903 **endo-** A word-initial combining element, derived from Greek *éndo(n)* 'within' (from *en* 'in, at' plus the adverbial suffix *-don*), used in its etymological and extended senses in Neo-Greek and Neo-Latin combinations: **endoabdominal, endocardial, endogastrectomy.** Also, **end-¹: endodontology.** Compare **en-¹.**

904 **endocrino-** A word-initial combining element, derived from Greek *en* 'in, within' plus the root of the verb *krínein* 'to separate' plus the combining vowel *-o-,* used in the sense of 'of or pertaining to internal secretion or to the bodily organs responsible for internal secretion' in Neo-Greek combinations: **endocrinogram, endocrinotherapy, endocrinotropic.** Also, **endocrin-: endocrinasthenia.** Compare **endo-.**

905 **endoperi-** A word-initial combining element, derived from Greek *endo-* 'within, inside' plus *peri* 'around,' used in two types of Neo-Greek combinations:
  1. those in which both **endo-** and **peri-** are to be understood as being separately joined to the combining root, e.g., **endopericardial** 'pertaining to both the *endocardium* and the *pericardium.*'
  2. those in which **endo-** is to be understood as modifying the combination of **peri-** plus the element to which it is joined, e.g. **endoperitoneal** 'inside the *peritoneum*': **endoperiarteritis, endoperimyocarditis, endoperineuritis.** Compare **endo-** and **peri-.**

906 **endothelio-** A word-initial combining element, derived from English *endotheli(um)* 'layer of simple cells lining the inner surface of the circulatory organs' (from Greek *endo-* 'within, inside' plus *thēl(ḗ)* 'nipple, teat' plus the Neo-Latin noun-forming suffix *-ium*) plus the combining vowel *-o-,* used in its etymological sense in Neo-Greek combinations: **endothelio-angiitis, endothelioblastoma, endotheliomyoma.** Also, **endotheli-: endotheliitis.** Compare **endo-** and **thel-.**

907 **engine-** A word-initial combining element, also occurring as a word, derived through Old French from Latin *ingen(ium)* 'natural ability,' hence, 'invention,' hence, 'mechanical contrivance,' used in the sense of 'mechanical contrivance, machine, esp. one producing motion' in combination with other English elements: **enginecounter, engineman, engine-turning.** Compare **in-²** and **genito-.**

908 **ennea-** A word-initial combining element, derived from Greek *ennéa* 'nine,' used in its etymological and extended senses in Neo-Greek combinations: **enneagynous, enneahedron, enneapennate.** Also, **enne-: enneander.** Related forms: **nine-, nona-, noon-.**

909 **eno-** A variant of **oeno-.**

910 **entero-** A word-initial combining element, derived from Greek *éntero(n)* 'intestine, gut, bowel' (from *ent(ós)* 'inside, within' plus the noun-forming suffix *-eron*), used in its etymological senses in biomedical terminology: **enteroantigen, enterobacteriotherapy, enteroptosis.** Also, **enter-: enterelcosis.** Compare **ento-.**

911   **ento-**   A word-initial combining element, derived from Greek *entó(s)* 'inside, within, between' (from *en* 'in' plus the adverbial suffix *-tos*), used in the sense of 'inner, inside' in Neo-Greek combinations: **entocone, entoderm, entoplastic.** Also, **ent-: entoptoscopy.** Compare **en-[1], entero-.**

912   **entomo-**   A word-initial combining element, derived from Greek *éntomo(s)* 'that which is cut up; a victim; an insect (whose body appears to be segmented)' (from *entémnein* 'to cut in, cut up' (from *en* 'in' plus *témnein* 'to cut')), used in the sense of 'of or pertaining to insects' in Neo-Greek combinations: **entomogenous, entomology, entomophobia.** Compare **en-[1]** and **tomo-.**

913   **entre-**   A word-initial combining element, derived from French *entre* 'between, among' (from Latin *inter* 'between, among, during, at intervals' (from *in* 'in, into' plus the adverbial suffix *-ter*)), appearing in its etymological and extended senses in borrowings from French: **entrecôte, entremets, entresol.** Compare **inter-.**

914   **eo-**   A word-initial combining element, derived from Greek *ēó(s)* 'daybreak, dawn, red of the dawn sky,' used chiefly in the sense of 'early, primeval' in Neo-Greek combinations: **Eocine, eohippus, eolithic.** Also, **eoso-: eosophobia.** Compare **eosino-.** Related form: **Austro-[1].**

915   **eosino-**   A word-initial combining element, derived from Greek *ēós* 'daybreak, dawn, red of the dawn sky' plus the suffix *-in* (used in naming chemical compounds) plus the combining vowel *-o-,* used in the sense of 'of or pertaining to the red stain or dye ($C_{20}H_8Br_4O_5$) or other red coal tar dye' in Neo-Greek combinations: **eosinocyte, eosinophil, eosinotactic.** Compare **eo-.**

916   **ep-**   A variant of **epi-.**

917   **ependymo-**   A word-initial combining element, derived from Scientific Latin *ependym(a)* 'membrane lining the central canal of the spinal cord and the ventricles of the brain' (from Greek *epéndyma* 'outer garment' (from *ep(i)* 'on, over' plus the root of the verb *endý(ein)* 'to put on, get dressed' plus the noun-forming suffix *-ma*)) plus the combining vowel *-o-,* used in its scientific sense in Neo-Greek combinations: **ependymoblast, ependymocytoma, ependymopathy.** Also, **ependym-: ependymitis.**

918 **epi-** A word-initial combining element, derived from Greek *epí* 'on, upon, in, near, by, against, over,' used in one or another of its etymological senses in borrowings from Greek and in Neo-Greek combinations: **epicenter, epigastric, epiphenomenon.** Also, **ep-: eparterial.** Related forms: **ob-, oc-, of-², op-³, opistho-.**

919 **epidermato-** A variant of **epidermo-.**

920 **epidermido-** A variant of **epidermo-.**

921 **epidermo-** A word-initial combining element, derived from Greek *epiderm(ís), epiderm(ídos)* 'outer skin' (from *epí* 'on, upon, over' plus *dérm(a), dérm(atos)* '(true) skin') plus the combining vowel *-o-*, used in its etymological sense in Neo-Greek combinations: **epidermodysplasia, epidermolysis, epidermomycosis.** Also, **epiderm-, epidermid-, epidermido-, epidermat-, epidermato-: epidermal, epidermidalization, epidermidolysis, epidermatic, epidermatoplasty.** Compare **epi-** and **derma-.**

922 **epididymo-** A word-initial combining element, derived from Greek *epididym(ís)* 'outer membrane of the testicle' (from *epí* 'on, upon, over' plus *dídym(os)* 'double, twin, testicle' (from *di-* 'two-' plus *dy-* 'two-' plus the noun-forming suffix *-mos*)) plus the combining vowel *-o-*, used in the sense of 'of or pertaining to the *epididymis,* the oblong organ which is attached to the posterior surface of each testicle' in biomedical combinations: **epididymodeferentectomy, epididymoorchitis, epididymovasectomy.** Also, **epididym-: epididymectomy.** Compare **epi-** and **duo-.**

923 **epiplo-** A word-initial combining element, derived from Greek *epíplo(on)* 'intestinal caul, omentum' (from *epí* 'on, upon, above' plus the suffix *-ploon* '-fold,' the *omentum* being a duplication, consisting of several folds, of the peritoneum), used in its etymological sense in biomedical combinations: **epiploenterocele, epiplomerocele, epiplosarcomphalocele.** Also, **epipl-: epiplomphalocele.**

924 **episio-** A word-initial combining element, derived from Greek *epís(e)ío(n)* 'pudenda, pubes,' used in the sense of 'of or pertaining to the vulva' in biomedical terminology: **epesio-elytrorrhaphy, epesioperineoplasty, epesiostenosis.**

925 **epithelio-** A word-initial combining element, derived from Scientific Latin *epitheli(um)* 'protective covering or lining of an internal or external bodily surface' (from Greek *epí* 'on, upon' plus *thēl(ḗ)* 'nipple, teat' plus the Scientific Latin noun-forming suffix *-ium*) plus the combining vowel -o-, used in its etymological sense in biomedical terminology: **epithelioceptor, epitheliofibril, epitheliomuscular.** Also, **epitheli-: epithelial.** Compare **epi-** and **thel-.**

926   **epsilon-** (E, ε)   A word-initial combining element, the fifth letter of the Greek alphabet, used chiefly to designate 'the fifth carbon atom in a straight chain compound or a derivative thereof in which the substitute group is attached to that atom' in chemical terminology. See **alpha-.**

927   **equi-**   A word-initial combining element, derived from Latin (a)equ(us) 'equal' plus the combining vowel -i-, appearing in its etymological sense in borrowings from Latin (and French) and in Neo-Latin combinations: **equidistant, equilibrium, equiprobabilism.** Also, **equ-: equal.**

928   **eremo-**   A word-initial combining element, derived from Greek érēmo(s) 'solitary, desolate,' used in its etymological and extended senses in Neo-Greek combinations: **eremobryoid, eremophobia,** *Eremopteris.* Related forms: **reti-, reticulo-, retino-.**

929   **ergasio-**   A word-initial combining element, derived from Greek ergasí(a) 'work, employment' (from érg(on) 'work' plus the agentive suffix -t(ēs) plus the noun-forming suffix -ia, thus, 'the state or condition of one who performs work') plus the combining vowel -o-, used in the sense of 'work' in Neo-Greek combinations: **ergasiology, ergasiomania, ergasiophobia.** Also, **ergas-, ergasi-: ergasiatrics, ergasidermatosis.** Compare **ergo-[1].**

930   **ergo-[1]**   A word-initial combining element, derived from Greek érgo(n) 'work,' used in its etymological and extended senses in Neo-Greek combinations: **ergograph, ergometer, ergonomics.** Also, **erg-: ergodic.** Compare **ergasio-.** Related forms: **organo-, work-.**

931   **ergo-[2]**   A word-initial combining element, derived from English ergo(t) 'fungus which infects cereal grasses and replaces their grain with long, stiff, sclerotial bodies' (from French ergot 'cock's spur'), used in the sense of 'of or pertaining to ergot' in biochemical terminology: **ergomonamine, ergonovine, ergosterol.** Also, **ergot-: ergotamine.**

932   **eri-**   A word-initial combining element, derived from Greek eri-, an intensifying prefix with no precise meaning, used in its etymological sense chiefly in Linnaean nomenclature: **eriglossate,** *Erignathus, Erirhinus.*

933   **erio-**   A word-initial combining element, derived from Greek *ério(n)* 'wool,' used in its etymological and extended senses in Neo-Greek combinations: **eriocarpous, eriometer, eriophyllous.**

934   **eroto-**   A word-initial combining element, derived from Greek *érō(s), érōt(os)* 'sexual passion or desire,' used in its etymological and extended senses in Neo-Greek and Neo-Latin combinations: **erotogenesis, erotographomania, erotosexual.** Also, **erot-: erotic.**

935   **erythro-**   A word-initial combining element, derived from Greek *erythró(s)* 'ruddy, red,' used in its etymological and extended senses in Neo-Greek and Neo-Latin combinations: ***Erythrobacillus,* erythrocatalysis, erythrodermatitis.** Also, **erythr-: erythralgia.** Related form: **red-².**

936   **eso-**   A word-initial combining element, derived from Greek *e(í)sō* 'within, inside' (from *eis* 'in, into' plus the adverbial suffix *-ō*), used in its etymological and extended senses in Neo-Greek and Neo-Latin combinations: **esocataphoria, esodeviation, esoethmoiditis.** Compare **eis-.**

937   **esophago-**   A word-initial combining element, derived from Greek *oisophágo(s)* 'gullet' (from *oís(ein)* 'to carry, bear' plus the combining vowel *-o-* plus *phag(eîn)* 'to eat,' thus, 'that which carries food; the path along which food travels from the mouth to the stomach'), used in its etymological sense in biomedical terminology: **esophagocele, esophagogasteroplasty, esophagoplication.** Also, **esophag-, oesophago-: esophagectomy, oesophagostomiasis.** Compare **phago-.**

938   **esthesio-**   A word-initial combining element, derived from Greek *aithēsi(s)* 'perception through one or another of the senses' plus the combining vowel *-o-,* used in its etymological and extended senses in Neo-Greek combinations: **esthesiomania, esthesiometer, esthesiophysiology.**

939   **eta-** (Η, η)   A word-initial combining element, the seventh letter of the Greek alphabet, used chiefly to designate 'the seventh carbon atom in a straight chain compound or a derivative thereof in which the substitute group is attached to that atom' in chemical terminology. See **alpha-.**

940   **ethmo-**   A word-initial combining element, derived from Greek *ēthmó(s)* 'strainer, sieve,' used in its etymological and extended senses in Neo-Greek and Neo-Latin combinations: **ethmocarditis, ethmocephalus, ethmofrontal.** Also, **ethm-: ethmoid.**

941   **ethno-**   A word-initial combining element, derived from Greek
éthno(s) 'group of people living together; community, family, race,'
used in its etymological and extended senses in Neo-Greek combinations: **ethnohistory, ethnolinguistics, ethnomusicology.** Also,
ethn-: ethnic. Related forms: **se-, self-, soli-².**

942   **etho-**   A word-initial combining element, derived from Greek
êtho(s), 'custom, usage,' used in its etymological and extended
senses in Neo-Greek combinations: **ethography, ethological, etho-
poetic.**

943   **ethyl-**   A word-initial combining element, also occurring as a word,
derived from Greek *aith(ér)* 'upper air, purer air,' hence, in
scientific terminology, 'volatile, clean-smelling, euphoria-produc-
ing liquid composed of alcohol and sulfuric acid' plus the suffix *-yl*
which is used in naming chemical radicals (from Greek *(h)ýl(ē)*
'wood; (basic) substance'), used in the sense of 'of, pertaining to,
containing, or derived from the chemical radical $(CH_3 \cdot CH_2)$' in
chemical terminology: **ethylamine, ethylbenzene, ethylbro-
moacetate.**

944   **etio-**   A word-initial combining element, derived from Greek *aitio(s)*
'causing, originating; that which causes or originates something,'
used in its etymological and extended senses in Neo-Greek combinations: **etiogenic, etiological, etiopathology.** Also, **aetio-: aetiological.**

945   **eu-**   A word-initial combining element, derived from Greek *eu-*
'well-, good-,' the combining form of the adverb *eû* 'well,' used in
its etymological and extended senses in borrowings from Greek
and in Neo-Greek and Neo-Latin combinations: **eugenics,
euphony, euthanasia.**

946   **Euro-**   A word-initial combining element, derived from English
Euro(pe) 'continent to the immediate west of Asia' (through Latin
from Greek *Eurōpē* 'Greek mainland' and, by extension, 'continent
to which the Greek mainland belongs'), used in its etymological
and extended senses in combination with other English elements:
Euro-American, Eurodollars, Euromarket. Also, **Eur-: Eurasian.**

947   **eury-**   A word-initial combining element, derived from Greek
eurý(s) 'wide, broad,' used in its etymological and extended senses
in Neo-Greek combinations: **eurycephalic, euryphotic, eurythermic.**

948   **euthy-**   A word-initial combining element, derived from Greek
euthý(s) 'straight,' used in its etymological and extended senses in

Neo-Greek combinations: **euthyneural, euthysymmetrical, euthytactic.**

949 even- A word-initial combining element, also occurring as a word, derived from Old English *efen* 'flat, level, uniform, equal,' used in its etymological and extended senses in combination with other English elements: **even-handed, even-minded, even-tempered.**

950 ever- A word-initial combining element, also occurring as a word, derived from Old English *æfr(e)* 'always, at all times,' used in its etymological and extended senses in combination with other English elements: **evergreen, everlasting, evermore.** Compare **every-.**

951 every- A word-initial combining element, also occurring as a word, derived from Old English *æfriċ,* a combination of *æfre* 'always' plus *(æl)ċ* 'each,' used in the sense of 'each, all' in combination with other English elements: **everyday, everyone, everywhere.** Compare **ever-.**

952 evil- A word-initial combining element, also occurring as a word, derived from Old English *yfel* 'bad' (perhaps from an Indo-European root meaning 'up from below; over,' the idea being, presumably, that *evil* is 'above and beyond' the norm), used in its etymological and extended senses in combination with other English elements: **evildoer, evil-eyed, evil-minded.** Related forms(?): **hyper-, hypo-, open-, over-, sub-, suc-, suf-, sup-, super-, supra-, sur-[1], sur-[2], sursum-, sus-, up-.**

953 ex-[1] A word-initial combining element, derived from Latin *ex* 'out of, out from, away from,' appearing in its etymological and extended senses in borrowings from Latin and in Neo-Latin combinations and used in the sense of 'former' in combination with other English elements: **exact, exculpate, ex-wife.** Compare **e-[1], ef-, extra-.** Related forms: **ec-, ecto-, ex-[2], exo-.**

954 ex-[2] A word-initial combining element, derived from Greek *ex* 'out of, away from,' appearing in its etymological and extended senses in borrowings from Greek and in Neo-Greek combinations in which the element to which it is joined begins with *h* or with a vowel: **exangia, exanthem, exeresis.** Compare **ec-, exo-.** Related forms: **e-[1], ef-, ex-[1], extra-.**

955 excito- A word-initial combining element, derived from Latin *excit(āre)* 'to summon forth, arouse, stimulate' (from *ex* 'out of, out from' plus *citāre* 'to call, summon, arouse') plus the combining vowel *-o-*, used in the sense of 'stimulating' in Neo-Latin and Neo-Greek combinations: **excitoanabolic, excitoglandular, excitosecretory.** Related forms: **cine-², kinesi-, kineto-, kino-.**

956 exhaust- A word-initial combining element, also occurring as a word, derived from Latin *exhaust(us)*, the past participle of the verb *exhaurīre* 'to empty out, drain out' (from *ex* 'out from, out of' plus *haurīre* 'to drain, spill'), used in the sense of 'that which empties out or is emptied out' in combination with other English elements: **exhaust-fan, exhaust-pipe, exhaust-valve.**

957 exo- A word-initial combining element, derived from Greek *éxō* 'on the outside; outside' (from *ex* 'out of, out from' plus the adverbial suffix *-ō*), used in its etymological and extended senses in Neo-Greek and Neo-Latin combinations: **exodeviation, exogenetic, exoskeleton.** Compare **ex-².**

958 express- A word-initial combining element, also occurring as a word, derived through Old French from Latin *express(us)*, the past participle of the verb *exprimere* 'to press out' and, by extension, 'to copy, describe' and, later, 'to design (for a special purpose, esp. for speed)' (from *ex* 'out of' plus *primere* 'to press'), used in one or another of its etymological senses in combination with other English elements: **express-bullet, express-car, expressman.** Compare **ex-¹** and **press-.**

959 extra- A word-initial combining element, also occurring as a word, derived from Latin *extrā* 'on the outside; beyond; besides' (from *ex* 'out of, away from' plus the adverbial suffix *-t(e)r* plus the ablative singular feminine ending *-ā*), used in its etymological and extended senses in a variety of combinations: **extrabold, extracystic, extramarital.** Also, **extro-: extrovert.** Compare **ex-¹.**

960 eye- A word-initial combining element, also occurring as a word, derived from Old English *ē(a)ǵe* 'organ of sight,' used in its etymological and extended senses in combination with other English elements: **eyebrow, eyeopener, eyestone.** Related forms: **ocelli-, oculo-, opo-¹, ophthalmo-, optico-.**

F

961 face- A word-initial combining element, also occurring as a word, derived through Old French from Latin *fac(i)ē(s)* 'form, external form, visage' (from an Indo-European root meaning 'form, make, set in place, do'), used chiefly in the sense of 'visage' and in extensions of this sense in combination with other English elements: **face-lift, face-saving, face-to-face.** Compare **facio-.**

962 facio- A word-initial combining element, derived from Latin *faci(ēs)* 'form, external form, visage' (from an Indo-European root meaning 'form, make, set in place, do') plus the combining vowel *-o-*, used in the sense of 'of or pertaining to the face' in biomedical terminology: **faciobrachial, faciocephalalgia, faciocervical.** Also, **faci-: facial.** Compare **face-.** Related forms: **do-, thec-.**

963 fair- A word-initial combining element, also occurring as a word, derived from Old English *fæġ(e)r* 'blemish free, comely,' used in its etymological and extended senses, chief among these being 'light,' in combination with other English elements: **fair-haired, fair-minded, fair-weather.**

964 fall- A word-initial combining element, also occurring as a word, derived from Old English *f(e)all(an)* 'to descend as a result of the force of gravity,' used in its etymological and extended senses in combination with other English elements: **fallfish, fall-gate, fallout.**

965 false- A word-initial combining element, also occurring as a word,

143

derived through Old English from Latin *fals(us)*, the past participle of the verb *fallere* 'to deceive,' used adjectivally in the sense of 'deceptive, untrue' in Latin as its reflex is today in combination with other English elements: **false-bottomed, false-hearted, falsework.**

966 fan-   A word-initial combining element, also occurring as a word, derived through Old English from Latin *van(nus)* 'tool used for winnowing grain,' used in the extended sense of 'device for stirring the air' and in extensions of this sense in combination with other English elements: **fanback, fanjet, fantail.**

967 fairy-   A word-initial combining element, also occurring as a word, derived from Old French *fai(e)rie* 'land of enchantment; enchantment' (from Latin *Fā(ta)* 'the Fates' plus the French noun-forming suffix *-erie*), used in the extended sense of 'small supernatural humanoid with magical powers' and in extensions of this sense in combination with other English elements: **fairy-bird, fairyland, fairy-stone.**

968 far-   A word-initial combining element, also occurring as a word, derived from Old English *feor(r)* 'to or at a great distance,' used in its etymological and extended senses in combination with other English elements: **faraway, far-famed, far-fetched.** Related forms: **first-, for-[1], fore-[3], forth-, par-[3], para-[1], per-, peri-, perisso-, pre-, primi-, pro-[1], pro-[2], pros-[1], proso-, proprio-, protero-, proto-, proximo-.**

969 farm-   A word-initial combining element, also occurring as a word, derived through Old French and Middle English from Late Latin *firm(a)* 'fixed payment, rent,' hence, 'land for which one pays rent,' hence, 'land on which crops and livestock are raised' (from Latin *firmāre* 'to make firm, confirm, fix'), used in the sense of 'land on which crops and livestock are raised' and in extensions of this sense in combination with other English elements: **farmhouse, farmland, farmyard.**

970 fascio-   A word-initial combining element, derived from Latin *fasci(a)* 'band, bandage' plus the combining vowel *-o-*, used in its etymological and extended senses, chief among these being 'of or pertaining to the *fascia*, the band or sheet of fibrous tissue providing a subcutaneous covering for the body,' in biomedical terminology: **fascioplasty, fasciorrhaphy, fasciotomy.** Also, **fasc-, fasci-, fascia-: fascitis, fascial, fasciagram.**

971 fast-   A word-initial combining element, also occurring as a word, derived from Old English *fæst* 'fixed' (later 'rapid'), used in its etymological and extended senses in combination with other English elements: **fastback, fast-breaking, fast-talk.**

972   **fat-**   A word-initial combining element, also occurring as a word, derived from Old English *fæt(t)* 'adipose; adipose matter,' used in its etymological and extended senses in combination with other English elements: **fatback, fathead, fat-soluble.** Related forms: **pimel-, pio-.**

973   **feather-**   A word-initial combining element, also occurring as a word, derived from Old English *feþer* 'epidermal appendage which, with others, forms the covering of birds,' used in its etymological and extended senses in combination with other English elements: **featherback, featherbrain, featherstitch.** Related forms: **pen-[1], penni-, pin-, pinnati-, pinni-, pterido-, ptero-, pterygo-, ptilo-.**

974   **febri-**   A word-initial combining element, derived from Latin *febr(is)* 'fever' plus the combining vowel *-i-*, used in its etymological and extended senses in biomedical terminology: **febricide, febrifugal, febriphobia.** Compare **fever-.**

975   **feed-**   A word-initial combining element, also occurring as a word, derived from Old English *fēd(an)* 'to give food to,' hence, 'food,' used in its etymological and extended senses in combination with other English elements: **feedback, feedbox, feedwater.** Compare **food-, foster-.**

976   **femoro-**   A word-initial combining element, derived from Latin *femur, femor(is)* 'thigh; upper part of the thigh' plus the combining vowel *-o-*, used in its etymological sense in biomedical combinations: **femorocaudal, femorocele, femorotibial.**

977   **femto-**   A word-initial combining element, derived from Danish *femten* 'fifteen' ('five' plus 'ten'), used in the sense of 'one quadrillionth (10^{-15}) of the unit of measurement named by the combining root' in scientific terminology: **femtoampere, femtojoule, femtovolt.** Related forms: **cinque-[1], cinque-[2], finger-, fist-, five-, penta-, quinque-, quint-; deca-, deci-, ten-[1].**

978   **fence-**   A word-initial combining element, also occurring as a word, derived from Middle English *(de)fens(e)* 'defense, esp. an enclosing wall' (through Old French from Latin *dēfens(us)*, the past participle of the verb *dēfendere* 'to ward off'), used in the sense of 'barrier made to enclose or define a yard or the like' and in extensions of

this sense in combination with other English elements: **fence-month, fence-sitter, fence-viewer.**

979   **ferment-**   A word-initial combining element, also occurring as a word, derived from Latin *ferment(um)* 'substance containing enzymes that break down carbohydrates,' used in its etymological and extended senses in a variety of combinations: **fermentdiagnosticum, fermentemia, ferment-oil.** Also, **fermento-: fermentogen.**

980   **ferri-**   A word-initial combining element, derived from Latin *ferr(um)* 'iron' plus the combining vowel *-i-*, used in the general sense of 'of, pertaining to, or containing iron' and in the specialized sense of 'of, pertaining to, or containing iron in its trivalent state' in Neo-Latin and Neo-Greek combinations: **ferrialbuminic, ferricyanogen, ferriferous.** Also, **ferr-[1]: ferric.** Compare **ferro-.**

981   **ferro-**   A word-initial combining element, derived from Latin *ferr(um)* 'iron' plus the combining vowel *-o-*, used in the general sense of 'of, pertaining to, or containing iron' and in the specialized sense of 'of, pertaining to, or containing iron in its divalent state' in Neo-Latin and Neo-Greek combinations: **ferrocyanogen, ferrometer, ferrotherapy.** Also, **ferr-[2]: ferrous.** Compare **ferri-.**

982   **feto-**   A word-initial combining element, derived from Latin *fēt(us)* 'produce, offspring' (from an Indo-European root meaning 'to suck, suckle') plus the combining vowel *-o-*, used in the sense of 'unborn offspring' in biomedical terminology: **fetography, fetometry, fetoplacental.** Also, **fet-, feti-: fetal, feticulture.** Related forms: **Fitz-(?), thel-, thely-[1].**

983   **fever-**   A word-initial combining element, also occurring as a word, derived through Old English from Latin *febr(is)* 'heightened body temperature,' used in its etymological and extended senses in combination with other English elements: **feverfew, feverweed, feverwort.** Compare **febri-.**

984   **fiber-**   A word-initial combining element, also occurring as a word, derived through Old French from Latin *fibr(a)* 'filament,' used in its etymological and extended senses in combination with other English elements: **fiberboard, fiberglass, fiberscope.** Also (chiefly British), **fibre-: fibreless.** Compare **fibro-.**

985   **fibrillo-**   A word-initial combining element, derived from Neo-Latin *fibrill(a)* 'small fiber or filament' (from Latin *fibr(a)* 'filament' plus the diminutive suffix *-illa*) plus the combining vowel *-o-*, used in the sense of 'minute filament or fiber' in biomedical terminology:

fibrilloblast, fibrillogenesis, fibrillolytic. Also, **fibrill-, fibrilo-: fibrillated, fibriloceptor.** Compare **fibro-.**

986   **fibrino-**   A word-initial combining element, also occurring as a word, derived from Latin *fibr(a)* 'filament' plus the suffix *-in* (which is used in naming chemical compounds) plus the combining vowel *-o-,* used in the sense of 'of or pertaining to *fibrin,* a fibrous protein found in the blood' in biomedical combinations: **fibrinogenic, fibrinoglobulin, fibrinokinase.** Compare **fibro-.**

987   **fibro-**   A word-initial combining element, derived from Latin *fibr(a)* 'filament' plus the combining vowel *-o-,* used in its etymological and extended senses in a variety of combinations: **fibroadipose, fibrofatty, fibrofibrous.** Compare **fiber-, fibrillo-, fibrino-.**

988   **fiddle-**   A word-initial combining element, also occurring as a word, derived through Old English from unattested Late Latin **vītula* 'small stringed instrument played with a bow' (from Latin *vītulārī* 'to celebrate (a victory)' (from *Vītula,* a goddess of victory and joy)), used in the sense of 'violin' and in extensions of this sense in combination with other English elements: **fiddleback, fiddlehead, fiddlewood.**

989   **field-**   A word-initial combining element, also occurring as a word, derived from Old English *feld* 'open land,' used in its etymological and extended senses in combination with other English elements: **fieldfare, fieldstone, fieldstrip.** Related forms: **flat-, floor-, palmati-, place-, placento-, plagio-, plain-, plano-¹, plano-², plasmo-, plasmodi-, plasto-, plate-, platino-, platy-.**

990   **figure-**   A word-initial combining element, also occurring as a word, derived through Old French from Latin *figūr(a)* 'form, shape,' used in its etymological and extended senses in combination with other English elements: **figure-ground, figurehead, figure-stone.**

991   **file-¹**   A word-initial combining element, also occurring as a word, derived from Latin *fīl(um)* 'thread, string' and, in Late Latin, 'wire or thread along which documents are strung for future reference,' used in the sense of 'container in which (ordered) documents are stored' and in extensions of this sense, chief among these being 'ordered series or procession,' in combination with other English elements: **file-card, file-closer, file-mark.** Compare **filo-.**

992   **file-²**   A word-initial combining element, also occurring as a word, derived from Old English *fēol* 'rasp' (from an Indo-European root meaning 'incise'), used in its etymological and extended senses in combination with other English elements: **file-cutter, file-finishing, filefish.** Related forms: **picro-, pigmento-, poikilo-.**

993 **film-** A word-initial combining element, also occurring as a word, derived from Old English *film(en)* 'membrane,' used in the extended sense of 'thin strip of emulsion-coated cellulose acetate or cellulose nitrate on which photographic images may be recorded' and in extensions of this sense in combination with other English elements: **film-goer, filmland, filmstrip.**

994 **filo-** A word-initial combining element, derived from Latin *fīl(um)* 'thread, string' plus the combining vowel *-o-,* used in its etymological and extended senses in Neo-Latin and Neo-Greek combinations: **filopodium, filopressure, filovaricosis.** Also, **fil-, fili-: filoma, filiform.** Compare **file-¹.**

995 **filter-** A word-initial combining element, also occurring as a word, derived through Old French from Latin *filtr(um)* 'felt' and, by extension, 'piece of felt (or the like) through which liquid may be strained,' used in the sense of 'strainer' in combination with other English elements: **filter-bed, filter-press, filter-pump.**

996 **fin-** A word-initial combining element, also occurring as a word, derived from Old English *fin(n)* 'winglike membranous appendage of the body of a fish,' used in its etymological and extended senses in combination with other English elements: **finback, finfoot, finweed.**

997 **fine-** A word-initial combining element, also occurring as a word, derived through Old French from Latin *fīn(is)* 'limit, boundary, end, highest point, greatest degree,' used in the extended sense of 'excellent, delicate, sharp, minute' in combination with other English elements: **fine-cut, fine-grained, finespun.**

998 **finger-** A word-initial combining element, also occurring as a word, derived from Old English *finger* 'digit of the hand' (from an Indo-European root meaning 'five'), used in its etymological sense in combination with other English elements: **fingerbreadth, fingernail, fingertip.** Related forms: **cinque-¹, cinque-², femto-, fist-, five-, penta-, quinque-, quint-.**

999 **Finno-** A word-initial combining element, derived from English *Finn(ish)* 'of or pertaining to a non-Indo-European Scandinavian people' (possibly a loan translation from one of the Scandinavian languages of Finnish *Suomi* 'Finn,' literally, '(person from the) swamp, fen') plus the combining vowel *-o-,* used in its etymological

sense in combination with other English elements: **Finno-American, Finno-Russo (War), Finno-Ugric.**

1000   **fire-**   A word-initial combining element, also occurring as a word, derived from Old English *fȳr* 'burning material; state of combustion,' used in its etymological and extended senses in combination with other English elements: **firebox, firebug, firecracker.** Related forms: **pyreto-, pyro-.**

1001   **first-**   A word-initial combining element, also occurring as a word, derived from Old English *fyr(e)st* 'ordinal corresponding to the number *one*,' literally, 'foremost' (from *for(e)*, *fyr-* '(be)fore-' plus the superlative suffix *-est*), used in its etymological and extended senses in combination with other English elements: **first-born, first-class, first-name.** Compare **fore-³.**

1002   **fish-**   A word-initial combining element, also occurring as a word, derived from Old English *fisć* 'water-dwelling vertebrate with gills,' used in its etymological and extended senses in combination with other English elements: **fisheye, fishhook, fishwife.** Related form: **pisci-.**

1003   **fissi-**   A word-initial combining element, derived from Latin *fiss(us)*, the past participle of the verb *findere* 'to split,' plus the combining vowel *-i-*, used in the sense of 'split, cloven, cleft' in Neo-Latin combinations: **fissilingual, fissiparous, fissirostral.** Also, **fiss-: fissile.**

1004   **fist-**   A word-initial combining element, also occurring as a word, derived from Old English *fȳst* 'clenched hand' (from an Indo-European root meaning 'five'), used in its etymological and extended senses in combination with other English elements: **fistfight, fistic, fistnote.** Related forms: **cinque-¹, cinque-², femto-, finger-, five-, penta-, quinque-, quint-.**

1005   **Fitz-**   A word-initial combining element, derived through Anglo-Norman from Latin *fīl(iu)s* 'son,' appearing in a number of English surnames in which its original sense was 'son of the person named by the combining root': **Fitzgerald, Fitzmorris, Fitzwilliam.** Related forms(?): **feto-, thel-, thely-¹.**

1006   **five-**   A word-initial combining element, also occurring as a word, derived from Old English *fīf* 'the cardinal number between *four* and *six*,' used in its etymological and extended senses in combination with other English elements: **five-and-ten, five-finger, five-gaited.** Related forms: **cinque-¹, cinque-², femto-, finger-, fist-, penta-, quinque-, quint-.**

1007   flag-   A word-initial combining element of obscure origin, also occurring as a word, perhaps derived from a blend of English *flap* and *fag* ('something hanging loose; a remnant'), used in the sense of 'banner, pennant' and in extensions of this sense in combination with other English elements: **flagfish, flagship, flag-waving.**

1008   flame-   A word-initial combining element, also occurring as a word, derived through Old French from Latin *flam(ma)* 'vapor or gas in a state of combustion,' used in its etymological and extended senses in combination with other English elements: **flamefish, flame-thrower, flame-tree.** Related forms: **black-, blue-, flavo-, phlogo-.**

1009   flannel-   A word-initial combining element, also occurring as a word, derived from Welsh *gwlanen* 'wool garment' (from *gwlān* 'wool'), used in the sense of 'fabric containing wool (or cotton, or both)' and in extensions of this sense in combination with other English elements: **flannelboard, flannelleaf, flannelmouth.** Related forms: **lani-, villi-, wool-.**

1010   flash-   A word-initial combining element, also occurring as a word, derived from Middle English *flask(ie)* 'sprinkle,' used in the sense of 'burst of water, light, etc.' in combination with other English elements: **flashback, flashcube, flashlight.**

1011   flat-   A word-initial combining element, also occurring as a word, derived from Old Norse *flat(r)* 'level, uncurved,' used in its etymological and extended senses in combination with other English elements: **flatbread, flatfoot, flatiron.** Related forms: **field-, floor-, palmati-, place-, placento-, plagio-, plain-, plano-[1], plano-[2], plasmo-, plasmodi-, plasto-, plate-, platino-, platy-.**

1012   flavo-   A word-initial combining element, derived from Latin *flāv(us)* '(reddish) yellow' plus the combining vowel *-o-*, used in its etymological and extended senses in Neo-Latin and Neo-Greek combinations: ***Flavobacterium,*** **flavoprotein, flavoxanthin.** Also, **flav-, flavi: flavism, flavicidin.** Related forms: **black-, blue-, flame-, phlogo-.**

1013   flea-   A word-initial combining element, also occurring as a word, derived from Old English *flēa(h)* 'parasitic insect of the order *Siphonaptera,*' used in its etymological and extended senses in combination with other English elements: **fleabag, flea-bitten, fleawort.**

1014   flesh-   A word-initial combining element, also occurring as a word, derived from Old English *flæsć* 'meat; muscle and fatty tissue,' used in its etymological and extended senses in combination with other English elements: **flesh-fly, fleshhook, fleshpot.**

1015   flint-   A word-initial combining element, also occurring as a word, derived from Old English *flint* 'variety of hard siliceous stone,' used in its etymological and extended senses in combination with other English elements: **flinthead, flintlock, flintstone.**

1016   float-   A word-initial combining element, also occurring as a word, derived from Old English *flot(ian)* 'to be buoyant,' used in its etymological and extended senses in combination with other English elements: **float-feed, floatplane, floatstone.** Related forms: **flood-, fly-¹, fly-², pluto-, pluvio-, pneumo-², pulmo-, pyelo-.**

1017   flood-   A word-initial combining element, also occurring as a word, derived from Old English *flōd* 'inundation; overflowing of water,' used in its etymological and extended senses in combination with other English elements: **floodgate, floodlight, floodwater.** Related forms: **float-, fly-¹, fly-², pluto-, pluvio-, pneumo-², pulmo-, pyelo-.**

1018   floor-   A word-initial combining element, also occurring as a word, derived from Old English *flōr* 'flat surface (of a room or the like) upon which one may walk,' used in its etymological and extended senses in combination with other English elements: **floorcloth, floorman, floorwalker.** Related forms: **field-, flat-, palmati-, place-, placento-, plagio-, plain-, plano-¹, plano-², plasmo-, plasmodi-, plasto-, plate-, platino-, platy-.**

1019   flori-   A word-initial combining element, derived from Latin *flō(s)*, *flōr(is)* 'flower' plus the combining vowel *-i-*, used in its etymological and extended senses in Neo-Latin combinations: **floribunda, floriculture, floriferous.** Also, **flor-: florist.** Compare **flour-, flower-.** Related forms: **folii-, phyllo-.**

1020   flour-   A word-initial combining element, also occurring as a word, originally simply a variant spelling of *flower* (from Latin *flō(s)*, *flōr(is)* 'blossom, flower'), used (as is the word *flowers* in chemical terminology today) in the sense of 'fine-ground (grain or other substance)' (from the metaphorical use of *flower/flour* to mean 'finest part') in combination with other English elements: **flour-emery, flour-gold, flour-mill.** Compare **flori-, flower-.**

1021   flower-   A word-initial combining element, also occurring as a word, derived through Old French from Latin *flō(s)*, *flōr(is)* 'blossom,' used in its etymological and extended senses in combination with other English elements: **flower-of-Jove, flowerpecker, flowerpot.** Compare **flori-, flour-.**

1022 fluid- A word-initial combining element, also occurring as a word, derived from Latin *fluid(us)* 'flowing' (from the verb *fluere* 'to flow'), used chiefly in the sense of 'liquid' in Neo-Latin and Neo-Greek combinations: **fluid-acet-extract, fluidism, fluidounce.** Also, **flui-: fluidram.** Compare **fluoro-.**

1023 fluoro- A word-initial combining element, derived from Neo-Latin *fluor* '*fluorite,* a common mineral (CaF_2) which melts easily and is used as a flux' (from Latin *flu(ere)* 'to flow' plus the noun-forming suffix *-or*) plus the combining vowel *-o-,* used in the sense of 'containing *fluorine* (F) (which is a constituent of *fluor)*' and '*fluorescent;* of or pertaining to *fluorescence* (which is so named because *fluor* is able to absorb light of one color and re-emit that light as another color)' in scientific terminology: **fluorocarbon, fluorometer, fluorophosphate.** Also, **fluo-, fluor-: fluoborate, fluoride.** Compare **fluid-.**

1024 fly-[1] A word-initial combining element, also occurring as a word, derived from Old English *flē(o)ġ(an)* 'to move through the air on wings,' used in its etymological and extended senses in combination with other English elements: **flyaway, fly-by-night, flywheel.** Compare **fly-[2].** Related forms: **float-, flood-, pluto-, pluvio-, pneumo-[2], pulmo-, pyelo-.**

1025 fly-[2] A word-initial combining element, also occurring as a word, derived from Old English *flē(o)ġ(e)*, *flȳġ(e)* 'winged insect of the order Diptera' (from Old English *flēogan* 'to move through the air on wings'), used in its etymological and extended senses in combination with other English elements: **flyblown, fly-fish, flypaper.** Compare **fly-[1].**

1026 fog- A word-initial combining element, also occurring as a word, perhaps derived from Danish *fog* 'shower, drift, storm' or perhaps derived as a back-formation to Middle English *foggy* 'boggy, marshy' (cf. Middle English *fogge* 'second growth of grass; winter meadow grass' (from one of the Scandinavian languages (cf. Norwegian *fogg* 'grass in a wet meadow'))), used in the sense of 'cloudlike mist near the surface of the earth' and in extensions of this sense in combination with other English elements: **fogbound, fogdog, foghorn.**

1027 folii- A word-initial combining element, derived from Latin *foli(um)* 'leaf' plus the combining vowel *-i-,* used in its etymological and extended senses in Neo-Latin combinations: **foliicolous, foliiferous, foliigerous.** Also, **foli-, folio-: foliaceous, foliosan.** Related forms: **flori-, flour-, flower-, phyllo-.**

1028 **folk-** A word-initial combining element, also occurring as a word, derived from Old English *folc* 'people,' used in its etymological and extended senses in combination with other English elements: **folklore, folk-rock, folkway.**

1029 **food-** A word-initial combining element, also occurring as a word, derived from Old English *fōd(a)* 'that which is eaten,' used in its etymological and extended senses in combination with other English elements: **food-fish, food-gathering, foodstuff.** Compare **feed-, foster-.**

1030 **fool-** A word-initial combining element, also occurring as a word, derived through Old French from Latin *foll(is)* 'bellows,' hence, 'windbag, silly person,' used in this last and extended senses in combination with other English elements: **foolhardy, fool-hen, foolstones.**

1031 **foot-** A word-initial combining element, also occurring as a word, derived from Old English *fōt* 'part of the leg below the ankle,' used in its etymological and extended senses in combination with other English elements: **footfall, foothill, footpad.** Related forms: **pedo-², pilot-, podo-.**

1032 **for-¹** A word-initial combining element, derived from Old English *fær-, for-,* a prefix with a wide variety of meanings, chief among these being 'refraining from or negation of' that which is expressed by the combining root, appearing in its etymological senses in inherited English combinations: **forbear, forbid, forsake.** Also, **fore-¹: forego.** Related forms: **far-, fore-³, forth-, par-³, para-¹, per-, peri-, perisso-, pre-, primi-, pro-¹, pro-², proprio-, pros-¹, proso-, protero-, proto-, proximo-.**

1033 **for-²** A word-initial combining element, derived from Latin *for(is)* 'out of doors; outside,' appearing in this latter and extended senses in a small number of borrowings from Latin through Old French: **forclose, forfeit, forjudge.** Also, **fore-²: foreclose.** Related forms: **door-, thyro-.**

1034 **for-³** A variant of **fore-³.**

1035 **force-** A word-initial combining element, also occurring as a word, derived through Middle French from Late Latin *fortia* 'power, violence' (from Latin *fort(is)* 'strong, powerful' plus the noun-forming suffix *-ia*), used in its etymological and extended senses in combination with other English elements: **force-feed, force-piece, force-out.**

1036   **fore-¹**   A variant of **for-¹.**

1037   **fore-²**   A variant of **for-².**

1038   **fore-³**   A word-initial combining element, also occurring as a word, derived from Old English *fore* '(in) front; earlier; first,' used in its etymological and extended senses in combination with other English elements: **forearm, foreman, foresee.** Also, **for-³: forgo** ('precede'). Compare **first-.** Related forms: **far-, for-¹, forth-, par-³, para-¹, per-, peri-, perisso-, pre-, primi-, pro-¹, pro-², proprio-, pros-¹, proso-, protero-, proto-, proximo-.**

1039   **form-¹**   A word-initial combining element, also occurring as a word, derived through Old French from Latin *form(a)* 'shape, figure' (possibly through Etruscan from Greek *morphē* 'shape, form'), used in its etymological and extended senses in combination with other English elements: **formboard, form-fitting, formwork.** Related form(?): **morpho-.**

1040   **form-²**   A word-initial combining element, derived from English *form(ic)* 'of or pertaining to ants' and, by extension, 'of or pertaining to the acid (HCOOH) (which is the basic component of the sting of an ant)' (from Latin *formīca* 'ant'), used in the sense of 'of, pertaining to, containing, or derived from (HCOOH)' in chemical terminology: **formaldehyde, formate, formamide.** Related form: **myrmeco-.**

1041   **forth-**   A word-initial combining element, also occurring as a word, derived from Old English *forþ* 'forward(s), onward(s),' appearing in its etymological and extended senses in a few inherited English combinations: **forthcoming, forthright, forthwith.** Related forms: **far-, first-, for-¹, fore-³, par-³, para-¹, per-, peri-, perisso-, pre-, primi-, pro-¹, pro-², proprio-, pros-¹, proso-, protero-, proto-, proximo-.**

1042   **foster-**   A word-initial combining element, also occurring as a word, derived from Old English *fōster* 'nourishment, feeding' and, by extension, 'care, rearing' (from Old English *fōd(a)* 'food' plus the instrumental case ending *-tr(om)*), used in reference to 'a familial relationship in which the person named by the combining root offers to, shares with, or receives parental care from another or others to whom that person is not related by blood' in combination with other English elements: **foster-brother, foster-child, foster-parent.** Compare **feed-, food-.**

1043 **foul-**   A word-initial combining element, also occurring as a word, derived from Old English *fūl* 'rotten, unclean,' used in its etymological and extended senses in combination with other English elements: **foulbrood, foulmouthed, foul-up.** Related form: **pyo-.**

1044 **four-**   A word-initial combining element, also occurring as a word, derived from Old English *f(ē)ow(e)r* 'the cardinal number between *three* and *five*,' used in its etymological and extended senses in combination with other English elements: **fourbagger, fourflusher, four-in-hand.** Related forms: **quadri-, quarter-, quarti-, square-, tetra-.**

1045 **fox-**   A word-initial combining element, also occurring as a word, derived from Old English *fox* 'mammal of the genus *Vulpes*,' used in its etymological and extended senses in combination with other English elements: **foxfire, foxhole, foxhound.**

1046 **Franco-**   A word-initial combining element, derived from Latin *Franc(us)* 'Frank(ish)' plus the combining vowel *-o-*, used in the sense of 'French' in a variety of combinations: **Franco-American, Francophone, Franco-Prussian.**

1047 **free-**   A word-initial combining element, also occurring as a word, derived from Old English *frē(o)* 'not in bondage,' used in its etymological and extended senses in combination with other English elements: **freeborn, free-for-all, freehand.**

1048 **frigo-**   A word-initial combining element, derived from Latin *frīg(us)* 'cold' plus the combining vowel *-o-*, used in its etymological sense in Neo-Latin and Neo-Greek combinations: **frigolabile, frigostabile, frigotherapy.**

1049 **frog-**   A word-initial combining element, also occurring as a word, derived from Old English *frog(ga)* 'amphibian of the order *Anura*,' used in its etymological and extended senses in combination with other English elements: **frogfish, froghopper, frogman.**

1050 **fronto-**   A word-initial combining element, derived from Latin *fron(s), front(is)* 'forehead' plus the combining vowel *-o-*, used in its etymological sense in biomedical terminology and in the extended sense of 'front, frontal zone' in meteorological terminology: **frontogenesis, frontomaxillary, frontonasal.** Also, **fronti-: frontipetal.**

1051 **frost-** A word-initial combining element, also occurring as a word, derived from Old English *forst, frost* 'frozen dew' (cf. Old English *frēosan* 'to freeze'), used in its etymological and extended senses in combination with other English elements: **frostbite, frost-itch, frostweed.**

1052 **fructo-** A word-initial combining element, derived from Latin *fruct(us)* 'fruit' plus the combining vowel *-o-*, used in its etymological sense and in the specialized sense of 'of, pertaining to, or containing *fructose,* the sugar $(C_6H_{12}O_6)$ (which is found in fruit)' in Neo-Latin and Neo-Greek combinations: **fructofuranose, fructopyranose, fructovegetative.** Also, **fructi-: fructiferous.** Compare **fructos-.**

1053 **fructos-** A word-initial combining element, derived from English *fructos(e)* 'fruit sugar $(C_6H_{12}O_6)$' (from Latin *fruct(us)* 'fruit' plus the suffix *-ose* which is used to designate 'carbohydrates, esp. sugars'), used in its etymological sense in chemical terminology: **fructosamine, fructosazone, fructosuria.** Compare **fructo-.**

1054 **full-** A word-initial combining element, also occurring as a word, derived from Old English *full* 'filled, complete,' used in its etymological and extended senses in combination with other English elements: **full-blooded, full-blown, full-time.** Related forms: **pleni-, pleo-, pluri-, poly-.**

1055 **fungi-** A word-initial combining element, derived from Latin *fung(us)* 'mushroom; vegetable organism of the division *fungi*' plus the combining vowel *-i-*, used in its etymological sense in Neo-Latin and Neo-Greek combinations: **fungicide, fungiform, fungitoxic.** Related form: **spongio-.**

1056 **fuso-** A word-initial combining element, derived from Latin *fūs(us)* 'spindle' plus the combining vowel *-o-*, used in the sense of 'spindlelike; of or pertaining to spindlelike bacteria' in Neo-Latin and Neo-Greek combinations: **fusocellular, fusospirillary, fusostreptococcicosis.** Also, **fusi-: fusiform.**

G

1057 **gain-** A word-initial combining element, derived from Old English *ġeġn, ġean* 'against,' appearing in its etymological sense in a few generally obsolete inherited combinations: **gaincome, gainsay, gainstand.**

1058 **Gal-** A word-initial combining element, derived from Irish Gaelic *gal(l)* 'stranger, foreigner, esp. English,' appearing in its etymological sense in a number of place names: **Galbally, Galwally, Galway.** Related form: **Gallo-.**

1059 **galacto-** A word-initial combining element, derived from Greek *gála, gálakt(os)* 'milk' plus the combining vowel *-o-*, used in its etymological and extended senses, chief among these being 'of or pertaining to *galactose* ($CH_2OH(CHOH)_4CHO$), an aldohexose which is obtained from milk sugar,' in Neo-Greek combinations: **galactoblast, galactopoietic, galactopyranose.** Also, **galact-: galactacrasia.** Compare **galactos-.** Related form(?): **lacto-.**

1060 **galactos-** A word-initial combining element, derived from English *galactos(e)* 'aldohexose ($CH_2OH(CHOH)_4CHO$) obtained from milk sugar' (from Greek *gála, gálakt(os)* 'milk' plus the suffix *-ose* which is used to designate 'carbohydrates, esp. sugars'), used in its etymological sense in chemical terminology: **galactosamine, galactosazone, galactosemia.** Compare **galacto-.**

1061 **gall-** A word-initial combining element, also occurring as a word,

157

derived from Old Norse *gall* 'bile' (from the Indo-European root which underlies English *gold* and *yellow,* bile being yellowish in color), used in its etymological and extended senses in combination with other English elements: **gallbladder, gallsickness, gallstone.** Related forms: **arseno-, chlor-¹, chlor-², chole-, choler-, glass-, gold-, golden-, yellow-.**

1062   Gallo-   A word-initial combining element, derived from Latin *Gall(us)* 'of or pertaining to Gaul, the region corresponding to modern-day France and Northern Italy' (from the Germanic root meaning 'foreigner, stranger' which underlies English *Wales, Welsh, Wallachian,* and *Walloon*) plus the combining vowel *-o-,* used in the sense of 'of or pertaining to France' in a variety of combinations: **Gallomania, Gallophobia, Gallo-Romance.** Also, **Gall-: Gallic.** Related form: **Gal-.**

1063   galvano-   A word-initial combining element, derived from (*Luigi*) *Galvan(i)* (1737–93) (whose experiments in physiology led to the invention of the electric cell) plus the combining vowel *-o-,* used in the sense of 'of or pertaining to electricity; producing or produced by an electric current, esp. one resulting from chemical action' in Neo-Greek and Neo-Latin combinations: **galvanocautery, galvanometer, galvanotropism.** Also, **galvan-: galvanism.**

1064   game-   A word-initial combining element, also occurring as a word, derived from Old English *game(n)* '(organized) sport or amusement,' used in its etymological and extended senses, chief among these being 'that which is hunted (for sport),' in combination with other English elements: **gamebag, gamecock, gamekeeper.**

1065   gameto-   A word-initial combining element, derived from Greek *gamet(ḗ)* 'wife' and *gamét(ēs)* 'husband' (from *gameîn* 'to marry') plus the combining vowel *-o-,* used chiefly in the extended sense of 'of or pertaining to a *gamete,* a mature reproductive cell' in Neo-Greek and Neo-Latin combinations: **gametocidal, gametocytemia, gametogenesis.** Also, **gamet-: gametic.** Compare **gamo-.**

1066   gamma- (Γ, γ)   A word-initial combining element, the third letter of the Greek alphabet, used chiefly to designate 'the third member of a series, esp. the third carbon atom (or its substitute) in a straight chain compound' in scientific terminology: **gammabufagin, gammagraphic, gamma-ray.** Also, **gamm-: gammexane.** See **alpha-.**

1067   gamo-   A word-initial combining element, derived from Greek *gámo(s)* 'wedding' (from *gameîn* 'to marry'), used in its etymological and extended senses, chief among these being 'of or pertaining to sexual union,' in Neo-Greek combinations: **gamogenesis, gamo-mania, gamophobia.** Also, **gam-: gamic.** Compare **gameto-.**

1068   **gang-**   A word-initial combining element, also occurring as a word, derived from Old English *gang* 'a going; passage; way' and, by extension, 'group (going together),' used in its etymological and extended senses in combination with other English elements: **gangland, gangplank, gangway.** Related form: **go-.**

1069   **ganglio-**   A word-initial combining element, derived from Greek *gánglio(n)* 'subcutaneous tumor on or about a tendon,' used in its etymological and extended senses, chief among these being 'of or pertaining to a mass of nerve tissue,' in biomedical terminology: **ganglioblast, ganglioneuroma, ganglionervous.** Also, **ganglion-, gangliono-: ganglionitis, ganglionoplegic.**

1070   **gar-**   A word-initial combining element, derived from Old English *gār* 'spear,' appearing in its etymological and extended senses in a small number of inherited combinations: **garbill, garlic, garfish.**

1071   **gas-**   A word-initial combining element, also occurring as a word, derived from Dutch *gas* 'expandable mobile substance which is neither solid nor liquid,' a term coined by the Flemish chemist J. B. van Helmont (1577–1644) and based on Greek *cháos* 'state of disorder,' used in its etymological and extended senses in combination with other English elements: **gasbag, gasholder, gaslight.** Also (in scientific terminology), **gasi-, gaso-, gazo-: gasiform, gasometer, gazogene.**

1072   **gastro-**   A word-initial combining element, derived from Greek *gast(ē̆)r, gastr(ós)* 'paunch, belly, womb' plus the combining vowel -*o*-, used in the sense of 'of or pertaining to the stomach or abdomen' in biomedical terminology: **gastrocolitis, gastrodiaphany, gastrotherapy.** Also, **gaster-, gastero-, gastr-: gasterasthenia, *Gasterophilus*, gastritis.**

1073   **gastroentero-**   See **gastro-** and **entero-.**

1074   **gastrohystero-**   See **gastro-** and **hystero-.**

1075   **gastrojejuno-**   See **gastro-** and **jejuno-.**

1076   **gate-**   A word-initial combining element, also occurring as a word, derived from Old English *ġeat* 'opening, passageway, esp. one which may be closed by means of a barrier,' hence, 'doorlike barrier,' used in its etymological and extended senses in combination with other English elements: **gate-crasher, gatefold, gatekeeper.**

1077 gear- A word-initial combining element, also occurring as a word, derived through Middle English from Old Norse *ger(vi)* 'equipment,' used in the specialized sense of 'device which meshes with another to transmit or receive force or motion' in combination with other English elements: **gearbox, gearshift, gearwheel.**

1078 gelo-¹ A word-initial combining element, derived from Greek *gélō(s)* 'laughter,' used in its etymological and extended senses in Neo-Greek combinations: *Gelochelidon,* **geloscopy, gelotherapy.**

1079 gelo-² A word-initial combining element, derived from Latin *gel(āre)* 'to freeze,' later, 'to congeal' plus the combining vowel -*o*-, used in a variety of senses, all having to do with 'congealing' or with '*gelatin,* a protein derived from the partial hydrolysis of animal skin, connective tissue, and bone,' chiefly in biochemical terminology: **gelodiagnosis, geloplasm, gelotripsy.** Also, **gel-: gelfoam.** Related forms: **cold-, cool-.**

1080 gem- A word-initial combining element, also occurring as a word, derived through Old French from Latin *gem(ma)* 'bud, jewel,' used in this latter sense in combination with other English elements: **gem-peg, gem-ring, gemstone.**

1081 genio- A word-initial combining element, derived from Greek *gén(e)io(n)* 'chin,' used in its etymological sense in biomedical terminology: **genioglossal, geniohyoid, genioplasty.** Also, **geni-: genial.** Compare **geny-.** Related form: **chin-¹.**

1082 genito- A word-initial combining element, derived from Latin *genet(ālia)* 'reproductive organs' (from an Indo-European root meaning 'beget, be born') plus the combining vowel -*o*-, used in its etymological and extended senses in biomedical terminology: **genitocrural, genitoinfectious, genitourinary.** Related forms: **geno-, gentle-, gonado-, gone-¹, gono-¹, king-, nevo-.**

1083 geno- A word-initial combining element, derived from Greek *géno(s)* 'race; line of descent' (from an Indo-European root meaning 'beget, be born'), used in the sense of 'of or pertaining to sexual relations, reproduction, or heredity' in Neo-Greek combinations: **genoblast, genodermatology, genophobia.** Also **gen-: genome.** Related forms: **genito-, gentle-, gonado-, gone-¹, gono-¹, king-, nevo-.**

1084 **gentle-**   A word-initial combining element, also occurring as a
word, derived through Old French from Latin *gentīl(is)* 'pertaining
or belonging to a clan; a kinsman' (from an Indo-European root
meaning 'beget, be born'), used in the extended senses of 'well-
born, well-bred' and 'mild-mannered, mild' in combination with
other English elements: **gentleman, gentle-voiced, gentlewoman.**
Related forms: **genito-, geno-, gonado-, gone-¹, gono-¹, king-, nevo-.**

1085 **genu-**   A word-initial combining element, derived from Latin *genū*
'knee,' used in its etymological sense in biomedical terminology:
genuclast, genucubital, genuflect. Related forms: **gony-, knee-.**

1086 **geny-**   A word-initial combining element, derived from Greek
gény(s) 'jaw, chin, cheek,' used in its etymological senses in
biomedical terminology: **genyantrum, genychiloplasty, genyplasty.**
Compare **genio-.** Related form: **chin-¹.**

1087 **geo-**   A word-initial combining element, derived from Greek *geō-*, a
combining form of *gê* 'land, earth,' used in the sense of 'of or
pertaining to the earth' in Neo-Greek and Neo-Latin combinations: **geochemistry, geodynamics, geonavigation.**

1088 **Germano-**   A word-initial combining element, derived from Latin
Germān(us) 'of or pertaining to the Teutonic people of central
Europe' (possibly from a Celtic word meaning 'neighbor' (cf. Old
Irish *gair* 'neighbor')), used in its etymological sense and, more
commonly, in the specialized sense of 'of or pertaining to *Germany*'
in a variety of combinations: **Germano-Italic, Germano-Prussian,
Germanophobia.** Also, **German-: Germanic.**

1089 **gero-**   A word-initial combining element, derived from Greek
gérō(n), géront(os) 'old man,' used in the sense of 'of or pertaining
to old age or to the aged' in Neo-Greek combinations: **geroderma,
geromarasmus, geromorphism.** Also, **ger-, geront-, geronto-: geriat-
rics, gerontopia, gerontotherapeutics.**

1090 **get-**   A word-initial combining element, also occurring as a word,
derived from Old Norse *get(a)* 'to obtain,' used in a variety of
extensions of its etymological sense in combination with other
English elements: **getaway, get-together, get-up.**

1091 **ghost-**   A word-initial combining element, also occurring as a word,
derived from Old English *gāst* 'spirit,' used in its etymological and
extended senses in combination with other English elements:
ghostland, ghost-word, ghostwriter.

1092 giga- A word-initial combining element, derived from Greek *gíga(s), gigant(os)* 'giant,' used in the extended sense of 'billion' in a variety of combinations: **gigacycle, gigahertz, gigameter.** Compare **giganto-.**

1093 giganto- A word-initial combining element, derived from Greek *gíga(s), gigant(os)* 'giant' plus the combining vowel *-o-,* used in the sense of 'giantlike, unusually large' in Neo-Greek combinations: **gigantoblast, gigantocyte, gigantosoma.** Also, **gigant-: gigantism.** Compare **giga-.**

1094 gill- A word-initial combining element, also occurring as a word, derived through Middle English from one of the Scandinavian languages (cf. Swedish *gàl* 'respiratory organ of a fish'), used in its etymological and extended senses in combination with other English elements: **gill-arch, gill-netter, gill-plate.** Related form: **cheilo-.**

1095 ginger- A word-initial combining element, also occurring as a word, derived, ultimately, from Sanskrit *śṛṅgavera* 'spicy root of the genus *Zingibar,* literally, 'horn-body' (from *śṛṅga* 'horn' plus *vera* 'body'), used in its etymological and extended senses in combination with other English elements: **gingerale, gingerbread, gingersnap.** Related forms: **caroten-, cerebello-, cerebro-, cervi-², cervico-, corneo-, corner-, cornu-, cranio-, hart's-, horn-, keratin-, kerato-.**

1096 gingivo- A word-initial combining element, derived from Latin *gingīv(a)* '(buccal) gum' plus the combining vowel *-o-,* used in the sense of 'of or pertaining to the gums' in biomedical terminology: **gingivoglossitis, gingivolabial, gingivostomatitis.** Also, **gingiv-: gingivectomy.**

1097 glass- A word-initial combining element, also occurring as a word, derived from Old English *glæs* 'brittle, translucent substance used in making windows, etc.' (from an Indo-European root meaning something on the order of 'shine'), used in its etymological sense in combination with other English elements: **glasshouse, glassmaking, glassware.** Related forms: **arseno-, chlor-¹, chlor-², chole-, choler-, gall-, gold-, golden-, yellow-.**

1098 glauco- A word-initial combining element, derived from Greek *glaukó(s)* 'silvery, gray, blue-green,' used in its etymological and extended senses in Neo-Greek combinations: **glaucogonidium, glaucolite, glaucopyrite.** Also, **glauc-, glaucon-, glaucos-: glaucoma, glauconite, glaucosuria.**

1099   glio-   A word-initial combining element, derived from Greek *gli(a)* 'glue' plus the combining vowel *-o-*, used in the sense of 'of or pertaining to a gluelike substance, esp. the *neuroglia*' in Neo-Greek combinations: **glioblastoma, gliocytoma, gliosarcoma.** Also, **gli-, glia-: glioma, gliacyte.** Related forms: **clod-, cloud-, club-, globe-.**

1100   globe-   A word-initial combining element, also occurring as a word, derived through Old French from Latin *glob(us)* 'ball, sphere,' used in its etymological and extended senses in combination with other English elements: **globefish, globeflower, globetrotter.** Related forms: **clod-, cloud-, club-, glio-.**

1101   glosso-   A word-initial combining element, derived from Greek *glôss(a)* 'tongue' and, by extension, 'speech, language' plus the combining vowel *-o-*, used in its etymological and extended senses in Neo-Greek combinations: **glossoepiglottic, glossophobia, glossospasm.** Also, **gloss-: glossanthrax.** Compare **glotto-.**

1102   glotto-   A word-initial combining element, derived from Attic Greek *glôtt(a)* 'tongue' and, by extension, 'speech, language' plus the combining vowel *-o-*, used in its etymological and extended senses in Neo-Greek combinations: **glottochronology, glottogony, glottology.** Also, **glott-: glottal.** Compare **glosso-.**

1103   gluco-   A word-initial combining element, derived from English *gluco(se)* 'the sugar ($C_6H_{12}O_6$),' a direct borrowing of the 1838 French coinage which was based on Greek *gleûkos* 'new sweet wine (in which the sugar in question is found)' and influenced by Greek *glyk$\acute{y}$(s)* 'sweet,' used in the sense of 'of, pertaining to, or derived from *glucose*' and, through confusion with the related form **glyco-,** in the sense of 'of or pertaining to sweetness or to one of the sugars other than glucose' in biochemical terminology: **glucofuranose, glucogenesis, glucoproteinase.** Also, **gluc-, glucos-: glucatonia, glucosazone.** Compare **glycero-, glyco-.**

1104   glycero-   A word-initial combining element, derived from (Homeric) Greek *glykeró(s)* 'sweet' (from *glyk-* plus the adjective-forming suffix *-eros*), used in the specialized sense of 'of or pertaining to the sweet, syrupy liquid ($CH_2OH \cdot CHOH \cdot CH_2OH$)' in chemical terminology: **glycerogelatin, glycerophilic, glycerophosphate.** Also, **glycer-: glyceraldehyde.** Compare **gluco-, glyco-.**

1105   glyco-   A word-initial combining element, derived from Greek *glyk($\acute{y}$s)* 'sweet' plus the combining vowel *-o-*, used in the specialized sense of 'of, pertaining to, or containing a sugar, esp. *glucose*' in biochemical terminology: **glycoformal, glycogenesis, glycometabolic.** Also, **glyc-: glycemia.** Compare **gluco-, glycero-.**

1106 gnatho- A word-initial combining element, derived from Greek *gnátho(s)* 'jaw,' used in its etymological and extended senses in Neo-Greek combinations: **gnathocephalus, gnathodynamics, gnathostatics.** Also, **gnath-: gnathalgia.**

1107 go- A word-initial combining element, also occurring as a word, derived from Old English *gā(n)* 'to proceed,' used in its etymological and extended senses in combination with other English elements: **go-ahead, go-cart, godown.** Related form: **gang-.**

1108 goat- A word-initial combining element, also occurring as a word, derived from Old English *gāt* 'female ruminant of the genus *Capra*,' used in the sense of 'ruminant (of either sex) of the genus *Capra*' and in extensions of this sense in combination with other English elements: **goatfish, goatherd, goatsucker.**

1109 God- A word-initial combining element, also occurring as a word, derived from Old English *god* 'deity, supreme being,' used in the sense of '(The) Supreme Being' and in extensions of this sense in combination with other English elements: **God-awful, Godforsaken, Godspeed.** Also, **god-[1], good-[1]: godsend, goodbye.** Compare **dad-, god-[2].**

1110 god-[1] A variant of **God-.**

1111 god-[2] A word-initial combining element, derived from Old English *god* 'deity, supreme being,' used in the specialized sense of 'person sponsoring or sponsored by another at baptism' in combination with other English elements: **godchild, godfather, godmother.** Compare **God-.**

1112 gold- A word-initial combining element, also occurring as a word, derived from Old English *gold* 'the mineral element (Au)' (from an Indo-European root meaning something on the order of 'shine'), used in its etymological and extended senses in combination with other English elements: **goldbrick, gold-dust, goldfinch.** Compare **golden-.** Related forms: **arseno-, chlor-[1], chlor-[2], chole-, choler-, gall-, glass-, yellow-.**

1113 golden- A word-initial combining element, also occurring as a word, derived from Old English *gylden* 'made of or resembling gold' (from *gold* plus the adjective-forming suffix *-en*), used in its etymological and extended senses in combination with other

English elements: **goldeneye, goldenrod, goldenseal.** Compare **gold-.**

1114 **gon-**[1] A variant of **gone-**[1].

1115 **gon-**[2] A variant of **gony-**.

1116 **gonado-** A word-initial combining element, derived from Neo-Latin *gona(s), gonad(is)* 'ovary or testis' (based on Greek *gónos* 'seed' and *gonē* 'that which begets; seed') plus the combining vowel *-o-,* used in its etymological sense in biomedical terminology: **gonadoinhibitory, gonadokinetic, gonadotherapy.** Also, **gonad-: gonadectomy.** Compare **gone-**[1], **gono-**[1].

1117 **gonato-** A variant of **gony-**.

1118 **gone-**[1] A word-initial combining element, derived from Greek *gonē* 'that which begets; seed,' used in the sense of 'of or pertaining to semen' in Neo-Greek combinations: **gonecystitis, goneitis, gonepoietic.** Also, **gon-**[1], **goni-: gonacratia, gonioma.** Compare **gonado-, gono-**[1]. Related forms: **genito-, geno-, gentle-, king-, nevo-.**

1119 **gone-**[2] A variant of **gony-**.

1120 **goni-** A variant of **gone-**[1].

1121 **gonio-** A word-initial combining element, derived from Greek *gōni(a)* 'angle' plus the combining vowel *-o-,* used in its etymological sense in Neo-Greek combinations: **goniocraniometry, goniometer, goniophotography.**

1122 **gono-**[1] A word-initial combining element, derived from Greek *góno(s)* 'that which begets; seed; that which is begotten,' used in the sense of 'of or pertaining to semen or to the reproductive organs (of either the male or female)' in biomedical terminology: **gonocytoma, gononephrotome, gonotoxemia.** Compare **gonado-, gone-**[1]. Related forms: **genito-, geno-, gentle-, king-, nevo-.**

1123 **gono-**[2] A variant of **gony-**.

1124 **gony-** A word-initial combining element, derived from Greek *góny, gón(atos)* 'knee,' used in its etymological sense in Neo-Greek combinations: **gonycampsis, gonycrotesis, gonyoncus.** Also, **gon-**[2], **gone-**[2], **gono-**[2], **gonyo-, gonat-, gonato-: gonarthrotomy, goneitis, gonocampsis, gonyocele, gonatagra, gonatocele.** Related forms: **genu-, knee-.**

1125 good-¹   A variant of **God-**.

1126 good-²   A word-initial combining element, also occurring as a word, derived from Old English *gōd* 'satisfactory; the opposite of bad,' used in its etymological and extended senses in combination with other English elements: **good-for-nothing, good-humored, good-looking.**

1127 goof-   A word-initial combining element, also occurring as a word, derived from Old French *gof(fe)* 'awkward,' used in its etymological and extended senses in combination with other English elements: **goofball, goof-off, goof-up.**

1128 goose-   A word-initial combining element, also occurring as a word, derived from Old English *gōs* 'bird of the genus *Anser*,' used in its etymological and extended senses in combination with other English elements: **gooseherd, gooseneck, goose-step.**

1129 Graeco-   A (chiefly British) variant of **Greco-**.

1130 gram-   A word-initial combining element, also occurring as a word, derived through French from Greek *grám(ma)* 'that which is written; a letter of the alphabet' and, in Late Greek, 'a measure of weight corresponding to the Latin *scrīpulum,* the smallest standard Roman unit of weight,' used in the extended sense of 'basic unit of mass in the metric system' in scientific terminology: **gram-ion, grammeter, gram-molecule.** Compare **grapho-**. Related form: **crab-¹**. [Note: **gram-** is not to be confused with the initial element of **gram-negative (Gram-negative)** and **gram-positive (Gram-positive)** which refer to a method of staining originated by Hans Christian Joachim *Gram.* (1853–1938)]

1131 grand-   A word-initial combining element, also occurring as a word, derived through French from Latin *grand(is)* 'great, large, full-grown,' used in two sorts of combination with other English elements:
  1. In the sense of 'great, large': **grand-guard, grand-scale, grand-stand.**
  2. In the sense of 'at one degree of kinship more remote than that named by the combining root': **grandchild, grandfather, grandniece.**

1132 granulo-   A word-initial combining element, derived from Late Latin *grānul(um)* 'particle, grain' (from *grān(um)* 'grain, kernel' plus the diminutive suffix *-ulum*) plus the combining vowel *-o-*, used in the sense of 'grainy, particulate' in Neo-Latin and Neo-

Greek combinations: **granuloadipose, granulocorpuscle, granuloplasm.** Also, **granul-, granuli-: granulate, granuliform.** Related form: **corn-.**

1133   **grape-**   A word-initial combining element, also occurring as a word, derived from Old French *grape* 'cluster of fruits of the vine of the genus *Vitis*' (from the verb *graper* 'to gather (fruit) with a grappling hook (or similar device)' (from a Germanic word meaning 'hook')), used in the sense of 'fruit of the vine of the genus *Vitis*' and in extensions of this sense in combination with other English elements: **grapefruit, grapeshot, grapevine.** Related forms: **cradle-, cramp-¹, cramp-², crank-, creeping-, crochet-, crook-, crop-.**

1134   **grapho-**   A word-initial combining element, derived from Greek *gráph(ein)* 'to scratch,' hence, 'to write, record' plus the combining vowel *-o-*, used in its etymological and extended senses in Neo-Greek and Neo-Latin combinations: **graphology, graphomotor, graphoscope.** Compare **gram-.** Related form: **crab-¹.**

1135   **grass-**   A word-initial combining element, also occurring as a word, derived from Old English *græs* 'green spiky plant(s) of the family *Gramineae*,' used in its etymological and extended senses in combination with other English elements: **grasshopper, grassland, grass-roots.** Related form: **green-.**

1136   **grave-**   A word-initial combining element, also occurring as a word, from Old English *græf* 'excavation (for burial),' used in its etymological sense in combination with other English elements: **graveclothes, gravedigger, gravestone.** Related form: **grub-.**

1137   **gravel-**   A word-initial combining element, also occurring as a word, derived from Old French *gravel(le)* 'coarse sand' (from *grave* 'sandy shore' (perhaps of Celtic origin) plus the diminutive suffix *-elle*), used in the sense of 'mixture of small stones (and sand)' and in extensions of this sense in combination with other English elements: **gravel-blind, graveldiver, gravelweed.**

1138   **gray-**   A word-initial combining element, also occurring as a word, derived from Old English *græg* 'color intermediate between black and white,' used in its etymological sense in combination with other English elements: **grayback, graybeard, graylag.** Also, **grey-: greyhound.**

1139   **great-**   A word-initial combining element, also occurring as a word, derived from Old English *grēat* 'large, important,' used in two different sorts of combination with other English elements:

1. In the sense of 'large': **great-circle, greatcoat, great-hearted.**
2. In the sense of 'at one degree of kinship more remote than that named by the combining root': **great-aunt, great-grandfather, great-great-granddaughter.** [Note: in this latter variety of combination, **great-** functions essentially as a loan translation of French *grand* (cf. **grand-**) with whose English reflex it is used interchangeably in the pairs **grandaunt/great-aunt, granduncle/great-uncle, grandniece/great-niece,** and **grandnephew/great-nephew. Great-** and **grand-** are otherwise in complementary distribution in kinship terminology, **grand-** being used to designate people 'at two generations' remove' from the subject, and **great-** being used to designate people 'at three (or more) generations' remove' from the subject.]

1140 **Greco-**   A word-initial combining element, derived through Latin from Greek *Graikó(s)* 'Greek,' used in its etymological sense in combination with other English elements: **Greco-Bactrian, Greco-Roman, Greco-Turkish.** Also (chiefly British), **Graeco-: Graeco-Roman.**

1141 **green-**   A word-initial combining element, also occurring as a word, derived from Old English *grēn(e)* 'verdant,' used in its etymological and extended senses in combination with other English elements: **greenback, greengrocer, greenhouse.** Related form: **grass-.**

1142 **grey-**   A variant of **gray-.**

1143 **ground-**   A word-initial combining element, also occurring as a word, derived from Old English *grund* 'foundation, surface of the earth,' used in its etymological and extended senses in combination with other English elements: **groundbreaking, groundkeeper, groundsill.**

1144 **grub-**   A word-initial combining element, also occurring as a word, derived from Middle English *grub(ben)* 'to dig' (whence Middle English *grubbe* 'wormlike insect larva'), used in its etymological and extended senses in combination with other English elements: **grubhook, grubstake, grubworm.** Related form: **grave-.**

1145 **guard-**   A word-initial combining element, also occurring as a word, derived through Old French from the Germanic word which underlies English *ward,* used in the sense of 'that which protects or watches over' and in extensions of this sense in combination with other English elements: **guardhouse, guardrail, guardroom.**

1146 **guide-**   A word-initial combining element, also occurring as a word, derived through Old French from the Proto-Germanic form which underlies English *wise,* used in the sense of 'that which directs' and in extensions of this sense in combination with other English elements: **guidebook, guideline, guidepost.** Related forms: **eido-, ideo-, story-, video-, visuo-.**

1147 guinea-   A word-initial combining element, also occurring as a word, derived from the 14th-century Portuguese rendering— *Guiné*—of the local name for a particular West African trading town (for which the surrounding area was named during the first days of European colonization of the region), used chiefly in the extended sense of 'of or from a vaguely distant land' in combination with other English elements: **guinea-fowl, guinea-hen, guinea-pig.** Also, **Guinea-: Guinea-worm.**

1148 gum-   A word-initial combining element, also occurring as a word, derived through Latin and Old French from Greek *kóm(mi)* 'sticky sap exuded by certain plants,' used in its etymological and extended senses in combination with other English elements: **gumdrop, gumshoe, gumwood.**

1149 gun-   A word-initial combining element, also occurring as a word, most probably derived through Middle English from Scandinavian *Gun(ne),* a pet form of the woman's name *Gunhild* (from Old Norse *gun(nr)* 'war' plus *hild(r)* 'war'), which might be applied to engines of war as speakers of English might refer to a howitzer as a *Big Bertha* or to a six-shooter as an *Old Betsy,* used in the sense of 'piece of ordnance; firearm' in combination with other English elements: **gunboat, gunfire, gun-shy.**

1150 gut-   A word-initial combining element, also occurring as a word, derived from Middle English *gut* 'drain, channel, intestine' (from Old English *geotan* 'to flow, drain'), used in the sense of 'intestine' and in extensions of this sense in combination with other English elements: **gutbucket, gut-scraper, gutwort.** Related forms: **chylo-, chymo-.**

1151 gutta-   A word-initial combining element, derived from Malay *gutta* '(plant) gum,' appearing in its etymological sense in a few borrowings from Malay: **gutta-percha, gutta-rambong, gutta-shea.**

1152 gutter-   A word-initial combining element, also occurring as a word, derived from Old French *g(o)ut(i)er* 'channel for receiving run-off water from a roof' (from *gout(e)* 'drop of liquid' plus the agentive suffix *-ier*), used in its etymological and extended senses in combination with other English elements: **gutter-flag, guttersnipe, gutter-spout.**

1153 gutturo-   A word-initial combining element, derived from Latin *guttur* 'throat' plus the combining vowel *-o-,* used in its etymological and extended senses in biomedical terminology: **gutturonasal, gutturophony, gutturotetany.** Also, **guttur-: guttural.**

1154 gymno-   A word-initial combining element, derived from Greek *gymnó(s)* 'unclad, naked,' used in its etymological and extended senses in Neo-Greek combinations: **gymnobacteria, gymnophobia, gymnosophist.** Related form: **nudi-.**

1155 gyn-   A variant of **gyno-.**

1156 gynaeco-   A (chiefly British) variant of **gyno-.**

1157 gynandro-   See **gyno-** and **andro-.**

1158 gyne-   A variant of **gyno-.**

1159 gyneco-   A variant of **gyno-.**

1160 gyno-   A word-initial combining element, derived from Greek *gyn(ē̆), gyn(aikós)* 'woman' plus the combining vowel *-o-,* used in the sense of 'of or pertaining to women or to the female sex' in Neo-Greek and Neo-Latin combinations: **gynogenesis, gynograph, gynoplastics.** Also, **gyn-, gynaeco-, gyne-, gynec-, gyneco-: gynandromorphism, gynaecophorus, gyneduct, gynecoid, gynecomania.**

1161 gyro-   A word-initial combining element, derived from Greek *gyró(s)* 'curved' and *gŷro(s)* 'ring, circle,' used in the sense of 'ringlike, rotating, convoluted' in a variety of combinations: **gyrocompass, gyroplane, gyrospasm.** Also, **gyr-: gyrencephalic.**

H

1162 **haem-**   A (chiefly British) variant of **hemo-**.

1163 **haemato-**   A (chiefly British) variant of **hemo-**.

1164 **hag-**   A word-initial combining element, also occurring as a word, derived from Middle English *hag(ge)* 'female evil spirit' (to which the Modern German cognate *Hexe* 'witch' may be compared), hence, 'ugly old woman,' used in this latter and extended senses in combination with other English elements: **hagborn, hagfish, hagseed.**

1165 **hagio-**   A word-initial combining element, derived from Greek *hágio(s)* 'sacred, holy,' used in its etymological and extended senses in Neo-Greek combinations: **hagiocracy, hagiographer, hagioscope.** Also, **hagi-: hagiarchy.**

1166 **hair-**   A word-initial combining element, also occurring as a word, derived from Old English *hær* 'filamentous outgrowth of an animal's body,' used in its etymological and extended senses in combination with other English elements: **hairball, hair-raising, hair-trigger.**

1167 **hal-**   A variant of **halo-**.

1168 **half-**   A word-initial combining element, also occurring as a word, derived from Old English *h(e)alf* '(being) one of two equal parts,'

171

used in its etymological and extended senses in combination with other English elements: **half-baked, half-breed, half-sister.**

1169 **halo-**   A word-initial combining element, derived from Greek *hál(s)*, *hal(ós)* 'salt' plus the combining vowel *-o-*, used in its etymological and extended senses in Neo-Greek and Neo-Latin combinations: **halobiotic, halogen, halosteresis.** Also, **hal-, hali-: halide, halisteresis.** Related forms: **sali-², salt-, sauce-.**

1170 **hammer-**   A word-initial combining element, also occurring as a word, derived from Old English *hamor, hamer* 'tool used for driving nails, beating metal, etc., having a solid head set at right angles to a handle,' used in its etymological and extended senses in combination with other English elements: **hammer-blow, hammer-head, hammertoe.**

1171 **hand-**   A word-initial combining element, also occurring as a word, derived from Old English *hand* 'extremity of the arm comprising the carpus, metacarpus, and fingers,' used in its etymological and extended senses in combination with other English elements: **handball, handkerchief, hand-me-down.**

1172 **hang-**   A word-initial combining element, also occurring as a word, derived from the fusion of three related verbs: Old English *hang(ian)* 'to be suspended,' Old Norse *hang(a)* 'to suspend,' and Old English *hōn* 'to suspend,' used in its etymological and extended senses in combination with other English elements: **hangdog, hangman, hangout.**

1173 **haplo-**   A word-initial combining element, derived from Greek *hapló(s)* 'single, simple,' literally, 'onefold,' used in its etymological and extended senses in Neo-Greek combinations: **haplobacteria, haplodermatitis, haplophase.** Also, **hapl-: haplopia.** Related forms: **hecto-, hendeca-, hetero-, homalo-, homeo-, homo-, simple-, single-, some-.**

1174 **hapto-**   A word-initial combining element, derived from Greek *hápt(ein)* 'to touch' plus the combining vowel *-o-*, used in the sense of 'of or pertaining to touch or contact' and in extensions of this sense in Neo-Greek combinations: **haptometer, haptophore, haptotaxis.** Also, **hapt-, hapte-: haptic, haptephobia.**

1175 **hard-**   A word-initial combining element, also occurring as a word, derived from Old English *h(e)ard* 'solid, not soft,' used in its etymological and extended senses in combination with other

English elements: **hard-boiled, hard-core, hard-hearted.** Related forms: **cancer-, carcino-, chancr-, karyo-.**

1176 hare-   A word-initial combining element, also occurring as a word, derived from Old English *har(a)* 'mammal of the genus *Lepus*,' used in its etymological and extended senses in combination with other English elements: **harebell, harebrained, harelip.**

1177 hart's-   A word-initial combining element, also occurring as a word, the possessive singular form of English *hart* (from Old English *heort* 'stag,' originally, 'horned animal') (from an Indo-European root meaning 'head, horn'), used in its etymological and extended senses in combination with other English elements: **hart's-clover, hart's-tongue, hart's-truffles.** Also, **harts-: hartshorn.** Related forms: **caroten-, cerebello-, cerebro-, cervi-², cervico-, corneo-, corner-, cornu-, cranio-, ginger-, horn-, keratin-, kerato-.**

1178 harvest-   A word-initial combining element, also occurring as a word, derived from Old English *hærfest* 'autumn,' used in the extended sense of 'the season in which crops are gathered; the gathering of crops' and in extensions of this sense in combination with other English elements: **harvestfish, harvestman, harvest-mouse.**

1179 hat-   A word-initial combining element, also occurring as a word, derived from Old English *hæt(t)* '(shaped) covering for the head,' used in its etymological sense in combination with other English elements: **hatband, hatpin, hatrack.**

1180 hatchet-   A word-initial combining element, also occurring as a word, derived from Old French *hachet(te)* 'hand ax,' literally, 'small ax' (from *hach(e)* 'ax' plus the diminutive suffix *-ette*), used in its etymological and extended senses in combination with other English elements: **hatchetfish, hatchet-faced, hatchet-shaped.** Related forms: **scab-, scapho-, scapulo-, scopi-.**

1181 haver-   A word-initial combining element, also occurring as a word, derived from Middle English *haver* 'oats,' used in its etymological and extended senses in combination with other English elements: **haverbread, havermeal, haversack.**

1182 hawk-   A word-initial combining element, also occurring as a word, derived from Old English *ha(fo)c* 'bird of prey of the family *Falconidae* or *Accipitridae*,' used in its etymological and extended senses in combination with other English elements: **hawkbill, hawk-eyed, hawkweed.**

1183   **hay-**   A word-initial combining element, also occurring as a word, derived from Old English *hēġ* 'grass which has been cut and dried (from *hēawan* 'to cut,' whence Modern English *hew*), used in its etymological and extended senses in combination with other English elements: **hayloft, haymaker, hayseed.**

1184   **he-**   A word-initial combining element, also occurring as a word, the third person singular masculine subject pronoun, used in the sense of 'male, masculine, resembling the male' in combination with other English elements: **he-huckleberry, he-man, he-wolf.** Compare **hind-.** Related form: **cis-.**

1185   **head-**   A word-initial combining element, also occurring as a word, derived from Old English *hēa(fo)d* 'the uppermost part of the human body which is joined to the neck and which contains the brain and the organs of taste, smell, sight, and hearing,' used in its etymological and extended senses in combination with other English elements: **headband, headmaster, headstrong.** Related forms: **capillar-(?), capilli-(?), capit-, scape-.**

1186   **heart-**   A word-initial combining element, also occurring as a word, derived from Old English *heort(e)* 'organ responsible for the circulation of the blood throughout the body (and formerly held to be the seat of the emotions),' used in its etymological and extended senses in combination with other English elements: **heartburn, heartwarming, heartworm.** Related forms: **cardio-, cordate-, core-[1].**

1187   **heat-**   A word-initial combining element, also occurring as a word, derived from Old English *hæt(u), hæt(e)* 'hotness,' used in its etymological sense in combination with other English elements: **heat-focus, heat-sink, heatstroke.** Compare **hot-.**

1188   **heath-**   A word-initial combining element, also occurring as a word, derived from Old English *hǣþ* 'uncultivated open land' and, later, 'plant (of the family *Ericaceae*) which grows on uncultivated open land,' used in both senses in combination with other English elements: **heathberry, heathbird, heath-pea.** Compare **heather-.**

1189   **heather-**   A word-initial combining element, also occurring as a word, derived from Old English *hǣþ* 'heath' plus the noun-forming suffix *-er,* used in the sense of 'plant of the family *Ericaceae* (which grows on a heath)' and in extensions of this sense in combination with other English elements: **heather-bell, heather-claw, heather-wool.** Compare **heath-.**

1190   **heavy-**   A word-initial combining element, also occurring as a word, derived from Old English *hefi(ġ)* 'weighty' (perhaps originally 'hard to lift or throw' (cf. Old English *hebban* 'to lift, throw,' whence Modern English *heave*)), used in its etymological and extended senses in combination with other English elements: **heavy-bearded, heavy-handed, heavyweight.**

1191 hebe-   A word-initial combining element, derived from Greek *hébē* 'youth, puberty, signs of puberty,' used in the sense of 'pubescent; of or pertaining to puberty or to the pubes' in Neo-Greek combinations: **hebeanthous, hebeosteotomy, hebephrenia.** Also, **heb-: hebosteotomy.**

1192 hecto-   A word-initial combining element, derived through French from Greek *hek(a)tó(n)* '(one) hundred' (from an Indo-European root meaning 'one' plus another meaning 'hundred'), used in its etymological sense and in the extended sense of 'many' in Neo-Greek combinations: **hectocotylus, hectograph, hectoliter.** Also, **hecato-, hecatom-, hecaton-, hect-, hekt-, hekto-: hecatophyllous, hecatompedon, hecatonstylon, hectare, hektare, hektometer.** Related forms: **haplo-, hendeca-, hetero-, homalo-, homeo-, homo-, simple-, single-, some; centi-, hundred.**

1193 hedge-   A word-initial combining element, also occurring as a word, derived from Old English *heġġ* 'row of bushes (acting as a boundary),' used in its etymological and extended senses in combination with other English elements: **hedgehog, hedgehop, hedgerow.**

1194 heel-   A word-initial combining element, also occurring as a word, derived from Old English *hēl(a)* 'hindmost part of the foot,' used in its etymological and extended senses in combination with other English elements: **heel-and-toe, heelpost, heeltap.**

1195 hekto-   A variant of **hecto-**.

1196 hel-[1]   A variant of **helo-[1]**.

1197 hel-[2]   A variant of **helo-[2]**.

1198 helico-   A word-initial combining element, derived from Greek *hélix, hélik(os)* 'that which is twisted, bent; spiral-shaped; a coil' and, by extension, 'snail' plus the combining vowel *-o-*, used in its etymological and extended senses in Neo-Greek and Neo-Latin combinations: **helicograph, helicogyrate, helicotrema.** Also, **heli-, helic-, helici-: helicline, helicopter, heliciform.** [Note: the **heli-** of

helipad and **heliport** represents an etymologically inaccurate abbreviation of the word *helicopter.*]

1199 **helio-** A word-initial combining element, derived from Greek *hḗlio(s)* '(the) sun,' used in its etymological and extended senses in Neo-Greek combinations: **heliocentric, heliometer, heliotropism.** Also, **heli-: helianthus.** Related forms: **sol-[1], south-, sun-.**

1200 **hell-** A word-initial combining element, also occurring as a word, derived from Old English *hel(l)* 'place (esp. a subterranean place) where evil-doers are sent to dwell as a punishment after death' (from an Indo-European root meaning 'cover(ed), conceal(ed),') used in its etymological and extended senses in combination with other English elements: **hellbent, hellcat, hellhound.** Related forms: **celli-, cello-, cellulo-, cilio-, coleo-, color-, hollow-.**

1201 **helmintho-** A word-initial combining element, derived from Greek *hélmin(s), hélminth(os)* 'worm' plus the combining vowel *-o-,* used in its etymological and extended senses in Neo-Greek and Neo-Latin combinations: **helminthochorton, helminthology, helminthophobia.** Also, **helminth-, helminthi-: helminthic, helminthicide.** Related forms: **ulo-[3], valvulo-, walk-(?), well-[2].**

1202 **helo-[1]** A word-initial combining element, derived from Greek *hêlo(s)* 'nail, stud, wart, corn,' used in its etymological and extended senses in Neo-Greek combinations: *Helobacterium,* **heloderm, helotomy.** Also, **hel-[1]: helodont.**

1203 **helo-[2]** A word-initial combining element, derived from Greek *hélo(s)* 'marsh, swamp,' used in its etymological and extended senses in Neo-Greek combinations: **helobious,** *Heloecetes, Helophilus.* Also, **hel-[2]: helodes.**

1204 **hem-[1]** A variant of **hemo-.**

1205 **hem-[2]** A variant of **hemi-.**

1206 **hemacyto-** See **hemo-** and **cyto-.**

1207 **hemangio-** See **hemo-** and **angio-.**

1208 **hemato-** A variant of **hemo-.**

1209 **hematocyto-** See **hemo-** and **cyto-.**

1210 **hemi-** A word-initial combining element, derived from Greek *hēmi-*

'half-,' used in its etymological and extended senses in a variety of combinations: **hemianopsia, hemidemisemiquaver, hemisphere.** Also, **hem-²: hemelytron.** Related forms: **semi-, sesqui-.**

1211 **hemihyper-**   See **hemi-** and **hyper-.**

1212 **hemo-**   A word-initial combining element, derived from Greek *haîm(a), haim(atos)* 'blood' plus the combining vowel *-o-,* used in its etymological and extended senses in Neo-Greek and Neo-Latin combinations: **hemoglobin, hemophobia, hemotoxin.** Also, **haem-, haema-, haemat-, haemati-, haemato-, haemo-, hem-, hema-, hemat-, hemati-, hemato-: haemangioma, haemachrome, haematoid, haematimeter, haematocyst, haemopoiesis, hemagglutinate, hemadromometer, hematemesis, hematimeter, hematocatharsis.**

1213 **hemocyto-**   See **hemo-** and **cyto-.**

1214 **hemoglobino-**   A word-initial combining element, derived from English *hemoglobin* 'oxygen-carrying protein of the red corpuscles' (from Greek *haîm(a)* 'blood' plus the combining vowel *-o-* plus Latin *glob(us)* 'sphere, ball' plus the protein-naming suffix *-in*) plus the combining vowel *-o-,* used in its etymological sense in biomedical terminology: **hemoglobinocholia, hemoglobinometer, hemoglobinopepsia.** Also, **hemoglobin-, hemoglobini-: hemoglobinemia, hemoglobiniferous.** Compare **hemo-, globe-.**

1215 **hen-**   A word-initial combining element, also occurring as a word, derived from Old English *hen(n)* 'female domestic fowl' (from *hana* 'cock' to which Latin *canere* 'to sing' may be compared), used in its etymological and extended senses in combination with other English elements: **henbane, henhouse, henpecked.**

1216 **hendeca-**   A word-initial combining element, derived from Greek *héndeka* 'eleven,' literally, 'one (and) ten,' used in its etymological sense in Neo-Greek combinations: **hendecahedron, hendecasemic, hendecasyllabic.** Also **hendec-: hendecandrous.** Related forms: **haplo-, hecto-, homalo-, homeo-, homo-, simple-, single-, some-; deca-, deci-, ten-¹.**

1217 **hepatico-**   A word-initial combining element, derived from Greek *hēpatikó(s)* 'of or belonging to the liver' (from *hêpa(r), hêpat(os)* 'liver' plus the adjective-forming suffix *-ikos*), used in its etymological sense and in the extended sense of 'of or pertaining to a *hepatic duct*' in biomedical terminology: **hepaticoenterostomy, hepaticojejunostomy, hepaticopulmonary.** Compare **hepato-.**

1218   hepato-   A word-initial combining element, derived from Greek *hêpa(r)*, *hêpat(os)* 'liver' plus the combining vowel *-o-*, used in its etymological sense in biomedical terminology: **hepatoenteric, hepatofugal, hepatopleural.** Also, **hepa-, hepar-, hepat-: hepaptosis, heparin, hepatectomy.** Compare **hepatico-.**

1219   hepta-   A word-initial combining element, derived from Greek *heptá* 'seven,' used in its etymological and extended senses in Neo-Greek combinations: **heptachromic, heptadactylism, heptahydrate.** Also, **hept-: heptaldehyde.** Related forms: **septi-², seven-.**

1220   herb-   A word-initial combining element, also occurring as a word, derived through Old French from Latin *herb(a)* 'grass, weed, flowering plant,' used in this last sense in combination with other English elements: **herb-doctor, herb-paris, herbwoman.**

1221   here-   A word-initial combining element, also occurring as a word, derived from Old English *hēr* 'in this place,' used in the sense of 'this place; this time' in combination with other English elements: **hereafter, herein, heretofore.**

1222   heredo-   A word-initial combining element, derived from Latin *hērē(s)*, *hērēd(is)* 'heir' (perhaps from an Indo-European root meaning 'grasp') plus the combining vowel *-o-*, used in the sense of 'congenital, inherited' in biomedical terminology: **heredoataxia, heredodegeneration, heredosyphilis.** Related form(?): **cheiro-.**

1223   hernio-   A word-initial combining element, derived from Latin *herni(a)* 'protruded viscus; rupture' plus the combining vowel *-o-*, used in the sense of 'protrusion of tissue or part of an organ through an abnormal opening in the surrounding walls' in biomedical terminology: **hernio-appendectomy, herniolaparotomy, herniopuncture.** Also, **herni-: herniated.** Related forms: **chord-, cord-².**

1224   herpeto-   A word-initial combining element, derived from Greek *herpató(n)* 'creeping thing; snake, reptile' (from the verb *hérpein* 'to creep, crawl' (from the Indo-European root which underlies English *serpent*)), used in its etymological and extended senses in Neo-Greek combinations: **herpetologic, *Herpetospondylia*, herpetotomy.**

1225   herring-   A word-initial combining element, also occurring as a word, derived from Old English *hæring* 'the fish *Clupea harengus*,' used in its etymological and extended senses in combination with other English elements: **herringbone, herring-buss, herring-driver.**

1226   hetero-   A word-initial combining element, derived from Greek *hétero(s)* 'one of two; the other (of two); other; different; unequal' (from an Indo-European root meaning 'one' plus the contrastive suffix *-teros*), used in its etymological and extended senses in Neo-Greek and Neo-Latin combinations: **heterodermic, heterogenetic, heterointoxication.** Also, **heter-: heteraxial.** Related forms: **haplo-, hecto-, hendeca-, homalo-, homeo-, homo-, simple-, single-, some-.**

1227　**hexa-**　A word-initial combining element, derived from Greek *héx* 'six' plus the combining vowel *-a-*, used in its etymological and extended senses in Neo-Greek and Neo-Latin combinations: **hexabasic, hexadecimal, hexavalent.** Also, **hex-: hexode.** Related forms: **sex-, six-.**

1228　**hi-**　A variant of **high-.**

1229　**hide-**　A word-initial combining element, also occurring as a word, derived from Old English *hȳd(an)* 'to conceal,' used in its etymological sense in combination with other English elements: **hide-and-seek, hideaway, hideout.**

1230　**hidro-**　A word-initial combining element, derived from Greek *hidró(s)* 'perspiration, sweat,' used in its etymological and extended senses, chief among these being 'of or pertaining to a sweat gland,' in Neo-Greek combinations: **hidroadenoma, hidrocystoma, hidroschesis.** Also, **hidr-, hidros-: hidradenoma, hidrosadenitis.** Related forms: **sudo-, sweat-.**

1231　**hiero-**　A word-initial combining element, derived from Greek *hieró(s)* 'sacred, holy,' used in its etymological and extended senses in a variety of combinations: **hierodeacon, hieroglyph, hierophobia.** Also, **hier-: hierarchy.**

1232　**high-**　A word-initial combining element, also occurring as a word, derived from Old English *hēah* 'lofty,' used in its etymological and extended senses in combination with other English elements: **highborn, highbrow, highlight.** Also, **hi-: hijack.**

1233　**hill-**　A word-initial combining element, also occurring as a word, derived from Old English *hyll* 'topographic elevation,' used in its etymological and extended senses in combination with other English elements: **hillbilly, hillside, hilltop.**

1234　**hind-**　A word-initial combining element, also occurring as a word, derived from Old English *hind(an)* 'at the back; from the rear' (from the Indo-European demonstrative pronoun which underlies English *he*), used in its etymological and extended senses in combination with other English elements: **hindbrain, hindgut, hindsight.** Compare **he-.** Related form: **cis-.**

1235   **hip-**   A word-initial combining element, also occurring as a word, derived from Old English *hyp(e)* 'top of the thigh projecting from the pelvis' (from an Indo-European root meaning 'bend'), used in its etymological sense in combination with other English elements: **hipbone, hiphuggers, hipshot.** Related forms: **cubo-, cup-, hop-[1].**

1236   **hippo-**   A word-initial combining element, derived from Greek *hippo(s)* 'horse,' used in its etymological and extended senses in Neo-Greek combinations: **hippocoprosterol, hippodrome, hippolith.** Also, **hipp-: hippuricase.**

1237   **Hispano-**   A word-initial combining element, derived from Latin *Hispān(us)* 'Spanish' plus the combining vowel *-o-,* used in the sense of 'native speaker of Spanish' in combination with other English elements: **Hispano-American, Hispano-Basque, Hispano-European.**

1238   **histio-**   A word-initial combining element, derived from Greek *histio(n),* a diminutive form of *histó(s)* 'web, cloth, tissue,' used in the sense of 'of or pertaining to (body) tissue' in biomedical terminology: **histioblastoma, histiocyte, histio-irritative.** Compare **histo-.**

1239   **histo-**   A word-initial combining element, derived from Greek *histó(s)* 'mast, beam' (from the verb meaning 'to stand'), hence, 'beam or warp of a loom,' hence, 'that which is woven; a web or tissue,' used in the sense of 'of or pertaining to (body) tissue' in biomedical terminology: **histofluorescence, histokinesis, histomorphology.** Also, **hist-: histaffine.** Compare **histio-.** Related forms: **stage-, stand-, stasi-, state-, stato-, stauro-, stern-[2](?), store-, stylo-.**

1240   **hit-**   A word-initial combining element, also occurring as a word, derived from Old Norse *hit(ta)* 'to encounter,' used in the sense of 'strike, encounter with force' and in extensions of this sense in combination with other English elements: **hit-and-run, hit-man, hit-or-miss.**

1241   **hodo-**   A word-initial combining element, derived from Greek *hodó(s)* 'way, road, path,' used in its etymological and extended senses in Neo-Greek combinations: **hodograph, hodology, hodoneuromere.** Also, **odo-: odometer.**

1242 **hog-**   A word-initial combining element, also occurring as a word, derived from Old English *hog(g)* 'swine, esp. a gelded pig' (probably from Celtic (cf. Welsh *hwch* 'sow' and Cornish *hoch* 'pig, hog' which are cognate with English *sow*), though it has also been suggested that *hog* is to be derived, alternatively, from the root which gives English *hack*), used in its etymological and extended senses in combination with other English elements: **hog-backed, hognut, hogtie.**

1243 **hold-**   A word-initial combining element, also occurring as a word, derived from Old English *h(e)ald(an)* 'to guard, keep fast, secure,' used in its etymological and extended senses in combination with other English elements: **hold-down, holdout, holdup.**

1244 **hollow-**   A word-initial combining element, also occurring as a word, derived through Middle English from Old English *holh* 'hole, cave' (from an Indo-European root meaning 'cover, conceal'), used in the sense of 'empty' and in extensions of this sense in combination with other English elements: **hollow-eyed, hollow-forge, hollowware.** Related forms: **celli-, cello-, cellulo-, cilio-, coleo-, color-, hell-.**

1245 **holo-**   A word-initial combining element, derived from Greek *hólo(s)* 'entire, whole, complete,' used in its etymological and extended senses in Neo-Greek combinations: **holoantigen, holographic, holosaccharide.** Also, **hol-: holistic.** Related forms: **safe-, solid-.**

1246 **homalo-**   A word-initial combining element, derived from Greek *homaló(s)* 'even, level, smooth' (from *homós* 'same'), used in the sense of 'flat, plane' in Neo-Greek combinations: **homalocephalus, homalographic, homalosternal.** Also, **homolo-: homolographic.** Compare **homo-.**

1247 **home-**   A word-initial combining element, also occurring as a word, derived from Old English *hām* 'dwelling,' used in its etymological and extended senses in combination with other English elements: **homebody, homeland, homemade.**

1248 **homeo-**   A word-initial combining element, derived from Greek *hómoio(s)* 'resembling, like, sharing in common' (from *homós* 'same'), used to express 'similarity' or 'sameness' in Neo-Greek and Neo-Latin combinations: **homeokinesis, homeo-osteopathy, homeotransplant.** Also, **homoeo-, homoio-: homoeomorphism, homoiostasis.** Compare **homo-.**

1249   homo-   A word-initial combining element, derived from Greek *homó(s)* 'same; one and the same' (from an Indo-European root meaning 'one'), used in its etymological and extended senses, among these being 'with the addition of one (CH_2) group to the compound named by the combining root,' in Neo-Greek and Neo-Latin combinations: **homocentric, homocinchonine, homosexual.** Also, **hom-: homodont.** Compare **homalo-, homeo-.** Related forms: **haplo-, hecto-, hendeca-, hetero-, simple-, single-, some-.**

1250   homoeo-   A variant of **homeo-.**

1251   homoio-   A variant of **homeo-.**

1252   homolo-   A variant of **homalo-.**

1253   honey-   A word-initial combining element, also occurring as a word, derived from Old English *huni(ġ)* 'sweet sticky liquid produced by bees from the nectar of flowers,' used in its etymological and extended senses in combination with other English elements: **honeycomb, honeydew, honeymoon.**

1254   hoof-   A word-initial combining element, also occurring as a word, derived from Old English *hōf* 'horny casing of the ends of the digits of such animals as the horse,' used in its etymological sense in combination with other English elements: **hoof-and-mouth (disease), hoofbeat, hoofprint.**

1255   hook-   A word-initial combining element, also occurring as a word, derived from Old English *hōk* 'curved implement for catching or suspending something,' used in its etymological and extended senses in combination with other English elements: **hooknose, hookup, hookworm.**

1256   hop-[1]   A word-initial combining element, also occurring as a word, derived from Old English *hop(pian)* 'to leap, spring' (from an Indo-European root meaning 'bend'), used in its etymological sense in combination with other English elements: **hop-o'-my-thumb, hopscotch, hoptoad.** Related forms: **cubo-, cup-, hip-.**

1257   hop-[2]   A word-initial combining element, also occurring as a word, derived from Middle Low German *hop(pe)* 'the plant *Humulus lupulus,*' used in its etymological and extended senses in combination with other English elements: **hophead, hopsacking, hoptree.**

1258   hormono-   A word-initial combining element, derived from English *hormon(e)* 'substance which is secreted into the body fluids by the endocrine glands and which affects the activities of certain organs' (from Greek *hormôn*, the present participle of the verb *hormân* 'to urge, set in motion') plus the combining vowel -*o*-, used in its etymological sense in biomedical terminology: **hormonogenesis, hormonopexic, hormonoprivia.** Also, **hormo-, hormon-: hormoprotein, hormonagogue.**

1259 **horn-** A word-initial combining element, also occurring as a word, derived from Old English *horn* 'bony, often curved growth on the heads of certain ungulates,' used in its etymological and extended senses in combination with other English elements: **hornbill, hornmad, hornworm.** Related forms: **caroten-, cerebello-, cerebro-, cervi-², cervico-, corneo-, corner-, cornu-, cranio-, ginger-, hart's-, keratin-, kerato-.**

1260 **horo-** A word-initial combining element, derived from Greek *hôr(a)* 'period of time, season, time' plus the combining vowel -*o*-, used in its etymological and extended senses in Neo-Greek combinations: **horography, horology, horoscope.** Compare **hour-.** Related form: **year-.** [Note: the **horo-** of **horograph** and **horotelic** and the **hor-** of **horopter** are derived not from *hôra* 'time' but, rather, from Greek *hóros* 'boundary.']

1261 **horse-** A word-initial combining element, also occurring as a word, derived from Old English *hors* 'the quadruped *Equus caballus*,' used in its etymological and extended senses in combination with other English elements: **horse-and-buggy, horselaugh, horsepower.**

1262 **hot-** A word-initial combining element, also occurring as a word, derived through Middle English from Old English *hāt* 'having a high temperature,' used in its etymological and extended senses in combination with other English elements: **hotbed, hotbox, hotshot.** Compare **heat-.**

1263 **hour-** A word-initial combining element, also occurring as a word, derived through Old French from Latin *hōr(a)* 'season, time, one twelfth of the day between sunrise and sunset' (from Greek *hôra* 'period of time, season, time'), used in the sense of 'one twenty-fourth of the solar day' and in extensions of this sense in combination with other English elements: **hour-bell, hourglass, hour-hand.** Compare **horo-.**

1264 **house-** A word-initial combining element, also occurring as a word, derived from Old English *hūs* 'building in which people live,' used in its etymological and extended senses in combination with other English elements: **housebreaker, housebroken, housefly.**

1265 **humero-** A word-initial combining element, derived from late Latin *humer(us)* 'shoulder, upper arm' (from Latin *umerus* 'shoulder, upper arm') plus the combining vowel *-o-*, used in the sense of 'of or pertaining to the bone which extends from the shoulder to the elbow' in Neo-Latin combinations: **humeroradial, humeroscapular, humeroulnar.** Also, **humer-: humeral.** Related form: **omo-.**

1266 **hundred-** A word-initial combining element, also occurring as a word, derived from Old English *hund* '100' plus *-red* 'number, reckoning, count,' used in its etymological and extended senses in combination with other English elements: **hundred-eyes, hundred-percenter, hundredweight.** Related forms: **centi-, hecto-.**

1267 **hyalo-** A word-initial combining element, derived from Greek *hýalo(s)* 'glass,' used in its etymological and extended senses, chief among these being 'of or pertaining to the *vitreous humor* or surrounding membrane,' in Neo-Greek and Neo-Latin combinations: **hyalomucoid, hyalophobia, hyaloplasm.** Also, **hyal-: hyalin.**

1268 **hydr-¹** A variant of **hydro-¹.**

1269 **hydr-²** A variant of **hydro-².**

1270 **hydro-¹** A word-initial combining element, derived from Greek *hydro-*, a combining form of *hýdōr* 'water,' used in its etymological and extended senses, chief among these being '(containing a) fluid,' in Neo-Greek and Neo-Latin combinations: **hydroappendix, hydroelectric, hydrotherapy.** Also, **hydr-¹: hydragogue.** Compare **hydro-².** Related forms: **wash-, water-, wet-, winter-.**

1271 **hydro-²** A word-initial combining element, derived from English *hydro(gen)* 'the chemical element (H) (which is so named because it combines with oxygen to form water)' (from Greek *hýd(ō)r* 'water' plus the combining vowel *-o-* plus the noun-forming suffix *-gen* 'producing'), used in its etymological sense in chemical terminology: **hydrocarbon, hydrochloric, hydroquinone.** Also, **hydr-²: hydracid.** Compare **hydro-¹.**

1272 **hydroxy-** See **hydro-²** and **oxy-².**

1273 **hydropneumo-** See **hydro-¹** and **pneumo-¹.**

1274 **hyeto-** A word-initial combining element, derived from Greek *hyetó(s)* 'rain,' used in its etymological sense in Neo-Greek combinations: **hyetograph, hyetology, hyetometer.** Also, **hyet-: hyetal.** Related form: **soup-.**

1275 **hygro-**   A word-initial combining element, derived from Greek *hygró(s)* 'wet, moist, fluid,' used in its etymological sense in Neo-Greek combinations: **hygrograph, hygrometer, hygrothermograph.**

1276 **hylo-**   A word-initial combining element, derived from Greek *hýl(ē)* 'wood' and, by extension, 'matter' plus the combining vowel *-o-*, used in both the sense of 'wood' and 'matter' in Neo-Greek combinations: **hylomorphic, hylophagous, hylozoism.** Also, **hyl-, hyle-: hyloma, hylephobia.**

1277 **hymeno-**   A word-initial combining element, derived from Greek *hymḗn, hymén(os)* 'skin, membrane' plus the combining vowel *-o-*, used in its etymological and extended senses, chief among these being 'membranous fold that occludes the external opening of the vagina,' in Neo-Greek combinations: **hymenology, Hymenoptera, hymenotome.** Also, **hymen-: hymenectomy.**

1278 **hyo-**   A word-initial combining element, derived from Greek *(h)y(psilón)* 'the letter *v*' (literally, '(plain) *v*') plus the combining vowel *-o-*, used chiefly in the sense of 'of or pertaining to the *hyoid* bone (which is so named because its shape resembles that of the Greek letter *v*)' in biomedical terminology: **hyobranchial, hyoglossal, hyomandibular.** Also, **hy-: hyodont.** Compare **upsilon-.**

1279 **hyp-**   A variant of **hypo-**.

1280 **hyper-**   A word-initial combining element, derived from Greek *hypér* 'over, above, beyond' (from an Indo-European root meaning 'up (from under)'), used in its etymological and extended senses, chief among these being 'excessive(ly)' and 'highest (of a series of chemical compounds),' in Neo-Greek and Neo-Latin combinations: **hyperactive, hyperchloric (acid), hyperplasmia.** Related forms: **evil-(?), over-, hypo-, sub-, suc-, suf-, sup-, super-, supra-, sur-¹, sur-², sursum-, sus-, up-.**

1281 **hypno-**   A word-initial combining element, derived from Greek *hýpno(s)* 'sleep,' used in its etymological and extended senses in Neo-Greek combinations: **hypnogenetic, hypnonarcoanalysis, hypnotherapy.** Also, **hypn-: hypnagogue.** Related form: **somni-.**

1282 **hypo-**   A word-initial combining element, derived from Greek *hypó* 'under, from under, beneath' (from an Indo-European root meaning '(up from) under'), used in its etymological and extended senses, chief among these being 'deficient, diminished' and, in reference to the principal element in a chemical compound, 'combined in the lowest state of valence,' in Neo-Greek and Neo-

Latin combinations: **hypoactivity, hypochlorite, hypocondylar.** Also, **hyp-: hypalgesic.** Related forms: **evil-(?), hyper-, open-, over-, sub-, suc-, suf-, sup-, super-, supra-, sur-¹, sur-², sursum-, sus-, up-.**

1283 **hypoglyco-** See **hypo-** and **glyco-.**

1284 **hypso-** A word-initial combining element, derived from Greek *hýpso(s)* 'height' (cf. *hýpsi* 'high, aloft'), used in its etymological and extended senses in Neo-Greek combinations: **hypsography, hypsometer, hypsophyll.** Also, **hyps-, hypsi-: hypsosis, hypsicephalic.**

1285 **hystero-** A word-initial combining element, derived from Greek *hystér(a)* 'womb' plus the combining vowel *-o-,* used in the sense of 'of or pertaining to the *uterus*' and in the specialized sense of 'of or pertaining to *hysteria,* a psychoneurosis originally thought to result from a disturbance of the uterine functions' in biomedical terminology: **hysterocarcinoma, hysteroepilepsy, hysterovaginoenterocele.** Also, **hyster-, hysteri-: hysterectomy, hysteriform.** Related forms(?): **utero-, ventro-, vesico-, vesiculo-.**

I

1286 **i-** A word-initial combining element, derived from Latin *i-*, a combining form of *in* 'not, un-,' appearing in its etymological sense in borrowings from Latin in which the element to which it is joined begins with *gn:* **ignoble, ignominious, ignore.** Compare **il-¹, im-¹, in-¹, ir-¹.** Related forms: **a-¹, an-¹, neutro-, never-, no-, non-¹, nulli-, un-¹.**

1287 **iatro-** A word-initial combining element, derived from Greek *iatró(s)* 'physician' (from a verb meaning 'to heal, cure'), used in its etymological and extended senses, chief among these being 'of or pertaining to medicine or its practice,' in Neo-Greek combinations: **iatrochemistry, iatrogenic, iatrology.** Also **iatr-: iatrarchy.**

1288 **ice-** A word-initial combining element, also occurring as a word, derived from Old English *īs* 'water in its solid state,' used in its etymological and extended senses in combination with other English elements: **iceberg, icebox, icebreaker.**

1289 **ichno-** A word-initial combining element, derived from Greek *íchno(s)* 'track, trace,' used in its etymological and extended senses, chief among these being 'of or pertaining to fossil footprints,' in Neo-Greek combinations: **ichnographic, ichnolite, ichnology.** Also, **ichn-: ichnite.**

1290 **ichor-** A word-initial combining element, also occurring as a word, derived from Greek *ichōr* 'fluid (distinct from blood) which flows

187

through the veins of the gods' and, by extension, 'watery part of blood or milk,' used in the sense of 'thin, serous or sanious fluid, esp. from a wound or sore' in biomedical combinations: **ichoremia, ichoroid, ichorrhea.**

1291 ichthyo- A word-initial combining element, derived from Greek *ichthý(s)* 'fish' plus the combining vowel *-o-*, used in its etymological and extended senses in Neo-Greek and Neo-Latin combinations: **ichthyology, ichthyophobia, ichthyosulfonate.** Also, **ichth-, ichthy-: ichthin, ichthyosis.**

1292 icono- A word-initial combining element, derived from Greek *(e)ikón* 'likeness' plus the combining vowel *-o-*, used in the sense of 'of or pertaining to a likness or image, esp. a holy one' in Neo-Greek combinations: **iconoclast, iconography, iconostasis.**

1293 icosa- A word-initial combining element, derived from Greek *(e)íkos(i)* 'twenty' plus the combining vowel *-a-*, used in its etymological sense in Neo-Greek combinations: **icosacolic, icosahedron, icosasemic.** Also, **icos-, icosi-: icosandrous, icosidodecahedron.**

1294 ictero- A word-initial combining element, derived from Greek *íktero(s)* 'jaundice,' used in its etymological sense in biomedical terminology: **icteroanemia, icterohemoglobinuria, icteromaturia.** Also, **icter-: icterepatitis.**

1295 ideo- A word-initial combining element, derived from Greek *idé(a)* 'form, appearance; class, species, model; general principle, idea' (from the verb *ideîn* 'to see' and, in the medio-passive, 'to appear') plus the combining vowel *-o-*, used in the sense of 'of, pertaining to, or resulting from mental activity, thinking, ideation' in Neo-Greek and Neo-Latin combinations: **ideoglandular, ideomotor, ideophrenia.** Compare **eido-.** Related forms: **guide-, story-, video-, visuo-.**

1296 idio- A word-initial combining element, derived from Greek *idio(s)* 'one's own,' used in its etymological and extended senses, chief among these being 'of or pertaining to the self; distinct, separate, alone,' in Neo-Greek and Neo-Latin combinations: **idio-agglutinin, idiohypnotism, idiomuscular.**

1297 igni- A word-initial combining element, derived from Latin *igni(s)* 'fire,' used in its etymological and extended senses, chief among these being 'of or pertaining to hot cautery,' in Neo-Latin combinations: **igniextirpation, ignigenous, ignipuncture.** Also, **ignis-: ignisation.**

1298   il-¹   A word-initial combining element, derived from Latin *il-*, a combining form of *in-* 'not, un-,' appearing in its etymological sense in borrowings from Latin in which the element to which it is joined begins with *l:* **illegal, illegible, illiterate.** Compare **i-, im-¹, in-¹, ir-¹.** Related forms: **a-¹, an-¹, neutro-, never-, no-, non-¹, nulli-, un-¹.**

1299   il-²   A word-initial combining element, derived from Latin *il-*, a combining form of *in* 'in, into,' appearing in its etymological and extended senses in borrowings from Latin in which the element to which it is joined begins with *l:* **illation, illuminate, illustrate.** Compare **im-², in-², ir-².** Related forms: **eis-, em-¹, en-¹, endo-, entero-, ento-, eso-, in-³.**

1300   ileo-   A word-initial combining element, derived from Late Latin *īle(um)* 'distal portion of the small intestine which extends from the cecum to the jejunum' (from Latin *īlium* 'lower abdomen; flank, groin') plus the combining vowel *-o-*, used in its Late Latin sense in biomedical terminology: **ileocecal, ileocolonic, ileosigmoid.** Also, **ile-: ileitis.** Compare **ilio-.**

1301   ilio-   A word-initial combining element, derived from Latin *īli(um)* 'lower abdomen; groin; flank' plus the combining vowel *-o-*, used in the sense of 'of or pertaining to the flank or haunch bone' in biomedical terminology: **iliofemoral, iliometer, iliosacral.** Also, **ili-: iliac.** Compare **ileo-.**

1302   ill-   A word-initial combining element, also occurring as a word, derived from Old Norse *īll(r)* 'evil, bad,' used in its etymological and extended senses in combination with other English elements: **ill-advised, ill-natured, ill-suited.**

1303   im-¹   A word-initial combining element, derived from Latin *im-*, a combining form of *in-* 'not, un-,' appearing in its etymological sense in borrowings from Latin in which the element to which it is joined begins with *b, m,* or *p:* **imbalance, immeasurable, impartial.** Compare **i-, il-¹, in-¹, ir-¹.** Related forms: **a-¹, an-¹, neutro-, never-, no-, non-¹, nulli-, un-¹.**

1304   im-²   A word-initial combining element, derived from Latin *im-*, a combining form of *in* 'in, into,' appearing in its etymological and extended senses in borrowings from Latin in which the element to which it is joined begins with *b, m,* or *p:* **imbibe, immanent,**

imposition. Compare em-², il-², in-², ir-². Related forms: eis-, em-¹, en-¹, endo-, entero-, ento-, eso-, in-³.

1305 **im-³** A variant of **em-²**

1306 **imido-** A word-initial combining element, an alteration of **amido-**, used in the sense of 'containing the bivalent group (=NH) (attached to an acid radical)' in chemical terminology: **imidogen, imidothiobiazoline, imidozanthin.** Also, **imid-: imidazoledione.** Compare **amido-**.

1307 **imino-** A word-initial combining element, an alteration of **amino-**, used in the sense of 'containing the bivalent group (=NH) (attached to a nonacid group)' in chemical terminology: **iminoacetonitrile, iminioethanol, iminourea.** Compare **amino-**.

1308 **immuno-** A word-initial combining element, derived from Latin *immūn(is)* 'unbound, free from, pure' plus the combining vowel -*o*-, used in the sense of 'of or pertaining to protection against or freedom from disease' in biomedical combinations: **immunochemsitry, immunology, immunoreaction.** Also, **immun-, immuni-: immunprotein, immunifacient.**

1309 **impari-** A word-initial combining element, derived from Latin *impār* 'unequal; uneven, odd (of numbers)' plus the combining vowel -*i*-, used in its etymological sense of 'odd-numbered' in Neo-Latin and Neo-Greek combinations: **imparidigitate, imparipennate, imparisyllabic.**

1310 **imper-** See **im-¹** and **per-**.

1311 **in-¹** A word-initial combining element, derived from Latin *in-* 'not-, un-,' used in its etymological sense in borrowings from Latin and in Neo-Latin combinations in which the element to which it is joined begins with a vowel or with a consonant other than *b, gn, l, m, p,* or *r:* **inappropriate, indirect, insist.** Compare **i-, il-¹, im-¹, ir-¹.** Related forms: **a-¹, an-¹, neutro-, never-, no-, non-¹, nulli-, un-¹.**

1312 **in-²** A word-initial combining element, derived from Latin *in* 'in, into, within,' appearing in its etymological and extended senses in borrowings from Latin and in Neo-Latin combinations in which the element to which it is joined begins with a vowel or with a consonant other than *b, l, m, p,* or *r:* **incapsulate, inductor, infection.** Compare: **en-², il-², im-², inter-, intero-, intra-, intro-, ir-².** Related forms: **eis-, em-¹, en-¹, endo-, entero-, ento-, eso-, in-³.**

1313   **in-³**   A word-initial combining element, derived from Old English *in* 'in, into,' used in its etymological and extended senses in combination with other English elements: **inbreeding, income, inmate.** Related forms: **eis-, em-¹, em-², en-¹, en-², endo-, entero-, ento-, entre-, eso-, il-², im-², in-², inter-, intero-, intra-, intro-, ir-².**

1314   **in-⁴**   A variant of **ino-.**

1315   **inac-**   See **in-¹** and **ac-.**

1316   **inad-**   See **in-¹** and **ad-.**

1317   **inch-**   A word-initial combining element, also occurring as a word, derived from Latin *unc(ia)* 'one twelfth' (from *ūnus* 'one'), used in the sense of 'one twelfth of a foot' and in extensions of this sense in combination with other English elements: **inchmeal, inch-pound, inchworm.** Compare **uni-.**

1318   **inciso-**   A word-initial combining element, derived from English *incis(al)* 'cutting' (from Latin *incīs(sus),* the past participle of the verb *incīdere* 'to cut into' (from *in* 'in, into' plus *caedere* 'to cut, hew'), plus the adjective-forming suffix *-al*) plus the combining vowel *-o-,* used in the sense of 'of or pertaining to the *incisal* wall of a tooth cavity' in Neo-Latin combinations: **incisolabial, incisolingual, incisoproximal.**

1319   **incom-**   See **in-¹** and **com-.**

1320   **incon-**   See **in-¹** and **con-.**

1321   **increto-**   A word-initial combining element, derived from English *incret(ion)* 'internal secretion' (from **in-²** plus *(se)cretion* (from Latin *sēcrētiō, sēcrētiōn(is)* 'a setting-aside, separation,' hence, 'the separation or elaboration of a substance through glandular activity')) plus the combining vowel *-o-,* used in the sense of 'of or pertaining to internal secretion, esp. by the endocrine glands' in biomedical terminology: **incretodiagnosis, incretogenous, incretotherapy.**

1322   **ind-**   A variant of **indo-.**

1323   **inde-**   See **in-¹** and **de-¹.**

1324   **indic-**   A variant of **indigo-.**

1325   **indican-**   A word-initial combining element, also occurring as a word, derived from **indic-,** a variant of **indigo-,** plus the adjective-forming suffix *-an*, used in the sense of 'of, pertaining to, or containing the indoxyl glycoside $(C_6H_4 \cdot NH \cdot CH:C \cdot O \cdot C_6H_{11}O_5)$ (which is derived from plants which yield *indigo*) or the indoxyl sulfate $(C_6H_4 \cdot NH \cdot CH \cdot CO \cdot SO_2 \cdot OK)$ (which is formed by the decomposition of tryptophan in the intestines)' in biochemical terminology: **indicanemia, indicanmeter, indicanuria.** Also, **indicano: indicanorachia.** Compare **indigo-.**

1326 **indigo-** A word-initial combining element, also occurring as a word, derived through Latin and Spanish from Greek (*phármakon*) *Indikó(n)* 'Indian (remedy, spice),' specifically, 'dark blue dye derived from plants of the genus *Indigofera* (which are native to India),' used in the sense of 'dark blue dye (derived from plants of the genus *Indigofera*); dark blue color; plant from which the dark blue dye called *indigo* is derived' and in extensions of this sense in a variety of combinations: **indigogen, indigolite, indigo-weed.** Also, **indic-, indico-, indig-: indican, indicophose, indiguria.** Compare **indican-, Indo-, indo-.**

1327 **indis-** See **in-¹** and **dis-².**

1328 **Indo-** A word-initial combining element, derived from Greek *Indó(s)* 'Indian' (from *Indós* 'the Indus River' (from Old Persian *Hindu,* equivalent to Sanskrit *sindhu* 'river, esp. the Indus River')), used in the sense of 'adjacent or pertaining to India' in combination with other English elements: **Indo-Chinese, Indo-European, Indonesian.** Compare **indigo-, indo-.**

1329 **indo-** A word-initial combining element, derived from English *ind(igo)* 'dark blue dye $(C_{16}H_{10}O_2N_2)$ which is derived from plants of the genus *Indigotera*' (ultimately from Greek (*phármakon*) *Indikón* 'Indian (remedy, spice),' specifically, 'dye from (Indian) plants of the genus *Indigofera*', used in the sense of 'of, pertaining to, containing, or derived from *indigo* $(C_{16}H_{10}O_2N_2)$)' in chemical terminology: **indoaniline, indodiazole, indophenol.** Also, **ind-: indoxyl.** Compare **indigo-, Indo-.**

1330 **inducte-** A word-initial combining element, derived from English *induct(ion)* 'appearance in a body of an electric current or of magnetic properties as the result of the proximity of another electric current or magnetic field' (from Latin *inductiō, inductiōn(is)* 'a bringing in' (from the verb *indūcere* 'to lead in(to), bring in(to)')), used in its etymological and extended senses in Neo-Latin and Neo-Greek combinations: **inductogram, inductopyrexia, inductotherm.**

1331   **inequi-**   See **in-**[1] and **equi-**.

1332   **inex-**   See **in-**[1] and **ex-**[1].

1333   **infero-**   A word-initial combining element, derived from Latin *infer(us)* 'below, underneath, lower' plus the combining vowel *-o-*, used in its etymological sense in Neo–Latin and Neo-Greek combinations: **inferobranchiate, inferolateral, inferomedian.** Compare **infra-**. Related form: **under-**.

1334   **infra-**   A word-initial combining element, derived from Latin *infrā* 'underneath, below' (from *(parte) inf(e)rā* 'on the lower (part, side)'), used in its etymological and extended senses in Neo-Latin and Neo-Greek combinations: **infradiaphragmatic, infrapatellar, infraversion.** Compare **infero-**.

1335   **infundibul-**   A word-initial combining element, derived from Latin *infundibul(um)* 'funnel,' literally, 'the (little) thing into which something is poured' (cf. *infundere* 'to pour into, pour out'), used chiefly in the sense of 'of or pertaining to a funnel-shaped organ of the body' in biomedical terminology: **infundibular, infundibulin, infundibuloma.** Also, **infundibuli-, infundibulo-: infundibuliform, infundibulopelvic.**

1336   **inguino-**   A word-initial combining element, derived from Latin *inguen, inguin(is)* 'groin' plus the combining vowel *-o-*, used in its etymological sense in biomedical terminology: **inguinoabdominal, inguinodynia, inguinoscrotal.**

1337   **ini-**   A word-initial combining element, derived from Greek *ini(on)* 'muscles between the occiput and the back' and, by extension, 'the back of the head, nape of the neck' (from *i(s), in(ós)* 'muscle' plus the noun-forming suffix *-ion*), used in the sense of 'of or pertaining to the occiput or to the occipital protuberance of the skull' and in extensions of this sense in Neo-Greek combinations: **iniac, iniencephaly, iniops.** Also, **inio-: iniodymus.** Compare **ino-**.

1338   **ink-**   A word-initial combining element, also occurring as a word, derived through Old French and Late Latin from Greek *énk(auston)* 'that which is burned in; colored wax which is painted onto a surface and fixed by the application of heat; (purple-red) fluid used in writing' (from the verb *enkaiein* 'to burn in; to paint with colored wax to be fixed by the application of heat'), used in the sense of 'fluid used in writing (with a pen) and printing (with a press or the like)' and in extensions of this sense in combination with other English elements: **inkberry, inkblot, inkwell.** Related form: **cauter-.**

1339   ino-   A word-initial combining element, derived from Greek *í(s),* *in(ós)* 'force, strength,' hence, 'seat of strength; muscle, sinew,' hence, 'fibrous vessel in a muscle,' hence, 'fiber' plus the combining vowel *-o-,* used chiefly in the sense of 'fiber, fibrous (growth)' and in extensions of this sense in Neo-Greek combinations: **inoblast, inocystoma, inolith.** Also, **in-⁴, inos-: inaxon, inositis.**

1340   insecti-   A word-initial combining element, derived from Latin *insect(um)* 'small invertebrate,' literally, 'that which is cut up, segmented (as the bodies of the first invertebrates to which the term was applied appeared to be)' (from the past participle of the verb *insecāre* 'to cut into, cut up') plus the combining vowel *-i-,* used in its etymological sense in Neo-Latin and Neo-Greek combinations: **insecticide, insectifuge, insectivorous.** Also, **insecto-: insectology.** Compare **entomo-.**

1341   insulin-   A word-initial combining element, also occurring as a word, derived from Latin *insul(a)* 'island' (here used in reference to the 'islands (islets) of Langerhans, irregular structures in the pancreas which produce the protein hormone *insulin* which is secreted into the blood where it regulates sugar metabolism') plus the suffix *-in* (which is used in naming chemical compounds), used in its etymological and extended senses in biochemical terminology: **insulinase, insulinemia, insulinlipodystrophy.** Also, **insul-, insulo-, insulino-: insulism, insulopathic, insulinogenesis.**

1342   inter-   A word-initial combining element, derived from Latin *inter* 'between' (from *in* 'in, within' plus the adverbial suffix *-ter*), used in its etymological and extended senses in a variety of combinations: **interchange, intercostal, interkinesis.** Compare **in-², intero-, intra-, intro-.**

1343   intero-   A word-initial combining element, derived from Neo-Latin *inter(us)* 'on the inside, internal' (by analogy to *exter, exterus* 'on the outside, external') plus the combining vowel *-o-,* used in its etymological and extended senses in Neo-Latin combinations: **interoceptor, interofection, interoinferiorly.** Compare **in-, inter-, intra-, intro-.**

1344   intra-   A word-initial combining element, derived from Latin *intrā* 'on the inside, within' (from **(parte) int(e)rā* 'on, at the inner (part)'), used in its etymological and extended senses in a variety of combinations: **intracavitary, intragalvanization, intraneural.** Compare **in-², inter-, intero-, intro-.**

1345   **intro-**   A word-initial combining element, derived from Latin *intrō* 'to, on the inside; within' (from **int(e)rō,* the masculine and neuter ablative singular form of unattested *interus, interum* 'inner'), used in its etymological and extended senses in a variety of combinations: **introflexion, introgastric, introvert.** Compare **in-², inter-, intero-, intra-.**

1346   **inul-**   A word-initial combining element, derived from Neo-Latin *Inul(a)* 'genus of composite-flowered plant' (perhaps from Greek *helénion* 'the composite-flowered plant *elecampane*'), used in the sense of 'of, pertaining to, derived from, or resembling *inulin,* the vegetable starch ($(C_6H_{10}O_5)_n$) which occurs in the rhizome of the *Inula helenium* and other composite-flowered plants' in chemical terminology: **inulase, inuloid, inulol.**

1347   **io-¹**   A variant of **ion-¹.**

1348   **io-²**   A variant of **iodo-.**

1349   **iodo-**   A word-initial combining element, derived from English *iod(ine)* 'the nonmetallic element (I)' (from Greek *iŏd(ēs)* 'violet-like' (from *io(n)* '(a) violet' plus the suffix *-oeidēs* '-like')—because the vapor of iodine is purple—plus the noun-forming suffix *-ine* (which is used in naming basic chemical substances)) plus the combining vowel *-o-,* used in the sense of 'of, pertaining to, derived from, or containing *iodine*' in biochemical terminology: **iodoform, iodohydrargyrate, iodotherapy.** Also, **io-², iod-: iocamfen, iodemia.** Compare **ion-¹.**

1350   **ion-¹**   A word-initial combining element, derived from Greek *ion* '(a) violet,' used in its etymological and extended senses in Neo-Greek and Neo-Latin combinations: *Ionidium,* **ionones,** *Ionornis.* Also, **io-¹, iono-¹: iolite, ionotherapy.** Compare **iodo-.**

1351   **ion-²**   A variant of **iono-².**

1352   **iono-¹**   A variant of **ion-¹.**

1353   **iono-²**   A word-initial combining element, derived from Greek *iōn, ión(tos),* the present participle of the verb *iénai* 'to go,' plus the combining vowel *-o-,* used in the specialized sense of 'of or pertaining to electrically charged particles which move through a solution or gas when an electrical force is applied to them' and in extensions of this sense in scientific terminology: **ionocolorimeter, ionophoresis, ionosphere.** Also, **ion-², ionto-: ionize, ionto-quantimeter.**

1354 **iota-** (I, ɩ) A word-initial combining element, the ninth letter of the Greek alphabet, used chiefly to designate 'the ninth carbon atom in straight chain compound or a derivative thereof in which the substitute group is attached to that atom' in chemical terminology. See **alpha-.**

1355 **ir-¹** A word-initial combining element, derived from Latin *ir-*, a combining form of *in-* 'not, un-,' appearing in its etymological sense in inherited combinations in which the element to which it is joined begins with *r:* **irrational, irreverent, irreconcilable.** Compare **i-, il-¹, im-¹, in-¹.** Related forms: **a-¹, an-¹, neutro-, never-, no-, non-¹, nulli-, un-¹.**

1356 **ir-²** A word-initial combining element, derived from Latin *ir-*, a combining form of *in* 'in, into,' appearing in its etymological and extended senses in inherited combinations in which the element to which it is joined begins with *r:* **irradiate, irradicate, irrigate.** Compare **il-², im-², in-².** Related forms: **eis-, em-¹, en-¹, endo-, entero-, ento-, eso-, in-³.**

1357 **ir-³** A variant of **irido-.**

1358 **irido-** A word-initial combining element, derived from Greek *îri(s), irid(os)* 'rainbow; any brightly colored circle around something, esp. the *iris* of the eye' plus the combining vowel *-o-*, used in its etymological and extended senses in Neo-Greek and Neo-Latin combinations: **iridochoroiditis, iridocyte, iridopupillary.** Also, **ir-³, iri-, irid-, iris-: iritis, iridesis, iridectomy, irisopsia.** Related form: **wire-.**

1359 **iron-** A word-initial combining element, also occurring as a word, derived from Old English *īren* 'the metallic element (Fe),' used in its etymological and extended senses in combination with other English elements: **ironclad, ironfisted, ironmaster.**

1360 **irre-** See **ir-¹** and **re-.**

1361 **is-** A variant of **iso-.**

1362 **isch-** A variant of **ischo-.**

1363 **ischi-** A variant of **ischio-.**

1364   **ischio-**   A word-initial combining element, derived from Greek *ischio(n)* 'hip-joint, hip,' used in the sense of 'of or pertaining to the hip, hip-bone, or *ischium,* the lower dorsal portion of the innominate bone' in biomedical terminology: **ischioanal, ischiodidymus, ischiopubiotomy.** Also, **ischi-: ischialgia.**

1365   **ischo-**   A word-initial combining element, derived from Greek *ísch(ein)* 'to check, stop, suppress' plus the combining vowel *-o-,* used in the sense of 'suppression' of that which is named by the element to which it is joined and in extensions of this sense in Neo-Greek combinations: **ischocholia, ischochymia, ischomenia.** Also, **isch-: ischemia.**

1366   **iso-**   A word-initial combining element, derived from Greek *íso(s)* 'equal (to), same (as),' used in its etymological and extended senses, chief among these being 'of the same species; of the same molecular formula,' in a variety of combinations: **isobody, isocomplement, isogenesis.** Also, **is-: isopters.**

1367   **isthmo-**   A word-initial combining element, derived from Greek *isthmó(s)* 'narrow passage or ridge,' used in the sense of 'narrow passage or strip (esp. of bodily tissue) connecting two larger entities' in Neo-Greek combinations: **isthmocholosis, isthmoparalysis, isthmospasm.** Also, **isthm-: isthmectomy.**

1368   **Italo-**   A word-initial combining element, derived from English *Ital(ian)* 'of or pertaining to Italy' (from Latin *Ītalia* 'the Italian people; the people inhabiting the Italic Peninsula' (from *Ītal(us)* 'Italian,' a term of ultimately obscure origin, plus the noun-forming suffix *-ia*) plus the adjective-forming suffix *-(a)n*), plus the combining vowel *-o-,* used in its etymological sense in a variety of combinations: **Italo-American, Italo-Byzantine, Italophile.**

1369   **ithy-**   A word-initial combining element, derived from Greek *ithý(s)* 'straight,' used in its etymological and extended senses in Neo-Greek combinations: **ithylordosis, ithykyphosis, ithyphallic.**

1370   **ivory-**   A word-initial combining element, also occurring as a word, derived through Old French from Latin *eboreus* 'made of *ivory,* the hard white substance which forms the main part of elephants' tusks' (probably ultimately of Near Eastern origin (cf. Egyptian *abu* and Coptic *ebu* 'elephant, ivory')), used in its etymological and extended senses in combination with other English elements: **ivory-billed (woodpecker), ivory-towerism, ivorytype.** Related form(?): **elephant-.**

J

1371 **jack-** A word-initial combining element, also occurring as a word, derived from the English name *Jack* (from *Joh*(*n*) or *Ja*(*n*) plus the diminutive suffix -*k*(*in*), perhaps also influenced by French *Jacques* 'James'), used in the sense of 'male' and in a variety of vague extensions of this sense in combination with other English elements: **jack-in-the-box, jackknife, jackstraw.** Also (chiefly British), **Jack-: Jack-a-lantern.** Related form: **Johnny.**

1372 **jail-** A word-initial combining element, also occurring as a word, derived through Old French from unattested Late Latin **gaviola,* a variant of **caveola,* a combination of Latin *cave*(*a*) 'enclosure, cage' (from an Indo-European root meaning 'hollow') plus the diminutive suffix -*ola,* used in the sense of 'of or pertaining to a prison' in combination with other English elements: **jailbait, jailbird, jailhouse.** Compare **cav-, cavern-.** Related forms: **celio-, celo-**[1].

1373 **jaw-** A word-initial combining element, derived from late Middle English *iaw*(*e*) 'bony framework forming the mouth and holding the teeth in vertebrates,' used in its etymological and extended senses in combination with other English elements: **jawbone, jawbreaker, jawfish.**

1374 **jejuno-** A word-initial combining element, derived from late Latin (*intestīnum*) *jējūn*(*um*) 'the fasting (intestine), the portion of the small intestine between the duodenum and the ileum' (so named because early anatomists typically found this organ to be empty in dissection) plus the combining vowel -o-, used in its etymological sense in biomedical terminology: **jejunocecostomy, jejunoileitis, jejunostomy.** Also, **jejun-: jejunectomy.**

1375   **jet-¹**   A word-initial combining element, also occurring as a word, derived through Old French from Latin *ja(c)t(āre)* 'to throw,' used in the extended sense of 'of or pertaining to the rapid expulsion of matter under pressure or to a vehicle whose engine develops thrust through such expulsion' in combination with other English elements: **jetliner, jetport, jet-propelled.**

1376   **jet-²**   A word-initial combining element, also occurring as a word, derived, ultimately, from Greek *gagát(ēs)* 'dark black gemstone,' literally, '(stone) from the Lycian town of *Gágai,*' used in its etymological and extended senses in combination with other English elements: **jet-black, jet-enameled (ware), jet-glass.**

1377   **Johnny-**   A word-initial combining element, also occurring as a common English pet name, from English *John* (ultimately from Hebrew *Yōhānān* 'the Lord is gracious' plus the diminutive suffix -*y,* used in the sense of '(a) male' and in a variety of vague extensions of this sense in combination with other English elements: **Johnny-come-lately, Johnny-jump-up, Johnny-on-the-spot.** Related form: **jack-.**

1378   **jump-**   A word-initial combining element, also occurring as a word of obscure origin, used in the sense of 'leap, spring' and in extensions of this sense in combination with other English elements: **jumpmaster, jump-off, jump-start.**

1379   **juris-**   A word-initial combining element, derived from Latin *jūris,* the genitive singular form of the noun *jūs* 'law,' used in its etymological sense in a few inherited combinations: **jurisconsult, jurisdiction, jurisprudence.**

1380   **juxta-**   A word-initial combining element, derived from Latin *juxtā* 'near, hard by' (from the Latin root *jug-* 'yoke, union'), used in its etymological and extended senses in a variety of combinations: **juxta-articular, juxta-epiphysial, juxtapose.** Also, **juxt-: juxtangina.** Related form: **zygo-¹.**

K

1381 **kaino-** A variant of **ceno-**[1].

1382 **kak-** A variant of **caco-**.

1383 **kali-** A word-initial combining element, derived, ultimately, from Arabic (*al-*)*qalīy* 'saltwort ash, potash' (from the verb *qalay* 'to fry'), used in the sense of 'of or pertaining to an *alkali*, esp. to the alkali metal *kalium* (an alternate name for *potassium*)' in chemical terminology: **kaliemia, kaligenous, kalimeter**. Also, **kalin-, kalio-**: **kalinite, kaliophilite**. Compare **alkali-**.

1384 **kappa-** (K, κ) A word-initial combining element, the tenth letter of the Greek alphabet, used chiefly to designate 'the tenth carbon atom in a straight chain compound or a derivative thereof in which the substitute group is attached to that atom' in chemical terminology. See **alpha-**.

1385 **karyo-** A word-initial combining element, derived from Greek *káryo*(*n*) 'nut, walnut' (from an Indo-European root meaning 'hard'), used chiefly in the extended sense of 'of or pertaining to a nucleus' in Neo-Greek combinations: **karyocyte, karyology, karyoplasm**. Also, **cary-, caryo-, kary-**: **caryopsis, caryocinesis, karyenchyma**. Related forms: **cancer-, carcino-, chancr-, hard-**.

1386 **kata-** A variant of **cata-**.

1387 **kato-** A word-initial combining element, derived from Greek *kátō* 'down, downwards, below, underneath,' the adverb corresponding to the preposition *katá* 'down, under,' used in its etymological and extended senses in Neo-Greek combinations: **katolysis, katophoria, katotropia.** Also, **cato-: catophoria.** Compare **cata-.**

1388 **kel-** A variant of **celo-²**.

1389 **keno-** A variant of **ceno-³**.

1390 **kentro-** A variant of **centro-.**

1391 **kephal-** A (chiefly British) variant of **cephalo-.**

1392 **keratin-** A word-initial combining element, also occurring as a word, derived from Greek *kéra(s), kérat(os)* 'horn' plus the suffix *-in* (which is used in naming proteins), used in the sense of 'of, pertaining to, containing, or derived from *keratin,* a highly insoluble scleroprotein which is the main constituent of horny tissues, the nails, and the organic matrix of tooth enamel' and in extensions of this sense in biochemical terminology: **keratinase, keratinoid, keratinose.** Compare **kerato-.**

1393 **kerato-** A word-initial combining element, derived from Greek *kéra(s), kérat(os)* 'horn' plus the combining element *-o-,* used in its etymological and extended senses, chief among these being 'of or pertaining to horny tissue, esp. the *cornea,* or to the scleroprotein *keratin,*' in Neo-Greek and Neo-Latin combinations: **keratoacanthoma, keratoconjunctivitis, keratodermia.** Also, **cerat-, cerato-, ker-, kera-, kerat-: ceratectomy, ceratohyoid, keroid, keraphyllocele, keratitis.** Compare **keratin-.** Related forms: **caroten-, cerebello-, cerebro-, cervi-², cervico-, corneo-, corner-, cornu-, cranio-, ginger-, hart's-, horn-.**

1394 **keri-** A variant of **cero-.**

1395 **kero-** A variant of **cero-.**

1396 **keto-** A word-initial combining element, derived from English *keto(ne)* 'chemical compound containing the carbonyl group (CO)' (from German *Keton* 'ketone' (from *(A)keton* 'acetone, the lowest of the ketone series')), used in its etymological sense in biochemical terminology: **ketogenesis, ketohexose, ketosteroid.** Also, **ket-: ketosis.** Compare **aceto-.**

1397 **kettle-** A word-initial combining element, also occurring as a word, derived through Old Norse from Latin *catill(us)* 'small dish or bowl,' used in the sense of 'bowl-shaped' in combination with other English elements: **kettle-bottom, kettledrum, kettle-hole.**

1398 **key-**   A word-initial combining element, also occurring as a word, derived from Old English used in its etymological and extended senses in combination with other English elements: **keyboard, keyhole, keynote.**

1399 **kick-**   A word-initial combining element, also occurring as a word, derived from Middle English *kik(en)* 'strike with the foot,' used in its etymological and extended senses in combination with other English elements: **kickback, kickoff, kickstand.**

1400 **kilo-**   A word-initial combining element, derived through French from Greek *chil(ioi)* 'thousand' plus the combining vowel *-o-*, used in its etymological sense in a variety of combinations: **kilocalorie, kilogram, kilovolt.** Compare **chili-.**

1401 **kine-¹**   A variant of **kino-.**

1402 **kine-²**   A variant of **cine-².**

1403 **kinesi-**   A word-initial combining element, derived from Greek *kinēs(is)* 'movement' (from the verb *kineîn* 'to move, set in motion') plus the combining vowel *-i-*, used in its etymological and extended senses, chief among these being 'of or pertaining to muscular activity,' in Neo-Greek combinations: **kinesiesthesiometer, kinesiodic, kinesitherapy.** Also, **cines-, kines-, kinesio-: cinesalgia, kinesiatrics, kinesiology.** Compare **cine-², kineto-, kino-.** Related form: **excito-.**

1404 **kineto-**   A word-initial combining element, derived from Greek *kinēt(ós)* 'moved, movable' (from the verb *kineîn* 'to move, set in motion') plus the combining vowel *-o-*, used in its etymological and extended senses, chief among these being 'of, pertaining to, characterized by, or resulting from motion,' in Neo-Greek combinations: **kinetocyte, kinetogenic, kinetoscope.** Also, **kinet-: kinetic.** Compare **cine-², kinesi-, kino-.** Related form: **excito-.**

1405 **king-**   A word-initial combining element, also occurring as a word, derived from Old English *cy(ni)ng* 'male monarch' (ultimately from an Indo-European root meaning 'beget, be born'), used in its etymological and extended senses in combination with other English elements: **king-cup, king-of-arms, kingpin.** Related forms: **genito-, geno-, gentle-, gonado-, gone-¹, gono-, nevo-.**

1406 kino- A word-initial combining element, derived from Greek *kin(eîn)* 'to move, set in motion' plus the combining vowel *-o-*, used in the sense of 'of or pertaining to movement' and in extensions of this sense in Neo-Greek and Neo-Latin combinations: **kinocilia, kinohapt, kinotoxin.** Also, **cin-, cine-¹, cino-, kin-, kine-¹: cinaesthesia, cineplasty, cinology, kinemia, kineplasty.** Compare **cine-², kinesi-, kineto-.** Related form: **excito-.**

1407 kio- A variant of **ciono-.**

1408 kiono- A variant of **ciono-.**

1409 klepto- A word-initial combining element, derived from Greek *klépt(ein)* 'to steal' plus the combining vowel *-o-*, used in the sense of 'of or pertaining to theft' and in extensions of this sense in Neo-Greek combinations: **kleptohemodeipnonism, kleptolagnia, kleptophobia.** Also, **clepto-: cleptomania.**

1410 knee- A word-initial combining element, also occurring as a word, derived from Old English *cnēo(w)* 'joint connecting the femur and tibia,' used in its etymological and extended senses in combination with other English elements: **kneecap, knee-deep, knee-jerk.** Related forms: **genu-, geny-.**

1411 knock- A word-initial combining element, also occurring as a word, derived from Old English *cnoc(ian)* 'to strike a blow' (from an Indo-European root meaning 'to form into a ball'), used in its etymological and extended senses in combination with other English elements: **knockabout, knock-knee, knockout.** Related forms: **knot-, knuckle-.**

1412 knot- A word-initial combining element, also occurring as a word, derived from Old English *cnot(ta)* 'lump; intertwining of a cord or cords (or the like) to form a tie' (from an Indo-European root meaning 'to form into a ball'), used in its etymological and extended senses in combination with other English elements: **knotgrass, knothead, knothole.** Related forms: **knock-, knuckle-.**

1413 know- A word-initial combining element, also occurring as a word, derived from Old English *(ġe)cnāw(an)* 'to recognize, perceive, be aware of,' used in its etymological and extended senses in combination with other English elements: **know-how, know-it-all, know-nothing.** Related forms: **n-, nor-¹, normo-, note-(?).**

1414 knuckle- A word-initial combining element, also occurring as a word, derived through Middle English from Middle Low German *knökel* 'bone joint' (from an Indo-European root meaning 'to form into a ball'), used in the sense of 'phalangeal joint' and in extensions of this sense in combination with other English elements: **knucklebone, knuckle-duster, knucklehead.** Related forms: **knock-, knot-.**

1415 **koilo-** A variant of **celo-**[1].

1416 **koino-** A variant of **ceno-**[2].

1417 **koly-** A word-initial combining element, derived from Greek *kōlý(ein)* 'to cut short, stop, hinder,' used in the sense of 'inhibiting' that which is named by the element to which it is joined in Neo-Greek combinations: **kolypeptic, kolyphrenia, kolyseptic.** Also, **coly-: colypeptic.**

1418 **koni-** A variant of **conio-**.

1419 **konio-** A variant of **conio-**.

1420 **kono-** A variant of **conio-**.

1421 **kopro-** A variant of **copro-**.

1422 **koro-** A variant of **core-**[2].

1423 **kreo-** A variant of **creo-**.

1424 **krymo-** A variant of **crymo-**.

1425 **kryo-** A variant of **cryo-**.

1426 **krypto-** A variant of **crypto-**.

1427 **ksi-** (Ξ, ξ) A variant of **xi-**.

1428 **kyano-** A variant of **cyano-**[1].

1429 **kymo-** A word-initial combining element, derived from Greek *kŷm(a), kŷm(atos)* 'anything swollen; swell, wave (of the sea); fetus, embryo; sprout' (from the verb *kŷein* 'to contain, swell') plus the combining vowel -*o-*, used in in its etymological and extended senses, chief among these being 'of or pertaining to (undulating) motion; wavelike,' in Neo-Greek combinations: **kymocyclograph, kymoscope, kymotrichous.** Also, **cym-, cyma-, cymato-, cymo-,** kymat-: **cymoid, cymagraph, cymatolite, cymophanous, kymatism.** Compare **cyo-, cyst-, cyto-.**

1430 kyno- A variant of **cyno-.**

1431 kyo- A variant of **cyo-.**

1432 kyrto- A variant of **cyrto-.**

L

1433 **L-** A word-initial combining element, an abbreviation of **l(evo)-**, used to designate 'the 'left-handed' enantiomer of an optical isomer,' as, e.g., **L-glyceraldehyde**; 'the highest-numbered asymmetric carbon atom in a carbohydrate,' as, e.g., **L-rhamnose**; and 'the lowest-numbered asymmetric carbon atom in an amino acid,' as, e.g., **L-threonine**. Compare L_g-, L_s-, l-, levo-.

1434 **L_g-** A variant of **L-**, used in carbohydrate nomenclature in naming substances 'of the same configurational family as **L-glyceraldehyde**,' as, e.g., **L_g-rhamnose**. Compare **L-**, **l-**, **levo-**.

1435 **L_s-** A variant of **L-**, used in amino acid nomenclature in naming substances 'of the same configurational family as **L-serine**,' as, e.g., **L_s-threonine**. Compare **L-**, **l-**, **levo-**.

1436 **l-** A word-initial combining element, an abbreviation of **l(evo)-**, used in two kinds of chemical term:

1. that in which **l-** refers to the 'counterclockwise direction in which the plane of polarized light rotates when passed through the substance named by the combining root,' as, e.g., **l-leucine,** and

2. that in which **l-**, followed by (+) or (−), refers to the 'counterclockwise or clockwise configurational family to which the substance named by the combining root belongs,' as, e.g., **l(+)-alanine** and **l(−)-cystine**. Compare **L-**, **L_g-**, **L_s-**, **levo-**.

207

1437 labio- A word-initial combining element, derived from Latin *labi(um)* 'lip' plus the combining vowel *-o-*, used in its etymological sense in biomedical terminology: **labio-alveolar, labioglossopharyngeal, labioplacement.** Also, **labi-: labial.** Related form: **lip-**[3].

1438 labyrinth- A word-initial combining element, also occurring as a word, derived from Greek *labýrinth(os)* 'maze,' used in its etymological and extended senses, chief among these being 'of or pertaining to the inner ear,' in Neo-Greek and Neo-Latin combinations: **labyrinthectomy, labyrinthitis, labyrinthodont.** Also, **labyrinthi-, labyrintho-: labyrinthibranchiate, labyrinthotomy.**

1439 lace- A word-initial combining element, also occurring as a word, derived through Old French from Latin *laque(us)* 'noose, snare,' used chiefly in the extended sense of 'of, pertaining to, or resembling ornamental netlike fabric' in combination with other English elements: **lace-fern, lacewing, lacework.**

1440 lack- A word-initial combining element, also occurring as a word, derived from Middle English *lak(ken)* 'to blame, be wanting,' used in this latter sense in combination with other English elements: **lackbrain, lack-Latin, lackluster.**

1441 lacrimo- A word-initial combining element, derived from Latin *lacrim(a)* 'tear(drop)' plus the combining vowel *-o-*, used in its etymological and extended senses in Neo-Latin and Neo-Greek combinations: **lacrimonasal, lacrimotome, lacrimotomy.** Also, **lachrym-, lacrim-, lacrym-, lacrymi-, lacrymo-: lachrymose, lacrimal, lacrymal, lacrymiform, lacrymonasal.** Related forms: **dacryo-, tear-.**

1442 lacto- A word-initial combining element, derived from Latin *lac, lact(is)* 'milk' plus the combining vowel *-o-*, used in its etymological and extended senses, chief among these being 'of or pertaining to *lactic acid* ($CH_3CHOHCOOH$) (which is found in sour milk),' in Neo-Latin and Neo-Greek combinations: **lactobacillin, lactobiose, lactoscope.** Also, **lact-, lacti-: lactose, lactimorbus.** Related form(?): **galacto-.**

1443 ladder- A word-initial combining element, also occurring as a word, derived from Old English *(h)lǣder* 'device consisting of parallel evenly spaced rungs for climbing or descending' (from an Indo-European root meaning 'slope'), used in its etymological and extended senses in combination with other English elements: **ladder-back, ladderman, ladder-stitch.** Related forms: **climato-, clino-**[1]**, clino-**[2]**.**

1444   lady-   A word-initial combining element, also occurring as a word, derived from Old English *hlǣ(f)diġe*, literally, 'loaf-kneader' (cf. Old English *dǣġe* 'kneader (of bread); dairy-woman; house-keeper'), used in the extended sense of 'woman (of rank)' and in extensions of this sense in combination with other English elements: **ladybug, lady-in-waiting, lady-killer.** Compare **dairy-, lady's-.**

1445   lady's-   A word-initial combining element, the possessive singular form of English *lady* 'woman (of rank)' from Old English *hlǣ(f)diġe*, literally, 'loaf-kneader'), appearing in its etymological sense in combination with other English elements in a number of plant names: **lady's-slipper, lady's-thumb, lady's-tresses.** Also, **lady-, ladies'-: lady-slipper, ladies'-tresses.** Compare **lady-.**

1446   laevo-   A variant of **levo-.**

1447   lalo-   A word-initial combining element, derived from Greek *lal(eîn)* 'to babble' plus the combining vowel *-o-,* used in its etymological and extended senses, chief among these being 'of or pertaining to a speech disorder, esp. stuttering' in Neo-Greek combinations: **lalo-neurosis, lalophobia, laloplegia.** Also, **lal-, lalio-: laliatry, laliophobia.**

1448   lambda-   (Λ, λ)   A word-initial combining element, the eleventh letter of the Greek alphabet, used chiefly to designate 'the eleventh carbon atom in a straight chain compound or a derivative thereof in which the substitute group is attached to that atom' in chemical terminology. See **alpha-.**

1449   lamb's-   A word-initial combining element, the possessive singular form of English *lamb* 'young sheep' (from Old English *lamb* 'young sheep'), used in its etymological and extended senses in combination with other English elements: **lamb's-quarters, lamb's-tongue, lamb's-wool.**

1450   lamelli-   A word-initial combining element, derived from Neo-Latin *lāmell(a)* 'thin plate' (from Latin *lām(ina)* 'thin plate or layer' plus the diminutive suffix *-ella*) plus the combining vowel *-i-,* used in its etymological and extended senses in Neo-Latin and Neo-Greek combinations: **lamellibranch, lamellicorn, lamelliform.** Also, **lamell-: lamellar.** Compare **lamin-.**

1451   lamin-   A word-initial combining element, derived from Latin *lāmin(a)* 'thin plate or layer,' used in its etymological and extended senses, chief among these being 'of or pertaining to a neurophysis of a vertebra,' in Neo-Latin and Neo-Greek combinations: **lami-**

nar, laminectomy, laminitis. Also, **lamina-, lamino-, lamn-: lamin-agraph, laminotomy, lamnectomy.** Compare **lamelli-**.

1452 **lamp-**   A word-initial combining element, also occurring as a word, derived through Late Latin and Old French from Greek *lamp(ás)* 'torch' (from the verb *lámpein* 'to shine, light up'), used in the extended sense of 'device for providing illumination' in combination with other English elements: **lamplight, lamppost, lampshade.** Compare **lampro-**.

1453 **lampro-**   A word-initial combining element, derived from Greek *lampró(s)* 'bright, clear' (from the verb *lámpein* 'to shine, light up'), used in its etymological and extended senses in Neo-Greek combinations: **lamprophony, lamprophyre, lamprotype.** Compare **lamp-**.

1454 **land-**   A word-initial combining element, also occurring as a word, derived from Old English *land* 'ground; country(side),' used in its etymological and extended senses in combination with other English elements: **landfall, landlady, landmark.**

1455 **laparo-**   A word-initial combining element, derived from Greek *lapár(a)* 'flank, loin' plus the combining vowel -*o*-, used in its etymological and extended senses, chief among these being 'of or pertaining to the *abdomen*,' in biomedical terminology: **laparocys-totomy, laparogastrotomy, laparomonodidymus.** Also, **lapar-: laparectomy.**

1456 **large-**   A word-initial combining element, also occurring as a word, derived through French from Latin *larg(a)* 'abundant,' used in the sense of 'big' in combination with other English elements: **large-hearted, large-minded, largemouth (bass).**

1457 **larvi-**   A word-initial combining element, derived from Linnaean Latin *larv(a)* 'insect in its grub stage' (from Latin *larva* 'mask' and, by extension, 'ghost,' the idea being that an insect in its grub stage is merely a ghost of its future self and does not resemble its future form) plus the combining vowel -*i*-, used in its Linnaean sense in Neo-Latin and Neo-Greek combinations: **larvicide, larviphagic, larviposition.** Also, **larv-: larvin.**

1458 **laryngo-**   A word-initial combining element, derived from Greek *láryn(x), láryng(os)* 'upper part of the windpipe, gullet' plus the combining vowel -*o*-, used in the sense of 'of or pertaining to the *larynx*, the musculocartilaginous structure below the tongue root and hyoid bone and above the trachea' in biomedical terminology:

laryngofissure, laryngoparalysis, laryngotracheobronchoscopy. Also,
laryng-: laryngitis.

1459   latero-   A word-initial combining element, derived from Latin
       lat(*us*), *later*(*is*) 'flank, side' plus the combining vowel -*o*-, used in
       the sense of 'of or pertaining to a side' in Neo-Latin combinations:
       latero-abdominal, lateroduction, lateroversion. Also, later-, lateri-:
       lateral, laterigrade.

1460   law-   A word-initial combining element, also occurring as a word,
       derived from Old English *la*(*g*)*u* 'code of rules' (literally, 'that
       which is laid down'), used in its etymological and extended senses
       in combination with other English elements: law-abiding, law-
       breaker, lawman. Related forms: lay-, lochio-, low-.

1461   lay-   A word-initial combining element, derived from Old English
       le(*ćgan*) 'to cause to lie; to set down,' used in a variety of
       extensions of its etymological sense in combination with other
       English elements: lay-by, layoff, lay-up. Related forms: law-,
       lochio-, low-.

1462   lead-   A word-initial combining element, also occurring as a word,
       derived from Old English *lēad* 'the base metal (Pb),' used in its
       etymological and extended senses in combination with other
       English elements: lead-pipe (cinch), leadplant, leadwort.

1463   leaf-   A word-initial combining element, also occurring as a word,
       derived from Old English *lēaf* 'flat structure which serves as the
       main organ of photosynthesis and transpiration in vascular plants,'
       used in its etymological and extended senses in combination with
       other English elements: leafhopper, leafstalk, leafworm.

1464   lease-   A word-initial combining element, also occurring as a word,
       derived through Old French from Latin *lax*(*āre*) 'to loose, let go,'
       used in the extended sense of 'of or pertaining to the contractual
       conveyance of property from one party to another for a specified
       period of time,' used in its etymological and extended senses in
       combination with other English elements: leaseback, leaseholder,
       lease-purchase.

1465   leather-   A word-initial combining element, also occurring as a
       word, derived from Old English *leðer-* 'tanned skin-, hide-,' used in
       its etymological and extended senses in combination with other
       English elements: leatherjacket, leatherneck, leatherwork.

1466   lecitho-   A word-initial combining element, derived from Greek *lékitho(s)* 'yolk of an egg,' used in its etymological and extended senses, chief among these being 'of or pertaining to the *ovum*,' in Neo-Greek and Neo-Latin combinations: **lecithoblast, lecithoprotein, lecithovitellin.** Also, **lecith-: lecithin.**

1467   **lee-**   A word-initial combining element, also occurring as a word, derived from Old English *hlē(ow)* 'shelter, covering,' used in the specialized sense of 'the side away from the wind; the side sheltered from the wind' in combination with other English elements in nautical terminology: **leeboard, lee-gage, leeway.**

1468   **left-**   A word-initial combining element, also occurring as a word, derived from Kentish *left* 'useless, insubstantial,' used in the extended sense of 'opposite to right' in combination with other English elements: **left-eyed (flounder), left-handed, left-laid.**

1469   **leg-**   A word-initial combining element, also occurring as a word, derived from Old Norse *leg(gr)* 'hollow bone; (lower) limb of the body,' used in this latter sense and in extensions of this sense in combination with other English elements: **leg-break, legman, leg-pull.**

1470   **leio-**   A word-initial combining element, derived from Greek *leîo(s)* 'smooth,' used in its etymological and extended senses in Neo-Greek and Neo-Latin combinations: **leiodermia, leiodystonia, leiomyofibroma.** Also, **lei-, li-, lio-: leiasthenia,** *Liodon*, **liomyoma.**

1471   **leip-**   A variant of **lipo-**[2].

1472   **lemon-**   A word-initial combining element, also occurring as a word, derived through Old French from Arabic *līmah* 'citrus fruit,' used in the specialized sense of 'the yellow citrus fruit *Citrus limonum*' and in extensions of this sense in combination with other English elements: **lemonade, lemonfish, lemon-grass.**

1473   **lenticulo-**   A word-initial combining element, derived from Latin *lenticul(āris)* 'lentil-shaped' (from *lenticula*, the diminutive form of *len(s)*, *lent(is)* 'lentil,' a term later used to refer to 'the (lentil-shaped) lens of the eye') plus the combining vowel *-o-*, used chiefly in the extended sense of 'of or pertaining to the *lenticular nucleus*, the (lentil-shaped) portion of the corpus striatum which is external to the third ventricle' in biomedical terminology: **lenticulo-optic, lenticulostriate, lenticulothalamic.** Also, **lenticul-: lenticular.**

1474   **lepido-**   A word-initial combining element, derived from Greek *lepi(s)*, *lepíd(os)* 'scale, rind, husk' (from the verb *lépein* 'to strip off') plus the combining vowel -o-, used in the sense of 'scale, flake' and in extensions of this sense in Neo-Greek combinations: *Lepidophyton,* lepidopterist, *Lepidoselaga.* Also, lepid-, lepo-: lepidoma, lepocyte. Compare lepto-.

1475 **lepto-**   A word-initial combining element, derived from Greek *leptó(s)* 'peeled, husked' (from the verb *lépein* 'to strip off') and, by extension, 'delicate, thin,' used chiefly in the sense of '(abnormally) thin, narrow, or delicate' and in extensions of this sense in Neo-Greek combinations: **leptochymia, leptocyte, leptodactylous.** Also, **lept-: leptandrin.** Compare **lepido-.**

1476 **letter-**   A word-initial combining element, also occurring as a word, derived through Old French from Latin *litter(a)* 'alphabetic sign' (which, in the plural, was also used in the sense of 'document; something written'), used in its etymological and extended senses in combination with other English elements: **letterhead, letter-perfect, letterpress.**

1477 **leuko-**   A word-initial combining element, derived from Greek *leukó(s)* 'light, clear, bright, white,' used chiefly in the sense of 'white' and in extensions of this sense, chief among these being 'of or pertaining to *white corpuscles* or to *leukocytes,* colorless ameboid cell masses,' in Neo-Greek and Neo-Latin combinations: **leukoderivative, leukodermia, leukosarcomatosis.** Also, **leuc-, leuco-, leuk-: leucitis, leucotomy, leukemia.** Related forms: **light-², luci-.**

1478 **leukocyto-**   A word-initial combining element, derived from English *leukocyt(e)* 'colorless ameboid cell mass' (from Greek *leukó(s)* 'clear, white' plus *kýt(os)* 'hollow vessel' and, by extension, 'cell') plus the combining vowel -o-, used in its etymological sense in biomedical combinations: **leukocytoblast, leukocytogenesis, leukocytolytic.** Also, **leucocyt-, leucocyto-, leukocyt-: leucocytosis,** *Leucocytozoon,* **leukocyturia.** Compare **leuko-** and **cyto-.**

1479 **levo-**   A word-initial combining element, derived from Latin *l(a)ev(us)* 'left' plus the combining vowel -o-, used in its etymological and extended senses, chief among these being 'of or pertaining to an enantiomorph which rotates towards the left,' in Neo-Latin and Neo-Greek combinations: **levocardia, levoglucose, levophobia.** Also, **L-, l-, laev-, laevo-, lev-: L-glyceraldehyde, l-leucine, laevulose, laevorotary, levulose.** Compare **levulos-.**

1480 **levulos-**   A word-initial combining element, derived from English *levulos(e)* 'fructose' (from Latin *l(a)ev(us)* 'left' plus the diminutive suffix -ul(e) plus the suffix -ose which is used in naming sugars, fructose being a levorotary ketose sugar), used in its etymological sense in chemical terminology: **levulosazone, levulosemia, levulosuria.** Also, **laevulos-: laevulosan.** Compare **levo-.**

1481 li-   A variant of **leio-.**

1482 lieno-   A word-initial combining element, derived from Latin *lien* 'spleen' plus the combining vowel *-o-*, used in its etymological sense in biomedical combinations: **lienocele, lienomyelomalacia, lienorenal.** Also, **lien-: lienitis.** Related forms: **splanchno-, spleno-.**

1483 life-   A word-initial combining element, also occurring as a word, derived from Old English *līf* 'animate existence,' used in its etymological and extended senses in combination with other English elements: **lifeblood, lifeboat, lifesaver.** Related forms: **lipo-[1], liver-.**

1484 light-[1]   A word-initial combining element, also occurring as a word, derived from Old English *lēoht, līht* 'not heavy,' used in its etymological and extended senses in combination with other English elements: **lightface, light-fingered, lightweight.** Related form: **lung-.**

1485 light-[2]   A word-initial combining element, also occurring as a word, derived from Old English *lēoht* 'illumination, brightness,' used in its etymological and extended senses in combination with other English elements: **lighthouse, lightstruck, light-year.** Related forms: **leuko-, luci-.**

1486 ligni-   A word-initial combining element, derived from Latin *lign(um)* 'wood' (from an Indo-European root meaning 'to gather together (as one might gather firewood)') plus the combining vowel *-i-*, used in its etymological sense in Neo-Latin combinations: **lignicole, ligniferous, lignivorous.** Also, **lign-: lignite.** Related form: **logo-.**

1487 lily-   A word-initial combining element, also occurring as a word, derived through Old French from Latin *līli(um)* 'plant of the family *Liliaceae*,' used in its etymological and extended senses in combination with other English elements: **lily-livered, lily-of-the-valley, lily-white.**

1488 lime-   A word-initial combining element, also occurring as a word, derived from Old English *līm* 'glue,' used in its etymological and extended senses, chief among these being 'calcium oxide (CaO),' in combination with other English elements: **limelight, limestone, lime-twig.**

1489 limno-   A word-initial combining element, derived from Greek *límn(ē)* 'pool, lake, marsh' plus the combining vowel *-o-*, used in its etymological and extended senses in Neo-Greek combinations: ***Limnocyon*, limnology, limnophilous.** Also, **limn-: limnemia.**

1490 line-   A word-initial combining element, also occurring as a word, derived from Latin *līne(a)* 'thread, string' (from *līneus* 'flaxen' (cf. *lāna* 'wool')), used in the extended sense of 'resembling a thread or string, esp. one which is taut' in combination with other English elements: **linebacker, lineman, line-up.** Related forms: **flannel-, villi-, wool-.**

1491 linguo-   A word-initial combining element, derived from Latin *lingu(a)* 'tongue' plus the combining vowel *-o-*, used in its etymological and extended senses in Neo-Latin combinations: **linguodental, linguodistal, linguoversion.** Also, **lingu-: lingual.** Related form: **tongue-.**

1492 lio-   A variant of **leio-.**

1493 lip-¹   A variant of **lipo-¹.**

1494 lip-²   A variant of **lipo-².**

1495 lip-³   A word-initial combining element, also occurring as a word, derived from Old English *lip(pa)* 'fleshy fold at the opening of the mouth,' used in its etymological and extended senses in combination with other English elements: **lip-fish, lip-read, lipstick.** Related form: **labio-.**

1496 lipo-¹   A word-initial combining element, derived from Greek *lipo(s)* 'fat,' used in its etymological and extended senses in Neo-Greek and Neo-Latin combinations: **lipoblastoma, lipoclasis, lipoferous.** Also, **lip-¹: lipectomy.** Related forms: **life-, liver-.**

1497 lipo-²   A word-initial combining element, derived from Greek *l(e)íp(ein)* 'to leave (behind), fail, lack' plus the combining vowel *-o-*, used chiefly in the sense of 'lacking' and in extensions of this sense in Neo-Greek combinations: **lipobranchiate, lipocephalous, lipogram.** Also, **leip-, lip-²: leiphemia, liparthritis.**

1498 litho-   A word-initial combining element, derived from Greek *litho(s)* 'stone,' used in its etymological and extended senses, chief among these being 'of or pertaining to a *calculus,*' in Neo-Greek combinations: **lithocystotomy, lithograph, lithosphere.** Also, **lith-: lithangiuria.**

1499 **liver-** A word-initial combining element, also occurring as a word, derived from Old English *lifer* 'bile-secreting organ which participates in the formation of blood and in the metabolism of fats, vitamins, and proteins,' used in its etymological and extended senses in combination with other English elements: **liverberry, liverleaf, liver-rot.** Related forms: **life-, lipo-¹.**

1500 **lobo-** A word-initial combining element, derived from Greek *lobó(s)* 'lower part of the ear or liver' (from an Indo-European root meaning something on the order of 'loose-hanging, flapping'), used in its etymological and extended senses in biomedical terminology: **lobocyte, lobostomy, lobotomy.** Also, **lob-: lobectomy.** Related forms: **slap-, sleep-.**

1501 **lochio-** A word-initial combining element, derived from Greek *lóchio(s)* 'of or pertaining to childbirth' and *lóchi(a)* 'vaginal discharge following childbirth' (from *lóchos* 'a lying in wait; a lying-in' (from the verb *légein* 'to lay, lie')), used in its etymological and extended senses in biomedical terminology: **lochiocolpos, lochiometritis, lochiorrhea.** Related forms: **law-, lay-, low-.**

1502 **lock-** A word-initial combining element, also occurring as a word, derived from Old English *loc* 'device for fastening a door or the like,' used in its etymological and extended senses in combination with other English elements: **lockjaw, locksmith, lockup.**

1503 **log-¹** A variant of **logo-.**

1504 **log-²** A word-initial combining element, also occurring as a word, derived from Middle English *log(ge)* 'bulky trunk of a felled tree,' used in its etymological and extended senses in combination with other English elements: **logjam, logroll, logwood.**

1505 **logo-** A word-initial combining element, derived from Greek *lógo(s)* 'word, saying, thought' (from an Indo-European root meaning 'to gather together,' the idea being that a word or saying was something that involved the gathering together of units of speech), used in its etymological and extended senses, chief among these being 'of or pertaining to speech,' in Neo-Greek combinations: **logokophosis, logomania, logoplegia.** Also, **log-¹: logasthenia.** Related form: **ligni-.**

1506 long- A word-initial combining element, also occurring as a word, derived from Old English *lang, long* 'great in length,' used in its etymological and extended senses in combination with other English elements: **longbow, long-suffering, long-winded.** Related form: **longi-.**

1507 longi- A word-initial combining element, derived from Latin *long(us)* 'long' plus the combining vowel *-i-,* used in its etymological sense in Neo-Latin combinations: **longilineal, longipedate, longiradiate.** Related form: **long-.**

1508 look- A word-initial combining element, also occurring as a word, derived from Old English *lōc(ian)* 'to regard,' used in its etymological and extended senses in combination with other English elements: **lookdown, look-in, lookout.**

1509 loose- A word-initial combining element, also occurring as a word, derived from Old Norse *lauss* 'unattached,' used in its etymological and extended senses in combination with other English elements: **loose-jointed, loose-leaf, loose-tongued.** Related forms: **lyo-, lyso-.**

1510 lopho- A word-initial combining element, derived from Greek *lópho(s)* 'ridge; crest,' used in its etymological and extended senses in Neo-Greek combinations: **lophobranch, lophophore, lophotrichous.** Also, **loph-: lophodont.**

1511 love- A word-initial combining element, also occurring as a word, derived from Old English *lof(u)* 'strong emotional attachment,' used in its etymological and extended senses in combination with other English elements: **lovebird, lovelock, lovesick.**

1512 low- A word-initial combining element, also occurring as a word, derived through Middle English from Old Norse *lá(gr)* 'not high,' used in its etymological and extended senses in combination with other English elements: **lowbrow, low-cost, low-down.** Related forms: **law-, lay-, lochio-.**

1513 loxo- A word-initial combining element, derived from Greek *loxó(s)* 'slanting, oblique,' used in its etymological and extended senses in Neo-Greek combinations: **loxodromic, loxolophodont, loxotomy.** Also, **lox-: loxophthalmus.**

1514 luci- A word-initial combining element, derived from Latin *lū(x), lūc(is)* 'brightness, light' plus the combining vowel *-i-,* used in its etymological sense in Neo-Latin and Neo-Greek combinations:

luciferase, lucifugal, lucipetal. Also, **luc-, luco-: Lucite, lucotherapy.**
Related forms: **leuko-, light-².**

1515 lumbo- A word-initial combining element, derived from Latin
lumb(us) 'loin' plus the combining vowel *-o-,* used in its etymological sense in biomedical terminology: **lumbocolostomy, lumbodorsal,
lumbodynia.** Also, **lumb-: lumbar.**

1516 lung- A word-initial combining element, also occurring as a word,
derived from Old English *lung(en)* 'organ of respiration' (from an
Indo-European root meaning 'light (in weight)'), used in its
etymological and extended senses in combination with other
English elements: **lungfish, lungworm, lungwort.** Related form:
light-¹.

1517 lute- A word-initial combining element, derived from Latin *lūte(us)*
'yellow, orange-yellow,' literally, 'of or pertaining to yellow-weed
(*lūtum*),' used in its etymological and extended senses, chief among
these being 'of or pertaining to the *corpus luteum,* a yellow ovarian
mass formed by a mature Graafian follicle,' in Neo-Latin and Neo-
Greek combinations: **luteectomy, lutein, luteose.** Also, **luteo-:
luteotropic.**

1518 ly- A variant of **lyo-.**

1519 lyco- A word-initial combining element, derived from Greek
lýko(s) 'wolf,' used in its etymological and extended senses in Neo-
Greek combinations: **lycomania, *Lycoperdon,* lycopodium.** Also,
lyc-, lycos-: lycanthropy, lycosid. Related form: **wolf-.**

1520 lymphadeno- See **lympho-** and **adeno-.**

1521 lymphangio- See **lympho-** and **angio-.**

1522 lympho- A word-initial combining element, derived from Latin
lymph(a) 'water' plus the combining vowel *-o-,* used in the extended
sense of 'of or pertaining to the *lymph,* a transparent fluid which is
derived from body tissue and conveyed to the bloodstream by the
lymphatic vessels' in biomedical terminology: **lymphoblastoma,
lymphoduct, lymphorrhea.** Also, **lymph-: lymphemia.**

1523 lymphocyto- See **lympho-** and **cyto-.**

1524 lyo- A word-initial combining element, derived from Greek *lý(ein)*
'to loosen, release, dissolve' plus the combining vowel *-o-,* used
chiefly in the sense of 'of or pertaining to solution' in Neo-Greek

and Neo-Latin combinations: **lyophilic, lyosorption, lyotropic.**
Also, **ly-: lyencephalous.** Compare **lyso-.** Related form: **loose-.**

1525   **lyso-**   A word-initial combining element, derived from Greek *lýs(is)* 'loosening, dissolution' (from the verb *lýein* 'to loosen, dissolve') plus the combining vowel *-o-,* used in its etymological and extended senses, chief among these being 'of or pertaining to the breaking down of cells by an antibody,' in biomedical terminology: **lysobacteria, lysoform, lysotype.** Also, **lys-, lysi-: lysin, lysimeter.** Compare **lyo-.** Related form: **loose-.**

M

1526 **m-**[1]   A variant of **meso-**.

1527 **m-**[2]   A variant of **meta-**.

1528 **Mac-**   A word-initial combining element, derived from Gaelic *mac* 'son,' appearing in a number of English surnames in which its original sense was 'son of the person named by the combining root': **MacArthur, MacDonald, Macmillan.** Also, **M'-, Mc-: M'Carthy, McCarthy.**

1529 **macro-**   A word-initial combining element, derived from Greek *makró(s)* 'long, tall, deep, large,' used in its etymological and extended senses in Neo-Greek combinations: **macrobiotic, macromania, macrophagocyte.** Also, **macr-: macropsia.**

1530 **mad-**   A word-initial combining element, also occurring as a word, derived through Middle English from Old English *(ġe)mǣd(d)* 'insane' (from an Indo-European root meaning 'change, move,' or the like, the idea being, presumably, that one who is *mad* is 'changed' from the norm), used in its etymological and extended senses in combination with other English elements: **madcap, mad-dog (skullcap), madhouse.** Related forms: **meato-, mis-**[1].

1531 **magneto-**   A word-initial combining element, derived from English *magnet* 'loadstone; body with the properties of a loadstone' (from Greek *(líthos) Magnḗtēs* 'Magnesian (stone),' Magnesia having

221

been a mineral-rich region of Thessaly) plus the combining vowel *-o-,* used in its etymological and extended senses in Neo-Greek and Neo-Latin combinations: **magnetoconstriction, magnetoelectric, magnetotherapy.** Also, **magnet-: magnetism.** Compare **mangano-.**

1532 magni- A word-initial combining element, derived from Latin *magn(us)* 'great' plus the combining vowel *-i-,* used in its etymological and extended senses in borrowings from Latin and in Neo-Latin and Neo-Greek combinations: **magnify, magniloquent, magniscope.** Also, **magn-: magnanimous.** Related forms: **maha-, master-, may-, mega-, megalo-.**

1533 maha- A word-initial combining element, derived from Sanskrit *mahā* 'great,' appearing in its etymological sense in borrowings from Sanskrit and Hindi: **mahamari, maharajah, Mahayana.** Also, **mah-: mahatma.** Related forms: **magni-, master-, may-, mega-, megalo-.**

1534 mail- A word-initial combining element, also occurring as a word, derived from Old French *mal(e)* 'bag, pouch,' used in the extended sense of 'of or pertaining to that which is sent by post'—originally, 'that which is carried in a bag or pouch'—in combination with other English elements: **mailbag, mailbox, mailman.**

1535 main- A word-initial combining element, also occurring as a word, derived from Old English *mæġ(e)n-* 'mighty, great' (cf. Old English *mæġen* 'power'), used in the sense of 'chief, principal' and in extensions of this sense in combination with other English elements: **mainmast, mainstay, mainstream.** Related form: **mechano-.**

1536 make- A word-initial combining element, also occurring as a word, derived from Old English *mac(ian)* 'to fashion, cause,' used in its etymological and extended senses in combination with other English elements: **make-believe, makeshift, make-up.** Related form: **match-[1].**

1537 mal- A word-initial combining element, derived through French from Latin *mal(us)* 'bad, evil, ill,' appearing in the sense of 'bad(ly)' in borrowings from French and in combination with other English elements: **maladjusted, malapropos, malfunction.** Compare **male-.**

1538 malaco- A word-initial combining element, derived from Greek *malakó(s)* 'soft,' used in its etymological and extended senses, chief among these being 'abnormal softening' and 'soft-bodied,' in Neo-Greek combinations: **malacology, malacoplakia, malacosarcosis.**

Also, **malac-, malako-: malacosteon, malakoplakia.** Related forms: **malt-, maltos-.**

1539 malario-   A word-initial combining element, derived from English *malari(a)* 'infectious disease caused by protozoa of the genus *Plasmodium* and transmitted by mosquitoes of the genus *Anopheles*' (from Italian *mal'aria,* literally, 'bad air') plus the combining vowel *-o-,* used in its etymological sense in biomedical terminology: **malariology, malariometry, malariotherapy.** Also, **malari-, malaria-: malarious, malariacidal.** Compare **mal-, aero-.**

1540 male-   A word-initial combining element, derived from Latin *male* 'badly, ill,' appearing in its etymological sense in inherited combinations: **malediction, malefactor, malevolence.** Compare **mal-.**

1541 malt-   A word-initial combining element, also occurring as a word, derived from Old English *m(e)alt* 'grain (esp. barley) which has germinated after soaking' (from an Indo-European root meaning 'soft'), used in its etymological and extended senses in chemical terminology: **maltase, maltine, maltose.** Also, **malto-: maltoflavin.** Compare **maltos-.** Related form: **malaco-.**

1542 maltos-   A word-initial combining element, derived from English *maltos(e)* 'the disaccharide ($C_{12}H_{22}O_{11} \cdot H_2O$) which results from the action of diastase (esp. from malt) on a starch' (from English *malt* plus the suffix *-ose* which is used in naming sugars), used in its etymological sense in chemical terminology: **maltosazone, maltoside, maltosuria.** Compare **malt-.**

1543 mammill-   A word-initial combining element, derived from Latin *ma(m)milla* 'breast, nipple' (from *mamm(a)* 'breast' plus the diminutive suffix *-illa*), used in the sense of 'nipple' and in extensions of this sense in biomedical terminology: **mammillate, mammillitis, mammilloid.** Also, **mammilli-: mammilliplasty.** Compare **mammo-.**

1544 mammo-   A word-initial combining element, derived from Latin *mamm(a)* 'breast' plus the combining vowel *-o-,* used in its etymological and extended senses in biomedical terminology: **mammogen, mammotomy, mammotropin.** Also, **mamm-, mammi-: mammose, mammilingus.** Compare **mammill-.**

1545 man-¹   A variant of **manu-.**

1546 man-²   A word-initial combining element, also occurring as a word, derived from Old English *man(n)* 'adult human,' used in its etymological sense and in the specialized sense of 'male adult human' in combination with other English elements: **man-eating, manhelper, manhunt.** Compare **woman-**.

1547   mandibulo-   A word-initial combining element, derived from Late Latin *mandibul(a)* 'jaw' (from the verb *mandere* 'to chew') plus the combining vowel -*o*-, used in the sense of 'of or pertaining to the *mandible,* the bone which forms the lower jaw' in biomedical terminology: **mandibulohyoid, mandibulomaxillary, mandibulopharyngeal.** Also, **mandibul-, mandibuli-: mandibular, mandibuliform.** Compare **mouth-**.

1548   mangano-   A word-initial combining element, derived through Late Latin and French from Greek *Magnēsi(os)* 'of or pertaining to the (mineral-rich) region of Thessaly called *Magnēsia,*' used in the sense of 'of, pertaining to, or containing the metallic element *manganese* (Mn)' in scientific terminology: **manganophyllite, manganosiderite, manganotantalite.** Also, **mangan-, mangani-: manganite, manganiferous.** Compare **magneto-**.

1549   mani-¹   A variant of **manu-**.

1550   mani-²   A variant of **many-**.

1551   manno-   A word-initial combining element, derived from English *manno(se)* 'the monosaccharide $(CH_2OH \cdot (CHOH)_4 \cdot CHO)$' (ultimately from Aramaic *mann(ā)* 'exudation of the *Tamarix gallica* or *Fraxinus ornus,* the miraculous food which fed the Israelites in the wilderness (Exodus 16:14-36)' plus the suffix -*ose* which is used in naming sugars), used in its etymological sense in chemical terminology: **mannocarolose, mannohydrazone, mannopyranose.** Also, **mannos-, mannoso-: mannosan, mannosocellulose.**

1552   mano-   A word-initial combining element, derived from Greek *manó(s)* 'thin, loose,' used in its etymological and extended senses in Neo-Greek combinations: **manometric, manoscopy, manoxylic.**

1553   manu-   A word-initial combining element, derived from Latin *manu(s)* 'hand,' used in its etymological and extended senses in a variety of combinations: **manufacture, manumotor, manustupration.** Also, **man-¹, mani-¹: manoptoscope, maniform.**

1554   many-   A word-initial combining element, also occurring as a word, derived from Old English *mani(ġ)* 'a great number of,' used in its etymological and extended senses in combination with other English elements: **many-one, many-sided, many-valued.** Also, **mani-²: manifold.**

1555 **market-** A word-initial combining element, also occurring as a word, derived through Old English from Latin *mercāt(us)* 'trade; place for trade to take place' (from the verb *mercārī* 'to trade, buy, sell' (from *merx* 'goods')), used in its etymological and extended senses in combination with other English elements: **market-fish, marketman, marketplace.** Related forms: **mercapto-, mercuro-.**

1556 **marrow-** A word-initial combining element, also occurring as a word, derived from Old English *mærh* 'soft substance which fills the cavities of bones,' used in its etymological and extended senses in combination with other English elements: **marrowbone, marrow-brain, marrowfat.**

1557 **maschal-** A word-initial combining element, derived from Greek *maschál(ē)* 'armpit,' used in its etymological and extended senses in biomedical combinations: **maschaladenitis, maschalephidrosis, maschaliatry.**

1558 **mast-** A variant of **masto-.**

1559 **master-** A word-initial combining element, also occurring as a word, derived through Old English from Latin *ma(gi)ster* 'chief, leader' (from an Indo-European root meaning 'great'), used in its etymological and extended senses in combination with other English elements: **master-at-arms, mastermind, masterpiece.** Related forms: **magni-, maha-, may-, mega-, megalo-.**

1560 **masto-** A word-initial combining element, derived from Greek *mastó(s)* 'breast,' used in its etymological sense in biomedical terminology: **mastocarcinoma, mastodynia, mastomenia.** Also, **mast-: mastectomy.** Compare **mastoid-.**

1561 **mastoid-** A word-initial combining element, also occurring as a word, derived from Greek *masto(e)id(és)* 'breast-shaped' (from *mast(ós)* 'breast' plus the adjective-forming suffix *-oeidēs* '-like'), used in the specialized sense of 'of or pertaining to the (breast-shaped) *mastoid process* of the temporal bone' in biomedical terminology: **mastoidalgia, mastoidectomy, mastoiditis.** Also, **mastoido-: mastoidotomy.** Compare **masto-.**

1562 **match-¹** A word-initial combining element, also occurring as a word, derived from Old English *(ġe)mæċċ(a)* 'mate, companion' (from an Indo-European root meaning 'to fashion, fit,' the idea being that a *mate* is 'one who is fitted with another'), used in its etymological and extended senses in combination with other

English elements: **matchboard, matchmaker, matchmark.** Related form: **make-.**

1563   **match-²**   A word-initial combining element, also occurring as a word, derived through Old French from Late Latin *myx(a)* 'lamp wick' (from Greek *mýxa* 'mucus,' hence 'nostril,' hence 'nozzle of a lamp'), used in the extended sense of 'piece of wood or the like which ignites when struck against an appropriate surface' and in extensions of this sense in combination with other English elements: **matchbook, matchbox, matchlock.** Compare **myxo-.**

1564   **matr-**   A variant of **metro-¹.**

1565   **matri-**   A word-initial combining element, derived from Latin *māt(e)r, mātr(is)* 'mother' plus the combining vowel *-i-*, used in its etymological and extended senses in Neo-Latin and Neo-Greek combinations: **matriarch, matrilineal, matrilocal.** Related forms: **metro-¹, metro-², mother-.**

1566   **matro-**   A variant of **metro-¹.**

1567   **maxillo-**   A word-initial combining element, derived from Latin *maxill(a)* 'jaw' plus the combining vowel *-o-*, used in its etymological and extended senses, chief among these being 'of or pertaining to the *maxilla,* one of the bones which forms the upper jaw in mammals,' in biomedical terminology: **maxillofacial, maxillomandibular, maxillopharyngeal.**

1568   **may-**   A word-initial combining element, derived through Old French from Latin *Mai(us) (mensis)* '(the month) belonging to the goddess *Maia*' (whose name is derived from an Indo-European root meaning 'great'), used in the sense of 'of or associated with the fifth month of the Christian calendar' in combination with other English elements: **mayflower, mayfly, maypole.** Also, **May-: Maypole.** Related forms: **magni-, maha-, master-, mega-, megalo-.**

1569   **mazo-**   A word-initial combining element, derived from Greek *mazó(s)* 'breast,' used in its etymological sense in biomedical terminology: **mazodynia, mazology, mazoplasia.**

1570   **Mc-**   A variant of **Mac-.**

1571   **me-**   A variant of **methyl-.**

1572   **meadow-**   A word-initial combining element, also occurring as a word, derived through Middle English from Old English *mædwa* 'open, grass-covered land(s),' literally, 'land that may be mowed,' used in its etymological and extended senses in combination with other English elements: **meadow-brown, meadow-grass, meadowlark.**

1573   **meat-¹**   A variant of **meato-**.

1574   **meat-²**   A word-initial combining element, also occurring as a word, derived from Old English *met(e)* 'food,' used in the specialized sense of '(edible) flesh' and in extensions of this sense in combination with other English elements: **meatball, meathead, meatman.**

1575   **meato-**   A word-initial combining element, derived from Latin *meāt(us)* 'passage' (from the verb *meāre* 'to go, pass') (from an Indo-European root meaning 'change, move, go') plus the combining vowel -*o*-, used in the sense of '(bodily) opening or canal' in biomedical terminology: **meatometer, meatorrhaphy, meatoscope.** Also, **meat-¹: meatal.** Related forms: **mad-, mis-¹.**

1576   **mechano-**   A word-initial combining element, derived from Greek *mēchan(ē)* 'contrivance, machine' plus the combining vowel -*o*-, used in the sense of 'of or pertaining to a machine or to the workings of a machine' and in extensions of this sense in Neo-Greek combinations: **mechanocyte, mechanogymnastics, mechanotherapy.** Also, **mechan-: mechanics.** Related form: **main-.**

1577   **medi-**   A word-initial combining element, derived from Latin *medi(us)* 'middle,' used in its etymological and extended senses in Neo-Latin combinations: **medifrontal, medipeduncle, meditemporal.** Also, **medio-: mediolateral.** Compare **mezzo-.** Related forms: **mesati-, mesio-, meso-, mid-, middle-.**

1578   **medico-**   A word-initial combining element, derived from Latin *medic(us)* 'physician' plus the combining vowel -*o*-, used in the sense of 'of or pertaining to the art of healing' in Neo-Latin and Neo-Greek combinations: **medicodental, medicomechanical, medicothorax.** Also, **medic-: medical.**

1579   **medio-**   A variant of **medi-**.

1580   **medullo-**   A word-initial combining element, derived from Latin *medull(a)* 'marrow' and, by extension, 'central part' plus the combining vowel -*o*-, used in its etymological and extended senses in biomedical terminology: **medulloarthritis, medulloculture, medullosuprarenoma.** Also, **medull-, medulli-: medullitis, medullispinal.**

1581 mega- A word-initial combining element, derived from Greek *méga(s)*, *megá(lē)* 'great, large,' used in its etymological and extended senses in a variety of combinations: **megabuck, megacecum, megacephalic.** Also, **meg-: megohm.** Compare **megalo-**. Related forms: **magni-, maha-, master-, may-**.

1582 megakaryo- A word-initial combining element, derived from English *megakaryo(cyte)* 'giant bone marrow cell' (from scientific Greek *méga(s)* 'large' plus *karyo(n)* 'nucleus' plus *-cyte* '-cell'), used in its etymological sense in biomedical combinations: **megakaryoblast, megakaryocytosis, megakaryophthisis.** Also, **megacaryo-: megacaryoblast.** Compare **mega-, karyo-, cyto-**.

1583 megalo- A word-initial combining element, derived from Greek *méga(s)*, *megál(ē)* 'great, large' plus the combining vowel *-o-*, used in its etymological and extended senses in Neo-Greek and Neo-Latin combinations: **megaloclitoris, megalocornea, megalomaniac.** Also, **megal-: megalerythema.** Compare **mega-**. Related forms: **magni-, maha-, master-, may-**.

1584 meio- A variant of **mio-**.

1585 mel-[1] A variant of **melo-[1]**.

1586 mel-[2] A variant of **melo-[2]**.

1587 melano- A word-initial combining element, derived from Greek *méla(s)*, *mélan(os)* 'black, dark' plus the combining vowel *-o-*, used in its etymological and extended senses, chief among these being 'strongly pigmented' and 'of or pertaining to (the pigment) dihydroxy indoxylic acid *melanin* $((OH)_2C_6H_2 \cdot CH \cdot C(COOH) \cdot NH)$,' in Neo-Greek and Neo-Latin combinations: **melanodermatitis, melanoflocculation, melanolaukoderma.** Also, **mela-, melam-, melan-, melas-, melen-: melaconite, *Melampus*, melancholic, melasicterus, melenemesis.**

1588 meli- A word-initial combining element, derived from Greek *méli*, *méli(tos)* 'honey,' used in its etymological and extended senses in Neo-Greek combinations: **melibiose, melicera, melilite.** Also, **melit-, melito-, melli-[2], mellit-, mellito-: melituria, melitophiline, mellilite, mellituria, mellitophiline.** Related form: **melli-[1]**.

1589 melli-[1] A word-initial combining element, derived from Latin *mel*, *mell(is)* 'honey' plus the combining vowel *-i-*, used in its etymological and extended senses in Neo-Latin combinations: **melliferous, mellifluence, *Mellisuga*.** Related form: **meli-**.

1590   melli-²   A variant of **meli-**.

1591   mellito-   A variant of **meli-**.

1592   melo-¹   A word-initial combining element, derived from Greek *mélo(s)* 'limb' and, by extension, '(metrical choral) song' (cf. the use of English *foot* to designate both the 'organ of the body' and the 'metrical unit'), used in its etymological and extended senses in borrowings from Greek and in Neo-Greek combinations: **melodidymus, melodrama, melomania**. Also, **mel-¹, melos-: melic, melosalgia.**

1593   melo-²   A word-initial combining element, derived from Greek *mêlo(n)* 'apple' and, by extension, 'cheek,' used in its etymological and extended senses in borrowings from Greek and in Neo-Greek combinations: **melocactus, melocoton, meloplasty**. Also, **mel-², melon-, melono-: melitis, *Melongenidae*, melonoplasty.**

1594   men-   A variant of **meno-**.

1595   meni-   A variant of **meno-**.

1596   meningo-   A word-initial combining element, derived from Greek *mênin(x), méning(os)* 'membrane' plus the combining vowel *-o-*, used in its etymological sense and in the specialized sense of 'of or pertaining to the *meninges*, the three membranes which envelop the spinal cord and the brain' in biomedical combinations: **meningocortical, meningomalacia, meningoradicular**. Also, **mening-, meninge-, meningeo-, meningi-: meningitis, meningeal, meningeocortical, meningioma.**

1597   meno-   A word-initial combining element, derived from Greek *mén, mēn(ós)* 'moon, (lunar) month' and, in the plural, 'menses' plus the combining vowel *-o-*, used in the sense of 'of or pertaining to the menses' in biomedical terminology: **menolipsis, menometrorrhagia, menopause**. Also, **men-, meni-: menhidrosis, menischesis**. Related forms: **metro-³, moon-**.

1598   ment-¹   A variant of **mento-**.

1599   ment-²   A variant of **menti-²**.

1600   menth-   A word-initial combining element, derived from Latin *mint(h)(a)* 'mint,' used in the sense of 'hydrocarbon derived from mint oil' in chemical terminology: **menthane, menthol, menthyl.**

1601 menti-¹ A variant of **mento-**.

1602 menti-² A word-initial combining element, derived from Latin *men(s), ment(is)* 'intellectual faculties; mind' plus the combining vowel *-i-*, used in its etymological sense in Neo-Latin and Neo-Greek combinations: **menticide, menticulture, mentimeter**. Also, **ment-²: mental²**. Related form: **monstri-**.

1603 mento- A word-initial combining element, derived from Latin *ment(um)* 'chin' plus the combining vowel *-o-*, used in its etymological sense in biomedical terminology: **mentoanterior, mentolabial, mentotransverse**. Also, **ment-¹, menti-¹: mental¹, mentigerous**.

1604 mer-¹ A variant of **mero-¹**.

1605 mer-² A variant of **mero-²**.

1606 mer-³ A variant of **mercuro-**.

1607 mer-⁴ A word-initial combining element, derived from Old English *mer(e)* 'pond, lake, sea,' used in its etymological sense in combination with other English elements: **mermaid, merman, merpeople**.

1608 mercapto- A word-initial combining element, derived from Late Latin *mer(curium) capt(ans)* 'quicksilver-capturing' (from Latin *Mercurius* 'the god (of commerce) Mercury,' later, 'the planet closest to the sun,' and, in Late Latin, 'the metallic element (Hg)' plus *captans,* the present participle of the verb 'to seize, capture') plus the combining vowel *-o-*, used in the sense of 'containing a member of the thiol group (-SH)' (because of the manner in which quicksilver (mercury) and the sulfurous members of the thiol group interact in combination) in chemical terminology: **mercaptomerin, mercaptophenyl, mercaptothiazole**. Also, **mercapt-: mercaptol**. Compare **mercuro-**. Related form: **market-**.

1609 mercuro- A word-initial combining element, derived from Late Latin *mercur(ius)* 'quicksilver, the metallic element (Hg)' (from Latin *Mercurius* 'the god of commerce (cf. *merx* 'goods'), later identified with the Greek god Hermes,' later, 'the planet closest to the sun') plus the combining vowel *-o-*, used in its late Latin sense in chemical terminology: **mercurochrome, mercurophen, mercurophylline**. Also, **mer-³, merco-, mercu-, mercur-: merbromin, mercocresols, mercupurin, mercurammonium**. Compare **mercapto-**. Related form: **market-**.

1610 mero-¹ A word-initial combining element, derived from Greek *méro(s)* 'part, portion,' used in its etymological and extended senses in Neo-Greek combinations: **meroacrania, merogenesis, meromicrosomia.** Also, **mer-¹, meri-: merergastic, merispore.**

1611 **mero-²** A word-initial combining element, derived from Greek *mēró(s)* 'thigh,' used in its etymological sense in biomedical combinations: **merocele, merocoxalgia, merosthenic.** Also, **mer-²: meralgia.**

1612 **merry-** A word-initial combining element, also occurring as a word, derived from Old English *myri(ġ)e* 'pleasing' 'perhaps' from an Indo-European root meaning 'short,' the idea being, presumably, that that which is of short duration is pleasing), used in the extended sense of 'joyous' and in extensions of this sense in combination with other English elements: **merry-go-round, merrymaker, merrythought.** Related forms(?): **brachio-, brachy-, brevi-.**

1613 **mes-** A variant of **meso-.**

1614 **mesati-** A word-initial combining element, derived from Greek *mé(s)sat(os)* 'middle,' literally, 'middlemost' (cf. *mésos* 'middle') plus the combining vowel *-i-,* used in the sense of 'medium-sized' in biomedical terminology: **mesaticephalic, mesatikerkik, mesatipelvic.** Compare **meso-.**

1615 **mesi-** A variant of **meso-.**

1616 **mesio-** A word-initial combining element, derived from Greek *més(os)* 'middle' plus the adjective-forming suffix *-ial,* used chiefly in the sense of 'closer to the center line of the dental arch' in the terminology of dentistry: **mesiobuccal, mesiolingual, mesioversion.** Compare **meso-.**

1617 **meso-** A word-initial combining element, derived from Greek *méso(s)* 'middle,' used in its etymological and extended senses in a variety of combinations: **Mesoamerica, meso-omentum, mesopneumon.** Also, **m-¹, mes-, mesi-: m-tartaric (acid), mesencephalon, mesiad.** Compare **mesati-, mesio-.** Related forms: **medi-, mezzo-, mid-, middle-.**

1618 **meta-** A word-initial combining element, derived from Greek *metá* 'between, among, along with, next to, over, behind, after,' used in its various etymological and extended senses, chief among these being 'changing, exchanging, changed' and, in chemical terminology, 'acid formed by the combination of one molecule of an oxide with one molecule of water,' 'benzene derivative in which two of

the hydrogen atoms have been replaced by other atoms or groups,'
and 'polymer,' in a variety of combinations: **metalinguistic, metameric, metasilicate.** Also, **m-², met-, meto-: m-dinitrobenzene, me-
tergasis, metoxenous.**

1619 metallo-   A word-initial combining element, derived from Greek
métallo(n) 'mine' and, by extension, 'mineral, metal,' used in this
latter sense in Neo-Greek combinations: **metallophobia, metalloporphyrin, metallotherapy.** Also, **metall-: metallesthesia.**

1620 meteoro-   A word-initial combining element, derived from Greek
metéōro(s) 'upraised, high,' hence, 'in the air,' hence, 'heavenly
body, atmospheric phenomenon' plus the combining vowel -*o*-,
used in this last and extended senses in Neo-Greek and Neo-Latin
combinations: **meteorology, meteorophobia, meteororesistant.**
Also, **meteor-: meteorism.**

1621 metepi-   See **met(a)-** and **epi-.**

1622 meth-   A variant of **methyl-.**

1623 methyl-   A word-initial combining element, also occurring as a
word, derived through French from Greek *méth(y)* 'mead, wine,
strong (alcoholic) drink' plus *(h)ýlē* 'wood, matter,' used in the
sense of 'of, pertaining to, containing, or derived from wood spirit
(CH_3)' in chemical terminology: **methylamine, methylguanidine,
methylmorphine.** Also, **me-, meth-: meprobamate, methane.**

1624 meto-   A variant of **meta-.**

1625 metopo-   A word-initial combining element, derived from Greek
métōpo(n) 'forehead' (from *met(á)* 'over' plus *ōp(s)* 'eye, face'), used
in its etymological sense in Neo-Greek combinations: **meto-
podynia, metopopagus, metopoplasty.** Also, **metop-: metopic.**

1626 metr-¹   A variant of **metro-¹.**

1627 metr-²   A variant of **metro-².**

1628 metr-³   A variant of **metro-³.**

1629 metro-¹   A word-initial combining element, derived from Greek
mḗt(ē)r, mēt(e)r(ós) 'mother' plus the combining vowel -*o*-, appearing in its etymological and extended senses in borrowings from
Greek and in Neo-Greek combinations: **metrocracy, metrocyte,**

metropolis. Also, **matr-, matro-, metr-¹: matronymic, matroclinous, metronymic.** Compare **metro-².** Related forms: **matri-, mother-.**

1630   **metro-²**   A word-initial combining element, derived from Greek *mḗtr(a)* 'womb' (cf. Greek *mḗtēr* 'mother') plus the combining vowel *-o-,* used in the sense of 'of or pertaining to the uterus' and in extensions of this sense in biomedical terminology: **metrofibroma, metroplasty, metrostaxis.** Also, **metr-², metra-: metritis, metratomy.** Compare **metro-¹.**

1631   **metro-³**   A word-initial combining element, derived from Greek *métro(n)* 'measure,' used in its etymological and extended senses in Neo-Greek combinations: **metrograph, metromania, metronome.** Also, **metr-³: metric.** Related forms: **meno-, moon-.**

1632   **mezzo-**   A word-initial combining element, derived from Italian *mezzo* 'middle' (from Latin *medius* 'middle'), appearing in its etymological and extended senses in a few borrowings from Italian: **mezzo-rilievo, mezzo-soprano, mezzotint.** Compare **medi-.**

1633   **mi-**   A variant of **mio-.**

1634   **micro-**   A word-initial combining element, derived from Greek *mikró(s)* 'small,' used in its etymological and extended senses, chief among these being 'one millionth,' in a variety of combinations: **microbacterium, microdot, microliter.** Also, **micr-: micracoustic.**

1635   **microbio-**   A word-initial combining element, derived from Greek *mikró(s)* 'small' plus *bío(s)* 'life,' used in the sense of 'of or pertaining to minute organisms' in Neo-Greek combinations: **microbiohemia, microbiology, microbiophobia.** Also, **microb-, microbi-: microbic, microbivorous.** Compare **micro-, bio-.**

1636   **mid-**   A word-initial combining element, also occurring as a word, derived from Old English *mid(d)* '(in the) middle (of),' used in its etymological and extended senses in combination with other English elements: **midair, midbrain, midwinter.** Compare **middle-.** Related forms: **medi-, mesati-, mesio-, meso-, mezzo-.**

1637   **middle-**   A word-initial combining element, also occurring as a word, derived from Old English *middel* 'having the same quantity on either side' (from Old English *midd* '(in the) middle (of)' plus the adjective-forming suffix *-el*), used in its etymological and extended senses in combination with other English elements: **middle-aged, middle-of-the-road, middleweight.** Compare **mid-.**

1638   **mil-¹**   A variant of **mille-**.

1639   **mil-²**   A variant of **milli-²**.

1640   **milk-**   A word-initial combining element, also occurring as a word, derived from Old English *milc* 'nutritive fluid secreted by the mammary glands of mammals,' used in its etymological and extended senses in combination with other English elements: **milkman, milksop, milkweed.**

1641   **mill-¹**   A variant of **mille-**.

1642   **mill-²**   A word-initial combining element, also occurring as a word, derived through Old English from Late Latin *mol(īnum)* 'building in which grain is ground' (cf. Latin *molere* 'to grind'), used in its etymological and extended senses in combination with other English elements: **millcake, milldam, millstone.** Related form: **mylo-**.

1643   **mille-**   A word-initial combining element, derived from Latin *mille* 'one thousand,' appearing in the sense of 'many' in borrowings from French and Italian and in Neo-Latin combinations: **millefiori, millepede, millepore.** Also, **mil-¹, mill-¹, milli-¹: milfoil, millennium, millipede.** Compare **milli-²**.

1644   **milli-¹**   A variant of **mille-**.

1645   **milli-²**   A word-initial combining element, derived from Latin *mill(e)* 'one thousand' plus the combining vowel -*i*-, used in the sense of 'one thousandth' in scientific terminology: **milliampere, millibar, millinormal.** Also, **mil-²: milammeter.** Compare **mille-**.

1646   **mine-**   A word-initial combining element, also occurring as a word, derived through Old French from one of the Celtic languages (cf. Gaelic *mein* and Welsh *mwyn* 'ore; (subterranean) source of ore'), used chiefly in the extended sense of 'subterranean or underwater explosive device used in warfare' in combination with other English elements: **minefield, minelayer, minesweeper.**

1647   **mini-**   A word-initial combining element, derived by abstraction from English *mini(ature)* 'small (likeness)' (from Latin *mināre* 'to illuminate, rubricate (with red lead)' (from *minium* 'red lead, cinnabar')) and influenced by *mini(mum)* 'least' (from Latin *minimum* 'least'), used in the sense of 'small, short' in combination with other English elements: **minibus, minicourse, miniskirt.** Related forms(?): **mio-², mis-²**.

1648   **mio-¹**   A variant of **myo-**.

1649   **mio-²**   A word-initial combining element, derived from Greek *m(e)iō̆(n)*, *m(e)îo(n)* 'less(er),' used in its etymological and extended senses, chief among these being 'diminished,' in Neo-Greek combinations: **miolecithal, mioplasmia, miophygmia**. Also, **meio-, meion-, mi-: meiophyly, meionite, miopus**. Related forms: **mini-(?), mis-²**.

1650   **mis-¹**   A word-initial combining element, derived from Old English *mis-* 'wrong(ly), bad(ly)' (from an Indo-European root meaning 'change, pass,' the idea being, presumably, that something which is wrongly or badly done represents a change or a turning from the norm), appearing in its etymological and extended senses, reinforced by **mis-²**, in combination with other English elements: **miscarry, misdeed, mislead**. Related forms: **mad-, meato-**.

1651   **mis-²**   A word-initial combining element, derived through Old French from Latin *mi(nu)s* 'less,' appearing in the sense of 'wrong(ly), bad(ly)' in borrowings from French and Latin: **misadventure, mischief, miscreant**. Related forms: **mini-(?), mio-**.

1652   **mis-³**   A variant of **miso-**.

1653   **miso-**   A word-initial combining element, derived from Greek *mîso(s)* 'hatred,' used in its etymological and extended senses in borrowings from Greek and in Neo-Greek combinations: **misocainia, misologia, misopedia**. Also, **mis-³: misanthropic**.

1654   **mito-**   A word-initial combining element, derived from Greek *míto(s)* 'thread,' used in its etymological and extended senses in Neo-Greek combinations: **mitochondria, mitogenetic, mitokinesis**. Also, **mit-: mitosis**.

1655   **mixo-**   A word-initial combining element, derived from Greek *mîx(is)* '(a) mingling' (from the verb *mignúnai* 'to mingle, combine') plus the combining vowel *-o-*, appearing in its etymological and extended senses in borrowings from Greek and in Neo-Greek combinations: **mixobarbaric, mixolydian (mode), mixoscopia**.

1656   **mock-**   A word-initial combining element, also occurring as a word, derived from Old French *moqu(er)* '(to) ridicule, make fun of,' used in the extended sense of 'imitation' and in extensions of this sense in combination with other English elements: **mock-apple, mock-heroic, mock-up**.

1657   **mogi-**   A word-initial combining element, derived from Greek *mógi(s)* 'with difficulty' (cf. Greek *mógos* 'toil'), used in its etymological and extended senses in Neo-Greek combinations: **mogiarthria, mogigraphia, mogilalia.**

1658 mon- A variant of **mono-.**

1659 money- A word-initial combining element, also occurring as a word, derived through Old French from Latin *monē(ta)* 'mint' (from *Monēta,* an epithet (of obscure origin) of the goddess Juno in whose Roman temple coins were minted), used in the sense of 'coin, currency' and in extensions of this sense in combination with other English elements: **moneybags, moneychanger, moneywort.**

1660 monkey- A word-initial combining element, also occurring as a word, perhaps derived from Middle Low German *Mon(e)ke,* the name of Martin the Ape's son in *The Story of Renard the Fox* (from Proto-Romance **mon(no)* 'simian creature' (possibly from Turkish *maimun* 'ape') plus a diminutive suffix), used chiefly in extensions of the sense of 'simian primate' in combination with other English elements: **monkey-bread, monkey-flower, monkeyshine.**

1661 mono- A word-initial combining element, derived from Greek *mono-,* a combining form of *móno(s)* 'single, only,' used in its etymological and extended senses in Neo-Greek and Neo-Latin combinations: **monobasic, monogametic, monoinfection.** Also, **mon-: monarch.**

1662 monstri- A word-initial combining element, derived from Latin *monstr(um), monstr(ī)* 'omen; supernatural manifestation,' hence, 'horrific supernatural being; supernatural manifestation' (ultimately from the verb *monēre* 'to warn,' literally, 'to make mindful of') plus the combining vowel *-i-,* used chiefly in the sense of 'of or pertaining to a fetus or an infant with substantial physical abnormalities' in Neo-Latin combinations: **monstricide, monstriferous, monstriparity.** Related form: **menti-².**

1663 moon- A word-initial combining element, also occurring as a word, derived from Old English *mōn(a)* 'the earth's natural satellite,' used in its etymological and extended senses in combination with other English elements: **moonbeam, mooncalf, moonflower.** Related forms: **meno-, metro-³.**

1664 morpho- A word-initial combining element, derived from Greek *morph(ḗ)* 'form, shape' plus the combining vowel *-o-,* used in its etymological and extended senses in Neo-Greek and Neo-Latin

combinations: **morphodifferentiation, morphogenetic, morphophoneme.** Related form(?): **form-**[1].

1665 **moss-**   A word-initial combining element, also occurring as a word,
derived from Old English *mos* 'bog' (from an Indo-European root
meaning 'wet'), used in the extended sense of 'green plant of the
class *Musci*' and in extensions of this sense in combination with
other English elements: **mossback, moss-grown, mosstrooper.**

1666 **mother-**   A word-initial combining element, also occurring as a
word, derived from Old English *mōdor* 'female parent,' used chiefly
in extensions of this sense in combination with other English
elements: **mother-in-law, motherland, mother-naked.** Related
forms: **matri-, metro-**[1]**, metro-**[2]**.**

1667 **motor-**   A word-initial combining element, also occurring as a word,
derived from Latin *mōtor* 'mover' (from *mōt(us)*, the past participle
of the verb *mōvēre* 'to move,' plus the agentive suffix *-or*), used in
the sense of 'that which produces motion' and in extensions of this
sense, chief among these being, 'of or pertaining to muscular
activity' and 'engine-powered,' in a variety of combinations:
motorbike, motorgraphic, motorpathy. Also, **moto-, motoro-:**
motofacient, motorogerminative.

1668 **mouse-**   A word-initial combining element, also occurring as a
word, derived from Old English *mūs* 'rodent of the genus *Mus*,'
used in its etymological and extended senses in combination with
other English elements: **mousefish, mousehole, mousetrap.** Related
forms: **musculo-, myelino-, myelo-, myo-.**

1669 **mouth-**   A word-initial combining element, also occurring as a
word, derived from Old English *mūþ* 'anterior opening of the
alimentary canal,' used in its etymological and extended senses in
combination with other English elements: **mouthbreeder, mouthpiece, mouthwash.** Related form: **mandibulo-.**

1670 **mu-** (M, μ)   A word-initial combining element, the twelfth letter of
the Greek alphabet, used chiefly as a designation of 'the twelfth
carbon atom in a straight chain compound or a derivative thereof
in which the substitute group is attached to that atom' in chemical
terminology. See **alpha-.**

1671 **muc-**   A variant of **muco-.**

1672 **muci-**   A variant of **muco-.**

1673 **mucino-** A word-initial combining element, derived from English *mucin* 'one of a number of nitrogenous glucoproteins or polysaccharides found in mucus secretions' (from Latin *mūc(us)* 'slimy substance produced by (nasal) membranes' plus the suffix *-in* which is used in naming enzymes) plus the combining vowel *-o-*, used in its etymological sense in biomedical combinations: **mucinoblast, mucinogen, mucinolytic.** Also, **mucin-: mucinuria.** Compare **muco-.**

1674 **muck-** A word-initial combining element, also occurring as a word, derived through Middle English from Old Norse *myki* 'dung' (from an Indo-European root meaning 'slime'), used in its etymological and extended senses in combination with other English elements: **muck-heap, muckrake, muckworm.** Related forms: **match-², mucino-, muco-, myco-¹, myco-², myxo-.**

1675 **muco-** A word-initial combining element, derived from Latin *mūc(us)* 'slimy substance produced by (nasal) membranes' plus the combining vowel *-o-*, used in its etymological and extended senses in biomedical combinations: **mucoprotein, mucopus, mucosanguinous.** Also, **muc-, muci-: mucin, muciform.** Compare **mucino-.** Related forms: **match², muck-, myco-¹, myco-², myxo-.**

1676 **mud-** A word-initial combining element, also occurring as a word, derived through Middle English from Middle Low German *mud(de)* 'soft, wet earth,' used in its etymological and extended senses in combination with other English elements: **mudcap, mudhole, mudslinging.**

1677 **multi-** A word-initial combining element, derived from Latin *multi-*, a combining form of *mult(us)* 'many,' used in its etymological sense in a variety of combinations: **multilateral, multiphase, multishot.**

1678 **musculo-** A word-initial combining element, derived through Old French from Latin *musc(u)l(us)* 'muscle,' literally, 'little mouse' (from *mūs* 'mouse' plus the diminutive suffix *-ulus,* the idea being that the visible movements of muscles resemble those of a mouse) plus the combining vowel *-o-*, used in its etymological sense in biomedical combinations: **musculocutaneous, musculodermic, musculoelastic.** Also, **muscul-: musculin.** Related forms: **mouse-, myelino-, myelo-, myo-.**

1679 **musico-** A word-initial combining element, derived from Greek *mousikó(s)* 'of or pertaining to the Muses, esp. the Muses of lyric poetry and song' (from *Moûs(a)* 'Muse' plus the adjective-forming suffix -*ikos*), used in the sense of 'of or pertaining to the art of combining sounds in sequence to produce aesthetic pleasure in the listener' in Neo-Greek combinations: **musicogenic, musicomania, musicotherapy.**

1680 **my-**[1] A variant of **myo-.**

1681 **my-**[2] A variant of **myi-.**

1682 **myc-** A variant of **myco-**[2].

1683 **myceto-** A variant of **myco-**[2].

1684 **myco-**[1] A word-initial combining element, derived from Greek *mŷko(s)* 'mucus' (from an Indo-European root meaning 'slime'), used in its etymological and extended sense in Neo-Greek combinations: **mycodermatitis, mycofibroma, mycopus.** Compare **myco-**[2], **myxo-.** Related forms: **mucino-, muck-, muco-.**

1685 **myco-**[2] A word-initial combining element, derived from Greek *mýk(ēs), mýk(ētos)* 'fungus, mushroom' (from an Indo-European root meaning 'slime,' the idea being, presumably, that mushrooms are slimy to the touch), used in its etymological sense in Neo-Greek and Neo-Latin combinations: **mycoagglutinin, mycohemia, mycology.** Also, **myc-, mycet-, myceto-: mycelium, mycethemia, mycetogenic.** Compare **myco-**[1], **myxo-.** Related forms: **mucino-, muck-, muco-.**

1686 **myel-** A variant of **myelo-.**

1687 **myelino-** A word-initial combining element, derived from English *myelin* 'lipoid substance sheathing certain nerve fibers; lipoid substance found in body tissue' (from Greek *myel(ós)* 'marrow' plus the suffix -*in* which is used in naming chemical compounds which are neither basic nor acidic) plus the combining vowel -*o*-, used in its etymological sense in biomedical terminology: **myelinoclasis, myelinogenesis, myelinolysin.** Also, **myelin-: myelinic.** Compare **myelo-.**

1688 **myelo-** A word-initial combining element, derived from Greek *myeló(s)* 'marrow' (from *mû(s)* 'muscle' plus the derivative suffix -*elos*), used in its etymological and extended senses, chief among these being 'of or pertaining to the spinal cord; of or pertaining to *myelin*,' in biomedical terminology: **myelocone, myelocyte, myelolysis.** Also, **myel-: myelatrophy.** Compare **myelino-, myo-.**

1689 myi- A word-initial combining element, derived from Greek *myî(a)* '(a) fly,' used in its etymological and extended senses in Neo-Greek combinations: *Myiadestes, Myiagra, Myiarchus.* Also, **my-²**, **myio-**: **myiasis, myiocephalon.**

1690 mylo- A word-initial combining element, derived from Greek *mýl(ē)* 'mill, molar' (from an Indo-European root meaning 'to grind') plus the combining vowel *-o-*, used chiefly with reference to 'the molar teeth' in Neo-Greek combinations: **myloglossus, mylohyoid, mylopharyngeus.** Also, **myl-**: **mylodont.** Related form: **mill-².**

1691 myo- A word-initial combining element, derived from Greek *mû(s)*, *my(ós)* 'mouse' and, by extension, 'muscle' (because the visible movement of a muscle resembles that of a mouse) plus the combining vowel *-o-*, used in both of its etymological senses in Neo-Greek combinations: **myoatrophy, myofibril, myomancy.** Also, **mio-¹**, **my-¹**: **miophone, myurous.** Compare **myelo-.** Related forms: **mouse-, musculo-.**

1692 myocardio- A word-initial combining element, derived from **myo-** plus **cardio-**, used in the sense of 'of or pertaining to the muscular substance of the heart' in biomedical combinations: **myocardiogram, myocardiograph, myocardiorrhaphy.** Also **myocardi-**: **myocarditis, myocardiosis.** Compare **myo-, cardio-.**

1693 myoneur- See **myo-** and **neur(o)-.**

1694 myri-¹ A variant of **myrio-.**

1695 myri-² A variant of **myria-².**

1696 myria-¹ A variant of **myrio-.**

1697 myria-² A word-initial combining element, derived from Greek *mýria* 'ten thousand' (from the nominative-accusative neuter plural form of *myríos* 'countless'), appearing in its etymological sense in borrowings from Greek and in Neo-Greek combinations: **myriagram, myrialiter, myriameter.** Also **myri-²**: **myriarch.** Compare **myrio-.**

1698 myringo- A word-initial combining element, derived from Scientific Latin *myring(a)* 'tympanic membrane' plus the combining vowel *-o-*, used in its etymological sense in biomedical terminology: **myringodermatitis, myringomycosis, myringoplasty.** Also, **myring-, myringod-**: **myringitis, myringodectomy.**

1699 **myrio-** A word-initial combining element, derived from Greek *myrío(s)* 'countless, innumerable' used in its etymological sense in Neo-Greek combinations: **myriophyllous, myriopod, myriosporous.** Also, **myri-¹, myria-¹: myriacanthous, myriapod.** Compare **myria-².**

1700 **myrmeco-** A word-initial combining element, derived from Greek *mýrmē(x), mýrmēk(os)* 'ant' plus the combining vowel *-o-,* used in its etymological sense in Neo-Greek combinations: **myrmecology, myrmecophagous, myrmecophile.** Also, **myrme-, myrmic-:** *Myrmeleon, Myrmicidae.* Related form: **form-².**

1701 **myro-** A word-initial combining element, derived from Greek *mýro(n)* 'unguent, perfume,' used in its etymological and extended senses in Neo-Greek combinations: **myrobalan, myropolist,** *Myroxylon.* Also, **myr-, myron-: myrosin, myronic.**

1702 **mytho-** A word-initial combining element, derived from Greek *mŷtho(s)* 'that which is delivered by word of mouth; story; legend,' used in its etymological and extended senses in Neo-Greek combinations: **mythology, mythomania, mythophobia.**

1703 **myxo-** A word-initial combining element, derived from Greek *mýx(a)* '(nasal) mucus' (from an Indo-European root meaning 'slime') plus the combining vowel *-o-,* used in its etymological and extended senses in biomedical terminology: **myxoblastoma, myxoglobulosis, myxorrhea.** Also, **myx-: myxedema.** Compare **match-², myco-¹, myco-².** Related forms: **mucino-, muck-, muco-.**

N

1704 **n-** A word-initial combining element, an abbreviation of English *n(ormal)*, used in the sense of 'normal (as opposed to isomeric)' in chemical terminology: **n-butane, n-butanol.** Compare **nor-[1], normo-.**

1705 **nail-** A word-initial combining element, also occurring as a word, derived from Old English *næ(ġe)l* 'horny covering of the finger or toe' and, by extension, 'metal spike,' used in its etymological and extended senses in combination with other English elements: **nailbone, nailbrush, nailhead.** Related form: **onycho-.**

1706 **nano-** A word-initial combining element, derived through Latin from Greek *nán(n)o(s)* 'dwarf,' used in its etymological and extended senses, chief among these being 'one billionth,' in a variety of combinations: **nanocormia, nanocurie, nanosecond.**

1707 **naphtho-** A word-initial combining element, derived through Latin from Greek *náphth(as)* 'volatile petroleum derivative' (perhaps from one of the Semitic languages (cf. Akkadian *nabāṭu* 'to ignite')) plus the combining vowel *-o-*, used in its etymological and extended senses, chief among these being 'of, pertaining to, containing, or derived from the coal-tar derivative *naphthol* $(C_{10}H_7 \cdot OH)$,' in chemical terminology: **naphthopyrine, naphthoquinone, naphthoresorcine.** Also, **naphth-: naphthamine.**

1708 **narco-** A word-initial combining element, derived from Greek *nárk(ē)* 'numbness' (from an Indo-European root meaning 'twist,

243

bind') plus the combining vowel *-o-*, used in its etymological and extended senses in biomedical terminology: **narcoanesthesia, narcomania, narcostimulant.** Also, **narc-: narcose.** Related form(?): **narrow-.**

1709 narrow- A word-initial combining element, also occurring as a word, derived from Old English *nearu* 'close, constricted' (perhaps from an Indo-European root meaning 'twist, bind'), used in its etymological and extended senses in combination with other English elements: **narrow-gage, narrow-minded, narrow-mouthed (toad).** Related form(?): **narco-.**

1710 naso- A word-initial combining element, derived from Latin *nās(us)* 'nose' plus the combining vowel *-o-*, used in its etymological sense in biomedical terminology: **nasoantritis, nasolabial, nasosinusitis.** Also, **nas-: nasal.** Related form: **nose-.**

1711 ne- A variant of **neo-.**

1712 near- A word-initial combining element, also occurring as a word, derived from Old Norse *náer* 'closer,' used in the sense of 'close' and in extensions of this sense in combination with other English elements: **nearby, near-hand, near-sighted.**

1713 neck- A word-initial combining element, also occurring as a word, derived from Old English *(h)nec(ca)* 'portion of the body between the head and the thorax' (perhaps from an Indo-European root meaning 'constriction'), used in its etymological and extended senses in combination with other English elements: **necklace, neckline, necktie.** Related forms(?): **nucleo-, nut-.**

1714 necro- A word-initial combining element, derived from Greek *nekró(s)* 'corpse,' used in its etymological and extended senses, chief among these being 'of or pertaining to death,' in a variety of combinations: **necrobiosis, necropyoculture, necrosadism.** Also, **necr-, necron-: necremia, necronectomy.** Related form: **noci-.**

1715 needle- A word-initial combining element, also occurring as a word, derived from Old English *nǣdl* 'thin pointed sewing implement' (from an Indo-European root meaning 'sew, spin'), used in its etymological and extended senses in combination with other English elements: **needlefish, needlepoint, needlework.** Related form: **nemato-.**

1716 nemato- A word-initial combining element, derived from Greek *nêma, némat(os)* 'that which is spun; thread' (from an Indo-

European root meaning 'sew, spin') plus the combining vowel *-o-,* used in the sense of 'of or pertaining to a threadlike structure, esp. a *nematode,* a threadlike endoparasite,' in Neo-Greek and Neo-Latin combinations: **nematocide, nematology, nematospermia.** Also, **nemat-, nemati-: nemathelminth, nematicide.** Related form: **needle-.**

1717 **neo-**   A word-initial combining element, derived from Greek *néo(s)* 'new,' used in its etymological and extended senses, chief among these being 'recent' and, in chemical terminology, 'isomer with a carbon atom attached to four other carbon atoms,' in a variety of combinations: **neoarsphenamine, Neo-Darwinism, neonatal.** Also, **ne-: neencephalon.** Related forms: **new-, news-, novo-.**

1718 **nephelo-**   A word-initial combining element, derived from Greek *nephél(ē)* 'cloud' plus the combining vowel *-o-,* used in its etymological and extended senses in Neo-Greek combinations: **nephelometer, nephelopsychosis, nephelosphere.** Also, **nephel-: nephelopia.**

1719 **nephro-**   A word-initial combining element, derived from Greek *nephró(s)* 'kidney,' used in its etymological sense in biomedical terminology: **nephroabdominal, nephrocirrhosis, nephrolith.** Also, **nephr-: nephritis.**

1720 **nervo-**   A word-initial combining element, derived from Latin *nerv(us)* 'sinew' and, by extension, 'nerve fiber' plus the combining vowel *-o-,* used in the sense of 'of or pertaining to a nerve or nerves' in Neo-Latin combinations: **nervocidine, nervomuscular, nervotabes.** Also, **nerv-, nervi-: nervine, nervimotor.** Related forms: **neuro-, neuron-.**

1721 **neuro-**   A word-initial combining element, derived from Greek *neûro(n)* 'sinew' and, by extension, 'nerve fiber,' used in the sense of 'of or pertaining to a nerve or nerves' in biomedical terminology: **neuroanastomosis, neuroceptor, neurohypophysis.** Also, **neur-, neuri-: neurectomy, neurimotor.** Compare **neuron-.** Related form: **nervo-.**

1722 **neuron-**   A word-initial combining element, also occurring as a word, derived from Greek *neûron* 'sinew' and, by extension, 'nerve fiber,' used in the sense of 'of or pertaining to a nerve cell or nerve cells' and in extensions of this sense in Neo-Greek combinations: **neuronagenesis, neuronatrophy, neuronitis.** Also, **neurono-: neuronotropic.** Compare **neuro-.** Related form: **nervo-.**

1723 neutro- A word-initial combining element, derived from Latin *neutr(um)* 'neither (of the two)' (from *ne* 'not' plus *utrum* 'either (of two)') plus the combining vowel *-o-*, used in its etymological and extended senses, chief among these being 'of or pertaining to *neutrophils,* cells which are readily stainable by neutral (neither acid nor basic) dies,' in Neo-Latin and Neo-Greek combinations: **neutroclusion, neutropenia, neutrosphere.** Also, **neutr-: neutral.** Compare **non-[1], nulli-.** Related forms: **a-[1], an-[1], i-, il-[1], im-[1], in-[1], ir-[1], never-, no-, un-[1].**

1724 never- A word-initial combining element, also occurring as a word, derived from Old English *nǣfre* 'at no time' (from *ne* 'not' plus *ǣfre* 'ever'), used in its etymological and extended senses in combination with other English elements: **nevermind, nevermore, never-never.** Compare **no-** and **ever-.** Related forms: **a-[1], an-[1], i-, il-[1], im-[1], in-[1], ir-[1], neutro-, non-[1], nulli-, un-[1].**

1725 nevo- A word-initial combining element, derived from Latin *n(a)ev(us)* 'birthmark, mole' (from an Indo-European root meaning 'beget, be born') plus the combining vowel *-o-*, used in its etymological and extended senses in biomedical terminology: **nevocarcinoma, nevolipoma, nevoxanthoendothelioma.** Also, **nev-: nevose.** Related forms: **genito-, geno-, gentle-, gonado-, gone-[1], gono-[1], king-.**

1726 new A word-initial combining element, also occurring as a word, derived from Old English *nē(o)w(e)* 'of recent origin,' used in its etymological and extended senses in combination with other English elements: **newborn, newcomer, newfangled.** Compare **news-.** Related forms: **neo-, novo-.**

1727 news- A word-initial combining element, also occurring as a word, the plural form of English *new* 'of recent origin' (from Old English *nē(o)w(e)* 'of recent origin'), modeled on Latin *nova* or French *nouvelles* 'new things; tidings (of new things),' used in the sense of 'tidings (of new things)' and in extensions of this sense in combination with other English elements: **newspaper, newsprint, newsreel.** Compare **new-.**

1728 nickel- A word-initial combining element, also occurring as a words, derived through Swedish from German (*Kupfer*)*nickel* 'the metallic element (Ni),' literally, 'copper-demon' (because nickel ore does not yield copper although it looks as though it should), used in its etymological and extended senses in combination with other English elements: **nickelodeon, nickel-plate, nickeltype.**

1729 **nidi-**   A word-initial combining element, derived from Latin *nīd(us)* 'nest' plus the combining vowel *-i-*, used in its etymological and extended senses in Neo-Latin combinations: **nidicolous, nidificate, nidifugous.** Also, **nid-: nidal.**

1730 **night-**   A word-initial combining element, also occurring as a word, derived from Old English *ni(e)ht* 'period between sunset and sunrise,' used in its etymological and extended senses in combination with other English elements: **nightcap, nightmare, nightshade.** Related forms: **noct-, nycto-.**

1731 **Nilo-**   A word-initial combining element, derived from Latin *Nīl(us)* '(the river) Nile' (perhaps from Old Egyptian *nwy* 'river') plus the combining vowel *-o-*, used in its etymological and extended senses in a variety of combinations: **Nilo-Hamitic, Nilometer, Nilo-Saharan.** Also, **nilo-: nilometer.**

1732 **nine-**   A word-initial combining element, also occurring as a word, derived from Old English *ni(ġo)n* 'the cardinal number between *eight* and *ten*,' used in its etymological and extended senses in combination with other English elements: **ninebark, ninepence, ninepins.** Related forms: **ennea-, nona-, noon-.**

1733 **nitro-**   A word-initial combining element, derived through French and Latin from Greek *nitro(n)* 'sodium carbonate, natron' (from Old Egyptian *ntr(j)* 'natron ($Na_2CO_3 \cdot 10H_2O$)'), used in the sense of 'containing the univalent group (NO_2)' in chemical terminology: **nitrobenzene, nitroglycerin, nitroprotein.** Also, **nitr-: nitrate.** Compare **nitroso-.**

1734 **nitroso-**   A word-initial combining element, derived from Neo-Latin *nitrōs(us)* 'full of sodium carbonate; full of natron' (from *nitr(um)*, a borrowing of Greek *nitro(n)* 'sodium carbonate; natron,' plus the suffix *-ōsus* 'full of') plus the combining vowel *-o-*, used in the sense of 'containing the group (-O:N)' and in extensions of this sense in chemical terminology: **nitrosobacteria, nitrosoindol, nitrososubstitution.** Also, **nitros-: nitrosamine.** Compare **nitro-.**

1735 **no-**   A word-initial combining element, derived from Old English *no-*, a combining form of *nān* 'none' (from *ne* 'not' plus *ān* 'one'), used in its etymological and extended senses in combination with other English elements: **no-account, nobody, no-hitter.** Compare **never-.** Related forms: **a-[1], an-[1], i-, il-[1], im-[1], in-[1], ir-[1], neutro-, non-[1], nulli-, un-[1].**

1736 **noci-**   A word-initial combining element, derived from Latin *noc(ēre)* 'to injure' plus the combining vowel *-i-,* used in the sense of 'injury, trauma' in biomedical terminology: **nociceptor, nocifensor, nociperception.** Related form: **necro-.**

1737 noct- A word-initial combining element, derived from Latin *no(x),* *noct(is)* 'night,' used in its etymological sense in Neo-Latin and Neo-Greek combinations: **noctalbuminuria, noctambulation, nocturia.** Also, **nocti-: noctiphobia.** Related forms: **night-, nycto-.**

1738 nomo- A word-initial combining element, derived from Greek *nómo(s)* 'custom, usage, law,' used in its etymological and extended senses in Neo-Greek combinations: **nomocanon, nomogenesis, nomotopic.** Also, **nom-: nomism.**

1739 non-[1] A word-initial combining element, derived through French from Latin *non* 'no, not' (from *ne* 'not' plus *ūn(us)* 'one'), used in its etymological and extended senses in borrowings from French and in combination with other English elements: **nonantigenic, nonconformist, nonstop.** Compare **neutro-, nulli-.** Related forms: **a-[1], an-[1], i-, il-[1], im-[1], in-[1], ir-[1], never-, no-, un-[1].**

1740 non-[2] A variant of **nona-.**

1741 nona- A word-initial combining element, derived from Latin *nōna* 'ninth,' used in its etymological sense and in the sense of 'nine' in Neo-Latin and Neo-Greek combinations: **nonacyclic, nonadecane, nonagon.** Also, **non-[2], noni-: nonyl, nonipara.** Compare **noon-.** Related forms: **ennea-, nine-.**

1742 noo- A word-initial combining element, derived from Greek *nóo(s)* 'mind, thought,' used in its etymological and extended senses in Neo-Greek combinations: **nookleptia, noopsyche, noothymopsychic.**

1743 noon- A word-initial combining element, also occurring as a word, derived through Old English from Latin *nōn(a hōra)* 'ninth (hour) (after sunrise),' hence, in Middle English, 'midday (meal),' hence, 'twelve p.m.,' used in the sense of 'midday' in combination with other English elements: **noonday, noontide, noontime.** Compare **nona-.**

1744 nor-[1] A word-initial combining element, an abbreviation of English *nor(mal)* 'ordinary, regular,' derived through French from Latin *normāl(is)* 'regular, standard' (from *norm(a)* 'standard, measure, rule' (from an Indo-European root meaning 'perceive, know') plus the adjective-forming suffix *-ālis*), used in the specialized sense of 'unaltered parent compound' in chemical terminology: **normo-adrenelin, noratropine, norleucine.** Compare **n-, normo-**. Related form(s): **know-, note-(?)**.

1745 **nor-²** A variant of **north-**.

1746 **nor'-** A variant of **north-**.

1747 **normo-** A word-initial combining element, derived from Latin *norm(a)* 'standard, measure, rule' (from an Indo-European root meaning 'perceive, know') plus the combining vowel *-o-,* used in the sense of 'standard, regular, usual' in Neo-Latin and Neo-Greek combinations: **normocytosis, normosexual, normothermia.** Also, **norm-: normergic.** Compare **n-, nor-¹.** Related form(s): **know-, note-(?).**

1748 **north-** A word-initial combining element, also occurring as a word, derived from Old English *norþ* 'the direction to the left as one faces the rising sun,' used in its etymological and extended senses in combination with other English elements: **northbound, northeast, Northfield.** Also, **nor-², nor'-: Norman, nor'easter.**

1749 **nos-** A variant of **noso-**.

1750 **nose-** A word-initial combining element, also occurring as a word, derived from Old English *nos(u)* 'organ of smell,' used in its etymological and extended senses in combination with other English elements: **nosebleed, nose-dive, nosegay.** Related form: **naso-**.

1751 **noso-** A word-initial combining element, derived from Greek *nóso(s)* 'sickness, disease,' used in its etymological sense in Neo-Greek combinations: **nosogenesis, nosology, nosophobia.** Also, **nos-: nosetiology.**

1752 **not-¹** A variant of **note-**.

1753 **not-²** A variant of **noto-**.

1754 **note-** A word-initial combining element, also occurring as a word, derived through French from Latin *not(a)* 'sign, mark' and, in the plural, 'writing' (perhaps from the verb *noscere* 'to perceive, know,' the idea being that a *sign* is that by which one perceives or makes something known), used in its etymological and extended senses in combination with other English elements: **notebook, notecase,**

noteworthy. Also, **not-**[1]: **notable.** Related forms(?): **know-, n-, nor-**[1], **normo-.**

1755   noto-   A word-initial combining element, derived from Greek *nôto(s)* '(the) back,' used in its etymological and extended senses, chief among these being 'of or pertaining to the spinal cord,' in Neo-Greek combinations: **notochord, notogenesis, notomyelitis.** Also, **not-**[2]: **notanencephalia.**

1756   novo-   A word-initial combining element, derived from Latin *nov(us)* 'new' plus the combining vowel *-o-*, used in its etymological and extended senses in a variety of combinations: **novobiocin, novoepinephrine, novoscope.** Also, **nov-, novi-: novepithel, novilunar.** Related forms: **neo-, new-, news-.**

1757   nu- (N, *ν*)   A word-initial combining element, the thirteenth letter of the Greek alphabet, used chiefly to designate 'the thirteenth carbon atom in a straight chain compound or a derivative thereof in which the substitute group is attached to that atom' in chemical terminology. See **alpha-.**

1758   nucleo-   A word-initial combining element, derived from Latin *nucle(us)* 'nut, kernel (of a nut)' (from *nu(x), nuc(is)* 'nut' plus the diminutive suffix *-(u)l(us)* plus the suffix *-eus* '(that which is) made of') plus the combining vowel *-o-*, used in the sense of 'kernel; central part' and in extensions of this sense, chief among these being 'central part of a cell,' in a variety of combinations: **nucleofugal, nucleohistone, nucleospindle.** Also, **nucle-, nuclei-: nuclease, nucleiform.** Related form(s): **neck-(?), nut-.**

1759   nudi-   A word-initial combining element, derived from Latin *nūd(us)* 'naked' plus the combining vowel *-i-*, used in its etymological and extended senses in Neo-Latin and Neo-Greek combinations: **nudibranch, nudicaul, nudipelliferous.** Also, **nud-, nudo-: nudism, nudophobia.** Related form: **gymno-.**

1760   nulli-   A word-initial combining element, derived from Latin *null(us)* 'not any; none' (from *ne* 'not' plus *ull(us)* 'any') plus the combining vowel *-i-*, used in its etymological and extended senses in Neo-Latin and Neo-Greek combinations: **nulliparous, nullipennate, nullisomatic.** Compare **neutro-, non-**[1]. Related forms: **a-**[1], **an-**[1], **i-, il-**[1], **im-**[1], **in-**[1], **ir-**[1], **never-, no-, un-**[1].

1761   nut-   A word-initial combining element, also occurring as a word, derived from Old English *(h)nut(u)* 'hard-shelled fruit,' used in its etymological and extended senses in combination with other

English elements: **nutcracker, nutgall, nutmeg.** Related form(s): **neck-(?), nucleo-.**

1762 nycto-   A word-initial combining element, a combining form of Greek *ný(x)*, *nykt(ós)* 'night' plus the combining vowel -*o*-, used in its etymological sense in Neo-Greek combinations: **nyctohemeral, nyctophobia, nyctophonia.** Also, **nyct-: nyctalopia.** Related forms: **night-, noct-.**

1763 nympho-   A word-initial combining element, a combining form of Greek *nýmph(ē)* '(young) bride; woman of marriageable age' and, in the plural, by extension, 'labia minora' plus the combining vowel -*o*-, used chiefly in this last and extended senses in Neo-Greek and Neo-Latin combinations: **nymphocaruncular, nymphomaniac, nymphotomy.** Also, **nymph-: nymphectomy.**

O

1764   **O'-**   A word-initial combining element, derived through Irish Gaelic from Old Irish *ui* 'descendant,' appearing in a number of Anglo-Irish surnames in which its original sense was 'son of the person named by the combining root': **O'Brian, O'Connor, O'Sullivan.**

1765   **o-¹**   A variant of **ortho-.**

1766   **o-²**   A variant of **oo-.**

1767   **oak-**   A word-initial combining element, also occurring as a word, derived from Old English *āc* 'tree of the genus *Quercus*,' used in its etymological and extended senses in combination with other English elements: **oak-apple, oak-leaved (geranium), oakmoss.**

1768   **ob-**   A word-initial combining element, derived from Latin *ob* 'toward, against, in front of,' appearing in its etymological and extended senses in inherited and Neo-Latin combinations: **object, obovate, obviate.** Compare **oc-, of-², op-³.** Related forms: **epi-, opistho-.**

1769   **obtusi-**   A word-initial combining element, derived from Latin *obtūs(us),* the past participle of the verb *obtundere* 'to blunt, dull' (from *ob-* 'against' plus *tundere* 'to beat, strike'), plus the combining vowel *-i-,* used in the sense of 'blunted, rounded, not acute' in Neo-Latin combinations: **obtusifolious, obtusilingual, obtusilobous.**

253

1770 oc-   A word-initial combining element, derived from Latin *oc-*, a combining form of *ob-* 'toward, against, in front of,' appearing in its etymological and extended senses in inherited combinations in which the element to which it is joined begins with *c:* **occidental, occult, occupy.** Compare **ob-, of-[2], op-[3].** Related forms: **epi-, opistho-.**

1771 occipito-   A word-initial combining element, derived from Latin *occipit(um)* 'back of the head' (from *oc-* 'against, in front of' plus a combining form of *caput, capitis* 'head') plus the combining vowel *-o-,* used in the sense of 'of or pertaining to the *occiput* or to the *occipital bone*' in biomedical terminology: **occipitoanterior, occipitofacial, occipitothalamic.** Also, **occipit-: occipital.** Compare **oc-** and **capit-.**

1772 ocelli-   A word-initial combining element, derived from Latin *ocell(us)* 'little eye,' a diminutive of *oculus* 'eye,' plus the combining vowel *-i-,* used in its etymological and extended senses, chief among these being 'spotted, dotted (as though with tiny eyes),' in Neo-Latin and Neo-Greek combinations: **ocellicyst, ocelliferous, ocelligerous.** Also, **ocell-: ocellated.** Compare **oculo-.**

1773 ochro-   A word-initial combining element, derived from Greek *ōchró(s)* 'pale, sallow; pale yellow,' used in its etymological and extended senses in Neo-Greek combinations: **ochrodermatitis, ochrometer, ochronosis.**

1774 octo-   A word-initial combining element, derived from Greek *octṓ* and Latin *octō* 'eight,' used in its etymological sense in Neo-Greek and Neo-Latin combinations: **octogynous, octolateral, octopod.** Also, **oct-, octa-, octi-, octon-: octodont, octastich, octiparous, octonocular.** Related form: **eight-.**

1775 oculo-   A word-initial combining element, derived from Latin *ocul(us)* 'eye' plus the combining vowel *-o-,* used in its etymological sense in biomedical combinations: **oculocephalogyric, oculomotor, oculoreaction.** Also, **ocul-: oculist.** Compare **ocelli-.** Related forms: **eye-, ophthalmo-, opo-[1], optico-.**

1776 ocy-   A word-initial combining element, derived from Greek *ōkẏ(s)* 'swift,' used in its etymological sense in Neo-Greek combinations: **ocydrome, *Ocyphaps, Ocypoda.***

1777 odd-   A word-initial combining element, also occurring as a word, derived from Old Norse *odd(a)-,* a combining form of *oddi* 'angle, point, third or uneven number,' used in the sense of 'uneven' and in extensions of this sense in combination with other English elements: **oddball, odd-pinnate, oddside.**

1778 **odo-** A variant of **hodo-**.

1779 **odonto-** A word-initial combining element, derived from Greek *od(oús)*, *odónt(os)* 'tooth' plus the combining vowel -*o*-, used in its etymological and extended senses in Neo-Greek combinations: **odontoblastoma, odontoiatria, odontosteophyte.** Also, **odont-: odontitis.** Related forms: **denti-, tooth-.**

1780 **odori-** A word-initial combining element, derived from Latin *odor*, *odōr(is)* '(a) smell' plus the combining vowel -*i*-, used in its etymological and extended senses in Neo-Latin and Neo-Greek combinations: **odoriferous, odorimeter, odoriphore.** Also, **odoro-: odorography.** Related forms: **olfacto-, osmo-¹, osphresio-, ozo-, ozono-.**

1781 **odyno-** A word-initial combining element, derived from Greek *odýn(ē)* 'pain' plus the combining vowel -*o*-, used in its etymological and extended senses in Neo-Greek combinations: **odynolysis, odynometer, odynophagia.** Also, **odyn-: odynphagia.**

1782 **oeco-** A variant of **eco-**.

1783 **oeno-** A word-initial combining element, derived from Greek *oîno(s)* 'wine,' used in its etymological and extended senses in Neo-Greek combinations: **oenology, oenomania, oenomel.** Also, **eno-, oen-: enology, oenanthol.** Related forms: **vine-, vini-, wine-.**

1784 **oesophago-** A variant of **esophago-**.

1785 **of-¹** A word-initial combining element, derived from Old English *of* '(away) from,' appearing in its etymological and extended senses chiefly in now-obsolete combinations with other English elements: **ofcome, offal, ofsake.** Compare **off-.** Related forms: **a-², ab-, abs-, after-, apo-.**

1786 **of-²** A word-initial combining element, derived from Latin *of-*, a combining form of *ob* 'toward, against, in front of,' appearing in its etymological and extended senses in inherited combinations in which the element to which it is joined begins with *f*: **offend, offer, offuscate.** Compare **ob-, oc-, op-³.** Related forms: **epi-, opistho-.**

1787 **off-** A word-initial combining element, derived from Old English *of* '(away) from,' used in its etymological and extended senses in combination with other English elements: **offbeat, off-color, off-shoot.** Compare **of-[1].**

1788 oiko- A variant of **eco-.**

1789 oil- A word-initial combining element, also occurring as a word, derived through Old French and Latin from Greek *él(aion)* 'liquid expressed from olives' (cf. Greek *elaia* 'olive tree'), used in its etymological and extended senses in combination with other English elements: **oilcan, oilcloth, oilfish.** Compare **eleo-, oleo-.**

1790 old- A word-initial combining element, also occurring as a word, derived from Old English *(e)ald* 'aged' (from an Indo-European root meaning 'to grow'), used in its etymological and extended senses in combination with other English elements: **old-fashioned, old-maidish, old-man's-beard.** Related form: **alti-.**

1791 oleo- A word-initial combining element, derived from Latin *ole(um)* '(olive) oil' (from Greek *élaion* '(olive) oil' (cf. Greek *elaía* 'olive tree') plus the combining vowel *-o-*, used in its etymological and extended senses in Neo-Latin and Neo-Greek combinations: **oleochrysotherapy, oleogranuloma, oleomargarine.** Also, **ole-: olein.** Compare **eleo-, oil-.** Related form: **olive-.**

1792 olfacto- A word-initial combining element, derived from Latin *olfact(us)*, the past participle of the verb *olfacere* 'to smell' (from the root underlying *odor* 'smell' plus *facere* 'to do, make'), plus the combining vowel *-o-*, used in the sense of 'of or pertaining to the sense of smell' in biomedical terminology: **olfactology, olfactometer, olfactophobia.** Also, **olfact-: olfactism.** Related forms: **odori-, osmo-[1], osphresio-, ozo-, ozono-.**

1793 oligo- A word-initial combining element, derived from Greek *olígo(s)* 'few, little,' used in its etymological and extended senses in Neo-Greek and Neo-Latin combinations: **oligocystic, oligodynamic, oligonatality.** Also, **olig-: oligarchy.**

1794 olive- A word-initial combining element, also occurring as a word, derived through Old French and Latin from Greek *elaía* 'the tree *Olea europaea*,' used in its etymological and extended senses in combination with other English elements: **oliveback, olive-green, olivewort.** Related forms: **eleo-, oil-, oleo-.**

1795 om- A variant of **omo-.**

1796 omega- (Ω, ω) A word-initial combining element, the twenty-fourth parameter:

letter of the Greek alphabet, used chiefly to designate 'the twenty-fourth carbon atom in a straight chain compound or a derivative thereof in which the substitute group is attached to that atom' and to indicate 'the substitution of an aromatic compound in a side chain group' in chemical terminology. See **alpha-**.

1797   **omento-**   A word-initial combining element, derived from Latin *ōment(um)* 'fat; adipose tissue' and, by extension, 'caul, intestines' plus the combining vowel *-o-*, used in the sense of 'of or pertaining to either pair of peritoneal folds which connect the stomach to the adjacent organs' in biomedical terminology: **omentofixation, omentosplenopexy, omentovolvulus**. Also, **oment-: omentectomy**.

1798   **omicron-** (O, o)   A word-initial combining element, the fifteenth letter of the Greek alphabet, used chiefly to designate 'the fifteenth carbon atom in a straight chain compound or a derivative thereof in which the substitute group is attached to that atom' in chemical terminology. See **alpha-**.

1799   **omni-**   A word-initial combining element, derived from Latin *omni(s)* 'all, every, the whole,' used in its etymological and extended senses in a variety of combinations: **omnidirectional, omnigraph, omnipresent**.

1800   **omo-**   A word-initial combining element, derived from Greek *ōmo(s)* 'shoulder,' used in its etymological and extended senses in biomedical terminology: **omocephalus, omoclavicular, omosternum**. Also, **om-: omalgia**. Related form: **humero-**.

1801   **omphalo-**   A word-initial combining element, derived from Greek *omphaló(s)* 'navel,' used in the sense of 'of or pertaining to the navel or to the umbilicus' in Neo-Greek combinations: **omphalocele, omphalogenesis, omphaloskepsis**. Also, **omphal-: omphaloncus**.

1802   **on-**   A word-initial combining element, also occurring as a word, derived from Old English *an, on* 'atop, in, into, to, towards,' used in its etymological and extended senses in combination with other English elements: **oncoming, ongoing, onlooker**. Compare **a-⁴**. Related forms: **ana-, ano-¹**.

1803   **onco-¹**   A word-initial combining element, derived from Greek *ónko(s)* 'bulk, mass' and, by extention, 'tumor' used in its etymological and extended senses in Neo-Greek combinations: **oncogenesis, oncography, oncology**. Also, **onc-: oncosis**.

1804 **onco-²** A word-initial combining element, derived from Greek *ónko(s)* 'barb, hook,' used in its etymological and extended senses in Neo-Greek combinations: **oncocerciasis,** *Oncorhynchus,* **onco-sphere.** Also, **oncho-: onchosphere.** Related forms: **Anglo-, ankylo-, unci-.**

1805 **one-** A word-initial combining element, also occurring as a word, derived from Old English *ān* 'first of the cardinal numbers; individual,' used in its etymological and extended senses in combination with other English elements: **one-bagger, one-horse, one-track.** Compare **any-.** Related forms: **eka-, inch-, uni-.**

1806 **oneiro-** A word-initial combining element, derived from Greek *óneiro(s)* '(a) dream,' used in its etymological and extended senses in Neo-Greek combinations: **oneirocritic, oneiromancy, oneiro-phrenia.** Also, **oneir-: oneirodynia.**

1807 **onomato-** A word-initial combining element, derived from Greek *ónoma, onómat(os)* 'name' plus the combining vowel *-o-,* used in its etymological and extended senses, chief among these being 'word,' in Neo-Greek combinations: **onomatology, onomatomania, onoma-tophobia.**

1808 **onycho-** A word-initial combining element, derived from Greek *óny(x), ónych(os)* 'nail, claw' plus the combining vowel *-o-,* used chiefly in the sense of 'of or pertaining to the nails of the digits' in Neo-Greek combinations: **onychograph, onychopathology, onycho-phagia.** Also, **onych-: onychitis.** Related form: **nail-.**

1809 **oo-** A word-initial combining element, derived from Greek *ōó(n)* 'egg,' used in its etymological and extended senses, chief among these being 'of or pertaining to an *ovum*,' in Neo-Greek combina-tions: **oocephalus, oogenesis, ooxanthine.** Also, **o-²: oidiomycosis.** Related forms: **avi-, egg-, ovario-, ovo-.**

1810 **oophoro-** A word-initial combining element, derived from Greek *ōophóro(s)* 'egg-bearing' (from *ōó(n)* 'egg' plus the suffix *-phoros* 'bearing, carrying' (from the verb *phoreîn,* the frequentative form of the verb *phérein* 'to bear, carry')), used in the extended sense of 'of or pertaining to the *ovary*' in biomedical terminology: **oophorocys-tectomy, oophoropeliopexy, oophorotomy.** Also, **oophor-: oophoritis.** Compare **oo-, phoro-.**

1811 **op-¹** A variant of **opo-¹.**

1812 **op-²** A variant of **opo-².**

1813 **op-³** A word-initial combining element, derived from Latin *op-*, a combining form of *ob* 'toward, against, in front of,' appearing in its etymological and extended senses in inherited combinations in which the element to which it is joined begins with *p:* **oppilate, oppose, oppress.** Compare **ob-, oc-, of-².** Related forms: **epi-, opistho-.**

1814 **open-** A word-initial combining element, also occurring as a word, derived from Old English *open* 'not covered; not closed' (ultimately from an Indo-European root meaning '(up from) under'), used in its etymological and extended senses in combination with other English elements: **open-air, open-and-shut, open-faced.** Related forms: **evil-(?), hyper-, hypo-, over-, sub-, suc-, suf-, sup-, super-, supra-, sur-¹, sur-², sursum-, sus-, up-.**

1815 **ophio-** A word-initial combining element, derived from Greek *ophio-*, a combining form of *óph(is), óph(eōs)* 'serpent, snake,' used in its etymological and extended senses in in borrowings from Greek and in Neo-Greek combinations: *Ophiocaryon,* **ophiocephaloid, ophiotoxin.** Also, **ophi-: ophicleide.**

1816 **ophthalmo-** A word-initial combining element, derived from Greek *ophthalmó(s)* 'eye,' used in its etymological and extended senses in a variety of combinations: **ophthalmocarcinoma, ophthalmofundoscope, ophthalmology.** Also, **ophthalm-: ophthalmectomy.** Compare **opo-¹, optico-.** Related forms: **eye-, ocelli-, oculo-.**

1817 **opistho-** A word-initial combining element, derived from Greek *ópisth(e(n))* 'behind' plus the combining vowel *-o-*, used in its etymological and extended senses in Neo-Greek combinations: **opisthobranch, opisthocomous, opisthogastric.** Also, **opisth-: opistharthrous.** Related forms: **epi-, ob-, oc-, of-², op-³.**

1818 **opo-¹** A word-initial combining element, derived from Greek *ōp(s), ōp(ós)* 'eye' and, by extension, 'face' plus the combining vowel *-o-*, used in its etymological and extended senses in Neo-Greek combinations: **opocephalus, opodidymus,** *Opomyza.* Also, **op-¹, opsi-¹, opso-¹: opalgia, opsialgia, opsoclonia.** Compare: **ophthalmo-, optico-.** Related forms: **eye-, ocelli-, oculo-.**

1819 **opo-²** A word-initial combining element, derived from Greek *opó(s)* 'juice,' used in its etymological and extended senses in Neo-Greek combinations: **opobalsamum, opopanax, opotherapy.** Also, **op-²: opium.**

1820 **opsi-¹** A variant of **opo-¹.**

1821 opsi-² A word-initial combining element, derived from Greek *ops(é)* 'late' plus the combining vowel *-i-*, used in its etymological and extended senses in Neo-Greek combinations: **opsigenes, opsimathy, opsiuria.** Also, **opso-²: opsomenorrhea.**

1822 opsino- A variant of **opsono-**.

1823 opso-¹ A variant of **opo-¹.**

1824 opso-² A variant of **opsi-².**

1825 opso-³ A variant of **opsono-**.

1826 opsono- A word-initial combining element, derived from English *opson(in)* 'antibody which renders bacteria susceptible to phagocytosis' (from Greek *ópson* 'boiled meat,' hence, 'something to accompany bread to make it more palatable,' hence, 'condiment, relish' plus the biochemical suffix *-in* which is used in naming antibiotics, the idea being that *opsonin* acts as a 'condiment' to make bacteria more 'palatable' to phagocytes) plus the combining vowel *-o-*, used in its etymological sense in biomedical terminology: **opsonocytophagic, opsonology, opsonotherapy.** Also, **opsino-, opso-³, opson-, opsoni-: opsinogenous, opsogen, opsonic, opsoniferous.**

1827 optico- A word-initial combining element, derived from Greek *optikó(s)* 'of or pertaining to sight,' used in its etymological and extended senses in Neo-Greek and Neo-Latin combinations: **opticociliary, opticokinetic, opticonasion.** Also, **opt-, opti-, optic-, opto-: optesthesia, optimeter, optical, optomeninx.** Compare: **ophthalmo-, opo-¹.** Related forms: **eye-, ocelli-, oculo-.**

1828 or- A variant of **oro-³.**

1829 orbito- A word-initial combining element, derived from Latin *orbit(a)* 'track, rut (made by a wheel)' (from *orbis* 'circle, disk') plus the combining vowel *-o-*, used chiefly in the extended sense of 'of or pertaining to the portion of the skull immediately surrounding the eye' and in extensions of this sense in Neo-Latin and Neo-Greek combinations: **orbitonasal, orbitostat, orbitotomy.** Also, **orbit-: orbital.**

1830 orchi- A variant of **orchio-**.

1831 orchido- A word-initial combining element, derived as though from Greek *órch(is), *órchid(os)* 'testicle' (cf. *órchis, órchios (órcheōs)* 'testicle') plus the combining vowel -*o*-, used in its etymological and extended senses in Neo-Greek combinations: **orchidocelioplasty, orchidoptosis, orchidotherapy**. Also, **orchid-: orchidectomy**. Compare **orchio-**.

1832   **orchio-**   A word-initial combining element, derived from Greek *órchi*(*s*), *órchi*(*os*) 'testicle' plus the combining vowel -*o*-, used in its etymological and extended senses in Neo-Greek combinations: **orchiocele, orchiomyeloma, orchiotomy**. Also, **orchi-: orchioscheocele**. Compare **orchido-**.

1833   **ordinato-**   A word-initial combining element, derived from Latin *ordināt*(*us*), the past participle of the verb *ordināre* 'to arrange, put in order,' plus the combining vowel -*o*-, used in the specialized sense of 'having rows of that which is named by the combining root' in Neo-Latin combinations: **ordinatoliturate, ordinatomaculate, ordinatopunctate**.

1834   **oreo-**   A variant of **oro-¹**.

1835   **organo-**   A word-initial combining element, derived from Greek *órgano*(*n*) 'instrument, tool' (cf. *érgon* 'work'), used in the extended sense of 'of or pertaining to a specific bodily part with a specific function or set of functions' and in extensions of this sense, chief among these being 'of or pertaining to an organized structure,' in Neo-Greek and Neo-Latin combinations: **organofaction, organogel, organogenesis**. Also, **organ-: organism**. Related forms: **ergasio-, ergo-¹, work-**.

1836   **ori-¹**   A variant of **oro-¹**.

1837   **ori-²**   A variant of **auri-²**.

1838   **ori-³**   A variant of **oro-³**.

1839   **ornitho-**   A word-initial combining element, derived from Greek *órni*(*s*), *órnith*(*os*) 'bird' plus the combining vowel -*o*-, used in its etymological and extended senses in Neo-Greek combinations: **ornithocephalous, ornithology, ornithopter**. Also, **ornith-: ornithine**.

1840   **oro-¹**   A word-initial combining element, derived from Greek *ór*(*os*), *ór*(*eos*) 'mountain' plus the combining vowel -*o*-, used in its etymological sense in Neo-Greek combinations: **orogeny, *Orohippus*, orology**. Also, **ore-, oreo-, ori-¹: *Oreodon*, oreography, *Oribates***.

1841   **oro-²**   A variant of **auri-²**.

1842   **oro-³**   A word-initial combining element, derived from Latin *ō(s)*, *ōr(is)* 'mouth, face' plus the combining vowel *-o-*, used in the sense of 'of or pertaining to the mouth' and in extensions of this sense in Neo-Latin and Neo-Greek combinations: **orolingual, oronasal, oropharynx.** Also, **or-, ori-³: oral, orinasal.** Compare **oscillo-.**

1843   **oro-⁴**   A word-initial combining element, derived from Greek *or(rh)ó(s)* 'whey, serum,' used in its etymological and extended senses in biomedical terminology: **orodiagnosis, oroimmunity, oromeningitis.** Also, **orrho-: orrhoreaction.** Related form: **sero-.**

1844   **ortho-**   A word-initial combining element, derived from Greek *orthó(s)* 'straight, correct, upright,' used in its etymological and extended senses, chief among these being 'normal' and, in chemical terminology, 'acid formed by the combination of an oxide with the greatest number of water molecules,' 'benzene derivative in which two contiguous hydrogen atoms have been replaced by other atoms or groups,' and 'isomer,' in a variety of combinations: **orthography, orthopedics, orthosilic (acid).** Also, **o-¹, orth-: o-dinitrobenzene, orthoptics.**

1845   **oscheo-**   A word-initial combining element, derived from Greek *óscheo(n)* 'scrotum,' used in its etymological sense in biomedical terminology: **oscheohydrocele, oscheolith, oscheoplasty.** Also, **osch-, osche-: oschelephantiasis, oscheitis.**

1846   **oscillo-**   A word-initial combining element, derived from Latin *oscill(āre)* 'to swing, vibrate' (from *oscillum*, a diminutive form of *ōs, ō(ris)*) 'mouth, face,' meaning 'small face' and, by extension, 'small mask of the god Bacchus' which was hung in Roman vineyards to propitiate the god of wine while frightening off grape-eating birds as it vibrated in the breeze) plus the combining vowel *-o*, used in its etymological and extended senses in Neo-Latin and Neo-Greek combinations: **oscillogram, oscillometer, oscilloscope.** Also, **oscill-: oscillopsia.** Compare: **oro-³.**

1847   **osmo-¹**   A word-initial combining element, derived from Greek *osm(ḗ)* 'odor, smell' plus the combining vowel *-o-*, used in the sense of 'of or pertaining to odors or to the sense of smell' in biomedical terminology: **osmoceptor, osmolagnia, osmometer¹.** Also, **osm-¹: osmidrosis.** Compare **osphresio-.** Related forms: **odori-, olfacto-, ozo-, ozono-.**

1848   **osmo-²**   A word-initial combining element, derived from Greek *ōsmó(s)* '(a) thrust, impulse,' used in its etymological and extended senses, chief among these being 'of or pertaining to *osmosis*, the passage through a semipermeable membrane of a solvent from the lesser-concentrated solution on one side of the membrane to the greater-concentrated solution on the other,' in Neo-Greek combinations: **osmometer²**, **osmophilic**, **osmotaxis**. Also, **osm-²**: **osmol**.

1849   **osphresio-**   A word-initial combining element, derived from Greek *ósphrēsi(s)* '(a) smell(ing)' plus the combining vowel *-o-*, used in the sense of 'of or pertaining to odor or to the sense of smell' in Neo-Greek combinations: **osphresiolagnia, osphresiology, osphresiophobia**. Compare **osmo-¹**. Related forms: **odori-, olfacto-, ozo-, ozono-**.

1850   **osphy-**   A word-initial combining element, derived from Greek *osphý(s)* 'loin,' used in its etymological sense in Neo-Greek combinations: **osphyalgia, osphyarthritis, osphyitis**. Also, **osphyo-**: **osphyomyelitis**.

1851   **osseo-**   A word-initial combining element, derived from Latin *osse(us)* 'bony' (from *os, oss(is)* 'bone' plus the adjective-forming suffix *-eus*), used in the sense of 'of or pertaining to bone' in biomedical terminology: **osseocartilaginous, osseofibrous, osseosonometer**. Also, **osse-**: **ossein**. Compare **ossi-**.

1852   **ossi-**   A word-initial combining element, derived from Latin *os, oss(is)* 'bone' plus the combining vowel *-i-*, used in its etymological sense in Neo-Latin and Neo-Greek combinations: **ossiferous, ossifluence, ossiform**. Compare **osseo-**. Related forms: **astragalo-, osteo-**.

1853   **osteo-**   A word-initial combining element, derived from Greek *ostéo(n)* 'bone,' used in its etymological sense in Neo-Greek and Neo-Latin combinations: **osteoarthrosis, osteocementum, osteomalacia**. Also, **ost-, oste-**: **ostalgia, osteoarthritis**. Related forms: **astragalo-, osseo-, ossi-**.

1854   **osteochondro-**   See **osteo-** and **chondro-**.

1855   **ot-**   A variant of **oto-**.

1856   **other-**   A word-initial combining element, also occurring as a word, derived from Old English *ōþer* 'the remaining one (of two),' used in its etymological and extended senses in combination with other English elements: **other-directed, otherwise, otherworldly**.

1857   **oto-**   A word-initial combining element, derived from Greek *o(ûs), ōt(ós)* 'ear' plus the combining vowel *-o-*, used in its etymological sense in biomedical terminology: **otocariasis, otoganglion, otolaryngology.** Also, **ot-: otitis.** Related forms: **auri-¹, auriculo-, ear-.**

1858 oul-¹   A variant of **ulo-¹.**

1859 oul-²   A variant of **ul-².**

1860 oulo-¹   A variant of **ulo-¹.**

1861 oulo-²   A variant of **ulo-³.**

1862 out-   A word-initial combining element, also occurring as a word, derived from Old English *ūt* 'away from inside,' used in its etymological and extended senses in combination with other English elements: **outcast, outlaw, outpost.**

1863 ov-   A variant of **ovo-.**

1864 ovario-   A word-initial combining element, derived from Neo-Latin *ōvāri(um)* 'ovary' (from *ōv(um)* 'egg' plus the noun-forming suffix *ārium*) plus the combining vowel *-o-*, used in its etymological and extended senses in biomedical terminology: **ovariodysneuria, ovariohysterectomy, ovariotherapy.** Compare **ovo-.**

1865 over-   A word-initial combining element, also occurring as a word, derived from Old English *ofer* 'above' (from an Indo-European root meaning 'up (from under)'), used in its etymological and extended senses in combination with other English elements: **overhang, overlook, overriding.** Related forms: **evil-(?), hypo-, hyper-, sub-, suc-, suf-, sup-, super-, supra-, sur-¹, sur-², sursum-, sus-, up-.**

1866 ovo-   A word-initial combining element, derived from Latin *ōv(um)* 'egg' plus the combining vowel *-o-*, used in its etymological and extended senses in Neo-Latin and Neo-Greek combinations: **ovocenter, ovocyte, ovoviviparous.** Also, **ov-, ovi-: oval, ovigerm.** Compare **ovario-.** Related forms: **avi-, egg-, oo-.**

1867 ox-¹   A variant of **oxal-.**

1868 ox-²   A variant of **oxy-².**

1869 ox-³   A word-initial combining element, also occurring as a word, derived from Old English *ox(a)* 'bovine mammal,' used in its etymological and extended senses in combination with other English elements: **oxblood, oxbow, oxpecker.**

1870   oxa-   A word-initial combining element, a variant of **oxy-²**, used in the specialized sense of 'containing an oxygen bridge; containing oxygen in place of carbon' in chemical terminology: **oxabicyclononane, oxamethane, oxaphor**. Also, **oxat-: oxatyl**. Compare **oxy-²**.

1871   oxal-   A word-initial combining element, derived through Latin from Greek *oxal(ís)* 'wood sorrel' (from *ox(ýs)* 'pointed, sharp, pungent, acidic,' the leaves of the wood sorrel being acidic to the taste), used in the extended sense of 'of, pertaining to, containing, or derived from *oxalic acid* ($HOOCCOOH \cdot 2H_2O$) (which was first discovered in the juice of the wood sorrel)' in chemical terminology: **oxalamide, oxalethyline, oxaluria**. Also, **ox-¹: oxamide**. Compare **oxy-¹**.

1872   oxat-   A variant of **oxa-**.

1873   oxi-   A variant of **oxy-²**.

1874   oxo-   A variant of **oxy-²**.

1875   oxy-¹   A word-initial combining element, derived from Greek *oxý(s)* 'pointed, sharp, pungent, acidic,' used in its etymological and extended senses in Neo-Greek combinations: **oxyblepsia, oxycephalic, oxyphonia**. Compare **oxal-, oxy-²**. Related forms: **acantho-, aceto-, acetyl-, acid-, acro-, acu-, acuti-, edge-, keto-**.

1876   oxy-²   A word-initial combining element, derived from French *oxy(gene)* 'the gaseous element (O),' a term coined by Lavoisier in 1786 and based on Greek *oxý(s)* 'pointed, sharp, acidic' plus *gene(á)* 'production,' the idea being that *oxygene*—'oxygen'—is a medium in which (some) substances will burn to produce oxides forming acidic solutions, used in its etymological and extended senses in biochemical terminology: **oxyhemaglobin, oxyluciferin, oxypurine**. Also, **ox-², oxi-, oxo-: oxide, oxigram, oxophenarsine (hydrochloride)**. Compare **oxa-, oxy-¹**.

1877   ozo-   A word-initial combining element, derived from Greek *óz(ein)* 'to smell' plus the combining vowel *-o-*, used in the sense of 'of or pertaining to odor or to the sense of smell' and in extensions of this sense in Neo-Greek combinations: **ozocerite, ozocrotous, ozogen**. Compare **ozono-**. Related forms: **odori-, olfacto-, osmo-¹, osphresio-**.

1878   ozono-   A word-initial combining element, from German *Ozon* 'allotropic oxygen (O_3),' a term coined by C. F. Schönbein in 1840 and based on Greek *ózon*, the present participle of the verb *ózein* 'to smell,' because of ozone's characteristic odor, used in its etymological sense in Neo-Greek combinations: **ozonolysis, ozonometer, ozonophore.** Also, **ozon-: ozonize.** Compare **ozo-.** Related forms: **odori-, olfacto-, osmo-[1], osphresio-.**

P

1879   **p-**   A variant of **para-**[1].

1880   **pachy-**   A word-initial combining element, derived from Greek *pachý(s)* 'large, thick,' used in its etymological and extended senses in Neo-Greek and Neo-Latin combinations: **pachydermatous, pachygnathous, pachyvaginalitis.** Also, **pach-, pacho-: pachemia, pachometer.**

1881   **pack-**   A word-initial combining element, also occurring as a word, derived from Middle English *pa(c)k* 'bundle,' used in its etymological and extended senses in combination with other English elements: **packhorse, packplane, packthread.**

1882   **paddle-**   A word-initial combining element, also occurring as a word, derived from Middle English *padel(l)* 'device for cleaning a ploughshare,' later, 'oar,' used in this latter sense and extended senses in combination with other English elements: **paddleboard, paddlefish, paddlewood.**

1883   **paedo-**   A variant of **pedo-**[1].

1884   **paido-**   A variant of **pedo-**[1].

1885   **palaeo-**   A variant of **paleo-**.

1886   **palato-**   A word-initial combining element, derived from Latin

267

palāt(um) 'roof of the mouth' plus the combining vowel *-o-,* used in its etymological sense in biomedical terminology: **palatoglossal, palatomaxillary, palatosalpingeus.** Also, **palat-: palatal.**

1887   **paleo-**   A word-initial combining element, derived from Greek *palaió(s)* 'old,' used in its etymological and extended senses, chief among these being 'primitive,' in Neo-Greek and Neo-Latin combinations: **paleobotany, paleocerebellum, paleopsychology.** Also, **palae-, palaeo-, pale-: palaeontography, palaeology, paleontology.** Related form: **tele-².**

1888   **palin-**   A word-initial combining element, derived from Greek *pálin* 'backwards, back, again,' used in its etymological and extended senses, chief among these being 'returning, repeating,' in inherited and Neo-Greek combinations: **palindrome, palingraphia, palinphrasia.** Also, **pali-, palim-: palirrhea, palimpsest.** Related forms: **coll-², collar-, cyclo-, polari-, teleo-³, telo-¹, wheel-.**

1889   **pallio-**   A word-initial combining element, derived from Latin *palli(um)* 'cloak' plus the combining vowel *-o-,* used in the sense of 'of or pertaining to a *mantle* (in any of its various physiological senses)' in Neo-Latin and Neo-Greek combinations: **palliobranchiate, palliocardiac, palliopedal.**

1890   **palmati-**   A word-initial combining element, derived from Latin *palmāt(us)* 'marked with the palm of the hand; adorned with palm leaves' (from an Indo-European root meaning 'flat, spread out') plus the combining vowel *-i-,* used chiefly in the sense of 'having five lobes which diverge from a common center (as fingers from an open palm)' and in extensions of this sense in botanical terminology: **palmatiform, palmatilobate, palmatisect.** Related forms: **field-, flat-, floor-, place-, placento-, plagio-, plain-, plano-¹, plano-², plasmo-, plasmodi-, plasto-, plate-, platino-, platy-.**

1891   **pan-¹**   A word-initial combining element, derived from Old English *pan(ne)* 'broad shallow container' (from an Indo-European root meaning 'flat, spread out'), used in its etymological and extended senses in combination with other English elements: **pancake, panfish, panhandle.** Related form: **petalo-.**

1892   **pan-²**   A word-initial combining element, derived from Greek *pân, pán(tos)* 'all, every,' used in its etymological and extended senses in a variety of combinations: **Pan-Africanism, panangiitis, pansinusitis.** Also, **pant-, panto-: pantalgia, pantophobic.**

1893   **pancreatico-**   A word-initial combining element, derived from Neo-

Latin *pancreatic(us)* 'of or pertaining to the *pancreas*' (from Greek *pánkrea(s), pankréat(os)* 'pancreas' plus the adjective-forming suffix *-ic(us)*) plus the combining vowel *-o-*, used in its etymological and extended senses, chief among these being 'of or pertaining to the *pancreatic duct*,' in biomedical terminology: **pancreaticoduodenal, pancreaticogastrostomy, pancreaticosplenic.** Compare **pancreo-.**

1894 pancreo- A word-initial combining element, derived from Greek *pánkre(as), pankré(atos)* 'pancreas' (from *pan* 'all' plus *kré(as)* 'flesh,' the idea being, apparently, to those who coined the word, that the *pancreas* is an organ composed entirely of glandular flesh) plus the combining vowel *-o-*, used in its etymological sense in biomedical terminology: **pancreolysis, pancreopathy, pancreoprivic.** Also, **pancre-, pancreat-, pancreato-: pancrealgia, pancreatectomy, pancreatoduodenostomy.** Compare **pan-²** and **creo-.**

1895 panto- A variant of **pan-².**

1896 papaver- A word-initial combining element, derived from Latin *papāver* 'poppy,' used in its etymological and extended senses, chief among these being 'of, pertaining to, containing, or derived from *opium*,' in botanical and chemical terminology: **papaveraldine, papaveramine, papaverosine.**

1897 paper- A word-initial combining element, also occurring as a word, derived through Old French and Latin from Greek *pápyr(os)* 'papyrus, an Egyptian rush from which material on which to write or draw may be made,' used in the sense of 'fibrous material on which to write or draw' and in extensions of this sense in combination with other English elements: **paperback, paperhanger, paperwork.**

1898 papillo- A word-initial combining element, derived from Latin *papill(a)* 'nipple' plus the combining vowel *-o-*, used in the sense of 'nipple-shaped elevation or growth' in biomedical terminology: **papillocarcinoma, papilloedema, papilloretinitis.** Also, **papill-, papilli-: papillitis, papilliform.** Compare **papulo-.**

1899 papulo- A word-initial combining element, derived from Latin *papul(a)* 'pimple, pustule' plus the combining vowel *-o-*, used in its etymological and extended senses in biomedical terminology: **papulopustular, papulosquamous, papulovesicular.** Also, **papul-, papuli-: papular, papuliferous.** Compare **papillo-.**

1900 par-¹ A variant of **para-¹.**

1901   **par-²**   A variant of **para-²**.

1902   **par-³**   A word-initial combining element, derived through French from Latin *per* 'through, from side to side, by, for,' appearing in its etymological and extended senses in borrowings from French: **paramour, parboil, parget.** Compare **per-**.

1903   **para-¹**   A word-initial combining element, derived from Greek *para-,* a combining form of *pará* 'beside, beyond, contrary to,' used in its etymological and extended senses, chief among these being 'resembling, partial, faulty' and, in chemical terminology, 'benzene derivative in which two opposite carbon atoms have been replaced by other atoms or groups,' 'characterized by an even rotational quantum number,' 'isomer, i.e., an arrangement of molecules which resembles another,' and 'polymer, i.e., an arrangement of molecules of the same type, one next to another,' in a variety of combinations: **paradichlorbenzene, paraformaldehyde, paramastoid.** Also, **p-, par-¹: p-dichlorbenzene, paraxial.** Related forms: **far-, first-, for-¹, fore-³, forth-, par-³, per-, peri-, perisso-, pre-, primi-, pro-¹, pro-², proprio-, pros-¹, proso-, protero-, proto-, proximo-**.

1904   **para-²**   A word-initial combining element, derived through French from Latin *parā(re)* 'to make ready, prepare' and, by extension, 'guard against, ward off,' appearing in this latter and extended senses in borrowings from French: **parachute, parapet, parasol.** Also, **par-²: parfleche.** Compare **para-³**.

1905   **para-³**   A word-initial combining element, derived through English from French *para(chute)* 'device used to retard a fall through the air' (from Latin *parā(re)* 'to prepare (against); guard against' plus French *chute* '(a) fall'), used in the sense of 'one who uses a parachute' in combination with other English elements: **paradoctor, paraglider, paratrooper.** Compare **para-²**.

1906   **parasito-**   A word-initial combining element, derived from Greek *parásito(s)* '(one) eating beside, with, or at the table of (someone else)' (from *pará* 'beside' plus *sîto(s)* 'grain, food'), used in the extended sense of 'of or pertaining to an organism which takes its nourishment from another without contributing to its host' in Neo-Greek and Neo-Latin combinations: **parasitogenic, parasitophobia, parasitotropic.** Also, **parasit-, parasiti-: parasitic, parasiticide.** Compare **para-¹** and **sito-**.

1907   **parathyro-**   See **para-¹** and **thyro-**.

1908   **parepi-**   See **par-¹** and **epi-**.

1909 **pari-** A word-initial combining element, derived from Latin *pār, par(is)* 'equal, even(-numbered)' plus the combining vowel *-i-*, used in its etymological and extended senses in Neo-Latin and Neo-Greek combinations: **paridigitate, paripinnate, parisyllabic.**

1910 **parieto-** A word-initial combining element, derived from Latin *pariē(s), pariet(is)* 'wall (of a house)' plus the combining vowel *-o-*, used in the extended sense of 'of or pertaining to the walls of a cavity or organ of the body' in biomedical terminology: **parieto-frontal, parietosphenoid, parietovisceral.** Also, **pariet-: parietal.**

1911 **parodont-** See **par(a)-**[1] and **odont(o)-.**

1912 **parrot-** A word-initial combining element, derived from French *P(i)errot,* a diminutive form of the name *Pierre* 'Peter,' used in the sense of '(domesticated) bird of the genus *Psittacus*' and in extensions of this sense in combinations with other English elements: **parrotbeak, parrot-coal, parrotfish.**

1913 **part-** A word-initial combining element, also occurring as a word, derived through Old French from Latin *par(s), part(is)* 'portion,' used in its etymological and extended senses in combination with other English elements: **part-score, part-time, partway.**

1914 **partheno-** A word-initial combining element, derived from Greek *parthéno(s)* 'maiden, virgin,' used in its etymological and extended senses in Neo-Greek combinations: **parthenogenesis, parthenology, parthenophobia.** Also, **partho-: parthogenesis.**

1915 **parvi-** A word-initial combining element, derived from Latin *parv(us)* 'small, little' plus the combining vowel *-i-*, used in its etymological and extended senses in Neo-Latin combinations: **parvicellular, parvipsoas, parvirostrate.** Also, **parvo-:** *Parvobacteriaceae.*

1916 **pass-** A word-initial combining element, also occurring as a word, derived from French *pass(er)* 'to move beyond' (from Latin *passus* 'step, pace'), used in the sense of 'that which allows one to move beyond' and in extensions of this sense in combination with other English elements: **passkey, passport, password.** Also, **pas-: pastime.** Compare **passe-.**

1917 **passe-** A word-initial combining element, derived from French *passe(r)* 'to go beyond' (from Latin *passus* 'step, pace'), appearing in its etymological and extended senses in borrowings from French: **passegarde, passement, passepied.** Compare **pass-.**

1918 passion-   A word-initial combining element, also occurring as a word, derived through French from late Latin *passio, passion(is)* 'martyrdom' (from the past participle of the Latin verb *patī* 'to suffer'), used in the specialized sense of 'the martyrdom of Christ' and in extensions of this sense in combination with other English elements: **passionflower, passionfruit, Passiontide.**

1919 patch-   A word-initial combining element, also occurring as a word, derived from Middle English *patch(e)* 'piece of cloth or the like (which is used to cover a hole),' used in its etymological and extended senses in combination with other English elements: **patchhead, patchstand, patchwork.** Related form(?): **piece-.**

1920 patho-   A word-initial combining element, derived from Greek *pátho(s)* 'suffering' and, by extension, 'disease,' used in this latter and extended senses in biomedical terminology: **pathocrinia, pathoformic, pathogenesis.** Also, **path-: pathergasia.**

1921 patri-   A word-initial combining element, derived from Latin *pat(e)r, patr(is)* and Greek *pat(ē̃)r, pat(é)r(os)* 'father' plus the combining vowel *-i-,* used in its etymological and extended senses in Neo-Latin and Neo-Greek combinations: **patriarch, patrilineal, patrimony.** Also, **patr-, patro-: patronymic, patroclinous.**

1922 pauci-   A word-initial combining element, derived from Latin *pauc(us)* 'few, little' plus the combining vowel *-i-,* used in its etymological sense in Neo-Latin combinations: **paucidentate, pauciflorous, pauciradiate.** Related forms: **poor-, pedo-[1].**

1923 pay   A word-initial combining element, also occurring as a word, derived through Old French from Latin *pā(cāre)* 'to pacify, appease' and, in Medieval Latin, 'to remunerate,' used in the sense of 'remuneration' and in extensions of this sense in combination with other English elements: **payload, paymaster, payoff.** Related form: **peace-.**

1924 pea-   A word-initial combining element, also occurring as a word, derived through late Latin from Greek *pí(sos)* 'variety of pulse,' used in its etymological and extended senses in combination with other English elements: **peamouth, peanut, peashooter.**

1925 peace-   A word-initial combining element, also occurring as a word, derived through Old French from Latin *pa(x), pāc(is)* 'tranquility,' used in its etymological and extended senses in combination with other English elements: **peacemaker, peace-pipe, peacetime.** Related form: **pay-.**

1926 peach-   A word-initial combining element, also occurring as a word, derived, ultimately, from Greek (*mêlon*) *pe*(*r*)*s*(*i*)*k*(*ón*) 'fruit of the *Amygdalus persica*,' literally, 'Persian (fruit),' used in its etymological and extended senses in combination with other English elements: **peach-black, peachblow, peachwort.**

1927 pearl-   A word-initial combining element, also occurring as a word, derived from Old French *perl*(*e*) 'round calcareous concretion formed by various species of mollusk' (perhaps from Latin *pirula* 'small pear' or from (unattested) **pernula* 'small ham,' the idea being, in the first case, that a pearl resembles a pear in shape and, in the second, that a mollusk shell resembles a ham), used in its etymological and extended senses in combination with other English elements: **pearlash, pearleye, pearlfish.**

1928 ped-¹   A variant of **pedo-¹.**

1929 ped-²   A variant of **pedo-².**

1930 pedi-¹   A variant of **pedo-¹.**

1931 pedi-²   A variant of **pedo-².**

1932 pedo-¹   A word-initial combining element, derived from Greek *paî*(*s*), *paid*(*ós*) 'child' (from an Indo-European root meaning 'little, few') plus the combining vowel -*o*-, used in its etymological and extended senses in Neo-Greek combinations: **pedobarometer, pedomorphism, pedophobia.** Also, **paed-, paedo-, paid-, paido-, ped-¹, pedi-¹: paederast, paedobaptist, paideutics, paidology, pediatrics, pediodontia.** Related forms: **pauci-, poor-.**

1933 pedo-²   A word-initial combining element, derived from Latin *pē*(*s*), *ped*(*is*) 'foot' plus the combining vowel -*o*-, used in its etymological sense in Neo-Latin and Neo-Greek combinations: **pedodynamometer, pedograph, pedopathy.** Also, **ped-², pedi-²: pedal, pedicure.** Related forms: **foot-, pilot-, podo-.**

1934 peep-   A word-initial combining element, also occurring as a word, derived from Middle English *pip*(*en*), a variant of *pik*(*en*) 'to peek,' used in its etymological and extended senses in combination with other English elements: **peephole, Peep-O'-Day (Boy), peepshow.**

1935 peg-   A word-initial combining element, also occurring as a word of uncertain origin, used in the sense of 'wooden nail or pin' and in extensions of this sense in combination with other English elements: **pegboard, pegbox, peg-legged.**

1936 pelo-   A word-initial combining element, derived from Greek *pēló(s)* 'earth, mud,' used in its etymological and extended senses in Neo-Greek combinations: **pelohemia, pelology, pelotherapy.**

1937 pelti-   A word-initial combining element, derived from Latin *pelt(a)* 'shield' (from Greek *péltē* 'shield') plus the combining vowel *-i-*, used in its etymological and extended senses in Neo-Latin combinations: **peltifolious, peltiform, peltinerved.** Compare **pelto-.**

1938 pelto-   A word-initial combining element, derived from Greek *pélt(ē)* 'shield' plus the combining vowel *-o-*, used in its etymological and extended senses in Neo-Greek combinations: *Peltocephalus, Peltochelys, Peltogaster.* Also, **pelt-:** *Peltops.* Compare **pelti-.**

1939 pelvi-   A word-initial combining element, derived from Latin *pelvi(s)* 'basin,' used in the sense of 'basin-shaped structure of the body' in biomedical terminology: **pelvicephalometry, pelvifixation, pelvirectal.** Also, **pelveo-, pelvio-, pelvo-: pelveoperitonitis, pelviolithotomy, pelvoscopy.**

1940 pen-¹   A word-initial combining element, also occurring as a word, derived through Old French from Latin *pen(na)* 'feather,' used in the extended sense of 'writing instrument (made from a quill)' and in extensions of this sense in combination with other English elements: **penknife, penman, penname.** Compare **penni-.**

1941 pen-²   A word-initial combining element, derived from Latin *p(a)en(e)* 'almost, nearly,' appearing in its etymological and extended senses in inherited and Neo-Latin combinations: **peninsula, peninvariant, penultimate.** Also, **pene-: penecontemporaneous.**

1942 penni-   A word-initial combining element, derived from Latin *penn(a)* 'feather' plus the combining vowel *-i-*, used in its etymological sense in Neo-Latin combinations: **penniform, pennigerous, penninerved.** Compare **pen-¹.** Related forms: **feather-, pin-, pinnati-, pinni-, pterido-, ptero-, pterygo-, ptilo-.**

1943 penny-   A word-initial combining element, also occurring as a word, derived from Old English *peni(ġ)* '(a) coin roughly corresponding, originally, to the Roman *dēnārius* (whence English *dime*),' used in its etymological and extended senses in combination with other English elements: **penny-a-liner, pennyweight, pennyworth.**

1944 pent-¹   A variant of **penta-.**

1945 pent-²   A variant of **pentos-.**

1946 penta-   A word-initial combining element, derived from Greek *penta-*, a combining form of *pént(e)* 'five,' used in its etymological and extended senses, chief among these being, in chemical terminology, 'having five atoms or groups of the sort named by the combining root,' in Neo-Greek combinations: **pentagon, pentamethylene, pentatonic**. Also, **pent-**[1], **pente-, pento-**[1]: **pentoxide, Pentecost, pentobarbital (calcium)**. Compare **pentos-**. Related forms: **cinque-**[1], **cinque-**[2], **femto-, finger-, fist-, five-, quinque-, quint-**.

1947 pento-[1]   A variant of **penta-**.

1948 pento-[2]   A variant of **pentos-**.

1949 pentos-   A word-initial combining element, derived from English *pentos(e)* 'the pentaglucose $(C_5H_{10}O_5)$' (from Greek *pént(e)* 'five' plus the suffix *-ose*—an abstraction from French *glucose*—which is used in naming sugars), used in its etymological sense in biochemical terminology: **pentosazon, pentosemia, pentosuria**. Also, **pent-**[2], **pento-**[2]: **pentnucleotide, pentolysis**. Compare **penta-**.

1950 pepper-   A word-initial combining element, also occurring as a word, derived, ultimately, from Sanskrit *pipal(lī)* 'berry; berry of the *Piper nigrum*,' used in this latter and extended senses in combination with other English elements: **pepperbox, peppercorn, peppermint**.

1951 pepto-[1]   A word-initial combining element, derived from Greek *pépt(ein)* 'to cook, boil, digest' plus the combining vowel *-o-*, used in the sense of 'of or pertaining to digestion' in Neo-Greek combinations: **peptocrinin, peptogaster, peptogenic**[1]. Also, **pept-**: **peptic**. Compare **pepto-**[2]. Related form: **cook-**.

1952 pepto-[2]   A word-initial combining element, derived from German *pepto(n)* 'peptone, a protein compound derived by acid or enzyme hydrolisis of a native protein' (from Greek *péptōn, pépton,* the present participle of the verb *péptein* 'to cook, boil, digest'), used in its etymological sense in biochemical terminology: **peptolysis, peptogenic**[2], **peptotoxin**. Also, **pepton-: peptonemia**. Compare **pepto-**[1].

1953 per-   A word-initial combining element, derived from Latin *per* 'through, throughout, by,' used in its etymological and extended senses, chief among these being 'completely, utterly' and, in chemical terminology, 'containing a large or maximum number of atoms or groups of atoms named by the combining root' and 'an

acid, oxide, or salt in which two oxygen atoms are joined together,'
in inherited and Neo-Latin combinations: **perchlorate, permeate,
persulfate.** Compare **par-³.** Related forms: **far-, first-, for-¹, fore-³,
forth-, para-¹, peri-, perisso-, pre-, primi-, pro-¹, pro-², proprio-,
pros-¹, proso-, protero-, proto-, proximo-.**

1954 **peri-** A word-initial combining element, derived from Greek *perí*
'around, near, about,' used in its etymological and extended senses,
chief among these being, 'surrounding that which is named by the
combining root,' in Neo-Greek and Neo-Latin combinations:
peribulbar, pericarp, periencephalitis. Related forms: **far-, first-,
for-¹, fore-³, forth-, par-³, para-¹, per-, perisso-, pre-, primi-, pro-¹,
pro-², proprio-, pros-¹, proso-, protero-, proto-, proximo-.**

1955 **pericardio-** A word-initial combining element, derived from Greek
perikárdio(s) 'membranous sac surrounding the heart' (from *perí*
'around' plus *kardía* 'heart'), used in its etymological sense in
biomedical terminology: **pericardiocentesis, pericardiomediastinitis,
pericardiosymphysis.** Also, **pericard-, pericardi-: pericardectomy,
pericardiectomy.** Compare **peri-, cardio-.**

1956 **perineo-** A word-initial combining element, derived from Greek
períneo(n) 'space between the scrotum or mons veneris and the
anus' (from *perí* 'around' plus *ineîn* 'to eliminate'), used in its
etymological sense in biomedical combinations: **perineocel, peri-
neoscrotal, perineotomy.**

1957 **periosteo-** A word-initial combining element, derived from Greek
periósteo(n) 'membrane surrounding a bone' (from *perí* 'around'
plus *ostéon* 'bone'), used in its etymological sense in biomedical
terminology: **periosteo-edema, periosteomedullitis, periosteophyte.**
Also, **periost-, perioste-: periostitis, periosteitis.** Compare **peri-** and
osteo-.

1958 **perisso-** A word-initial combining element, derived from Greek
perissó(s) 'extraordinary, odd, odd-numbered,' used in its etymological and extended senses in Neo-Greek combinations: **perisso-
dactyl, perissology, perissosyllabic.** Also, **periss-: perissad.** Related
forms: **far-, first-, for-¹, fore-³, forth-, par-³, para-¹, per-, peri-, pre-,
primi-, pro-¹, pro-², proprio-, pros-¹, proso-, protero-, proto-, prox-
imo-.**

1959 **peritoneo-** A word-initial combining element, derived from Greek
peritónaio(n) 'membrane surrounding the lower viscera' (from the
verb *periteínein* 'to stretch around' (from *perí* 'around' plus *teínein*
'to stretch, extend')), used in its etymological sense in biomedical

combinations: **peritoneocentesis, peritoneomuscular, peritone-opathy.** Also, **periton-, peritone-: peritonitis, peritonealgia.** Compare **peri-** and **tono-.**

1960 **pero-** A word-initial combining element, derived from Greek *pēró(s)* 'maimed, crippled,' used in its etymological and extended senses, chief among these being 'deformed,' in biomedical combinations: **perobrachius, peropus, perosplanchnia.**

1961 **pesti-** A word-initial combining element, derived from Latin *pesti(s)* 'plague,' used in its etymological and extended senses in Neo-Latin combinations: **pesticide, pestiduct, pestiferous.**

1962 **petalo-** A word-initial combining element, derived from Greek *pétalo(n)* 'leaf' (from the adjective *pétalos* 'flat, spread out'), used in its etymological and extended senses in Neo-Greek combinations: **petalobacteria, petalomania, petalostichous.** Also, **petal-:** *Petalodus.* Related form: **pan-¹.**

1963 **petro-** A word-initial combining element, derived from Greek *pétr(a)* 'rock, stone' plus the combining vowel *-o-,* used in its etymological and extended senses in Neo-Greek and Neo-Latin combinations: **petrochemical, petroglyph, petrosphere.** Also, **petr-, petri-: petroleum, petrifaction.**

1964 **phaco-** A word-initial combining element, derived from Greek *phakó(s)* 'lentil,' used in the extended sense of 'of or pertaining to the *lens* of the eye (which is so called because of its resemblance in appearance to a lentil)' in biomedical terminology: **phacocystitis, phacoglaucoma, phacolysis.** Also, **phac-, phak-, phako-: phacitis, phakitis, phakoscope.**

1965 **phaeno-** A variant of **pheno-¹.**

1966 **phaeo-** A word-initial combining element, derived from Greek *phaió(s)* 'dusky,' literally, 'having the color of the twilight sky' (from *phôs (pháos)* 'light, daylight'), used in its etymological and extended senses in Neo-Greek combinations: **phaeophyl, phaeopus,** *Phaeosporae.* Also, **pheo-: pheochrome.** Compare **photo-.**

1967 **phago-** A word-initial combining element, derived from Greek *phag(eîn)* 'to eat' plus the combining vowel *-o-,* used in its etymological and extended senses in Neo-Greek combinations: **phagocaryosis, phagomania, phagotherapy.** Also, **phage-: phagelysis.**

1968 **phako-** A variant of **phaco-.**

1969 phalang- A word-initial combining element, derived from Greek *phálan(x), phálang(os)* 'line of battle; truncheon; bone between two joints of a finger or toe,' used in this last and extended senses in biomedical combinations: **phalangectomy, phalangitis, phalangosis.** Also, **phalango-: phalangophalangeal.**

1970 phallo- A word-initial combining element, derived from Greek *phalló(s)* 'penis,' used in its etymological sense in Neo-Greek combinations: **phallocampsis, phalloplasty, phallorrhagia.** Also, **phall-, phalle-: phallic, phallephoric.** Related form: **ball-.**

1971 phanero- A word-initial combining element, derived from Greek *phaneró(s)* 'apparent, visible' (from *phaínesthai* 'to appear, be visible,' literally, 'to come to light'), used in its etymological and extended senses in Neo-Greek combinations: **phanerogenetic, phaneromania, phaneroplasm.** Also, **phaner-: phanerosis.** Related forms: **phaeo-, pheno-¹, pheno-², phenol-, phenyl-, photo-.**

1972 pharmaco- A word-initial combining element, derived from Greek *phármako(n)* 'drug, medicine,' used in its etymological sense in Neo-Greek combinations: **pharmacodiagnosis, pharmacomania, pharmacotherapy.** Also, **pharmac-: pharmacist.**

1973 pharyngo- A word-initial combining element, derived from Greek *pháryn(x), pháryng(os)* 'opening of the windpipe and gullet; throat,' used in the sense of 'of or pertaining to the *pharynx,* the section of the body which extends from the nasal cavities to the esophagus' in biomedical combinations: **pharyngoglossal, pharyngomaxillary, pharyngospasm.** Also, **pharyng-: pharyngitis.**

1974 pheno-¹ A word-initial combining element, derived from Greek *phaín(ein)* 'to show, make apparent' (cf. *phaínesthai* 'to appear,' literally, 'to come to light') plus the combining vowel *-o-,* used in the sense of 'showing, making evident' and in extensions of this sense in Neo-Greek combinations: **phenocryst, phenology, pheno-type.** Compare **pheno-².** Related forms: **phaeo-, phanero-, phenol-, phenyl-, photo-.**

1975 pheno-² A word-initial combining element, derived from French *(acide) phén(ique)* 'phenol (C_6H_5OH)' (based on Greek *phaínein* 'to show,' literally, 'to bring to light,' phenol having originally been extracted from illuminating gas) plus the combining vowel *-o-,* used in the sense of 'of, pertaining to, containing, or derived from *benzene*' in chemical terminology: **phenobarbital, phenothiazine, phenoxanthein.** Also, **phen-: phenoxycaffeine.** Compare **pheno-¹, phenol-, phenyl-.**

1976 phenol- A word-initial combining element, also occurring as a word, derived from **pheno-²** plus the suffix *-ol* which is used in naming compounds made up of one or more hydroxyl groups joined to a hydrocarbon group, used in the sense of 'of, pertaining to, containing, or derived from *phenol* (C_6H_5OH)' in biochemical terminology: **phenolemia, phenolphthalein, phenolquinine.** Compare **pheno-².**

1977 phenyl- A word-initial combining element, also occurring as a word, derived from **pheno-²** plus the suffix *-yl* which is used in naming chemical radicals, used in the sense of 'of, pertaining to, containing, or derived from *phenyl* (C_6H_5)' in chemical terminology: **phenylcarbinol, phenylethylamine, phenylquinoline.** Also, ϕ: ϕ-**carbinol.** Compare **pheno-², hylo-.** See **phi-.**

1978 pheo- A variant of **phaeo-.**

1979 phi- (Φ, ϕ) A word-initial combining element, the twenty-first letter of the Greek alphabet, used chiefly as a designation of 'the twenty-first carbon atom in a straight chain compound or a derivative thereof in which the substitute group is attached to that atom' and as an abbreviatory symbol for '**phenyl-**' in chemical terminology. See **alpha-, phenyl-.**

1980 philo- A word-initial combining element, derived from Greek *phílo(s)* 'beloved, loving,' used in this latter and extended senses in Neo-Greek combinations: **philodendron, philology, philopatridomania.** Also, **phil-: philanthropy.**

1981 phlebo- A word-initial combining element, derived from Greek *phlé(ps)*, *phleb(ós)* 'vein' (from the verb *phleîn* 'to flow') plus the combining vowel *-o-*, used in its etymological sense in Neo-Greek combinations: **phlebocarcinoma, phlebolith, phlebotropism.** Also, **phleb-: phlebitis.**

1982 phlogo- A word-initial combining element, derived from Greek *phló(x)*, *phlog(ós)* 'fire, flame' plus the combining vowel *-o-*, used chiefly in the sense of 'of or pertaining to inflammation' in Neo-Greek combinations: **phlogocyte, phlogogenic, phlogoxelotism.** Also, **phlog-: phlogistic.** Related forms: **black-, blue-, flame-, flavo-.**

1983 phono- A word-initial combining element, derived from Greek *phōn(ḗ)* 'sound, tone (esp. of the voice)' plus the combining vowel *-o-*, used in its etymological and extended senses in Neo-Greek and Neo-Latin combinations: **phonograph, phonophobia, phonoreceptor.** Also, **phon-: phonautograph.**

1984 **phoro-** A word-initial combining element, derived from Greek *phóro(s)*, a verbal noun formed to the verb *phérein* 'to bear, carry,' used in the sense of 'bearing or carrying that which is named by the combining root' and in extensions of this sense in Neo-Greek combinations: **phoroblast, phorology, phorometer.** Also, **phor-: phoria.** Related form: **birth-.**

1985 **phos-** A variant of **photo-.**

1986 **phosph-[1]** A variant of **phosphor-.**

1987 **phosph-[2]** A variant of **phosphat-.**

1988 **phosphat-** A word-initial combining element, derived from English *phosphat(e)* 'salt of phosphoric acid' (from **phosph-[1]** (**phosphoro-**) plus the suffix *-ate* which is used in naming salts of acids), used in its etymological sense in biochemical terminology: **phosphatemia, phosphatidosis, phosphatine.** Also, **phosph-[2], phosphata-, phosphato-, phospho-[2]: phosphuria, phosphatagenic, phosphatoptosis, phosphocreatinase.** Compare **phosphor-.**

1989 **phospho-[1]** A variant of **phosphor-.**

1990 **phospho-[2]** A variant of **phosphat-.**

1991 **phosphor-** A word-initial combining element, derived from **phos-** (**photo-**) plus **phor(o)-,** used in the sense of 'of, pertaining to, containing, or derived from the nonmetallic element *phosphorus* (P) (so named because phosphorus—literally, 'light-bearer'—glows in the dark)' in biochemical terminology: **phosphorenesis, phosphorhidrosis, phosphoruria.** Also, **phosph-[1], phospho[1], phosphoro-: phosphite, phospholipid, phosphorolysis.** Compare **phosphat-; photo-** and **phoro-.**

1992 **photo-** A word-initial combining element, derived from Greek *phô̂(s), phōt(ós)* 'light, daylight' plus the combining vowel *-o-,* used in its etymological and extended senses, chief among these being 'of or pertaining to *photography,* the recording of images on light-sensitive surfaces,' in a variety of combinations: **photoelectron, photomontage, photosynthesis.** Also, **phos-, phot-: phosgenic, photopsia.** Compare **phaeo-.** Related forms: **phanero-, pheno-[1], pheno-[2], phenol-, phenyl-.**

1993 **phren-[1]** A variant of **phreno-.**

1994 **phren-[2]** A variant of **phrenico-.**

1995 **phrenico-** A word-initial combining element, derived from English *phrenic* 'of or pertaining to the diaphragm or to the mind' (from Greek *phrēn* 'midriff; diaphragm; seat of human emotional and mental activity' plus the adjective-forming suffix *-ic*) plus the combining vowel *-o-*, used in the specialized sense of 'of or pertaining to the *phrenic nerve,* a branch of the fourth cervical nerve which is distributed through the thorax to the diaphragm' in biomedical terminology: **phreniconeurectomy, phrenicotomy, phrenicotripsy.** Also, **phren-², phrenic-: phrenectomy, phrenicectomy.** Compare **phreno-.**

1996 **phreno-** A word-initial combining element, derived from Greek *phrēn* 'midriff; diaphragm; seat of human emotional and mental activity' plus the combining vowel *-o-*, used in the sense of 'of or pertaining to the diaphragm' and 'of or pertaining to the mind' and in extensions of these two senses in biomedical terminology: **phrenoglottic, phrenology, phrenosterol.** Also, **phren-¹: phrenic.** Compare **phrenico-.**

1997 **phryno-** A word-initial combining element, derived from Greek *phrŷno(s)* 'toad,' used in its etymological and extended senses in Neo-Greek combinations: **phrynoderma, phrynolysine, *Phrynosoma.*** Also, **phryn-: phrynin.**

1998 **phthisio-** A word-initial combining element, derived from Greek *phthísi(s)* 'decay, wasting away' (from the verb *phthiein* 'to waste away') plus the combining vowel *-o-*, used in its etymological and extended senses, chief among these being 'of or pertaining to *tuberculosis* ('consumption'),' in Neo-Greek combinations: **phthisiogenesis, phthisiology, phthisiotherapy.** Also, **phthis-: phthisic.**

1999 **phyco-** A word-initial combining element, derived from Greek *phŷko(s)* 'seaweed,' used in its etymological and extended senses in Neo-Greek combinations: **phycochrome, phycology, *Phycomycetes.***

2000 **phyllo-** A word-initial combining element, derived from Greek *phýllo(n)* 'leaf,' used in its etymological and extended senses in Neo-Greek combinations: **phyllochlorin, phyllodineous, phyllophagous.** Also, **phyll-: *Phyllanthus.*** Related forms: **flori-, flour-, flower-, folii-.**

2001 **phylo-** A word-initial combining element, derived from Greek *phyl(ē̂)* 'community of individuals; tribe' plus the combining vowel *-o-*, used in its etymological and extended senses in Neo-Greek combinations: **phylobiology, phylogenesis, *Phyloptera.*** Related forms: **bond-, physali-, physico-, physio-, phyto-.**

2002 phys-   A variant of **physio-**.

2003 physali-   A word-initial combining element, derived from Greek *physalí(s)* 'bubble,' used in its etymological and extended senses in Neo-Greek and Neo-Latin combinations: **physaliferous, physaliform, physaliphore**. Also, **physalo-**: *Physaloptera.* Related forms: **bond-, phylo-, physico-, physio-, phyto-**.

2004 physico-   A word-initial combining element, derived from Greek *physikó(s)* 'natural, inborn' (from *phýs(is)* 'nature, inborn quality' plus the adjective-forming suffix *-ikós*), used in its etymological and extended senses, chief among these being 'bodily,' in Neo-Greek and Neo-Latin combinations: **physicochemical, physicomental, physicotherapy**. Also, **physic-**: **physical**. Compare **physio-**.

2005 physio-   A word-initial combining element, derived from Greek *phýsi(s)* 'nature, inborn quality' plus the combining vowel *-o-*, used in the sense of 'of or pertaining to nature or to *physiology,* the science which is concerned with the natural functions of living organisms' in Neo-Greek and Neo-Latin combinations: **physiogenesis, physiomedical, physiopsychic**. Also, **phys-**: **physiatrics**. Compare **physico-**. Related forms: **bond-, phylo-, physali-, phyto-**.

2006 physo-   A word-initial combining element, derived from Greek *phûs(a)* 'breath, wind' plus the combining vowel *-o-*, used in the sense of 'of or pertaining to air or gas' and in extensions of this sense in Neo-Greek combinations: **physocele, physohematometra, physopyosalpinx**.

2007 phyto-   A word-initial combining element, derived from Greek *phytó(n)* '(a) plant,' literally, 'that which has grown,' used in its etymological and extended senses in Neo-Greek and Neo-Latin combinations: **phytochemistry, phytocide, phytoparasite**. Also, **phyt-, phyton-**: **phytalbumin, phytoncide**. Related forms: **bond-, phylo-, physali-, physico-, physio-**.

2008 pi- (Π, π)   A word-initial combining element, the sixteenth letter of the Greek alphabet, used chiefly to designate 'the sixteenth carbon atom in a straight chain compound or a derivative thereof in which the substitute group is attached to that atom' in chemical terminology. See **alpha-**.

2009 pick-   A word-initial combining element, also occurring as a word, derived from Old English *pīc* 'point, pointed tool,' used in its etymological and extended senses, chief among these being '(to) probe (with a pointed object), pluck,' in combination with other

English elements: **pickaxe, picklock, pickpocket.** Related forms: **pico-, pitch-¹.**

2010 **pico-** A word-initial combining element, derived from Spanish *pico* 'beak, tip, peak' and, by extension, 'large quantity,' used in the specialized sense of 'one trillionth' in the terminology of the metric system: **picofarad, picometer, picosecond.** Related forms: **pick-, pitch-¹.**

2011 **picro-** A word-initial combining element, derived from Greek *pikró(s)* 'sharp, bitter' (from an Indo-European root meaning 'incise'), used in its etymological and extended senses, chief among these being 'of, pertaining to, containing or derived from *picric acid* $(C_6H_2(NO_2)_3OH)$ (which is so named for its bitterness),' in Neo-Greek and Neo-Latin combinations: **picroformal, picrogeusia, picrotoxin.** Also, **picr-: picrin.** Related forms: **file-², pigmento-, poikilo-.**

2012 **piece-** A word-initial combining element, also occurring as a word, derived from Old French *piece* 'portion,' used in its etymological and extended senses in combination with other English elements: **piece-dyed, piecemeal, piecework.** Related form(?): **patch-.**

2013 **piezo-** A word-initial combining element, derived from Greek *piéz(ein)* 'to press' plus the combining vowel *-o-*, used in the sense of 'of or pertaining to pressure' in Neo-Greek combinations: **piezoelectricity, piezometer, piezotherapy.** Also, **piez-: piezallochromy.**

2014 **pig-** A word-initial combining element, also occurring as a word, derived from Middle English *pig(ge)* '(young) swine,' used in its etymological and extended senses in combination with other English elements: **pigboat, pigheaded, pigskin.**

2015 **pigeon-** A word-initial combining element, also occurring as a word, derived from Old French *pijon* 'young bird' (from onomatopoeic Latin *pīpiāre* 'to peep'), used in the sense of 'bird of the family *Columbidae*' and in extensions of this sense in combination with other English elements: **pigeonhole, pigeon-toed, pigeonwing.** Related form: **pipe-.**

2016 **pigmento-** A word-initial combining element, derived from Latin *pigment(um)* 'paint' (from an Indo-European root meaning 'incise,' hence, 'tattoo') plus the combining vowel *-o-*, used chiefly in the extended sense of 'of or pertaining to natural bodily coloring' in Neo-Latin and Neo-Greek combinations: **pigmentogenesis, pig-**

mentolysin, pigmentophore. Also, **pigment-: pigmentation.** Related forms: **file-², picro-, poikilo-.**

2017 **pilo-**   A word-initial combining element, derived from Latin *pil(us)* 'hair' plus the combining vowel *-o-*, used in its etymological and extended senses in Neo-Latin and Neo-Greek combinations: **pilobezoar, piloerection, pilology.** Also, **pili-: piliform.**

2018 **pilot-**   A word-initial combining element, also occurring as a word, derived through French from unattested Greek **pēdōt(ēs)* 'steersman' (from *pēdón* 'flat part of an oar; rudder'), used in its etymological and extended senses in combination with other English elements: **pilotfish, pilothouse, pilotweed.** Related forms: **foot-, pedo-², podo-.**

2019 **pimel-**   A word-initial combining element, derived from Greek *pimel(ḗ)* '(soft) fat,' used in its etymological and extended senses in Neo-Greek combinations: **pimelitis, pimeloma, pimeluria.** Also, **pimele-, pimelo-:** *Pimelepterus*, **pimelopterygium.** Compare **pio-.** Related form: **fat-.**

2020 **pin-**   A word-initial combining element, also occurring as a word, derived from Latin *pin(na)* 'feather' and, by extension in Late Latin, 'pointed peg used as a fastener,' used in this latter and extended senses in combination with other English elements: **pinball, pincushion, pinpoint.** Compare **pinni-.**

2021 **pinch-**   A word-initial combining element, also occurring as a word, derived through Anglo-Norman French from unattested Latin **pinctiāre* 'to nip,' used in its etymological and extended senses in combination with other English elements: **pinchbottle, pinchcock, pinchpenny.**

2022 **pine-**   A word-initial combining element, also occurring as a word, derived from Latin *pīn(us)* 'coniferous tree of the genus *Pinus*,' used in its etymological and extended sense in combination with other English elements: **pineapple, pinedrops, pinesap.**

2023 **pinnati-**   A word-initial combining element, derived from Latin *pinnāt(us)* 'feathered' (from *pinna* 'feather') plus the combining vowel *-i-*, used chiefly in the extended sense of 'featherlike' in Neo-Latin combinations: **pinnatilobate, pinnatipartite, pinnatisect.** Compare **pinni-.**

2024 **pinni-**   A word-initial combining element, derived from Latin *pinn(a)* 'feather' plus the combining vowel *-i-*, used in its etymological and extended senses, chief among these being 'fin,' in Neo-Latin combinations: **pinniform, pinninerved, pinnitarsal.** Compare **pin-, pinnati-.** Related forms: **feather-, pen-¹, penni-, pterido-, ptero-, pterygo-, ptilo-.**

2025 **pio-** A word-initial combining element, derived from Greek *píō(n)* 'fat,' used in its etymological and extended senses in Neo-Greek combinations: **pio-epithelium,** *Piophila,* **pioscope.** Also, **pi-², pion-: piorthopnea, pionemia.** Compare **pimel-.** Related form: **fat-.**

2026 **pipe-** A word-initial combining element, derived, ultimately, from Latin *pīp(āre)* 'to chirp, peep,' used chiefly in the extended sense of 'tube, esp. one through which tobacco smoke may be drawn (which is so named because of its resemblance to a tube through which musical tones may be produced)' in combination with other English elements: **pipe-clay, pipefish, pipestone.** Related form: **pigeon-.**

2027 **piper-** A word-initial combining element, derived from Latin *piper* 'pepper' (from Sanskrit *pippalī* 'berry; peppercorn'), used in its etymological and extended senses, chief among these being 'of, pertaining to, containing, or derived from *piperine* ($C_{17}H_{19}NO_3$), an extract of black pepper,' in Neo-Latin and Neo-Greek combinations: **piperazine, piperidine, piperism.**

2028 **pisci-** A word-initial combining element, derived from Latin *pisci(s)* 'fish,' used in its etymological sense in Neo-Latin combinations: **piscicolous, pisciculture, pisciform.** Related form: **fish-.**

2029 **pistol-** A word-initial combining element, also occurring as a word, derived through French from Czech *pištal(a)* 'pipe,' used in the extended sense of 'handgun (so named because of the shape of its barrel)' in combination with other English elements: **pistol-grip, pistol-handle, pistol-whip.**

2030 **pit-** A word-initial combining element, also occurring as a word, derived from Old English *pyt(t)* '(deep) hole in the ground,' used in its etymological and extended senses in combination with other English elements: **pitfall, pitman, pitsaw.**

2031 **pitch-¹** A word-initial combining element, also occurring as a word, derived from Middle English *piht(e)* 'thrust,' used in its etymological and extended senses in combination with other English elements: **pitchfork, pitchman, pitch-out.** Related forms: **pick-, pico-.**

2032 **pitch-²** A word-initial combining element, derived through Old

English from Latin *pi(x), pic(is)* 'tar,' used in its etymological and extended senses in combination with other English elements: **pitch-black, pitchblende, pitch-dark.**

2033 place- A word-initial combining element, also occurring as a word, derived through Old French and Latin from Greek *plateîa (hodós)* 'broad (way),' *plateîa* being the feminine form corresponding to (masculine) *platýs* 'flat, broad,' used in a variety of extensions of its etymological sense, chief among these being 'space, position,' in combination with other English elements: **place-kick, placeman, place-name.** Compare **platy-.**

2034 placento- A word-initial combining element, derived from Latin *placent(a)* 'flat cake' plus the combining vowel *-o-,* used in the extended sense of 'cakelike mass, esp. the uterine organ which connects the mother to the child by way of the umbilical cord' in biomedical terminology: **placentocytotoxin, placentogenesis, placentopathy.** Also, **placent-, placenta-: placentitis, placentapepton.** Related forms: **field-, flat-, floor-, palmati-, place-, plagio-, plain-, plano-[1], plano-[2], plasmo-, plasmodi-, plasto-, plate-, platino-, platy-.**

2035 plagio- A word-initial combining element, derived from Greek *plágio(s)* 'sideways, slanting, sloping,' used in its etymological and extended senses in Neo-Greek combinations: **plagiocephalic, plagioclase, plagiotropism.** Also, **plagi-: plagiodont.** Related forms: **field-, flat-, floor-, palmati-, place-, placento-, plain-, plano-[1], plano-[2], plasmo-, plasmodi-, plasto-, plate-, platino-, platy-.**

2036 plain- A word-initial combining element, also occurring as a word, derived through Old French from Latin *plān(us)* 'flat, level,' used chiefly in the extended sense of 'straightforward, simple' in combination with other English elements: **plainchant, plainclothes, plainspoken.** Compare **plano-[1].**

2037 plan-[1] A variant of **plano-[1].**

2038 plan-[2] A variant of **plano-[2].**

2039 plano-[1] A word-initial combining element, derived from Latin *plān(us)* 'flat, level' plus the combining vowel *-o-,* used in its etymological and extended senses in Neo-Latin and Neo-Greek combinations: **planocellular, planoconvex, planography.** Also, **plan-[1], plani-: *Planorbis,* planigram.** Compare **plain-.** Related forms: **field-, flat-, floor-, palmati-, place-, placento-, plagio-, plano-[2], plasmo-, plasmodi-, plasto-, plate-, platino-, platy-.**

2040 **plano-²** A word-initial combining element, derived from Greek *pláno(s)* '(a) wandering' (from an Indo-European root meaning 'flat, spread out,' the idea being, presumably, that to wander is to spread out), used in its etymological and extended senses in inherited and Neo-Greek combinations: **planoblast, planocyte, planotopokinesia.** Also, **plan-²: planet.** Related forms: **field-, flat-, floor-, palmati-, place-, placento-, plagio-, plain-, plano-¹, plasmo-, plasmodi-, plasto-, plate-, platino-, platy-.**

2041 **plasmo-** A word-initial combining element, derived from Greek *plásm(a)*, *plásm(atos)* 'that which is formed or molded' (from the verb *plássein* 'to form, mold' which is itself derived from an Indo-European root meaning 'flat, spread out') plus the combining vowel *-o-*, used in the extended sense of 'medium in which matter is suspended to form a colloid' and in extensions of this sense, chief among these being 'of or pertaining to *protoplasm,* the colloidal substance which forms the basis of plant and animal life,' in Neo-Greek combinations: **plasmogen, plasmolysis, plasmosphere.** Also, **plasm-, plasma-, plasmat-, plasmato-: plasmic, plasmapheresis, plasmatic, plasmatorrhexis.** Compare **plasmodi-, plasto-.** Related forms: **field-, flat-, floor-, palmati-, place-, placento-, plagio-, plain-, plano-¹, plano-², plate-, platino-, platy-.**

2042 **plasmodi-** A word-initial combining element, derived from **plasm(o)-** plus the noun-forming suffix *-ode* (from Greek *-o(ei)dē(s)* '-like') plus the noun-forming suffix *-i(um),* used in its etymological and extended senses in Neo-Greek and Neo-Latin combinations: **plasmodiblast, plasmodicide, plasmoditrophoblast.** Compare **plasmo-.**

2043 **plasto-** A word-initial combining element, derived from Greek *plastó(s)* 'molded, formed' (from the verb *plássein* 'to mold, form' (from an Indo-European root meaning 'spread out; flat')), used in its etymological and extended senses, chief among these being 'forming, able to form or to be formed,' in Neo-Greek combinations: **plastochondria, plastodynamia, plastotype.** Also, **plast-: plastic.** Compare **plasmo-, plasmodi-.** Related forms: **field-, flat-, floor-, palmati-, place-, placento-, plagio-, plain-, plano-¹, plano-², plate-, platino-, platy-.**

2044 **plate-** A word-initial combining element, also occurring as a word, derived through Old French and Late Latin from Greek *platý(s)* 'flat,' used in the sense of 'flat object' in combination with other English elements: **plate-dog, plateholder, platelayer.** Compare **platy-.**

2045 **platino-** A word-initial combining element, derived from Neo-Latin *platin(um)* 'the silvery metallic element (Pt)' (from Spanish *platin(a)*, a diminutive form of *plata* 'silver,' originally, '(thin) sheet of metal' (through Late Latin from Greek *platýs* 'spread out, flat')) plus the combining vowel -*o*-, used in its etymological and extended senses in a variety of combinations: **platinocyanide, platinogold, platinotype**. Also, **platin-: platinic**. Compare **platy-**.

2046 **platy-** A word-initial combining element, derived from Greek *platý(s)* 'flat, broad, wide,' used in its etymological and extended senses in Neo-Greek combinations: **platycrania, platyhelminth, platyspondylisis**. Compare **place-, plate-, platino-**. Related forms: **field-, flat-, floor-, palmati-, placento-, plagio-, plain-, plano-[1], plano-[2], plasmo-, plasmodi-, plasto-**.

2047 **play-** A word-initial combining element, also occurring as a word, derived from Old English *pleġ(an)* 'to exercise oneself, esp. as a diversion from work,' used in its etymological and extended senses in combination with other English elements: **play-act, playboy, playmate**.

2048 **plecto-** A word-initial combining element, derived from Greek *plektó(s)* 'plaited, twisted,' used in its etymological and extended senses in Neo-Greek combinations: *Plectocomia*, **plectognath, plectospondylous**. Also, **pleco-: plecolepidous**. Related form: **plici-**.

2049 **pleio-** A variant of **pleo-**.

2050 **pleni-** A word-initial combining element, derived from Latin *plēn(us)* 'full' plus the combining vowel -*i*-, used in its etymological and extended senses in Neo-Latin combinations: **plenicorn, plenilunar, plenipotentiary**. Related forms: **full-, pleo-, pluri-, poly-**.

2051 **pleo-** A word-initial combining element, derived from Greek *ple(i)ō(n)*, the comparative form of *polýs* 'many,' used in the sense of 'more, greater (in number), supernumerary' and in extensions of this sense in Neo-Greek combinations: **pleochromatic, pleomastia, pleomorphism**. Also, **pleio-, pleon-, plio-: pleiomorphic, pleonotia, Pliocene**. Compare **poly-**.

2052 **plesio-** A word-initial combining element, derived from Greek *plēsio(s)* 'near' (from an Indo-European root meaning 'thrust,' the idea being, presumably, that that which is near is as though thrust into proximity), used chiefly in the extended sense of 'resembling that which is named by the combining root' in Neo-Greek

combinations: *Plesiochelys,* **plesiomorphous, plesiosaurus.** Also,
plesi-: *Plesiarctomys.* Related form: **push-.**

2053   **pleuro-**   A word-initial combining element, derived from Greek
pleur(á) 'rib, side' and, by extension, 'the membrane which lines the
chest cavity' plus the combining vowel *-o-,* used in its etymological
senses in biomedical terminology: **pleurocentesis, pleurolysis,
pleurosomus.** Also, **pleur-: pleuritis.**

2054   **plici-**   A word-initial combining element, derived from Latin *plic(a)*
'(a) fold' plus the combining vowel *-o-,* used in its etymological and
extended senses in Neo-Latin combinations: **plicidentine, pliciform,**
Plicipennes. Related form: **plecto.**

2055   **plio-**   A variant of **pleo-.**

2056   **plow-**   A word-initial combining element, also occurring as a word,
derived from Old Norse *plô(gr)* 'device for cutting furrows in the
earth,' used in its etymological sense in combination with other
English elements: **plowboy, plowland, plowshare.** Also (chiefly
British), **plough-: ploughboy.**

2057   **plug-**   A word-initial combining element, also occurring as a word,
derived from Middle Dutch *plug(ge)* 'stopper,' used in its etymological and extended senses in combination with other English
words: **plugboard, plughole, plugugly.**

2058   **plumbo-**   A word-initial combining element, derived from Latin
plumb(um) 'lead, the metallic element (Pb)' plus the combining
vowel *-o-,* used in its etymological sense in biochemical terminology: **plumbocalcite, plumbogummite, plumbotherapy.** Also, **plumb-,
plumbi-: plumbite, plumbiferous.**

2059   **plumi-**   A word-initial combining element, derived from Latin
plūm(a) 'feather' plus the combining vowel *-i-,* used in its etymological and extended senses in Neo-Latin combinations: **plumicorn,
plumigerous, plumiped.**

2060   **pluri-**   A word-initial combining element, derived from Latin *plu(s),*
plūr(is) 'more' plus the combining vowel *-i-,* used in its etymological and extended senses, chief among these being 'several,' in Neo-
Latin and Neo-Greek combinations: **pluridyscrinia, plurigravida,
pluriresistant.** Also, **plur-: plural.** Related forms: **full-, pleni-, pleo-,
poly-.**

2061   **pluto-**   A word-initial combining element, derived from Greek *ploûto(s)* 'wealth' (from an Indo-European root meaning 'flow, float'), used in its etymological and extended senses in Neo-Greek combinations: **plutocrat, plutology, plutomania.** Also, **plut-: plutarchy.** Related forms: **float-, flood-, fly-¹, fly-², pluvio-, pneumo-², pulmo-, pyelo-.**

2062   **pluvio-**   A word-initial combining element, derived from Latin *pluvi(a)* 'rain' plus the combining vowel *-o-,* used in its etymological sense in Neo-Latin and Neo-Greek combinations: **pluviograph, pluviometer, pluvioscope.** Also, **pluvi-: pluvial.** Related forms: **float-, flood-, fly-¹, fly-², pluto-, pneumo-², pulmo-, pyelo-.**

2063   **pneo-**   A word-initial combining element, derived from Greek *pno(ḗ)* 'air, vapor, breath' (cf. *pneîn* 'to blow, breathe') plus the combining vowel *-o-,* used chiefly in the sense of 'of or pertaining to respiration' in Neo-Greek combinations: **pneodynamics, pneogaster, pneograph.** Related form: **pneumato-.**

2064   **pneum-¹**   A variant of **pneumato-.**

2065   **pneum-²**   A variant of **pneumo-².**

2066   **pneumato-**   A word-initial combining element, derived from Greek *pneûma, pneúmat(os)* 'wind, air, breath, respiration' (cf. *pneîn* 'to blow, breathe'), used in its etymological and extended senses in Neo-Greek combinations: **pneumatodyspnea, pneumatology, pneumatometer.** Also, **pneum-¹, pneuma-, pneumat-, pneumo-¹: pneumarthrosis, pneumascope, pneumathemia, pneumohemia.** Related form: **pneo-.**

2067   **pneumo-¹**   A variant of **pneumato-.**

2068   **pneumo-²**   A word-initial combining element, derived from Greek *pneúmō(n)* 'lung,' a variant of *pleúmōn* (from an Indo-European root meaning 'flow, float' (cf. Greek *pleîn* 'to sail')), the change of *pleúmōn* to *pneúmōn* being by analogy to derivatives of the (etymologically unrelated) verb *pneîn* 'to blow, breathe' (cf. **pneo-, pneumato-**), used in its etymological sense in biomedical terminology: **pneumoalveolography, pneumochirurgia, pneumopexy.** Also, **pneum-², pneumon-, pneumono-: pneumectomy, pneumonia, pneumonocirrhosis.** Related forms: **float-, flood-, fly-¹, fly-², pluto-, pluvio-, pulmo-, pyelo-.**

2069   **pneumohydro-**   A word-initial combining element, derived from **pneumo-¹ (pneumato-)** plus **hydro-¹,** used in the sense of 'of or pertaining to a collection of gas and fluid in that region of the body which is named by the combining root': **pneumohydrometra, pneumohydropericadrium, pneohydrothorax.** Compare **pneumato-, hydro-**[1].

2070 **pneumono-**   A variant of **pneumo-**[2].

2071 **pocket-**   A word-initial combining element, also occurring as a word, derived from Old (North) French *poque* 'pouch' plus the diminutive suffix *-et,* used in the specialized sense of 'small pouch sewn into a garment' and in extensions of this sense in combination with other English elements: **pocketbook, pocket-handkerchief, pocketknife.**

2072 **podo-**   A word-initial combining element, derived from Greek *po(ús), pod(ós)* 'foot' plus the combining vowel *-o-,* used in its etymological and extended senses in Neo-Greek combinations: **podobromidrosis, pododerm, podograph.** Also, **pod-: podiatry.** Related forms: **foot-, pilot-, pedo-**[2].

2073 **poecilo-**   A variant of **poikilo-.**

2074 **poikilo-**   A word-initial combining element, derived from Greek *poikílo(s)* 'mottled, variegated' and, by extension, 'various' (from an Indo-European root meaning 'incise,' hence, 'tattoo'), used in its etymological and extended senses, chief among these being 'irregular, abnormal,' in Neo-Greek combinations: **poikiloblast, poikilocytosis, poikilothermal.** Also, **poecil-, poecilo-, poikil-: poecilonomy, poecilocytosis, poikilergasia.** Related forms: **file-**[2]**, picro-, pigmento-.**

2075 **point-**   A word-initial combining element, also occurring as a word, derived through Old French from the substantive use of Latin *pun(c)t(a)* and *pun(c)t(um),* forms (of different grammatical genders) of the past participle of the verb *pungere* 'to pierce,' *puncta* having been used in the sense of 'sharp end (of a piercing instrument),' while *punctum* was used to mean 'small mark (as might be made by the sharp end of a piercing instrument),' used in its etymological and extended senses in combination with other English elements: **point-blank, point-set, point-to-point.**

2076 **polari-**   A word-initial combining element, derived from English *polar(ization)* '(production of) the condition in which light or other radiant waves vibrate in a single plane, ellipse, or circle' (from Neo-Latin *polār(is)* 'of or pertaining to a *pole*' (from Latin *pol(us)* 'pole; either extremity of an axis through a sphere' plus the adjective-forming suffix *-āris*) plus the (English) verb-forming suffix -*iz*(*e*) plus the noun-forming suffix -*ation*) plus the combining vowel -*i*-, used in its etymological sense in variety of combinations: **polarimeter, polariscope, polaristrobometer.** Also, **polaro-: polarogram.** Related forms: **coll-², collar-, cyclo-, palin-, teleo-³, telo-¹, wheel-.**

2077 **polio-** A word-initial combining element, derived from Greek *polió*(*s*) 'gray,' used in its etymological and extended senses, chief among these being 'of or pertaining to the gray matter of the nervous system,' in biomedical terminology: **poliocidal, poliomyelopathy, poliothrix.**

2078 **polioencephalo-** A word-initial combining element, derived from polio- plus **encephalo-,** used in the sense of 'of or pertaining to the gray matter of the brain' in biomedical terminology: **polioencephalomeningomyelitis, polioencephalopathy, polioencephalotropic.** Also, **polioencephal-: polioencephalitis.** Compare **polio-, encephalo-.**

2079 **poly-** A word-initial combining element, derived from Greek *polý*(*s*) 'many,' used in its etymological and extended senses, chief among these being 'excessive, supernumerary,' in Neo-Greek and Neo-Latin combinations: **polyceptor, polychromatic, polyorchidism.** Compare **pleo-.** Related forms: **full-, pleni-, pluri-.**

2080 **pomi-** A word-initial combining element, derived from Latin *pōm*(*um*) 'fruit, fruit-tree' plus the combining vowel -*i*-, used in its etymological and extended senses in Neo-Latin and Neo-Greek combinations: **pomiculture, pomiferous, pomiform.** Also, **pomo-: pomology.**

2081 **pono-** A word-initial combining element, derived from Greek *póno*(*s*) 'toil, pain,' used in its etymological and extended senses in Neo-Greek combinations: **ponograph, ponopalmosis, ponophobia.**

2082 **poor-** A word-initial combining element, also occurring as a word, derived through Old French from Latin *pau*(*pe*)*r* 'of little means,' used in its etymological and extended senses in combination with other English elements: **poorhouse, poor-mouth, poor-spirited.** Related forms: **pauci-, pedo-¹.**

2083 **pop-** A word-initial combining element of onomatopoeic origin, also occurring as a word, used in the sense of 'making a sharp explosive sound' and in extensions of this sense in combination with other English elements: **popcorn, popeyed, popgun.**

2084   **por-**   A variant of **poro-**.

2085   **pori-**   A variant of **poro-**.

2086   **pork-**   A word-initial combining element, also occurring as a word, derived through Old French from Latin *porc(us)* 'hog, swine,' used in its etymological and extended senses in combination with other English elements: **porkchop, porkfish, porkpie (hat)**.

2087   **porno-**   A word-initial combining element, derived from Greek *pórn(ē)* 'prostitute' (from a verb meaning 'to export, sell,' prostitutes in ancient Greece having largely been victims of the slave trade) plus the combining vowel *-o-*, used in its etymological and extended senses in Neo-Greek combinations: **pornocracy, pornography, pornolagnia**.

2088   **poro-**   A word-initial combining element, derived through Old French and Latin from Greek *póro(s)* 'passageway,' used chiefly in the extended sense of 'of or pertaining to a *pore*, a small orifice' in Neo-Greek and Neo-Latin combinations: **porocephalosis, poroplastic, porotomy**. Also, **por-, pori-: poradenitis, poriferous**. Related form: **porte-**.

2089   **porphyr-**   A word-initial combining element, derived from Greek *porphýr(a)* 'purple-fish (*Purpura murex*),' hence, 'purple dye (obtained from the purple-fish),' hence 'purple,' used in this last and extended senses in Neo-Greek combinations: **porphyria, porphyrin, porphyropsin**. Also, **porph-, porpho-: porphin, porphobilin**.

2090   **porte-**   A word-initial combining element, derived from French *porte(r)* 'to carry' (from Latin *portāre* 'to convey, carry'), appearing in the sense of 'carrying that which is named by the combining root' and in extensions of this sense in borrowings from French: **porte-acid, porte-aiguille, porte-noeud**. Also, **port-: portmanteau**. Related form: **poro-**.

2091   **post-¹**   A word-initial combining element, derived from Latin *post* 'behind, after,' used in its etymological senses in a variety of combinations: **postcerebellar, postdiastolic, postwar**. Compare **postero-**.

2092   **post-²**   A word-initial combining element, derived through Old French from Latin *pos(i)t(us)*, the past participle of the verb *ponere* 'to put, place,' used in the specialized sense of 'of or pertaining to the mail' (from the use of *positus* as '(military) position or station,' hence, 'station to which or from which (military) dispatches are to be carried,' hence, 'dispatch, mail'), used in this last and extended senses in combination with other English elements: **postcard, posthaste, postmaster.**

2093 postero- A word-initial combining element, derived from Latin *poster(us)* 'following' (from *post* 'behind, after') plus the combining vowel *-o-*, used in the sense of 'behind, rear, dorsal' in Neo-Latin combinations: **posteroanterior, posterolateral, posteroparietal.** Compare **post-¹**.

2094 pot- A word-initial combining element, also occurring as a word, derived from Old English *pot(t)* '(round) container,' used in its etymological and extended senses in combination with other English elements: **potbelly, potboiler, potluck.**

2095 potamo- A word-initial combining element, derived from Greek *potamó(s)* 'river,' used in its etymological and extended senses in Neo-Greek combinations: *Potamogale,* **potamography, potamology.** Also, **potam-: potamic.**

2096 power- A word-initial combining element, also occurring as a word, derived from Old French *poeir* 'to be able,' used in the sense of 'ability, authority, self-sufficiency' and in extensions of this sense in combination with other English elements: **powerboat, power-dive, powerhouse.**

2097 prae- A variant of **pre-**.

2098 pre- A word-initial combining element, derived from Latin *pr(a)e* 'before; in front of,' used in its etymological and extended senses in a variety of combinations: **precirrhosis, preconscious, prewar.** Also, **prae-: praecordial.** Related forms: **far-, first-, for-¹, fore-³, forth-, par-³, para-¹, peri-, perisso-, primi-, pro-¹, pro-², proprio-, pros-¹, proso-, protero-, proto-, proximo-.**

2099 presby- A word-initial combining element, derived from Greek *présby(s)* 'old, aged,' used in its etymological and extended senses in Neo-Greek combinations: **presbyacusia, presbyopic, presbysphacelus.**

2100 press- A word-initial combining element, also occurring as a word, derived through Old French from Latin *press(āre)* 'to bear down on or against' (from *press(us),* the past participle of the verb *premere* 'to press,' plus the endings of the first conjugation class), used chiefly in the extended sense of 'of or pertaining to a *printing press* (which, in its earliest form, was a device that forced inked type against paper to create a printed image)' and in extensions of this sense in combination with other English elements: **pressman, pressmark, pressroom.** Related form: **presso-.**

2101 **presso-** A word-initial combining element, derived from Latin *press(ūra)* 'pressure' (from *press(us)*, the past participle of the verb *premere* 'to press,' plus the noun-forming suffix *-ūra*) plus the combining vowel *-o-*, used in its etymological and extended senses in Neo-Latin and Neo-Greek combinations: **pressometer, pressoreceptor, pressosensitive.** Also, **pressi-: pressinervoscopy.** Related form: **press-.**

2102 **primi-** A word-initial combining element, derived from Latin *prīm(us)* 'first, foremost' plus the combining vowel *-i-*, used in its etymological and extended senses in Neo-Latin combinations: **primigenial, primigravida, primiparous.** Also, **prim-, primo-: primordial, primogeniture.** Related forms: **far-, first-, for-[1], fore-[3], forth-, par-[3], para-[1], per-, peri-, perisso-, pre-, pro-[1], pro-[2], proprio-, pros-[1], proso-, protero-, proto-, proximo-.**

2103 **pro-[1]** A word-initial combining element, derived from Greek *pró* 'before, in front of,' used in its etymological and extended senses, chief among these being 'anterior, earlier,' in Neo-Greek combinations: **proatlas, procephalic, proptosis.** Related forms: **far-, first-, for-[1], fore-[3], forth-, par-[3], para-[1], per-, peri-, perisso-, pre-, primi-, pro-[2], proprio-, pros-[1], proso-, protero-, proto-, proximo-.**

2104 **pro-[2]** A word-initial combining element, derived from Latin *prō* 'before, in front of, for,' appearing in its etymological and extended senses, chief among these being 'in favor of that which is named by the combining root,' in a variety of combinations: **proceed, progenitor, pro-war.** Compare **proprio-.** Related forms: **far-, first-, for-[1], forth-, par-[3], para-[1], per-, peri-, perisso-, pre-, primi-, pro-[1], pros-[1], proso-, protero-, proto-, proximo-.**

2105 **procto-** A word-initial combining element, derived from Greek *prōktó(s)* 'anus,' used in its etymological and extended senses in biomedical terminology: **proctoclysis, proctocolitis, proctology.** Also, **proct-: proctatresia.**

2106 **proli-** A word-initial combining element, derived from Latin *prōl(ēs)* 'offspring' plus the combining vowel *-i-*, used in its etymological sense in Neo-Latin combinations: **prolicide, proliferous, proligerous.**

2107 **prop-** A word-initial combining element, derived from English *prop(ionic acid)* 'the fatty acid $(CH_3CH_2CO_2H)$' (from Greek *pró* 'before, in front of' plus *píōn* 'fat' plus the (English) adjective-forming suffix *-ic,* propionic acid being so named because it is the first in order of the fatty acids), used in the sense of 'of, pertaining to, containing, or derived from *proprionic acid*' in chemical terminology: **propamidine, propane, propene.** Compare **pro-[1]** and **pio-.**

2108 **proprio-** A word-initial combining element, derived from Latin *propri(us)* '(one's) own; individual' (from *prō prī(vō)* '(for the) individual,' *prīvō* being the ablative singular form of *prīvus* 'individual' (whose original meaning was on the order of 'being before, in front of,' hence, 'being apart from others') plus the combining vowel *-o-,* used in its etymological and extended senses in Neo-Latin combinations: **proprioceptor, propriodentium, propriospinal.** Compare **pro-[2].** Related forms: **far-, first-, for-[1], fore-[2], forth-, par-[3], para-[1], per-, peri-, perisso-, pre-, primi-, pro-[1], pros-[1], proso-, protero-, proto-, proximo-.**

2109 **propyl-** A word-initial combining element, also occurring as a word, derived from **prop-** plus the suffix *-yl* (which is used in naming chemical radicals (from Greek *(h)ýl(ē)* 'wood, matter')), used in the sense of 'of, pertaining to, containing, or derived from the univalent radical (C_3H_7)' in chemical terminology: **propylamine, propylene, propylthiouracil.** Compare **prop-** and **hylo-.**

2110 **pros-[1]** A word-initial combining element, derived from Greek *prós* 'from, toward, at, near, beside,' appearing in its etymological and extended senses in borrowings from Greek and in Neo-Greek combinations: **proselyte, prosenchyma, prosody.** Compare **proso-.** Related forms: **far-, first-, for-[1], fore-[3], forth-, par-[3], para-[1], per-, peri-, perisso-, pre-, primi-, pro-[1], pro-[2], proprio-, protero-, proto-, proximo-.**

2111 **pros-[2]** A variant of **proso-.**

2112 **proso-** A word-initial combining element, derived from Greek *prósō* 'forward, further' (from *prós* 'from, toward, at, near, beside' plus the adverb-forming suffix *-ō*), appearing chiefly in the sense of 'anterior, forward' in borrowings from Greek and in Neo-Greek combinations: **prosocoele, prosodemic, prosogaster.** Also, **pros-[2]: prosencephalon.** Compare **pros-[1].**

2113 **prosopo-** A word-initial combining element, derived from Greek *prōsōpo(n)* 'face, countenance' (from *prós* 'near, at' plus *ōp(s), ōp(ós)* 'face'), used in its etymological and extended senses in Neo-Greek and Neo-Latin combinations: **prosopoanoschisis, prosopodiplegia,**

prosopopilar. Also, **prosop-: prosopectasia.** Compare **pros-**[1] and **opo-**[1].

2114   **prostato-**   A word-initial combining element, derived from Greek *prostát(ēs)* 'one who stands before, in front of' (from the past participle of the verb *proistánai* 'to stand in front' (from *pró* 'before, in front of' plus *histánai* 'to stand')) plus the combining vowel *-o-,* used in the extended sense of 'of or pertaining to the *prostate gland* (which is so named because it 'stands before' the mouth of the bladder)' in biomedical terminology: **prostatocystitis, prostatolithotomy, prostatovesiculitis.** Also, **prostat-: prostatectomy.** Compare **pro-**[1], **stato-**.

2115   **prot-**   A variant of **proto-**.

2116   **prote-**   A variant of **proteino-**.

2117   **proteino-**   A word-initial combining element, derived from English *protein* 'organic nitrogenous compound which is a principal, essential component of cell protoplasm' (from French *protéine,* a term coined by G. J. Mulder in 1838 and based on Greek *prōte(îos)* 'in first place; primary' (from *prôtos* 'first') plus the noun-forming suffix *-in(e)* which is used in naming basic substances) plus the combining vowel *-o-,* used in its etymological and extended senses in Neo-Greek and Neo-Latin combinations: **proteinochrome, proteinogenous, proteinotherapy.** Also, **prote-, protein-, proteini-, proteo-: proteuric, proteinphobia, proteinivorous, proteopeptic.** Compare **proto-**.

2118   **protero-**   A word-initial combining element, derived from Greek *prótero(s)* 'former, earlier, older,' used in its etymological and extended senses in Neo-Greek combinations: **proterobase, proteroglyph,** *Proterosaurus.* Also, **proter-: proterandry.** Related forms: **far-, first-, for-**[1], **fore-**[3], **forth-, par-**[3], **para-**[1], **per-, peri-, perisso-, pre-, primi-, pro-**[1], **pro-**[2], **proprio-, pros-**[1], **proso-, proto-, proximo-**.

2119   **proto-**   A word-initial combining element, derived from Greek *prôto(s)* 'first,' used in its etymological and extended senses in a variety of combinations: **Proto-Indo-European, prototype, protovertebra.** Also, **prot-: protalbumose.** Related forms: **far-, first-, for-**[1], **fore-**[3], **forth-, par-**[3], **para-**[1], **per-, peri-, perisso-, pre-, primi-, pro-**[1], **pro-**[2], **proprio-, pros-**[1], **proso-, protero-, proximo-**.

2120   **protozoo-**   A word-initial combining element, derived from **proto-** plus **zoo-,** used in the sense of 'of or pertaining to *protozoa,* primitive, single-celled organisms' and in extensions of this sense in Neo-Greek and Neo-Latin combinations: **protozoology, protozoophage, protozootherapy.** Also, **protozo-, protozoa-: protozoiasis, protozoacide.** Compare **proto-, zoo-.**

2121 **proximo-**   A word-initial combining element, derived from Latin *proxim(us)* 'nearest, next' plus the combining vowel *-o-*, used in its etymological and extended senses in Neo-Latin and Neo-Greek combinations: **proximoataxia, proximobuccal, proximoceptor.** Also, **proxim-: proximad.** Related forms: **far-, first-, for-[1], fore-[3], forth-, par-[3], para-[1], per-, peri-, perisso-, pre-, primi-, pro-[1], pro-[2], proprio-, pros-[1], proso-, protero-, proto-.**

2122 **psammo-**   A word-initial combining element, derived from Greek *psámmo(s)* 'sand,' used in its etymological and extended senses in Neo-Greek combinations: **psammocarcinoma, psammosarcoma, psammotherapy.** Also, **psamm-, psamme-: psammite, psammead.** Related forms: **ammo-, sand-.**

2123 **pseudo-**   A word-initial combining element, derived from Greek *pseud(és)* 'counterfeit, false' plus the combining vowel *-o-*, used in its etymological and extended senses, chief among these being 'simulating that which is named by the combining root,' in a variety of combinations: **pseudoalveolar, pseudocodein, pseudorickets.** Also, **pseud-, psi- (ψ): pseudacromegaly, ψ-aconitine, psicaine.**

2124 **psi- (Ψ, ψ)**   A word-initial combining element, the twenty-third letter of the Greek alphabet, used chiefly as a designation of 'the twenty-third carbon atom in a straight chain compound or a derivative thereof in which the substitute group is attached to that atom' and as an abbreviatory symbol for '**pseud(o)**' in chemical terminology. Compare **pseudo-.** See **alpha-.**

2125 **psilo-**   A word-initial combining element, derived from Greek *psiló(s)* 'bare, smooth, plain, mere,' used in its etymological and extended senses in Neo-Greek combinations: *Psiloceras,* **psilodermatous, psilomelane.** Also, **psil-: psilanthropy.**

2126 **psor-**   A word-initial combining element, derived from Greek *psôr(a)* 'itch, mange,' used in its etymological and extended senses in Neo-Greek combinations: **psoriasis, psoric, psorophthalmia.** Also, **psoro-: psorocomium.**

2127 **psycho-**   A word-initial combining element, derived from Greek *psych(é)* 'breath, spirit, mind' plus the combining vowel *-o-*, used in the sense of 'of or pertaining to the conscious and unconscious life of the mind' in a variety of combinations: **psychobabble, psychoreaction, psychotherapy.** Also, **psych-: psychlampsia.**

2128   **psychro-**   A word-initial combining element, derived from Greek *psychró(s)* 'cold,' used in its etymological sense in Neo-Greek combinations: **psychroalgia, psychrometer, psychrophobia.**

2129   **pter-**   A variant of **ptero-.**

2130   **pterido-**   A word-initial combining element, derived from Greek *ptéri(s), ptérid(os)* 'fern' (from *pter(ón)* 'feather, wing') plus the combining vowel *-o-,* used in its etymological sense in Neo-Greek combinations: **pteridology, pteridomania, pteridophyte.** Compare **ptero-.**

2131   **ptero-**   A word-initial combining element, derived from Greek *pteró(n)* 'feather, wing,' used in its etymological and extended senses in Neo-Greek combinations: **pterodactyl, pterography, pteropod.** Also, **pter-: pterin.** Compare **pterido-, pterygo-.** Related forms: **feather-, pen-[1], penni-, pin-, pinnati-, pinni-, ptilo-.**

2132   **pterygo-**   A word-initial combining element, derived from Greek *ptéry(x), ptéryg(os)* 'wing' (from *pter(ón)* 'feather, wing') plus the combining vowel *-o-,* used in its etymological and extended senses, chief among these being 'wing-shaped, featherlike,' in Neo-Greek and Neo-Latin combinations: **pterygoblast, pterygomaxillary, pterygosphenoid.** Compare **ptero-.**

2133   **ptilo-**   A word-initial combining element, derived from Greek *ptílo(n)* 'feather, wing,' used in its etymological and extended senses in Neo-Greek combinations: *Ptilocerus, Ptilogonys,* **ptilolite.** Also, **ptil-, ptilono-:** *Ptilichthys, Ptilonopus.* Related forms: **feather-, pen-[1], penni-, pin-, pinnati-, pinni-, pterido-, ptero-, pterygo-.**

2134   **ptyalo-**   A word-initial combining element, derived from Greek *ptýalo(n)* 'spittle, saliva,' used in its etymological and extended senses in Neo-Greek and Neo-Latin combinations: **ptyalogenic, ptyalolithotomy, ptyaloreaction.** Also, **ptya-, ptyal-: ptyalith, ptyalectasis.** Related form: **spit-.**

2135   **pubo-**   A word-initial combining element, derived from Latin *pūb(ēs), pūb(is)* 'mature, adult,' hence, 'sign of (sexual) maturity, esp. the growth of pubic hair,' plus the combining vowel *-o-,* used chiefly in the extended sense of 'of or pertaining to the pubic bone' in biomedical terminology: **pubococcygeus, pubofemoral, puboprostatic.** Also, **pub-, pubio-: pubetrotomy, pubioplasty.**

2136 pull-   A word-initial combining element, also occurring as a word, derived from Old English *pull(ian)* 'to pluck, tug at,' used in its etymological and extended senses in combination with other English elements: **pullback, pull-in, pullover.**

2137 pulmo-   A word-initial combining element, derived from Latin *pulmō, pulmō(nis)* 'lung,' used in its etymological and extended senses in biomedical terminology: **pulmoaortic, pulmogram, pulmometer.** Also, **pulmon-, pulmono-: pulmonectomy, pulmonoperitoneal.** Related forms: **float-, flood-, fly-¹, fly-², pluto-, pluvio-, pneumo-², pneumono-, pyelo-.**

2138 pulp-   A word-initial combining element, also occurring as a word, derived from Latin *pulp(a)* 'flesh,' used in its etymological and extended senses, chief among these being 'of or pertaining to the tissue contained in a tooth,' in a variety of combinations: **pulpalgia, pulpitis, pulpwood.** Also, **pulpi-, pulpo-: pulpiform, pulpotomy.**

2139 pump-   A word-initial combining element, also occurring as a word of uncertain origin, used in the sense of 'mechanical device for transferring water (or gas) through a tube from a source to a destination' and in extensions of this sense in combination with other English elements: **pump-action, pumpman, pumpwell.**

2140 punch-   A word-initial combining element, also occurring as a word of uncertain origin, used in the sense of 'poke, hit (with a fist)' and in extensions of this sense in combination with other English elements: **punchball, punchboard, punch-drunk.**

2141 pupillo-   A word-initial combining element, derived from Latin *pūpill(a)* 'little girl; doll' and by extension, 'pupil (of the eye)' (presumably because of the small image which one may see reflected therein), from *pūp(a)* 'girl' plus the diminutive suffix *-illa* plus the combining vowel *-o-,* used in its extended sense in biomedical terminology: **pupillometer, pupillomotor, pupilloscope.** Also, **pupill-: pupillatonia.**

2142 push-   A word-initial combining element, also occurring as a word, derived through Old French from Latin *pu(l)s(āre)* 'to strike repeatedly; to impel' (from an Indo-European root meaning 'thrust'), used in the sense of 'thrust' and in extensions of this sense in combination with other English elements: **push-button, pushcart, pushpin.** Related form: **plesio-.**

2143 put-   A word-initial combining element, also occurring as a word, derived from Old English *put(en)* 'to thrust, push,' used in a variety of extensions of this sense in combination with other English elements: **put-down, put-on, put-upon.**

2144   **py-**   A variant of **pyo-.**

2145   **pycno-**   A word-initial combining element, derived from Greek *pyknó(s)* 'close, compact, thick, fast,' used in its etymological and extended senses in Neo-Greek combinations: **pycnometer, pycnometochia, pycnospore.** Also, **pycn-, pykn-, pykno-: pycnodont, pyknemia, pyknocardia.**

2146   **pyelo-**   A word-initial combining element, derived from Greek *pýelo(s)* 'basin, tub' (from an Indo-European root meaning 'flow, float'), used in the extended sense of 'of or pertaining to the (basin-shaped) renal pelvis' in biomedical terminology: **pyelocystitis, pyelofluoroscopy, pyelogram.** Also, **pyel-: pyelitis.** Related forms: **float-, flood-, fly-¹, fly-², pluto-, pluvio-, pneumo-², pulmo-.**

2147   **pygo-**   A word-initial combining element, derived from Greek *pyg(ē̆)* 'rump, buttocks' plus the combining vowel *-o-,* used in its etymological and extended senses in Neo-Greek combinations: **pygoamorphus, pygodidymus, pygopod.** Also, **pyg-: pygist.**

2148   **pykno-**   A variant of **pycno-.**

2149   **pyloro-**   A word-initial combining element, derived from Greek *pylōró(s)* 'gatekeeper' and, by extension, 'lower gastric orifice through which the contents of the stomach enter the duodenum,' used in this latter sense in biomedical terminology: **pylorodilator, pylorogastrectomy, pylorospasm.** Also, **pylor-, pylori-: pyloralgia, pyloristenosis.**

2150   **pyo-**   A word-initial combining element, derived from Greek *pŷo(n)* 'pus,' used in its etymological and extended senses in biomedical terminology: **pyoculture, pyochezia, pyoderma.** Also, **py-: pyarthrosis.** Related form: **foul-.**

2151   **pyocyano-**   A word-initial combining element, derived from **pyo-** plus **cyan(o)-¹,** used in the sense of 'of, pertaining to, containing, or derived from *pyocyanin,* a blue antibiotic pigment' in biochemical terminology: **pyocyanobacterin, pyocyanogenic, pyocyanolysin.** Also, **pyocyan-: pyocyanase.** Compare **pyo-, cyano-¹.**

2152   **pyopneumo-**   See **pyo-** and **pneumo-¹.**

2153   **pyr-**   A variant of **pyro-.**

2154 pyreto-   A word-initial combining element, derived from Greek *pyretó(s)* 'burning heat, fever' (from *pŷr* 'fire'), used in the sense of 'of or pertaining to fever' in Neo-Greek combinations: **pyretogenetic, pyretology, pyretotyphosis.** Also, **pyret-: pyretic.** Compare **pyro-.**

2155 pyro-   A word-initial combining element, derived from Greek *pŷr* 'fire' plus the combining vowel *-o-*, used in its etymological and extended senses, chief among these being 'heat; produced by heating,' in Neo-Greek and Neo-Latin combinations: **pyroform, pyrogenic, pyromania.** Also, **pyr-: pyrazoline.** Compare **pyreto-.** Related form: **fire-.**

Q

2156 quadri-   A word-initial combining element, derived from Latin *quadri-*, a combining form of *quattuor* 'four,' appearing in its etymological and extended senses in borrowings from Latin and in Neo-Latin and Neo-Greek combinations: **quadriceps, quadrilateral, quadriplegia.** Also, **quadr-, quadru-: quadrangle, quadruped.** Compare **square-.** Related forms: **four-, quarter-, quarti-, tetra-.**

2157 quanti-   A word-initial combining element, derived from Latin *quant(us)* 'how much; as much as' plus the combining vowel *-i-*, used in the sense of 'amount' and in extensions of this sense in Neo-Latin and Neo-Greek combinations: **quantification, quantimeter, quantivalence.** Related forms: **quasi-, what-, when-, where-, who-.**

2158 quarter-   A word-initial combining element, also occurring as a word, derived through Old French from Latin *quartār(ius)* 'fourth part' (from *quart(us)* 'one fourth' plus the noun-forming suffix *-ārius*), used in its etymological and extended senses in combination with other English elements: **quarterback, quarterdeck, quartertone.** Compare **quarti-.**

2159 quarti-   A word-initial combining element, derived from Latin *quart(us)* 'fourth' plus the combining vowel *-i-*, used in its etymological and extended senses in Neo-Latin combinations: **quartiporous, quartisect, quartisternal.** Also, **quart-: quartinvariant.** Compare **quarter-.** Related forms: **four-, quadri-, square-, tetra-.**

303

2160 **quasi-** A word-initial combining element, derived from Latin *quasi* 'as though; somewhat like,' used in its etymological and extended senses in a variety of combinations: **quasifaithful, quasifatal, quasiheroic.** Related forms: **quanti-, what-, when-, where-, who-; so-.**

2161 **querc-** A word-initial combining element, derived from Latin *querc(us)* 'oak,' used to designate 'any of a variety of chemical substances derived from oak bark or acorns' in chemical terminology: **quercetin, quercin, quercite.** Compare **cork-.**

2162 **quick-** A word-initial combining element, also occurring as a word, derived from Old English *cwic(u)* 'alive,' used in a variety of extensions of its etymological sense, chief among these being 'lively, fast,' in combination with other English elements: **quickfreeze, quicksand, quickset.** Related forms: **bio-, vita-[1], vivi-, zoo-.**

2163 **quill-** A word-initial combining element, also occurring as a word of uncertain origin, used in the sense of 'resembling the hollow stem of a feather' in combination with other English elements: **quillback, quillfish, quillwort.**

2164 **quin-[1]** A variant of **quint-.**

2165 **quin-[2]** A word-initial combining element, derived through Spanish from Quechua *kina* '(tree) bark,' used in the specialized sense of 'of, pertaining to, containing, or derived from one or another of the alkaloids contained in the bark of trees of the genus *Cinchona*' in chemical terminology: **quinamidine, quinidine, quinine.** Also, **chin-[2], chino-, quino-: chinine, chinoform, quinoform.**

2166 **quinque-** A word-initial combining element, derived from Latin *quinque* 'five,' appearing in its etymological sense in borrowings from Latin and in Neo-Latin and Neo-Greek combinations: **quinquecuspid, quinquesyllable, quinquevalent.** Also, **quin-[1], quinqu-: quincunx, quinquennial.** Compare **cinque-[1], cinque-[2], quint-.** Related forms: **femto-, finger-, fist-, five-, penta-.**

2167 **quint-** A word-initial combining element, derived from Latin *quint(us)* 'fifth' (from *quin(que)* 'five' plus the ordinal-forming suffix *-tus*), used in its etymological and extended senses in Neo-Latin combinations: **quintessence, quintillion, quintroon.** Also, **quinti-, quintu-: quintipara, quintuplicate.** Compare **quinque-.**

R

2168 **race-** A word-initial combining element, also occurring as a word, derived from Old Norse *rás* 'rush, run,' used in the extended sense of 'contest of speed' in combination with other English elements: **racecourse, racehorse, racetrack.**

2169 **rachio-** A word-initial combining element, derived from Greek *rháchi(s), rháchi(os)* 'backbone, spine' plus the combining vowel *-o-*, used in its etymological and extended senses in biomedical terminology: **rachiocampsis, rachiomyelitis, rachioresistance.** Also, **rach-, rachi-, rachis-, rhach-, rhachi-, rhachio-: rachitis, rachialgia, rachisagra, rhachitis, rhachialgia, rhachiomyelitis.**

2170 **radiculo-** A word-initial combining element, derived from Latin *rādīcul(a)* 'little root' (from *rādi(x), rādīc(is)* 'root' plus the diminutive suffix *-ula*) plus the combining vowel *-o-*, used in the specialized sense of 'of or pertaining to nerve roots' in biomedical terminology: **radiculoganglionitis, radiculomedullary, radiculoneuropathy.** Also, **radicul-: radiculectomy.** Related forms: **rami-, rhizo-(?), root-.**

2171 **radio-** A word-initial combining element, also occurring as a word, derived from Latin *radi(us)* 'rod, spoke (of a wheel), ray (of light)' plus the combining vowel *-o-*, used in a variety of extensions of its etymological sense, chief among these being 'of or pertaining to the *radius,* the thicker, shorter bone of the forearm;' 'of or pertaining to the sending out of rays, whether of light, heat, or some other

305

form of energy, as x rays or gamma rays;' 'of or pertaining to the transmission of signals by means of 'wireless' waves;' and 'of or pertaining to *radioactivity,* the spontaneous breaking up of an atomic nucleus with the emission of rays in the form of charged particles,' in Neo-Latin and Neo-Greek combinations: **radiocarpal, radioisotope, radiolocation.** Also, **radi-: radiate.**

2172   **rag-**   A word-initial combining element, derived from Old Norse *ròg(g)* 'shagginess,' used in the extended sense of 'scrap of cloth' and in extensions of this sense in combination with other English elements: **ragbag, ragman, ragweed.**

2173   **rail-**   A word-initial combining element, also occurring as a word, derived through Old French from Latin *rē(gu)l(a)* 'straight stick, bar,' used in its etymological and extended senses in combination with other English elements: **railhead, rail-splitter, railway.** Related forms: **recti-, recto-, right-.**

2174   **rain-**   A word-initial combining element, also occurring as a word, derived from Old English *re(ġ)n* 'condensed atmospheric vapor falling to the earth as drops of water,' used in its etymological and extended senses in combination with other English elements: **rainbow, raincoat, rainwash.**

2175   **rami-**   A word-initial combining element, derived from Latin *rām(us)* 'branch' plus the combining vowel *-o-,* used in its etymological and extended senses in Neo-Latin combinations: **ramicolous, ramicorn, ramiflorous.** Also, **ram-: ramose.** Related forms: **radiculo-, rhizo-(?), root-.**

2176   **rani-**   A word-initial combining element, derived from Latin *rān(a)* 'frog' plus the combining vowel *-i-,* used in its etymological sense in Neo-Latin combinations: ***Raniceps,* raniform, ranivorous.**

2177   **rat-**   A word-initial combining element, derived from Old English *ræt* 'larger rodent of the genus *Mus*,' used in its etymological and extended senses in combination with other English elements: **ratfink, ratfish, rattrap.**

2178   **rattle-**   A word-initial combining element, also occurring as a word of uncertain origin, used in the sense of 'making a succession of popping sounds' and in extensions of this sense in combination with other English elements: **rattlebox, rattlebrained, rattlesnake.**

2179   **raw-**   A word-initial combining element, also occurring as a word, derived from Old English *(h)r(ē)aw* 'uncooked' (from an Indo-

European root meaning '(uncooked) flesh,' used in its etymological and extended senses in combination with other English elements: **rawboned, rawhide, raw-pack (method).** Related forms: **creatin-, creo-.**

2180   **razor-**   A word-initial combining element, also occurring as a word, derived from Old French *rasor* 'instrument used for shaving' (from Latin *rās(us)*, the past participle of the verb *rādere* 'to scrape'), used in the extended sense of 'resembling an instrument for shaving (in form or sharpness)' in combination with other English elements: **razorback, razor-billed (auk), razorfish.**

2181   **re-**   A word-initial combining element, derived from Latin *rĕ-* 'back, against, again, in return,' appearing in its etymological and extended senses in a variety of combinations: **react, reflect, reword.** Also, **red-¹: redaction.** Compare **retro-.**

2182   **ready-**   A word-initial combining element, also occurring as a word, derived, ultimately, from Old English *(ġe)rǣd(e)* 'prepared (for a ride),' hence, 'prepared,' used in this latter and extended senses in combination with other English elements: **ready-made, ready-mix, ready-to-wear.** Related form: **road-.**

2183   **rect-¹**   A variant of **recti-.**

2184   **rect-²**   A variant of **recto-.**

2185   **recti-**   A word-initial combining element, derived from Latin *rect(us)* 'in a straight line; straight; correct' plus the combining vowel *-i-*, used in its etymological and extended senses in Neo-Latin combinations: **rectification, rectilinear, rectirostral.** Also, **rect-¹: rectangle.** Compare **recto-.** Related forms: **rail-, right-.**

2186   **recto-**   A word-initial combining element, derived from Neo-Latin *rect(um intestinum)* 'straight (intestine),' that is, 'the part of the large intestine which ends at the anus,' plus the combining vowel *-o-*, used in its etymological and extended senses in biomedical terminology: **rectoabdominal, rectocele, rectophobia.** Also, **rect-²: rectitis.** Compare **recti-.** Related forms: **rail-. right-.**

2187   **red-¹**   A variant of **re-.**

2188   **red-²**   A word-initial combining element, derived from Old English *rē(a)d* 'the color of blood,' used in its etymological and extended senses in combination with other English elements: **redbait, red-breast, red-hot.** Related form: **erythro-.**

2189 **reflexo-** A word-initial combining element, derived from English *reflex* 'involuntary response to a stimulus' (from Latin *reflex(us)*, the past participle of the verb *reflectere* 'to turn back, bring back' (from *re-* 'back, again' plus *flectere* 'to bend, turn')) plus the combining vowel *-o-*, used in its etymological and extended senses in biomedical terminology: **reflexogenic, reflexograph, reflexotherapy.**

2190 **reni-** A word-initial combining element, derived from Latin *rēn(ēs)* 'kidneys' plus the combining vowel *-i-*, used in its etymological and extended senses in biomedical terminology: **renicardiac, reniform, renipuncture.** Also, **ren-, reno-: renal, renogastric.**

2191 **reti-** A word-initial combining element, derived from Latin *rēt(e)*, *rēt(is)* 'net' plus the combining vowel *-o-*, used in its etymological and extended senses, chief among these being 'of or pertaining to a network,' in Neo-Latin combinations: **retiform, retisolution, retispersion.** Also, **reto-: retoperithelium.** Compare **reticulo-, retino-.** Related form: **eremo-.**

2192 **reticulo-** A word-initial combining element, derived from Latin *rēticul(um)* 'small net' (from *rēt(e)* 'net' plus the combining vowel *-i-* plus the diminutive suffix *-culum*) plus the combining vowel *-o-*, used in the extended sense of 'of or pertaining to a netlike structure or to a network' and in extensions of this sense in Neo-Latin and Neo-Greek combinations: **reticulocytopenia, reticuloendothelial, reticulopod.** Also, **reticul-: reticular.** Compare **reti-.**

2193 **retino-** A word-initial combining element, derived from Late Latin *retin(a)* 'innermost tunic of the eye' (from Latin *rēt(e)* 'net' plus the noun-forming suffix *-ina* '-like') plus the combining vowel *-o-*, used in its etymological sense in biomedical terminology: **retinodialysis, retinomalacia, retinopapillitis.** Also, **retin-: retinitis.** Compare **reti-.**

2194 **reto-** A variant of **reti-.**

2195 **retro-** A word-initial combining element, derived from Latin *retrō* 'backward, behind' (from *re-* 'back, against, again, in return' plus the element *-trō* (derived by abstraction from such adverbs as *ultrō* 'at a distance' and *citrō* 'to this side')), used in its etymological and extended senses, chief among these being 'posterior,' in Neo-Latin and Neo-Greek combinations: **retrobuccal, retrograde, retropharyngitis.** Also, **retr-: retrad.** Compare **re-.**

2196 **rhabdo-** A word-initial combining element, derived from Greek *rhábdo(s)* 'rod, stick, strip, stripe,' used in its etymological and extended senses, chief among these being 'rod-shaped, striated,' in Neo-Greek combinations: **rhabdomancy, rhabdomyoblastoma, rhabdophobia**. Also, **rhabd-: rhabdite**.

2197   **rhach-**   A variant of **rachio-**.

2198   **rhampho-**   A word-initial combining element, derived from Greek *rhámpho(s)* 'curved beak' (from an Indo-European root meaning 'turn, bend'), used in its etymological and extended senses in Neo-Greek combinations: ***Rhamphocoelus*, rhamphorhynchine, rhamphotheca**. Also, **rhamph-: *Rhamphalcyon***. Related forms: **rhombo-, vermi-, vertebro-, worm-, wrist-**.

2199   **rheo-**   A word-initial combining element, derived from Greek *rhéo(s)* 'that which flows' (from *rheîn* 'to flow'), used in its etymological and extended senses, chief among these being 'of or pertaining to an electrical current,' in Neo-Greek combinations: **rheobase, rheology, rheotaxis**. Also, **rhe-: rheostosis**. Compare **rheumato-**. Related form: **rhythmo-**.

2200   **rheumato-**   A word-initial combining element, derived from Greek *rheûma, rheúmat(os)* 'that which flows; flux' (from *rheîn* 'to flow') plus the combining vowel *-o-*, used chiefly in the extended sense of 'of or pertaining to *rheumatism*, a disease characterized by inflammation of the joints and muscles'—originally, 'disease characterized by a discharge of one or another of the body's "humors"'—in biomedical terminology: **rheumatocelis, rheumatology, rheumatopyra**. Also, **rheum-, rheuma-, rheumat-: rheumarthritis, rheumapyra, rheumatalgia**. Compare **rheo-**. Related form: **rhythmo-**.

2201   **rhino-**   A word-initial combining element, derived from Greek *rhí(s), rhin(ós)* 'nose' plus the combining vowel *-o-*, used in its etymological and extended senses in Neo-Greek and Neo-Latin combinations: **rhinochiloplasty, rhinolalia, rhinoreaction**. Also, **rhin-: rhinallergosis**.

2202   **rhipido-**   A word-initial combining element, derived from Greek *rhipí(s), rhipîd(os)* 'fan' plus the combining vowel *-o-*, used chiefly in the extended sense of 'fanlike; having a fanlike structure' in zoological terminology: **rhipidoglossate, *Rhipidogorgia*, *Rhipidopterygia***. Also, **rhipi-, rhipid-: *Rhipicera*, rhipidura**.

2203   **rhizo-**   A word-initial combining element, derived from Greek *rhíz(a)* 'root' plus the combining vowel *-o-*, used in its etymological and extended senses in Neo-Greek combinations: **rhizomelic,**

rhizoneure, rhizotomist. Also, **rhiz-: rhizodontropy.** Related forms(?): **radiculo-, rami-, root-.**

2204 **rho-** (P, ρ) A word-initial combining element, the seventeenth letter of the Greek alphabet, used chiefly to designate 'the seventeenth carbon atom in a straight chain compound or a derivative thereof in which the substitute group is attached to that atom' in chemical terminology. See **alpha-.**

2205 **rhodo-** A word-initial combining element, derived from Greek *rhódo(n)* '(a) rose,' used chiefly in the extended sense of 'roselike, rose-colored, red' in Neo-Greek combinations: **rhodocyte, rhododendron, rhodophane.** Also, **rhod-: rhodanic.** Related form: **rose-.**

2206 **rhombo-** A word-initial combining element, derived from Greek *rhómbo(s)* 'that which may be turned or spun around; magician's circle; equilateral parallelogram in which only the opposite angles are equal' (from an Indo-European root meaning 'turn, bend'), used chiefly in the sense of 'equilateral parallelogram in which only the opposite angles are equal' and in extensions of this sense in Neo-Greek combinations: **rhombocoele, rhombogenic, rhombohedron.** Also, **rhomb-, rhombi-: rhombic, rhombicuboctahedron.** Related forms: **rhampho-, vermi-, vertebro-, worm-, wrist-.**

2207 **rhyncho-** A word-initial combining element, derived from Greek *rhýncho(s)* 'beak, snout,' used in its etymological and extended senses in Neo-Greek combinations: ***Rhynchobdella, Rhynchocyon,*** **rhynchophorous.** Also, **rhynch-: rhynchodont.**

2208 **rhythmo-** A word-initial combining element, derived from Greek *rhythmó(s)* 'regularly recurring motion; measured motion' (from an Indo-European root meaning 'flow'), used in its etymological and extended senses in Neo-Greek combinations: **rhythmometer, rhythmophone, rhythmotherapy.** Related forms: **rheo-, rheumato-.**

2209 **rib-** A word-initial combining element, also occurring as a word, derived from Old English *rib(b)* 'curved bone extending from a vertebra towards the sternum,' used in the extended sense of 'resembling a curved bone' in combination with other English elements: **ribband, ribgrass, ribwort.**

2210 **ribo-** A word-initial combining element, derived from English *ribo(se)* 'arabinose, the aldopentose ($CH_2OH(CHOH)_3CHO$)' (from German *Ribonsäure,* itself a rendering of English *arabin(ose)* (from (*gum*) *arab(ic)* plus the suffixes *-in* and *-ose*) plus *Säure* 'acid'), used in the sense of 'of, pertaining to, containing, or derived from *ribose*' in chemical terminology: **ribodesose, riboflavin, ribonuclease.**

2211   **right-**   A word-initial combining element, also occurring as a word, derived from Old English *riht* 'straight, true, just, correct,' used in its etymological and extended senses in combination with other English elements: **right-angled, right-handed, right-minded.** Related forms: **rail-, recti-, recto-.**

2212   **ring-**   A word-initial combining element, also occurring as a word, derived from Old English (*h*)*ring* 'circle,' used in its etymological and extended senses in combination with other English elements: **ringbolt, ringleader, ringworm.** Related forms: **curb-, curvi-, crown-.**

2213   **rip-**   A word-initial combining element, also occurring as a word of uncertain origin, used in the sense of 'tear, rend' and in extensions of this sense in combination with other English elements: **rip-roaring, ripsaw, ripsnorter.**

2214   **river-**   A word-initial combining element, also occurring as a word, derived through Old French from Latin **rīpār(ia)*, the (unattested) feminine-gender form of *rīpārius* 'of or pertaining to a (stream) bank' (from *rīp(a)* 'bank (of a stream)' plus the adjective-forming suffix *-ārius*), used in the sense of '(large) natural stream' in combination with other English elements: **riverbed, riverhead, riverweed.** Related form: **rope-.**

2215   **road-**   A word-initial combining element, also occurring as a word, derived from Old English *rād* '(a) riding,' used in the extended sense of 'open way designed to accommodate travelers' and in extensions of this sense in combination with other English elements: **roadbed, roadblock, roadrunner.** Related form: **ready-.**

2216   **rock-**   A word-initial combining element, also occurring as a word, derived through dialectal Old French from Late Latin *roc(ca)* 'stone,' used in its etymological and extended senses in combination with other English elements: **rock-bound, rockfish, rockweed.**

2217   **roentgeno-**   A word-initial combining element, derived from English *roentgen* 'international unit of x or gamma radiation' (from (*Wilhelm Conrad*) *Röntgen* (1845–1923) who first discovered x rays) plus the combining vowel *-o-*, used in the sense of 'of or pertaining to x rays' in a variety of combinations: **roentgenocinematography, roentgenolucent, roentgenotherapy.** Also, **roentgen-: roentgenopaque.**

2218   roll-   A word-initial combining element, also occurring as a word, derived through Old French from (unattested) Latin *ro(tu)l(āre)* 'to turn like a wheel' (from *rotul(a)* 'little wheel' (from *rot(a)* 'wheel' plus the diminutive suffix *-ula*) plus the endings of the first conjugation class), used in its etymological and extended senses in combination with other English elements: **rollaway, roll-back, roll-top (desk)**. Compare **roti-**.

2219   root-   A word-initial combining element, derived from Old Norse *rót* 'the part of a plant through which it draws nutrients from the surrounding soil,' used in its etymological and extended senses in combination with other English elements: **rootstalk, rootstock, rootworm**. Related forms: **radiculo-, rami-, rhizo-(?)**.

2220   rope-   A word-initial combining element, also occurring as a word, derived from Old English *rāp* '(wound) cord,' used in its etymological and extended senses in combination with other English elements: **ropedancer, ropewalk, ropeway**. Related form: **river-**.

2221   rose-   A word-initial combining element, also occurring as a word, derived from Latin *ros(a)* 'plant of the genus *Rosa* or its flower,' used in its etymological and extended senses, chief among these being 'of the color of a rose; red,' in combination with other English elements: **rosebush, rosefish, rosewood**. Related form: **rhodo-**.

2222   rostro-   A word-initial combining element, derived from Latin *rostr(um)* 'beak' plus the combining vowel *-o-*, used in its etymological and extended senses in Neo-Latin and Neo-Greek combinations: **rostroantennary, rostrobranchial, rostrolateral**. Also, **rostr-, rostri-: rostrad, rostriform**.

2223   roti-   A word-initial combining element, derived from Latin *rot(a)* 'wheel' plus the combining vowel *-i-*, used in its etymological and extended senses in Neo-Latin combinations: ***Rotifera*, rotiform, rotispinalis**. Also, **rot-: rotate**. Compare **roll-, round-**.

2224   rough-   A word-initial combining element, also occurring as a word, derived from Old English *rūh* 'not smooth,' used in its etymological and extended senses in combination with other English elements: **rough-and-tumble, roughcast, roughdry**.

2225   round-   A word-initial combining element, also occurring as a word, derived through Old French from Latin *ro(t)und(us)* 'circular, spherical' (from *rota* 'wheel'), used in its etymological and extended senses in combination with other English elements: **round-about, Roundhead, roundhouse.** Compare **roti-.**

2226 **rudder-** A word-initial combining element, also occurring as a word, derived from Old English *roper* 'steering oar,' used in the sense of 'mounted device for steering a (sea-going) vessel' and in extensions of this sense in combination with other English elements: **rudderfish, rudderhead, rudderpost.** Compare **Russo-.**

2227 **run-** A word-initial combining element, also occurring as a word, derived from Old English *rin(nan)* 'to move forward quickly on foot,' used in a variety of extended senses, all having something to do with 'movement,' in combination with other English elements: **runaround, run-in, runway.**

2228 **Russo-** A word-initial combining element, derived from English *Russ(ian)* 'of or pertaining to Russia' (through Late Latin from Old Russian *Rus'* 'Norsemen, i.e., Scandinavian conquerors who founded the first Russian principalities' (from Old Norse *Róps(menn)* 'Oars(men), Sea-farers')) plus the combining vowel *-o-*, used in its etymological sense in a variety of combinations: **Russo-Japanese (War), Russophile, Russophobia.** Compare **rudder-.**

S

2229 saber- A word-initial combining element, also occurring as a word, derived through French and German from Hungarian *szabl(ya)* 'curved cavalry sword,' used in the sense of 'swordlike' in combination with other English elements: **saberbill, saber-fish, saber-toothed (tiger).** Also (chiefly British), **sabre-: sabre-fish.**

2230 sacc- A variant of **sacco-.**

2231 saccharo- A word-initial combining element, derived, ultimately, from Sanskrit *śa(r)kar(ā)* 'gravel, grit' and, by extension, '(candied) sugar' plus the combining vowel *-o-,* used in the sense of 'of, pertaining to, containing, or resembling sugar' in Neo-Greek and Neo-Latin combinations: **saccharobacillus, saccharogalactorrhea, saccharomycetic.** Also, **sacchar-: saccharose.** Compare **sucr-, sugar-.**

2232 sacco- A word-initial combining element, derived through Latin and Greek from one of the Semitic languages (cf. Hebrew *saq* 'bag'), used in its etymological and extended senses in Neo-Greek and Neo-Latin combinations: **saccobranchiate, saccocirrus, saccophore.** Also, **sacc-, sacci-: saccate, sacciform.**

2233 sacro- A word-initial combining element, derived from Latin (*os*) *sacr(um)* 'sacred (bone)' plus the combining vowel *-o-,* used in the sense of 'of or pertaining to the *sacrum,* the triangular bone which forms the posterior section of the pelvis (and which was at one

315

time used sacrificially)' in biomedical terminology: **sacrococcyx, sacrodynia, sacroiliac.** Also, **sacr-, sacri-: sacralgia, sacriplex.**

2234 **saddle-** A word-initial combining element, also occurring as a word, derived from Old English *sadol* 'seat for a rider on an animal's back,' used in its etymological and extended senses in combination with other English elements: **saddlebag, saddleback, saddlecloth.** Related forms: **set-², sit-.**

2235 **safe-** A word-initial combining element, also occurring as a word, derived through Old French from Latin *sa(l)v(us)* 'in good health; uninjured,' used in its etymological and extended senses in combination with other English elements: **safe-conduct, safekeeping, safelight.** Related forms: **holo-, solid-.**

2236 **sail-** A word-initial combining element, also occurring as a word, derived from Old English *se(ġe)l* 'shaped piece of canvas (or the like) which is fastened to a mast (or the like) and is designed to catch the wind, thereby propelling the vessel to which it is fitted,' used in its etymological and extended senses in combination with other English elements: **sailboat, sailcloth, sailfish.**

2237 **sal-¹** A variant of **salicyl-.**

2238 **sal-²** A variant of **sali-².**

2239 **sales-** A word-initial combining element, also occurring as a word, derived from Old Norse *sal(a)* 'act of selling' plus the English plural marker *-s,* used in the sense of 'of, pertaining to, or facilitating selling' in combination with other English elements: **salesclerk, salesmanship, salesroom.**

2240 **sali-¹** A variant of **salicyl-.**

2241 **sali-²** A word-initial combining element, derived from Latin *sal, sal(is)* 'salt' plus the combining vowel *-i-,* used in its etymological and extended senses in Neo-Latin and Neo-Greek combinations: *Salicornia,* **saliferous, salimeter.** Also, **sal-²: saline.** Compare **sauce-.** Related forms: **halo-, salt-.**

2242 **salicyl-** A word-initial combining element, also occurring as a word, derived from Latin *sali(x), salic(is)* 'willow' plus the suffix *-yl* (which is used in naming chemical radicals), used in the sense of 'of, pertaining to, containing, or derived from *salicylic acid* ($C_7H_6O_3$) (which is obtained from the bark of the willow)' in chemical terminology: **salicylamide, salicylanilide, salicylquinine.** Also, **sal-¹, sali-¹, salo-: salunguene, saliphen, saloquinine.**

2243 **salpingo-** A word-initial combining element, derived from Greek *sálpin(x), sálping(os)* 'trumpet' plus the combining vowel *-o-*, used chiefly in the extended sense of 'of or pertaining to a tube, esp. a fallopian tube, oviduct, or eustachian tube' in biomedical terminology: **salpingocatheterism, salpingo-oophorectomy, salpingoovariotomy.** Also, **salping-: salpingitis.**

2244 **salt-** A word-initial combining element, also occurring as a word, derived from Old English *s(e)alt* 'sodium chloride,' used in its etymological and extended senses in combination with other English elements: **saltbox, saltbush, saltcellar.** Related forms: **halo-, sali-², sauce-.**

2245 **sand-** A word-initial combining element, also occurring as a word, derived from Old English *sand* 'fine rock particles,' used in its etymological and extended senses in combination with other English elements: **sandbag, sandbox, sandhog.** Related forms: **ammo-, psammo-.**

2246 **sangui-** A word-initial combining element, derived from Latin *sangui(s), sangui(nis)* 'blood,' used in its etymological sense in biomedical combinations: **sanguicolous, sanguimotor, sanguivorous.** Also, **sanguin-, sanguino-: sanguinous, sanguinopoietic.**

2247 **sap-¹** A word-initial combining element, derived from Old English *sæp* 'plant juice,' used in its etymological and extended senses in combination with other English elements: **saphead, sapsucker, sapwood.**

2248 **sap-²** A variant of **sapon-.**

2249 **sap-³** A variant of **sapro-.**

2250 **sapon-** A word-initial combining element, derived from Latin *sāpō, sāpōn(is)* 'soap,' used in its etymological and extended senses in Neo-Latin and Neo-Greek combinations: **saponaceous, *Saponaria,* saponin.** Also, **sap-², sapo-, saponi-: *Sapindus,* sapogenin, saponification.** Related form: **soap-.**

2251 **sapro-** A word-initial combining element, derived from Greek *sapró(s)* 'rotten, putrid,' used in its etymological and extended senses in Neo-Greek combinations: **saprogenic, saprophyte, saprozoic.** Also, **sap-³, sapr-: sapine, saprine.** Related form: **septico-.**

2252 **sarco-** A word-initial combining element, derived from Greek
sár(x), sark(ós) 'flesh' plus the combining vowel *-o-,* used in its
etymological and extended senses, chief among these being 'of or
pertaining to muscle tissue,' in Neo-Greek combinations: **sarco-
genic, sarcolemma, sarcoplasm.** Also, **sarc-: sarcosis.**

2253 **satin-** A word-initial combining element, also occurring as a word,
derived through Old French from the Arabic rendering of the
native name of the Chinese city of *Tseutung* (from which the cloth
was first imported), used in the sense of 'silken cloth' and in
extensions of this sense in combination with other English elements: **satinflower, satinpod, satinwood.**

2254 **sauce-** A word-initial combining element, also occurring as a word,
derived through Old French from Latin *sals(a)* '(that which has
been) salted' (from *sal* 'salt'), used in the extended sense of
'(semiliquid) condiment' and in extensions of this sense in combination with other English elements: **sauceboat, saucebox, saucepan.**
Compare **sali-².**

2255 **sauro-** A word-initial combining element, derived from Greek
saûro(s) 'lizard,' used in its etymological and extended senses in
Neo-Greek combinations: ***Saurobatrachia,* saurognathous, sauro-
phagous.** Also, **saur-: saurodont.**

2256 **saw-** A word-initial combining element, also occurring as a word,
derived from Old English *sa(g)u* 'toothed cutting tool,' used in its
etymological and extended senses in combination with other
English elements: **sawbones, sawdust, sawfish.** Related forms: **saxi-,
sickle-, skin-.**

2257 **saxi-** A word-initial combining element, derived from Latin
sax(um) 'rough stone, broken rock' (from an Indo-European root
meaning 'to cut, sever') plus the combining vowel *-i-,* used in its
etymological and extended senses in Neo-Latin combinations:
saxicavous, saxicolous, saxifrage. Related forms: **saw-, sickle-,
skin-.**

2258 **scab-** A word-initial combining element, also occurring as a word,
derived from Old Norse *skab(br)* 'disease of the skin' (from an
Indo-European root meaning 'cut, scrape,' hence, 'itch'), used in its
etymological and extended senses in combination with other
English elements: **scabland, scab-mite, scabwort.** Related forms:
hatchet, scapho-, scapulo-, scopi-.

2259 **scape-** A word-initial combining element, derived from English (e)scape 'get away from' (through Old French from unattested Late Latin *excappāre 'to get away from,' literally, 'to remove one's cloak (whether to leave it in the hands of one's assailants or simply to disencumber oneself)' (from Latin ex- 'from, out from' plus capp(a) '(hooded) cloak' (from the root underlying Latin caput 'head') plus the endings of the first conjugation class), appearing in its etymological and extended senses in combination with a few other English elements: scape-gallows, scapegoat, scapegrace. Related forms: capillar-(?), capilli-(?), capit-, head-.

2260 scapho- A word-initial combining element, derived from Greek skápho(s) 'trench; deep vessel; ship's hull' (from an Indo-European root meaning 'cut, scrape,' hence, 'hollow out'), used chiefly in the sense of 'hull-shaped, esp. the hull-shaped (scaphoid) bone' in Neo-Greek and Neo-Latin combinations: scaphocephalic, scapho-cuneiform, scaphognathite. Related forms: hatchet-, scab-, scapulo-, scopi-.

2261 scapulo- A word-initial combining element, derived from Latin scapul(a) 'shoulder (blade)' (from an Indo-European root meaning 'cut, scrape,' the shoulder blade being shaped like an blade of an ax) plus the combining vowel -o-, used in its etymological sense in biomedical combinations: scapuloanterior, scapulohumeral, scapulothoracic. Also, scapul-: scapulectomy. Related forms: hatch-et, scab-, scapho-, scopi-.

2262 scare- A word-initial combining element, derived from Old Norse skír(ra) 'frighten,' used in its etymological and extended senses in combination with other English elements: scarecrow, scarehead, scaremonger.

2263 scato- A word-initial combining element, derived from Greek sk(ôr), skat(ós) 'dung' plus the combining vowel -o-, used in its etymological sense in Neo-Greek combinations: scatology, scato-mancy, scatophagy. Also, scat-, scor-: scatacratia, scoracratia. Related form: sterco-.

2264 scatter- A word-initial combining element, also occurring as a word of uncertain origin, used in the sense of 'disperse' and in extensions of this sense in combination with other English elements: scatterbrained, scattergood, scattershot.

2265 schisto- A word-initial combining element, derived from Greek schistó(s), the past participle of the verb schízein 'to split, cleave,' used in its etymological and extended senses in Neo-Greek combinations: **schistocelia, schistoglossia, schistosomiasis.** Also, **schist-: schistasis.** Compare **schizo-.** Related form: **shin-.**

2266 **schizo-** A word-initial combining element, derived from Greek *schíz(ein)* 'to split, cleave' plus the combining vowel *-o-,* used in the sense of 'split, divided' and in extensions of this sense in Neo-Greek and Neo-Latin combinations: **schizocephalia, schizophreniform, schizothorax.** Also, **schiz-: schizaxon.** Compare **schisto-.** Related form: **shin-.**

2267 **school-** A word-initial combining element, also occurring as a word, derived through Latin from Greek *schol(ḗ)* 'leisure time; learning (done at leisure); place in which learning occurs,' used in this last sense in combination with other English elements: **schoolbook, schoolteacher, schoolwork.**

2268 **scia-** A variant of **skia-.**

2269 **scilli-** A word-initial combining element, derived through Latin from Greek *skill(a)* 'squill' plus the combining vowel *-i-,* used in the sense of 'derived from squill' in chemical terminology: **scillipicrin, scilliroside, scillitoxin.** Also, **scill-: scillonin.**

2270 **sclero-** A word-initial combining element, derived from Greek *sklēró(s)* 'hard,' used in its etymological and extended senses, chief among these being 'of or pertaining to the *sclera,* the hard covering of the eyeball,' in biomedical terminology: **scleroconjunctivitis, scleroderma, scleroprotein.** Also, **scler-, skler-: sclerectasia, sklerema.** Related form: **skeleto-.**

2271 **scolec-** A word-initial combining element, derived from Greek *skṓle(x), skṓlēk(os)* 'worm' (from an Indo-European root meaning 'bend, curve'), used in its etymological and extended senses in Neo-Greek and Neo-Latin combinations: **scolecine, colecitis, scolecophidian.** Also, **scoleci-, scoleco-: scoleciform, scolecology.** Related forms: **scolio-, skel-.**

2272 **scolio-** A word-initial combining element, derived from Greek *skolió(s)* 'bent, crooked,' used in its etymological and extended senses in Neo-Greek combinations: **scoliokyphosis, scoliopathexis, scoliorachitic.** Also, **scoli-, skoli-: scoliodontia, skoliosis.** Related forms: **scolec-, skel-.**

2273 **scopi-** A word-initial combining element, derived from Latin *scōp(ae)* 'thin branches,' hence, 'broom' (from an Indo-European root meaning 'cut, scrape') plus the combining vowel *-i-,* used in its etymological and extended senses in Neo-Latin combinations: **scopiferous, scopiform, scopiped.** Related forms: **hatchet-, scab-, scapho-, scapulo-.**

2274   **scopo-¹**   A variant of **scopol-.**

2275   **scopo-²**   A word-initial combining element, derived from Greek *skop(eîn)* 'to observe, examine' plus the combining vowel -*o*-, used in its etymological and extended senses in Neo-Greek combinations: **scopograph, scopophilia, scopophobia.** Also, **skopo-: skopometer.** Related form: **spectro-.**

2276   **scopol-**   A word-initial combining element, derived from Neo-Latin *Scopol(ia)* 'genus of plants resembling beladonna' (named after Johann Antoni *Scopoli* (1723–1788)), used in the sense of 'of or pertaining to the alkaloid derivative ($C_{17}H_{23}NO_2$) of plants of the genus *Scopolia*' in chemical terminology: **scopolamine, scopoleine, scopoline.** Also, **scop-, scopo-¹: scopine, scopomorphinism.**

2277   **scor-**   A variant of **scato-.**

2278   **score-**   A word-initial combining element, also occurring as a word, derived from Old Norse *skor* 'notch, tally' (from an Indo-European root meaning 'cut, scrape'), used in the sense of 'tally' in combination with other English elements: **scoreboard, scorecard, scorekeeper.** Related forms: **carni-, core-², cork-(?), cortico-, screw-, scrofulo-, sharp-, shirt-, short-.**

2279   **scoto-**   A word-initial combining element, derived from Greek *skóto(s)* 'darkness,' used in its etymological and extended senses in Neo-Greek combinations: **scotodinia, scotographic, scotophobia.** Also, **scot-: scotopia.** Related form: **shadow-.**

2280   **screw-**   A word-initial combining element, derived from Old French *(e)scrou(e)* 'hole in which a threaded fastener is seated' (from a combination of Latin *scrōbis* 'ditch, furrow' and *scrōfa* 'sow' (both from an Indo-European root meaning 'cut, scrape'), the idea being that the hole in which a threaded fastener is seated resembles a furrow of a shape reminiscent of the twisted tail of a pig), used in the extended sense of 'threaded fastener' and in extensions of this sense in combination with other English elements: **screwball, screwdriver, screwworm.** Related forms: **carni-, core-², cork-(?), cortico-, score-, scrofulo-, sharp-, shirt-, short-.**

2281   **scrofulo-**   A word-initial combining element, derived from Late Latin *scrōful(a)* 'breeding sow' (from *scrōf(a)* 'sow' (from an Indo-

European root meaning 'cut, scrape,' the sow being so named because of its characteristic furrowing behavior) plus the diminutive suffix *-ula*) plus the combining vowel *-o-*, used in the extended sense of 'of or pertaining to *scrofula*, a tubercular swelling, esp. of the lymphatic glands (and so named, perhaps, because the swelling resembles the shape of a sow)' and in extensions of this sense in biomedical terminology: **scrofuloderma, scrofulophyma, scrofulotuberculosis.** Also, **scroful-: scrofulide.** Related forms: **carni-, core-[2], cork-(?), cortico-, score-, screw-, sharp-, shirt-, short-.**

2282 se- A word-initial combining element, derived from Latin *sē* 'by itself; apart from,' appearing in its etymological and extended senses in borrowings from Latin: **secede, seduce, separate.** Related forms: **ethno-, self-, soli-[2].**

2283 sea- A word-initial combining element, also occurring as a word, derived from Old English *sǣ* 'ocean,' used in its etymological and extended senses in combination with other English elements: **seadog, seaplane, seashore.**

2284 sebo- A word-initial combining element, derived from Latin *sēb(um)* 'tallow, suet' plus the combining vowel *-o-*, used in its etymological and extended senses, chief among these being 'of or pertaining to a suetlike secretion of the body,' in Neo-Latin and Neo-Greek combinations: **sebocystoma, sebolith, seborrhea.** Also, **seb-, sebi-: sebaceous, sebiagogic.**

2285 second- A word-initial combining element, also occurring as a word, derived through Old French from Latin *secund(us)*, the future participle of the verb *sequī* 'to follow,' used in the sense of 'following; coming after the first' and in extensions of this sense in combination with other English elements: **second-class, second-hand, secondstory (man).** Related forms: **sign-, socio-.**

2286 secreto- A word-initial combining element, derived from Latin *sēcrēt(us)*, the past participle of the verb *sēcernere* 'to set aside' (from *sē* 'by itself' plus *cernere* 'to separate') plus the combining vowel *-o-*, used in the sense of 'of or pertaining to the glandular extraction or elaboration of a natural substance' in biomedical combinations: **secretodermatosis, secretoinhibitory, secretomotor.** Also, **secret-: secretagogue.**

2287 seismo- A word-initial combining element, derived from Greek *seismó(s)* '(a) shaking, vibration,' used in its etymological and extended senses in Neo-Greek combinations: **seismograph, seismology, seismometer.** Also, **seism-: seismesthesia.**

2288   **seleno-**   A word-initial combining element, derived from Greek *sēlén(ē)* '(the) moon' plus the combining vowel *-o-*, used in its etymological and extended senses in Neo-Greek combinations: **selenography, selenology, selenoplegia**. Also, **selen-: selenol**.

2289   **self-**   A word-initial combining element, also occurring as a word, derived from Old English *self* 'non-other,' used in its etymological and extended senses in combination with other English elements: **self-abuse, self-hypnosis, self-respect**. Related forms: **ethno-, se-, soli-[2]**.

2290   **semeio-**   A variant of **semio-**.

2291   **semi-**   A word-initial combining element, derived from Latin *sēmi-* 'half-,' used in its etymological and extended senses, chief among these being 'partly-,' in a variety of combinations: **semicomatose, semilunar, semivalent**. Related forms: **hemi-, sesqui-**.

2292   **semio-**   A word-initial combining element, derived from Greek *sēm(e)îo(n)* 'mark, sign; that by which something is known,' used in its etymological and extended senses in Neo-Greek combinations: **semiography, semiology, *Semioptera***. Also, **semeio-: semeiological**.

2293   **sensi-**   A word-initial combining element, derived from Latin *sens(us)*, the past participle of the verb *sentīre* 'to perceive, feel,' plus the combining vowel *-i-*, used in the sense of 'of or pertaining to the feelings or perceptions' in Neo-Latin and Neo-Greek combinations: **sensiferous, sensigerous, sensimeter**. Also, **sens-: sensate**. Compare **sensori-**.

2294   **sensori-**   A word-initial combining element, derived as though from Latin **sensōri(us)* 'of or pertaining to sensation or to the senses' (cf. Late Latin *sensōrium* 'seat of sensation'), used in its etymological sense in biomedical terminology: **sensorimetabolism, sensorimotor, sensorivascular**. Also, **senso-: sensomotor**. Compare **sensi-**.

2295   **sept-[1]**   A variant of **septico-**.

2296   **sept-[2]**   A variant of **septi-[2]**.

2297   **sept-[3]**   A variant of **septo-[2]**.

2298   **septa-**   A variant of **septi-[2]**.

2299   **septi-[1]**   A variant of **septico-**.

2300   **septi-²**   A word-initial combining element, derived from Latin *sept(em)* 'seven' plus the combining vowel -*i*-, used in its etymological and extended senses in Neo-Latin combinations: **septigravida, septilateral, septivalent.** Also, **sept-², septa-: septangle, septavalent.** Related forms: **hepta-, seven-.**

2301   **septico-**   A word-initial combining element, derived from Greek *sēptikó(s)* 'rotten, putrid' (from the verb *sēpein* 'to make rotten'), used in the sense of 'of, pertaining to, causing, or resulting from putrefaction' and in extensions of this sense in Neo-Greek and Neo-Latin combinations: **septicophlebitis, septicopyemia, septicozymoid.** Also, **sept-¹, septi-¹, septic-, septo-¹: septemia, septimetritis, septicemia, septometer¹.**

2302   **septo-¹**   A variant of **septico-.**

2303   **septo-²**   A word-initial combining element, derived from Latin *s(a)ept(a)* 'fence, wall, enclosure' plus the combining vowel -*o*-, used in the sense of 'partition' and in extensions of this sense in Neo-Latin and Neo-Greek combinations: **septomarginal, septometer-², septonasal.** Also, **sept-³: septal.**

2304   **seri-¹**   A variant of **sero-.**

2305   **seri-²**   A word-initial combining element, derived through Latin from Greek *sēri(kos)* 'silken,' literally, 'of or pertaining to the *Sēres,* the Asian people from whom the Greeks first obtained silk,' used in its etymological and extended senses in Neo-Greek and Neo-Latin combinations: **sericulture,** *Serilophus,* **seriscission.** Also, **seric-, serico-: sericite,** *Sericostoma.* Compare **silk-.**

2306   **sero-**   A word-initial combining element, derived from Latin *ser(um)* 'whey' plus the combining vowel -*o*-, used chiefly in the extended sense of 'of or pertaining to clear animal fluid' in biomedical terminology: **serofibrinous, serohepatitis, serosanguinous.** Also, **ser-, seri-¹: seralbumin, seriflux.** Related form: **oro-⁴.**

2307   **sesqui-**   A word-initial combining element, derived from Latin *sesqui* 'half again,' used in the sense of 'one and a half' and in extensions of this sense in a variety of combinations: **sesquibasic, sesquipedalian, sesquisalt.** Related forms: **hemi-, semi-.**

2308   **set-¹**   A variant of **seti-.**

2309   **set-²**   A word-initial combining element, also occurring as a word, derived from Old English *set(tan)* 'to cause to sit,' hence, 'to place,' used in this latter and extended senses in combination with other English elements: **setback, setscrew, setup.** Compare **sit-.** Related form: **saddle-.**

2310 **seti-**   A word-initial combining element, derived from Latin *s(a)et(a)* 'bristle' plus the combining vowel *-i-*, used in its etymological and extended senses in Neo-Latin combinations: **setiferous, setiform, setirostral.** Also, **set-¹: setaceous.**

2311 **seven-**   A word-initial combining element, derived from Old English *se(o)fon* 'the cardinal number between *six* and *eight*,' used in its etymological and extended senses in combination with other English elements: **sevenbark, seven-up, seven-year (itch).** Related forms: **hepta-, septi-².**

2312 **sex-**   A word-initial combining element, derived from Latin *sex* 'six,' used in its etymological and extended senses in Neo-Latin combinations: **sexcentenary, sexdigitate, sexradiate.** Also, **sexa-, sexi-: sexadecimal, sexivalent.** Related forms: **hexa-, six-.**

2313 **shadow-**   A word-initial combining element, also occurring as a word, derived through Middle English from Old English *scĕ(e)adu* 'darkness; dark image cast by an object intercepting light,' used in its etymological and extended senses in combination with other English elements: **shadowbox, shadowgraph, shadowland.** Related form: **scoto-.**

2314 **shake-**   A word-initial combining element, also occurring as a word, derived from Old English *scĕ(e)ac(an)* 'to move, agitate,' used in its etymological and extended senses in combination with other English elements: **shakedown, shakefork, shake-up.**

2315 **sharp-**   A word-initial combining element, also occurring as a word, derived from Old English *scĕ(e)arp* 'keen, acute' (from an Indo-European root meaning 'cut'), used in its etymological and extended senses in combination with other English elements: **sharp-fanged, sharpshooter, sharp-tongued.** Related forms: **carni-, core-², cork-(?), cortico-, score-, screw-, scrofulo-, shirt-, short-.**

2316 **she-**   A word-initial combining element, also occurring as a word, derived through Middle English from Old English *sīo* 'feminine singular demonstrative pronoun,' used in the sense of 'female' and, by extension, 'lesser' in combination with other English elements: **she-devil, she-oak, she-wolf.**

2317 **sheep-**   A word-initial combining element, also occurring as a word, derived from Old English *scēp* 'mammal of the genus *Ovis*,' used in its etymological and extended senses in combination with other English elements: **sheepberry, sheep-dip, sheepdog.**

2318   **shell-**   A word-initial combining element, also occurring as a word, derived from Old English *scell* 'husk, scale; hard outer covering,' used in its etymological and extended senses in combination with other English elements: **shellback, shellfire, shellfish.**

2319   **shin-**   A word-initial combining element, also occurring as a word, derived from Old English *scin(u)* 'anterior part of the leg between the ankle and the knee' (from an Indo-European root meaning 'bend, curve'), used in its etymological and extended senses in combination with other English elements: **shinbone, shindig, shinleaf.** Related forms: **schisto-, schizo-.**

2320   **ship-**   A word-initial combining element, also occurring as a word, derived from Old English *scip* '(large) sea-going vessel,' used in its etymological and extended senses in combination with other English elements: **shipload, shipmate, ship-to-shore (radio).**

2321   **shirt-**   A word-initial combining element, also occurring as a word, derived from Old English *scyrt(e)* 'undergarment serving to cover the upper half of the body' (from an Indo-European root meaning 'cut,' the idea being that this article of clothing—like the cognate *skirt*—was made from a piece of cut cloth), used in the sense of 'garment serving to cover the upper half of the body' and in extensions of this sense in combination with other English elements: **shirtband, shirttail, shirtwaist.** Related forms: **carni-, core-², cork-(?), cortico-, score-, screw-, scrofulo-, sharp-, short-.**

2322   **shoe-**   A word-initial combining element, also occurring as a word, derived from Old English *scō(h)* 'covering for the foot,' used in its etymological sense in combination with other English elements: **shoehorn, shoelace, shoestring.**

2323   **shop-**   A word-initial combining element, also occurring as a word, derived from Old English *sc(e)op(pa)* 'booth, stall,' used in the sense of 'of or pertaining to a building in which goods are offered for sale' and in extensions of this sense in combination with other English elements: **shopkeeper, shoplifter, shoptalk.**

2324   **short-**   A word-initial combining element, also occurring as a word, derived from Old English *sc(e)ort* 'not long' (from an Indo-European root meaning 'cut'), used in its etymological and extended senses in combination with other English elements: **short-**

change, shortcut, short-lived. Related forms: **carni-, core-[2], cork-(?), cortico-, score-, screw-, scrofulo-, sharp-, shirt-.**

2325   **shot-**   A word-initial combining element, also occurring as a word, derived from Old English *sć(e)ot* 'that which is speedily sent forth' (from *sćēotan* 'to speedily send forth; to shoot'), used in its etymological and extended senses in combination with other English elements: **shotgun, shot-peen, shot-putter.** Related form: **shut-.**

2326   **shovel-**   A word-initial combining element, also occurring as a word, derived from Old English *sćofl* 'spade, hoe,' used in the sense of 'spadelike' and extensions of this sense in combination with other English elements: **shovelboard, shovelhead, shovelnose.**

2327   **show-**   A word-initial combining element, also occurring as a word, derived from Old English *sć(ē)aw(ian)* 'to look at,' used in the extended sense of 'to cause to look at; to exhibit' and in extensions of this sense in combination with other English elements: **show-boat, showdown, show-stopper.**

2328   **shut-**   A word-initial combining element, also occurring as a word, derived from Old English *sćyt(tan)* 'to fasten (by shooting a bolt),' used in the extended sense of 'close(d)' and in extensions of this sense in combination with other English elements: **shut-eye, shutoff, shutout.** Related form: **shot-.**

2329   **sialo-**   A word-initial combining element, derived from Greek *sialo(n)* 'saliva,' used in its etymological and extended senses, chief among these being 'of or pertaining to the salivary glands,' in Neo-Greek combinations: **sialoadenotomy, sialodochoplasty, sialo-lithotomy.** Also, **sial-: sialadenitis.**

2330   **sick-**   A word-initial combining element, also occurring as a word, derived from Old English *sē(o)c* 'ill,' used in its etymological and extended senses in combination with other English elements: **sickbay, sickbed, sickroom.**

2331   **sickle-**   A word-initial combining element, also occurring as a word, derived through Old English from Latin *secul(a)* 'reaping hook' (from *sec(āre)* 'to cut' plus the diminutive noun-forming suffix *-ula*), used in its etymological and extended senses in combination with other English elements: **sicklebill, sickle-hocked, sickleweed.** Related forms: **saw-, saxi-, skin-.**

2332   **side-**   A word-initial combining element, also occurring as a word, derived from Old English *sīde* 'long surface; aspect to the left or right of center,' used in its etymological and extended senses in combination with other English elements: **sidearm, sidecar, sidelight.**

2333 sidero-   A word-initial combining element, derived from Greek *sidēro(s)* 'iron,' used in its etymological and extended senses in Neo-Greek and Neo-Latin combinations: **siderodromophobia, siderofibrosis, siderophone.** Also, **sider-: siderosis.**

2334 sight-   A word-initial combining element, also occurring as a word, derived from Old English *sihþ* 'that which is seen; vision,' used in its etymological and extended senses in combination with other English elements: **sighthole, sight-read, sightseeing.**

2335 sigma- (Σ, σ)   A word-initial combining element, the eighteenth letter of the Greek alphabet, used chiefly to designate 'the eighteenth carbon atom in a straight chain compound or a derivative thereof in which the substitute group is attached to that atom' in chemical terminology. See **alpha-.** Compare **sigmoido-.**

2336 sigmoido-   A word-initial combining element, derived from Greek *sigmo(e)id(ēs)* 'shaped like the letter *sigma* (Σ)' plus the combining vowel *-o-,* used in the sense of 'of or pertaining to the *sigmoid flexure,* the S-shaped bend in the colon,' in biomedical terminology: **sigmoidopexy, sigmoidoscope, sigmoidostomy.** Also, **sigmo-, sigmoid-: sigmoscope, sigmoidectomy.** Compare **sigma-.**

2337 sign-   A word-initial combining element, also occurring as a word, derived through Old French from Latin *sign(um)* 'mark, token, indication' (from an Indo-European root meaning 'follow,' a *sign* having originally been, presumably, 'a directive which one is to follow'), used in its etymological and extended senses in combination with other English elements: **signboard, sign-off, signpost.** Related forms: **second-, socio-.**

2338 silico-   A word-initial combining element, derived from Neo-Latin *silic(a)* 'the crystalline compound (SiO_2) (which occurs as, among other things, flint, quartz, and sand)' (from Latin *sil(ex)*, *silic(is)* 'flint') plus the combining vowel *-o-*, used in the sense of 'of, pertaining to, or containing *silica* or *silicon,* the element (Si) whose dioxide is *silica,*' in a variety of combinations: **silicoanthracosis, silicofluoride, silicotungstate.** Also, **silic-: silicate.**

2339 silk-   A word-initial combining element, also occurring as a word, derived, ultimately, from Greek *sēr(i)k(ós)* 'silken,' literally, 'of or pertaining to the *Sēres,* the Asian people from whom the Greeks first obtained *silk,* a soft fiber spun by the larvae of certain moths,' used in its etymological and extended senses in combination with other English elements: **silkscreen, silk-stocking, silkworm.** Compare **seri-².**

2340 **silver-** A word-initial combining element, derived, ultimately, from Akkadian *sarpu* 'refined form of the metallic element (Ag)' (from *sarāpu* 'to refine'), used in its etymological and extended senses in combination with other English elements: **silverleaf, silverside, silversmith.**

2341 **simple-** A word-initial combining element, also occurring as a word, derived through Old French from Latin *simpl(us)* 'single, uncomplicated' (from a combination of two Indo-European roots, the first meaning 'one' and the other meaning 'fold,' the historical sense of *simple* being 'onefold'), used in its etymological and extended senses in combination with other English elements: **simple-faced. simple-hearted, simple-minded.** Related forms: **haplo-, hecto-, hendeca-, hetero-, homalo-, homeo-, homo-, single-, some-.**

2342 **sin-¹** A variant of **sinap-.**

2343 **sin-²** A variant of **sino-.**

2344 **sinap-** A word-initial combining element, derived from Greek *sinap(i)* 'mustard,' used in its etymological and extended senses in Neo-Greek and Neo-Latin combinations: **sinapine, sinapism, sinapolin.** Also, **sin-¹, sinapi-: sinalbin, sinapiscopy.**

2345 **single-** A word-initial combining element, also occurring as a word, derived through Old French from Latin *sing(u)l(us)* 'individual, separate' (from an Indo-European root meaning 'one'), used in its etymological and extended senses in combination with other English elements: **single-breasted, single-handed, singlestick.** Related forms: **haplo-, hecto-, hendeca-, hetero-, homalo-, homeo-, homo-, simple-, some-.**

2346 **sinistro-** A word-initial combining element, derived from Latin *sinist(e)r, sinistr(a), sinistr(um)* 'left, on the left' plus the combining vowel *-o-,* used in its etymological and extended senses in Neo-Latin and Neo-Greek combinations: **sinistrocardia, sinistromanual, sinistrophobia.** Also, **sinistr-: sinistrosis.**

2347 **Sino-** A word-initial combining element, derived, ultimately, from (Mandarin) Chinese *Ch'in²* 'China' plus the combining vowel *-o-,* used in its etymological and extended senses in a variety of combinations: **Sinology, Sinophobia, Sino-Tibetan.**

2348   **sino-**   A word-initial combining element, derived from Latin *sin(us)* 'hollow, basin; curved or bent surface' plus the combining vowel *-o-,* used in its etymological and extended senses, chief among these being 'of or pertaining to a cavity of the body,' in Neo-Latin and Neo-Greek combinations: **sino-auricular, sinobronchitis, sinospiral.** Also, **sinu-, sinus, sinuso-: sinuventricular, sinusitis, sinusotomy.**

2349   **siphono-**   A word-initial combining element, derived from Greek *siphōn, siphōn(os)* 'hollow reed; tube' plus the combining vowel *-o-,* used in its etymological and extended senses in Neo-Greek combinations: **siphonognathoid, siphonophore, siphonostele.** Also, **siphon-:** *Siphonaptera.*

2350   **sit-**   A word-initial combining element, also occurring as a word, derived from Old English *sit(tan)* 'to be seated; to seat oneself,' used in its etymological and extended senses in combination with other English elements: **sit-down, sitfast, sit-up.** Compare **set-².** Related form: **saddle-.**

2351   **sito-**   A word-initial combining element, derived from Greek *sîto(s)* 'grain,' hence, 'food,' used in this latter and extended senses in Neo-Greek combinations: **sitomania, sitophobia, sitotherapy.** Also, **siti-, sitio-: sitieirgeia, sitiophobia.**

2352   **six-**   A word-initial combining element, also occurring as a word, derived from Old English *s(e)ix* 'the cardinal number between *five* and *seven,*' occurring in its etymological and extended senses in combination with other English elements: **six-gun, six-pack, sixpenny.** Related forms: **hexa-, sex-.**

2353   **skel-**   A word-initial combining element, derived from Greek *skél(os)* 'leg,' used in its etymological sense in Neo-Greek combinations: **skelalgia, skelasthenia, skelatony.** Related forms: **scolec-, scolio-.**

2354   **skeleto-**   A word-initial combining element, derived from Greek *(sôma) skeletó(n)* 'dried up (body),' used in the extended sense of 'of or pertaining to the bony framework of an animal' in Neo-Greek combinations: **skeletogenous, skeletography, skeletology.** Also, **skele-, skelet-: skeletopia, skeletin.** Related form: **sclero-.**

2355   **skew-**   A word-initial combining element, also occurring as a word, derived from dialectal Old French (*e*)*sku*(*er*) 'to avoid,' hence, in Middle English, 'to move to the side,' used in the sense of 'off-center' and in extensions of this sense in combination with other English elements: **skewback, skewbald, skew-symmetrical.**

2356 **skia-** A word-initial combining element, derived from Greek *skiá* 'shadow, shade,' used in its etymological and extended senses, chief among these being 'of or pertaining to roentgen rays,' in Neo-Greek combinations: **skiabaryt, skiagraph, skiascope.** Also, **scia-: scialyscope.**

2357 **skin-** A word-initial combining element, also occurring as a word, derived from Old Norse *skin*(*n*) 'stripped hide of an animal; derma' (from an Indo-European root meaning 'cut'), used in its etymological and extended senses in combination with other English elements: **skin-deep, skin-dive, skinflint.** Related forms: **saw-, saxi-, sickle-.**

2358 **skip-** A word-initial combining element, also occurring as a word of obscure origin, used in the sense of 'spring lightly' and in extensions of this sense in combination with other English elements: **skip-bomb, skipdent, skipjack.**

2359 **skler-** A variant of **sclero-.**

2360 **skoli-** A variant of **scolio-.**

2361 **skopo-** A variant of **scopo-.**

2362 **sky-** A word-initial combining element, also occurring as a word, derived from Old Norse *ský* 'cloud,' used in the extended sense of 'celestial vault' and in extensions of this sense in combination with other English elements: **skydive, sky-high, skylark.**

2363 **slap-** A word-initial combining element, also occurring as a word, derived from Low German *slap*(*p*) 'smacking blow with the flat of the hand' (from an Indo-European root meaning something on the order of 'loose-hanging, flapping'), used in its etymological and extended senses in combination with other English elements: **slapdash, slapjack, slapshot.** Related forms: **lobo-, sleep-.**

2364 **sleep-** A word-initial combining element, also occurring as a word, derived from Old English *slēp* 'normal state of unconsciousness' (from an Indo-European root meaning something on the order of 'loose-hanging, flapping'), used in its etymological sense in combination with other English elements: **sleep-in, sleepwalking, sleep-wear.** Related forms: **lobo-, slap-.**

2365 **slip-**   A word-initial combining element, also occurring as a word, derived from Middle Low German *slip(pen)* 'to slide (away),' used in its etymological and extended senses in combination with other English elements: **slipknot, slipstitch, slip-up.**

2366 **slow-**   A word-initial combining element, also occurring as a word, derived from Old English *slāw* 'not fast,' used in its etymological and extended senses in combination with other English elements: **slowdown, slowpoke, slow-witted.**

2367 **small-**   A word-initial combining element, also occurring as a word, derived from Old English *smæl* 'little in extent or size,' used in its etymological and extended senses in combination with other English elements: **small-minded, smallpox, small-time.**

2368 **smoke-**   A word-initial combining element, also occurring as a word, derived from Old English *smoc(a)* 'vapor consisting of partially combusted matter,' used in its etymological and extended senses in combination with other English elements: **smokehouse, smokejack, smokestack.**

2369 **smooth-**   A word-initial combining element, also occurring as a word, derived from late Old English *smōþ* 'having an even surface,' used in its etymological and extended senses in combination with other English elements: **smoothbore, smooth-faced, smoothhound.**

2370 **snail-**   A word-initial combining element, also occurring as a word, derived from Old English *snæ(ġe)l* 'shell-bearing gastropod' (from an Indo-European root meaning 'creep(er)'), used in its etymological and extended senses in combination with other English elements: **snailfish, snailflower, snail-paced.** Related form: **snake-.**

2371 **snake-**   A word-initial combining element, also occurring as a word, derived from Old English *snac(a)* 'reptile of the suborder *Serpentes*' (from an Indo-European root meaning 'creep(er)'), used in its etymological and extended senses in combination with other English elements: **snakebite, snakefish, snakeroot.** Related form: **snail-.**

2372 **snap-**   A word-initial combining element, also occurring as a word, derived from Middle Low German *snap(pen)* 'to catch quickly,' used in its etymological and extended senses in combination with other English elements: **snapdragon, snap-on, snapshot.**

2373   **snow-** A word-initial combining element, also occurring as a word, derived from Old English *snāw* 'precipitation in the form of crystalline flakes,' used in its etymological and extended senses in combination with other English elements: **snowball, snowbell, snowshed.**

2374   **so-** A word-initial combining element, also occurring as a word, derived from Old English *swā* 'in such a way,' used in its etymological and extended senses in combination with other English elements: **so-and-so, so-called, soever.** Related form: **quasi-.**

2375   **soap-** A word-initial combining element, also occurring as a word, derived from Old English *sāp(e)* 'detergent compound of a fatty acid (or the like) and an alkali,' used in its etymological and extended senses in combination with other English elements: **soapbox, soapstone, soapsuds.** Related form: **sapon-.**

2376   **socio-** A word-initial combining element, derived from Latin *soci(us)* 'companion, partner, ally' (from an Indo-European root meaning 'follow(er)') plus the combining vowel *-o-*, used in the sense of 'of or pertaining to interpersonal relationships' in Neo-Latin and Neo-Greek combinations: **socioeconomic, sociology, sociometric.** Also, **soci-: social.** Related forms: **second-, sign-.**

2377   **sodio-** A word initial combining element, derived from Late Latin *sod(a)* 'glasswort, saltwort,' hence, 'sodium carbonate (which may be derived from the ashes of burned glasswort or saltwort)' (from Arabic *suwwād* 'glasswort') plus the Scientific Latin noun-forming suffix *-i(um)* (which is used in naming metallic elements) plus the combining vowel *-o-*, used in the sense of 'of, pertaining to, or containing the element *sodium* (Na) (which forms the metallic base of sodium carbonate)' in chemical terminology: **sodio-cupric (chloride), sodio-malonic, sodiotartrate.** Also, **sod-, sodi-, sodo-: sodemia, sodiarsphenamine, sodophthalyl.**

2378   **soft-** A word-initial combining element, also occurring as a word, derived from Old English *sōft(e)* 'agreeable, mild,' used in the extended sense of 'not hard' and in extensions of this sense in combination with other English elements: **softball, softboiled, softhearted.**

2379   **sol-¹** A word-initial combining element, derived from Latin *sol, sōl(is)* '(the) sun,' appearing in its etymological sense in inherited and Neo-Latin combinations: **solar, sol-lunar, solstice.** Also, **soli-¹, solo-: soliform, solograph.** Related forms: **helio-, south-, sun-.**

2380 sol-² A variant of **soli-²**.

2381 sole- A word-initial combining element, also occurring as a word, derived, ultimately, from Latin *sol*(*um*) 'lowest part; bottom (of the foot),' used in its etymological senses in combination with other English elements: **solepiece, soleplate, soleprint.**

2382 soleno- A word-initial combining element, derived from Greek *sōlḗn, sōlḗn*(*os*) 'channel, pipe' plus the combining vowel -*o*-, used in its etymological and extended senses in Neo-Greek combinations: **solenoconch, solenoglyph, solenostomous.** Also, **solen-: solenite.**

2383 soli-¹ A variant of **sol-¹**.

2384 soli-² A word-initial combining element, derived from Latin *sōl*(*us*) 'single, sole, only' plus the combining vowel -*i*-, used in its etymological and extended senses in Neo-Latin and Neo-Greek combinations: ***Solibranchia,* solifidian, soliloquy.** Also, **sol-²: solipsist.** Related forms: **ethno-, se-, self-.**

2385 soli-³ A variant of **solid-**.

2386 solid- A word-initial combining element, also occurring as a word, derived through Old French from Latin *solid*(*us*) 'whole,' hence, 'firm, sound,' used in its etymological and extended senses in combination with other English elements: **solid-looking, solid-state, solidungulate.** Also, **soli-³: soliped.** Related forms: **holo-, safe-.**

2387 solo- A variant of **sol-¹**.

2388 somato- A word-initial combining element, derived from Greek *sôma, sômat*(*os*) 'body, mass' (from an Indo-European root meaning 'swell') plus the combining vowel -*o*-, used in its etymological and extended senses in Neo-Greek and Neo-Latin combinations: **somatoceptor, somatogenesis, somatomegaly.** Also, **som-, soma-, somat-, somo-: somasthenia, somaplasm, somatesthesia, somopsychosis.** Related forms: **thimble-, thumb-, tuberculo-, tyro-.**

2389 some- A word-initial combining element, also occurring as a word, derived from Old English *sum* 'a certain' (from an Indo-European root meaning 'one'), used in its etymological and extended senses in combination with other English elements: **somebody, somehow, something.** Related forms: **haplo-, hecto-, hendeca-, hetero-, homalo-, homeo-, homo-, simple-, single-.**

2390   **somni-**   A word-initial combining element, derived from Latin *somn(us)* 'sleep' plus the combining vowel *-i-*, used in its etymological and extended senses in Neo-Latin and Neo-Greek combinations: **somniferous, somniloquist, somnipathy.** Also, **somn-, somno-: somnambulist, somnocinematograph.** Related form: **hypno-**.

2391   **sou'-**   A variant of **south-**.

2392   **soup-**   A word-initial combining element, also occurring as a word, derived from Old French *soup(e)* 'bread to be dipped in a broth; broth,' used in this latter and extended senses in combination with other English elements: **soup-and-fish, soupbone, soupspoon.** Related form: **hyeto-**.

2393   **sour-**   A word-initial combining element, also occurring as a word, derived from Old English *sūr* 'acetic, tart,' used in its etymological and extended senses in combination with other English elements: **sourball, sourdough, sourpuss.**

2394   **south-**   A word-initial combining element, also occurring as a word, derived from Old English *sūþ* 'the direction to the right as one faces the rising sun' (from an Indo-European root meaning '(the) sun'), used in its etymological and extended senses in combination with other English elements: **southbound, southpaw, Southport.** Also, **sou'-: sou'wester.** Related forms: **helio-, sol-¹, sun-**.

2395   **space-**   A word-initial combining element, also occurring as a word, derived through Old French from Latin *spat(ium)* 'extent, distance, room' (from an Indo-European root meaning 'stretch'), used in its etymological and extended senses in combination with other English elements: **spacecraft, spaceman, space-time.** Related forms: **span-², spasmo-, spider-, spin-²**.

2396   **spade-**   A word-initial combining element, also occurring as a word, derived from Old English *spad(u)* 'digging tool (with a wedge-shaped blade)' (from an Indo-European root meaning 'wedge'), used in its etymological and extended senses in combination with other English elements: **spadefish, spadefoot, spadework.** Related form: **spheno-**.

2397   **span-¹**   A variant of **spano-**.

2398   **span-²**   A word-initial combining element, also occurring as a word, derived from Old English *span(n)* 'distance between the tip of the thumb and the tip of the little finger when the hand is spread out' (from an Indo-European root meaning 'stretch'), used in the sense of 'short expanse' and in extensions of this sense in combination with other English elements: **spanpiece, spanrail, spanworm.** Related forms: **space-, spasmo-, spider-, spin-².**

2399 **spano-** A word-initial combining element, derived from Greek *spanó(s)* 'scarce,' used in its etymological and extended senses in Neo-Greek combinations: **spanogyny, spanomenorrhea, spanopnea.** Also, **span-¹: spanemia.**

2400 **spark-** A word-initial combining element, also occurring as a word, derived from Old English *sp(e)arc(a)* 'fiery particle,' used chiefly in the sense of 'electrical discharge' and in extensions of this sense combination with other English elements: **spark-killer, sparkoven, sparkplug.**

2401 **spasmo-** A word-initial combining element, derived from Greek *spasmó(s)* 'tension, convulsion' (from the verb *spân* 'to draw tight' (from an Indo-European root meaning 'stretch')), used in the sense of 'of or pertaining to a sudden, involuntary contraction' and in extensions of this sense in Neo-Greek combinations: **spasmogenic, spasmolygmus, spasmophemia.** Also, **spasm-: spasmalgin.** Related forms: **space-, span-², spider-, spin-².**

2402 **spatter-** A word-initial combining element, also occurring as a word of probably onomatopoeic origin, used in the sense of 'splash with droplets' and in extensions of this sense in combination with other English elements: **spatterdash, spatterdock, spatterware.**

2403 **spear-** A word-initial combining element, also occurring as a word, derived from Old English *sper(e)* 'weapon with a long shaft and pointed tip,' used in its etymological and extended senses in combination with other English elements: **spearfish, spearhead, spearmint.**

2404 **spectro-** A word-initial combining element, derived from Latin *spectr(um)* 'image, apparition' (from an Indo-European root meaning 'look, see') plus the combining vowel *-o-,* used in its etymological and extended senses, chief among these being 'of or pertaining to the range of wavelengths of refracted and diffracted electromagnetic vibrations,' in Neo-Latin and Neo-Greek combinations: **spectrocolorimeter, spectrophobia, spectroscope.** Also, **spectr-: spectral.** Related form: **scopo-².**

2405 **speed-** A word-initial combining element, also occurring as a word, derived from Old English *spēd* 'quickness,' used in its etymological and extended senses in combination with other English elements: **speedball, speedboat, speedway.**

2406 **spermato-** A word-initial combining element, derived from Greek *spérma, spérmat(os)* 'seed' plus the combining vowel *-o-,* used in its etymological and extended senses, chief among these being, 'of or pertaining to semen,' in Neo-Greek and Neo-Latin combinations: **spermatoblast, spermatogenesis, spermatoschesis.** Also, **sperm-, spermat-, spermi-, spermo-: spermacrasia, spermatovum, spermicidal, spermocytoma.** Related form: **sporo-.**

2407 **sphaer-** A variant of **sphero-.**

2408 **spheno-** A word-initial combining element, derived from Greek *sphēn, sphēn(ós)* 'wedge' plus the combining vowel *-o-,* used in its etymological and extended senses, chief among these being 'of or pertaining to the *sphenoid* bone, a wedge-shaped bone found at the base of the skull,' in Neo-Greek and Neo-Latin combinations: **sphenofrontal, sphenometer, sphenotresia.** Also, **sphen-: sphenethmoid.** Related form: **spade-.**

2409 **sphero-** A word-initial combining element, derived from Greek *sphaîr(a)* 'ball, globe' plus the combining vowel *-o-,* used in its etymological and extended senses in Neo-Greek combinations: **spherocylinder, spherocyte, spherometer.** Also, **sphaer-, sphaero-, spher-: sphaerenchyma, *Sphaerogaster,* spherical.**

2410 **sphinctero-** A word-initial combining element, derived from Greek *sphinktḗr, sphinktḗr(os)* 'that which binds,' hence, 'muscle which closes an aperture of the body' (from the verb *sphingein* 'to bind, draw tight') plus the combining vowel *-o-,* used in its latter and extended senses in Neo-Greek combinations: **sphincterolysis, sphincteroscope, sphincterotomy.** Also, **sphincter-: sphincteralgia.**

2411 **sphygmo-** A word-initial combining element, derived from Greek *sphygmó(s)* '(throbbing) pulse,' used in its etymological and extended senses in Neo-Greek and Neo-Latin combinations: **sphygmocardiograph, sphygmosignal, sphygmotonometer.** Also, **sphygm-: sphygmic.**

2412 **spiculi-** A word-initial combining element, derived from Latin *spīcul(um)* 'little sharp point' (from *spīc(a)* 'point, spike' plus the diminutive suffix *-ulum*) plus the combining vowel *-i-,* used in the sense of 'needle' and in extensions of this sense in Neo-Latin combinations: **spiculiferous, spiculiform, spiculigenous.** Related form: **spino-.**

2413   **spider-**   A word-initial combining element, also occurring as a word, derived from Old English *spiþr(a)* 'arachnid of the order *Araneae*' (from an Indo-European root meaning 'stretch,' hence, 'spin'), used in its etymological and extended senses in combination with other English elements: **spiderhunter, spiderweb, spiderwood**. Related forms: **space-, span-², spasmo-, spin-².**

2414   **spin-¹**   A variant of **spino-**.

2415   **spin-²**   A word-initial combining element, also occurring as a word, derived from Old English *spin(nan)* 'to draw and twist into thread' (from an Indo-European root meaning 'stretch'), used chiefly in extensions of the sense of 'twist or rotate (quickly)' in combination with other English elements: **spin-dry, spin-off, spinproof**. Related forms: **space-, span-², spasmo-, spider-.**

2416   **spino-**   A word-initial combining element, derived from Latin *spīn(a)* 'thorn, prickle' and, by extension, 'backbone' plus the combining vowel *-o-*, used in its etymological and extended senses, chief among these being 'of or pertaining to the *spinal cord*,' in Neo-Latin and Neo-Greek combinations: **spinobulbar, spinocellular, spinoneural**. Also, **spin-¹, spini-: spinalgia, spinifugal**. Related form: **spiculi-.**

2417   **spir-¹**   A variant of **spiro-¹**.

2418   **spir-²**   A variant of **spiro-²**.

2419   **spiri-**   A variant of **spiro-²**.

2420   **spiro-¹**   A word-initial combining element, derived from Latin *spīr(āre)* 'to breathe' plus the combining vowel *-o-*, used in its etymological and extended senses in Neo-Latin and Neo-Greek combinations: **spirometer, spirophore, spiroscope**. Also, **spir-¹: spirant.**

2421   **spiro-²**   A word-initial combining element, derived from Greek *sp(e)îr(a)* (and Latin *spīr(a)*) 'coil' plus the combining vowel *-o-*, used in its etymological and extended senses in Neo-Greek and Neo-Latin combinations: **spirofibrillae, spirospartae, spirozooid**. Also, **spir-², spiri-: spiral, spirignath.**

2422   **spirochet-**   A word-initial combining element, derived from Greek *sp(e)îr(a)* 'coil' plus the combining vowel *-o-* plus *chait(ē)* '(long flowing) hair,' hence, 'hair, bristle,' used in the sense of 'of or pertaining to *spirochetes,* coil-shaped microorganisms' in biomedical terminology: **spirochetal, spirochetemia, spirocheturia.** Also, **spirochaet-, spirocheta-, spirocheti-, spirocheto-:** *Spirochaetaceae,* **spirochetalytic, spirocheticidal, spirochetogenous.** Compare **spiro-², chaeto-.**

2423 **spit-**   A word-initial combining element, also occurring as a word, derived from Old English (*ge*)*spit*(*tan*) 'to eject saliva,' used in its etymological and extended senses in combination with other English elements: **spit-and-polish, spitball, spitfire.** Related form: **ptyalo-.**

2424 **splanchno-**   A word-initial combining element, derived from Greek *splánchn*(*a*) 'viscera' plus the combining vowel *-o-*, used in its etymological and extended senses in biomedical terminology: **splanchnocele, splanchnodiastasis, splanchnopleural.** Also, **splanchn-: splanchnodynia.** Related forms: **lieno-, spleno-.**

2425 **spleno-**   A word-initial combining element, derived from Greek *splēn, splēn*(*ós*) 'spleen' plus the combining vowel *-o-*, used in its etymological and extended senses in biomedical terminology: **splenocleisis, splenomedullary, splenonephroptosis.** Also, **splen-: splenatrophy.** Related forms: **lieno-, splanchno-.**

2426 **split-**   A word-initial combining element, also occurring as a word, derived from Middle Dutch *split*(*ten*) 'to break apart (by running aground); cleave,' used in its etymological and extended senses in combination with other English elements: **split-face, split-level, split-off.**

2427 **spodo-**   A word-initial combining element, derived from Greek *spodó*(*s*) 'ashes,' used in its etymological and extended senses, chief among these being 'of or pertaining to waste materials,' in Neo-Greek combinations: **spodogram, spodophagous, spodophorous.**

2428 **spondylo-**   A word-initial combining element, derived from Greek *sp*(*h*)*óndylo*(*s*) 'vertebra,' used in its etymological and extended senses, chief among these being, 'of or pertaining to the spinal column,' in Neo-Greek combinations: **spondylodesis, spondylomalacia, spondylotherapy.** Also, **spondyl-: spondylitis.**

2429 **spongio-**   A word-initial combining element, derived from Greek *spongi*(*á*) and Latin *spongi*(*a*) 'sponge' plus the combining vowel *-o-*, used in its etymological and extended senses in Neo-Greek and Neo-Latin combinations: **spongioblast, spongiopilin, spongioplasm.** Also, **spongi-, spongo-: spongiform, spongosterol.** Related form: **fungi-.**

2430 **sporo-** A word-initial combining element, derived from Greek *spóro(s)* 'a sowing,' hence, 'that which is sown or which results from sowing; seed,' used chiefly in the sense of 'of or pertaining to a *spore*, the reproductive element of any of a variety of lower organisms' in Neo-Greek and Neo-Latin combinations: **sporoblast, sporoduct, sporoplasm.** Also, **spor-, spori-: sporont, sporicidal.** Related form: **spermato-.**

2431 **sports-** A word-initial combining element, also occurring as a word, derived from Old French (*de*)*sport*(*er*) 'to divert, amuse' (from Latin *dis-* 'away' plus *portāre* 'to carry') plus the (English) plural marker of nouns, *-s*, used in the sense of 'of or pertaining to athletic competition (as a diversion or amusement)' in combination with other English elements: **sportscast, sportsman, sportswear.** Compare **des-, porte-.**

2432 **spot-** A word-initial combining element, also occurring as a word of obscure origin, used in the sense of 'speck, blot' and in extensions of this sense in combination with other English elements: **spot-check, spotlight, spot-weld.**

2433 **spring-** A word-initial combining element, also occurring as a word, derived from Old English *spring*(*an*) 'to issue forth,' used in a variety of extensions of its etymological sense in combination with other English elements: **springboard, springlock, springtime.**

2434 **squamo-** A word-initial combining element, derived from Latin *squām*(*a*) 'layer, scale' plus the combining vowel *-o-*, used in its etymological and extended senses, chief among these being 'of or pertaining to the *squama temporalis*, the platelike portion of the temporal bone,' in Neo-Latin and Neo-Greek combinations: **squamocellular, squamopetrosal, squamosphenoid.** Also, **squam-: squamate.**

2435 **square-** A word-initial combining element, also occurring as a word, derived through Old French from (unattested) Late Latin **(e)xquadr(āre)* 'to make to have (four) sides at right angles' (from *ex-* 'from, out of' plus *quadr(a)* 'equilateral rectangle' (from an Indo-European root meaning 'four') plus the endings of the first conjugation class), used in the sense of 'resembling an equilateral rectangle' in combination with other English elements: **square-dance, squareface, square-rigged.** Compare **ex-[1]** and **quadri-.**

2436 **squaw-** A word-initial combining element, also occurring as a word, derived from one of the Algonquian languages (cf. Massachusetts *squa* 'woman'), used in the sense of 'of or pertaining to a

North American Indian woman' and in extensions of this sense in combination with a few English elements: **squawbush, squawfish, squawroot.**

2437 stage- A word-initial combining element, also occurring as a word, derived from Old French (*e*)*stage* 'dwelling, situation' (from (unattested) Late Latin **staticum* 'station; standing place' (from the verb *stāre* 'to stand')), used chiefly in the extended sense of 'of or pertaining to the theater' in combination with other English elements: **stagecoach, stagehand, stagestruck.** Related forms: **histio-, histo-, stand-, stasi-, state-, stato-, stauro-, stern-²(?), store-, stylo-.**

2438 stair- A word-initial combining element, derived from Old English *staǣ(ǵe)r* 'flight of steps,' used in its etymological sense in combination with other English elements: **staircase, stairhead, stairwell.** Related form: **sticho-.**

2439 stand- A word-initial combining element, also occurring as a word, derived from Old English *stand(an)* 'to assume an erect position,' used in its etymological and extended senses in combination with other English elements: **standby, standpipe, stand-up.** Related forms: **histio-, histo-, stage-, stasi-, state-, stato-, stauro-, stern-²(?), store-, stylo-.**

2440 stann- A word-initial combining element, derived from Late Latin *stann(um)* 'tin,' the word originally having been used to designate 'an alloy of lead and silver,' used chiefly in the sense of 'of, pertaining to, containing, or derived from *stannic acid,* a compound of tetravalent tin' in chemical terminology: **stannane, stannate, stannite.**

2441 staphylo- A word-initial combining element, derived from Greek *staphyl(ē)* 'bunch of grapes,' hence, 'the uvula (which resembles a grape hanging from a stock)' plus the combining vowel *-o-,* used chiefly in the sense of 'resembling a bunch of grapes,' 'of or pertaining to the uvula,' and 'of or pertaining to *staphylococci,* grape-shaped bacteria occurring in irregular clusters' in Neo-Greek and Neo-Latin combinations: **staphylocoagulase, staphylopharyngorrhaphy, staphylotomy.** Also, **staphyl-: staphyline.**

2442 star- A word-initial combining element, also occurring as a word, derived from Old English *steor(ra)* 'self-luminous celestial body,' used in its etymological and extended senses in combination with other English elements: **starfish, starflower, stargazer.** Related form: **astro-.**

2443   stasi-   A word-initial combining element, derived from Greek *stási(s)* '(a) standing' (from the verb *histánai* 'to stand'), used in its etymological and extended senses in Neo-Greek combinations: **stasibasiphobia, stasimetry, stasimorphy.** Also, **staso-: stasophobia.** Related forms: **histio-, histo-, stage-, stand-, state-, stato-, stauro-, stern-²(?), store-, stylo-.**

2444   stat-   A variant of **stato-.**

2445   state-   A word-initial combining element, also occurring as a word, derived from Latin *stat(us)* 'standing, position,' hence, 'organization' (from the verb *stāre* 'to stand'), used in its etymological and extended senses in combination with other English elements: **statecraft, state-of-the-art, stateside.** Related forms: **histio-, histo-, stage-, stand-, stasi-, stato-, stauro-, stern-²(?), store-, stylo-.**

2446   stato-   A word-initial combining element, derived from Greek *statό(s)* 'placed, standing' (from the verb *histánai* 'to stand'), used in a variety of extensions of its etymological sense, chief among these being 'of or pertaining to equilibrium,' in Neo-Greek combinations: **statoblast, statocyst, statometer.** Also, **stat-: static.** Related forms: **histio-, histo-, stage-, stand-, stasi-, state-, stauro-, stern-²(?), store-, stylo-.**

2447   stauro-   A word-initial combining element, derived from Greek *staurό(s)* 'upright stake' (from an Indo-European root meaning 'stand'), hence, 'rood, cross,' used in the sense of 'cross-shaped, crosslike, crossed' in Neo-Greek combinations: **staurolite, *Stauromedusae,* stauroplegia.** Also, **staur-: stauraxonial.** Related forms: **histio-, histo-, stage-, stand-, stasi-, state-, stato-, stern-²(?), store-, stylo-.**

2448   steam-   A word-initial combining element, also occurring as a word, derived from Old English *stēam* 'vapor resulting from the application of heat to water,' used in its etymological and extended senses in combination with other English elements: **steamboat, steamfitter, steamroller.**

2449   steato-   A word-initial combining element, derived from Greek *stéa(r), stéat(os)* 'suet, tallow, fat' plus the combining vowel *-o-*, used in its etymological and extended senses in Neo-Greek and Neo-Latin combinations: **steatolysis, steatonecrosis, steatopygia.** Also, **stear-, steari-, stearo-, steat-: stearentin, steariform, stearodermia, steatitis.**

2450   steel-   A word-initial combining element, also occurring as a word, derived from Old English *stēl(i)* 'durable alloy of lead and carbon,' used in its etymological and extended senses in combination with other English elements: **steelhead, steelworker, steelyard.**

2451 **stego-**   A word-initial combining element, derived from Greek *stég(ein)* 'to cover' plus the combining vowel *-o-,* used in the sense of 'covered' and in extensions of this sense in Neo-Greek combinations: **stegocarpous, stegocephalous,** *Stegosaurus.* Also, **steg-: stegodon.**

2452 **steno-**   A word-initial combining element, derived from Greek *stenó(s)* 'narrow,' used in its etymological and extended senses, chief among these being 'constricted, contracted,' in Neo-Greek combinations: **stenobregmate, stenography, stenophotic.** Also, **sten-: stenopeic.**

2453 **step-¹**   A word-initial combining element, derived from Old English *stē(o)p-* 'degree of kinship resulting from the remarriage of a parent' (from an Indo-European root meaning 'push, hit' which seems to have been specialized in Germanic to mean 'bereave(d)'), used in its etymological sense in combination with other English elements: **stepchild, stepfather, stepsister.** Related forms: **tympano-, type-, typo-.**

2454 **step-²**   A word-initial combining element, also occurring as a word, derived from Old English *step(pan)* 'to lift the foot up and put it down again (as in walking or dancing),' used in its etymological and extended senses in combination with other English elements: **step-down, stepladder, step-up.**

2455 **sterco-**   A word-initial combining element, derived from Latin *sterc(us), sterc(oris)* 'dung, excrement' plus the combining vowel *-o-,* used in its etymological and extended senses in Neo-Latin and Neo-Greek combinations: **stercobilin, stercolith, stercoporphyrin.** Also, **stercor-, stercoro-: stercoremia, stercorolith.** Related form: **scato-.**

2456 **stereo-**   A word-initial combining element, derived from Greek *stereó(s)* 'stiff, hard, solid,' used in its etymological and extended senses, chief among these being 'three-dimensional' and 'fixed,' in Neo-Greek and Neo-Latin combinations: **stereoblastula, stereofluoroscopy, stereotype.** Also, **stere-: stereopsis.**

2457 **stern-¹**   A variant of **sterno-.**

2458 **stern-²**   A word-initial combining element, also occurring as a word, probably derived from Old Norse *stjōrn* 'rudder, steering' (perhaps from an Indo-European root meaning 'stand'), used in the sense of 'rear part of a sea-going vessel' in combination with other English elements: **sternforemost, sternpost, sternson.** Related forms(?): **histio-, histo-, stage-, stand-, stasi-, state-, stato-, stauro-, store-, stylo-.**

2459   sterno-   A word-initial combining element, derived from Greek *stêrno(n)* 'chest, breast' (from an Indo-European root meaning 'spread out'), used in its etymological and extended senses, chief among these being 'of or pertaining to the *sternum,* the breast-bone,' in Neo-Greek and Neo-Latin combinations: **sternoclavicular, sternodymia, sternoxiphopagus.** Also, **stern-**[1]: **sternalgia.** Related forms: **strato-, straw-, street-.**

2460   stetho-   A word-initial combining element, derived from Greek *stêtho(s)* 'chest, breast,' used in its etymological and extended senses in Neo-Greek combinations: **stethograph, stethomenia, stethoscope.** Also, **steth-: stethalgia.**

2461   stheno-   A word-initial combining element, derived from Greek *sthéno(s)* 'strength,' used in its etymological and extended senses in Neo-Greek combinations: **sthenometer, sthenophotic, sthenopyra.** Also, **sthen-: sthenic.**

2462   stib-   A word-initial combining element, derived from Latin *stib(ium)* 'antimony,' used in its etymological and extended senses in chemical terminology: **stibacetin, stibamine, stiburea.**

2463   sticho-   A word-initial combining element, derived from Greek *sticho(s)* 'line, row,' used in its etymological and extended senses in Neo-Greek combinations: **stichochrome, stichometry, stichomythia.** Related form: **stair-.**

2464   stick-   A word-initial combining element, also occurring as a word, derived from Old English *stic(ian)* 'to pierce; to cause to adhere' and *stic(ca)* 'rod; thin piece of wood,' literally, 'that with which one may pierce or cause to adhere,' used in its etymological and extended senses in combination with other English elements: **stickball, stick-in-the-mud, stickpin.**

2465   stink-   A word-initial combining element, also occurring as a word, derived from Old English *stinc(an)* 'to give off an offensive odor,' used in its etymological and extended senses in combination with other English elements: **stinkbug, stinkpot, stinkweed.**

2466   **stock-**   A word-initial combining element, also occurring as a word, derived from Old English *stoc(c)* '(tree) trunk,' used in its etymological and extended senses, chief among these being 'supply, esp. of something of (monetary) value, such as cattle, or a token thereof (from the English practice of recording the borrowing of money from an individual by the State by notching a stick and then splitting the stick along the notches and giving the lender half of the stick as a receipt to be matched against the half kept by the Exchequer when the loan was to be repaid),' in combination with other English elements: **stockbroker, stock-still, stockyard.**

2467   **stomato-**   A word-initial combining element, derived from Greek *stóma, stómat(os)* 'mouth' plus the combining vowel *-o-,* used in its etymological and extended senses in Neo-Greek combinations: **stomatodysodia, stomatolalia, stomatoplasty.** Also, **stom-, stoma-, stomat-: stomal, stomatomy, stomatalgia.**

2468   **stone-**   A word-initial combining element, also occurring as a word, derived from Old English *stān* 'rock,' used in its etymological and extended senses in combination with other English elements: **stone-deaf, stonechat, stonecutter.**

2469   **stop-**   A word-initial combining element, also occurring as a word, derived from Old English *-stop(pian)* 'to plug,' used in its etymological and extended senses, chief among these being 'arrest,' in combination with other English elements: **stopcock, stopgap, stoplight.** Related form: **stypt-.**

2470   **store-**   A word-initial combining element, also occurring as a word, derived through Old French from Latin *(in)staur(āre)* 'to repair, renew,' literally, 'to set up' (from an Indo-European root meaning 'stand'), used in a variety of extensions of its etymological sense, chief among these being 'supply' and 'establishment in which supplies are offered for sale,' in combination with other English elements: **store-bought, storefront, storehouse.** Related forms: **histio-, histo-, stage-, stand-, stasi-, state-, stato-, stauro-, stern-²(?), stylo-.**

2471   **story-**   A word-initial combining element, also occurring as a word, derived through Old French and Latin from Greek *(hi)storí(a)* 'observation, learning,' hence, 'narrative of that which one has observed or learned' (from an Indo-European root meaning 'know, observe'), used in this latter and extended senses in combination with other English elements: **storyboard, storybook, storyteller.** Related forms: **eido-, guide-, ideo-, video-, visuo-.**

2472 straight- A word-initial combining element, also occurring as a word, derived from Middle English *streġt,* the past participle of the verb *strecche* 'to stretch,' used in the extended sense of 'not curved' and in extensions of this sense in combination with other English elements: **straight-arm, straightforward, straightway.**

2473 strap- A word-initial combining element, also occurring as a word, a variant of *strop* (from Middle Low German *strop* 'band of rope' (from an Indo-European root meaning 'twist(ed)')), used in its etymological and extended senses in combination with other English elements: **straphanger, strap-hinge, strap-laid.** Related forms: **strepho-, strepsi-, strepto-¹, strepto-².**

2474 strato- A word-initial combining element, derived from Latin *strāt(us), strāt(a), strāt(um)* 'stretched, spread out' plus the combining vowel *-o-,* used in the extended sense of 'layer; cloud layer' in Neo-Latin and Neo-Greek combinations: **strato-cirrus, stratocumulus, stratosphere.** Also, **strati-: stratigram.** Compare **street-.** Related forms: **sterno-, straw-.**

2475 straw- A word-initial combining element, also occurring as a word, derived from Old English *str(ē)aw* 'cereal stocks or stems,' literally, 'that which is strewn' (from an Indo-European root meaning 'spread'), used in its etymological and extended senses in combination with other English elements: **strawberry, strawboard, straw-hat.** Related forms: **sterno-, strato-, street-.**

2476 street- A word-initial combining element, also occurring as a word, derived from Late Latin *(via) strāt(a)* 'extended (road),' used in the sense of 'road' and in extensions of this sense in combination with other English elements: **streetcar, streetlight, streetwalker.** Compare **strato-.**

2477 strepho- A word-initial combining element, derived from Greek *stréph(ein)* 'to twist' plus the combining vowel *-o-,* used in the sense of 'twisted' and in extensions of this sense in Neo-Greek combinations: **strephopodia, strephosymbolia, strephotome.** Also, **streph-: strephexopodia.** Compare **strepsi-, strepto-¹, strepto-².** Related form: **strap-.**

2478 strepsi- A word-initial combining element, derived from Greek *strépsi(s)* '(a) twisting' (from the verb *stréphein* 'to twist'), used in its etymological and extended senses in Neo-Greek combinations: **strepsiceros, strepsinema, strepsipterous.** Compare **strepho-, strepto-¹, strepto-².** Related form: **strap-.**

2479   **strepto-**[1]   A word-initial combining element, derived from Greek *streptó(s)*, the past participle of the verb *stréphein* 'to twist,' used in its etymological and extended senses in Neo-Greek and Neo-Latin combinations: **streptobacillus, streptomicrodactyly,** *Streptomyces.* Compare **strepho-, strepsi-.** Related form: **strap-.**

2480   **strepto-**[2]   A word-initial combining element, derived from English *strepto(coccus)* 'spherical bacterium occurring in cellular chains' (from Greek *streptó(s)* 'twisted,' hence 'chain,' plus *kókk(os)* 'kernel,' hence, 'spheroid'), used in its etymological and extended senses in biomedical terminology: **streptodermatitis, streptokinase, streptoleukocidin.** Compare **strepto-**[1], **cocc(o)-.**

2481   **strike-**   A word-initial combining element, also occurring as a word, derived from Old English *stric(an)* 'to stroke' and, by extension, 'to hit,' used in extensions of this latter sense, chief among these being 'of or pertaining to the refusal to work (as a means of 'hitting' one's employer),' in combination with other English elements: **strikebound, strikebreaker, strikeout.** Related form: **strio-.**

2482   **string-**   A word-initial combining element, derived from Old English *streng* 'cord, line' (from an Indo-European root meaning 'tight'), used in its etymological and extended senses in combination with other English elements: **stringboard, stringhalt, stringholder.** Related form: **strong-.**

2483   **strio-**   A word-initial combining element, derived from Latin *stri(a)* 'furrow' (from an Indo-European root meaning 'stroke, rub, streak') plus the combining vowel *-o-*, used in the sense of 'furrowed, grooved' and in extensions of this sense in Neo-Latin and Neo-Greek combinations: **striocellular, striomuscular, striospinoneural.** Also, **stri-: striate.** Related form: **strike-.**

2484   **strong-**   A word-initial combining element, also occurring as a word, derived from Old English *strong* 'powerful' (from an Indo-European root meaning 'tight'), used in its etymological and extended senses in combination with other English elements: **strong-arm, strongbox, strong-willed.** Related form: **string-.**

2485   **strumi-**   A word-initial combining element, derived from Latin *strūm(a)* 'scrofulous tumor; swollen gland' plus the combining vowel *-i-*, used in its etymological and extended senses in biomedical terminology: **strumiferous, strumiform, strumiprivous.** Also, **strum-, strumo-: strumitis, strumoderma.**

2486   **stump-**   A word-initial combining element, also occurring as a word, derived from Middle Low German *stump* 'part from which the rest has been broken off,' used in its etymological and extended senses in combination with other English elements: **stumpfoot, stumpjump (plow), stumpsucker.**

2487 stylo- A word-initial combining element, derived from Greek *stŷlo(s)* 'pillar' (from an Indo-European root meaning 'stand'), used in the sense of 'of or pertaining to a pillarlike implement or structure, esp. the *styloid process* of the temporal bone,' in Neo-Greek and Neo-Latin combinations: **stylohyal, stylomandibular, stylostixis.** Also, **styl-, styli-: stylet, styliform.** Related forms: **histio-, histo-, stage-, stand-, stasi-, state-, stato-, stauro-, stern-²(?), store-.**

2488 stypt- A word-initial combining element, derived from Greek *stypt(ikós)* 'astringent' (from the verb *stýphein* 'to contract, be astringent'), used in its etymological and extended senses in biochemical terminology: **styptase, stypticin, styptol.** Related form: **stop-.**

2489 styr- A word-initial combining element, derived from Greek *stýr(ax)* 'storax, an aromatic resin,' used in its etymological and extended senses in chemical terminology: **styrene, styrol, styrone.**

2490 sub- A word-initial combining element, derived from Latin *sub* 'under, below, behind, near' (from an Indo-European root meaning '(up from) under'), used in its etymological and extended senses in a variety of combinations: **subabdominal, subclinical, subglossitis.** Compare **suc-, suf-, sup-, sur-¹, sursum-, sus-.** Related forms: **evil-(?), hyper-, hypo-, open-, over-, super-, supra-, sur-², up-.**

2491 subin- See **sub-** and **in-².**

2492 suc- A word-initial combining element, derived from Latin *suc-,* a combining form of *sub* 'under, below, behind, near' (from an Indo-European root meaning '(up from) under'), appearing in its etymological and extended senses in inherited combinations in which the element to which it is joined begins with *c:* **succeed, succentor, succinct.** Compare **sub-, suf-, sup-, sur-¹, sursum-, sus-.** Related forms: **evil-(?), hyper-, hypo-, open-, over-, super-, supra-, sur-², up-.**

2493 succin- A word-initial combining element, derived from Latin *succin(um)* 'amber,' used in the sense of 'of, pertaining to, containing, or derived from *succinic acid* ($C_4H_6O_4$) (which is found in amber)' in chemical terminology: **succinate, succinchlorimide, succinylsulfathiazole.** Also, **succino-: succinoresinol.**

2494 **sucr-** A word-initial combining element, derived from French *sucr(e)* 'sugar' (through Italian, Arabic, and Persian from Sanskrit *śa(r)k(a)r(ā)* 'gravel, sugar' and, by extension, '(candied) sugar'), used in its etymological and extended senses in chemical terminology: **sucrase, sucrol, sucrose.** Compare **saccharo-, sugar-.**

2495 **sudori-** A word-initial combining element, derived from Latin *sūdor, sūdōr(is)* 'sweat' plus the combining vowel *-i-*, used in its etymological sense in biomedical terminology: **sudoriceratosis, sudoriferous, sudoriparous.** Also, **sudo-, sudor-: sudomotor, sudoresis.** Related form: **sweat-.**

2496 **suf-** A word-initial combining element, derived from Latin *suf-*, a combining form of *sub* 'under, below, behind, near' (from an Indo-European root meaning '(up from) under'), appearing in its etymological and extended senses in inherited combinations in which the element to which it is joined begins with *f*: **suffer, suffix, suffocate.** Compare **sub-, suc-, sup-, sur-[1], sursum-, sus-.** Related forms: **evil-(?), hyper-, hypo-, open-, over-, super-, supra-, sur-[2], up-.**

2497 **sugar-** A word-initial combining element, also occurring as a word, derived through Old French, ultimately from Sanskrit *śa(r)kar(ā)* 'gravel' and, by extension, 'the (granular) disaccharide ($C_{12}H_{22}O_{11}$),' used in this latter and extended senses in combination with other English elements: **sugar-coated, sugarhouse, sugarplum.** Compare **sucr-.** Compare **saccharo-, sucr-.**

2498 **sulf-** A word-initial combining element, derived through Old French from Latin *sulf(ur), sulph(ur)* 'brimstone; the nonmetallic element (S),' used in the sense of 'of, pertaining to, containing, or derived from *sulfur*' in chemical terminology: **sulfate, sulfide, sulfoxide.** Also, **sulfa-, sulfo-, sulfur-, sulph-, sulpha-, sulpho-, sulphur-: sulfamethazine, sulfosalt, sulfuryl, sulphate, sulphamide, sulphopurpuric, sulphurate.** Compare **sulfon-.**

2499 **sulfon-** A word-initial combining element, derived from **sulf-** plus the suffix *-one* (which is used in naming chemical compounds containing oxygen), used to designate 'a chemical compound containing a *sulfonyl group* (SO_2) attached to two carbon atoms' in chemical terminology: **sulfonamide, sulfonethylmethane, sulfonmethane.** Also, **sulphon-: sulphonate.** Compare **sulf-.**

2500 **sulfur-** A variant of **sulf-.**

2501 **sulph-** A variant of **sulf-**.

2502 **sulpha-** A variant of **sulf-**.

2503 **sulpho-** A variant of **sulf-**.

2504 **sulphon-** A variant of **sulfon-**.

2505 **sulphur-** A variant of **sulf-**.

2506 **sun-** A word-initial combining element, also occurring as a word, derived from Old English *sun(ne)* '(the) day star,' used in its etymological and extended senses in combination with other English elements: **sunburn, sundowner, sunflower.** Related forms: **helio-, sol-[1], south-**.

2507 **sup-** A word-initial combining element, derived from Latin *sup-*, a combining form of *sub* 'under, below, behind, near' (from an Indo-European root meaning '(up from) under'), appearing in its etymological and extended senses in inherited combinations in which the element to which it is joined begins with *p:* **supplement, supplicate, suppose.** Compare **sub-, suc-, suf-, sur-[1], sursum-, sus-**. Related forms: **evil-(?), hyper-, hypo-, open-, over-, super-, supra-, sur-[2], up-**.

2508 **super-** A word-initial combining element, derived from Latin *super* 'above, over, more than' (from an Indo-European root meaning 'up (from under)'), used in its etymological and extended senses, chief among these being 'excessive(ly),' in a variety of combinations: **superalbal, superalkalinity, superman.** Compare **supra-, sur-[2]**. Related forms: **evil-(?), hyper-, hypo-, open-, over-, sub-, suc-, suf-, sup-, sur-[1], sursum-, sus-, up-**.

2509 **supra-** A word-initial combining element, derived from Latin *supr(ā)* 'above; on the upper side' (from *sup(e)r* 'over, above' plus the adverb-forming suffix *-ā*), used in its etymological and extended senses in Neo-Latin and Neo-Greek combinations: **suprabuccal, suprahepatic, supramolecular.** Compare **super-**.

2510 **sur-[1]** A word-initial combining element, derived from Latin *sur-*, a combining form of *sub* 'under, below, behind, near' (from an Indo-European root meaning '(up from) under'), appearing in its etymological and extended senses in inherited combinations in which the element to which it is joined begins with *r:* **surrection, surreptitious, surrogate.** Compare **sub-, suc-, suf-, sup-, sursum-,**

sus-. Related forms: **evil-(?)**, **hyper-**, **hypo-**, **open-**, **over-**, **super-**, **supra-**, **sur-²**, **up-**.

2511 **sur-²** A word-initial combining element, derived from French *sur* 'over, above, excessive(ly)' (from Latin *super* 'over, above'), appearing in its etymological and extended senses in borrowings from French and in a variety of other combinations: **surbase, surexcitation, surrealism.** Compare **super-**.

2512 **sursum-** A word-initial combining element, derived from Latin *sursum* 'from below; up(wards)' (from *su(b)* 'under, below' plus *(vo)rsum* 'turned'), used in its etymological and extended senses in Neo-Latin combinations: **sursumduction, sursumvergence, sursumversion.** Compare **sub-**.

2513 **sus-** A word-initial combining element, derived from Latin *sus-*, a combining form of *sub* 'under, below, behind, near' (from an Indo-European root meaning '(up from) under'), appearing in its etymological and extended senses in inherited combinations in which the element to which it is joined begins with *c, p,* or *t:* **susceptible, suspend, sustain.** Compare **sub-, suc-, suf-, sup-, sur-¹, sursum-**. Related forms: **evil-(?)**, **hyper-**, **hypo-**, **open-**, **over-**, **super-**, **supra-**, **sur-²**, **up-**.

2514 **sweat-** A word-initial combining element, also occurring as a word, derived from Old English *swǣt(an)* 'to perspire,' used in its etymological and extended senses in combination with other English elements: **sweatband, sweatbox, sweatshop.** Related form: **sudori-**.

2515 **sweep-** A word-initial combining element, also occurring as a word, derived from Old English *swāp(an)* 'to clear away (with a broom or the like),' used in its etymological and extended senses in combination with other English elements: **sweepback, sweep-second, sweepstakes.**

2516 **sweet-** A word-initial combining element, also occurring as a word, derived from Old English *swēt(e)* 'pleasing,' used in its etymological and extended senses, chief among these being 'sugary,' in combination with other English elements: **sweetbriar, sweetbread, sweetmeat.**

2517 **switch-** A word-initial combining element, also occurring as a word of uncertain origin whose original sense seems to have been 'flexible twig,' used chiefly in the sense of 'device that facilitates a change of direction' and in extensions of this sense in combination with other English elements: **switchblade, switchboard, switchyard.**

2518 sword- A word-initial combining element, also occurring as a word, derived from Old English *sword* 'weapon with a long blade with a sharpened edge and point,' used in its etymologica! and extended senses in combination with other English elements: **swordfish, swordplay, swordtail.**

2519 syl- A word-initial combining element, derived from Greek *syl-*, a combining form of *sýn* 'with, together with,' appearing in its etymological and extended senses in inherited combinations in which the element to which it is joined begins with *l:* **syllable, syllepsis, syllogism.** Compare **sym-, syn-, sys-.**

2520 sym- A word-initial combining element, derived from Greek *sym-*, a combining form of *sýn* 'with, together with,' appearing in its etymological and extended senses in inherited combinations in which the element to which it is joined begins with *b, m,* or *p:* **symbiotic, symmetrical, symphonic.** Compare **syl-, syn-, sys-.**

2521 sympathetico- A word-initial combining element, derived from Greek *sympathētikó(s)* 'sharing feelings' (from *sýn* 'with, together with' plus *páth(os)* 'pain, feeling' plus the adjective-forming suffix *-ikós),* used in the extended sense of 'of or pertaining to the *sympathetic nervous system,* a part of the autonomic nervous system which controls a variety of involuntary bodily functions' in biomedical terminology: **sympatheticomimetic, sympatheticoparalytic, sympatheticotonic.** Also, **sympath-, sympatheo-, sympathet-, sympathetic-, sympatheto-: sympathectomy, sympatheoneuritis, sympathetectomy, sympatheticalgia, sympathetoblast.** Compare **sym-, patho-.**

2522 symphysio- A word-initial combining element, derived from Greek *sýmphysi(s)* '(a) growing together; fusion' (from *sýn* 'with, together with' plus *phý(esthai)* 'to grow' plus the noun-forming suffix *-sis)* plus the combining vowel *-o-,* used in its etymological and extended senses, chief among these being 'of or pertaining to a *symphysis,* the line of fusion or point of articulation between once-distinct bones,' in Neo-Greek combinations: **symphysiolysis, symphysiorrhaphy, symphysiotomy.** Also, **symphys-, symphyseo-, symphysi-, symphyso-: symphysic, symphyseorrhaphy, symphysial, symphysodactylia.** Compare **sym-, physio-.**

2523 syn- A word-initial combining element, derived from Greek *sýn* 'with, together with,' appearing in its etymological and extended senses in inherited, Neo-Greek, and Neo-Latin combinations: **syndactylia, syndrome, synreflexia.** Compare **syl-, sym-, sys-.**

2524 **synchro-**   A word-initial combining element, derived from Greek *sýnchro(nos)* 'simultaneous' (from *sýn* 'with, together with' plus *chrónos* 'time'), used in its etymological and extended senses in a variety of combinations: **synchrocyclotron, synchroflash, synchromesh.** Also, **synchron-: synchronism.** Compare **syn-, chrono-.**

2525 **syncytio-**   A word-initial combining element, derived from **syn-** plus **cytio-**, used in the sense of 'of or pertaining to a *syncytium,* a polynuclear protoplasmic mass produced by the merger of cells' in biomedical terminology: **syncytiolysin, syncytiotoxin, syncytiotrophoblast.** Also, **syncyt-, syncyti-, syncyto-: syncytoid, syncytial, syncytotoxin.** Compare **syn-, cyto-.**

2526 **syndesmo-**   A word-initial combining element, derived from Greek *sýndesmo(s)* 'that which binds together; band, bond' (from *sýn* 'with, together with' plus *desmó(s)* 'bond'), used in the sense of 'of or pertaining to connective tissue, esp. ligaments' in biomedical terminology: **syndesmochorial, syndesmology, syndesmoplasty.** Also, **syndesm-: syndesmitis.** Compare **syn-, desmo-.**

2527 **syphilo-**   A word-initial combining element, derived from Latin *Syphil(us)*, the eponymous hero of Girolamo Fracastoro's 1530 poem *Syphilus sive Morbus Gallicus* ('Syphilus, or, the French Disease'), plus the combining vowel *-o-*, used in the sense of 'of or pertaining to *syphilus,* a venereal disease (of which Fracastoro's hero was a victim) which is caused by the microorganism *Treponema pallidum*' in biomedical terminology: **syphilogenesis, syphilophobia, syphilotherapy.** Also, **syphi-, syphil-, syphili-: syphitoxin, syphilionthus, syphiliphobia.**

2528 **syringo-**   A word-initial combining element, derived from Greek *sŷrin(x), sýring(os)* 'pipe, tube' plus the combining vowel *-o-*, used in its etymological and extended senses, chief among these being 'of or pertaining to a cavity or fistula,' in Neo-Greek and Neo-Latin combinations: **syringobulbia, syringopontia, syringotomy.** Also, **syring-: syringectomy.**

2529 **sys-**   A word-initial combining element, derived from Greek *sys-*, a combining form of *sýn* 'with, together with,' appearing in its etymological and extended senses in inherited combinations in which the element to which it is joined begins with *s*: **syssarcosis, syssiderite, syssomus.** Compare **syl-, sym-, syn-.**

T

2530 **table-** A word-initial combining element, also occurring as a word, derived through Old French from Latin *tab(u)l(a)* 'board; counter' used chiefly in this latter and extended senses in combination with other English elements: **tablecloth, table-hop, tablespoon.**

2531 **tachy-** A word-initial combining element, derived from Greek *tachý(s)* 'swift,' used in its etymological and extended senses in Neo-Greek combinations: **tachyauxesis, tachycardia, tachyphrenia.**

2532 **taeni-** A variant of **teni-**.

2533 **tail-** A word-initial combining element, also occurring as a word, derived from Old English *tæ(ġe)l* 'posterior appendage (of an animal),' used chiefly in the sense of 'rear, hind' and in extensions of this sense in combination with other English elements: **tailback, tailgate, taillight.**

2534 **take-** A word-initial combining element, also occurring as a word, derived from Old Norse *tak(a)* 'to seize, grasp,' used in a variety of extensions of its etymological sense in combination with other English elements: **takedown, take-home (pay), takeoff.**

2535 **talo-** A word-initial combining element, derived from Latin *tāl(us)* 'ankle bone' plus the combining vowel *-o-*, used in its etymological sense in biomedical terminology: **talocrural, talofibular, taloscaph-oid.** Also, **tal-: talalgia.**

355

2536   tann-   A word-initial combining element, derived from *tann(in)* ($C_{14}H_{10}O_9$) (from Old French *tann(er)* 'to tan (hide)' plus the suffix *-in* which is used in naming nonbasic chemical compounds, tannin being an astringent suitable for use in tanning hides), used in its etymological and extended senses in chemical terminology: **tannalbin, tannargan, tannase.** Also, **tanni-: tannigen.**

2537   tapho-   A word-initial combining element, derived from Greek *tápho(s)* 'grave, tomb,' used in its etymological and extended senses in Neo-Greek combinations: **taphophilia, taphophobia,** *Taphozous.*

2538   tarso-   A word-initial combining element, derived from Greek *tarsó(s)* 'reed mat; flat surface,' hence, 'flat of the foot; wing,' used in the sense of 'of or pertaining to the instep of the foot or to the edge of the eyelid' in biomedical terminology: **tarsoclasis, tarsomalacia, tarsotibial.** Also, **tars-: tarsalgia.**

2539   tau- (T, τ)   A word-initial combining element, the nineteenth letter of the Greek alphabet, used chiefly to designate 'the nineteenth carbon atom in a straight chain compound or a derivative thereof in which the substitute group is attached to that atom' in chemical terminology. See **alpha-.**

2540   tauro-   A word-initial combining element, derived from Greek *taûro(s)* 'bull,' used in its etymological sense in Neo-Greek combinations: **tauromachic, tauromorphous, taurophobia.**

2541   taurochol-   A word-initial combining element, derived from Greek *taûro(s)* 'bull' plus *chól(os)* 'bile,' used in the sense of 'of or pertaining to *taurocholic acid* ($C_{26}H_{45}NO_7S$) (which was first found in ox bile)' in chemical terminology: **taurocholaneresis, taurocholanopoiesis, taurocholemia.** Compare **tauro-, chol(e)-.**

2542   tauto-   A word-initial combining element, derived from Greek *tautó* 'the same' (from the definite article *to* plus the reflexive pronoun *autó*), used in its etymological and extended senses in Neo-Greek combinations: **tautology, tautomenial, tautomeral.** Compare **auto-**[1].

2543   tax-[1]   A word-initial combining element, derived through Old French from Latin *tax(āre)*, the frequentative form of *tangere* 'to touch,' hence, 'to appraise,' used in the sense of 'assessed payment' in combination with other English elements: **tax-deductible, tax-exempt, taxpayer.** Compare **taxi-**[1].

2544   tax-[2]   A variant of **taxi-**[2].

2545   **taxi-¹**   A word-initial combining element, also occurring as a word, derived from French *taxi(mètre)* 'device for calculating a distance traveled (in a vehicle for hire) and the corresponding fare due' (from *tax(e)* 'tariff' (from Latin *tax(āre)*, the frequentative form of *tangere* 'to touch,' hence, 'to appraise') plus the combining vowel *-i-* plus *mètre* 'meter' (from Greek *métr(on)* 'measure')), used in the sense of 'vehicle for hire' and in extensions of this sense in combination with other English elements: **taxicab, taxiplane, taxiway.** Compare **tax-¹, metro-³.**

2546   **taxi-²**   A word-initial combining element, derived from Greek *táxi(s)* 'arrangement, order(ing),' used in its etymological and extended senses in Neo-Greek and Neo-Latin combinations: **taxiarch, taxicorn, taxidermic.** Also, **tax-², taxo-: taxeme, taxonomy.**

2547   **tea-**   A word-initial combining element, also occurring as a word, derived, ultimately, from Amoy Chinese *t'e* 'the plant *Thea chinensis* or *Camellia sinensis* or the beverage made from its leaves,' used in its etymological and extended senses in combination with other English elements: **teaberry, teahouse, teakettle.** Related form: **theo-².**

2548   **tear-**   A word-initial combining element, also occurring as a word, derived from Old English *tēar* 'drop of the watery substance secreted by the lacrimal glands,' used in its etymological sense in combination with other English elements: **teardrop, tear-jerker, tear-stained.** Related forms: **dacryo-, lacrimo-.**

2549   **techno-**   A word-initial combining element, derived from Greek *téchn(ē)* 'art, handicraft,' hence, 'method of making or doing' plus the combining vowel *-o-*, used in its etymological and extended senses in Neo-Greek combinations: **technocausis, technology, technopsychology.**

2550   **tel-¹**   A variant of **telo-¹.**

2551   **tel-²**   A variant of **tele-².**

2552   **tele-¹**   A variant of **telo-¹.**

2553   **tele-²**   A word-initial combining element, derived from Greek *têle* 'far away,' used in its etymological and extended senses in Neo-Greek and Neo-Latin combinations: **telekinesis, telescope, television.** Also, **tel-², teleo-², telo-²: telesthesia, teleotherapeutics, teloreceptor.** Related form: **paleo-.**

2554   tele-³   A variant of **teleo-³**.

2555   tele-⁴   A word-initial combining element, derived from English *tele*(*vision*) 'the long-distance transmission of images via radiowaves to an apparatus that converts these waves back into images' (from **tele-²** plus *vision* (from Latin *vīsiō, vīsiōn*(*is*) 'act of seeing; that which is seen')), used in its etymological and extended senses in combination with other English elements: **telecast, teleplay, teletranscription**. Compare **tele-², visuo-**.

2556   telei-   A variant of **teleo-³**.

2557   teleo-¹   A variant of **telo-¹**.

2558   teleo-²   A variant of **tele-²**.

2559   teleo-³   A word-initial combining element, derived from Greek *téle*(*i*)*o*(*s*) 'ended, complete' (from *télos* 'end'), used in its etymological and extended senses in Neo-Greek combinations: **teleobranchiate, teleomitosis, teleosaur**. Also, **tele-³, telei-: teleorganic, teleianthus**. Compare **telo-¹**.

2560   telo-¹   A word-initial combining element, derived from Greek *télo*(*s*) 'end, extremity, completion,' used in its etymological and extended senses in Neo-Greek combinations: **telobiosis, telodendron, telophase**. Also, **tel-¹, tele-¹, teleo-¹: telangiectasia, teleneuron, teleology**. Compare **teleo-³**. Related forms: **coll-², collar-, cyclo-, palin-, polari-, wheel-**.

2561   telo-²   A variant of **tele-²**.

2562   temporo-   A word-initial combining element, derived from Latin *temp*(*us*), *tempor*(*is*) 'side of the head near the eye; temple' plus the combining vowel *-o-*, used in its etymological sense in biomedical terminology: **temporofacial, temporopontile, temporosphenoid**.

2563   ten-¹   A word-initial combining element, also occurring as a word, derived from Old English *tēn*(*e*) 'the cardinal number between *nine* and *eleven*,' used in its etymological and extended senses in combination with other English elements: **ten-gallon (hat), tenpenny (nail), tenpin**. Related forms: **deca-, deci-**.

2564   ten-²   A variant of **teni-**.

2565   ten-³   A variant of **teno-**.

2566   **tendo-**   A word-initial combining element, derived from Late Latin *tendō, tendōn(is)* 'cord of tissue connecting muscle to bone' (from *tendere* 'to stretch'), used in its etymological sense in biomedical terminology: **tendolysis, tendosynovitis, tendovaginitis.** Compare **tensio-.** Related forms: **teni-, teno-, tetano-, tono-.**

2567   **teni-**   A word-initial combining element, derived through Latin from Greek *tainí(a)* 'ribbon, band,' and, by extension, 'tapeworm,' used in its etymological and extended senses in Neo-Greek and Neo-Latin combinations: **tenial, tenicide, tenifugal.** Also, **taen-, taeni-, taenia-, taenio-, ten-², tenia-, tenio-: taeniasis, taeniform, taeniacide, taenioglossate, teniasis, teniacide, teniotoxin.** Related forms: **tendo-, teno-, tensio-, tetano-, tono-.**

2568   **teno-**   A word-initial combining element, derived from Greek *ténō(n), téno(ntos),* the present participle of the verb *ténein* 'to stretch,' used in the sense of 'that which stretches' and, by extension, 'tendon' in Neo-Greek and Neo-Latin combinations: **tenodesis, tenoplastic, tenosuspension.** Also, **ten-³, tenon-, tenont-, tenonto-: tenalgia, tenonitis, tenontectomy, tenontomyotomy.** Compare **tetano-.** Related forms: **tendo-, teni-, tensio-, tono-.**

2569   **tensio-**   A word-initial combining element, derived from Latin *tensiō, tensiō(nis)* '(a) stretching, tautness' (from *tens(us),* the past participle of the verb *tendere* 'to stretch,' plus the noun-forming element *-iō, -iōn(is)),* used in its etymological and extended senses in Neo-Latin and Neo-Greek combinations: **tensio-active, tensiometer, tensiophone.** Compare **tendo-.** Related forms: **teni-, teno-, tetano-, tono-.**

2570   **ter-**   A word-initial combining element, derived from Latin *ter* 'thrice,' used in the sense of 'three' and in extensions of this sense in Neo-Latin and Neo-Greek combinations: **tercentenary, teroxide, tervalent.** Related forms: **testi-(?), third-, three-, tri-, triple-, triplo-, trit-.**

2571   **tera-**   A word-initial combining element, derived from Greek *téra(s), téra(tos)* 'omen, marvel, monster,' used in the sense of 'one trillion' (as an extension of the sense of 'monster') in scientific terminology: **teracycle, terahertz, teraohm.** Compare **terato-.**

2572   **terato-**   A word-initial combining element, derived from Greek *téra(s), térat(os)* 'omen, marvel, monster' plus the combining vowel *-o-,* used in this last and extended senses, chief among these being 'of or pertaining to malformation, esp. of a fetus,' in Neo-Greek combinations: **teratoblastoma, teratogenetic, teratophobia.** Also, **terat-: teratism.** Compare **tera-.**

2573 **testi-** A word-initial combining element, derived from Latin *testi(s)* 'male gonad' (possibly from a specialized use—as 'witness to a person's virility'—of Latin *testis* 'witness,' originally, 'third party'), used in its etymological and extended senses, chief among these being 'gonad-shaped,' in biomedical terminology: **testibrachium, testicond, testitoxicosis.** Also, **test-, testo-: testitis, testopathy.** Related forms(?): **ter-, third-, three-, tri-, triple-, triplo-, trit-.**

2574 **tetano-** A word-initial combining element, derived from Greek *tétano(s)* 'tension, esp. a convulsive tension' (from *tetanós,* the perfect participle of the verb *ténein* 'to stretch'), used in its etymological and extended senses, chief among these being 'of or pertaining to muscle spasm or to *tetanus,* an infectious disease characterized by muscle spasm,' in Neo-Greek and Neo-Latin combinations: **tetanometer, tetanomotor, tetanotoxine.** Also, **tetan-, tetani-: tetanic, tetaniform.** Compare **teno-.** Related forms: **tendo-, teni-, tensio-, tono-.**

2575 **tetra-** A word-initial combining element, derived from Greek *tetra-,* a combining form of *téttares* 'four,' used in its etymological sense and extended senses in Neo-Greek and Neo-Latin combinations: **tetrabasic, tetradactylous, tetravaccine.** Also, **tetr-: tetratomic.** Related forms: **four-, quadri-, quarter-, quarti-, square-.**

2576 **thalamo-** A word-initial combining element, derived through Latin from Greek *thálamo(s)* 'inner room,' used chiefly in the sense of 'of or pertaining to the *thalamus,* the middle part of the diencephalon which relays sensory impulses to the cerebral cortex' in biomedical terminology: **thalamocrural, thalamolenticular, thalamotomy.** Also, **thalam-: thalamencephalon.**

2577 **thalasso-** A word-initial combining element, derived from Greek *thálass(a)* 'sea' plus the combining vowel *-o-,* used in its etymological and extended senses in Neo-Greek combinations: **thalassographic, thalassometer, thalassotherapy.** Also, **thalass-, thalassi-, thalassio-: thalassic, *Thalassicolla,* thalassiophyte.**

2578 **thallo-** A word-initial combining element, derived from Greek *thalló(s)* 'young branch, shoot' (from *thállein* 'to sprout, bloom'), used chiefly in two extensions of its etymological sense, 'of or pertaining to a *thallus,* a simple plant body with undifferentiated root, stem, and leaf' and 'of, pertaining to, or containing *thallium* (Tl), an element named for its green spectral line,' in a variety of combinations: **thallogen, thallophyte, thallotoxicosis.** Also, **thal-, thall-: thalgrain, thallic.**

2579   **thanato-**   A word-initial combining element, derived from Greek *thánato(s)* 'death,' used in its etymological and extended senses in Neo-Greek combinations: **thanatobiologic, thanatognomic, thanatomania.** Also, **thanat-: thanatophidial.**

2580   **the-¹**   A variant of **theo-¹.**

2581   **the-²**   A variant of **theo-².**

2582   **thec-**   A word-initial combining element, derived from Greek *thēk(ē)* 'box, case in which to place things' (from an Indo-European root meaning 'set in place'), used in a variety of extensions of its etymological sense, chief among these being 'sac, socket, sheath,' in Neo-Greek and Neo-Latin combinations: **thecate, thecitis, thecodont.** Also, **theca-, theci-, theco-: thecaspore, theciform, thecosome.** Related forms: **do-, face-, facio-.**

2583   **thel-**   A word-initial combining element, derived from Greek *thēl(ē)* 'nipple,' used in its etymological and extended senses in Neo-Greek combinations: **thelalgia, thelerethism, thelitis.** Also, **thele-, thelo-, thely-²: theleplasty, thelorrhagia, thelyplasty.** Compare **thely-¹.** Related form(s): **feto-, Fitz-(?).**

2584   **thely-¹**   A word-initial combining element, derived from Greek *thêly(s)* 'female,' used in its etymological and extended senses in Neo-Greek combinations: **thelyblastic, thelykinin, thelytocia.** Compare **thel-.** Related form(s): **feto-, Fitz-(?).**

2585   **thely-²**   A variant of **thel-.**

2586   **theo-¹**   A word-initial combining element, derived from Greek *theó(s)* 'god,' appearing in its etymological and extended senses in inherited and Neo-Greek combinations: **theogony, theomachy, theomorphism.** Also, **the-¹: theist.** Compare **theo-³.**

2587   **theo-²**   A word-initial combining element, derived from English *theo(phylline)* 'the alkaloid $(C_7H_8N_4O_2 \cdot H_2O)$' (from Late Latin *the(a)* 'tea' plus Greek *phýll(on)* 'leaf' plus the suffix *-ine* which is used in naming chemical substances, theophylline being easily derived from tea leaves), used in its etymological sense in chemical terminology: **theocine, theoglycinate, theopropanol.** Also, **the-²: thephorine.** Compare **tea-** and **phyllo-.**

2588 **theo-³** A word-initial combining element, derived from English *theo*(*bromine*) 'the alkaloid $(C_7H_8N_4O_2)$' (from *Theobrom*(*a*), literally, 'food of the gods' (from Greek *theó*(*s*) 'god' plus *brôma* 'food'), used in the sense of 'genus of trees that includes the *cacao* (from whose beans theobromine is easily derived),' plus the suffix *-ine* which is used in naming chemical compounds), used in its etymological sense in chemical terminology: **theocalcine, theophen, theophorine.** Also, **theon-: theonacete.** Compare **theo-¹.**

2589 **there-** A word-initial combining element, also occurring as a word, derived from Old English *þēr* 'to or at that place,' used in its etymological and extended senses in combination with other English elements: **thereabout, thereafter, therein.**

2590 **therio-** A word-initial combining element, derived from Greek *thērío*(*n*) 'wild beast; animal' (from *thḗr* 'wild beast; animal' plus the diminutive suffix *-ion*), used in its etymological and extended senses in Neo-Greek combinations: **theriopod, theriotherapy, theriotomy.** Also, **theri-: therianthropic.** Compare **thero-.**

2591 **thermo-** A word-initial combining element, derived from Greek *thermó*(*s*) 'hot' and *thérm*(*ē*) 'heat' plus the combining vowel *-o-*, used in its etymological and extended senses in a variety of combinations: **thermobiotic, thermolabile, thermomassage.** Also, **therm-, thermi-: thermanesthesia, thermifugin.**

2592 **thero-** A word-initial combining element, derived from Greek *thḗr* 'wild beast, animal' plus the combining vowel *-o-*, used in its etymological and extended senses in Neo-Greek combinations: **therology, theromorph, theropod.** Also, **ther-: theriatrics.** Compare **therio-.**

2593 **theta-** (Θ, θ) A word-initial combining element, the eighth letter of the Greek alphabet, used chiefly to designate 'the eighth carbon atom in a straight chain compound or a derivative thereof in which the substitute group is attached to that atom' in chemical terminology. See **alpha-.**

2594 **thi-** A variant of **thio-.**

2595 **thick-** A word-initial combining element, also occurring as a word, derived from Old English *þic*(*ce*) 'dense,' used in its etymological and extended senses in combination with other English elements: **thickhead, thickset, thick-skinned.**

2596 **thigmo-** A word-initial combining element, derived from Greek *thígm(a)* 'touch; that which is touched' plus the combining vowel *-o-*, used in its etymological and extended senses in Neo-Greek combinations: **thigmocyte, thigmotaxis, thigmotropic.** Also, **thigm-: thigmesthesia.** Related forms: **dairy-, lady-, lady's-.**

2597   **thimble-**   A word-initial combining element, also occurring as a word, derived from Old English *þýmel* 'fingerstall; protective finger cap used in sewing' (from *þūm(a)* 'thumb' plus the suffix *-el* which was used to denote '(an) instrument, appliance'), used in the sense of 'thimblelike' and in extensions of this sense in combination with other English elements: **thimbleberry, thimblerig, thimbleweed.** Compare **thumb-.**

2598   **thio-**   A word-initial combining element, derived from Greek *th(e)îo(n)* 'brimstone, sulfur' (from an Indo-European root meaning 'breath, smoke, dust'), used in its etymological and extended senses in Neo-Greek and Neo-Latin combinations: ***Thiobacillus,* thiobarbital, thioglucose.** Also, **thi, thion-: thiemia, thionic.** Related forms: **deer-, dust-, thym-[1], thymo-[2], typhl-[1], typhlo-[2], typho-.**

2599   **third-**   A word-initial combining element, also occurring as a word, derived from Old English *þird(da),* a variant of *þrid(da)* 'the ordinal corresponding to the cardinal number *three,*' used in its etymological and extended senses in combination with other English elements: **third-degree, thirdhand, third-rate.** Compare **three-.**

2600   **thorac-**   A variant of **thoraco-.**

2601   **thoracico-**   A word-initial combining element, derived from Greek *thōrakikó(s)* 'of or pertaining to the chest' (from *thōra(x), thōrak(os)* 'breastplate; chest' plus the adjective-forming suffix *-ikós*), used in its etymological sense in biomedical terminology: **thoracicoabdominal, thoracicoacromialis, thoracicohumeral.** Compare **thoraco-.**

2602   **thoraco-**   A word-initial combining element, derived from Greek *thōra(x), thōrak(os)* 'breastplate,' hence, 'that which is covered by a breastplate; chest' plus the combining vowel *-o-,* used in the sense of 'of or pertaining to the chest' in biomedical terminology: **thoracocautery, thoracogastrodidymus, thoracolumbar.** Also, **thorac-: thoracaorta.** Compare **thoracico-.**

2603   **thorough-**   A word-initial combining element, also occurring as a word, derived from Old English *þur(u)h* 'through,' used in its etymological and extended senses, chief among these being 'with complete accomplishment,' in combination with other English elements: **thoroughbred, thoroughfare, thoroughgoing.** Compare **through-.**

2604 thread- A word-initial combining element, also occurring as a word, derived from Old English *þrǣd* 'fine string of spun fibers' (from an Indo-European root meaning 'twist, turn, bore'), used in its etymological and extended senses in combination with other English elements: **threadbare, threadfin, threadworm.** Related forms: **drill-, traumato-, trypano-, turn-.**

2605 three- A word-initial combining element, also occurring as a word, derived from Old English *þrī* 'the cardinal number between *two* and *four*,' used in its etymological and extended senses: **three-bagger, threepenny, three-piece** (suit). Compare **third-.** Related forms: **ter-, testi-(?), tri-, triple-, triplo-, trit-.**

2606 thrombo-[1] A word-initial combining element, derived from Greek *thrómbo(s)* 'lump, clot,' used in its etymological and extended senses in Neo-Greek combinations: **thromboblast, thrombogenesis, thrombopathy.** Also, **thromb-**[1]: **thrombectomy.**

2607 thrombo-[2] A word-initial combining element, derived from English *thrombo(cyte)* 'blood platelet' (cf. **thrombocyto-**), used in its etymological and extended senses in biomedical combinations: **thrombopenia, thrombophthisis, thrombopoiesis.** Also, **thromb-**[2]: **thrombasthenia.** Compare **thrombocyto-.**

2608 thrombocyto- A word-initial combining element, derived from **thrombo-**[1] plus **cyto-,** used in the sense of 'of or pertaining to *blood platelets,* protoplasmic disks involved in the coagulation of blood' in biomedical terminology: **thrombocytocrit, thrombocytolysis, thrombocytopenia.** Compare **thrombo-**[1], **cyto-.**

2609 through- A word-initial combining element, also occurring as a word, derived from Old English *þurh* 'from one end to the other,' used in its etymological and extended senses in combination with other English elements: **through-composed, throughout, throughway.** Also, **thru-: thruway.** Compare **thorough-.** Related form: **trans-.**

2610 thumb- A word-initial combining element, derived from Old English *þūm(a)* 'digit of the hand which is thickest at the nail' (from an Indo-European root meaning 'swell, swollen'), used in its etymological and extended senses in combination with other English elements: **thumbnail, thumbnut, thumbtack.** Compare **thimble-.** Related forms: **somato-, tuberculo-, tyro-.**

2611   **thunder-**   A word-initial combining element, also occurring as a word, derived from Old English *þunor* 'sound that accompanies lightning,' used in its etymological and extended senses in combination with other English elements: **thunderbird, thunderclap, thundercloud.**

2612   **thym-**[1]   A word-initial combining element, derived through Old French and Latin from Greek *thým(on)* 'aromatic herb of the genus *Thymus*' (from an Indo-European root meaning 'breath, smoke'), used in the sense of 'of or pertaining to chemical derivatives of *thyme*' in chemical terminology: **thymacetin, thymene, thymol.** Also, **thymo-**[1]: **thymoform.** Compare **thymo-**[2]. Related forms: **deer-, dust-, thio-, typhl-**[1]**, typhlo-**[2]**, typho-.**

2613   **thym-**[2]   A variant of **thymo-.**

2614   **thymo-**[1]   A variant of **thym-**[1].

2615   **thymo-**[2]   A word-initial combining element, derived from Greek *thýmo(s)* 'glandular excrescence found in the anterior mediastinal cavity' (from *thýmon* 'thyme' (because the thymus is said to resemble a bunch of thyme in its shape)), used in its etymological and extended senses in Neo-Greek and Neo-Latin combinations: **thymocrescin, thymolysis, thymotropism.** Also, **thym-**[2]: **thymectomy.** Compare **thym-**[1].

2616   **thyro-**   A word-initial combining element, derived from Greek (*chóndros*) *thyr(e)o(eidḗs)* 'thyroid (cartilage),' literally, 'shield-shaped (cartilage)' (from *thyre(ós)* 'shield'—originally, 'large stone placed against a door (*thýra*) to keep it closed'—plus the adjective-forming suffix *-eidḗs* '-like'), used in the sense of 'of or pertaining to the thyroid gland' and in extensions of this sense in biomedical terminology: **thyrofissure, thyroglossal, thyrotoxin.** Also, **thyr-, thyre-, thyreo-, thyroid-, thyroido-: thyremphraxis, thyrein, thyreoitis, thyroidectomy, thyroidotoxin.** Related forms: **door-, for-**[2].

2617   **tibio-**   A word-initial combining element, derived from Latin *tībi(a)* '(larger) shinbone' plus the combining vowel *-o-*, used in its etymological and extended senses in biomedical terminology: **tibiocalcanean, tibiofibular, tibioscapular.** Also, **tibi-: tibialgia.**

2618   **tide-**   A word-initial combining element, also occurring as a word, derived from Old English *tīd* 'period of time' (from an Indo-European root meaning 'divide'), hence, 'regular rising and falling of the sea,' used in this latter and extended senses in combination

with other English elements: **tidehead, tidemark, tidewater.** Related
forms: **demo-, time-.**

2619 **tie-** A word-initial combining element, also occurring as a word,
derived from Old English *tī(ġ)an* 'to fasten, bind,' used in its
etymological and extended senses in combination with other
English elements: **tie-and-dye, tieclasp, tie-up.** Related form: **tow-.**

2620 **tight-** A word-initial combining element, also occurring as a word,
derived from Old Norse *þét(tr)* 'impermeable,' used in the sense of
'close, constricted' and in extensions of this sense in combination
with other English elements: **tight-fisted, tightrope, tightwad.**

2621 **timber-** A word-initial combining element, also occurring as a
word, derived from Old English *timber* 'building,' hence, 'building
material, esp. wood,' used in this latter and extended senses in
combination with other English elements: **timber-hitch, timberjack,
timberland.**

2622 **time-** A word-initial combining element, also occurring as a word,
derived from Old English *tīm(a)* 'measure or period of duration'
(from an Indo-European root meaning 'divide'), used in its etymological and extended senses in combination with other English
elements: **time-consuming, time-lag, timeserver.** Related forms:
demo-, tide-.

2623 **tin-** A word-initial combining element, also occurring as a word,
derived from Old English *tin* 'the malleable metallic element (Sn),'
used in its etymological and extended senses in combination with
other English elements: **tinfoil, tinhorn, tinsmith.**

2624 **tip-** A word-initial combining element, also occurring as a word,
derived from Old Norse *typ(pi)* 'apex,' used in its etymological and
extended senses in combination with other English elements:
tipburn, tiptoe, tiptop. Related form: **top-[2].**

2625 **to-** A word-initial combining element, also occurring as a word,
derived from Old English *tō* 'towards,' hence, 'for the purpose of,'
used in its etymological and extended senses in combination with
other English elements: **to-and-fro, today, to-do.**

2626 **toad-** A word-initial combining element, also occurring as a word,
derived from Old English *tād(a)* 'amphibian of the genus *Bufo*,'
used in its etymological and extended senses in combination with
other English elements: **toadeater, toadflax, toadstool.**

2627 **toco-** A word-initial combining element, derived from Greek *tóko(s)* 'childbirth,' used in its etymological and extended senses in Neo-Greek combinations: **tocodynagraph, tocomania, tocophobia.** Also, **toko-: tokodynamograph.**

2628 **toe-** A word-initial combining element, also occurring as a word, derived from Old English *tā* 'digit of the foot,' used in its etymological and extended senses in combination with other English elements: **toe-dance, toehold, toenail.**

2629 **toko-** A variant of **toco-**.

2630 **tol-** A variant of **tolu-**.

2631 **toll-** A word-initial combining element, also occurring as a word, derived through Old English and Late Latin from Greek *tél(os)* 'tax, duty,' used in its etymological and extended senses in combination with other English elements: **tollgate, tollhouse, tollkeeper.**

2632 **tolu-** A word-initial combining element, derived from Spanish (*Santiago de*) *Tolú*, a town in Colombia to which the *Myrospermum toluiferum* tree is native, used in the sense of 'of, pertaining to, or derived from the balsam found in the *Myrospermum toluiferum*' in chemical terminology: **toluene, toluol, toluyl.** Also, **tol-: tolyl.**

2633 **tom-** A word-initial combining element, derived from the English proper noun *T(h)om(as)* (from Aramaic *t'ōmə* 'twin'), used in the sense of 'male, masculine' and in extensions of this sense in combination with other English elements: **tomboy, tomcat, tomfoolery.**

2634 **tomo-** A word-initial combining element, derived from Greek *tómo(s)* '(a) cut, cutting,' used in its etymological and extended senses in Neo-Greek combinations: **tomography, tomomania, tomotocia.**

2635 **ton-** A variant of **tono-**.

2636 **tongue-** A word-initial combining element, also occurring as a word, derived from Old English *tunge* 'muscular organ in the mouth used in tasting, swallowing, and speaking,' used in its etymological and extended senses in combination with other English elements: **tongue-and-groove, tongue-lash, tongue-tied.** Related form: **linguo-.**

2637 **tono-** A word-initial combining element, derived from Greek *tóno(s)* 'that which stretches or may be stretched; tension' and, by extension, 'sound, tone,' used in its etymological and extended senses in Neo-Greek and Neo-Latin combinations: **tonofibril, tonometer, tonoscope.** Also, **ton-, tonon-: tonaphasia, tononoscillograph.** Related forms: **tendo-, teni-, teno-, tensio-, tetano-.**

2638 **tonsillo-** A word-initial combining element, derived from Latin *tonsill(a)* 'tonsil' plus the combining vowel *-o-*, used in its etymological sense in biomedical terminology: **tonsillohemisporosis, tonsillomycosis, tonsilloprive.** Also, **tonsil-, tonsill-: tonsillith, tonsillitis.**

2639 **tool-** A word-initial combining element, also occurring as a word, derived from Old English *tōl* 'implement, esp. handheld,' used in its etymological and extended senses in combination with other English elements: **toolbox, toolmaker, toolshed.**

2640 **tooth-** A word-initial combining element, also occurring as a word, derived from Old English *tōþ* 'bonelike structure rooted in the jaw,' used in its etymological and extended senses in combination with other English elements: **toothache, toothpick, toothwort.** Related forms: **denti-, odonto-.**

2641 **top-¹** A variant of **topo-.**

2642 **top-²** A word-initial combining element, also occurring as a word, derived from Old English *top(p)* 'crest, summit,' used in its etymological and extended senses in combination with other English elements: **topflight, topgallant, top-heavy.** Related form: **tip-.**

2643 **topo-** A word-initial combining element, derived from Greek *tópo(s)* 'locality,' used in its etymological and extended senses in Neo-Greek and Neo-Latin combinations: **topognosis, topology, topovaccinotherapy.** Also, **top-¹: tophyperperidrosis.**

2644 **touch-** A word-initial combining element, also occurring as a word, derived through Old French from Proto-Romance **tocc(āre)* 'to strike, knock,' used in the sense of 'come into contact; bring into contact' and in extensions of this sense in combination with other English elements: **touch-and-go, touchback, touchstone.**

2645 **tow-** A word-initial combining element, also occurring as a word, derived from Old English *to(gian)* 'to drag (a vessel) with a rope,' used in its etymological and extended senses in combination with

other English elements: **towboat, towline, towpath.** Related form:
tie-.

2646 **tox-¹** A variant of **toxico-.**

2647 **tox-²** A variant of **toxin-.**

2648 **toxi-¹** A variant of **toxico-.**

2649 **toxi-²** A variant of **toxin-.**

2650 **toxico-** A word-initial combining element, derived through Latin
from Greek (*phármakon*) *toxikó(n)* 'poison to be smeared on
arrowheads,' the original meaning of *toxikón* being 'of or pertaining to the bow (and arrow)' (from *tóx(on)* 'bow' plus the adjective-
forming suffix *-ikón*), used in the sense of 'of or pertaining to
poison' in biomedical terminology: **toxicoderma, toxicology, toxicomania.** Also, **tox-¹, toxi-¹, toxic-, toxo-¹: toxenzyme, toxicide,**
Toxicophidia, **toxogen.** Compare **toxin-.**

2651 **toxin-** A word-initial combining element, also occurring as a word,
derived from **tox-¹** plus the suffix *-in* which is used in naming
chemical substances, used in the sense of 'poisonous substance of
animal or vegetable origin' in biomedical terminology: **toxinantitoxin, toxinemia, toxinosis.** Also, **tox-², toxi-², toxini-, toxino-,
toxo-²: toxemia, toxigenic, toxinicide, toxinotherapy, toxoinfection.**
Compare **toxico-.**

2652 **toxo-¹** A variant of **toxico-.**

2653 **toxo-²** A variant of **toxin-.**

2654 **tra-** A variant of **trans-.**

2655 **trach-** A variant of **tracheo-.**

2656 **trachelo-** A word-initial combining element, derived from Greek
tráchēlo(s) 'throat, neck,' used in this latter and extended senses in
biomedical terminology: **trachelobregmatic, trachelocystitis,
trachelo-occipitalis.** Also, **trachel-: trachelagra.**

2657 **tracheo-** A word-initial combining element, derived through Latin
from Greek (*artēría*) *trache(îa)* 'windpipe'—literally, 'rough (artery,
windpipe)' (from *trachýs, tracheîa, trachý* 'rough')—plus the combining vowel *-o-,* used in the sense of 'of or pertaining to the
windpipe' in biomedical terminology: **tracheofissure, tracheo-**

malacia, tracheostenosis. Also, **trach-, trache-, trachea-: trachitis,
tracheitis, tracheaectasy.**

2658 **trade-** A word-initial combining element, also occurring as a word,
derived from Middle Low German *trade* 'path, track,' used in the
extended sense of 'continuing practice of a profession or business'
and in extensions of this sense in combination with other English
elements: **trade-in, trade-last, trademark.** Related forms: **dromo-,
trap-.**

2659 **trago-** A word-initial combining element, derived from Greek
trágo(s) 'goat,' appearing in its etymological and extended senses in
borrowings from Greek and Neo-Greek combinations: **tragomaschalia, tragophony, tragopodia.** Also, **trag-: tragacanth.**

2660 **train-** A word-initial combining element, also occurring as a word,
derived from Old French *train(e)* 'that which trails or drags,' used
in its etymological and extended senses, chief among these being
'of or pertaining to a series of railroad cars coupled together (and
pulled by an engine),' in combination with other English elements:
trainbearer, trainmaster, trainsick.

2661 **trans-** A word-initial combining element, derived from Latin *trans*
'beyond, on the far side of; across, over, through,' used in its
etymological and extended senses, chief among these being, in
chemical terminology, 'axially stereoisomeric form of the compound named by the combining root' and, in astronomical terminology, 'farther from the sun than the planet named by the
combining root,' in a variety of combinations: **transaminase,
translucent, transplutonian.** Also, **tra-: traduce.** Related forms:
thorough-, through-.

2662 **transverso-** A word-initial combining element, derived from Latin
transvers(us) 'lying crosswise' (from *trans* 'across' plus *versus,* the
past participle of the verb *vertere* 'to turn') plus the combining
vowel *-o-,* used in the sense of 'that which lies crosswise or
traverses' and in extensions of this sense in Neo-Latin and Neo-
Greek combinations: **transversocostal, transversospinalis, transversotomy.** Also, **transvers-: transversectomy.** Compare **trans-.**

2663 **trap-** A word-initial combining element, also occurring as a word,
derived from Old English *træp(pe)* 'snare' (from an Indo-European
root meaning something on the order of 'move ahead,' a trap being
something into which its victim is supposed to unsuspectingly
'move ahead'), used in its etymological and extended senses in

combination with other English elements: **trapball, trap-door (spider), trapshooting.** Related forms: **dromo-, trade-.**

2664 **traumato-** A word-initial combining element, derived from Greek *traûma, traúmat(os)* 'injury, wound' (from an Indo-European root meaning 'twist, turn, bore') plus the combining vowel *-o-*, used in its etymological and extended senses in Neo-Greek combinations: **traumatogenic, traumatopathy, traumatotherapy.** Also, **traum-, trauma-, traumat-: traumasthenia, traumatherapy, traumatic.** Related forms: **drill-, thread-, trypano-, turn-.**

2665 **tre-** A variant of **tri-.**

2666 **tree-** A word-initial combining element, also occurring as a word, derived from Old English *trē(o)* 'tall perennial plant with a single wooden stem' (from an Indo-European root meaning something on the order of 'solid, steadfast'), used in its etymological and extended senses in combination with other English elements: **treefish, treehopper, treetop.** Related forms: **dendro-, duro-, true-.**

2667 **tremo-** A word-initial combining element, derived from Latin *tremo(r)* '(a) trembling, shaking,' used in its etymological sense in Neo-Latin and Neo-Greek combinations: **tremograph, tremolabile, tremophobia.** Also, **tremor-: tremorgram.**

2668 **tri-** A word-initial combining element, derived from Greek *tri-*, a combining form of *treîs, tría* 'three' and *trís* 'thrice,' and from Latin *tri-*, a combining form of *trēs, tria* 'three,' used in its etymological and extended senses in a variety of combinations: **triangle, tricycle, trioxide.** Also, **tre-, tria-, trio-, tris-: tredecaphobia, triakaidekaphobia, triocephalus, trisnitrate.** Compare **triple-, triplo-, trit-.** Related forms: **ter-, testi-(?), third-, three-.**

2669 **tribrom-** See **tri-** and **brom(o)-².**

2670 **trich-** A variant of **tricho-.**

2671 **trichlor-** See **tri-** and **chlor-².**

2672 **tricho-** A word-initial combining element, derived from Greek *t(h)rí(x), trich(ós)* 'hair (of a person or beast)' plus the combining vowel *-o-*, used in its etymological and extended senses in a variety of combinations: **trichobezoar, trichofibroacanthoma,** *Trichomonas.* Also, **trich-: trichitis.**

2673 **triethyl-** See **tri-** and **ethyl-.**

2674 **trigono-**   A word-initial combining element, derived from Greek *trígōno(s)* 'triangular' (from *tri-* 'three-' plus *gôn(ía)* 'angle'), used in its etymological and extended senses in Neo-Greek combinations: **trigonocephalic, trigonometric, trigonotome.** Also, **trigon-: trigonitis.** Compare **tri-, gonio-.**

2675 **trihydroxy-**   See **tri-, hydro-²,** and **oxy-².**

2676 **triketo-**   See **tri-** and **keto-.**

2677 **trimethyl-**   See **tri-** and **methyl-.**

2678 **trinitro-**   See **tri-** and **nitro-.**

2679 **trio-**   A variant of **tri-.**

2680 **triphenyl-**   See **tri-** and **phenyl-.**

2681 **triple-**   A word-initial combining element, also occurring as a word, derived through Old French from Latin *tripl(us)* 'threefold,' used in its etymological and extended senses in combination with other English elements: **triple-decker, triple-header, tripletail.** Compare **tri-.**

2682 **triplo-**   A word-initial combining element, derived from Greek *tripló(os)* 'triple,' literally, 'threefold,' used in its etymological and extended senses in Neo-Greek combinations: **triploblastic, triplokoria, *Triplopus*.** Also, **tripl-: triplopia.** Compare **tri-.**

2683 **tris-**   A variant of **tri-.**

2684 **trit-**   A word-initial combining element, derived from Greek *trit(os)* 'third' (from *tr(e)î(s), trí(a)* 'three' plus the ordinal-forming suffix *-tos*), used in its etymological and extended senses in Neo-Greek combinations: **tritanopia, tritopine, tritoxide.** Also, **trito-: tritocone.** Compare **tri-.**

2685 **trocho-**   A word-initial combining element, derived from Greek *trochó(s)* 'that which is round(ed),' used in its etymological and extended senses in Neo-Greek combinations: **trochocardia, trochocephalia, trochophore.** Also, **troch-: trochiscus.**

2686 **trop-¹**   A variant of **tropo-¹.**

2687 **trop-²**   A word-initial combining element, derived from English *(a)trop(ine)* 'the poisonous alkaloid ($C_{17}H_{23}NO_3$) which is found in belladonna and related plants' (through German from Neo-Latin *Atrop(a)* 'genus to which belladonna belongs' (from Greek *Átropos* 'the Fate who cuts the thread of life spun and measured off by her two sisters,' literally, 'inflexible, unbending' (from *a(n)*- 'not, un-' plus *trópos* '(a) turn(ing)')) plus the noun-forming suffix *-in(e)* which is used in naming chemical substances), used in the sense of 'derived from atropine' in chemical terminology: **tropeine, tropidine, tropine.** Also, **tropa-, tropo-²: tropacocaine, tropococaine.** Compare **a-¹, tropo-¹.**

2688   **tropho-**   A word-initial combining element, derived from Greek *troph(ḗ)* 'food, nourishment' plus the combining vowel *-o-*, used in its etymological and extended senses in Neo-Greek combinations: **trophoblastic, trophodynamics, trophospongium.**

2689   **tropo-¹**   A word-initial combining element, derived from Greek *trópo(s)* '(a) turn(ing), direction,' used in its etymological and extended senses, chief among these being 'of or pertaining to a change, esp. in temperature or atmosphere,' in Neo-Greek combinations: **tropometer, tropopause, troposphere.** Also **trop-¹: tropic.**

2690   **tropo-²**   A variant of **trop-².**

2691   **true-**   A word-initial combining element, also occurring as a word, derived from Middle English *trȳ(w)e* 'steadfast,' used in its etymological and extended senses in combination with other English elements: **true-blue, trueborn, truelove.** Also, **tru-: truism.** Related forms: **dendro-, duro-, tree-.**

2692   **trumpet-**   A word-initial combining element, also occurring as a word, derived from (Old) French *trompet(te)* 'soprano musical instrument (of the brass family),' used in the sense of 'resembling a *trompette*' in combination with other English elements: **trumpetfish, trumpet-leaf, trumpetwood.**

2693   **trypano-**   A word-initial combining element, derived from Greek *trýpano(n)* 'auger, borer,' used chiefly in the sense of 'of, pertaining to, or resembling *trypanosomes,* parasitic protozoa of the genus *Trypanosoma*'—literally, 'auger-bodied'—in Neo-Greek and Neo-Latin combinations: **trypanocide, trypanolysis, *Trypanoplasma.*** Also, **trypan-: *Trypanophis.*** Related forms: **drill-, thread-, traumato-, turn-.**

2694   **tub-**   A variant of **tubo-.**

2695   **tuberculo-**   A word-initial combining element, derived from Latin *tūbercul(us)* 'little tumor' (from *tūber* 'lump, tumor' plus the diminutive suffix *-culus*) plus the combining vowel *-o-*, used in its etymological and extended senses, chief among these being 'of or pertaining to *tuberculosis,* an infectious disease characterized by the formation of caseous nodules in body tissue,' in Neo-Latin and Neo-Greek combinations: **tuberculocele, tuberculomania, tuberculotherapy.** Also, **tubercul-, tuberculi-: tuberculase, tuberculigenous.** Related forms: **somato-, thimble-, thumb-, tyro-.**

2696 tubo- A word-initial combining element, derived from Latin *tub(us)* 'tube' (from *tuba* 'trumpet') plus the combining vowel *-o-*, used in its etymological and extended senses, chief among these being 'of or pertaining to an oviduct,' in Neo-Latin and Neo-Greek combinations: **tuboligamentous, tubo-ovariotomy, tubotorsion.** Also, **tub-: tubal.** Compare **tubulo-.**

2697 tubulo- A word-initial combining element, derived from Latin *tubul(us)* 'small tube' (from *tub(us)* 'tube' plus the diminutive suffix *-ulus*) plus the combining vowel *-o-*, used in its etymological and extended senses in Neo-Latin and Neo-Greek combinations: **tubulocyst, tubulodermoid, tubuloracemose.** Also, **tubul-: tubular.** Compare **tubo-.**

2698 turbo- A word-initial combining element, derived from English *turb(ine)* 'waterwheel or other power-generating rotary mechanism' (through French from Latin *turb(ō), turbin(is)* 'that which spins or whirls') plus the combining vowel *-o-*, used in its etymological and extended senses in combination with other English elements: **turbo-electric, turbofan, turbojet.**

2699 turkey- A word-initial combining element, also occurring as a word, derived from English *turkey (cock)* 'guinea fowl, a bird first brought to Europe from Africa through *Turkey* by the Portuguese,' used in the sense of 'American bird of the genus *Meleagris*' and in extensions of this sense in combination with other English elements: **turkeyfish, turkey-pen, turkey-trot.**

2700 turn- A word-initial combining element, also occurring as a word, derived through Old French and Old English from Latin *torn(āre)* 'to round off (on a lathe)' (cf. *tornus* 'lathe' (from Greek *tórnos* 'carpenter's device for drawing a circle')), used in its etymological and extended senses in combination with other English elements: **turnabout, turnover, turnpike.** Related forms: **drill-, thread-, traumato-, trypano-.**

2701 turtle- A word-initial combining element, also occurring as a word of obscure origin, used in the sense of 'resembling a marine tortoise' in combination with other English elements: **turtleback, turtlehead, turtleneck.**

2702   **tway-**   A variant of **twi-.**

2703   **twelve-**   A word-initial combining element, also occurring as a word, derived from Old English *twelf(e)* 'the cardinal number between *eleven* and *thirteen*' (from Proto-Germanic **twa-lif* 'two-left (over),' i.e., 'two left over when ten is taken away'), used in its etymological and extended senses in combination with other English elements: **twelvemonth, twelvepenny, twelve-tone.** Compare **two-.**

2704   **twi-**   A word-initial combining element, derived from Old English *twi-,* a combining form of *twā* 'two,' appearing in its etymological and extended senses in a few inherited combinations: **twibill, twifoil, twilight.** Also, **tway-: twayblade.** Compare **two-.**

2705   **twin-**   A word-initial combining element, also occurring as a word, derived from Old English *(ġe)twin(n)* 'double,' used in its etymological and extended senses in combination with other English elements: **twinberry, twinborn, twin-screw.** Compare **two-.**

2706   **two-**   A word-initial combining element, also occurring as a word, derived from Old English *twā* 'the cardinal number between *one* and *three*,' used in its etymological and extended senses in combination with other English elements: **two-bit, twofer, two-step.** Compare **twelve-, twi-, twin-.** Related forms: **bi-[1], bin-, bis-, di-[1], dicho-, diplo-, dis-[1], double-, dui-, duo-.**

2707   **tympano-**   A word-initial combining element, derived from Greek *týmpano(n)* 'kettledrum' (from an Indo-European root meaning 'push, hit'), used in a variety of extensions of its etymological sense, chief among these being 'of or pertaining to the *tympanum,* the eardrum,' in Neo-Greek and Neo-Latin combinations: **tympanohyal, tympanolabyrinthopexy, tympanotemporal.** Also, **tympan-, tympani-: tympanitis, tympanichord.** Related forms: **step-[1], type-, typo-.**

2708   **type-**   A word-initial combining element, also occurring as a word, derived through Late Latin from Greek *týp(os)* '(a) blow,' hence, '(a) stamp,' hence, 'image (made by a stamp),' hence, 'model,' used in a variety of its etymological and extended senses in combination with other English elements: **typecast, typeface, typewriter.** Compare **typo-.**

2709   typh-   A variant of **typho-**.

2710   typhl-¹   A word-initial combining element, derived from Greek *typhló(s)* 'blind' (from *tŷph(os)* 'smoke, cloud' plus the noun- and adjective-forming suffix *-los*), used in its etymological and extended senses in Neo-Greek combinaions: **Typhlophthalmi, Typhlops, typhlosis**. Also, **typhlo-¹: typhlology**. Compare **typhlo-², typho-**.

2711   typhl-²   A variant of **typhlo-²**.

2712   typhlo-¹   A variant of **typhl-¹**.

2713   typhlo-²   A word-initial combining element, derived from Greek *typhló(s)* 'blind,' used in the specialized sense of 'of or pertaining to the *cecum* ('blind gut')' in Neo-Greek combinations: **typhlocolitis, typhlolithiasis, typhlostomy**. Also, **typhl-²: typhlitis**. Compare **typhl-¹, typho-**.

2714   typho-   A word-initial combining element, derived from Greek *tŷpho(s)* 'smoke, cloud,' hence, 'clouding of the mind; stupor resulting from a fever,' used in the sense of 'of or pertaining to *typhoid fever*' in biomedical terminology: **typhobacillosis, typhomania, typhorubeloid**. Also, **typh-: typhemia**. Compare **typhl-¹, typhlo-²**. Related forms: **deer-, dust-, thio-, thym-¹, thymo-²**.

2715   typo-   A word-initial combining element, derived from Greek *týpo(s)* '(a) blow,' hence, '(a) stamp,' hence, 'image made with a stamp,' hence, 'model,' used in a variety of its etymological and extended senses in Neo-Greek combinations: **typographic, typology, typothetae**. Compare **type-**. Related forms: **step-¹, tympano-**.

2716   tyro-   A word-initial combining element, derived from Greek *tyró(s)* 'cheese' (from an Indo-European root meaning 'swell'), used in its etymological and extended senses in Neo-Greek and Neo-Latin combinations: **tyrocidine, tyrogenous, tyrotoxin**. Also, **tyr-: tyremesis**. Related forms: **somato-, thimble-, thumb-, tuberculo-**.

U

2717   **ul-¹**   A variant of **ulo-¹**.

2718   **ul-²**   A word-initial combining element, derived from Greek (*o*)*ul*(*ḗ*) 'scar,' used in its etymological and extended senses in Neo-Greek combinations: **ulectomy-², ulerythema, ulosis.** Also, **oul-², ule-, ulo-²: oulectomy-², ulegyria, ulotomy-².**

2719   **ulno-**   A word-initial combining element, derived from Latin *uln*(*a*) 'elbow' and, by extension, 'arm' plus the combining vowel *-o-*, used in the sense of 'of or pertaining to the larger bone of the forearm' in biomedical terminology: **ulnocarpal, ulnometacarpal, ulnoradial.** Also, **uln-: ulnar.**

2720   **ulo-¹**   A word-initial combining element, derived from Greek (*o*)*ûl*(*a*) '(the) gums' plus the combining element *-o-*, used in its etymological sense in biomedical terminology: **ulocarcinoma, uloglossitis, ulotomy-¹.** Also, **oul-¹, oulo-¹, ul-¹: oulectomy-¹, oulorrhagia, ulectomy-¹.**

2721   **ulo-²**   A variant of **ul-²**.

2722   **ulo-³**   A word-initial combining element, derived from Greek (*o*)*ûlo*(*s*) 'woolly, curly' (from an Indo-European root meaning 'turn, roll'), used in its etymological and extended senses in Neo-Greek combinations: ***Ulophocinae, Ulothrix,* ulotrichous.** Also,

377

oulo-²: oulopholite. Related forms: **helmintho-, valvulo-, walk-(?), well-².**

2723   **ultra-**   A word-initial combining element, derived from Latin *ultrā* 'beyond, farther, above, exceeding,' used in its etymological and extended senses in a variety of combinations: **ultrabrachycephalic, ultracrepidarian, ultra-red.** Related forms: **allelo-, allo-, allotrio-, alter-.**

2724   **un-¹**   A word-initial combining element, derived from Old English *un-* 'not, contrary to that which is specified by the combining root,' used in its etymological sense in combination with other English elements: **unfriendly, unnatural, unreasonable.** Related forms: **a-¹, an-¹, i-, il-¹, im-¹, in-¹, ir-¹, neutro-, never-, no-, non-¹, nulli-.**

2725   **un-²**   A word-initial combining element, derived from Old English *un-, on-* 'depriving of or reversing that which is expressed by the combining root,' used in its etymological and extended senses in combination with other English elements: **undress, unlock, unsheathe.** Related forms: **ante-, antero-, anti-, end-².**

2726   **un-³**   A variant of **uni-**.

2727   **unci-**   A word-initial combining element, derived from Latin *unc(us)* 'hook' plus the combining vowel *-i-*, used in its etymological and extended senses in Neo-Latin combinations: **unciform, uncipressure, uncirostrate.** Also, **unc-**: *Uncaria.* Related forms: **Anglo-, ankylo-, onco-².**

2728   **under-**   A word-initial combining element, also occurring as a word, derived from Old English *under* 'below,' used in its etymological and extended senses in combination with other English elements: **underestimate, underground, underhanded.** Related forms: **infero-, infra-.**

2729   **uni-**   A word-initial combining element, derived from Latin *ūn(us)* 'one' plus the combining vowel *-i-*, used in its etymological and extended senses in Neo-Latin and Neo-Greek combinations: **unicycle, uniform, unilateral.** Also, **un-³: unanimous.** Compare **inch-**. Related forms: **any, eka-, one-.**

2730   **up-**   A word-initial combining element, also occurring as a word, derived from a combination of Old English *up(p)* 'elevated (motion)' and *up(pe)* 'elevated (position),' used in its etymological and extended senses in combination with other English elements: **upbringing, upheaval, upside-down.** Related forms: **evil-(?), hyper-,**

hypo-, open-, over-, sub-, suc-, suf-, sup-, super-, supra-, sur-¹, sur-²,
sursum-, sus-.

2731 **upsilon-** (Υ, υ) A word-initial combining element, the twentieth
letter of the Greek alphabet, used chiefly to designate 'the twentieth carbon atom in a straight chain compound or a derivative
thereof in which the substitute group is attached to that atom' in
chemical terminology. See **alpha-**. Compare **hyo-**.

2732 **ur-¹** A variant of **uro-¹**.

2733 **ur-²** A variant of **uro-²**.

2734 **uran-** A variant of **urano-**.

2735 **uranisco-** A word-initial combining element, derived from Greek
(*o*)*uranísko*(*s*) 'roof of the mouth,' literally, 'little vault of heaven'
(from *ouran*(*ós*) 'vault of heaven' plus the diminutive suffix *-iskos*),
used in its etymological and extended senses in biomedical terminology: **uraniscochasma, uraniscolalia, uraniscoplasty**. Also, **uranis-
con-: uranisconitis**. Compare **urano-**.

2736 **urano-** A word-initial combining element, derived from Greek
(*o*)*uranó*(*s*) 'vault of heaven,' hence, 'the sky; Uranus, the sky god;
the roof of the mouth,' used in its various etymological and
extended senses in Neo-Greek combinations: **uranophobia, ura-
noplastic, uranoscope**. Also, **uran-: uranism**. Compare **uranisco-**.

2737 **urea-** A word-initial combining element, also occurring as a word,
derived from scientific Latin *urea* 'carbamide ($NH_2CO \cdot NH_2$), the
principal constituent of urine' (from **ur(e)-¹** plus the noun- and
adjective-forming suffix *-ea*), used in its etymological and extended
senses in Neo-Latin and Neo-Greek combinations: **ureabromine,
ureagenetic, ureameter**. Also, **ure-, ureo-: ureal, ureosecretory**.
Compare **uro-¹**.

2738 **uretero-** A word-initial combining element, derived from Greek
(*o*)*urētḗr* 'urinary duct between the kidney and the bladder' (from
oure(*în*) 'to urinate' (from *oûron* 'urine') plus the agentive suffix
-tēr) plus the combining vowel *-o-*, used in its etymological sense in
biomedical terminology: **ureterocervical, ureterodialysis, ureterovaginal**. Also, **ureter-: ureteralgia**. Compare **uro-¹**.

2739 **ureterocysto-** See **uretero-** and **cyst(o)-**.

2740 **ureteropyelo-** See **uretero-** and **pyelo-**.

2741 urethro- A word-initial combining element, derived from Greek (*o*)*uréthr*(*a*) 'duct through which urine is expelled from the bladder' (from *oure*(*în*) 'to urinate' (from *oûron* 'urine') plus the noun-forming suffix -*thra*) plus the combining vowel -*o*-, used in its etymological and extended senses in biomedical terminology: **urethrobulbar, urethrograph, urethroprostatic.** Also, **urethr-: urethratresia.** Compare **uro-**[1].

2742 urethrocysto- See **urethro-** and **cyst(o)-**.

2743 urico- A word-initial combining element, derived from (*o*)*urētikó*(*s*) 'of or pertaining to urine' (from *oûr*(*on*) 'urine' plus the adjective-forming suffix -*ikós*), used chiefly in the sense of 'of, pertaining to, or containing *uric acid*' in biochemical terminology: **uricocholia, uricolysis, uricometer.** Also, **uri-, uric-: urisolvent, uricase.** Compare **uro-**[1].

2744 urino- A word-initial combining element, derived from Latin *ūrīn*(*a*) 'urine' plus the combining vowel -*o*-, used in its etymological and extended senses in Neo-Latin and Neo-Greek combinations: **urinocryoscopy, urinoglucosometer, urinosexual.** Also, **urin-, urina-, urini-: urinemia, urinaserum, uriniparous.** Related forms: **urea-, uretero-, urethro-, urico-, uro-**[1].

2745 uro-[1] A word-initial combining element, derived from Greek (*o*)*ûro*(*n*) 'urine,' used in its etymological and extended senses in Neo-Greek and Neo-Latin combinations: **urocrisia, urofuscohematin, urophobia.** Also, **ur-**[1]**, urono-: uremia, uronology.** Compare **urea-, uretero-, urethro-, urico-.** Related form: **urino-.**

2746 uro-[2] A word-initial combining element, derived from Greek (*o*)*ur*(*á*) 'tail' plus the combining vowel -*o*-, used in its etymological and extended senses in Neo-Greek combinations: **urochord, uropod, uropygium.** Also, **ur-**[2]**: *Urapterix.***

2747 urobilin- A word-initial combining element, also occurring as a word, derived from **uro-**[1] plus **bili-** plus the suffix -*in* which is used in naming chemical substances, used in the sense of 'of, pertaining to, or containing *urobilin* ($C_{35}H_{44}O_8N_4$), a substance produced by the oxidation of bilirubin and found in urine and feces' in biochemical terminology: **urobilinemia, urobilinicterus, urobilinuria.** Also, **urobilino-: urobilinogen.** Compare **uro-**[1]**, bili-**.

2748 urono- A variant of **uro-**[1].

2749 utero- A word-initial combining element, derived from Latin *uter(us)* 'womb' plus the combining vowel -*o*-, used in its etymological sense in biomedical terminology: **uteroabdominal, uterolith, uterothermometry**. Also, **uter-: uteritis**. Related forms(?): **hystero-, ventriculo-, ventro-, vesico-, vesiculo-**.

2750 **uveo-** A word-initial combining element, derived from Late Latin *ūve(a)* 'grapelike' (from *ūv(a)* 'grape' plus the adjective-forming suffix -*ea*) plus the combining vowel -*o*-, used in the sense of 'of or pertaining to the *uvea*, the (grapelike) surface of the iris of the eye' and in extensions of this sense in biomedical terminology: **uveoparotid, uveoplasty, uveoscleritis**. Also, **uve-: uveitis**.

2751 **uvio-** A word-initial combining element, derived from English *u(ltra)vio(let)* 'of or pertaining to that part of the visible spectrum just beyond the violet' (from **ultra-** plus *violet* 'purple'), used in its etymological sense in a variety of combinations: **uviofast, uviometer, uvioresistant**. Also, **uvi-: uviol**. Compare **ultra-**.

V

2752 **vaccino-** A word-initial combining element, derived from English *vaccin(e)* 'suspension of killed or attenuated microorganisms administered orally or by injection for the prevention or treatment of infectious disease' (from Scientific Latin (*vīrus*) *vaccīnus* 'cow(pox) (medicinal liquid, virus)' (from *vacc(a)* 'cow' plus the adjective-forming suffix *-īnus*)) plus the combining vowel *-o-*, used in its etymological and extended senses in biomedical terminology: **vaccinogen, vaccinophobia, vaccinostyle.** Also, **vacci-, vaccin-, vaccini-: vaccigenous, vaccination, vaccinifer.**

2753 **vag-** A variant of **vago-.**

2754 **vagino-** A word-initial combining element, derived from Latin *vāgīn(a)* 'scabbard, sheath,' hence, 'canal connecting the vulva and the cervix uteri in the female' plus the combining vowel *-o-*, used in this latter sense in biomedical terminology: **vaginoabdominal, vaginometer, vaginovesical.** Also, **vagin-, vagini-: vaginitis, vaginicoline.**

2755 **vago-** A word-initial combining element, derived from Scientific Latin (*nervus*) *vag(us)* 'unsettled, wandering (nerve), the tenth and longest of the cranial nerves' plus the combining vowel *-o-*, used in its etymological sense in biomedical terminology: **vagogram, vagosympathetic, vagotonic.** Also, **vag-: vagitis.**

2756 **valvulo-** A word-initial combining element, derived from Scientific

383

Latin *valvul(a)* '(little) valve' (from Latin *valv(a)* 'one of the leaves of a folding door' (from *volvere* 'to turn, roll') plus the diminutive suffix *-ula*) plus the combining vowel *-o-*, used in the sense of 'of or pertaining to a *valve*, a doorlike structure in a passageway that hinders or prevents the reflux of its contents' in Neo-Latin and Neo-Greek combinations: **valvuloplasty, valvulotome, valvulotomy.** Also, **valvul-: valvulitis.** Related forms: **helmintho-, ulo-³, walk-(?), well-².**

2757 **vapori-** A word-initial combining element, derived from Latin *vapor, vapōr(is)* 'steam' plus the combining vowel *-i-*, used in its etymological and extended senses in Neo-Latin and Neo-Greek combinations: **vaporiferous, vaporiform, vaporimeter.** Also, **vapo-, vapor-: vapotherapy, vaporize.**

2758 **varico-** A word-initial combining element, derived from Latin *vari(x), varic(is)* 'swollen vein' plus the combining vowel *-o-*, used in its etymological and extended senses in biomedical terminology: **varicoblepharon, varicocele, varicophlebitis.** Also, **varic-: varicosis.**

2759 **vas-** A variant of **vaso-.**

2760 **vasculo-** A word-initial combining element, derived from Latin *vascul(um)* '(small) vessel' (from *vas* 'vessel' plus the diminutive suffix *-culum*) plus the combining vowel *-o-*, used in its etymological and extended senses in Neo-Latin and Neo-Greek combinations: **vasculogenesis, vasculomotor, vasculotoxic.** Also, **vascul-: vasculitis.** Compare **vaso-.**

2761 **vaso-** A word-initial combining element, derived from Latin *vas, vās(is)* 'vessel' plus the combining vowel *-o-*, used in its etymological and extended senses, chief among these being 'of or pertaining to a blood vessel,' in Neo-Latin and Neo-Greek combinations: **vasodilator, vasoganglion, vasomotor.** Also, **vas-, vasi-: vasalgia, vasifactive.** Compare **vasculo-.**

2762 **veno-** A word-initial combining element, derived from Latin *vēn(a)* 'blood vessel, vein' plus the combining vowel *-o-*, used in its etymological sense in biomedical terminology: **venoclysis, venogram, venostasis.** Also, **ven-, vene-, veni-: venectomy, venepuncture, venisuture.**

2763 **ventri-** A variant of **ventro-.**

2764 **ventriculo-** A word-initial combining element, derived from Latin *ventricul(us)* '(little) belly,' hence, 'ventricle, a small cavity, esp. of the heart or brain' (from *vent(e)r, ventr(is)* 'belly' plus the diminutive suffix *-culus*) plus the combining vowel *-o-*, used in this latter sense in biomedical terminology: **ventriculocisternostomy, ventriculopuncture, ventriculoscope.** Also, **ventricul-: ventriculitis.** Compare **ventro-.**

2765   **ventro-**   A word-initial combining element, derived from Latin *vent(e)r, ventr(is)* 'belly' plus the combining vowel *-o-*, used in its etymological and extended senses in biomedical terminology: **ventrocystorrhaphy, ventrolateral, ventroptosis.** Also, **ventr-, ventri-: ventral, ventricumbent.** Compare **ventriculo-.** Related forms(?): **hystero-, utero-, vesico-, vesiculo-.**

2766   **ver-**   A variant of **veri-.**

2767   **veratr-**   A word-initial combining element, derived from Scientific Latin *Verātr(um)* 'genus of hellebore' (from Latin *verātrum* 'hellebore'), used in the sense of 'of, pertaining to, containing, or derived from *veratrine,* a mixture of alkaloids derived from plants of the genus *Veratrum*' in chemical terminology: **veratralbine, veratridine, veratroidine.**

2768   **veri-**   A word-initial combining element, derived from Latin *vēri,* a combining form of *vēr(us)* 'true, genuine,' appearing in its etymological and extended senses in borrowings from Latin: **veridical, veriloquent, verisimilar.** Also, **ver-: veracious.**

2769   **vermi-**   A word-initial combining element, derived from Latin *vermi(s)* 'worm' (from an Indo-European root meaning 'bend, turn'), used in its etymological sense in Neo-Latin and Neo-Greek combinations: **vermicide, vermifuge, vermiphobia.** Also, **vermo-: vermography.** Related forms: **rhampho-, rhombo-, vertebro-, worm-, wrist-.**

2770   **vertebro-**   A word-initial combining element, derived from Latin *vertebr(a)* 'joint, esp. of the spinal column' (from *verte(re)* 'to turn' plus the noun-forming suffix *-bra*) plus the combining vowel *-o-*, used in its etymological and extended senses in biomedical terminology: **vertebrochondral, vertebrofemoral, vertebrosacral.** Also, **vertebr-: vertebrectomy.** Related forms: **rhampho-, rhombo-, vermi-, worm-, wrist-.**

2771   **vesico-**   A word-initial combining element, derived from Latin *vēsīc(a)* 'bladder' plus the combining vowel *-o-*, used in its etymological and extended senses, chief among these being 'of or pertaining to a blister,' in biomedical terminology: **vesico-**

cavernous, vesicocervical, vesicoclysis. Also, vesic-: vesicant. Compare vesiculo-. Related forms(?): hystero-, utero-, ventriculo-, ventro-.

2772 **vesiculo-** A word-initial combining element, derived from Latin *vēsīcul(a)* '(small) blister,' literally, 'small bladder' (from *vēsīc(a)* 'bladder' plus the diminutive suffix *-ula*) plus the combining vowel *-o-*, used in its etymological and extended senses in biomedical terminology: **vesiculogram, vesiculopapular, vesiculotomy**. Also, **vesicul-, vesiculi-: vesiculectomy, vesiculiform**. Compare **vesico-**.

2773 **vibro-** A word-initial combining element, derived from Latin *vibr(āre)* 'to quiver, oscillate' plus the combining vowel *-o-*, used in its etymological and extended senses in a variety of combinations: **vibrocardiogram, vibromasseur, vibrophone**. Also, **vibr-: vibrissa**. Related form: **whip-**.

2774 **vice-** A word-initial combining element, derived through Old French from Latin *vice,* the ablative singular form of *vicis* 'change, succession, position, place,' used in the sense of 'one who is a deputy of or a stand-in for the person named by the combining root' and in extensions of this sense in a variety of combinations: **vicegerent, vicereine, viceroy**. Related form: **weak-**.

2775 **video-** A word-initial combining element, derived from Latin *vidē(re)* 'to see' plus the combining vowel *-o-*, used in the sense of 'of or pertaining to the transmission of images by means of television' in a variety of combinations: **videogenic, videognosis, video-tape**. Compare **visuo-**. Related forms: **eido-, guide-, ideo-, story-**.

2776 **villi-** A word-initial combining element, derived from Latin *vill(us)* 'tuft of hair, fleece' plus the combining vowel *-i-*, used in the extended sense of 'of or pertaining to a *villus,* a small protrusion, esp. arising from a mucous membrane' in biomedical terminology: **villiferous, villikinin, villioma**. Also, **vill-: villoma**. Related forms: **flannel-, line-, wool-**.

2777 **vin-** A variant of **vini-**.

2778 **vine-** A word-initial combining element, also occurring as a word, derived through Old French from Latin *vīne(a)* 'garden of grape-bearing plants' (from *vīn(um)* 'wine' plus the adjective-forming suffix *-ea*), used in the sense of 'of or pertaining to grape-bearing plants (for use in making wine)' in combination with other English elements: **vinedresser, vineland, vineyard**. Compare **vini-**.

2779   **vini-**   A word-initial combining element, derived from Latin *vīn(um)* 'wine' plus the combining vowel *-i-,* used in its etymological and extended senses in Neo-Latin and Neo-Greek combinations: **viniculture, viniferous, vinificator.** Also, **vin-, vino-: vinyl, vinometer.** Compare **vine-, wine-.** Related form: **oeno-.**

2780   **viscero-**   A word-initial combining element, derived from Latin *viscer(a)* '(larger) internal organs of the body' plus the combining vowel *-o-,* used in its etymological and extended senses in biomedical terminology: **viscerography, visceromotor, visceroptosis.** Also, **viscer-, visceri-: visceralgia, viscerimotor.**

2781   **visco-**   A word-initial combining element, derived from Late Latin *viscō(sus)* 'sticky' (from Latin *visc(um)* 'mistletoe' and, by extension, 'birdlime (made from mistletoe berries)' plus the adjective-forming suffix *-ōsus* 'full of or characterized by that which is named by the combining root'), used in its etymological and extended senses in a variety of combinations: **viscogel, viscometer, viscosaccharase.** Also, **visc-, viscos-, viscosi-: viscin, viscosity, viscosimeter.**

2782   **visuo-**   A word-initial combining element, derived from Latin *vīsu(s)* '(a) looking, sight' (from the past participle of the verb *vidēre* 'to see') plus the combining vowel *-o-,* used in the sense of 'of or pertaining to sight' in Neo-Latin and Neo-Greek combinations: **visuo-auditory, visuognosis, visuosensory.** Also, **visu-: visual.** Compare **video-.**

2783   **vit-¹**   A variant of **vita-¹.**

2784   **vit-²**   A variant of **vitamino-.**

2785   **vita-¹**   A word-initial combining element, derived from Latin *vīta* 'life,' used in its etymological and extended senses in a variety of combinations: **vitaglass, vitagraph, vitascope.** Also, **vit-¹, vito-: vital, vitodynamic.** Related forms: **bio-, quick-, vivi-, zoo-.**

2786   **vita-²**   A variant of **vitamino-.**

2787   **vitamino-**   A word-initial combining element, derived from German *Vitamin(e)* 'organic substance occurring in food and essential for the body's normal metabolic functioning' (from Latin *vīt(a)* 'life' plus German *Amine* 'amine') plus the combining vowel *-o-,* used in its etymological and extended senses in biochemical terminology: **vitaminogenic, vitaminology, vitaminoscope.** Also, **vit-², vita-², vita-**

min-²: **vitagonist, vitameter, vitaminoid.** Compare **vit(a)-¹** and **amino-.**

2788 **vitello-**   A word-initial combining element, derived from Latin *vitell(us)* 'yolk' plus the combining vowel *-o-*, used in its etymological and extended senses in Neo-Latin and Neo-Greek combinations: **vitellogenesis, vitellolutein, vitellorubin.** Also, **vitell-: vitellase.**

2789 **vito-**   A variant of **vita-¹.**

2790 **vivi-**   A word-initial combining element, derived from Latin *vīv(us)* 'alive, living' plus the combining vowel *-i-*, used in its etymological and extended senses in Neo-Latin and Neo-Greek combinations: **vividialysis, viviparous, vivisection.** Also, **vivo-: vivosphere.** Related forms: **bio-, quick-, vita-¹, zoo-.**

2791 **volt-**   A word-initial combining element, also occurring as a word, derived from (*Alessandro*) *Volt(a),* the name of an early investigator of the nature of electricity, used in the sense of 'of or pertaining to the unit of electromotive force necessary to cause one ampere of current to counter one ohm of resistance' in scientific terminology: **voltage, voltammeter, voltmeter.** Also, **volta-: voltameter.**

2792 **vulvo-**   A word-initial combining element, derived from Latin *vulv(a)* 'covering,' hence, 'womb' plus the combining vowel *-o-*, used in the sense of 'of or pertaining to the external genital organs of the female' in biomedical terminology: **vulvocrural, vulvo-uterine, vulvovaginal.** Also, **vulv-: vulvitis.**

W

2793 **waist-** A word-initial combining element, also occurring as a word, derived from Middle English *wast* '(the) part of the body between the bottom of the rib cage and the top of the pelvis' (perhaps from an Indo-European root meaning 'grow, increase,' the idea being, presumably, that this portion of the human anatomy is the one which most obviously continues to expand as one grows older), used in its etymological and extended senses in combination with other English elements: **waistband, waistcloth, waistcoat.** Related forms(?): **auxano-, auxo-.**

2794 **walk-** A word-initial combining element, also occurring as a word, derived from Old English *w(e)alc(an)* 'to roll, move about,' hence, 'to go (on foot),' used in this last and extended senses in combination with other English elements: **walk-on, walkout, walk-way.** Related forms(?): **helmintho-, ulo-³, valvulo-, well-².**

2795 **wall-** A word-initial combining element, also occurring as a word, derived, ultimately, from Latin *vall(um)* 'palisaded rampart' (from *vallus* 'stake'), used chiefly in the extended sense of 'of or pertaining to an upright structure designed to enclose an area' and in extensions of this sense in combination with other English elements: **wallboard, wallflower, wallpaper.**

2796 **war-** A word-initial combining element, also occurring as a word, derived through Anglo-Norman from a Germanic form meaning 'confusion, strife' (cf. Old High German *werra* 'confusion, dis-

389

cord'), used in the sense of 'prolonged hostilities between opposing armies' and in extensions of this sense in combination with other English elements: **warhead, war-horse, warlord.**

2797   **wash-**   A word-initial combining element, also occurring as a word, derived from Old English *wasć(an)* 'to cleanse with water' (from an Indo-European root meaning 'water, wet'), used in its etymological and extended senses in combination with other English elements: **washcloth, washout, washroom.** Related forms: **hydro-[1], water-, wet-, winter-.**

2798   **waste-**   A word-initial combining element, also occurring as a word, derived through dialectal Old French from Latin *vast(um)* 'harsh, empty land,' used in its etymological and extended senses in combination with other English elements: **wastebasket, wasteland, wastepile.**

2799   **watch-**   A word-initial combining element, also occurring as a word, derived from Old English *wæć(ćan)* 'to be awake; to stay awake,' used in a variety of extensions of its etymological sense, chief among these being '(being on the) look-out' and 'of or pertaining to a mechanical time-keeping device worn on the wrist or carried in the pocket,' (originally, 'alarm-clock'), in combination with other English elements: **watchdog, watchmaker, watchtower.**

2800   **water-**   A word-initial combining element, also occurring as a word, derived from Old English *wæter* 'the liquid (H_2O),' used in its etymological and extended senses in combination with other English elements: **watercool, watercress, watermelon.** Related forms: **hydro-[1], wash-, wet-, winter-.**

2801   **watt-**   A word-initial combining element, also occurring as a word, derived from (*James*) *Watt* (1736–1819), the name of the inventor of the modern condensing steam engine, used in the sense of 'of or pertaining to the unit of power equal to one joule per second' in scientific terminology: **watt-hour, wattmeter, watt-second.**

2802   **wave-**   A word-initial combining element, also occurring as a word, derived from a combination of Middle English *wave(n)* 'to move back and forth' (from Old English *wafian* 'to move (the hands) back and forth') and *waġe, wawe* 'movement in which water rises (and then falls)' (cf. Old English *wagian* 'to sway back and forth'), used chiefly in the sense of 'of or pertaining to an oscillating telegraphic signal' and in extensions of this sense in combination with other English elements: **waveband, waveguide, wavelength.** Related form: **web-.**

2803   wax-   A word-initial combining element, also occurring as a word, derived from Old English *wæx* 'tallowlike substance produced by bees,' used in the extended sense of 'of or pertaining to a tallowlike substance similar to that produced by bees' in combination with other English elements: **waxberry, waxwing, waxwork.**

2804   way-   A word-initial combining element, also occurring as a word, derived from Old English *we(ġ)* 'route of travel,' used in its etymological and extended senses in combination with other English elements: **waybill, wayside, wayworn.**

2805   weak-   A word-initial combining element, also occurring as a word, derived through Middle English from Old Norse *veik(r)* 'pliant,' used in its etymological and extended senses in combination with other English elements: **weakfish, weak-kneed, weak-minded.** Related form: **vice-.**

2806   weather-   A word-initial combining element, also occurring as a word, derived from Old English *weder* 'atmospheric condition' (from an Indo-European root meaning '(to) blow'), used in its etymological and extended senses in combination with other English elements: **weather-beaten, weatherboard, weatherman.** Related forms: **wind-, window-, wing-.**

2807   web-   A word-initial combining element, also occurring as a word, derived from Old English *web(b)* 'woven fabric; spider's woven net,' used in the sense of 'resembling a spider's woven net' in combination with other English elements: **webfoot, web-toed, webworm.** Related form: **wave-.**

2808   well-¹   A word-initial combining element, derived from Old English *wel(l)* 'in good manner or measure,' used in its etymological and extended senses in combination with other English elements: **well-bred, well-heeled, well-wisher.** Also, **wel-: welfare.**

2809   well-²   A word-initial combining element, also occurring as a word, derived from Old English *well(a)* 'spring,' hence, 'pit from which spring water may be obtained' (from an Indo-European root meaning 'roll, turn'), used in its etymological and extended senses in combination with other English elements: **wellhead, wellhole, wellspring.** Related forms: **helmintho-, ulo-³, valvulo-, walk-(?).**

2810   wet-   A word-initial combining element, also occurring as a word, derived from Old English *wæt* 'moist, moistened,' used in its etymological and extended senses in combination with other

English elements: **wetback, wet-blanket, wet-nurse.** Related forms: **hydro-¹, wash-, water-, winter-.**

2811 whale- A word-initial combining element, also occurring as a word, derived from Old English *hwæl* 'marine mammal of the order *Cetacea*,' used in its etymological and extended senses in combination with other English elements: **whaleback, whaleboat, whalebone.**

2812 what- A word-initial combining element, also occurring as a word, derived from Old English *hwæt,* the neuter interrogative and relative pronoun, appearing in its etymological and extended senses in a few inherited combinations: **whatever, whatnot, whatsoever.** Related forms: **quanti-, quasi-, when-, where-, who-.**

2813 wheel- A word-initial combining element, also occurring as a word, derived from Old English *hwē(o)l* 'disk or circle which rotates on an axle,' used in its etymological and extended senses in combination with other English elements: **wheelbarrow, wheelchair, wheelwright.** Related forms: **coll-², collar-, cyclo-, palin-, polari-, teleo-³, telo-¹.**

2814 when- A word-initial combining element, also occurring as a word, derived from Old English *hwen(ne)* 'at which time,' appearing in its etymological and extended senses in combination with other English elements: **whenever, when-issued, whensoever.** Related forms: **quanti-, quasi-, what-, where-, who-.**

2815 where- A word-initial combining element, also occurring as a word, derived from Old English *hwær* 'in which place,' used in its etymological and extended senses in combination with other English elements: **whereabouts, whereas, whereby.** Related forms: **quanti-, quasi-, what-, when-, who-.**

2816 whip- A word-initial combining element, also occurring as a word, derived from Middle English *hwip(pen)* 'to move quickly,' hence, 'to lash' (probably from Middle Low German or Middle Dutch *wippen* 'to vacillate'), used in its etymological and extended senses in combination with other English elements: **whipcord, whiplash, whipsaw.** Related form: **vibro-.**

2817 whirl- A word-initial combining element, also occurring as a word, derived from Old Norse *hvir(f)l(a)* 'to turn about,' used in the sense of 'turning about quickly' in combination with other English elements: **whirlabout, whirlpool, whirlwind.** Related form: **carpo-¹.**

2818   **white-**   A word-initial combining element, also occurring as a word, derived from Old English *hwīt* 'light achromatic color,' used in its etymological and extended senses in combination with other English elements: **whitebait, white-collar, white-out.**

2819   **who-**   A word-initial combining element, also occurring as a word, derived from Old English *hwā* 'which person,' used in its etymological and extended senses in combination with other English elements: **whodunit, whoever, whoso.** Related forms: **quanti-, quasi-, what-, when-, where-.**

2820   **whole-**   A word-initial combining element, also occurring as a word, derived from Old English *hāl* 'complete, undivided,' used in its etymological and extended senses in combination with other English elements: **wholehearted, wholesale, whole-wheat.**

2821   **whore-**   A word-initial combining element, also occurring as a word, derived from Old English *hōre* 'prostitute,' used in its etymological and extended senses in combination with other English elements: **whorehouse, whoremonger, whoreson.**

2822   **wide-**   A word-initial combining element, also occurring as a word, derived from Old English *wīd* 'broad, extensive from side to side' (from an Indo-European root meaning 'apart'), used in its etymological and extended senses in combination with other English elements: **wide-awake, wide-eyed, widespread.** Related form: **with-.**

2823   **wild-**   A word-initial combining element, also occurring as a word, derived from Old English *wild(e)* 'existing in its natural state,' used in its etymological and extended senses in combination with other English elements: **wildcat, wildflower, wild-goose (chase).**

2824   **wind-**   A word-initial combining element, also occurring as a word, derived from Old English *wind* 'vigorously moving air,' used in its etymological and extended senses in combination with other English elements: **windbag, windburn, windfall.** Related forms: **weather-, window-, wing-.**

2825   **window-**   A word-initial combining element, also occurring as a word, derived from Old Norse *vindau(ga)* '(an) opening in a wall through which fresh air may pass,' literally, 'wind-eye' (from *vind(r)* 'wind' plus *auga* 'eye'), used in its etymological and extended senses in combination with other English elements: **window-dressing, windowpane, window-shop.** Related forms: **weather-, wind-, wing-; eye-, ocelli-, oculo-, opo-[1], ophthalmo-, optico-.**

2826 wine- A word-initial combining element, also occurring as a word, derived through Old English from Latin *vīn(um)* 'alcoholic beverage made from the fermented juice of grapes,' used in its etymological and extended senses in combination with other English elements: **wineglass, winepress, wineskin.** Compare **vini-**.

2827 wing- A word-initial combining element, also occurring as a word, derived from Old Norse *væng(r)* 'organ of flight' (from the Indo-European root which underlies English *weather* and *wind*), used in its etymological and extended senses in combination with other English elements: **wingback, wingover, wingspan.** Related forms: **weather-, wind-, window-.**

2828 winter- A word-initial combining element, also occurring as a word, derived from Old English *winter* '(the) season between fall and spring,' used in its etymological and extended senses in combination with other English elements: **winterberry, winterkill, wintertime.** Related forms: **hydro-[1], wash-, water-, wet-.**

2829 wire- A word-initial combining element, also occurring as a word, derived from Old English *wīr* 'thin rod-shaped piece of metal' (from an Indo-European root meaning 'twist, turn'), used in its etymological and extended senses in combination with other English elements: **wire-draw, wire-haired, wiretap.** Related form: **irido-.**

2830 with- A word-initial combining element, also occurring as a word, derived from Old English *wiþ* 'opposing, away from' and, later, 'accompanying,' used chiefly in its earlier etymological and extended senses in combination with other English elements: **withdraw, withhold, without.** Related form: **wide-.**

2831 wolf- A word-initial combining element, also occurring as a word, derived from Old English *wulf* 'the doglike animal *Canis lupus*,' used in its etymological and extended senses in combination with other English elements: **wolfberry, wolf-boy, wolfhound.** Related form: **lyco-.**

2832 woman- A word-initial combining element, also occurring as a word, derived from Old English *wī(f)man(n)* 'adult female human being' (from *wīf* 'adult female human being' plus *man(n)* 'person'), used in its etymological sense in combination with other English elements: **woman-chaser, woman-hater, womanpower.** Compare **man-[2]**.

2833 wood- A word-initial combining element, also occurring as a word, derived from Old English *wud(u)* 'tree,' hence, 'group of trees growing in the same vicinity' and 'material of which a tree is composed,' used in its etymological and extended senses in combination with other English elements: **woodblock, woodpecker, woodpile.**

2834   **wool-**   A word-initial combining element, also occurring as a word, derived from Old English *wul(l)* 'fleece,' used in its etymological and extended senses in combination with other English elements: **woolgathering, woolgrower, woolskin.** Related forms: **flannel-, line-, villi-.**

2835   **word-**   A word-initial combining element, also occurring as a word, derived from Old English *word* 'discrete sound or group of sounds conveying a meaning,' used in its etymological and extended senses in combination with other English elements: **word-blind, word-of-mouth, wordplay.**

2836   **work-**   A word-initial combining element, also occurring as a word, derived from Old English *w(e)orc* 'that which is done; that which one does; labor,' used in its etymological and extended senses in combination with other English elements: **workbook, workday, workhorse.** Related forms: **ergasio-, ergo-[1], organo-.**

2837   **world-**   A word-initial combining element, also occurring as a word, derived from Old English *w(e)or(o)ld* 'human life,' literally, 'man's age' (from *wer* 'man' plus *ald, old* 'age'), hence, 'human society,' hence, 'the place in which human society exists, i.e., the earth, the universe,' used in its etymological and extended senses in combination with other English elements: **world-shaking, world-weary, worldwide.**

2838   **worm-**   A word-initial combining element, also occurring as a word, derived from Old English *wyrm* 'serpent, helminth' (from an Indo-European root meaning 'turn, bend'), used in the sense of 'helminth' and in extensions of this sense in combination with other English elements: **worm-eaten, wormhole, wormwood.** Related forms: **rhampho-, rhombo-, vermi-, vertebro-, wrist-.**

2839   **wrist-**   A word-initial combining element, also occurring as a word, derived from Old English *wrist* 'joint between the hand and the forearm' (from an Indo-European root meaning 'turn, bend'), used in its etymological sense in combination with other English elements: **wristband, wristdrop, wristlock.** Related forms: **rhampho-, rhombo-, vermi-, vertebro-, worm-.**

2840 write-   A word-initial combining element, also occurring as a word, derived from Old English *wrīt(an)* 'to inscribe,' used in its etymological and extended senses in combination with other English elements: **write-in, write-off, write-up.**

X

2841 **x-**   A word-initial combining element, the twenty-fourth letter of the English alphabet, used chiefly in the sense of 'unknown (quantity)' and 'shaped like the letter *x*' in combination with other English elements: **x-high, x-ray, x-stretcher.**

2842 **xantho-**   A word-initial combining element, derived from Greek *xanthó(s)* 'yellow,' used in its etymological and extended senses in Neo-Greek and Neo-Latin combinations: **xanthochromatic, xanthofibroma, xanthoprotein.** Also, **xan-, xanth-, zanth-, zantho-: xanchromatic, xanthemia, zanthine, zanthoxylum.**

2843 **xeno-**   A word-initial combining element, derived from Greek *xéno(s)* 'foreign(er),' used in its etymological and extended senses in Neo-Greek combinations: **xenodiagnosis, xenoparasite, xenophobia.** Also, **xen-: xenenthesis.**

2844 **xero-**   A word-initial combining element, derived from Greek *xēró(s)* 'dry,' used in its etymological and extended senses in Neo-Greek and Neo-Latin combinations: **xeroderma, xerography, xerophagia.** Also, **xer-: xerophthalmia.**

2845 **xi-** (Ξ, ξ)   A word-initial combining element, the fourteenth letter of the Greek alphabet, used chiefly to designate 'the fourteenth carbon atom in a straight chain compound or a derivative thereof in which the substitute group is attached to that atom' in chemical terminology. Also, **ksi-.** See **alpha-.**

2846 xipho- A word-initial combining element, derived from Greek *xipho(s)* 'sword,' used chiefly in the sense of 'of or pertaining to the *xiphoid process,* a sword-shaped bone which forms part of the sternum' in biomedical terminology: **xiphocostal, xiphodidymus, xiphopagotomy.** Also, **xiph-, xiphi-: xiphoid, xiphisternum.**

2847 xylo- A word-initial combining element, derived from Greek *xýlo(n)* 'wood,' used in its etymological and extended senses in Neo-Greek combinations: **xylograph, xylophone, xylopyranose.** Also, **xyl-: xylanthrax.**

Y

2848 yard- A word-initial combining element, also occurring as a word, derived from Old English *ġerd* 'staff, rod,' used in the extended sense of 'spar set at right angles to a mast' and 'unit of measurement equal to three feet' in combination with other English elements: **yardarm, yard-of-ale, yardstick.**

2849 year- A word-initial combining element, also occurring as a word, derived from Old English *ġēar* 'period of time spanning the four seasons,' used in its etymological and extended senses in combination with other English elements: **yearbook, year-end, yearling.** Related forms: **horo-, hour-.**

2850 yellow- A word-initial combining element, also occurring as a word, derived from Old English *ġe(o)lu* 'color of gold,' used in its etymological and extended senses in combination with other English elements: **yellow-bellied, yellowjacket, yellowweed.** Related forms: **arseno-, chlor-¹, chlor-², chole-, choler-, gall-, glass-, gold-, golden-.**

2851 yester- A word-initial combining element, derived from Old English *ġe(o)str(an)* 'the day before today,' used in the sense of 'of or pertaining to the period of time before the present one named by the combining root' and in extensions of this sense in combination with other English elements: **yesterday, yesterweek, yesteryear.**

Z

2852   **zantho-**   A variant of **xantho-**.

2853   **zeta-** (Z, ζ)   A word-initial combining element, the sixth letter of the Greek alphabet, used chiefly to designate 'the sixth carbon atom in a straight chain compound or a derivative thereof in which the substitute group is attached to that atom' in chemical terminology. See **alpha-**.

2854   **zo-**   A variant of **zoo-**.

2855   **zoni-**   A word-initial combining element, derived through Latin from Greek *zôn(ḗ)* 'girdle, belt,' plus the combining vowel *-i-*, used in its etymological and extended senses, chief among these being 'of or pertaining to an area with definable boundaries, esp. an encircling area,' in Neo-Greek and Neo-Latin combinations: **zoniferous, zonifugal, zoniferous.** Also, **zon-, zono-: zonesthesia, zonociliate.**

2856   **zoo-**   A word-initial combining element, derived from Greek *zôo(n)* 'living being, animal,' used in its etymological and extended senses in Neo-Greek and Neo-Latin combinations: **zoo-agglutinin, zoogeography, zoopharmacy.** Also, **zo-: zoanthropic.** Related forms: **bio-, quick-, vita-[1], vivi-**.

2857   **zygo-[1]**   A word-initial combining element, derived from Greek *zygó(n)* 'yoke,' used in the sense of 'yoked, joined' and in extensions of that sense in Neo-Greek combinations: **zygodactyly, zygoneure, zygoplast**. Also, **zyg-: zygapophysis**. Compare **zygomatico-**. Related form: **juxta-**.

2858   **zygo-²**   A variant of **zygomatico-**.

2859   **zygomatico-**   A word-initial combining element, derived from Greek *zýgōma, zygṓmat(os)* 'the malar bone or the arch that the malar bone forms with the other bones to which it is connected' (from *zyg(ón)* 'yoke' plus the noun-forming suffix *-ōma* which denotes 'swelling,' the zygoma being so named because it 'yokes' the bones of the face together with those of the skull) plus the adjective-forming suffix *-ic* plus the combining vowel *-o-*, used in its etymological sense in biomedical terminology: **zygomaticofacial, zygomaticofrontal, zygomaticosphenoid**. Also, **zygo-²: zygomaxillary**. Compare **zygo-¹**.

2860   **zymo-**   A word-initial combining element, derived from Greek *zým(ē)* 'leaven' plus the combining vowel *-o-*, used chiefly in the sense of 'of or pertaining to fermentation or to enzymes' in Neo-Greek and Neo-Latin combinations: **zymochemistry, zymoexcitator, zymogenic**. Also, **zym-: zymase**.

Index

Index

405

acetyloxyphenol, 17
acetylsulfathiazole, 17
achroa-, 22
achroacytosis, 22
achromo-, 19, 20, 22
achroo-, 18
achrooamyloid, 22
achroocytosis, 22
achroodextrin, 22
áchroo(s), 22
acid, 23
'acid', 2210
acid-, 12, 16, 25, 28, 29,
868, 1875
acidalbumin, 23
acid-fast, 23
acidi-, 23
'acidic', 1871, 1875, 1876
acidimeter, 23
acido-, 23
acidocytopenia, 23
acidosis, 23
acīd(us), 23
'acorn', 31, 204
acouesthesia, 24
acoulalion, 24
acoumeter, 24
acouo-, 24
acouophonia, 24
acouto-, 24
acoutometer, 24
acquire, 11
acr-, 25
'acrid', 246
acro-, 12, 16, 23, 26, 28,
29, 868, 1875
acro-ataxia, 25
acromioclavicular, 26
acromiohumeral, 26
acromion, 26
acromiothoracic, 26
acronyx, 25
acroparalysis, 25
acrophobia, 25
'across', 764, 768, 769,
2661, 2662
actin-, 27
actini-, 27
actiniform, 27
actinism, 27
actinochemistry, 27
actinogenesis, 27
actinotoxemia, 27

'act of seeing', 2555
acu-, 12, 16, 23, 25, 29,
868, 1875
acuclosure, 28
acūere, 29
acupuncture, 28
acu(s), 28
acusection, 28
'acute', 2315
acuti-, 12, 16, 23, 25, 28,
868, 1875
acutifoliate, 29
acutilingual, 29
acutilobate, 29
acūt(us), 29
ad, 6, 11, 30, 34, 35, 43,
45, 50, 95, 128, 136,
159, 168
ad-, 6, 11, 35, 41, 43, 50,
95, 128, 136, 159, 168,
1316
ad-, 41
adamant(is), 767
adámant(os), 767
adamās, 767
address, 30
adēn, 31
aden-, 31
adeno-, 1520
adenocarcinoma, 31
adenoid, 31
adenology, 31
adén(os), 31
adenovirus, 31
adep(s), 33
adhere, 30
'adhesion', 45, 111
α-dinitrophenol, 71
adip-, 33
adipic, 33
adip(is), 33
adipocellular, 33
adipofibroma, 33
adipolysis, 33
adipos-, 33
'adipose', 972
'adipose matter', 972
'adipose tissue', 1797
adiposuria, 33
adjective, 30
admire, 30
adnectere, 34
adnex(a), 34

adnexectomy, 34
adnexitis, 34
adnexo-, 34
adnexogenesis, 34
adnexorganogenic, 34
adopt, 30
adren-, 35
adrenal glands, 35
adrenic, 35
adrenocortical, 35
adrenopause, 35
adrenotoxin, 35
'adult', 2135
'adult human', 1546
'adult (male) person', 848
'adult person', 848
advertise, 30
aedoeocephalus, 36
aedoeoptosis, 36
aedoeotomy, 36
æf, 4
ǣfre, 950, 951, 1724
ǣfrić, 951
æfter, 42
aego-, 873
aegobronchophony, 37
Aegocerus, 37
aegophonic, 37
ǣl, 869
ælf, 887
aelur-, 38
aeluro-, 889
aelurophile, 38
aelurophobia, 38
aeluropodous, 38
aeluropsis, 38
æniġ, 125
āēr, 39, 48
aer-, 39
aerenchyma, 39
aeri-, 39
aeriform, 39
āer(is), 39
aero-, 48, 98, 1539
aerocystography, 39
aero-embolism, 39
aeropause, 39
aér(os), 39
aetio-, 944
aetiological, 944
af-, 6, 11, 30, 43, 50, 95,
128, 136, 159, 168

algiovascular, 58
algo-, 57, 58
algolagnia, 59
algometer, 59
algophobia, 59
álgo(s), 57, 58, 59
ali-, 195, 196
aliform, 60
alinasal, 60
alinjection, 54
-*ālis)*, 1744
alisphenoid, 60
'alive', 2162, 2790
alk-[1], 54
alk-[2], 64
alkal-, 64
alkalemia, 64
alkali, 64, 1383
alkali-, 63, 1383
alkaligenous, 64
alkalimeter, 64
alkalipenia, 64
alkalo-, 64
alkalotherapy, 64
alkamine, 62
alkargen, 64
al-koh'l, 54, 62
Alk(ohol), 62
alkozide, 62
alkyl, 62
(e)all, 65
'all', 951, 1799, 1892, 1894
all-[2], 69
allant-, 67
allantiasis, 67
allantochorion, 67
allantoinuria, 67
allantois, 67
allânt(os), 67
allantotoxicon, 67
allâ(s), 67
allelo-, 69, 72, 2723
allelocatalysis, 68
allelomorph, 68
allēlō(n), 68
allelotaxis, 68
allergy, 69
alleviate, 50
allheal, 65
all-important, 65
allo-, 66, 68, 70, 72, 2723
allocentric, 69

allolalia, 69
állos, 68, 69, 70
'allotment', 523
allotransplantation, 69
allotri-, 70
allotrio-, 69, 72, 2723
allotriogeustia, 70
allotriolith, 70
allotriophagy, 70
allótrio(s), 70
allotriuria, 70
'allotropic oxygen', 1878
allow, 50
alloy, 50
all-purpose, 65
'ally', 2376
'almond', 91
'almond-shaped organ', 91
'almost', 1941
'aloft', 1284
'alone', 1296
'along with', 1618
'alongside', 311
alpha-, 71, 230, 444, 740,
   926, 939, 1066, 1354,
   1384, 1448, 1670, 1757,
   1796, 1798, 1979, 2008,
   2124, 2204, 2335, 2539,
   2593, 2731, 2845, 2853
'alphabetic sign', 1476
alpha-brass, 71
alpha-ray, 71
alt-, 73
altazimuth, 73
alter, 72
alter-, 69, 2723
alterative, 72
altercation, 72
alteregoism, 72
alti-, 1790
altigraph, 73
altimeter, 73
altivolant, 73
alto-, 73
altocumulus, 73
alt(us), 73
'alum', 74
alūm(en), 74
aluminate, 74
alūmin(is), 74
aluminite, 74

aluminize, 74
alumino-, 74
aluminosilicate, 74
aluminum, 74
'aluminum', 74
alveol-, 75
alveolectomy, 75
alveoloclasia, 75
alveolodental, 75
alveolotomy, 75
alveol(us), 75
'always', 950, 951
am-, 892
amail, 81
amb-, 77
'amber', 883, 2493
ambi-, 79, 88
ambi-, 77
ambidextrous, 77
ambient, 77
ambilateral, 77
ambivalent, 77
amblyaphia, 78
amblygeustia, 78
amblypod, 78
amblý(s), 78
ambō, 77, 79
ambo-, 77, 89
amboceptor, 79
ambomalleal, 79
ambosexual, 79
ambush, 892
ameb-, 80
ameba-, 87
amebacide, 80
amebadiastase, 80
amebaism, 80
amebi-, 80
amebiasis, 80
amebiform, 80
amebo-, 80
amebocyte, 80
ameloblast, 81
amelodental, 81
amelogenesis, 81
amid-, 82
amidase, 82
amide, 82
amido-, 83, 85, 765, 1306
amidobenzene, 82
amidohexose, 82
amidopyrine, 82

amin-, 83
aminase, 83
amine, 83
'amine', 2787
Amine, 2787
amino-, 82, 85, 766, 1307,
  2787
aminoacidemia, 83
aminobenzene, 83
aminopeptidase, 83
ammo-, 2122, 2245
Ammobium, 84
ammochryse, 84
Ammocrypta, 84
ammon-, 85
Ámmōn, 85
ammonemia, 85
ammoni-, 82, 83
ammonia, 82, 83, 85
(*sal*) *ammoni*(*acus*), 85
ammoniemia, 85
ammonification, 85
ammonirrhea, 85
'ammonium chloride
  (NH₄Cl)', 85
ammono-, 85
ammonolysis, 85
ámmo(*s*), 84
amniocentesis, 86
amnío(*n*), 86
amnion-, 86
amnionitis, 86
amnioplastin, 86
amniorrhexis, 86
amnós, 86
amoeb-, 80
amoeba-, 80
amoeba-movement, 80
amoebi-, 80
amoebiform, 80
amoebo-, 80
Amoebobacter, 80
amoeboid, 80
amoibḗ, 80
'among', 897, 913, 1618
amorphous, 2
'amount', 2157
amph-, 88
ampheclesis, 88
amphí, 88
amphi-, 77, 89
amphibious, 88
amphiblastic, 88

amphicentric, 88
ámphō, 88, 89
ampho-, 79, 88
amphodiplopia, 89
amphogenic, 89
amphotony, 89
Amūn, 85
'amuse', 2431
amygdal-, 91
amygdalase, 91
amygdál(*ē*), 91
amygdalolith, 91
amygdalophenin, 91
amygdalothrypsis, 91
Amygdalus persica, 1926
amyl, 92
amyl-, 92
amylemia, 92
amyloclastic, 92
amylodextrin, 92
amyloprolamine, 92
ámylos, 92
amyl(*um*), 92
amyoesthesis, 93
amyoplasia, 93
amyostasia, 93
ān, 5, 125, 1735, 1802,
  1805
an-¹, 2, 98, 105, 109, 110,
  115, 1286, 1298, 1303,
  1311, 1355, 1723, 1724,
  1735, 1739, 1760, 2724
an-², 6, 11, 30, 41, 43, 50,
  128, 136, 159, 168
an-³, 97
a(*n*)-, 2, 13, 22, 44, 92, 93,
  94, 95, 115, 116, 164,
  165, 169, 170, 174, 197,
  2687
-(*a*)*n*, 1325, 1368
aná, 97, 99, 106, 113
ana-, 96, 100, 106, 113,
  1802
anabiosis, 97
anabolism, 97
anachoresis, 97
analgesic, 94
anaphylact-, 99
anaphylactia, 99
anaphylactogen, 99
anaphylactogenesis, 99
anaphylactotoxin, 99

anaphylaxis, 99
anarchy, 94
anatémnein, 100
Anatidae, 838
'anatomical cul-de-sac',
  391
anatomicomedical, 100
anatomicopathological,
  100
anatomicosurgical, 100
anatomikó(*s*), 100
anatomy, 100
anchyl-, 111
anchylo-, 111
anchyloblepharon, 111
anchylosis, 111
'ancient', 140
ancyclostomiasis, 111
ancyl-, 111
ancylo-, 111
ancylotic, 111
andr-, 103
andranatomy, 103
andro-, 1157
androgalactozemia, 103
androgen, 103
andrology, 103
andr(*ós*), 103
anemopathy, 104
anemophilous, 104
anemophobia, 104
ánemo(*s*), 104
an(*ḗr*), 103
anerythropsia, 97
-*āneum*, 317
aneurysm, 106
aneurysm-, 106
aneúrysm(*a*), 106
aneurysmectomy, 106
aneurysmograph, 106
aneurysmoplasty, 106
aneurysmotomy, 106
anew, 4
ang(*e*)*îo*(*n*), 107, 461
angi-, 107
angiectomy, 107
angio-, 461, 1207, 1521
angioblast, 107
angiocarditis, 107
angioscopy, 107
'angle', 1121, 1777, 2674
'angle(d)', 348

Anglo-, 111, 1804, 2727
Anglo-American, 108
Anglophobe, 108
Anglo-Saxon, 108
Angl(us), 108
Anguilla, 869
angul, 108
Angul, 108
ani-, 114
anilinction, 114
'animal', 737, 2590, 2592, 2856
'animal hide', 306
'animate existence', 1483
'ankle bone', 166, 2535
ankyl-, 111
ankýl(ē), 111
ankylo-, 101, 102, 108, 1804, 2727
ankylochilia, 111
ankyloglossia, 111
ankylomele, 111
ankylurethria, 111
annihilate, 95
annotate, 95
announce, 95
annul-, 114
Annulaceae, 112
annulet, 112
annulose, 112
annul(us), 112
ánō, 113
ano-¹, 97, 1802
ano-², 112
anoderm, 114
anodyne, 94
'anoint', 662
'Anointed One', 475
anomal-, 115
anomalogonatous, 115
anomalopia, 115
anŏmalo(s), 115
anomaloscope, 115
anomalotrophy, 115
anomocarpous, 116
Anomoean, 116
anomophyllous, 116
ánomo(s), 116
anoneme, 113
anoopsia, 113
anoperineal, 114
Anopheles, 1539
anorectal, 114

'another', 68, 69, 70
anotropia, 113
Anser, 1128
'ant', 1040, 1700
ant-, 123
antacid, 123
ante, 118, 119
ante-, 119, 123, 902, 2725
antefebrile, 118
antenuptial, 118
anteposition, 118
anter(ior), 119
'anterior', 2103, 2112
'anterior surface of the chest', 279
antero-, 118, 123, 902, 2725
anterograde, 119
antero-internal, 119
anteroposterior, 119
anth-, 120
anthema, 120
anthobian, 120
anthocarpous, 120
anthophore, 120
ántho(s), 120
anthra-, 121
anthrac-, 121
anthracene, 121
anthracometer, 121
anthraconecrosis, 121
anthracosilicosis, 121
ánthrak(os), 121
anthraquinone, 121
ánthra(x), 121
anthropogenesis, 122
anthropolatry, 122
anthropophage, 122
ánthrōpo(s), 122
anti, 123, 899
anti-, 117, 118, 899, 902, 2725
antiblastic, 123
anti-intellectual, 123
antimatter, 123
'antimony', 2462
'antimony sulfide', 54, 62
antíos, 899
antr-, 124
antritis, 124
antrodynia, 124
ántro(n), 124

antronasal, 124
antroscope, 124
Anura, 1049
ān(us), 112, 114
'anus', 2105
any, 2729
'any', 125, 1760
any-, 878, 1805
anybody, 125
anyhow, 125
'anything swollen', 1429
anyway, 125
aort-, 126
aortarctia, 126
aort(ē), 126
aortico-, 126
aorticorenal, 126
aorto-, 156
aortoclasia, 126
aortolith, 126
aortosclerosis, 126
ap-, 128, 133
ap-¹, 131
ap-², 6, 11, 30, 41, 43, 50, 95, 133, 136, 159, 168
'ap-²', 133
apandria, 131
'apart', 730, 742, 803, 2822
'apart from', 2282
'ape', 1660
aperture, 3
ap(ex), 130
'apex', 2624
aphasia, 2
'Aphrodite', 711
apiary, 129
apic-, 130
apical, 130
apic(is), 130
apicoectomy, 130
apicosan, 129
apicostome, 130
apicotomy, 130
apiculture, 129
api(s), 129
A-plant, 1
apó, 131, 132
apo-, 3, 8, 10, 42, 127, 132, 1785
apoatropine, 131
apocoptic, 131

apolegamy, 131
aponeur-, 132
aponeurectomy, 132
aponeurology, 132
aponeurorrhaphy, 132
aponeúrō(sis), 132
aponeurotomy, 132
apparatus, 128
'apparent', 1971
'apparition', 2404
'appear', 874, 1295, 1971, 1974
'appearance', 1295
'appease', 1923
append, 128
append-, 133
'appendages', 34
appendalgia, 133
appendic-, 133
appendic(is), 133
appendicitis, 133
appendicocecostomy, 133
appendicolithiasis, 133
appendicopathy, 133
appendi(x), 133
'apple', 1593
'appliance', 2597
'appraise', 2543, 2545
'approach', 588
approve, 128
aqu-, 135
aqua, 135
aquacade, 135
aqualung, 135
aquaplane, 135
aqueduct, 135
aqui-, 135
aquifer, 135
aquila, 856
(avis) aquila, 856
ar-, 6, 11, 30, 41, 43, 50, 95, 128, 159, 168
ar-, 136
-ar, 318
(gum) arab(ic), 2210
arabin(ose), 2210
'arabinose', 2210
arachn-, 137
aráchn(ē), 137
arachnid, 137
arachnodactylia, 137
arachnogastria, 137
arachnolysin, 137

àràhkunem, 610
araió(s), 147
Araneae, 2413
'arch', 269, 334
arch-[1], 141
arch-[2], 140, 141, 145, 146
archa-, 140
archae-, 140
archaeal, 140
archaeo-, 139, 141, 142, 143, 146
archaeological, 140
archaeopteryx, 140
Archaeozoic, 140
archaic, 140
archaîo(s), 140
archamphiaster, 141
archangel, 139
archdeacon, 139
archḗ, 141
arche-[1], 138, 139, 140, 144, 146
arche-[2], 140
archebiosis, 141
archecentric, 141
'arched', 334, 607
'arched roof', 334
archenemy, 139
archeo-, 140
archeology, 140
archespore, 141
archetype, 140
archi-[1], 141
archi-[2], 139
archiblast, 141
architect, 139
archo-, 139, 140, 141
archocele, 146
archoptoma, 146
archorrhea, 146
archó(s), 139, 146
'(measured) area', 590
areocardia, 147
areocentric, 148
areographic, 148
areology, 148
areometry, 147
areostyle, 147
Áré(s), 148.
argentaffine, 149
argenti-, 149
argentic, 149

argentiferous, 149
argentite, 149
argento-, 149
argentophil, 149
argent(um), 149
argyranthous, 150
argyremia, 150
argyro-, 150
argyron, 150
argyrophil, 150
árgyr(os), 150
-āris, 350, 2076
arise, 7
aristo-, 152, 153, 157, 158
aristocrat, 151
aristogenics, 151
áristo(s), 151
aristotype, 151
ārium, 1864
-ārius, 320, 628, 2158, 2214
(e)arm, 152
'arm', 152, 272, 882, 2719
arm-[1], 151, 153, 157, 158
arm-[2], 151, 152, 157, 158
arma, 153
arm(āre), 153
armband, 152
armchair, 152
arm(er), 153
armhole, 152
armiger, 153
armistice, 153
'armpit', 60, 1557
army, 153
'army', 512
'aromatic resin', 229
'around', 77, 88, 497, 905, 1954, 1955, 1956, 1957, 1959
'arouse', 955
arraign, 136
arrange, 136
'arrange', 591, 825, 826, 1833
'arrangement', 169, 2546
arrest, 136
'arrest', 435, 2469
árrhen, 154
arrhenoblastoma, 154
arrhenogenic, 154
arrhenotoky, 154

'arrive', 588
ar(s), 158
ars-, 155
arsen-, 155
arsenic, 155
arsenic, 155
arsen(ikón), 155
arseno, 155
arseno-, 457, 462, 1061,
1097, 1112, 2850
arseno-autohemotherapy,
155
arsenobenzol, 155
arsenoresistant, 155
arsphenamine, 155
'art', 158, 2549
'art of healing', 1578
arteri-, 156
artērí(a), 156
arteriectasia, 156
arterio-, 126
arterioatony, 156
arteriogenesis, 156
arteriosclerosis, 156
'arteriosclerosis', 171
'artery', 156
arthr-, 157
arthritis, 157
arthro-, 151, 152, 153, 158
arthroclasia, 157
arthroendoscopy, 157
árthro(n), 157
arthropathy, 157
arti-, 151, 152, 153, 157
artifact, 158
artifex, 158
artificial, 158
art(is), 158
as-, 6, 11, 30, 41, 43, 50,
95, 128, 136, 168
as-, 159
ascariasis, 160
ascaricide, 160
ascarid-, 160
ascaridosis, 160
ascariosis, 160
ascend, 6
'ascend', 528
ascocarp, 161
ascogonium, 161
Ascomycetes, 161
ashamed, 7
'ashes', 2427

A-ship, 1
askarí(dos), 160
askarí(s), 160
askó(s), 161
asleep, 5.1
'as much as', 2157
asperg(ere), 163
aspergillar, 163
aspergillin, 163
aspergillo-, 163
aspergillomycosis, 163
aspergillosis, 163
Aspergillus, 163
aspiration, 6
assemble, 159
'assembly of people', 641
assent, 159
'assessed payment', 2543
assimilate, 159
asthen-, 164
asthen(és), 164
asthenobiosis, 164
asthenocoria, 164
asthenophobia, 164
asthenopia, 164
astigmagraph, 165
astigmat-, 165
astigmatism, 165
astigmatism, 165
astigmato-, 165
astigmatoscope, 165
astigmia, 165
astigmic, 165
astigmo-, 165
astigmometer, 165
'as though', 2160
astragal-, 166
astragalar, 166
astragalo-, 1852, 1853
astragalocalcanean, 166
astragalomancy, 166
astrágalo(s), 166
astragaloscaphoid, 166
astride, 5.2
astringent, 6
'astringent', 2488
astro-, 2442
astrocyte, 167
astrology, 167
ástro(n), 167
astrophysics, 167
asunder, 5.1

'asunder', 730, 742, 753,
762, 776, 795
asymmetry, 2
at, 30
'at', 877, 891, 897, 899,
903, 2110, 2112, 2113
at-, 6, 11, 41, 43, 50, 95,
128, 136, 159
at-, 168
'at a distance', 2195
'at a good bargain', 434
'at a good price', 434
'at a great bargain', 434
'at a great distance', 968
'at a great price', 434
'at all times', 950
atax-, 169
ataxaphasia, 169
ataxi-, 169
ataxía, 169
ataxiadynamia, 169
ataxiagraph, 169
ataxiamnesic, 169
ataxiaphasia, 169
ataxio-, 169
ataxiophemia, 169
ataxo-, 169
ataxophobia, 169
-ate, 1988
atel-, 170
atelectasis, 170
atel(és), 170
atelocardia, 170
ateloencephalia, 170
ateloprosopia, 170
at good cheape, 434
at greate cheape, 434
'Athenian', 176
ather-, 171
athér(ē), 171
atherocheuma, 171
atherogenesis, 171
atheroma, 171
atheronecrosis, 171
'at intervals', 913
-ation, 2076
atlant-, 172
atlantal, 172
atlantoaxial, 172
atlantodidymus, 172
atlantomastoid, 172
Átlant(os), 172

'Atlas', 172
Átlas, 172
atlo-, 172
atlodidymus, 172
atm-, 173
atmiatrics, 173
atmocausis, 173
atmograph, 173
atmó(s), 173
atmosphere, 173
'atmosphere', 39, 48
'atmospheric condition', 2806
'atmospheric phenomenon', 1620
'at no time', 1724
atomic, 1
atomic energy, 1
'atop', 1802
atret-, 174
atretocephalus, 174
atretogastria, 174
atretometria, 174
atretopsia, 174
átrēto(s), 174
atrionector, 175
atriotomy, 175
atrioventricular, 175
atrium, 175
Atrop(a), 2687
'atropine', 2687
Átropos, 2687
'attach', 34, 151, 152, 153, 157, 158
'attack', 435
attempt, 168
attend, 168
'at the back', 1234
'at the table of', 1906
attic, 176
attic-, 176
atticitis, 176
atticoantrotomy, 176
atticomastoid, 176
atticotomy, 176
Attic(us), 176
attract, 168
-*ātus*, 621
'at which time', 2814
'Au', 1112
audi-, 177
audiclave, 177
audiology, 177

audiometry, 177
audio-visual, 177
audī(re), 177
auga, 2825
'auger', 2693
'auger-bodied', 2693
aur-[1], 180
aur-[2], 181
aural, 180
auri-[1], 178, 182, 183, 857, 1857
auri-[2], 179, 184, 1837, 1841
auriargentiferous, 181
auricul-, 182
auricul(a), 182
auriculid, 182
auriculo-, 180, 857, 1857
auriculocranial, 182
auriculotemporal, 182
auriculoventricular, 182
auride, 181
aurilave, 180
auriphrygia, 181
auripuncture, 180
auri(s), 180, 182
auriscope, 180
aurivorous, 181
auro-[1], 180
auro-[2], 181
aurocephalous, 181
aurometer, 180
aur(um), 181
auster, 188
Austr-[1], 187
Austr-[2], 188
Australia, 188
Austrasia, 187
austr(ī), 188
Austr(ia), 187
'Austria', 187
austro-, 188
Austro-[1], 185, 914
Austro-[2], 186
Austro-Asiatic, 188
Austrocolumbia, 188
Austro-Germanic, 187
Austro-Hungarian, 187
austromancy, 188
Austronesian, 188
Austro-Prussian, 187
aut-, 189

autarcesis, 189
'authority', 2096
autó, 2542
auto-[1], 190, 2542
auto-[2], 189
autoanalysis, 189
autoblood, 189
autobus, 190
autocade, 190
autologous, 189
auto(mobile), 190
'automobile', 357
'automotive', 190
autó(s), 189, 190
autotruck, 190
'autumn', 1178
aux-, 193
auxán(ein), 192
auxano-, 193, 2793
auxanogram, 192
auxanography, 192
auxanology, 192
aúx(ein), 192, 193
auxesis, 193
auxi-, 193
auxilytic, 193
auxo-, 191, 192, 2793
auxocardia, 193
auxodrome, 193
auxoflore, 193
avert, 3
avi-, 871, 1809, 1866
aviation, 194
aviculture, 194
avifauna, 194
avi(s), 194
avoid, 3
'avoid', 2355
awash, 5.2
'away', 7, 10, 753, 762, 776, 795, 2431
'away from', 3, 8, 10, 131, 729, 854, 896, 953, 954, 959, 1785, 1787, 2830
'away from inside', 1862
'awkward', 1127
'ax', 1180
*ax-, 60
axi-, 195
axifugal, 195
axio-, 60, 196
axiobuccal, 195

boviculture, 268
bovid, 268
bovine, 268
'bovine mammal', 1869
bov(is), 225, 268
bovo-, 268
bovovaccination, 268
Bovril, 268
'bow', 882, 2650
bowdrill, 269
'bowel', 910
bowgrace, 270
bowknot, 269
'bowl', 86, 690, 799
'bowl-shaped', 1397
bowman, 270
bowsprit, 270
bowstring, 269
'box', 355, 376, 378, 2582
boxcar, 271
boxhead, 271
box-spring, 271
'box-tree', 271
'boxwood', 271
'Br', 287
-bra, 2770
brachi-, 272
brachialgia, 272
brachio-, 273, 282, 1612
brachiocrural, 272
brachiocyrtosis, 272
brachiō(n), 272
brachiopod, 272
brachy-, 272, 282, 1612
brachybasia, 273
brachydactylia, 273
brachymorphic, 273
brachý(s), 272, 273
Brachyura, 650
brād, 284
bradycardia, 274
bradycrotic, 274
bradylexia, 274
bradý(s), 274
bræ(ǧe)n, 275
'brain', 413, 414, 900
brainchild, 275
brainpan, 275
brainwash, 275
'branch', 2175
branchi-, 276
bránchi(a), 276
branchiform, 276

branchiogenous, 276
branchiopneustic, 276
branchiostegal, 276
'brand', 165
'branding iron', 388
'brass', 424
Brassica, 569
brēad, 277
'bread to be dipped', 2392
breadbasket, 277
breadboard, 277
breadfruit, 277
'break apart', 2426
'break down', 661
breakdown, 278
'breakdown in mental health', 661
'breaking down of cells', 1525
breakthrough, 278
breakwater, 278
'breast', 1543, 1544, 1560, 1561, 1569, 2459, 2460
breastbone, 279
'breastbone', 2459
breast-feed, 279
breast-hook, 279
'breastplate', 2601, 2602
'breast-shaped', 1561
'breath', 104, 737, 847, 2006, 2063, 2066, 2127, 2598, 2612
'breathe', 2063, 2066, 2068, 2420
brēč, 280
brec(an), 278
breechblock, 280
breechcloth, 280
breechloader, 280
'breeding sow', 2281
brēost, 279
breph-, 281
brephic, 281
brephoplastic, 281
brephopolyscaria, 281
brépho(s), 281
brephotrophic, 281
'Bretonese', 400
brevi-, 272, 273, 1612
brevicaudate, 282
brevicollis, 282
brevipennate, 282

brevi(s), 282
brid(d), 240, 241
'(young) bride', 1763
bridgehead, 283
bridgeman, 283
bridgework, 283
'bright', 519, 1453, 1477
'brightness', 1485, 1514
'brimstone', 2498, 2598
'bring back', 2189
'bring in(to)', 1330
'bring into agreement', 595
'bring into contact', 2644
'bring to light', 1975
'bring together', 547
'bringing in', 1330
'bristle', 421, 2310, 2422
'broad', 106, 947, 2033, 2046, 2822
broadax, 284
broadband, 284
'broad shallow container', 1891
broadside, 284
'broad (way)', 2033
broce, 296
bro(i)sse, 296
'broken rock', 2257
brōm, 294
brom-¹, 286
brom-², 287
brôma, 285, 2588
broma-, 285
bromacetone, 287
bromatherapy, 285
bromatology, 285
brômat(os), 285
bromatotherapy, 285
bromatotoxin, 285
brom(e), 294
bromidrosis, 286
bromine, 287
bromo-¹, 287
brom(o)-², 286, 2669
bromobenzylcyanide, 287
bromohyperhidrosis, 286
bromomenorrhea, 286
bromomethylethyl, 287
bromophenol, 287
bromopnea, 286
brôm(os), 286, 287

carcino-, 344, 1175, 1385
carcinogenic, 360
carcinology, 360
carcinolysin, 360
card-, 362, 373
'(playing) card', 373
'card wool', 367
cardboard, 361
card-carrying, 361
card(e), 361
cardi-, 362
cardialgia, 362
Cardiff, 356
cardio, 1692
cardio-, 13, 621, 622,
  1186, 1692, 1955
cardio-accelerator, 362
cardiocentesis, 362
cardiokinetic, 362
carditis, 362
cardsharp, 361
'care', 1042
carefree, 363
caretaker, 363
careworn, 363
cari(er), 371
Carlisle, 356
carload, 357
carman, 357
carn-, 364
Carnarvon, 356
carne-, 364
carneous, 364
carni-, 623, 624, 632,
  2278, 2280, 2281, 2315,
  2321, 2324
carniferrin, 364
carnigen, 364
carnine, 364
carn(is), 364
carnivorous, 364
carno-, 364
carnophobia, 364
car(ō), 364
carōt(a), 365
caroten-, 414, 417, 418,
  629, 657, 1095, 1177,
  1259, 1393
carotene, 365
carotenemia, 365
carotenoid, 365
carotenosis, 365
carotin-, 365

carotinase, 365
carp-, 369
carpere, 367
carpet(a), 367
carpetbag, 367
carpet-cut, 367
carpetweed, 367
carpholite, 368
carphology, 368
carphosiderite, 368
carpitis, 369
carpo-¹, 366, 2817
carpocarpal, 369
carpogonium, 370
carpopedal, 369
carpophagous, 370
carpophore, 370
carpoptosis, 369
carport, 357
carr, 357
'carriage', 372
'(horse-drawn) carriage',
  546
'carrot', 365
car(rus), 357, 371
'carry', 937, 1810, 1984,
  2090, 2431
carry-, 357
carryall, 371
carry-back, 371
'carrying', 1810, 2090
carry-over, 371
'cart', 371, 546
cart-horse, 372
'cartilage', 468
'(ring-shaped) cartilage',
  670
cartload, 372
carto-, 361, 432
cartogram, 373
cartography, 373
cartomancy, 373
cartwright, 372
cary-, 1385
caryo-, 1385
caryocinesis, 1385
caryopsis, 1385
case-², 355, 378, 383
case-³, 437
casebook, 375
casebound, 376
casefy, 377

caseharden, 376
casein, 377
caseload, 375
caseo-, 377
caseogenous, 377
caseose, 377
cās(eus), 377, 437
caseworker, 375
caseworm, 376
cash-, 355, 376, 383
cashbook, 378
cashbox, 378
cashdrawer, 378
'casing', 890
'cask', 690
cass(ier), 378
'cast', 775
castaway, 379
cast(en), 379
cast-iron, 379
'castle', 356
cast-off, 379
cās(us), 375
'cat', 38
cat-², 382
cata-, 381, 386, 1386,
  1387
catabatic, 382
catalysis, 382
catamnesis, 382
cataphasia, 382
catcall, 380
catch-, 376, 378
'catch quickly', 2372
catchall, 383
catch-as-catch-can, 383
catch-cord, 383
'categorization', 512
caten-, 423
catēn(a), 384, 423
catenane, 384
catenate, 384
catenoid, 384
'caterpillar', 340
catfish, 380
catill(us), 1397
catnap, 380
cato-, 1387
catophoria, 1387
catoptromancy, 386
catoptrophobia, 386
catoptroscope, 386

'central part', 622, 1580,
  1758
centre-, 406
centreboard, 406
centri-, 407
centrifugal, 407
centro-, 406, 1390
centrocecal, 407
centrodorsal, 407
centroosteosclerosis, 407
cent(um), 405
centuple, 405
cephal-, 408
cephalalgia, 408
cephalo-, 15, 900, 1391
cephalodymia, 408
cephalogyric, 408
cephalomotor, 408
cer-¹, 415
ceraceous, 415
cerat-, 1393
ceratectomy, 1393
cerato-, 1393
ceratohyoid, 1393
cercocystitis, 412
cercolabine, 412
cercomonad, 412
cereal, 410
'cereal stocks or stems',
  2475
cerebell-, 413
cerebellar, 413
cerebelli-, 413
cerebellifugal, 413
cerebello-, 365, 414, 417,
  418, 629, 657, 1095,
  1177, 1259, 1393
cerebelloolivary, 413
cerebellopontile, 413
cerebellospinal, 413
cerebell(um), 413
cerebr-, 414
cerebrasthenia, 414
cerebri-, 414
cerebriform, 414
cerebro-, 365, 413, 417,
  418, 629, 657, 1095,
  1177, 1259, 1393
cerebrocentric, 414
cerebrology, 414
cerebroocular, 414
cerebr(um), 413, 414
Cer(ēs), 410

'Ceres', 410
cerite, 410
cerium, 410
cernere, 2286
cero-, 409, 1394, 1395
cerolysin, 415
ceromel, 415
ceroplasty, 415
'certain', 2389
cerv-, 417
cervanthropy, 417
cervi-¹, 418
cervi-², 365, 414, 418, 629,
  657, 1095, 1177, 1259,
  1393
cervic-, 418
cervical, 418
cervicaprine, 417
cervici-, 418
cervicide, 417
cerviciplex, 418
cervīc(is), 418
cervico-, 365, 414, 416,
  417, 629, 657, 1095,
  1177, 1259, 1393
cervicoaxillary, 418
cervicobuccal, 418
cervicoplasty, 418
cervicorn, 417
Cervidae, 737
cervimeter, 418
cervi(x), 418
cerv(us), 417
cess(o), 419
cesspipe, 419
cesspit, 419
cesspool, 419
(sē)cess(us), 419
Cetacea, 2811
cetacean, 420
cetane, 420
ceto-, 420
cetochelid, 420
cetyl, 420
ch, 761
chaet-, 421
chaet(a), 421
chaeti-, 421
chaetiferous, 421
chaeto-, 2422
chaetodont, 421
chaetognath, 421

chaetophorous, 421
chaetotaxy, 421
chaff-flower, 422
chaff-seed, 422
chaffweed, 422
'chain', 384, 2480
chain-, 384
chainbreak, 423
chainsmoke, 423
chainstitch, 423
chait(ē), 421, 2422
chalc-, 426
chalcanthite, 424
chalco-, 424
chalcone, 424
chalcopyrite, 424
chalcosis, 424
'chalk', 339
chalk-¹, 322
chalk-², 424
chalkboard, 425
chalkitis, 424
chalk-line, 425
chalk(ós), 424
chalkstone, 425
chamae-, 429
chamaecephaly, 427
chamaelirium, 427
chamaeprosopy, 427
chamai, 427
'chamber', 395, 397
'(dark) chamber', 337
chamber-, 334, 337
chamberlain, 428
chambermaid, 428
chamber-pot, 428
chambre, 428
chame-, 427
chamecephalous, 427
chancr-, 344, 360, 1175,
  1385
chancr(e), 430
chancrelle, 430
chancri-, 430
chancriform, 430
chancroid, 430
chancrous, 430
'change', 80, 1530, 1575,
  1650, 2689, 2774
'changed', 1530, 1618
changeling, 431
changemaker, 431

chrŏs, 22
chrys-, 478
chrysanthemum, 478
chrysocreatinine, 478
chrysoderma, 478
chrysó(s), 478
chrysotherapy, 478
chuck-a-luck, 479
chuck-farthing, 479
chuckhole, 479
churchgoer, 480
churchman, 480
churchwarden, 480
chute, 1905
chyl-, 481
chyle, 481
chylemia, 481
chyli-, 481
chylifaction, 481
chylo-, 482, 1150
chylocyst, 481
chyloderma, 481
chylomediastinum, 481
chylό(s), 481
chym-, 482
chymase, 482
chyme, 482
chymeîa, 442
chymi-, 482
chymification, 482
chymo-, 481, 1150
chymopapain, 482
chymorrhea, 482
chymό(s), 482
chymotrypsin, 482
čîcen, 446
cicon-, 483
cicōni(a), 483
Ciconiidae, 483
ciconiiform, 483
ciconiine, 483
ciconine, 483
cider-brandy, 484
cider-mill, 484
cider-press, 484
čild, 448
cili-, 485
ciliectomy, 485
cilio-, 395, 570, 582, 1200, 1244
ciliogenesis, 485
cilioretinal, 485
ciliospinal, 485

cili(um), 485
cīm(ex), 486
cimici-, 486
cimicid, 486
cimicifugin, 486
cimicine, 486
cīmic(is), 486
cimicosis, 486
cin-, 1406
cinaesthesia, 1406
cinch-, 488
cinchamidine, 488
cincho-, 488
cinchon-, 488
cinchon(a), 488
Cinchona, 488, 2165
cinchonamine, 488
cinchonate, 488
cinchonine, 488
cinchonism, 488
cinchono-, 488
cinchonology, 488
cinchophen, 488
cine-[1], 1406
cine-[2], 955, 1402, 1403, 1404, 1406
cinefluorography, 490
cinema-, 490
cinemascopia, 490
cinemat-, 490
cinematic, 490
cinemato-, 490
cine(matograph), 490
cinematoradiography, 490
cineplasty, 1406
cineradiography, 490
cineroentgenography, 490
cines-, 1403
cinesalgia, 1403
cin(n), 451
cinn-, 492
'cinnabar', 1647
cinnaldehydum, 492
cinnamate, 492
cinnamic acid, 492
cinnamo-, 492
cinnamol, 492
Cinnamomum, 492
cinnamoyl, 492
cinnamyl, 492
cino-, 1406
cinology, 1406

cinq-, 494
cinqfoil, 494
cinque-[1], 977, 998, 1004, 1006, 1946, 2166
cinque-[2], 977, 998, 1004, 1006, 1946, 2166
cinquecento, 495
cinquedea, 495
cinquefoil, 494
cinque-pace, 494
cinque-port, 494
cion-, 496
cionectomy, 496
ciono-, 1407, 1408
cionoptosis, 496
cionorrhaphy, 496
cionotome, 496
ćip(p), 453
cipri-, 711
cipriphobia, 711
'circle', 497, 590, 704, 1161, 1829, 2212
'circular', 2225
circum, 497
circum-, 670
circumcorneal, 497
circumnavigate, 497
circumvallate, 497·
circus, 497
cirr-, 498
cirri-, 498
cirrigerous, 498
cirrocumulus, 498
cirropodous, 498
cirrose, 498
cirrostomous, 498
cirr(us), 498
cirs-, 499
cirsocele, 499
cirsodesis, 499
cirsomphalos, 499
cirsotome, 499
cis, 500
cis-, 1184, 1234
cisalpine, 500
cisatlantic, 500
cisvestitism, 500
citāre, 955
cite(t), 502
'citizenship', 502
citrate, 501
citrine, 501

climatometer, 527
climb, 528
climb(an), 528
climbing-fern, 528
climbing-fish, 528
climbing-irons, 528
climo-, 527
climograph, 527
clin-, 530
clinic, 530
clino-[1], 527, 530, 1443
clino-[2], 527, 529, 1443
Clinocoris, 530
clinodactyly, 529
clinomania, 530
clinoscope, 529
clinostatism, 529
clinotherapy, 530
clipboard, 531
clip-fed, 531
clip-on, 531
clisto-, 521
clistocarp, 521
clitor-, 533
clitorid-, 514, 515, 520,
   521, 538
clitoridauxe, 533
clitoridectomy, 533
clitoriditis, 533
'clitoris', 533
clitorism, 533
clitoro-, 533
clitorotomy, 533
'cloak', 456, 1889
cloak-, 535
cloak-and-dagger, 534
cloak-bag, 534
cloakroom, 534
clocca, 534, 535
clock-, 534
clockmaker, 535
clockwise, 535
'clockwise', 718.2
'clockwise direction',
   718.1
clockwork, 535
clod-, 541, 542, 1099,
   1100
clod(de), 536, 541
clodhopper, 536
clodpate, 536
clodpoll, 536
clog-almanac, 537

clog-burnisher, 537
clog-dance, 537
clog(ge), 537
'close', 514, 515, 533,
   1709, 1712, 2145, 2620
close-, 514, 515, 520, 521,
   533
'close(d)', 521, 2328
close-fertilization, 538
closefisted, 538
close-fitting, 538
'closer', 1712
'closet', 395, 397
'clot', 2606
'cloth', 1238
cloth-, 540
clothbound, 539
'clothes', 825
clothes-, 539
clotheshorse, 540
clothesline, 540
clothespin, 540
cloth-stitch, 539
cloth-yard, 539
'clotting of the blood',
   547
'cloud', 1718, 2362, 2710,
   2714
cloud-, 536, 542, 1099,
   1100
'cloud layer', 2474
cloudburst, 541
cloud-capped, 541
'clouding of the mind',
   2714
cloudland, 541
'cloudlike mist', 1026
'cloven', 1003
'club', 516
club-, 536, 541, 1099,
   1100
clubfoot, 542
'clubfoot', 317
clubhouse, 542
clubroot, 542
clūd, 541
Clupea harengus, 1225
'cluster of grapes', 266
'clustering (male) blos-
   som', 297
clyp(pan), 531
(ġe)cnāw(an), 1413

cnemapophysis, 543
cnemi-, 543
cnemial, 543
cnemidium, 543
cnemitis, 543
cnemo-, 543
cnemoscoliosis, 543
cnēo(w), 1410
cnid-, 544
cnidoblast, 544
cnidocyst, 544
cnidophore, 544
cnidosis, 544
cnoc(ian), 1411
cnot(ta), 1412
co-, 565, 586, 592, 614
co-, 545
'CO', 1396
coach-and-four, 546
coachman, 546
coachwork, 546
coactive, 545
coagulability, 547
coāgul(āre), 547
coagulin, 547
coagulo-, 547
coagulose, 547
coaguloviscosimeter, 547
coāgulum, 547
'coal', 121, 564
coal-, 564
coalbin, 548
coalfish, 548
coalmouse, 548
'coarse sand', 1137
coast-, 638
coastguardsman, 549
coastline, 549
coastward, 549
'coat', 534
coatdress, 550
coatroom, 550
coattail, 550
cocaine, 551
cocainidine, 551
cocainine, 551
cocainism, 551
cocaino-, 551
cocainomaniac, 551
cocc-, 552
coccal, 552
cocci-, 552

cradle-, 654, 655, 658, 665, 672, 673, 674, 1133
cradle-cap, 653
cradle-scythe, 653
cradlesong, 653
cradol, 653
cræt, 372
crāma, 662
cramp-[1], 653, 655, 658, 665, 672, 673, 674, 1133
cramp-[2], 653, 654, 658, 665, 672, 673, 674, 1133
cramp-bark, 655
cramp-bone, 655
cramp-drill, 654
cramp-iron, 654
cramp-joint, 654
cramp-stone, 655
cran, 656
cranc-, 658
crancstæf, 658
crane-fly, 656
crane-ladle, 656
crane-necked, 656
crani-, 657
craniamphitomy, 657
cranio-, 365, 414, 417, 418, 629, 1095, 1177, 1259, 1393
cranio-acromial, 657
craniobuccal, 657
craniodidymus, 657
crank-, 653, 654, 655, 665, 672, 673, 674, 1133
crankcase, 658
crankpin, 658
crankshaft, 658
cras(c)h(en), 659
cras(en), 659, 661
crash-, 661, 725
crash-dive, 659
crash-land, 659
crash-pad, 659
cratto, 653
crauno-, 666
craunotherapy, 666
'craw of a bird', 674
crāw(e), 676
'crawl', 1224
crazy-, 659

crazy-bone, 661
crazyweed, 661
crazywork, 661
cre-, 667
crea-, 667
'cream', 723
cream-, 475
cream-colored, 662
creamcups, 662
creamware, 662
creatin-, 667, 2179
creatinase, 663
creatinemia, 663
creatinuria, 663
creato-, 667
creatotoxism, 667
creatoxin, 667
creep, 665
'creep', 1224
'creep(er)', 2370, 2371
creeping-, 653, 654, 655, 658, 672, 673, 674, 1133
'creeping thing', 1224
creeping-disk, 665
creeping-jenny, 665
creeping-sailor, 665
creno-, 660
crenology, 666
crenotherapy, 666
Crenothrix, 666
creo-, 663, 664, 1423, 1894, 2179
creodont, 667
crēop(an), 665
creophagy, 667
creosote, 667
creotoxin, 667
cre(s)m(e), 662
'crest', 633, 677, 1510, 2642
'crested lark', 633
crestfallen, 668
crestfish, 668
crest-tile, 668
(se)cretion, 1321
crib, 669
crib-dam, 669
crib-strap, 669
cribwork, 669
cric-, 670
crico-, 497

cricoarytenoid, 670
cricoderma, 670
cricoid, 670
cricotracheotomy, 670
criocephalous, 671
criocerate, 671
criosphinx, 671
'crippled', 1960
crist(a), 668
crochet, 672
crochet-, 653, 654, 655, 658, 665, 673, 674, 1133
crochet-needle, 672
crochet-type, 672
crochetwork, 672
crook, 654
crook-, 653, 655, 658, 665, 672, 674, 1133
crookback, 673
'crooked', 111, 334, 343, 658, 665, 677, 692, 693, 2272
crookneck, 673
crook-rafter, 673
crop-, 653, 654, 655, 658, 665, 672, 673, 1133
crop-duster, 674
crop-eared, 674
cropland, 674
crop(p), 674
'cross', 678, 757, 758, 2447
cross-, 678
cross-bearer, 675
crossbones, 675
crosscurrent, 675
'crossed', 445, 2447
'crossing', 445
'crosslike', 678, 2447
'cross-shaped', 2447
'crow', 616
crowbar, 676
'crowd', 646
crowfoot, 676
crowhop, 676
'crowlike', 616
crown-, 693, 2212
crown-of-jewels, 677
crownpiece, 677
crownwork, 677
'crow's beak', 616

'division (of the Roman
  citizenry)', 512
d-menthol, 718.1, 760
'do', 228, 961, 962, 1792
do-, 962, 2582
do(c)g(a), 810
dochó(s), 464
dock(e), 808
'docked', 579
dockside, 808
dockwalloper, 808
dockyard, 808
'document', 1476
dodec-, 809
dodeca-, 843
dodecahedron, 809
dodecapetalous, 809
dodecarchy, 809
dodecasyllabic, 809
dofe, 817
'dog', 709
dogbane, 810
dogcatcher, 810
do-gooder, 807
dogtooth, 810
do-it-yourself, 807
dolich-, 811
dolichocephalic, 811
dolichofacial, 811
dolichó(s), 811
dolichosigmoid, 811
dolichuranic, 811
'doll', 2141
dollar-a-year (man), 812
dollarbird, 812
dollarfish, 812
'dolt', 536
-don, 903
dó(n), 807
Don Qui(xote), 813
'done', 2836
donkey-, 817
donkey-engine, 813
donkey-pump, 813
donkey-rest, 813
do-nothing, 807
'door', 814
door-, 1033, 2616
doorbell, 814
'doorlike barrier', 1076
doorstop, 814
door-to-door, 814
dōr, 814

dor(e), 814
dors-, 815
'dorsal', 2093
dorsalgia, 815
dorsi-, 815
dorsiflexion, 815
dorsoanterior, 815
dorsolumbar, 815
dorsomesial, 815
dors(um), 815
'dot', 165
'dotted', 1772
'double', 88, 232, 238,
  243, 761, 789, 794, 922,
  2705
double-, 232, 761, 794,
  839, 842, 2706
double-barreled, 816
double-decker, 816
doublethink, 816
'doubly', 232, 243
dovecote, 817
dovetail, 817
dovewood, 817
'do well', 228
'down', 382, 1387
downfall, 818
downhearted, 818
'downwards', 748, 1387
downwind, 818
draft-, 820, 823
draft-hole, 819
draft-hook, 819
draft-horse, 819
'drag', 819, 823
drag-, 819, 823
'drag with a rope', 2645
drag(a), 820
drag(an), 819, 820, 823
drag-chain, 820
draghound, 820
dragnet, 820
dragonfly, 821
dragonhead, 821
dragonroot, 821
'drags', 2660
draht, 819
'drain', 956, 1150
drain-, 835
'drain out', 956
drainboard, 822
drainfield, 822

drainspout, 822
drákōn, 821
dramʹeîn, 831
'draw', 490, 819
draw-, 819, 820
'draw tight', 2401, 2410
'draw together', 607
drawbridge, 823
drawknife, 823
'drawn', 819
draw-sheet, 823
drēa(h)n(ian), 822
'dream', 1806
dreamboat, 824
dreamland, 824
dream-world, 824
drēm, 824
dress-, 792, 826
dress, 826
dress(er), 825, 826
dressing-, 792, 825
dressing-gown, 826
dressing-knife, 826
dressing-room, 826
dressmaker, 825
dress-spur, 825
dress-up, 825
'dried up (body)', 2354
drīf(an), 827, 829, 830
drift, 827
'drift', 1026
drift-, 829, 830
driftbolt, 827
driftfish, 827
driftwood, 827
drill-, 2604, 2664, 2693,
  2700
drill(en), 828
drillmaster, 828
drill-press, 828
drillstock, 828
'drinking vessel', 690
drit, 793
drive, 830
drive, 830
'drive', 827, 881
drive-, 827
drive-in, 829
'driven', 827
'driven herd', 827
'driven snow', 827
driveway, 829

ē(a)d-, 867
ē(a)ge, 960
eagle-eyed, 856
eagle-ray, 856
eaglestone, 856
'ear', 180, 182, 1857
ear-, 180, 1857
earache, 857
'eardrum', 2707
ēar(e), 857
earflap, 857
'earlier', 1038, 2103, 2118
'early', 914
'early stage of development', 281
earshot, 857
'earth', 1087, 1936, 2837
earthmover, 858
earthquake, 858
earthwork, 858
'eastern', 187
'Eastern Kingdom', 187
'eat', 285, 937, 1967
'eaten', 1029
'eating beside', 1906
'eating with', 1906
eboreus, 1370
ebu, 885, 1370
ec-, 854, 865, 870, 953, 954
eccentric, 859
e(ć)ǵ, 868
echidn-, 860
échidn(a), 860
echidnase, 860
Echidnophaga, 860
echidnotoxin, 860
echidnovaccine, 860
echin-, 861
echinochrome, 861
echinococciasis, 861
Echinodermata, 861
echinophthalmia, 861
echîno(s), 861
ēchố, 862
echo-, 864
echoacousia, 862
echomimia, 862
echopraxis, 862
eco-, 1782, 1788
eco-², 862
economy, 863
ecophobia, 863

ecophony, 862
ecosphere, 863
ecphylactic, 859
ect-, 865
ectethmoids, 865
ecthyreosis, 859
ecto-, 854, 859, 870, 953
ectodermal, 865
ectoglobular, 865
ectonuclear, 865
ectrodactylia, 866
ectrogenic, 866
ectromelic, 866
edge-, 12, 16, 23, 25, 28, 29, 1875
edge-grained, 868
Edgewater, 868
Edgewood, 868
Edmund, 867
educate, 854
Edward, 867
Edwin, 867
eelback, 869
eelgrass, 869
eelpout, 869
ef-, 854, 859, 953, 954
ef-, 870
efen, 949
efflorescence, 870
effort, 870
effusion, 870
egg, 871
'egg', 1809, 1810, 1864, 1866
egg-, 194, 1809, 1866
'egg-bearing', 1810
eggbeater, 871
eggnog, 871
eggplant, 871
'egg white', 53
egō, 872
ego-², 37
egoaltruistic, 872
egobronchophony, 37
egocentric, 872
egotheism, 872
'Egypt', 442
'Egypt mixture', 442
eht(a), 876
eid-, 874
-eidḗs, 2616
eido-, 1146, 1295, 2471, 2775

eidogen, 874
eidograph, 874
eidoptometry, 874
eîdo(s), 874
eidoscope, 874
eigen, 875
eigenfunction, 875
eigenvalue, 875
eigenvector, 875
eight, 1732, 2311
'eight', 1774
eight-, 1774
eightball, 876
eightfoil, 876
eightscore, 876
eis, 877, 936
eis-, 891, 897, 936, 1299, 1304, 1312, 1313, 1356
eisanthema, 877
eisegesis, 877
e(i)sō, 936
eisodic, 877
'either (of two)', 1723
'eject saliva', 2423
ek-, 859, 865, 866
eka, 878
eka-, 1805, 2729
eka-iodine, 878
ektitrőskein, 866
ektó(s), 865
éktrō(ma), 866
éktrō(sis), 866
ēl, 869
-el, 1637, 2597
elaeo-, 884
elaeoplast, 884
elaia, 884, 1789, 1791, 1794
elaio-, 884
élaion, 1789, 1791
elaiopathy, 884
elasmobranch, 881
elasmognathous, 881
elasmó(s), 881
Elasmosaurus, 881
elaúnein, 881
'elbow', 882, 2719
elbow-board, 882
elbow-grease, 882
elbowroom, 882
elecampane, 1346

everywhere, 951
evil, 952
'evil', 1302, 1537
evil-(?), 1280, 1282, 1814,
1865, 2490, 2492, 2496,
2507, 2508, 2510, 2513,
2730
evildoer, 952
evil-eyed, 952
evil-minded, 952
'evil spirit', 744
ex, 854, 859, 870, 953,
954, 955, 956, 957, 958,
959
ex-, 2259, 2435
ex-¹, 854, 859, 870, 954,
958, 959, 2435
ex-², 854, 859, 870, 953,
957
exact, 953
exacto-, 490
'examine', 2275
exangia, 954
exanthem, 954
*excappāre, 2259
'excavation (for burial)',
1136
'exceeding', 2723
'excellent', 997
'excessive', 2079
'excessive(ly)', 1280, 2508,
2511
'exchange', 80, 431
'exchanging', 1618
excit(āre), 955
'excite', 46
excito-, 1403, 1404, 1406
excitoanabolic, 955
excitoglandular, 955
excitosecretory, 955
'excrement', 793, 2455
exculpate, 953
'exercise oneself', 2047
exeresis, 954
exhaurīre, 956
exhaust-fan, 956
exhaust-pipe, 956
exhaust(us), 956
exhaust-valve, 956
'exhibit', 2327
'exist', 259
éxō, 957
exo-, 854, 870, 953, 954

exodeviation, 957
exogenetic, 957
exoskeleton, 957
'explosive device', 258,
1646
'export', 2087
express-bullet, 958
express-car, 958
expressman, 958
express(us), 958
exprimere, 958
'extend', 1959
'extended (road)', 2476
'extent', 2395
exter, 1343
'external', 1343
'external ear', 182
'external form', 961, 962
exterus, 1343
extrā, 959
extra-, 859, 953, 954
extrabold, 959
extracystic, 959
extramarital, 959
'extraordinary', 1958
'extreme', 25
'extreme coldness', 681
'extremity', 902, 2560
'extremity of the heart',
126
'extremity of the lower
jaw', 451
extro-, 959
extrovert, 959
ex-wife, 953
ex-, 1332
'eye', 1625, 1772, 1775,
1816, 1818, 2825
eye-, 1775, 1816, 1818,
1827, 2825
eyebrow, 960
'eyelash', 485
'eyelash(es)', 250
'eyelid', 250, 485
'eyelid(s)', 250
eyeopener, 960
eyestone, 960

F

f, 41, 586, 776, 870, 1786,
2496
'F', 1023

'fabric containing wool',
1009
'face', 962, 1625, 1818,
1842, 1846, 2113
face-, 807, 962, 2582
face-lift, 961
facere, 1792
face-saving, 961
face-to-face, 961
faci-, 962
facial, 962
faci(ēs), 961, 962
'facing', 605, 606
facio-, 807, 961, 2582
faciobrachial, 962
faciocephalalgia, 962
faciocervical, 962
fǽǵ(e), 963
fǽr-, 1032
fǽst, 971
fǽt(t), 972
fag, 1007
fai(e)rie, 967
'fail', 1497
'fail to reach', 756
fair-haired, 963
fair-minded, 963
fair-weather, 963
fairy-bird, 967
fairyland, 967
fairy-stone, 967
Falconidae, 1182
'fall', 375, 1905
'(a) fall', 375
'fall behind', 756
fallere, 965
fallfish, 964
fall-gate, 964
'fallopian tube', 2243
fallout, 964
'falls', 832
'false', 2123
false-bottomed, 965
false-hearted, 965
falsework, 965
fals(us), 965
'family', 941
'fan', 2202
fanback, 966
fanjet, 966
'fanlike', 2202
fantail, 966

fluorine, 1023
fluorite, 1023
fluoro-, 1022
fluorocarbon, 1023
fluorometer, 1023
fluorophosphate, 1023
'flux', 2200
'fly', 1689
fly-[1], 1016, 1017, 1025,
 2061, 2062, 2068, 2137,
 2146
fly-[2], 1016, 1017, 1024,
 2061, 2062, 2068, 2137,
 2146
flyaway, 1024
flyblown, 1025
fly-by-night, 1024
fly-fish, 1025
flȳg̃(e), 1025
flypaper, 1025
flywheel, 1024
'focal point', 165
'focus', 165
fōd(a), 1029, 1042
'fodder', 264, 566
fog, 1026
fogbound, 1026
fogdog, 1026
fogg, 1026
fogge, 1026
foggy, 1026
foghorn, 1026
folc, 1028
'fold', 2054, 2341
'-fold', 923
foli-, 1027
foliaceous, 1027
folii-, 1019, 2000
foliicolous, 1027
foliiferous, 1027
foliigerous, 1027
folio-, 1027
foliosan, 1027
foli(um), 1027
folklore, 1028
folk-rock, 1028
folkway, 1028
foll(is), 1030
'follow', 2285, 2337
'follow(er)', 2376
'following', 42, 2093, 2285

'food', 285, 566, 975,
 1042, 1574, 1906, 2351,
 2588, 2688
food-, 975, 1042
'food of the gods', 2588
food-fish, 1029
food-gathering, 1029
foodstuff, 1029
foolhardy, 1030
fool-hen, 1030
foolstones, 1030
foot, 1592
'foot', 214, 215, 216, 1933,
 2072
foot-, 1933, 2018, 2072
footfall, 1031
foothill, 1031
footpad, 1031
'for', 1902, 2104
for-, 1032
for-[1], 968, 1036, 1038,
 1041, 1903, 1953, 1954,
 1958, 2098, 2102, 2103,
 2104, 2108, 2110, 2118,
 2119, 2121
for-[2], 814, 1037, 2616
for-[3], 1038
forbear, 1032
forbid, 1032
'force', 1339
force-feed, 1035
force-out, 1035
force-piece, 1035
forclose, 1033
forćyppian, 453
fore, 1001, 1038
'(be)fore-', 1001
fore-[1], 1032
fore-[2], 1033, 2108
fore-[3], 968, 1001, 1032,
 1034, 1041, 1903, 1953,
 1954, 1958, 2098, 2102,
 2103, 2110, 2118, 2119,
 2121
forearm, 1038
'forearm', 882
foreclose, 1033
forego, 1032
'forehead', 1050, 1625
'foreign', 70
'foreign(er)', 1058, 1062,
 2843
foreman, 1038

'foremost', 1001, 2102
'foremost person', 139,
 146
foresee, 1038
forfeit, 1033
forgo, 1038
for(is), 1033
forjudge, 1033
'form', 792, 825, 826, 874,
 961, 962, 990, 1039,
 1295, 1664, 2041, 2043
form-[1], 1664
form-[2], 1700
'form into a ball', 1411,
 1412, 1414
form(a), 1039
formaldehyde, 1040
formamide, 1040
formate, 1040
'formative', 141
formboard, 1039
'formed', 2041, 2043
'former', 953, 2118
form-fitting, 1039
form(ic), 1040
formīca, 1040
'forming', 2043
formwork, 1039
forsake, 1032
forst, 1051
forþ, 1041
forth-, 968, 1032, 1038,
 1903, 1953, 1954, 1958,
 2098, 2102, 2103, 2104,
 2108, 2110, 2118, 2119,
 2121
forthcoming, 1041
'for the purpose of', 2625
forthright, 1041
forthwith, 1041
fortia, 1035
fort(is), 1035
'forward', 2112
'forward end of a boat',
 270
'forward(s)', 1041
'fossil footprints', 1289
fōster, 1042
foster-, 975, 1029
foster-brother, 1042
foster-child, 1042
foster-parent, 1042
fōt, 1031

galactopyranose, 1059
galactos-, 1059
galactosamine, 1060
galactosazone, 1060
galactos(e), 1059, 1060
galactosemia, 1060
gálakt(os), 1059, 1060
Galbally, 1058
gall, 1058, 1061
'gall', 461, 462, 463, 464,
  465, 466, 467
gall-, 155, 457, 462, 1097,
  1112, 2850
Gall-, 1062
gallbladder, 1061
'gallbladder', 463
Gallic, 1062
Gallo-, 1058
Gallomania, 1062
Gallophobia, 1062
Gallo-Romance, 1062
'gallows tree', 675, 678
gallsickness, 1061
gallstone, 1061
'gallstone(s)', 465
Gall(us), 1062
(Luigi) Galvan(i), 1063
galvan-, 1063
galvanism, 1063
galvanocautery, 1063
galvanometer, 1063
galvanotropism, 1063
Galwally, 1058
Galway, 1058
gam-, 1067
gāmāl, 335
gamebag, 1064
gamecock, 1064
gameîn, 1065, 1067
gamekeeper, 1064
game(n), 1064
gamet-, 1065
gamete, 1065
gamét(ēs), 1065
gametic, 1065
gameto-, 1067
gametocidal, 1065
gametocytemia, 1065
gametogenesis, 1065
gamic, 1067
gamm-, 1066
gamma-, 71
gammabufagin, 1066

gammagraphic, 1066
gamma-ray, 1066
gammexane, 1066
gamo-, 44, 1065
gamogenesis, 1067
gamomania, 1067
gamophobia, 1067
gámo(s), 44, 1067
gā(n), 1107
gang, 1068
gang-, 1107
gangland, 1068
ganglioblast, 1069
gánglio(n), 1069
ganglion-, 1069
ganglionervous, 1069
ganglioneuroma, 1069
ganglionitis, 1069
gangliono-, 1069
ganglionoplegic, 1069
gangplank, 1068
gangway, 1068
gār, 1070
garbill, 1070
garfish, 1070
'garland', 677
garlic, 1070
'garment', 539, 540
'garments', 540
gas, 1071
'gas', 173, 1008, 2006
gasbag, 1071
gasholder, 1071
gasi-, 1071
gasiform, 1071
gaslight, 1071
gaso-, 1071
gasometer, 1071
gāst, 1091
gast(ế)r, 1072
gaster-, 1072
gasterasthenia, 1072
gastero-, 1072
Gasterophilus, 1072
gastr-, 1072
gastritis, 1072
gastro-, 1073, 1074, 1075
gastrocolitis, 1072
gastrodiaphany, 1072
gastr(ós), 1072
gastrotherapy, 1072
gāt, 1108
'gate', 814

gate-crasher, 1076
gatefold, 1076
gatekeeper, 1076
'gatekeeper', 2149
'gather (fruit)', 1133
'gather together', 1486,
  1505
'gathering of crops', 1178
'Gaul', 1062
*gaviola, 1372
gazo-, 1071
gazogene, 1071
gê, 1087
ġean, 1057
ġēar, 2849
gearbox, 1077
gearshift, 1077
gearwheel, 1077
ġeat, 1076
ġeġn, 1057
gel-, 1079
gel(āre), 1079
gelatin, 1079
'gelded pig', 1242
gelfoam, 1079
gelo-², 567, 609
Gelochelidon, 1078
gelodiagnosis, 1079
geloplasm, 1079
gélō(s), 1078
geloscopy, 1078
gelotherapy, 1078
gelotripsy, 1079
gem(ma), 1080
gem-peg, 1080
gem-ring, 1080
gemstone, 1080
gen-, 1083
-gen, 701, 1271
gene(á), 1876
gén(e)io(n), 1081
'general principle', 1295
genet(ália), 1082
geni-, 1081
genial, 1081
genio-, 451, 1086
genioglossal, 1081
geniohyoid, 1081
genioplasty, 1081
'genitals', 36
genito-, 907, 1083, 1084,
  1118, 1122, 1405, 1725

glôtt(a), 1102
glottal, 1102
glotto-, 1101
glottochronology, 1102
glottogony, 1102
glottology, 1102
'glowing piece of wood',
    548
gluc-, 1103
glucatonia, 1103
gluco-, 1104, 1105
glucofuranose, 1103
glucogenesis, 1103
glucoproteinase, 1103
glucos-, 1103
glucosazone, 1103
glucose, 1103, 1105, 1949
'glue', 45, 573, 578, 1099,
    1488
'glue to', 45
'gluelike substance', 1099
glüten, 45
glütinis, 45
glyc-, 1105
glycemia, 1105
glycer-, 1104
glyceraldehyde, 1104
glycero-, 1103, 1105
glycerogelatin, 1104
glycerophilic, 1104
glycerophosphate, 1104
glyco-, 1103, 1104, 1283
glycoformal, 1105
glycogenesis, 1105
glycometabolic, 1105
glyk-, 1104
glykeró(s), 1104
glyk(ýs), 1103, 1105
gn, 545, 1286, 1311
gnath-, 1106
gnathalgia, 1106
gnathocephalus, 1106
gnathodynamics, 1106
gnátho(s), 1106
gnathostatics, 1106
'go', 214, 215, 216, 1353,
    1575
go-, 1068
go-ahead, 1107
'go beyond', 1917
'goat', 37, 354, 2659
goatfish, 1108
goatherd, 1108

goatsucker, 1108
go-cart, 1107
'god', 2586, 2588
God, 722
God-, 722, 1110, 1111,
    1125
gōd, 1109, 1111, 1126
god-¹, 1109
god-², 1109
God-awful, 1109
godchild, 1111
godfather, 1111
Godforsaken, 1109
godmother, 1111
'god of war', 148
'(lesser) god or goddess',
    744
godown, 1107
godsend, 1109
Godspeed, 1109
gof(fe), 1127
'go in different direc-
    tions', 804, 805
'going', 1068
gold, 1061, 1112, 1113
'gold', 155, 181, 478
gold-, 155, 457, 462, 1061,
    1097, 1113, 2850
goldbrick, 1112
gold-dust, 1112
golden, 462
'golden', 478
golden-, 155, 457, 1061,
    1097, 1112, 2850
goldeneye, 1113
goldenrod, 1113
goldenseal, 1113
goldfinch, 1112
gon-¹, 1118
gon-², 1124
gonacratia, 1118
gonad-, 1116
gonadectomy, 1116
gonad(is), 1116
gonado-, 1082, 1083,
    1084, 1118, 1122, 1405,
    1725
gonadoinhibitory, 1116
gonadokinetic, 1116
gonadotherapy, 1116
'gonad-shaped', 2573
gonarthrotomy, 1124

gona(s), 1116
gonat-, 1124
gonatagra, 1124
gonato-, 1124
gonatocele, 1124
gón(atos), 1124
gonḗ, 1116, 1118
gone-¹, 1082, 1083, 1084,
    1114, 1116, 1120, 1122,
    1405, 1725
gone-², 1124
gonecystitis, 1118
goneitis, 1118, 1124
gonepoietic, 1118
goni-, 1118
gôn(ía), 1121, 2674
gonio-, 2674
goniocraniometry, 1121
gonioma, 1118
goniometer, 1121
goniophotography, 1121
gono-, 1405
gono-¹, 1082, 1083, 1084,
    1116, 1118, 1725
gono-², 1124
gonocampsis, 1124
gonocytoma, 1122
gononephrotome, 1122
góno(s), 1116, 1122
gonotoxemia, 1122
góny, 1124
gony-, 1085, 1115, 1117,
    1119, 1123
gonycampsis, 1124
gonycrotesis, 1124
gonyo-, 1124
gonyocele, 1124
gonyoncus, 1124
'good', 228
good-¹, 1109
'good-', 945
goodbye, 1109
good-for-nothing, 1126
good-humored, 1126
good-looking, 1126
'goods', 1555, 1609
goofball, 1127
goof-off, 1127
goof-up, 1127
'go (on foot)', 2794
gooseherd, 1128
gooseneck, 1128

goose-step, 1128
gōrāl, 617, 618
gōs, 1128
Gossypium, 639
gout(e), 1152
g(o)ut(i)er, 1152
Graeco-, 1140
Graeco-Roman, 1140
græf, 1136
grǣ́ǵ, 1138
græs, 1135
Graikó(s), 1140
'grain', 410, 468, 626,
   1132, 1906, 2351
'grain (esp. barley)', 1541
'grainy', 1132
gram-, 650, 1130, 1134
Gram, 1130
Gramineae, 1135
gram-ion, 1130
grám(ma), 1130
grammeter, 1130
gram-molecule, 1130
gram-negative (Gram-neg-
   ative), 1130
gram-positive (Gram-posi-
   tive), 1130
grand, 1139
grand-, 1139.2
grandaunt/great-aunt,
   1139.2
grandchild, 1131.2
grandfather, 1131.2
grand-guard, 1131.1
grand(is), 1131
grandnephew/great-
   nephew, 1139.2
grandniece, 1131.2
grandniece/great-niece,
   1139.2
grand-scale, 1131.1
grandstand, 1131.1
granduncle/great-uncle,
   1139.2
granul-, 1132
'granular', 468
granulate, 1132
granuli-, 1132
granuliform, 1132
granulo-, 626
granuloadipose, 1132
granulocorpuscle, 1132
granuloplasm, 1132

grānul(um), 1132
grān(um), 1132
grape, 1133
'grape', 2750
grape-, 653, 654, 655, 658,
   665, 672, 673, 674
'grape-bearing plants',
   2778
grapefruit, 1133
'grapelike', 2750
graper, 1133
'grape-shaped bacteria',
   2441
grapeshot, 1133
grapevine, 1133
-graph, 490
gráph(ein), 490, 1134
grapho-, 650, 1130
graphology, 1134
graphomotor, 1134
graphoscope, 1134
'grasp', 439, 1222, 2534
'grasp firmly', 511
'grass', 264, 1220
grass-, 1141
grasshopper, 1135
'grass in a wet meadow',
   1026
grassland, 1135
grass-roots, 1135
'grate', 513
grave, 1137
'grave', 2537
grave-, 1144
graveclothes, 1136
gravedigger, 1136
'gravel', 2231, 2494, 2497
gravel-blind, 1137
graveldiver, 1137
gravel(le), 1137
gravelweed, 1137
gravestone, 1136
'gray', 1098, 2077
gray-, 1142
grayback, 1138
graybeard, 1138
graylag, 1138
'gray matter', 2077, 2078
grēat, 1139
'great', 1131, 1131.1,
   1532, 1533, 1535, 1559,
   1568, 1581, 1583
great-, 1139.2

Great-, 1139.2
'great artery', 126
great-aunt, 1139.2
great-circle, 1139.1
greatcoat, 1139.1
'greater (in number)',
   2051
'greatest degree', 997
great-grandfather, 1139.2
great-great-granddaughter,
   1139.2
great-hearted, 1139.1
'great in length', 1506
'great number of', 1554
Greco-, 1129
Greco-Bactrian, 1140
Greco-Roman, 1140
Greco-Turkish, 1140
'Greek', 1140
'Greek mainland', 946
green-, 1135
greenback, 1141
greengrocer, 1141
greenhouse, 1141
grēn(e), 1141
grey-, 1138
greyhound, 1138
'grief', 363
'grind', 1642, 1690
'gristle', 468
'grit', 2231
'groat', 468
'groats', 171
'groin', 1300, 1301, 1336
'grooved', 265, 2483
'ground', 214, 215, 216,
   858, 1454
groundbreaking, 1143
groundkeeper, 1143
groundsill, 1143
'(organized) group', 646
'group (going together)',
   1068
'group of people living
   together', 941
'grow', 73, 192, 193, 259,
   1790, 2522, 2793
'growing together', 2522
'grown', 2007
'growth', 192, 193
'growth of pubic hair',
   2135

hebeosteotomy, 1191
hebephrenia, 1191
hebosteotomy, 1191
hecato-, 1192
hecatom-, 1192
hecatompedon, 1192
hecaton-, 1192
hecatonstylon, 1192
hecatophyllous, 1192
hect-, 1192
hectare, 1192
hecto-, 405, 1173, 1195,
 1216, 1226, 1249, 1266,
 2341, 2345, 2389
hectocotylus, 1192
hectograph, 1192
hectoliter, 1192
hedgehog, 1193
'hedgehog', 861
hedgehop, 1193
hedgerow, 1193
'heel', 317, 318, 321
'heel bone', 317
heel-and-toe, 1194
heelpost, 1194
heeltap, 1194
hefi(ġ), 1190
hēġ, 1183
heġġ, 1193
'he-goat', 300
he-huckleberry, 1184
'height', 1284
'heightened body temper-
 ature', 983
'heir', 1222
hek(a)tó(n), 1192
hekt-, 1192
hektare, 1192
hekto-, 1192
hektometer, 1192
hel-[1], 1202
hel-[2], 1203
hēl(a), 1194
helénion, 1346
heli-, 1198, 1199
helianthus, 1199
helic-, 1198
helici-, 1198
heliciform, 1198
helicline, 1198
helicograph, 1198
helicogyrate, 1198
helicopter, 1198

helicopter, 1198
helicotrema, 1198
hélik(os), 1198
helio-, 2379, 2394, 2506
heliocentric, 1199
heliometer, 1199
hēlio(s), 1199
heliotropism, 1199
helipad, 1198
heliport, 1198
hélix, 1198
hel(l), 1200
hell-, 395, 485, 570, 582,
 1244
hellbent, 1200
hellcat, 1200
'hellebore', 2767
hellhound, 1200
'helmet', 633
hélmin(s), 1201
'helminth', 2838
helminth-, 1201
helminthi-, 1201
helminthic, 1201
helminthicide, 1201
helmintho-, 2722, 2756,
 2794, 2809
helminthochorton, 1201
helminthology, 1201
helminthophobia, 1201
hélminth(os), 1201
helo-[1], 1196
helo-[2], 1197
Helobacterium, 1202
helobious, 1203
heloderm, 1202
helodes, 1203
helodont, 1202
Heloecetes, 1203
Helophilus, 1203
hélo(s), 1202, 1203
helotomy, 1202
hem-, 1212
hem-[2], 1210
'hem in', 514, 515, 538
hema-, 1212
hemadromometer, 1212
hemagglutinate, 1212
he-man, 1184
hemat-, 1212
hematemesis, 1212
hemati-, 1212

hematimeter, 1212
hemato-, 1212
hematocatharsis, 1212
hemelytron, 1210
hemi-, 1205, 1211, 2291,
 2307
hēmi-, 1210
hemianopsia, 1210
hemidemisemiquaver,
 1210
hemisphere, 1210
hemo-, 1162, 1163, 1204,
 1206, 1207, 1208, 1209,
 1213, 1214
hemoglobin, 1212
hemoglobin, 1214
hemoglobin-, 1214
hemoglobinemia, 1214
hemoglobini-, 1214
hemoglobiniferous, 1214
hemoglobinocholia, 1214
hemoglobinometer, 1214
hemoglobinopepsia, 1214
hemophobia, 1212
hemotoxin, 1212
'hemp', 347
henbane, 1215
'hence', 2447, 2618
hendec-, 1216
hendeca-, 1173, 1192,
 1226, 1249, 2341, 2345,
 2389
hendecahedron, 1216
hendecandrous, 1216
hendecasemic, 1216
hendecasyllabic, 1216
héndeka, 1216
henhouse, 1215
hen(n), 1215
henpecked, 1215
heort, 1177
heort(e), 1186
hepa-, 1218
hepaptosis, 1218
hêpa(r), 1217, 1218
hepar-, 1218
heparin, 1218
hepat-, 1218
hepatectomy, 1218
hepatic duct, 1217
hepatico-, 1218
hepaticoenterostomy, 1217

hotbox, 1262
'hot cautery', 1297
'hotness', 1187
hotshot, 1262
hour-, 1260, 2849
hour-bell, 1263
hourglass, 1263
hour-hand, 1263
'house', 211, 863
housebreaker, 1264
housebroken, 1264
housefly, 1264
'household', 863
'householder', 259
'housekeeper', 1444
'how much', 2157
'hue', 582
'hull', 632
'hull-shaped', 2260
'human being', 122
'human life', 2837
'human society', 2837
humer-, 1265
humeral, 1265
humero-, 1800
humeroradial, 1265
humeroscapular, 1265
humeroulnar, 1265
humer(us), 1265
'humming sound', 258
Humulus lupulus, 1257
hund, 1266
hundred, 1192
'hundred', 405, 1192
'(one) hundred', 1192
hundred-, 405
hundred-eyes, 1266
hundred-percenter, 1266
'hundredth', 405
hundredweight, 1266
huni(ġ), 1253
'hunted (for sport)', 1064
'hurt', 866
hūs, 1264
'husband', 1065
'husk', 332, 556, 1474,
   2318
'husk (of grain)', 422
'husked', 1475
hvir(f)l(a), 2817
hwā, 2819
hwæl, 2811
hwær, 2815

hwæt, 2812
hwch, 1242
hwen(ne), 2814
hwē(o)l, 2813
hwip(pen), 2816
hwīt, 2818
hy-, 1278
hyal-, 1267
hyalin, 1267
hyalomucoid, 1267
hyalophobia, 1267
hyaloplasm, 1267
hýalo(s), 1267
hȳd(an), 1229
hýd(ō)r, 1270, 1271
hydr-[1], 1270
hydr-[2], 1271
hydracid, 1271
hydragogue, 1270
hydro-, 55, 738, 781
hydro-, 1270
hydro-[1], 109, 1268, 1271,
   1273, 2069, 2797, 2800,
   2810, 2828
hydro-[2], 1269, 1270, 1272,
   2675
hydroappendix, 1270
hydrocarbon, 1271
hydrochloric, 1271
hydroelectric, 1270
hydro(gen), 1271
hydroquinone, 1271
hydrotherapy, 1270
hyet-, 1274
hyetal, 1274
hyeto-, 2392
hyetograph, 1274
hyetology, 1274
hyetometer, 1274
hyetó(s), 1274
hygrograph, 1275
hygrometer, 1275
hygró(s), 1275
hygrothermograph, 1275
hyl-, 1276
hyle-, 1276
hylephobia, 1276
hyll, 1233
hylo-, 1977, 2109
hyloma, 1276
hylomorphic, 1276
hylophagous, 1276

hylozoism, 1276
hymḗn, 1277
hymen-, 1277
hymenectomy, 1277
hymenology, 1277
Hymenoptera, 1277
hymén(os), 1277
hymenotome, 1277
hyo-, 2731
hyobranchial, 1278
hyodont, 1278
hyoglossal, 1278
hyoid, 1278
hyomandibular, 1278
hyp-, 1282
hypalgesic, 1282
hyp(e), 1235
hypér, 1280
hyper-, 952, 1211, 1282,
   1814, 1865, 2490, 2492,
   2496, 2507, 2508, 2510,
   2513, 2730
hyperactive, 1280
hyperchloric (acid), 1280
hyperplasmia, 1280
hypn-, 1281
hypnagogue, 1281
hypno-, 2390
hypnogenetic, 1281
hypnonarcoanalysis, 1281
hýpno(s), 1281
hypnotherapy, 1281
hypó, 1282
hypo-, 952, 1279, 1280,
   1283, 1814, 1865, 2490,
   2492, 2496, 2507, 2508,
   2510, 2513, 2730
hypoactivity, 1282
hypochlorite, 1282
hypocondylar, 1282
hyps-, 1284
hýpsi, 1284
hypsi-, 1284
hypsicephalic, 1284
hypsography, 1284
hypsometer, 1284
hypsophyll, 1284
hýpso(s), 1284
hypsosis, 1284
hyster-, 1285
hystér(a), 1285
hysterectomy, 1285

hysteri-, 1285
hysteria, 1285
hysteriform, 1285
hystero-, 1074, 2749,
2765, 2771
hysterocarcinoma, 1285
hysteroepilepsy, 1285
hysterovaginoenterocele,
1285

I

i-, 2, 94, 1298, 1303, 1311,
1355, 1723, 1724, 1735,
1739, 1760, 2724
i-, 1286
'I', 872
-ia, 236, 394, 584, 929,
1035, 1368
-ia-, 169
-ial, 1616
iatr-, 1287
iatrarchy, 1287
iatrochemistry, 1287
iatrogenic, 1287
iatrology, 1287
iatró(s), 1287
iaw(e), 1373
-ic, 1, 443, 883, 1995,
2107, 2859
'(clear) ice', 683
iceberg, 1288
icebox, 1288
icebreaker, 1288
'icelike', 683
ichn-, 1289
ichnite, 1289
ichnographic, 1289
ichnolite, 1289
ichnology, 1289
íchno(s), 1289
ichôr, 1290
ichoremia, 1290
ichoroid, 1290
ichorrhea, 1290
ichth-, 1291
ichthin, 1291
ichthy-, 1291
ichthyology, 1291
ichthyophobia, 1291
ichthyosis, 1291
ichthyosulfonate, 1291
ichthý(s), 1291
iconoclast, 1292

iconography, 1292
iconostasis, 1292
icos-, 1293
icosacolic, 1293
icosahedron, 1293
icosandrous, 1293
icosasemic, 1293
icosi-, 1293
icosidodecahedron, 1293
icter-, 1294
icterepatitis, 1294
icteroanemia, 1294
icterohemoglobinuria,
1294
icteromaturia, 1294
-ic(us), 1893
-ide, 82, 702
idé(a), 1295
'idea', 1295
'ideation', 1295
ideîn, 874, 1295
ideo-, 874, 1146, 2471,
2775
ideoglandular, 1295
ideomotor, 1295
ideophrenia, 1295
idio-agglutinin, 1296
idiohypnotism, 1296
idiomuscular, 1296
idio(s), 1296
iénai, 1353
-ier, 378, 436, 1152
-iğ, 125
igniextirpation, 1297
ignigenous, 1297
ignipuncture, 1297
igni(s), 1297
ignis-, 1297
ignisation, 1297
'ignite', 1707
ignoble, 1286
ignominious, 1286
ignore, 1286
-ikón, 2650
(e)ikôn, 1292
-ikós, 1217, 1679, 2004,
2521, 2601, 2743
(e)íkos(i), 1293
íktero(s), 1294
il-, 1298, 1299
il-[1], 2, 94, 1286, 1303,
1311, 1355, 1723, 1724,
1735, 1739, 1760, 2724

il-[2], 877, 891, 897, 898,
1304, 1312, 1313, 1356
ile-, 1300
ileitis, 1300
ileo-, 1301
ileocecal, 1300
ileocolonic, 1300
ileosigmoid, 1300
īle(um), 1300
ili-, 1301
iliac, 1301
ilio-, 1300
iliofemoral, 1301
iliometer, 1301
iliosacral, 1301
īli(um), 1300, 1301
'ill', 1537, 1540, 2330
'ill-', 853
-illa, 985, 1543, 2141
ill-advised, 1302
illation, 1299
illegal, 1298
illegible, 1298
illiterate, 1298
ill-natured, 1302
īll(r), 1302
ill-suited, 1302
illuminate, 1299
'illuminate', 1647
'illumination', 1485
-ill(us), 163
illustrate, 1299
im-, 892, 1303, 1304
im-[1], 2, 94, 1286, 1298,
1310, 1311, 1355, 1723,
1724, 1735, 1739, 1760,
2724
im-[2], 877, 891, 892, 897,
1299, 1312, 1313, 1356
im-[3], 892
'image', 1292, 2404, 2708,
2715
imbalance, 1303
imbed, 892
imbibe, 1304
imid-, 1306
imidazoledione, 1306
imido-, 82
imidogen, 1306
imidothiobiazoline, 1306
imidozanthin, 1306

jetliner, 1375
jetport, 1375
jet-propelled, 1375
'jewel', 1080
'Joachimsthal', 812
John, 1371, 1377
Johnny, 1371
Johnny-come-lately, 1377
Johnny-jump-up, 1377
Johnny-on-the-spot, 1377
'joined', 2857
'joining', 645
'joint', 111, 157, 2770
'joyous', 1612
jug-, 1380
'juice', 481, 482, 1819
'juice of pressed apples',
  484
jumpmaster, 1378
jump-off, 1378
jump-start, 1378
jūris, 1379
jurisconsult, 1379
jurisdiction, 1379
jurisprudence, 1379
jūs, 1379
'just', 2211
juxt-, 1380
juxtā, 1380
juxta-, 2857
juxta-articular, 1380
juxta-epiphysial, 1380
juxtangina, 1380
juxtapose, 1380

K

Kaffa, 561
kaíein, 388
kaino-, 402
kainophobia, 402
kainó(s), 402
kak-, 313
kakergasia, 313
kako-, 313
kakó(s), 313
kakotrophy, 313
kali-, 64
kaliemia, 1383
kaligenous, 1383
kalimeter, 1383
kalin-, 1383
kalinite, 1383
kalio-, 1383

kaliophilite, 1383
kalium, 1383
kalli-, 327
kállos, 327
kalós, 327
kályk(os), 332
kalýptein, 333
kalyptó(s), 333
kály(x), 332
kamára, 334, 428
kamp(ế), 340
kámptein, 342
kamptó(s), 342
kampýlo(s), 343
kánnab(is), 347
kántho(s), 348, 349
kapnó(s), 353
kappa-, 71
kāpūr, 339
kardía, 13, 362, 1955
karkíno(s), 360
kárphein, 368
kárpho(s), 368
karpó(s), 369, 370
kary-, 1385
karyenchyma, 1385
karyo-, 344, 360, 374,
  1175, 1582
karyocyte, 1385
karyology, 1385
karyo(n), 1385, 1582
karyoplasm, 1385
katá, 382, 386, 1387
kata-, 382
kataphylaxis, 382
kátō, 1387
kato-, 382, 385
katolysis, 1387
katophoria, 1387
kátoptro(n), 386
katotropia, 1387
kauló(s), 387
kautếr, 388
kédros, 501
'keen', 2315
'keep away', 56
'keep fast', 1243
kel-, 399
kēl(ế), 399
kelectome, 399
kelo-, 399
kelotomy, 399

Kelt(oí), 400
keno-, 404
kenophobia, 404
kenó(s), 404
kentro-, 407
kentrokinesia, 407
kéntr(on), 406, 407
kephal-, 408
kephal(ế), 408, 900
kephalin, 408
kephalo-, 408
kephalogram, 408
ker-, 1393
kera-, 1393
keraphyllocele, 1393
kéra(s), 1392, 1393
kerat-, 1393
keratin, 1392, 1393
keratin-, 365, 414, 417,
  418, 629, 657, 1095,
  1177, 1259, 1393
keratinase, 1392
keratinoid, 1392
keratinose, 1392
keratitis, 1393
kerato-, 365, 411, 414,
  417, 418, 629, 657,
  1095, 1177, 1259, 1392
keratoacanthoma, 1393
keratoconjunctivitis, 1393
keratodermia, 1393
kérat(os), 1392, 1393
keri-, 415
keritherapy, 415
kérko(s), 412
'kernel', 552, 1132, 1758,
  2480
kero-, 415
keroid, 1393
kēró(s), 415
kerosene, 415
ket-, 1396
keto-, 12, 16, 23, 25, 28,
  29, 868, 1875, 2676
ketogenesis, 1396
(A)keton, 1396
ketohexose, 1396
Keton, 1396
keto(ne), 1396
'ketone', 1396
kêt(os), 420
ketosis, 1396

ketosteroid, 1396
kettle-bottom, 1397
kettledrum, 1397
'kettledrum', 2707
kettle-hole, 1397
'key', 515, 520, 533
keyboard, 1398
keyhole, 1398
'keylike shape', 515
keynote, 1398
khmi, 442
kickback, 1399
kickoff, 1399
kickstand, 1399
'kidney', 1719
'kidneys', 35, 2190
-*k-ie*, 813
kiid(ē), 544
kik(en), 1399
kilo-, 449
kilocalorie, 1400
kilogram, 1400
kilovolt, 1400
(*al*)*kīm(īyā*), 442
kin-, 1406
-*k(in)*, 1371
kina, 2165
kine-[1], 1406
kine-[2], 490
kin(eîn), 490, 1403, 1404, 1406
kinēma, 490
kinemato-, 490
kinematograph, 490
kinēmat(os), 490
kinemia, 1406
kineplasty, 1406
kines-, 1403
kinescope, 490
kinesi-, 490, 491, 955, 1404, 1406
kinesiatrics, 1403
kinesiesthesiometer, 1403
kinesio-, 1403
kinesiodic, 1403
kinesiology, 1403
kinēs(is), 1403
kinesitherapy, 1403
kinet-, 1404
kinetic, 1404
kineto-, 490, 955, 1403, 1406
kinetocyte, 1404

kinetogenic, 1404
kinēt(ós), 1404
kinetoscope, 1404
'king', 435, 436
king-, 1082, 1083, 1084, 1118, 1122, 1725
'king dies', 435
king-cup, 1405
'kingdom', 187
king-of-arms, 1405
kingpin, 1405
kino-, 487, 489, 490, 493, 955, 1401, 1403, 1404
kinocilia, 1406
kinohapt, 1406
kinotoxin, 1406
'kinsman', 1084
kio-, 496
kiōn, 496
kiono-, 496
kionocranial, 496
kiotome, 496
kirsó(s), 499
kládo(s), 504
klamp(e), 507
klásma, 510
klásmat(os), 510
kleidó(s), 520
kleíein, 533
kleís, 520, 533
kleistó(s), 521
kl(e)itoríd(os), 533
kl(e)itorí(s), 533
klépt(ein), 1409
klepto-, 522
kleptohemodeipnonism, 1409
kleptolagnia, 1409
kleptophobia, 1409
klêro(s), 523
klêthr(a), 513
klíma, 527
klímat(os), 527
klindro(s), 705
klín(ē), 530
klinesthai, 529, 530
klock(e), 535
klub(ba), 542
'kneader (of bread)', 723, 1444
'knee', 1085, 1124
knee-, 1085, 1124

kneecap, 1410
knee-deep, 1410
knee-jerk, 1410
knēm(ē), 543
'knife', 687
'knock', 2644
knock-, 1412, 1414
knockabout, 1411
knock-knee, 1411
knockout, 1411
knökel, 1414
knot-, 1411, 1414
knotgrass, 1412
knothead, 1412
knothole, 1412
'knotty stick', 516
'know', 1744, 1747, 1754, 2471
know-, 1744, 1747, 1754
know-how, 1413
know-it-all, 1413
know-nothing, 1413
'knuckle', 598
knuckle-, 1411, 1412
knucklebone, 1414
knuckle-duster, 1414
knucklehead, 1414
'knucklelike knob', 598
kochlí(as), 554
Kocs, 546
kocs(i czeker), 546
koil-, 398
koilí(a), 394
koilo-, 398
koîlo(s), 394, 398
koilosternia, 398
koino-, 403
koinó(s), 403
koinotropic, 403
kókk(os), 552, 2480
kókky(gos), 553
kókky(x), 553
koleó(s), 570
kóll(a), 573, 578
kólon, 566, 571
kólo(s), 579
kólpo(s), 583
koly-, 585
kōlý(ein), 1417
kolypeptic, 1417
kolyphrenia, 1417

lactobiose, 1442
lactoscope, 1442
lactose, 1442
ladder-, 527, 529
ladder-back, 1443
ladderman, 1443
ladder-stitch, 1443
ladies'-, 1445
ladies'-tresses, 1445
lady, 1445
lady-, 723, 1445, 2596
ladybug, 1444
lady-in-waiting, 1444
lady-killer, 1444
lady's-, 723, 1444, 2596
lady-slipper, 1445
lady's-slipper, 1445
lady's-thumb, 1445
lady's-tresses, 1445
(h)læder, 1443
laev-, 1479
laevo-, 1479
laevorotary, 1479
laevulos-, 1480
laevulosan, 1480
laevulose, 1479
l(a)ev(us), 1479, 1480
lá(gr), 1512
la(g)u, 1460
'laid crosswise', 445
'laid down', 1460
'lake', 1489, 1607
lak(ken), 1440
lal-, 1447
l(+)-alanine, 1436.2
lal(eîn), 1447
laliatry, 1447
lalio-, 1447
laliophobia, 1447
laloneurosis, 1447
lalophobia, 1447
laloplegia, 1447
lamb, 1449
'lamb', 86
lambda-, 71
lamb's-quarters, 1449
lamb's-tongue, 1449
lamb's-wool, 1449
lamell-, 1450
lāmell(a), 1450
lamellar, 1450
lamelli-, 1451
lamellibranch, 1450

lamellicorn, 1450
lamelliform, 1450
lamin-, 1450
lāmin(a), 1450, 1451
lamina-, 1451
laminagraph, 1451
laminar, 1451
laminectomy, 1451
laminitis, 1451
lamino-, 1451
laminotomy, 1451
lamn-, 1451
lamnectomy, 1451
lamp-, 1453
lamp(ás), 1452
lámpein, 1452, 1453
lamplight, 1452
lamppost, 1452
lampro-, 1452
lamprophony, 1453
lamprophyre, 1453
lampró(s), 1453
lamprotype, 1453
lampshade, 1452
'lamp wick', 1563
lāna, 1490
land, 1454
'land', 473, 1087
'(one's) land', 644
landfall, 1454
landlady, 1454
landmark, 1454
'land of black earth', 442
'land of enchantment', 967
'land that may be mowed', 1572
lang, 1506
'language', 1101, 1102
lani-, 1009
'lap', 583
lapar-, 1455
lapár(a), 1455
laparectomy, 1455
laparocystotomy, 1455
laparogastrotomy, 1455
laparomonodidymus, 1455
laque(us), 1439
'lard', 33
larg(a), 1456
'large', 235, 1131, 1131.1, 1139, 1529, 1581, 1582, 1583, 1880

'large fish', 420
large-hearted, 1456
large-minded, 1456
largemouth (bass), 1456
'large quantity', 2010
'large town', 502
larv-, 1457
larva, 1457
larvicide, 1457
larvin, 1457
larviphagic, 1457
larviposition, 1457
laryng-, 1458
laryngitis, 1458
laryngofissure, 1458
laryngoparalysis, 1458
láryng(os), 1458
laryngotracheobronchoscopy, 1458
larynx, 1458
'lash', 2816
'late', 1821
later-, 1459
lateral, 1459
lateri-, 1459
laterigrade, 1459
later(is), 1459
latero-abdominal, 1459
lateroduction, 1459
lateroversion, 1459
'lathe', 2700
'lattice', 513
'lattice(d)', 513
'latticelike', 513
lat(us), 1459
'laughter', 1078
lauss, 1509
'law', 116, 1379, 1738
law-, 1461, 1501, 1512
law-abiding, 1460
lawbreaker, 1460
'lawless', 116
lawman, 1460
lax(āre), 1464
'lay', 1501
lay-, 1460, 1501, 1512
'lay straight', 792, 825, 826
lay-by, 1461
'layer', 2434, 2474
'layer of hard tissue', 401

layoff, 1461
lay-up, 1461
l(−)-cystine, 1436.2
lēad, 1462
'lead', 2058
'lead in(to)', 1330
'leader', 139, 146, 1559
lead-pipe (cinch), 1462
leadplant, 1462
leadwort, 1462
lēaf, 1463
'leaf', 1027, 1962, 2000, 2587
leafhopper, 1463
leafstalk, 1463
leafworm, 1463
'leap', 1256, 1378
'learning', 2471
'learning (done at leisure)', 2267
leaseback, 1464
leaseholder, 1464
lease-purchase, 1464
'least', 1647
'leather', 306, 471, 474
leatherjacket, 1465
leatherneck, 1465
leatherwork, 1465
'leave (behind)', 1497
'leaven', 2860
le(ćgan), 1461
lecith-, 1466
lecithin, 1466
lecithoblast, 1466
lecithoprotein, 1466
lecithovitellin, 1466
leeboard, 1467
lee-gage, 1467
leeway, 1467
left, 1468
'left', 1479, 1480, 2346
left-eyed (flounder), 1468
left-handed, 1468
'left-handed', 1433
left-laid, 1468
'leg', 2353
leg-break, 1469
légein, 1501
'legend', 1702
leg(gr), 1469
legman, 1469
leg-pull, 1469
lei-, 1470

leiasthenia, 1470
leio-, 1481, 1492
leiodermia, 1470
leiodystonia, 1470
leiomyofibroma, 1470
leîo(s), 1470
leip-, 1497
l(e)íp(ein), 1497
leiphemia, 1497
'leisure time', 2267
lékitho(s), 1466
'lemon tree', 501
lemonade, 1472
lemonfish, 1472
lemon-grass, 1472
lens, 1473, 1964
'lens the eye', 1473
lenticul-, 1473
lenticula, 1473
lenticular, 1473
lenticular nucleus, 1473
lenticul(āris), 1473
lenticulo-optic, 1473
lenticulostriate, 1473
lenticulothalamic, 1473
'lentil', 1473, 1964
'lentil-shaped', 1473
lent(is), 1473
lēoht, 1484, 1485
lépein, 1474, 1475
lepid-, 1474
lepido-, 1475
lepidoma, 1474
Lepidophyton, 1474
lepidopterist, 1474
lepíd(os), 1474
Lepidoselaga, 1474
lepí(s), 1474
lepo-, 1474
lepocyte, 1474
lept-, 1475
leptandrin, 1475
lepto-, 1474
leptochymia, 1475
leptocyte, 1475
leptodactylous, 1475
leptó(s), 1475
Lepus, 1176
'less', 1651
'lesser', 1649, 2316
'let go', 1464
leðer-, 1465

'letter of the alphabet', 1130
'letter *v*', 1278
letterhead, 1476
letter-perfect, 1476
letterpress, 1476
leuc-, 1477
leucitis, 1477
leuco-, 1477
leucocyt-, 1478
leucocyto-, 1478
leucocytosis, 1478
Leucocytozoon, 1478
leucotomy, 1477
leuk-, 1477
leukemia, 1477
leuko-, 1478, 1485, 1514
leukocyt-, 1478
leukocyt(e), 1478
leukocytes, 1477
leukocytoblast, 1478
leukocytogenesis, 1478
leukocytolytic, 1478
leukocyturia, 1478
leukoderivative, 1477
leukodermia, 1477
leukó(s), 1477, 1478
leukosarcomatosis, 1477
lev-, 1479
'level', 949, 1011, 1246, 2036, 2039
levo-, 1433, 1434, 1435, 1436, 1436.2, 1446, 1480
levocardia, 1479
levoglucose, 1479
levophobia, 1479
levulos-, 1479
levulosazone, 1480
levulose, 1479
levulos(e), 1480
levulosemia, 1480
levulosuria, 1480
L$_g$-, 1433, 1436.2
L-glyceraldehyde, 1433, 1434, 1479
L$_g$-rhamnose, 1434
λ-hydroxy, 71
li-, 1470
-*līc*, 210
'lie', 1501
'lie down', 529, 530

lockjaw, 1502
locksmith, 1502
lockup, 1502
'lofty', 73, 1232
lof(u), 1511
log-¹, 1505
logasthenia, 1505
log(ge), 1504
logjam, 1504
logo-, 1486, 1503
logokophosis, 1505
logomania, 1505
logoplegia, 1505
lógo(s), 1505
logroll, 1504
logwood, 1504
'loin', 1455, 1515, 1850
long, 1506
'long', 811, 1507, 1529
long-, 1507
longbow, 1506
longi-, 1506
longilineal, 1507
longipedate, 1507
longiradiate, 1507
long-suffering, 1506
'long surface', 2332
long(us), 1507
long-winded, 1506
'look', 2404
'look at', 2327
lookdown, 1508
look-in, 1508
'looking', 2782
lookout, 1508
'loop', 111
'loose', 1464, 1552
loose-, 1524, 1525
'loose-hanging', 1500,
    2363, 2364
loose-jointed, 1509
loose-leaf, 1509
'loosen', 1524, 1525
'loosening', 1525
loose-tongued, 1509
loph-, 1510
lophobranch, 1510
lophodont, 1510
lophophore, 1510
lópho(s), 1510
lophotrichous, 1510
'Lord is gracious', 1377
-*los*, 2710

'lot', 523
lovebird, 1511
lovelock, 1511
lovesick, 1511
'loving', 1980
'low', 427
low-, 1460, 1461, 1501
'low temperature', 567
lowbrow, 1512
low-cost, 1512
low-down, 1512
'lower', 1333
'lower abdomen', 1300,
    1301
'lower extremity of the
    windpipe', 126
'lower position', 818
'lowest part', 2381
lox-, 1513
loxodromic, 1513
loxolophodont, 1513
loxophthalmus, 1513
loxó(s), 1513
loxotomy, 1513
L-rhamnose, 1433
L$_s$-, 1433, 1436.2
L-serine, 1435
L$_s$-threonine, 1435
L-threonine, 1433
luc-, 1514
luci-, 1477, 1485
luciferase, 1514
lucifugal, 1514
lucipetal, 1514
lūc(is), 1514
Lucite, 1514
luco-, 1514
lucotherapy, 1514
lumb-, 1515
lumbar, 1515
lumbocolostomy, 1515
lumbodorsal, 1515
lumbodynia, 1515
lumb(us), 1515
'lump', 1412, 2606, 2695
'lump (of dirt)', 536
'lump (of earth)', 541
'lung', 2068, 2137
lung-, 1484
lung(en), 1516
lungfish, 1516
lungworm, 1516
lungwort, 1516

luteectomy, 1517
lutein, 1517
luteo-, 1517
luteose, 1517
luteotropic, 1517
lūte(us), 1517
lūtum, 1517
lū(x), 1514
ly-, 1524
lyc-, 1519
lycanthropy, 1519
lyco-, 2831
lycomania, 1519
Lycoperdon, 1519
lycopodium, 1519
lycos-, 1519
lycosid, 1519
lýein, 1524, 1525
lyencephalous, 1524
'lying crosswise', 2662
'lying-in', 1501
'lying in wait', 1501
lýko(s), 1519
lymph, 1522
lymph-, 1522
lymph(a), 1522
lymphemia, 1522
lympho-, 1520, 1521, 1523
lymphoblastoma, 1522
lymphoduct, 1522
lymphorrhea, 1522
lyo-, 1509, 1518, 1525
lyophilic, 1524
lyosorption, 1524
lyotropic, 1524
lys-, 1525
lysi-, 1525
lysimeter, 1525
lysin, 1525
lýs(is), 1525
lyso-, 1509, 1524
lysobacteria, 1525
lysoform, 1525
lysotype, 1525

M

m, 30, 586, 592, 761, 891,
    892, 1303, 1304, 1311,
    1312, 2520
m-¹, 1617
m-², 1618

melodrama, 1592
melomania, 1592
mêlo(n), 1593
melon-, 1593
Melongenidae, 1593
melono-, 1593
melonoplasty, 1593
meloplasty, 1593
mélo(s), 1592
melos-, 1592
melosalgia, 1592
'membrane', 471, 474,
    993, 1277, 1596
'membrane surrounding
    the fetus in utero', 86
mên, 1597
men-, 1597
menhidrosis, 1597
meni-, 1597
mening-, 1596
meninge-, 1596
meningeal, 1596
meningeo-, 1596
meningeocortical, 1596
meninges, 1596
meningi-, 1596
meningioma, 1596
meningitis, 1596
meningocortical, 1596
meningomalacia, 1596
meningoradicular, 1596
mêning(os), 1596
mênin(x), 1596
menischesis, 1597
meno-, 1594, 1595, 1631,
    1663
menolipsis, 1597
menometrorrhagia, 1597
menopause, 1597
mên(ós), 1597
men(s), 1602
'menses', 1597
ment-¹, 1603
ment-², 1602
mental¹, 1603
mental², 1602
'mental activity', 1295
menthane, 1600
menthol, 1600
menthyl, 1600
menti-¹, 1603
menti-², 1599, 1662
menticide, 1602

menticulture, 1602
mentigerous, 1603
mentimeter, 1602
ment(is), 1602
mento-, 1598, 1601
mentoanterior, 1603
mentolabial, 1603
mentotransverse, 1603
ment(um), 1603
meprobamate, 1623
mer-¹, 1610
mer-², 1611
mer-³, 1609
meralgia, 1611
merbromin, 1609
mercapt-, 1608
mercapto-, 1555, 1609
mercaptol, 1608
mercaptomerin, 1608
mercaptophenyl, 1608
mercaptothiazole, 1608
mercārī, 1555
mercāt(us), 1555
merco-, 1609
mercocresols, 1609
mercu-, 1609
mercupurin, 1609
mercur-, 1609
mercurammonium, 1609
mer(curium) capt(ans),
    1608
mercur(ius), 1609
Mercurius, 1608, 1609
mercuro-, 1555, 1606,
    1608
mercurochrome, 1609
mercurophen, 1609
mercurophylline, 1609
'Mercury', 1608
mer(e), 1607
'mere', 2125
merergastic, 1610
meri-, 1610
merispore, 1610
mermaid, 1607
merman, 1607
mero-¹, 1604
mero-², 1605
meroacrania, 1610
merocele, 1611
merocoxalgia, 1611
merogenesis, 1610

meromicrosomia, 1610
mēró(s), 1610, 1611
merosthenic, 1611
merpeople, 1607
merry-(?), 272, 273
merry-go-round, 1612
merrymaker, 1612
merrythought, 1612
merx, 1555, 1609
mes-, 1617
mesati-, 1577, 1617, 1636
mesaticephalic, 1614
mesatikerkik, 1614
mesatipelvic, 1614
mesencephalon, 1617
mesi-, 1617
mesiad, 1617
mesio-, 1577, 1617, 1636
mesiobuccal, 1616
mesiolingual, 1616
mesioversion, 1616
meso-, 1526, 1577, 1613,
    1614, 1615, 1616, 1636
Mesoamerica, 1617
meso-omentum, 1617
mesopneumon, 1617
méso(s), 1614, 1616, 1617
'mess', 419
mé(s)sat(os), 1614
'Messiah', 475
met-, 1618
met(á), 1618, 1625
meta-, 1527, 1621, 1624
'metal', 1619
metalinguistic, 1618
metall-, 1619
metallesthesia, 1619
métallo(n), 1619
metallophobia, 1619
metalloporphyrin, 1619
metallotherapy, 1619
'metal plate', 881
'metal spike', 1705
metameric, 1618
metasilicate, 1618
met(e), 1574
meteor-, 1620
meteorism, 1620
meteorology, 1620
meteorophobia, 1620
meteororesistant, 1620
metéōro(s), 1620

miopus, 1649
'mirror', 386
mis-, 1650
mis-¹, 1530, 1575
mis-², 1647, 1649, 1650
mis-³, 1653
misadventure, 1651
misanthropic, 1653
'miscarriage', 866
miscarry, 1650
'miscarry', 866
mischief, 1651
miscreant, 1651
misdeed, 1650
mislead, 1650
miso-, 1652
misocainia, 1653
misologia, 1653
misopedia, 1653
mîso(s), 1653
'mistletoe', 2781
mit-, 1654
'mite', 14
mitochondria, 1654
mitogenetic, 1654
mitokinesis, 1654
mito(s), 1654
mitosis, 1654
mîx(is), 1655
mixobarbaric, 1655
mixolydian (mode), 1655
mixoscopia, 1655
'Mn', 1548
mōbile, 190
mōbil(is), 190
mock-apple, 1656
mock-heroic, 1656
mock-up, 1656
'model', 1295, 2708, 2715
mōdor, 1666
mogiarthria, 1657
mogigraphia, 1657
mogilalia, 1657
mógi(s), 1657
mógos, 1657
'moist', 1275, 2810
'moistened', 2810
'molar', 1690
'molar teeth', 1690
'mold', 2041, 2043
'molded', 2041, 2043
'mole', 1725
molere, 1642

mol(īnum), 1642
mon-, 1661
mōn(a), 1663
monarch, 1661
Mon(e)ke, 1660
monēre, 1662
monē(ta), 1659
Monēta, 1659
'money', 378
moneybags, 1659
'money-box', 378
moneychanger, 1659
moneywort, 1659
monkey-bread, 1660
monkey-flower, 1660
monkeyshine, 1660
*mon(no), 1660
mono-, 1658
mono-, 1661
monobasic, 1661
monogametic, 1661
monoinfection, 1661
móno(s), 1661
'monster', 2571, 2572
monstr(ī), 1662
monstri-, 1602
monstricide, 1662
monstriferous, 1662
monstriparity, 1662
monstr(um), 1662
'(lunar) month', 1597
'moon', 1597, 2288
moon-, 1597, 1631
moonbeam, 1663
mooncalf, 1663
moonflower, 1663
moqu(er), 1656
'more', 2051, 2060
'more remote', 803
'more than', 2508
morph(ḗ), 1039, 1664
morpho-, 1039
morphodifferentiation, 1664
morphogenetic, 1664
morphophoneme, 1664
'morsel (of food)', 277
mos, 1665
-mos, 922
'moss', 297
mossback, 1665
moss-grown, 1665

mosstrooper, 1665
'mother', 1565, 1629, 1630
mother-, 1565, 1629
mother-in-law, 1666
motherland, 1666
mother-naked, 1666
'motion', 490, 1404
'(undulating) motion',
    1429
'motion picture camera or
    projector', 490
'motion picture photogra-
    phy', 490
moto-, 1667
motofacient, 1667
mōtor, 1667
motor-, 896
motorbike, 1667
motorgraphic, 1667
motoro-, 1667
motorogerminative, 1667
motorpathy, 1667
'mottled', 2074
mōt(us), 1667
'mountain', 1840
Moûs(a), 1679
'mouse', 1678, 1691
mouse-, 1678, 1691
mousefish, 1668
mousehole, 1668
mousetrap, 1668
mousikó(s), 1679
'mouth', 299, 1842, 1846,
    2467
mouth-, 1547
mouthbreeder, 1669
mouthpiece, 1669
mouthwash, 1669
'movable', 190, 1404
'move', 490, 896, 1403,
    1404, 1406, 1530, 1575,
    1667, 2314
'move about', 2794
'move ahead', 2663
'move back and forth',
    2802
'move beyond', 1916
'moved', 1404
'movement', 490, 1403,
    1406, 2227
'move out or away', 896
'move quickly', 2816

myring-, 1698
myring(a), 1698
myringitis, 1698
myringod-, 1698
myringodectomy, 1698
myringodermatitis, 1698
myringomycosis, 1698
myringoplasty, 1698
myrio-, 1694, 1696, 1697
myriophyllous, 1699
myriopod, 1699
myrío(s), 1697, 1699
myriosporous, 1699
myrme-, 1700
myrmeco-, 1040
myrmecology, 1700
myrmecophagous, 1700
myrmecophile, 1700
mýrmēk(os), 1700
Myrmeleon, 1700
mýrmē(x), 1700
myrmic-, 1700
Myrmicidae, 1700
myrobalan, 1701
mýro(n), 1701
myron-, 1701
myronic, 1701
myropolist, 1701
myrosin, 1701
Myrospermum toluiferum,
2632
Myroxylon, 1701
mý(s), 93
mythology, 1702
mythomania, 1702
mythophobia, 1702
mýtho(s), 1702
myurous, 1691
myx-, 1703
mýx(a), 1563, 1703
myxedema, 1703
myxo-, 1563, 1674, 1675,
1684, 1685
myxoblastoma, 1703
myxoglobulosis, 1703
myxorrhea, 1703

N

n, 71, 95
n-, 1413, 1744, 1747, 1754
(er)n, 211
'=NH', 82, 83, 85, 1306,
1307

'NH₂CO·NH₂', 2737
'NO₂', 1733
'Na', 2377
nabātu, 1707
'Na₂CO₃·10H₂O', 1733
nǣdl, 1715
nǣfre, 1724
næ(ge)l, 1705
náer, 1712
n(a)ev(us), 1725
'nail', 1202, 1808
nail-, 1808
nailbone, 1705
nailbrush, 1705
nailhead, 1705
'nails of the digits', 1808
'naked', 209, 1154, 1759
'name', 1807
nān, 1735
nán(n)o(s), 1706
nanocormia, 1706
nanocurie, 1706
nanosecond, 1706
'nape of the neck', 1337
naphth-, 1707
naphthamine, 1707
náphth(as), 1707
naphthol, 1707
naphthopyrine, 1707
naphthoquinone, 1707
naphthoresorcine, 1707
narc-, 1708
narco-, 1709
narcoanesthesia, 1708
narcomania, 1708
narcose, 1708
narcostimulant, 1708
nárk(ē), 1708
'narrow', 1475, 2452
narrow-, 1708
narrow-gage, 1709
narrow-minded, 1709
narrow-mouthed (toad),
1709
'narrow passage or ridge',
1367
'narrow passage or strip',
1367
nas-, 1710
nasal, 1710
naso-, 1750
nasoantritis, 1710

nasolabial, 1710
nasosinusitis, 1710
nās(us), 1710
'native', 189
'native speaker of Span-
ish', 1237
'nativity', 242
'natron', 1733, 1734
'natural', 189, 2004
'natural ability', 907
'natural bodily coloring',
2016
'(large) natural stream',
2214
'nature', 2004, 2005
'navel', 1801
n-butane, 1704
n-butanol, 1704
ne, 1723, 1724, 1735,
1739, 1760
ne-, 1717
'near', 6, 11, 30, 34, 35,
41, 43, 45, 50, 95, 128,
136, 159, 168, 219, 877,
891, 897, 899, 918,
1380, 1954, 2052, 2110,
2112, 2113, 2490, 2492,
2496, 2507, 2510, 2513
nearby, 1712
'nearest', 2121
near-hand, 1712
'nearly', 1941
near-sighted, 1712
nearu, 1709
(h)nec(ca), 1713
'neck', 418, 574, 575, 750,
2656
neck-(?), 1758, 1761
'neck chain', 575
necklace, 1713
neckline, 1713
necktie, 1713
necr-, 1714
necremia, 1714
necro-, 1736
necrobiosis, 1714
necron-, 1714
necronectomy, 1714
necropyoculture, 1714
necrosadism, 1714
nectere, 34
'needle', 28, 2412

nitr-, 1733
nitrate, 1733
nitro-, 784, 1734, 2678
nitrobenzene, 1733
nitrogen, 197
nitroglycerin, 1733
nitro(n), 1733, 1734
nitroprotein, 1733
nitros-, 1734
nitrosamine, 1734
nitroso-, 1733
nitrosobacteria, 1734
nitrosoindol, 1734
nitrososubstitution, 1734
nitrōs(us), 1734
nitr(um), 1734
'no', 1739
no-, 2, 94, 1286, 1298,
    1303, 1311, 1355, 1723,
    1724, 1739, 1760, 2724
no-, 1735
'no longer alive', 731
no-account, 1735
nobody, 1735
noc(ēre), 1736
noci-, 1714
nociceptor, 1736
nocifensor, 1736
nociperception, 1736
noct-, 1730, 1762
noctalbuminuria, 1737
noctambulation, 1737
nocti-, 1737
noctiphobia, 1737
noct(is), 1737
nocturia, 1737
no-hitter, 1735
nom-, 1738
nomism, 1738
nomo-, 116
nomocanon, 1738
nomogenesis, 1738
nómo(s), 116, 1738
nomotopic, 1738
non, 1739
non-¹, 2, 94, 1286, 1298,
    1303, 1311, 1355, 1723,
    1724, 1735, 1760, 2724
non-², 1741
nōna, 1741
nona-, 908, 1732, 1740,
    1743
nōn(a hōra), 1743

nonacyclic, 1741
nonadecane, 1741
nonagon, 1741
nonantigenic, 1739
nonconformist, 1739
'none', 1735, 1760
noni-, 1741
nonipara, 1741
'nonmilled substance', 92
'non-other', 2289
nonstop, 1739
nonyl, 1741
nookleptia, 1742
noon-, 908, 1732, 1741
noonday, 1743
noontide, 1743
noontime, 1743
noopsyche, 1742
nóo(s), 1742
'noose', 1439
noothymopsychic, 1742
nor'-, 1748
nor-¹, 1413, 1704, 1747,
    1754
nor-², 1748
noratropine, 1744
nor'easter, 1748
norleucine, 1744
norm-, 1747
norm(a), 1744, 1747
nor(mal), 1704, 1744
'normal', 1704, 1844
normāl(is), 1744
Norman, 1748
normergic, 1747
normo-, 1413, 1704, 1744,
    1754
normoadrenelin, 1744
normocytosis, 1747
normosexual, 1747
normothermia, 1747
'Norsemen', 2228
norþ, 1748
north-, 1745, 1746
northbound, 1748
northeast, 1748
Northfield, 1748
nos-, 1751
noscere, 1754
'nose', 1710, 2201
nose-, 1710
nosebleed, 1750

nose-dive, 1750
nosegay, 1750
nosetiology, 1751
noso-, 1749
nosogenesis, 1751
nosology, 1751
nosophobia, 1751
nóso(s), 1751
'nostril', 1563
nos(u), 1750
'not', 1, 13, 22, 44, 92, 93,
    94, 115, 116, 174, 197,
    730, 753, 762, 767, 776,
    795, 1286, 1298, 1303,
    1355, 1723, 1724, 1735,
    1739, 1760, 2687, 2724
'not-', 1311
not-¹, 1754
not-², 1755
not(a), 1754
notable, 1754
'not acute', 1769
notanencephalia, 1755
'not any', 1760
'notch', 2278
'not closed', 1814
'not covered', 1814
'not curved', 2472
note-, 1413, 1744, 1747,
    1752
notebook, 1754
notecase, 1754
noteworthy, 1754
'not fast', 2366
'not good', 202
'not hard', 2378
'not heavy', 1484
'not high', 1512
'not in bondage', 1047
'not light', 724
'not long', 2324
noto-, 1753
'not obscure', 519
notochord, 1755
notochord, 469
notogenesis, 1755
notomyelitis, 1755
nôto(s), 1755
'not smooth', 2224
'not soft', 1175
'nourishment', 1042, 2688
nouvelles, 1727

nov-, 1756
nova, 1727
novepithel, 1756
novi-, 1756
novilunar, 1756
novo-, 1717, 1726
novobiocin, 1756
novoepinephrine, 1756
novoscope, 1756
nov(us), 1756
no(x), 1737
'nozzle of a lamp', 1563
ntr(j), 1733
nu-, 71
nuc(is), 1758
nucle-, 1758
nuclease, 1758
nuclei-, 1758
nucleiform, 1758
nucleo-, 1713, 1761
nucleofugal, 1758
nucleohistone, 1758
nucleospindle, 1758
nucle(us), 1758
'nucleus', 1385, 1582
nud-, 1759
nudi-, 1154
nudibranch, 1759
nudicaul, 1759
nudipelliferous, 1759
nudism, 1759
nudo-, 1759
nudophobia, 1759
nūd(us), 1759
nulli-, 2, 94, 1286, 1298,
    1303, 1311, 1355, 1723,
    1724, 1735, 1739, 2724
nulliparous, 1760
nullipennate, 1760
nullisomatic, 1760
null(us), 1760
'number', 1266
'numbness', 1708
'nut', 1385, 1758
nut-, 1713, 1758
nutcracker, 1761
nutgall, 1761
nutmeg, 1761
(h)nut(u), 1761
nu(x), 1758
nwy, 1731
nyct-, 1762
nyctalopia, 1762

nycto-, 1730, 1737
nyctohemeral, 1762
nyctophobia, 1762
nyctophonia, 1762
nykt(ós), 1762
nymph-, 1763
nýmph(ē), 1763
nymphectomy, 1763
nymphocaruncular, 1763
nymphomaniac, 1763
nymphotomy, 1763
ný(x), 1762

O

o-¹, 1844
o-², 1809
-ō, 113, 936, 957, 2112
'-O:N', 1734
'O₃', 1876, 1878
'oak', 624, 2161
oak-apple, 1767
oak-leaved (geranium),
    1767
oakmoss, 1767
'oak tree', 836
'oar', 1882
'Oars(men)', 2228
'oats', 1181
ob, 1768, 1786, 1813
ob-, 918, 1770, 1786,
    1813, 1817
ob-, 1769, 1770
object, 1768
'oblique', 1513
obovate, 1768
O'Brian, 1764
'observation', 2471
'observe', 2275, 2471
'obstruction', 893
'obtain', 1090
obtundere, 1769
obtusifolious, 1769
obtusilingual, 1769
obtusilobous, 1769
obtūs(us), 1769
obviate, 1768
oc-, 918, 1768, 1771,
    1786, 1813, 1817
oc-, 1770, 1771
-(o)ca, 564
occidental, 1770
occipit-, 1771

occipital, 1771
occipital bone, 1771
'occipital protuberance',
    1337
occipitoanterior, 1771
occipitofacial, 1771
occipitothalamic, 1771
occipit(um), 1771
occiput, 1771
'occiput', 1337
occult, 1770
occupy, 1770
'ocean', 2283
ocell-, 1772
ocellated, 1772
ocelli-, 960, 1775, 1816,
    1818, 1827, 2825
ocellicyst, 1772
ocelliferous, 1772
ocelligerous, 1772
ocell(us), 1772
ochrodermatitis, 1773
ochrometer, 1773
ochronosis, 1773
ōchró(s), 1773
O'Connor, 1764
oct-, 1774
octa-, 1774
octastich, 1774
octi-, 1774
octiparous, 1774
octō, 1774
octo-, 876
octodont, 1774
octogynous, 1774
octolateral, 1774
octon-, 1774
octonocular, 1774
octopod, 1774
ocul-, 1775
oculist, 1775
oculo-, 960, 1772, 1816,
    1818, 1827, 2825
oculocephalogyric, 1775
oculomotor, 1775
oculoreaction, 1775
ocul(us), 1772, 1775
ocydrome, 1776
Ocyphaps, 1776
Ocypoda, 1776
'odd', 1958
odd(a)-, 1777

oddball, 1777
oddi, 1777
'odd-numbered', 1309,
  1958
'odd (of numbers)', 1309
odd-pinnate, 1777
oddside, 1777
-*ode*, 2042
o-dinitrobenzene, 1844
odo-, 1241
odometer, 1241
odont-, 1779
odontitis, 1779
odonto-, 746, 1911, 2640
odontoblastoma, 1779
odontoiatria, 1779
odónt(os), 1779
odontosteophyte, 1779
odor, 1780, 1792
'odor', 1847, 1849, 1877
odori-, 1792, 1847, 1849,
  1877, 1878
odoriferous, 1780
odorimeter, 1780
odoriphore, 1780
odōr(is), 1780
odoro-, 1780
odorography, 1780
'odors', 1847
od(oús), 1779
odyn-, 1781
odýn(ē), 1781
odynolysis, 1781
odynometer, 1781
odynophagia, 1781
odynphagia, 1781
oeco-, 863
oecology, 863
-*o(ei)dē(s)*, 474, 578, 616,
  1349, 1561, 2042
oen-, 1783
oenanthol, 1783
oeno-, 909, 2779
oenology, 1783
oenomania, 1783
oenomel, 1783
oesophago-, 937
oesophagostomiasis, 937
of, 4, 1785, 1787
'of', 4
of-, 1786
of-¹, 3, 8, 10, 42, 131,
  1787

of-², 918, 1768, 1770,
  1813, 1817
'(house) of the Lord', 480
ofcome, 1785
ofer, 1865
off-, 3, 8, 10, 42, 131,
  1785
offal, 1785
offbeat, 1787
'off-center', 2355
off-color, 1787
offend, 1786
offer, 1786
offshoot, 1787
'offspring', 982, 2106
offuscate, 1786
'of little means', 2082
'of one another', 68
'of or pertaining to the
  planet Mars', 148
'of or pertaining to the
  sweet', 1104
ofsake, 1785
'of recent origin', 1726,
  1727
'o heal', 1287
oidiomycosis, 1809
oiko-, 863
oikophobia, 863
oíko(s), 863
'oil', 359, 884
'(olive) oil', 884, 1791
oil-, 884, 1791, 1794
oilcan, 1789
oilcloth, 1789
oilfish, 1789
oîno(s), 1783
ois(ein), 937
oisophágo(s), 937
ōký(s), 1776
-*ol*, 359, 1976
-*ola*, 1372
old, 2837
'old', 1887, 2099
old-, 73
'old age', 1089
Old Betsy, 1149
'older', 2118
old-fashioned, 1790
old-maidish, 1790
'old man', 1089
old-man's-beard, 1790

ole-, 1791
Olea europaea, 1794
olein, 1791
oleo-, 359, 884, 1789,
  1794
oleochrysotherapy, 1791
oleogranuloma, 1791
oleomargarine, 1791
ole(um), 359, 1791
olfacere, 1792
olfact-, 1792
olfactism, 1792
olfacto-, 1780, 1847, 1849,
  1877, 1878
olfactology, 1792
olfactometer, 1792
olfactophobia, 1792
olfact(us), 1792
olig-, 1793
oligarchy, 1793
oligocystic, 1793
oligodynamic, 1793
oligonatality, 1793
olígo(s), 1793
olive-, 884, 1791
'olive tree', 1789, 1791
oliveback, 1794
olive-green, 1794
olivewort, 1794
oln, 882
-*ol(us)*, 291
om-, 1800
-*ōma*, 2859
omalgia, 1800
omega-, 71
'omen', 1662, 2571, 2572
oment-, 1797
omentectomy, 1797
omentofixation, 1797
omentosplenopexy, 1797
omentovolvulus, 1797
ōment(um), 923, 1797
'omentum', 923
omicron-, 71
omnidirectional, 1799
omnigraph, 1799
omnipresent, 1799
omni(s), 1799
omo-, 26, 1265, 1795
omocephalus, 1800
omoclavicular, 1800
ōmo(s), 26, 1800

opo-², 1812
opobalsamum, 1819
opocephalus, 1818
opodidymus, 1818
Opomyza, 1818
opopanax, 1819
ōp(ós), 1818, 1819, 2113
opotherapy, 1819
oppilate, 1813
oppose, 1813
'opposing', 123, 764, 769, 899, 2830
'opposite', 804, 899
'(territory) opposite facing', 644
'opposite of bad', 1126
'opposite of white', 247
'opposite to', 123
'opposite to right', 1468
oppress, 1813
ōp(s), 1625, 1818, 2113
ops(é), 1821
opsi-¹, 1818
opsi-², 1824
opsialgia, 1818
opsigenes, 1821
opsimathy, 1821
opsino-, 1826
opsinogenous, 1826
opsiuria, 1821
opso-¹, 1818
opso-², 1821
opso-³, 1826
opsoclonia, 1818
opsogen, 1826
opsomenorrhea, 1821
ópson, 1826
opson-, 1826
opsoni-, 1826
opsonic, 1826
opsoniferous, 1826
opsonin, 1826
opsono-, 1822, 1825
opsonocytophagic, 1826
opsonology, 1826
opsonotherapy, 1826
opt-, 1827
optesthesia, 1827
opti-, 1827
optic-, 1827
optical, 1827
optico-, 386, 960, 1775, 1816, 1818, 2825

opticociliary, 1827
opticokinetic, 1827
opticonasion, 1827
optikó(s), 1827
optimeter, 1827
opto-, 1827
optomeninx, 1827
op(tós), 386
or-, 1842
-or, 1023, 1667
oral, 1842
'orange or red pigment', 365
'orange-yellow', 1517
orbis, 1829
orbit-, 1829
orbit(a), 1829
orbital, 1829
orbitonasal, 1829
orbitostat, 1829
orbitotomy, 1829
orchi-, 1832
orchid-, 1831
orchidectomy, 1831
orchido-, 1832
orchidocelioplasty, 1831
orchidoptosis, 1831
*órchid(os), 1831
orchidotherapy, 1831
orchio-, 1830, 1831
orchiocele, 1832
orchiomyeloma, 1832
órchi(os), 1832
órchios (órcheōs), 1831
orchioscheocele, 1832
orchiotomy, 1832
órchi(s), 1831, 1832
'order', 169, 825, 2546
'ordered series or procession', 991
ordināre, 1833
'ordinary', 1744
ordinatoliturate, 1833
ordinatomaculate, 1833
ordinatopunctate, 1833
ordināt(us), 1833
'ore', 1646
ore-, 1840
oreo-, 1840
Oreodon, 1840
oreography, 1840
ór(eos), 1840

organ-, 1835
'organic appendage', 133
organism, 1835
'organization', 2445
'organized structure', 1835
organo-, 930, 2836
organofaction, 1835
'organ of hearing', 857
'organ of respiration', 1516
'organ of sight', 960
'organ of smell', 1750
'organ of the body', 1592
organogel, 1835
organogenesis, 1835
órgano(n), 1835
ori-¹, 1840
ori-², 181
ori-³, 1842
Oribates, 1840
'origin', 141
'original', 141
'originating', 944
orinasal, 1842
oriole, 181
ō(ris), 1842, 1846
'ornamental netlike fabric', 1439
órni(s), 1839
ornith-, 1839
ornithine, 1839
ornithocephalous, 1839
ornithology, 1839
ornithopter, 1839
órnith(os), 1839
oro-¹, 1834, 1836
oro-², 181
oro-³, 1828, 1838, 1846
oro-⁴, 2306
orodiagnosis, 1843
orogeny, 1840
Orohippus, 1840
oroide, 181
oroimmunity, 1843
orolingual, 1842
orology, 1840
oromeningitis, 1843
oronasal, 1842
oropharynx, 1842
ór(os), 1840
'orpiment', 155

passio, 1918
passionflower, 1918
passionfruit, 1918
passion(is), 1918
Passiontide, 1918
passkey, 1916
passport, 1916
passus, 590, 1916, 1917
password, 1916
pastime, 1916
patch-, 2012
patch(e), 1919
patchhead, 1919
patchstand, 1919
patchwork, 1919
pat(e)r, 1921
pat(é)r(os), 1921
'path', 1241, 2658
path-, 1920
pathergasia, 1920
patho-, 2521
pathocrinia, 1920
pathoformic, 1920
pathogenesis, 1920
páth(os), 1920, 2521
patī, 1918
patr-, 1921
patriarch, 1921
patrilineal, 1921
patrimony, 1921
patr(is), 1921
patro-, 1921
patroclinous, 1921
patronymic, 1921
pauci-, 1932, 2082
paucidentate, 1922
pauciflorous, 1922
pauciradiate, 1922
pauc(us), 1922
'paunch', 1072
pau(pe)r, 2082
pa(x), 1925
pay-, 1925
payload, 1923
paymaster, 1923
payoff, 1923
'Pb', 1462, 2058
p-dichlorbenzene, 1903
peace-, 1923
peacemaker, 1925
peace-pipe, 1925
peacetime, 1925
peach-black, 1926

peachblow, 1926
peachwort, 1926
'peak', 2010
peamouth, 1924
peanut, 1924
pearlash, 1927
pearleye, 1927
pearlfish, 1927
peashooter, 1924
'pebble', 617, 618
'peculiar', 875
ped-[1], 1932
ped-[2], 1933
pedal, 1933
pedi-[1], 1932
pedi-[2], 1933
pediatrics, 1932
pedicure, 1933
pediodontia, 1932
ped(is), 1933
pedo-[1], 1883, 1884, 1922,
   1928, 1930, 2082
pedo-[2], 1031, 1929, 1931,
   2018, 2072
pedobarometer, 1932
pedodynamometer, 1933
pedograph, 1933
pedomorphism, 1932
pēdón, 2018
pedopathy, 1933
pedophobia, 1932
*pēdót(ēs), 2018
'peek', 1934
'peeled', 1475
'peep', 2015, 2026
peephole, 1934
Peep-O'-Day (Boy), 1934
peepshow, 1934
pegboard, 1935
pegbox, 1935
peg-legged, 1935
pelohemia, 1936
pelology, 1936
pēló(s), 1936
pelotherapy, 1936
pelt-, 1938
pelt(a), 1937
pélt(ē), 1937, 1938
pelti-, 1938
peltifolious, 1937
peltiform, 1937
peltinerved, 1937

pelto-, 1937
Peltocephalus, 1938
Peltochelys, 1838
Peltogaster, 1938
Peltops, 1938
pelveo-, 1939
pelveoperitonitis, 1939
pelvicephalometry, 1939
pelvifixation, 1939
pelvio-, 1939
pelviolithotomy, 1939
pelvirectal, 1939
pelvi(s), 1939
pelvo-, 1939
pelvoscopy, 1939
pen-[1], 973, 1942, 2024,
   2131, 2133
pend(ere), 133
pene-, 1941
penecontemporaneous,
   1941
peni(ġ), 1943
peninsula, 1941
peninvariant, 1941
'penis', 1970
penknife, 1940
penman, 1940
penn(a), 1940, 1942
penname, 1940
'pennant', 1007
penni-, 973, 1940, 2024,
   2131, 2133
penniform, 1942
pennigerous, 1942
penninerved, 1942
penny-a-liner, 1943
pennyweight, 1943
pennyworth, 1943
pent-[1], 1946
pent-[2], 1949
penta-, 977, 998, 1004,
   1006, 1944, 1947, 1949,
   2166
penta-, 1946
pentagon, 1946
pentamethylene, 1946
pentatonic, 1946
pént(e), 1946, 1949
pente-, 1946
Pentecost, 1946
pentnucleotide, 1949
pento-[1], 1946

phagocaryosis, 1967
phagomania, 1967
phagotherapy, 1967
phainein, 1974, 1975
phainesthai, 1971, 1974
phaió(s), 1966
phak-, 1964
phakitis, 1964
phako-, 1964
phakó(s), 1964
phakoscope, 1964
'phalangeal joint', 1414
phalangectomy, 1969
phalangitis, 1969
phalango-, 1969
phalangophalangeal, 1969
phálang(os), 1969
phalangosis, 1969
phálan(x), 1969
phall-, 1970
phalle-, 1970
phallephoric, 1970
phallic, 1970
phallo-, 205
phallocampsis, 1970
phalloplasty, 1970
phallorrhagia, 1970
phalló(s), 1970
phaneîn, 768
phaner-, 1971
phanero-, 1974, 1992
phanerogenetic, 1971
phaneromania, 1971
phaneroplasm, 1971
phaneró(s), 1971
phanerosis, 1971
pharmac-, 1972
pharmacist, 1972
pharmacodiagnosis, 1972
pharmacomania, 1972
pharmacotherapy, 1972
phármako(n), 1972
pharyng-, 1973
pharyngitis, 1973
pharyngoglossal, 1973
pharyngomaxillary, 1973
pháryng(os), 1973
pharyngospasm, 1973
pharynx, 1973
phen-, 1975
(acide) phén(ique), 1975
pheno-[1], 768, 1965, 1971, 1975, 1992

pheno-[2], 1971, 1974, 1976, 1977, 1992
phenobarbital, 1975
phenocryst, 1974
phenol, 359, 1976
'phenol', 1975
phenol-, 1971, 1974, 1975, 1992
phenolemia, 1976
phenology, 1974
phenolphthalein, 1976
phenolquinine, 1976
phenothiazine, 1975
phenotype, 1974
phenoxanthein, 1975
phenoxycaffeine, 1975
phenyl, 1977
phenyl-, 788, 1971, 1974, 1975, 1979, 1992, 2680
phenylcarbinol, 1977
phenylethylamine, 1977
phenylquinoline, 1977
pheo-, 1966
pheochrome, 1966
phérein, 1810, 1984
φ-carbinol, 1977
phil-, 1980
philanthropy, 1980
philodendron, 1980
philology, 1980
philopatridomania, 1980
phílo(s), 1980
phleb-, 1981
phlebitis, 1981
phlebocarcinoma, 1981
phlebolith, 1981
phleb(ós), 1981
phlebotropism, 1981
'phlegm', 249
phleîn, 1981
phlé(ps), 1981
phlog-, 1982
phlogistic, 1982
phlogo-, 247, 254, 1008, 1012
phlogocyte, 1982
phlogogenic, 1982
phlog(ós), 1982
phlogoxelotism, 1982
phló(x), 1982
phon-, 1983
phonautograph, 1983

phōn(é̄), 1983
phonograph, 1983
phonophobia, 1983
phonoreceptor, 1983
phor-, 1984
phoreîn, 1810
phoria, 1984
phoro-, 242, 1810, 1991
phoroblast, 1984
phorology, 1984
phorometer, 1984
phóro(s), 1984
-phoros, 1810
phō̂(s), 1992
phos-, 1992
phō̂s (pháos), 1966
phos- (photo-), 1991
phosgenic, 1992
phosph-[1], 1988, 1991
phosph-[2], 1988
phat-, 1987, 1990, hosp.ph
phosphata-, 1988
phosphatagenic, 1988
phosphat(e), 1988
phosphatemia, 1988
phosphatidosis, 1988
phosphatine, 1988
phosphato-, 1988
phosphatoptosis, 1988
phosphite, 1991
phospho[1], 1991
phospho-[2], 1988
phosphocreatinase, 1988
phospholipid, 1991
phosphor-, 1986, 1988, 1989
phosphorenesis, 1991
phosphorhidrosis, 1991
phosphoro-, 1988, 1991
phosphorolysis, 1991
phosphoruria, 1991
phosphorus, 1991
phosphuria, 1988
phot-, 1992
photo-, 1966, 1971, 1974, 1985, 1991
photoelectron, 1992
photography, 1992
photomontage, 1992
photopsia, 1992
phōt(ós), 1992
photosynthesis, 1992

pilot-, 1031, 1933, 2072
pilotfish, 2018
pilothouse, 2018
pilotweed, 2018
pil(us), 2017
pimel-, 972, 2025
pimel(ḗ), 2019
pimele-, 2019
Pimelepterus, 2019
pimelitis, 2019
pimelo-, 2019
pimeloma, 2019
pimelopterygium, 2019
pimeluria, 2019
'pimple', 1899
pin-, 973, 1942, 2024,
    2131, 2133
pinball, 2020
pinchbottle, 2021
pinchcock, 2021
pinchpenny, 2021
*pinctiāre, 2021
pincushion, 2020
pineapple, 2022
pinedrops, 2022
pinesap, 2022
pinn(a), 2020, 2023, 2024
pinnati-, 973, 1942, 2024,
    2131, 2133
pinnatilobate, 2023
pinnatipartite, 2023
pinnatisect, 2023
pinnāt(us), 2023
pinni-, 973, 1942, 2020,
    2023, 2131, 2133
pinniform, 2024
pinninerved, 2024
pinnitarsal, 2024
pinpoint, 2020
pīn(us), 2022
Pinus, 2022
pio-, 972, 2019, 2107
pio-epithelium, 2025
piŏn, 2025, 2107
pion-, 2025
pionemia, 2025
Piophila, 2025
piorthopnea, 2025
pioscope, 2025
pipal(lī), 1950
pīp(āre), 2026
'pipe', 2029, 2382, 2528
pipe-, 2015

pipe-clay, 2026
pipefish, 2026
pip(en), 1934
piper, 2027
Piper nigrum, 1950
piperazine, 2027
piperidine, 2027
piperine, 2027
piperism, 2027
pipestone, 2026
pīpiāre, 2015
pippalī, 2027
pirula, 1927
pisci-, 1002
piscicolous, 2028
pisciculture, 2028
pisciform, 2028
pisci(s), 2028
pi(sos), 1924
pištal(a), 2029
pistol-grip, 2029
pistol-handle, 2029
pistol-whip, 2029
'pit', 265
pitch-1, 2009, 2010
pitch-black, 2032
pitchblende, 2032
pitch-dark, 2032
pitchfork, 2031
pitchman, 2031
pitch-out, 2031
pitfall, 2030
pitman, 2030
pitsaw, 2030
'pitted', 265
'pivot', 60
'pivotal point', 60
pi(x), 2032
'place', 473, 591, 2092,
    2309, 2774
place-, 989, 1011, 1018,
    1890, 2034, 2035, 2039,
    2040, 2041, 2043, 2046
'placed', 2446
'place for computation',
    643
'place for trade', 1555
place-kick, 2033
placeman, 2033
place-name, 2033
placent-, 2034
placent(a), 2034

placenta-, 2034
placentapepton, 2034
placentitis, 2034
placento-, 989, 1011,
    1018, 1890, 2035, 2039,
    2040, 2041, 2043, 2046
placentocytotoxin, 2034
placentogenesis, 2034
placentopathy, 2034
plagi-, 2035
plagio-, 989, 1011, 1018,
    1890, 2034, 2039, 2040,
    2041, 2043, 2046
plagiocephalic, 2035
plagioclase, 2035
plagiodont, 2035
plágio(s), 2035
plagiotropism, 2035
'plague', 1961
'plain', 792, 2125
plain-, 989, 1011, 1018,
    1890, 2034, 2035, 2039,
    2040, 2041, 2043, 2046
plainchant, 2036
plainclothes, 2036
plain-spoken, 2036
'plaited', 2048
plan-1, 2039
plan-2, 2040
'plane', 1246
planet, 2040
'planet Mars', 148
plani-, 2039
planigram, 2039
plano-1, 989, 1011, 1018,
    1890, 2034, 2035, 2036,
    2037, 2040, 2041, 2043,
    2046
plano-2, 989, 1011, 1018,
    1890, 2034, 2035, 2038,
    2039, 2041, 2043, 2046
planoblast, 2040
planocellular, 2039
planoconvex, 2039
planocyte, 2040
planography, 2039
Planorbis, 2039
pláno(s), 2040
planotopokinesia, 2040
'plant', 264, 2007
'plant juice', 2247
'plant life', 264

pluvi-, 2062
pluvi(a), 2062
pluvial, 2062
pluvio-, 1016, 1017, 1024,
2061, 2068, 2137, 2146
pluviograph, 2062
pluviometer, 2062
pluvioscope, 2062
pneîn, 2063, 2066, 2068
pneo-, 2066, 2068
pneodynamics, 2063
pneogaster, 2063
pneograph, 2063
pneohydrothorax, 2069
pneum-¹, 2066
pneum-², 2068
pneûma, 2066
pneuma-, 2066
pneumarthrosis, 2066
pneumascope, 2066
pneumat-, 2066
pneumathemia, 2066
pneumato-, 2063, 2064,
2067, 2068, 2069
pneumatodyspnea, 2066
pneumatology, 2066
pneumatometer, 2066
pneúmat(os), 2066
pneumectomy, 2068
pneumo-¹, 1273, 2066,
2069, 2152
pneumo-², 1016, 1017,
1024, 2061, 2062, 2065,
2070, 2137, 2146
pneumoalveolography,
2068
pneumochirurgia, 2068
pneumohemia, 2066
pneumohydrometra, 2069
pneumohydropericadrium,
2069
pneúmōn, 2068
pneumon-, 2068
pneumonia, 2068
pneumono-, 2068, 2137
pneumonocirrhosis, 2068
pneumopexy, 2068
pno(ė̃), 2063
pocketbook, 2071
pocket-handkerchief, 2071
pocketknife, 2071
pod-, 2072
podiatry, 2072

podo-, 1031, 1933, 2018
podobromidrosis, 2072
pododerm, 2072
podograph, 2072
pod(ós), 2072
poecil-, 2074
poecilo-, 2074
poecilocytosis, 2074
poecilonomy, 2074
poeir, 2096
pofamic, 2095
poikil-, 2074
poikilergasia, 2074
poikilo-, 992, 2011, 2016,
2073
poikiloblast, 2074
poikilocytosis, 2074
poikilo(s), 2074
poikilothermal, 2074
'point', 406, 407, 628,
1777, 2009, 2412
'point of a compass', 406,
407
point-blank, 2075
'pointed', 12, 16, 23, 25,
28, 29, 1871, 1875,
1876
'pointed protuberance',
628
'pointed tool', 2009
point-set, 2075
point-to-point, 2075
'poison', 2650
'poisonous substance',
2651
'poke', 2140
polari-, 574, 704, 1888,
2560, 2813
polarimeter, 2076
polār(is), 2076
polariscope, 2076
polaristrobometer, 2076
polar(ization), 2076
polaro-, 2076
polarogram, 2076
pole, 2076
'pole', 2076
polio-, 2078
poliocidal, 2077
polioencephal-, 2078
polioencephalitis, 2078
polioencephalomeningo-
myelitis, 2078

polioencephalopathy, 2078
polioencephalotropic, 2078
poliomyelopathy, 2077
polió(s), 2077
poliothrix, 2077
pol(us), 2076
poly-, 1054, 2050, 2051,
2060
polyceptor, 2079
polychromatic, 2079
'polymer', 1618, 1903
polyorchidism, 2079
polý(s), 2051, 2079
pomiculture, 2080
pomiferous, 2080
pomiform, 2080
pomo-, 2080
pomology, 2080
pōm(um), 2080
'pond', 1607
ponere, 591, 2092
ponograph, 2081
ponopalmosis, 2081
ponophobia, 2081
póno(s), 2081
'pool', 1489
poor-, 1922, 1932
poorhouse, 2082
poor-mouth, 2082
poor-spirited, 2082
popcorn, 2083
popeyed, 2083
popgun, 2083
'poppy', 1896
poque, 2071
por-, 2088
poradenitis, 2088
porc(us), 2086
pore, 2088
pori-, 2088
poriferous, 2088
porkchop, 2086
porkfish, 2086
porkpie (hat), 2086
pórn(ē), 2087
pornocracy, 2087
pornography, 2087
pornolagnia, 2087
poro-, 2084, 2085, 2090
porocephalosis, 2088
poroplastic, 2088

póro(s), 2088
porotomy, 2088
porph-, 2089
porphin, 2089
porpho-, 2089
porphobilin, 2089
porphýr(a), 2089
porphyria, 2089
porphyrin, 2089
porphyropsin, 2089
'porridge', 171
port-, 2090
portāre, 2090, 2431
porte-, 2088, 2431
porte-acid, 2090
porte-aiguille, 2090
porte-noeud, 2090
porte(r), 2090
'portion', 364, 1610, 1913, 2012
portmanteau, 2090
'position', 2033, 2445, 2774
'(military) position', 2092
positus, 2092
'-possessing', 621
post, 2091, 2093
post-¹, 2093
postcard, 2092
postcerebellar, 2091
postdiastolic, 2091
'posterior', 2195
'posterior appendage', 2533
postero-, 2091
posteroanterior, 2093
posterolateral, 2093
posteroparietal, 2093
poster(us), 2093
posthaste, 2092
postmaster, 2092
postwar, 2091
potam-, 2095
potam, 2095
Potamogale, 2095
potamography, 2095
potamology, 2095
potamó(s), 2095
'potash', 64, 1383
potassium, 1383
potbelly, 2094
potboiler, 2094
potluck, 2094

pot(t), 2094
'pouch', 306, 713, 1534, 2071
'pour', 442, 481, 482
'pour into', 1335
'pour out', 1335
po(ús), 2072
'powder derived by sublimation', 54, 62
'powdery white limestone', 425
'power', 613, 852, 1035, 1535
powerboat, 2096
power-dive, 2096
'powerful', 1035, 2484
powerhouse, 2096
pr(a)e, 2098
prae-, 2098
praecordial, 2098
'prayer', 221
pre-, 968, 1032, 1038, 1041, 1903, 1953, 1954, 1958, 2097, 2102, 2103, 2104, 2108, 2110, 2118, 2119, 2121
'precede', 1038
precirrhosis, 2098
preconscious, 2098
'pregnancy', 710
premere, 2100, 2101
'preparation of food', 608
'prepare', 825, 826, 1904
'prepare (against)', 1905
'prepared', 2182
'prepared (for a ride)', 2182
presbyacusia, 2099
presbyopic, 2099
présby(s), 2099
presbysphacelus, 2099
'presence of nitrogen', 197
'preserving or giving life', 197
'press', 507, 958, 2013, 2100, 2101
press-, 958, 2101
'press out', 958
press(āre), 2100
pressi-, 2101
pressinervoscopy, 2101
pressman, 2100

pressmark, 2100
presso-, 2100
pressometer, 2101
pressoreceptor, 2101
pressosensitive, 2101
pressroom, 2100
press(ūra), 2101
'pressure', 212, 2013, 2101
press(us), 2100, 2101
'prevailing weather', 527
prewar, 2098
'price', 434
'prick', 165
'pricker', 12
'prickle', 2416
'prickly seed case', 305
prim-, 2102
'primary', 2117
primere, 958
'primeval', 914
primi-, 968, 1032, 1038, 1041, 1903, 1953, 1954, 1958, 2098, 2103, 2104, 2108, 2110, 2118, 2119, 2121
primigenial, 2102
primigravida, 2102
primiparous, 2102
'primitive', 141, 1887
primo-, 2102
primogeniture, 2102
primordial, 2102
prīm(us), 2102
'principal', 1535
'print type', 591
printing press, 2100
'prison', 1372
'private tutor', 546
prīvō, 2108
prīvus, 2108
'privy', 419
pró, 2103, 2104, 2107, 2114
pro-¹, 968, 1032, 1038, 1041, 1903, 1953, 1954, 1958, 2098, 2102, 2104, 2107, 2108, 2110, 2114, 2118, 2119, 2121
pro-², 968, 1032, 1038, 1041, 1903, 1953, 1954, 1958, 2098, 2102, 2103, 2108, 2110, 2118, 2119, 2121

prō prī(vō), 2108
proatlas, 2103
'probe', 2009
proceed, 2104
'proceed', 1107
procephalic, 2103
proct-, 2105
proctatresia, 2105
proctoclysis, 2105
proctocolitis, 2105
proctology, 2105
Procyon lotor, 610
'produce', 982
'produce a current of air',
253
'produced by heating',
2155
'produces motion', 1667
'producing', 1271
'-producing', 701
'production', 1876
'profound', 736
progenitor, 2104
proistánai, 2114
prōktó(s), 2105
prōl(ēs), 2106
prolicide, 2106
proliferous, 2106
proligerous, 2106
prop-, 2109
propamidine, 2107
propane, 2107
'propel', 829, 830
'propelling', 830
propene, 2107
prop(ionic acid), 2107
proprio, 968
proprio-, 1032, 1038,
1041, 1903, 1953, 1954,
1958, 2098, 2102, 2103,
2104, 2110, 2118, 2119,
2121
proprioceptor, 2108
propriodentium, 2108
proprionic acid, 2107
propriospinal, 2108
propri(us), 2108
proptosis, 2103
propylamine, 2109
propylene, 2109
propylthiouracil, 2109
prós, 2110, 2112, 2113
pros-¹, 2119

pros-¹, 968, 1032, 1038,
1041, 1903, 1953, 1954,
1958, 2098, 2102, 2103,
2104, 2108, 2112, 2113,
2118, 2121
pros-², 2112
proselyte, 2110
prosencephalon, 2112
prosenchyma, 2110
prósō, 2112
proso-, 968, 1032, 1038,
1041, 1903, 1953, 1954,
1958, 2098, 2102, 2103,
2104, 2108, 2110, 2111,
2118, 2119, 2121
prosocoele, 2112
prosodemic, 2112
prosody, 2110
prosogaster, 2112
prosop-, 2113
prosopectasia, 2113
prosopoanoschisis, 2113
prosopodiplegia, 2113
prōsōpo(n), 2113
prosopopilar, 2113
'prosperity', 867
prostat-, 2114
prostate gland, 2114
prostatectomy, 2114
prostát(ēs), 2114
prostatocystitis, 2114
prostatolithotomy, 2114
prostatovesiculitis, 2114
'prostitute', 2087, 2821
prot-, 2119
protalbumose, 2119
prote-, 2117
'protection against dis-
ease', 1308
'protects', 1145
protein, 2117
protein-, 2117
protéine, 2117
proteini-, 2117
proteinivorous, 2117
proteino-, 2116
proteinochrome, 2117
proteinogenous, 2117
proteinotherapy, 2117
proteinphobia, 2117
prōte(îos), 2117
proteo-, 2117

proteopeptic, 2117
proter-, 2118
proterandry, 2118
protero, 968, 1032
protero-, 1041, 1903,
1953, 1954, 1958, 2098,
2100, 2102, 2103, 2104,
2108, 2119, 2121
protero-, 1038
proterobase, 2118
proteroglyph, 2118
prótero(s), 2118
Proterosaurus, 2118
proteuric, 2117
proto, 968, 1032
proto-, 1038, 1041, 1903,
1953, 1954, 1958, 2098,
2100, 2102, 2103, 2104,
2108, 2115, 2117, 2118,
2120, 2121
Proto-Indo-European,
2119
protoplasm, 2041
prôto(s), 2117, 2119
prototype, 2119
protovertebra, 2119
protozo-, 2120
protozoa, 2120
protozoa-, 2120
protozoacide, 2120
protozoiasis, 2120
protozoology, 2120
protozoophage, 2120
protozootherapy, 2120
'protruded viscus', 1223
'protrusion of tissue',
1223
pro-war, 2104
proxim-, 2121
proximad, 2121
proximo-, 968, 1032,
1038, 1041, 1903, 1953,
1954, 1958, 2098, 2100,
2103, 2104, 2108, 2118,
2119
proximoataxia, 2121
proximobuccal, 2121
proximoceptor, 2121
proxim(us), 2121
psamm-, 2122
psamme-, 2122
psammead, 2122

'put away', 9
put-down, 2143
put(en), 2143
'put in order', 825, 826,
1833
put-on, 2143
'put on', 917
'putrefaction', 2301
'putrid', 2251, 2301
'put together', 591
put-upon, 2143
py-, 2150
pyarthrosis, 2150
pycn-, 2145
pycno-, 2148
pycnodont, 2145
pycnometer, 2145
pycnometochia, 2145
pycnospore, 2145
pyel-, 2146
pyelitis, 2146
pyelo-, 1016, 1017, 1024,
2061, 2062, 2068, 2137,
2740
pyelocystitis, 2146
pyelofluoroscopy, 2146
pyelogram, 2146
pýelo(s), 2146
pyg-, 2147
pyg(é), 2147
pygist, 2147
pygoamorphus, 2147
pygodidymus, 2147
pygopod, 2147
pykn-, 2145
pyknemia, 2145
pykno-, 2145
pyknocardia, 2145
pyknó(s), 2145
pylor-, 2149
pyloralgia, 2149
pylori-, 2149
pyloristenosis, 2149
pylorodilator, 2149
pylorogastrectomy, 2149
pylōró(s), 2149
pylorospasm, 2149
pyo-, 1043, 2144, 2151,
2152
pyochezia, 2150
pyoculture, 2150
pyocyan-, 2151
pyocyanase, 2151

pyocyanin, 2151
pyocyanobacterin, 2151
pyocyanogenic, 2151
pyocyanolysin, 2151
pyoderma, 2150
pŷo(n), 2150
pŷr, 2154, 2155
pyr-, 2155
pyrazoline, 2155
pyret-, 2154
pyretic, 2154
pyreto-, 1000, 2155
pyretogenetic, 2154
pyretology, 2154
pyretó(s), 2154
pyretotyphosis, 2154
pyro-, 1000, 2153, 2154
pyroform, 2155
pyrogenic, 2155
pyromania, 2155
pyt(t), 2030

Q

qahwah, 561
qalay, 64, 1383
(al-)qalīy, 64, 1383
qāneh, 346
qinnāmōn, 492
qu, 11
quadr-, 2156
quadr(a), 2435
quadrangle, 2156
quadri-, 1044, 2159, 2435,
2575
quadri-, 2156
quadriceps, 2156
quadrilateral, 2156
quadriplegia, 2156
quadru-, 2156
quadruped, 2156
quanti-, 2160, 2812, 2814,
2815, 2819
quantification, 2157
quantimeter, 2157
quantivalence, 2157
quant(us), 2157
'quarry-stone', 401
quart-, 2159
quartār(ius), 2158
quarter-, 1044, 2156,
2159, 2575
quarterback, 2158

quarterdeck, 2158
quartertone, 2158
quarti-, 1044, 2156, 2158,
2575
quartinvariant, 2159
quartiporous, 2159
quartisect, 2159
quartisternal, 2159
quart(us), 2158, 2159
quasi, 2160
quasi-, 2157, 2374, 2812,
2814, 2815, 2819
quasifaithful, 2160
quasifatal, 2160
quasiheroic, 2160
quattuor, 2156
quercetin, 2161
quercin, 2161
quercite, 2161
querc(us), 624, 2161
Quercus, 1767
Quercus suber, 624
quick-, 239, 2785, 2790,
2856
quick-freeze, 2162
'quickness', 2405
quicksand, 2162
quickset, 2162
'quicksilver', 1609
'quicksilver-capturing',
1608
quillback, 2163
quillfish, 2163
quillwort, 2163
quin-[1], 2166
quin-[2], 452
quinamidine, 2165
quincunx, 2166
quinidine, 2165
quinine, 2165
quino-, 2165
quinoform, 2165
quinqu-, 2166
quin(que), 494, 495, 2166,
2167
quinque-, 494, 495, 977,
998, 1004, 1006, 1946,
2167
quinquecuspid, 2166
quinquennial, 2166
quinquesyllable, 2166
quinquevalent, 2166

reflexograph, 2189
reflexotherapy, 2189
reflex(us), 2189
'refraining from', 1030
'refusal to work', 2481
'regard', 1508
regiō, 644
re(ĝ)n, 2174
rē(gu)l(a), 2173
'regular', 1744, 1747
'regularly recurring motion', 2208
'relationship of contrast or mutuality', 68
'release', 1524
'relish', 1826
'remaining one', 1856
'remnant', 1007
'removal', 729
'remove liquid', 822
'remove one's cloak', 2259
'remunerate', 1923
'remuneration', 1923
ren-, 2190
renal, 2190
'(basin-shaped) renal pelvis', 2146
'rend', 2213
rēn(ēs), 35, 2190
'renew', 2470
reni-, 35
renicardiac, 2190
reniform, 2190
renipuncture, 2190
'rennet', 547
reno-, 2190
renogastric, 2190
'rent', 969
'repair', 2470
'repeating', 1888
'repetition', 862
'reproduction', 613, 1083
'reproductive organs', 1082, 1122
'reptile', 1224
'resembling', 1248, 1903
'resembling the male', 1184
'resound', 652
'respiration', 173, 2063, 2066
'respiratory organ of a fish', 1094

'restlessness', 46
'resulting from', 866
rēt(e), 2191, 2192, 2193
reti-, 928, 2192, 2193, 2194
reticul-, 2192
reticular, 2192
reticulo-, 928, 2191
reticulocytopenia, 2192
reticuloendothelial, 2192
reticulopod, 2192
rēticul(um), 2192
retiform, 2191
retin-, 2193
retin(a), 2193
retinitis, 2193
retino-, 928, 2191
retinodialysis, 2193
retinomalacia, 2193
retinopapillitis, 2193
'retinue', 646
rēt(is), 2191
retisolution, 2191
retispersion, 2191
reto-, 2191
retoperithelium, 2191
retr-, 2195
retrad, 2195
'retreat', 419
retrō, 2195
retro-, 2181
retrobuccal, 2195
retrograde, 2195
retropharyngitis, 2195
'return', 80
'returned sound', 862
'returning', 1888
'reversal', 729
'reversed', 69
reword, 2181
rhabd-, 2196
rhabdite, 2196
rhabdomancy, 2196
rhabdomyoblastoma, 2196
rhabdophobia, 2196
rhábdo(s), 2196
rhach-, 2169
rhachi-, 2169
rhachialgia, 2169
rhachio-, 2169
rhachiomyelitis, 2169
rháchi(os), 2169

rháchi(s), 2169
rhachitis, 2169
rhamph-, 2198
Rhamphalcyon, 2198
rhampho-, 2206, 2769, 2770, 2838, 2839
Rhamphocoelus, 2198
rhamphorhynchine, 2198
rhámpho(s), 2198
rhamphotheca, 2198
rhe-, 2199
rheîn, 2199, 2200
rheo-, 2200, 2208
rheobase, 2199
rheology, 2199
rhéo(s), 2199
rheostosis, 2199
rheotaxis, 2199
rheum-, 2200
rheûma, 2200
rheuma-, 2200
rheumapyra, 2200
rheumarthritis, 2200
rheumat-, 2200
rheumatalgia, 2200
rheumatism, 2200
rheumato-, 2199, 2208
rheumatocelis, 2200
rheumatology, 2200
rheumatopyra, 2200
rheúmat(os), 2200
rhin-, 2201
rhinallergosis, 2201
rhinochiloplasty, 2201
rhinolalia, 2201
rhinoreaction, 2201
rhin(ós), 2201
rhipi-, 2202
Rhipicera, 2202
rhipid-, 2202
rhipidoglossate, 2202
Rhipidogorgia, 2202
Rhipidopterygia, 2202
rhipîd(os), 2202
rhipidura, 2202
rhipi(s), 2202
rhi(s), 2201
rhiz-, 2203
rhiz(a), 2203
rhizo-(?), 2170, 2175, 2219
rhizodontropy, 2203
rhizomelic, 2203

roper, 2226
Róps(menn), 2228
roti-, 2218, 2225
Rotifera, 2223
rotiform, 2223
rotispinalis, 2223
'rotten', 1043, 2251, 2301
rotul(a), 2218
*ro(tu)l(āre), 2218
ro(t)und(us), 2225
'rough', 2657
'rough (artery)', 2657
rough-and-tumble, 2224
roughcast, 2224
roughdry, 2224
'rough stone', 2257
round-, 2223
roundabout, 2225
'round(ed)', 607, 1769, 2685
'rounded outward', 607
Roundhead, 2225
roundhouse, 2225
'round off', 2700
'round plate', 796, 799
'route of travel', 2804
'row', 2463
'row of bushes', 1193
'royal dwelling or retinue', 646
'royalty', 677
(vo)rsum, 2512
'rub', 2483
'rubricate (with red lead)', 1647
'rudder', 2018, 2458
rudder-, 2228
rudderfish, 2226
rudderhead, 2226
rudderpost, 2226
'ruddy', 935
rūh, 2224
'rule', 116, 1744, 1747
'rump', 2147
'run', 831, 2168
runaround, 2227
run-in, 2227
runway, 2227
'rupture', 1223
'rural land', 644
Rus', 2228
'rush', 2168
'Russia', 2228

Russ(ian), 2228
Russo-, 2226
Russo-Japanese (War), 2228
Russophile, 2228
Russophobia, 2228
'rut', 1829

S

s, 159, 761, 795, 855, 2529
-s, 877, 2239, 2431
'S', 2498
'SO$_2$', 2499
saberbill, 2229
saber-fish, 2229
saber-toothed (tiger), 2229
sabre-, 2229
sabre-fish, 2229
'sac', 463, 713, 720, 2582
sacc-, 2232
saccate, 2232
sacchar-, 2231
saccharo-, 2494, 2497
saccharobacillus, 2231
saccharogalactorrhea, 2231
saccharomycetic, 2231
saccharose, 2231
sacci-, 2232
sacciform, 2232
sacco-, 2230
saccobranchiate, 2232
saccocirrus, 2232
saccophore, 2232
'sack', 161, 203
'sack in which spores are formed', 161
sacr-, 2233
sacralgia, 2233
'sacred', 1165, 1231
'sacred (bone)', 2233
sacri-, 2233
sacriplex, 2233
sacrococcyx, 2233
sacrodynia, 2233
sacroiliac, 2233
sacrum, 2233
(os) sacr(um), 2233
saddle-, 2309, 2350
saddleback, 2234
saddlebag, 2234
saddlecloth, 2234

sadol, 2234
sǣ, 2283
sǣp, 2247
s(a)ept(a), 2303
s(a)et(a), 2310
safe-, 1245, 2386
safe-conduct, 2235
safekeeping, 2235
safelight, 2235
sa(g)u, 2256
'sail', 2068
sailboat, 2236
sailcloth, 2236
sailfish, 2236
sal, 2241, 2254
sal-^{1}, 2242
sal-^{2}, 2241
sal(a), 2239
salesclerk, 2239
salesmanship, 2239
salesroom, 2239
sali-^{1}, 2242
sali-^{2}, 1169, 2238, 2244, 2254
salic(is), 2242
Salicornia, 2241
salicyl-, 2237, 2240
salicylamide, 2242
salicylanilide, 2242
salicylic acid, 2242
salicylquinine, 2242
saliferous, 2241
salimeter, 2241
saline, 2241
saliphen, 2242
sal(is), 2241
'saliva', 2134, 2329
'salivary glands', 2329
sali(x), 2242
'sallow', 1773
salo-, 2242
saloquinine, 2242
salping-, 2243
salpingitis, 2243
salpingocatheterism, 2243
salpingo-oophorectomy, 2243
salpingoovariotomy, 2243
sálping(os), 2243
sálpin(x), 2243
sals(a), 2254
'salt', 1169, 2241, 2254

sitophobia, 2351
sîto(s), 1906, 2351
sitotherapy, 2351
sit(tan), 2350
'situation', 2437
sit-up, 2350
six, 1006, 2311
'six', 1227, 2312
six-, 1227, 2312
six-gun, 2352
six-pack, 2352
sixpenny, 2352
'six-sided solid', 685
skab(br), 2258
skápho(s), 2260
skat(ós), 2263
skel-, 2271, 2272
skelalgia, 2353
skelasthenia, 2353
skelatony, 2353
skele-, 2354
skelet-, 2354
skeletin, 2354
skeleto-, 2270
skeletogenous, 2354
skeletography, 2354
skeletology, 2354
(sōma) skeletó(n), 2354
skeletopia, 2354
skél(os), 2353
skewback, 2355
skewbald, 2355
skew-symmetrical, 2355
skiá, 2356
skia-, 2268
skiabaryt, 2356
skiagraph, 2356
skiascope, 2356
skill(a), 2269
'skin', 471, 474, 696, 751, 1277
skin-, 2256, 2257, 2331
'(true) skin', 471, 921
skin-deep, 2357
skin-dive, 2357
skinflint, 2357
skin(n), 2357
skip-bomb, 2358
skipdent, 2358
skipjack, 2358
skir(ra), 2262
skirt, 2321
skler-, 2270

sklerema, 2270
sklēró(s), 2270
skṓlēk(os), 2271
skṓle(x), 2271
skoli-, 2272
skolió(s), 2272
skoliosis, 2272
skop(eîn), 2275
skopo-, 2275
skopometer, 2275
skor, 2263, 2278
skóto(s), 2279
skrabbe, 651
(e)sku(er), 2355
'skull', 657
ský, 2362
'sky', 2736
skydive, 2362
sky-high, 2362
skylark, 2362
slag, 833
'slander', 757, 758
'slanderer', 757, 758
'slant(ed)', 348
'slanting', 1513, 2035
slap-, 1500, 2364
slapdash, 2363
slapjack, 2363
slap(p), 2363
slapshot, 2363
slāw, 2366
'sleep', 1281, 2390
sleep-, 1500, 2363
sleep-in, 2364
sleepwalking, 2364
sleepwear, 2364
slēp, 2364
'slice', 695
'slide (away)', 2365
'slight', 147
'slime', 1674, 1684, 1685, 1703
'slimy substance', 1673, 1675
slipknot, 2365
slip(pen), 2365
'slipper', 321
slipstitch, 2365
slip-up, 2365
'slope', 527, 529, 530, 1443
'sloping', 2035
'slow', 213, 274

slowdown, 2366
slowpoke, 2366
slow-witted, 2366
'smacking blow', 2363
smæl, 2367
'small', 273, 1634, 1635, 1647, 1915
'small ax', 1180
'small bladder', 2772
'small cavity', 75
'small cell', 396
'small closed space', 395
'small dish or bowl', 1397
'small end branch', 291
'small (esp. glandular) cavity', 682
'small face', 1846
'small fiber', 985
'small ham', 1927
'small hook (used in knitting)', 672
'small insect', 302
'small invertebrate', 1340
'small (likeness)', 1647
'small mark', 2075
'small mask', 1846
small-minded, 2367
'small net', 2192
'small orifice', 2088
'small pear', 1927
'small pouch', 2071
smallpox, 2367
'small rounded mass', 468
'small sea-going vessel', 255
'small storeroom', 396, 397
small-time, 2367
'small tube', 2697
'smash', 659
'smell', 1780, 1792, 1847, 1877, 1878
'smell(ing)', 1849
smoc(a), 2368
'smoke', 173, 353, 737, 847, 2598, 2612, 2710, 2714
smokehouse, 2368
smokejack, 2368
smokestack, 2368
'smooth', 115, 1246, 1470, 2125

tél(os), 170, 2559, 2560, 2631
témnein, 912
'temple', 2562
tempor(is), 2562
temporofacial, 2562
temporopontile, 2562
temporosphenoid, 2562
temp(us), 2562
ten, 1732
'ten', 733, 809, 844, 977
ten-¹, 733, 734, 977, 1216
ten-², 2567
ten-³, 2568
'ten thousand', 1697
tenalgia, 2568
tendere, 2566, 2569
'tendinous end of a
  muscle', 132
tendō, 2566
tendo-, 2567, 2568, 2569,
  2574, 2637
tendolysis, 2566
'tendon', 132, 2568
tendōn(is), 2566
tendosynovitis, 2566
tendovaginitis, 2566
'tendril', 498
tēn(e), 2563
ténein, 2568, 2574
ten-gallon (hat), 2563
teni-, 2532, 2564, 2566,
  2568, 2569, 2574, 2637
tenia-, 2567
teniacide, 2567
tenial, 2567
teniasis, 2567
tenicide, 2567
tenifugal, 2567
tenio-, 2567
teniotoxin, 2567
teno-, 2565, 2566, 2567,
  2569, 2574, 2637
tenodesis, 2568
ténō(n), 2568
'tenon', 507
tenon-, 2568
tenonitis, 2568
tenont-, 2568
tenontectomy, 2568
tenonto-, 2568
tenontomyotomy, 2568
téno(ntos), 2568

tenoplastic, 2568
tenosuspension, 2568
tenpenny (nail), 2563
tenpin, 2563
tensiō, 2569
tensio-, 2566, 2567, 2568,
  2574, 2637
tensio-active, 2569
tensiometer, 2569
'tension', 2401, 2574,
  2637
tensiō(nis), 2569
tensiophone, 2569
tens(us), 2569
ter, 2570
ter-, 2573, 2605, 2668
-*tēr*, 388, 913, 959, 1342,
  2738
tera-, 2572
teracycle, 2571
terahertz, 2571
teraohm, 2571
téra(s), 2571, 2572
terat-, 2572
teratism, 2572
terato-, 2571
teratoblastoma, 2572
teratogenetic, 2572
teratophobia, 2572
térat(os), 2571, 2572
tercentenary, 2570
'terminus', 902
-*teros*, 1226
teroxide, 2570
terra, 644
'terrible', 785
'territory', 743
tervalent, 2570
-*t(ēs)*, 929
test-, 2573
testi-(?), 2570, 2605, 2668
testibrachium, 2573
'testicle', 205, 922, 1831,
  1832
testicond, 2573
testis, 2573
'testis', 1116
testitis, 2573
testitoxicosis, 2573
testo-, 2573
testopathy, 2573
tetan-, 2574

tetani-, 2574
tetanic, 2574
tetaniform, 2574
tetano-, 2566, 2567, 2568,
  2569, 2637
tetanometer, 2574
tetanomotor, 2574
tetanós, 2574
tetanotoxine, 2574
tetanus, 2574
tetr-, 2575
tetra-, 1044, 2156, 2159
tetra-, 2575
tetrabasic, 2575
tetradactylous, 2575
tetratomic, 2575
tetravaccine, 2575
téttares, 2575
'Teutonic people', 1088
th, 761
(*Joachims*)*t(h)aler*, 812
thal-, 2578
thalam-, 2576
thalamencephalon, 2576
thalamocrural, 2576
thalamolenticular, 2576
thálamo(s), 2576
thalamotomy, 2576
thalamus, 2576
thalass-, 2577
thálass(a), 2577
thalassi-, 2577
thalassic, 2577
Thalassicolla, 2577
thalassio-, 2577
thalassiophyte, 2577
thalassographic, 2577
thalassometer, 2577
thalassotherapy, 2577
thalgrain, 2578
thall-, 2578
thállein, 2578
thallic, 2578
thallium, 2578
thallogen, 2578
thallophyte, 2578
thalló(s), 2578
thallotoxicosis, 2578
thallus, 2578
thanat-, 2579
thanatobiologic, 2579
thanatognomic, 2579

'towards', 1802, 2625
towboat, 2645
towline, 2645
towpath, 2645
tox-¹, 2650, 2651
tox-², 2651
toxemia, 2651
toxenzyme, 2650
toxi-¹, 2650
toxi-², 2651
toxic-, 2650
toxicide, 2650
toxico-, 2646, 2648, 2651, 2652
toxicoderma, 2650
toxicology, 2650
toxicomania, 2650
Toxicophidia, 2650
toxigenic, 2651
toxikón, 2650
(phármakon) toxikó(n), 2650
toxin-, 2647, 2649, 2650, 2653
toxinantitoxin, 2651
toxinemia, 2651
toxini-, 2651
toxinicide, 2651
toxino-, 2651
toxinosis, 2651
toxinotherapy, 2651
toxo-¹, 2650
toxo-², 2651
toxogen, 2650
toxoinfection, 2651
tóx(on), 2650
tra-, 2661
'trace', 1289
trach-, 2657
trache-, 2657
trachea-, 2657
tracheaectasy, 2657
tracheîa, 2657
(artēría) trache(îa), 2657
tracheitis, 2657
trachel-, 2656
trachelagra, 2656
trachelobregmatic, 2656
trachelocystitis, 2656
trachelo-occipitalis, 2656
tráchēlo(s), 2656
tracheo-, 2655
tracheofissure, 2657

tracheomalacia, 2657
tracheostenosis, 2657
trachitis, 2657
trachý, 2657
trachýs, 2657
'track', 1289, 1829, 2658
trade, 2658
'trade', 434, 1555
trade-, 831, 2663
trade-in, 2658
trade-last, 2658
trademark, 2658
traduce, 2661
træp(pe), 2663
trag-, 2659
tragacanth, 2659
tragomaschalia, 2659
tragophony, 2659
tragopodia, 2659
trágo(s), 2659
'trails', 2660
'train', 357
trainbearer, 2660
train(e), 2660
trainmaster, 2660
trainsick, 2660
'train soldiers', 828
'tranquility', 1925
trans, 2661, 2662
trans-, 2609, 2654, 2662
transaminase, 2661
'transcript', 613
translucent, 2661
'transparent', 683, 768
transplutionan, 2661
transvers-, 2662
transversectomy, 2662
transversocostal, 2662
transversospinalis, 2662
transversotomy, 2662
transvers(us), 2662
trap-, 831, 2658
trapball, 2663
trap-door (spider), 2663
trapshooting, 2663
traum-, 2664
traûma, 2664
'trauma', 1736
trauma-, 2664
traumasthenia, 2664
traumat-, 2664
traumatherapy, 2664

traumatic, 2664
traumato-, 828, 2604, 2693, 2700
traumatogenic, 2664
traumatopathy, 2664
traúmat(os), 2664
traumatotherapy, 2664
'traverses', 2662
tre-, 2668
tredecaphobia, 2668
'tree', 745, 836, 2833
tree-, 745, 846, 2691
treefish, 2666
treehopper, 2666
treetop, 2666
tr(e)î(s), 2668, 2684
'trembling', 2667
tremograph, 2667
tremolabile, 2667
tremophobia, 2667
tremo(r), 2667
tremor-, 2667
tremorgram, 2667
'trench', 2260
trē(o), 2666
Treponema pallidum, 2527
trēs, 2668
trētós, 174
tri-, 2570, 2573, 2605, 2665, 2669, 2671, 2673, 2674, 2675, 2676, 2677, 2678, 2679, 2680, 2681, 2682, 2683, 2684
tri-, 2668, 2674
trí(a), 2668, 2684
tria-, 2668
triakaidekaphobia, 2668
triangle, 2668
'triangular', 2674
'tribe', 2001
trich-, 2672
trichitis, 2672
tricho-, 2670
trichobezoar, 2672
trichofibroacanthoma, 2672
Trichomonas, 2672
trich(ós), 2672
tricycle, 2668
trigon-, 2674
trigonitis, 2674
trigonocephalic, 2674

'turning about quickly',
  2817
'turn like a wheel', 2218
turnover, 2700
turnpike, 2700
turtleback, 2701
turtlehead, 2701
turtleneck, 2701
-tus, 2167
twā, 2704, 2706
*twa-lif, 2703
tway-, 2704
twayblade, 2704
twelf(e), 2703
'twelve', 809, 844, 845
twelve-, 232, 238, 243,
  761, 794, 839, 842,
  2706
'twelve p.m.', 1743
twelvemonth, 2703
twelvepenny, 2703
twelve-tone, 2703
'twenty', 1293
twi-, 232, 238, 243, 761,
  794, 839, 842, 2702,
  2706
twi-, 2704
twibill, 2704
'twice', 232, 243, 761, 794
'twice as large', 816
'twice as much', 816
twifoil, 2704
twilight, 2704
'twin', 922, 2633
(ǵe)twin(n), 2705
twin-, 232, 238, 243, 761,
  794, 839, 842, 2706
twinberry, 2705
twinborn, 2705
twin-screw, 2705
'twist', 369, 1708, 1709,
  2477, 2478, 2479, 2604,
  2664, 2829
'twisted', 1198, 2048,
  2473, 2477, 2480
'twisting', 2478
two, 2605
'two', 77, 79, 88, 89, 231,
  809, 839, 842, 844,
  2704
two-, 231, 232, 238, 243,
  761, 794, 839, 842,
  2703, 2704, 2705

'two-', 922
two-bit, 2706
'two by two', 238
twofer, 2706
'twofold', 232, 243, 789,
  816
'two-left (over)', 2703
two-step, 2706
'two (together)', 238
tympan-, 2707
tympani-, 2707
'tympanic membrane',
  1698
tympanichord, 2707
tympanitis, 2707
tympano-, 2453, 2715
tympanohyal, 2707
tympanolabyrinthopexy,
  2707
týmpano(n), 2707
tympanotemporal, 2707
tympanum, 2707
type-, 2453, 2707, 2715
typecast, 2708
typeface, 2708
typewriter, 2708
typh-, 2714
typhemia, 2714
typhl-¹, 737, 847, 2598,
  2612, 2712, 2713, 2714
typhl-², 2713
typhlitis, 2713
typhlo-¹, 2710
typhlo-², 737, 847, 2598,
  2612, 2710, 2711, 2714
typhlocolitis, 2713
typhlolithiasis, 2713
typhlology, 2710
Typhlophthalmi, 2710
Typhlops, 2710
typhló(s), 2710, 2713
typhlosis, 2710
typhlostomy, 2713
typho-, 737, 847, 2598,
  2612, 2709, 2710, 2713
typhobacillosis, 2714
typhoid fever, 2714
typhomania, 2714
typhorubeloid, 2714
týpho(s), 2710, 2714
typo-, 2453, 2707, 2708
typographic, 2715
typology, 2715

týpo(s), 2708, 2715
typothetae, 2715
typ(pi), 2624
tyr-, 2716
tyremesis, 2716
tyro-, 310, 2388, 2610,
  2695
tyrocidine, 2716
tyrogenous, 2716
tyró(s), 308, 309, 310,
  2716
tyrotoxin, 2716

U

'ugly old woman', 1164
ui, 1764
ul-¹, 2720
ul-², 1859, 2721
-ula, 355, 397, 2170, 2218,
  2281, 2331, 2756, 2772
(o)ûl(a), 2720
'ulcer', 430
'(syphilitic) ulcer', 430
ule-, 2718
-ul(e), 1480
(o)ul(ḗ), 2718
ulectomy-¹, 2720
ulectomy-², 2718
ulegyria, 2718
ulerythema, 2718
ull(us), 1760
uln-, 2719
uln(a), 882, 2719
ulnar, 2719
ulnocarpal, 2719
ulnometacarpal, 2719
ulnoradial, 2719
ulo-¹, 1858, 1860, 2717
ulo-², 2718
ulo-³, 1201, 1861, 2756,
  2794, 2809
ulocarcinoma, 2720
uloglossitis, 2720
Ulophocinae, 2722
(o)ûlo(s), 2722
ulosis, 2718
Ulothrix, 2722
ulotomy-¹, 2720
ulotomy-², 2718
ulotrichous, 2722
ultrā, 2723

ureterodialysis, 2738
ureterovaginal, 2738
urethr-, 2741
(o)urḗthr(a), 2741
urethratresia, 2741
urethro-, 2742, 2744, 2745
urethrobulbar, 2741
urethrograph, 2741
urethroprostatic, 2741
(o)urētikó(s), 2743
'urge', 1258
uri-, 2743
uric-, 2743
uric acid, 2743
uricase, 2743
urico-, 2744, 2745
uricocholia, 2743
uricolysis, 2743
uricometer, 2743
urin-, 2744
ūrīn(a), 2744
urina-, 2744
'urinary duct', 2738
urinaserum, 2744
'urinate', 2738, 2741
'urine', 2738, 2741, 2743,
    2744, 2745
urinemia, 2744
urini-, 2744
uriniparous, 2744
urino-, 2745
urinocryoscopy, 2744
urinoglucosometer, 2744
urinosexual, 2744
urisolvent, 2743
uro-¹, 2732, 2737, 2738,
    2741, 2743, 2744, 2747,
    2748
uro-², 2733
urobilin, 2747
urobilinemia, 2747
urobilinicterus, 2747
urobilino-, 2747
urobilinogen, 2747
urobilinuria, 2747
urochord, 2746
urocrisia, 2745
urofuscohematin, 2745
(o)ûro(n), 2738, 2741,
    2743, 2745
urono-, 2745
uronology, 2745
urophobia, 2745

uropod, 2746
uropygium, 2746
Ursus, 223
'usage', 942, 1738
'useless', 1468
'usual', 1747
ūt, 1862
uter-, 2749
uteritis, 2749
utero-, 1285, 2765, 2771
uteroabdominal, 2749
uterolith, 2749
uterothermometry, 2749
uter(us), 1285, 2749
'uterus', 1630
utrum, 1723
'utterly', 730, 753, 762,
    764, 776, 795, 1953
ūv(a), 2750
uve-, 2750
uvea, 2750
uveitis, 2750
uveoparotid, 2750
uveoplasty, 2750
uveoscleritis, 2750
uvi-, 2751
uviofast, 2751
uviol, 2751
uviometer, 2751
uvioresistant, 2751
'uvula', 496, 2441

V

v, 3, 8, 30
vacc(a), 2752
vacci-, 2752
vaccin-, 2752
vaccination, 2752
vaccin(e), 2752
vaccingenous, 2752
vaccini-, 2752
vaccinifer, 2752
vaccinogen, 2752
vaccinophobia, 2752
vaccinostyle, 2752
(vīrus) vaccīnus, 2752
'vacillate', 2816
væng(r), 2827
vag-, 2755
vagin-, 2754
vāgīn(a), 2754
'vagina', 570, 583, 890

'vaginal discharge', 1501
vagini-, 2754
vaginicoline, 2754
vaginitis, 2754
vaginoabdominal, 2754
vaginometer, 2754
vaginovesical, 2754
vagitis, 2755
vago-, 2753
vagogram, 2755
vagosympathetic, 2755
vagotonic, 2755
'vaguely distant land',
    1147
(nervus) vag(us), 2755
vall(um), 2795
vallus, 2795
valv(a), 2756
valve, 2756
'(little) valve', 2756
valvul-, 2756
valvul(a), 2756
valvulitis, 2756
valvulo-, 1201, 2722, 2794,
    2809
valvuloplasty, 2756
valvulotome, 2756
valvulotomy, 2756
van(nus), 966
vapo-, 2757
vapor, 2757
'vapor', 173, 353, 1007,
    2063
vapor-, 2757
vaporiferous, 2757
vaporiform, 2757
vaporimeter, 2757
vapōr(is), 2757
vaporize, 2757
vapotherapy, 2757
varic-, 2758
varic(is), 2758
varicoblepharon, 2758
varicocele, 2758
varicophlebitis, 2758
varicosis, 2758
'variegated', 2074
'variety of pulse', 1924
'various', 2074
vari(x), 2758
'varix', 499
vas, 2760, 2761

viniferous, 2779
vinificator, 2779
vino-, 2779
vinometer, 2779
vīn(um), 2778, 2779, 2826
vinyl, 2779
'violence', 1035
violet, 2751
'violet', 1349, 1350
'violetlike', 1349
'violin', 988
'viper', 860
'virgin', 1914
'visage', 961, 962
visc-, 2781
viscer-, 2780
viscer(a), 2780
'viscera', 2424
visceralgia, 2780
visceri-, 2780
viscerimotor, 2780
viscerography, 2780
visceromotor, 2780
visceroptosis, 2780
viscin, 2781
viscogel, 2781
viscometer, 2781
viscos-, 2781
viscosaccharase, 2781
viscosi-, 2781
viscosimeter, 2781
viscosity, 2781
viscō(sus), 2781
visc(um), 2781
'visible', 1971
vīsiō, 2555
vision, 2555
'vision', 2334
'vision in sleep', 824
vīsiōn(is), 2555
visu-, 2782
visual, 2782
visuo-, 874, 1146, 1295,
    2471, 2555, 2775
visuo-auditory, 2782
visuognosis, 2782
visuosensory, 2782
vīsu(s), 2782
vit-[1], 2785
vit-[2], 2787
vīt(a), 2785, 2787
vita-[1], 239, 2162, 2783,
    2787, 2789, 2790, 2856

vita-[2], 2787
vitaglass, 2785
vitagonist, 2787
vitagraph, 2785
vital, 2785
vitameter, 2787
vitamin-[2], 2787
Vitamin(e), 2787
vitamino-, 2784, 2786
vitaminogenic, 2787
vitaminoid, 2787
vitaminology, 2787
vitaminoscope, 2787
vitascope, 2785
vitell-, 2788
vitellase, 2788
vitellogenesis, 2788
vitellolutein, 2788
vitellorubin, 2788
vitell(us), 2788
Vitis, 1133
vito-, 2785
vitodynamic, 2785
vitreous humor, 1267
*vītula, 988
Vītula, 988
vītulārī, 988
vivi-, 239, 2162, 2785,
    2856
vividialysis, 2790
viviparous, 2790
vivisection, 2790
vivo-, 2790
vivosphere, 2790
vīv(us), 2790
volta-, 2791
(Alessandro) Volt(a), 2791
voltage, 2791
voltameter, 2791
voltammeter, 2791
voltmeter, 2791
volvere, 2756
'vomit', 895
'vomiting', 895
Vulpes, 1045
vulv-, 2792
vulv(a), 2792
'vulva', 924
vulvitis, 2792
vulvocrural, 2792
vulvo-uterine, 2792
vulvovaginal, 2792

W

wǣć(ćan), 2799
wǣt, 2810
wǣter, 2800
wǣx, 2803
wafian, 2802
wagian, 2802
'wagon', 357, 371
waist-, 193
waistband, 2793
waistcloth, 2793
waistcoat, 2793
Wales, 1062
walk-(?), 1201, 2722,
    2756, 2809
'walk(ing)', 216
walk-on, 2794
walkout, 2794
walkway, 2794
'wall', 2303
'wall (of a house)', 1910
Wallachian, 1062
wallboard, 2795
wallflower, 2795
Walloon, 1062
wallpaper, 2795
'walnut', 1385
'wandering', 2040, 2755
'war', 1149
ward, 1145
'ward off', 56, 978, 1904
warhead, 2796
war-horse, 2796
warlord, 2796
'warm', 680
'warn', 1662
'warp of a loom', 1239
'wart', 1202
wasć(an), 2797
wash-, 1270, 2800, 2810,
    2828
washcloth, 2797
washout, 2797
washroom, 2797
wast, 2793
'waste away', 1998
wastebasket, 2798
wasteland, 2798
'waste materials', 2427
wastepile, 2798
'wasting away', 1998
watchdog, 2799